DATE DUE

FOUNDED BY BURNS MANTLE

THE BEST PLAYS THEATER YEARBOOK 2007–2008

JEFFREY ERIC JENKINS
Editor

○○○○○
○○○○○ THE BEST PLAYS
○○○○○ THEATER YEARBOOK
○○○○○
○○○○○

Editorial research and data compilation
for *The Best Plays Theater Yearbook 2007–2008*
has been partly underwritten by a generous grant from
the Harold and Mimi Steinberg Charitable Trust.

Carole A. Krumland, James D. Steinberg, Michael A. Steinberg,
Seth M. Weingarten, William D. Zabel
Directors

THE BEST PLAYS
THEATER YEARBOOK
2007–2008

EDITED BY

JEFFREY ERIC JENKINS

Illustrated with production photographs

LIMELIGHT EDITIONS

AN IMPRINT OF HAL LEONARD CORPORATION
NEW YORK

ISBN: 978-0-87910-366-8

ISSN: 1942-339X

Printed in the United States of America

Published in 2009 by
Limelight Editions
An Imprint of Hal Leonard Corporation
7777 West Bluemound Road
Milwaukee, WI 53213

Trade Book Division Editorial Offices
19 West 21st Street, New York, NY 10010
www.limelighteditions.com

INTRODUCTION

A S WE PORE over the statistics of the theater season under review and add our research of earlier years to the mix, an astonishing fact arises from the result: neither *South Pacific* nor *Gypsy*—both of which received outstanding revivals this season—were chosen as Best Plays for their respective seasons (1948–49 and 1958–59). Sitting as virtual bookends to the decade of the Korean War and the Eisenhower administration, these two works were shining examples of theater art—and its possibility—in a time often cited as the "Golden Era" of the Broadway musical.

Despite record attendance figures in recent years and the collection of many millions of dollars at the box office, an increasingly figurative term given the rise of online ticketing through the internet, Broadway attendance has become the purview of those who can afford tickets that run to $100 or more. At the end of the 2007–2008 season, *Variety* reported that the average ticket price was $73.55, down $2.72 from its all-time high the previous year. If one figures on a family of four who may wish to have dinner in the Theater District, may need to park a vehicle and may desire a souvenir of the experience, a trip to Broadway can easily run $500 or more. Even in flush times, which these are not, that is a significant amount of money for a family evening. Although ticket prices today are roughly consonant with those of the Golden Era—the median four-person family income in the tri-state area rose by multiples of 22 to 28 between 1949 and 2007 while top Broadway ticket prices increased by a factor of a little more than 20—the perception of tickets at $100 or more raises concerns of accessibility from many corners. New Yorkers in the know, of course, are aware of ticket-buying clubs that make extremely low-price tickets available to their members, but it is difficult to imagine that Broadway's core audience of tourists and tri-state residents might easily avail themselves of such bargains.

Setting aside the commercial details of attendance and income for the moment, it is worth considering what constitutes a Best Play as we launch into the seasonal narrative that comprises the *Best Plays Theater Yearbook*.

The absence of *South Pacific* and *Gypsy* from the master Best Plays list implies that the respective editors of those past volumes (John Chapman and Louis Kronenberger) found something lacking in the now-classic musicals. Chapman admitted that *South Pacific* was a "fine musical" but found it not to be the "real work of art" of Rodgers and Hammerstein's *Carousel* and *Oklahoma!* It is tempting to suspect that Chapman took the idea of "play" too seriously, but a review of Best Plays during his tenure as editor demonstrates that he managed to pick such divergent musicals as Rodgers and Hammerstein's *Allegro* (1947–48), *Lost in the Stars* by Maxwell Anderson and Kurt Weill (1949–50) and *Guys and Dolls* by Jo Swerling, Abe Burrows and Frank Loesser (1950–51). The works that bumped *South Pacific* from the list included such titles as Sidney Kingsley's melodramatic *Detective Story* and Robert E. McEnroe's *The Silver Whistle*, but that season's honorees also included plays such as Arthur Miller's *Death of a Salesman* and Maxwell Anderson's *Anne of the Thousand Days*.

A decade later, Kronenberger declined to pick *Gypsy* by Arthur Laurents, Jule Styne and Stephen Sondheim because the musical "hardly seemed worthy" of the critical plaudits it received on its opening. Kronenberger gave most credit for *Gypsy*'s success to director-choreographer Jerome Robbins and star Ethel Merman (who nonetheless saw the Tony Award go to Mary Martin that year for *The Sound of Music*). Unwilling to let it go at that, Kronenberger further noted that Laurents's book was a "touch commonplace and more than a touch repetitious," that Styne's score was "nowhere noteworthy" and Sondheim's lyrics were "largely routine." These hasty judgments must give pause to any historian who hopes to construct a reliable narrative from a theater season of the recent past. In the ensuing decades, *South Pacific* and *Gypsy* became touchstones of American musical theater, embedding themselves in our consciousness largely through their memorable songs but also in the ways that each musical plucks emotional and spiritual chords that are distinctly American.

In *South Pacific*, Rodgers, Hammerstein and Joshua Logan crafted a poignant and deeply disconcerting story regarding the human cost of war and racial prejudice. At a time when African-American veterans of the recent world war returned to find themselves continuing to be treated as second- or third-class citizens, *South Pacific* raised the hackles of some members of the Establishment. When the show previewed in Boston, according to critic Elliot Norton in an interview published in *Under the Copper Beech* (Foundation ATCA, 2004), "the audience froze [after 'You've Got to Be Carefully Taught']. You could almost feel the chill and I talked to some people afterwards—bigoted people who hated the show, believe it or not." Norton told Bill Gale that he subsequently tried to get Logan to "tone it down a little," but that the director intensely disagreed. (Norton came to believe that Logan was correct to stay with his instinct.) Although it is often said that there are no atheists in foxholes, *South Pacific* made its first audiences question whether the same held true for racists—and it raised these questions less than a year after President Truman issued an executive order requiring the "equality of treatment and opportunity for all persons in the Armed Services." Although it nearly cost him his presidency that year, Truman effectively began the desegregation of the military. As a result of Truman's actions, the US military is now the most egalitarian institution in American life. But when *South Pacific* opened in 1949, issues of racial prejudice were not a common topic for mass entertainment.

In the case of *Gypsy*, sometimes described as the perfect show-business musical, it is easy to discern the ways in which the work echoes familiar elements in the American psyche. Much has been made, for instance, of the American Dream—particularly in cultural products emanating from 20th-century popular fiction, Hollywood films and 1950s women's magazines. The "dream" has become a cultural Rorschach test in which almost anyone can define his or her deepest desires as related to it. Mama Rose's ambition for her daughters and, by extension, herself, mark this musical as a tale—which has more than a little in common with Bertolt Brecht's *Mother Courage and Her Children*—of continual adaptation to attain a measure of success. That it results in a young woman, Louise, converting herself into a commodity, Gypsy Rose Lee, presented to satisfy what theorists call the "male gaze" only heightens the paradox of what some women encounter on the path to material success without the direct support of a dominant male figure. Indeed, Mama Rose's grasping nature also aligns to a large extent with the fame-at-any-cost ethos so prevalent in American reality television today.

Should *Gypsy* have been overlooked by editor Kronenberger in favor of Shimon Wincelberg's *Kataki*, which played 20 performances on Broadway? Judging from the e-mail received and chatter on theater websites after we announce the 10 Best Plays of a given season, this is the type of question on the minds of many theater lovers. The answer, of course, is complex: We choose three dozen or so finalists, which are then discussed with nearly two dozen theater critics and writers, including the *Best Plays* editorial board, former essayists and other top theater writers. For the season just past, we considered 48 plays for a place on the *Best Plays* list. Although we sometimes wish there were enough space to honor 15 Best Plays, we cannot. Did we choose the "correct" 10 plays? Have we overlooked the next *South Pacific* or *Gypsy*? Read on and decide for yourself.

II

AS WE EXAMINE the list of this season's 10 Best Plays (and one Special Citation), it is natural to wonder what these choices tell us about the 2007–2008 theater season in New York. We often find that there is a narrative thread to be teased from the fabric of our choices, but occasionally that thread is rather more tortured than teased. It is, however, our mission to construct a second-draft of recent theater history—with journalism, a craft in seemingly inexorable decline, as the first. Amid the growing elimination of theater critic positions (and shrinking arts coverage) at daily newspapers around the US, it sometimes feels as though *Best Plays* may soon be the last publication of mainstream critical perspective on theater to appear in print. In the meantime, however, we have 11 New York theater works from the season under consideration to explore.

There was a great deal of unhappiness lodged in the works we celebrate in this volume. Could it be that we have chosen these works because they reflect our sense of insecurity at a time of war and growing economic calamity? In *Adding Machine*, Jason Loewith and Joshua Schmidt's musical adaptation of Elmer Rice's 1923 play *The Adding Machine*, the talented duo have tapped Rice's key thematics regarding the ways in which guilt may prevent sentient creatures from pursuing what anthropologist Joseph Campbell called their "bliss." Performed in 90 intermissionless minutes, Loewith and Schmidt's work unearthed the essence of Rice's expressionistic classic in near operatic form. Despite the use of Rice's work as a springboard, the creators made *Adding Machine* a new entity of its own—and converted some detractors of the original. Essayist Jeffrey Sweet unfolds the results of their work.

Leo Tolstoy's aphorism about family happiness that begins *Anna Karenina*—"Happy families are all alike; every unhappy family is unhappy in it own way" (Constance Garnett translation)—seems to bear weight once again with the productions of *August: Osage County* by Tracy Letts and *Dividing the Estate* by Horton Foote. In *August*, which first came to life at Chicago's Steppenwolf Theatre Company, an extended family in Oklahoma gathers to mourn its patriarch as it tries to contain its drug-addled matriarch. Playwright Letts shows that he has learned well the lessons of Eugene O'Neill, Arthur Miller and Sam Shepard, with a side helping from the king of trash-talk television, Jerry Springer. Chris Jones, who observed the play's development from Chicago to New York, takes note of this Pulitzer Prize-winning play.

The unhappiness at the core of Horton Foote's *Dividing the Estate* is less about familial chaos and more about the sense of entitlement that runs through a Texas family. Foote's play, which is set during the oil bust of the late 1980s, centers on a family, featured in other plays of his, who were once wealthy landowners and farmers. In the straitened circumstances of 1987, the family discovers that the land is worth much less than they hoped and that their free-spending ways are about to end. Essayist Garrett Eisler draws parallels between Foote's characters and the challenging economic climate now facing millions of Americans.

Plays by two women, Sarah Ruhl and Kate Fodor, examine the nature of love and loss in works that share an elegiac underpinning. In Ruhl's *eurydice*, the title character attains a kind of grace as she leaves behind her beloved and travels to the Underworld where she encounters her dead father. Essayist Celia Wren makes the water-drenched voyage with Eurydice and discovers that in our world today "comic desolation" may at times resemble a "leaky faucet." John Istel makes a similar journey in his essay on Fodor's *100 Saints You Should Know*, yet another Steppenwolf gift to New York. In *100 Saints*, however, Fodor tracks the paths of several characters seeking solace and understanding: a sexually confused priest questions his faith and befriends a working-class mother, a teenage boy tries to fit into his own skin but makes a fateful choice to engage with the working-class mother's daredevil daughter. These lives intersect and diverge in the course of the play. Ultimately, however, Istel finds that the playwright's art lies in how she allows "each point of view" to radiate "its own profoundly human value and worth."

Evil rears its head in ways banal and Biblical in plays by Adam Bock and Conor McPherson. Bock, who captured the attention of audiences and critics with *The Thugs* during the 2006–07 season, is honored for *The Receptionist*. Essayist David Cote argues that the two plays combined, which are one-acts of roughly 50 and 80 minutes, might make for a "darkly funny evening of post-September 11 paranoia." Cote explores Bock's deployment of the banality that overlays a corporate culture in which torture is the service provided by a commercial entity. In *The Receptionist*, Bock demonstrates what is possible (and probable?) in a society whose moral compass has gone haywire. Playwright McPherson dabbles with a more familiar image of evil. Amid a houseful of alcoholics on Christmas Eve, the Devil comes to call and collect the debt of a soul owed by one of the men.

Essayist Charles McNulty considers McPherson's narrative style and how the playwright's perspective echoes literary classics as he grapples with the essence of "Hell" and the desire for grace.

Master playwrights Tom Stoppard and Edward Albee each make their ninth appearance in the *Best Plays* series. Stoppard's ideological sequel to last season's *The Coast of Utopia* charts the crushing oppression and decline of Soviet-style Communism in *Rock 'n' Roll*. Appropriating popular music and art movements of the latter part of the 20th century, Stoppard shows the naivete of those who believe that ideals of freedom and revolution in popular culture can overcome the personal betrayals elicited by totalitarian regimes and their secret police. Essayist Charles Wright argues that Stoppard's characters are "superbly shaded" and that, despite the intellectual debate at the play's core, the author's work is marked by "increasing poignance and variety of emotion." Albee's *Peter and Jerry* (retitled in 2008 as *At Home at the Zoo*) receives a Special Citation in this volume partly because one half of the piece is the revised version of the playwright's 1958 play, *The Zoo Story*. Essayist Michael Sommers details the dark humor that Albee evokes as he "completes" a play that long has been a classic in American colleges and on American stages.

It is entirely fitting to end our brief introduction to the Best Plays honored herein with questions that relate to everything we do in this series: What is history and who owns it? Aaron Sorkin's *The Farnsworth Invention*, which was criticized for not hewing strictly to the facts of Philo T. Farnsworth's life and career, is a Best Play that raises one such question. After surviving a stagehands' strike while in previews, the creative team faced a *New York Post* piece on factual inaccuracies in the play just a few days before opening. Sorkin was accused of taking liberties with certain events, including a dramatized court case that did not end as depicted in the play. Other elements such as Farnsworth's well-documented drinking problems and his eventual loss of control over his invention, were challenged for the way they were handled. Some who were interviewed in the *Post* article had a significant financial stake in Farnsworth-influenced projects unrelated to the play. Sorkin confronted his accusers in an open letter and the contretemps devolved into "he said, he said." But for 104 performances, Sorkin's trademark dialogue and crisp narrative style held sway on Broadway in a fascinating tale that was itself an interrogation of the way history is often written by the victors, implicitly criticizing the tactics employed by those victors. Essayist Christopher Rawson digs into the piece and finds a story in which neither of the play's narrators is completely reliable—which may well have been Sorkin's point all along.

David Henry Hwang's *Yellow Face* also challenges the ways in which history is constructed. In Hwang's case, however, the story is more personal than it was for Sorkin. Hwang unspools the threads of his own life through a character named "DHH," whose father shares initials with the playwright's late father, a prominent banker. In *Yellow Face* the tale told centers on a prominent Asian-American writer who finds himself speaking for an entire community of Asian-American theater workers. As the play unfolds, often in comic fashion, DHH confronts a variety of issues that relate to personal and ethnic identity. He also learns that life in the public square all-too-easily spins out of control when the agendas of others—newspaper reporters, unemployed actors, government regulators—come into conflict with one's own sense of reality. Essayist Dan Bacalzo finds that Hwang "explodes notions of truth and authenticity," exposing them as "subjective and prone to manipulation."

In creating narratives that interrogate the nature of storytelling even as they reconstruct narratives beloved by various interest groups, Sorkin and Hwang have both demonstrated that compelling playwriting need not be hostage to linearity—as long as the writing possesses wit, clarity, perspective and humanity. Indeed, it is fair to argue that all of this year's honorees—whether exploring dyfunctional characters in decline, societies gone mad or the reliability of narrative—tell us something about what it means to be a human being in ways that are fresh and, often, exhilarating.

In addition to the plays celebrated in these essays, we also hope that readers enjoy the volume's expanded statistics and index. Whenever possible we track all Broadway and Off Broadway revivals back to their original presentations in New York, around the country and abroad. In the case of William Shakespeare and others of his ilk, we employ George C.D. Odell's *Annals of the New York Stage*—which links with the *Best Plays Theater Yearbook* series to chronicle New York theater back to the 18th century. We also use the archives of *The New York Times* and other major publications as we attempt to locate plays in their original contexts.

With our colleagues in the American Theatre Critics Association, we also keep close tabs on new plays developing in theaters across the US. Through the Harold and Mimi Steinberg Charitable Trust, we recognize the honorees of the Steinberg/ATCA New Play Award and Citations. The Steinberg Charitable Trust, which has supported the *Best Plays Theater Yearbook* series since 2001, recently renewed its support of our editorial research and data compilation mission for an additional five years, which will help keep this publication in print until at least 2013. We extend our deepest thanks to the Trust and its board (William D. Zabel, Carole A.

Krumland, James D. Steinberg, Michael A. Steinberg and Seth M. Weingarten) for making *Best Plays Theater Yearbook* a priority for their support.

Honorees for the 2008 Steinberg/ATCA New Play Award and Citations are Moisés Kaufman's *33 Variations*, which won the Steinberg top prize ($25,000). Kaufman's play is discussed by Nelson Pressley. The 2008 Steinberg/ATCA New Play Citations (along with $7,500 each) went to Sarah Ruhl for *Dead Man's Cell Phone* (detailed here by Peter Marks), and to Deborah Zoe Laufer for *End Days* (essay by Christine Dolen).

III

AS WE MOVE forward with the 89th volume of this chronicle of theater in the United States, we celebrate the beginning of a reinvigorated partnership with Limelight Editions, now under the management of publisher John Cerullo.

The collection of data for a volume such as this relies on the labors of many people. Our thanks to Sylviane Gold for her remarkably thorough essay on Off Off Broadway theater. Sheryl Arluck continues as an invaluable compiler and assistant editor of the Off Off Broadway section, among other duties for the series. Jennifer Ashley Tepper expands her portfolio to include the USA, Cast Replacements and Touring, and In Memoriam sections. Jonathan Dodd, the longtime publisher of the *Best Plays* series, continues to provide important background information and good advice. Thanks as well to our friend and colleague Robert Brustein for generously continuing as consulting editor to the series.

We are also deeply indebted to all of the press representatives who assisted in the gathering of information for this volume, but we particularly acknowledge Adrian Bryan-Brown and Chris Boneau of Boneau/Bryan-Brown for their unflagging support of the series and its editors.

Thanks also are due to the members of the *Best Plays Theater Yearbook*'s editorial board, who give their imprimatur to our work by their presence on the masthead. With this edition we welcome Misha Berson to the editorial board as we wish our longtime colleague and friend Tish Dace a happy and well-deserved retirement. We are grateful as well to those who have offered and provided extra support and assistance to this edition: Charles Wright, Christopher Rawson (Theater Hall of Fame Awards), Caldwell Titcomb (Elliot Norton Awards), David A. Rosenberg (Connecticut Critics' Circle Awards), Bill Hirschman (Steinberg/ATCA New Play Award and Citations) and Edwin Wilson and Mimi Kilgore (Susan Smith Blackburn Prize).

We especially note the ongoing joint efforts of the *Best Plays* editorial team and the research department of the The Broadway League—which changed its name from the League of American Theatres and Producers on December 18, 2007—over the past several years. First with Stephen Greer, later Neal Freeman and now with Jennifer Stewart, we have worked since 2002 to correct the records of the Internet Broadway Database (www.ibdb.com) as well as past errors made in the pages of *Best Plays*. Our thanks and compliments to our friends at the League for their cooperation in this long-term project of correcting the historical record.

We congratulate and thank all of the Best Plays honorees who made the 2007–08 season so invigorating to contemplate. Edward Albee, Adam Bock, Kate Fodor, Horton Foote, David Henry Hwang, Tracy Letts, Jason Loewith, Conor McPherson, Sarah Ruhl, Joshua Schmidt, Aaron Sorkin and Tom Stoppard all enriched our lives during the season under review. The photographers who capture theatrical images on film and help keep those ephemeral moments alive for historical perspective are also due thanks for their generous contributions to the greater body of theatrical work. Building on our work from past years, we have included credits with each photograph and indexed the photographers' names for easier reference. Similarly, we continue offering biographical information about each of this volume's essayists and editors.

A personal note: In addition to serving as editor of this series, I teach full-time in the Drama Department at New York University's Tisch School of the Arts. Although I am blessed with superb students who inspire me to strive for excellence in my teaching, research, editing and writing, I also have the support and friendship of as fine a faculty of artists and scholars as I have had the honor to know. Each member of the faculty has provided the kind of encouragement one needs to keep in print an annual compendium of critical perspective and historical reference that runs more than 500 pages. Thanks to all of my colleagues for their advocacy, especially to the senior academic faculty: Awam Amkpa, Una Chaudhuri, Laura Levine, Carol Martin and Robert Vorlicky. For the season under review, I especially thank our department chair, Kevin Kuhlke, and our director of theater studies, Edward Ziter, for their continuing support of my work as a teacher, researcher and writer. Thanks also to Dan Dinero, my graduate assistant during the season under review, for helping to make my work more manageable.

My wife, Vivian Cary Jenkins, continues to serve the theater and *Best Plays Theater Yearbook* as a tracker of what is happening in the New York theater. Despite facing challenges that would utterly stymie someone made of lesser stuff, she continues to contribute in ways large and small to the success of the series even as she has collaborated this season with the brilliant theater artist, Ping Chong. Although I repeat these thanks each year, one thing remains true: It is largely through her consistent efforts that this series continues to appear.

JEFFREY ERIC JENKINS
NEW YORK

Contents

THE SEASON
ON AND OFF
BROADWAY

THE SEASON:
BROADWAY AND OFF BROADWAY

○ ○ ○ ○ ○ *By Jeffrey Eric Jenkins* ○ ○ ○ ○ ○

IN ANY NEW YORK theater season, there are numerous story lines worth pursuing in the chase to construct a "second draft" of theater history. The 2007–2008 season was no exception with a flowering of productions that gave overdue prominence to African-American artists, a stagehands' strike that shuttered most of Broadway for 19 performances entering the busiest time of the year, charges and countercharges of historical revisionism surrounding *The Farnsworth Invention* (a Best Play), outstanding musical revivals that recalled the Golden Era and new musicals that offered hope for creative evolution. Despite that rising hope, however, when the 2008 Tony Awards were bestowed at the end of the season, half of all the prizes went to revivals of plays and musicals—including most of the acting and design awards. This celebration of past accomplishment has been a source of anxiety in past versions of these essays due to Broadway's continued locus as a theatrical museum where innovation often takes a backseat to commerce.

Over the past decade, however, the definition of "commerce" has become somewhat flexible as nonprofit theaters have evolved into dominant players in the commercial theater landscape. Indeed, it was Lincoln Center Theater's sumptuous revival of *South Pacific* that snagged the lion's share of honors with seven 2008 Tony Awards, a record number for a musical revival. (Since the 2005 Tony Awards, musicals and plays have separate sets of design awards so they no longer compete across theatrical forms.)

Theater columnist Michael Riedel reported in the *New York Post* during the 2008 Tony Award voting season that commercial producers were dissatisfied with "unfair" advantages enjoyed by nonprofit entities. These benefits include lower pay scales for union artists, subsidies from contributors and reduced rates for advertising in certain media. The Tony Awards, which honored "outstanding contributions" to the theater season in its early years—the *New York Times* noted in 1948 that "citations refrained from

BROADWAY SEASON 2007–2008

Productions in a continuing run on May 31, 2008 in bold
Plays honored as Best Plays selections in italics
Best Plays from prior seasons are noted with a volume date in italics

NEW PLAYS (7)
Mauritius (Manhattan Theatre Club)
Rock 'n' Roll
The Farnsworth Invention
August: Osage County
The Seafarer
Is He Dead?
November

NEW MUSICALS (8)
Xanadu
Young Frankenstein
The Little Mermaid
Passing Strange *06–07*
In the Heights
A Catered Affair
Cry-Baby
Glory Days

PLAY REVIVALS (13)
Old Acquaintance
  (Roundabout Theatre Company)
The Ritz 74–75 (Roundabout)
Pygmalion (Roundabout)
Cyrano de Bergerac
Cymbeline (Lincoln Center Theater)

PLAY REVIVALS *(cont'd)*
The Homecoming 66–67
Come Back, Little Sheba 49–50
  (Manhattan)
Cat on a Hot Tin Roof *54–55*
Macbeth
The Country Girl *50–51*
Les Liaisons Dangereuses *86–87*
  (Roundabout)
Boeing-Boeing
Top Girls (Manhattan)

MUSICAL REVIVALS (5)
Grease
Dr. Seuss's How the Grinch
  Stole Christmas!
Sunday in the Park
  With George *83–84* (Roundabout)
Gypsy
South Pacific (Lincoln)

SOLO PERFORMANCES (2)
A Bronx Tale
Thurgood

SPECIALTIES (1)
The 39 Steps (Roundabout)

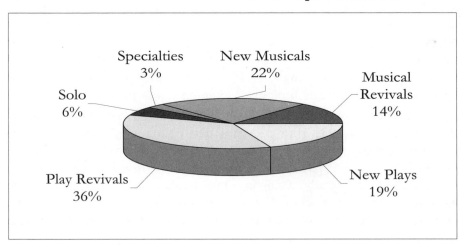

Specialties 3%
New Musicals 22%
Musical Revivals 14%
Solo 6%
Play Revivals 36%
New Plays 19%

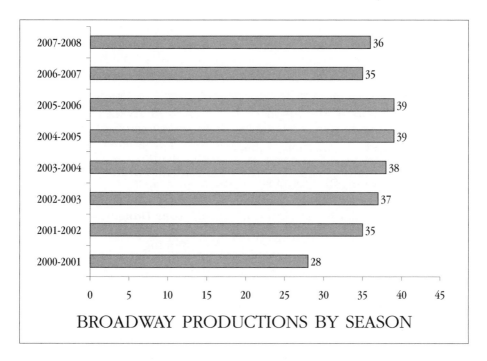

BROADWAY PRODUCTIONS BY SEASON

using the words 'best' or 'first,' employing such terms as 'outstanding' and 'distinguished' instead"—gradually shifted their emphasis to "best" and are now considered the imprimatur of Broadway success. With the Tonys' stamp of approval often—but not always—comes a lift in ticket sales that can forestall an early closing. From the perspective of commercial producers, Tony Awards are much more crucial to the survival of presenters operating with higher costs and a reduced margin for error.

To some extent, however, the Tony Award angst of commercial producers exists in a false binary. While it is true that nonprofit theaters enjoy certain financial advantages, the lines between commercial and nonprofit theater have blurred for more than 40 years, most significantly since the Arena Stage production of *The Great White Hope* moved to a commercial Broadway production in 1968. Over the past several decades, many productions have moved from development in nonprofit theaters to commercial runs. Riedel noted in his article that Rocco Landesman, one of the most powerful commercial producers in the world, has himself enjoyed numerous successes sparked by nonprofit collaborations.

The gold standard among nonprofit-commercial relationships, of course, was the development of *A Chorus Line* (1975), which stabilized the Public Theater's fiscal health for many years. More of the time, however, commercial producers have provided "enhancement money" to develop works in nonprofit theaters that producers can later move to a commercial run—if all goes well. Although enhancement arrangements are often more "miss" than "hit," there are such varied models as *Rent, Spring Awakening, LoveMusik* and *The Drowsy Chaperone.* In March 2007, producer Carole Shorenstein Hays told Campbell Robertson of the *New York Times* that she was reconsidering her involvement in enhancement arrangements, "I'm kind of folding my hands . . . because I think it does start polluting everything." Hays was referring to a concern she and others share that enhancement money has, in Robertson's formulation, caused the "specter of a commercial transfer to hover over the artistic process." Robertson noted, however, that Hays was in the minority in eschewing these deals.

With regard to the perceived need for Tony Awards, however, it is also possible that producers are driven more by ego than by financial circumstance. Six months or so before his unexpected death in September 2007, producer Jay Harris—a passionate advocate who was also a true gentlemen of the theater—told of conversations with "several producers" who were investing in "five or six shows" in order to improve their odds for a Tony Award. (It was stunning, in 2007, to see dozens of producers flood the stage when *Spring Awakening* received the Tony Award for best musical—a stark comment on the millions of dollars necessary to mount a Broadway musical.) There are also more than a few Tony Awards given to productions and performers who have departed shows before the awards are given. At the 2008 Tony Awards that capped the season under review, the women who received honors for best actress (Deanna Dunagan) and best featured actress (Rondi Reed) in a play (*August: Osage County*, a Best Play), had departed their show earlier that day. Similarly, Jim Norton received the Tony for best featured actor in a play for *The Seafarer* (a Best Play), which had closed more than two months earlier. (It should be noted that all of the nominees in Norton's category were from shows that had been closed for months.) Lest one think that 2008 was anomalous, one needs look no further than 2007 when the superb revival of *Journey's End* received the best play-revival Tony a few hours after its final performance. Despite the quality of the work onstage, producers could not keep that World War I drama playing because audiences averaged 37 percent of the theater's capacity for the entire run. In fact, 10 of 25 competitive 2007 Tony Awards were given to entities that were out of business before the ceremony. Of the other 15 honorees at the 2007 Tony Awards, five more departed the Broadway boards in the first weeks of this season.

For those who decry the advantage enjoyed by such nonprofit companies as Lincoln Center Theater, Roundabout Theatre Company and Manhattan Theatre Club—all of which control Broadway venues—it is worth considering whether any commercial producer could (or would) have underwritten the risk involved with either Tom Stoppard's epic *The Coast of Utopia* or the lavish revival of *South Pacific*. For those two productions Lincoln Center received 14 Tony Awards over two seasons, setting records each time. As for the Tony Awards themselves—financial outcomes and revival celebrations aside—one may take a "glass half full" approach to the 2007–08 season and note that half of all 2008 Tony Awards went to new works and that all awards were spread among nine different shows, which represented a more than a third of nominated productions.

End of the Great 'White' Way?

ARTISTS OF COLOR have long commented—some more pointedly than others—on Broadway's "Great White Way" moniker. Memory recalls John Leguizamo ad-libbing on artists of color missing from Broadway—"No wonder they call it the Great *White* Way"— in his solo piece, *Freak* (1998). Was it during the segment when he spoke about Morales in *A Chorus Line* and how young Leguizamo felt the character spoke directly to him? Memory is unreliable, however, and the line appears nowhere in the published texts for *Freak* or his later Broadway piece, *Sexaholix* (2001). This season, in a February 2008 interview with Atlanta's *Insite* magazine, Charles S. Dutton—the superb interpreter of August Wilson's characters—was asked about creative freedom in the theater as opposed to film. Dutton affirmed that the theater is "halfway less racist," but, he added, "They don't call it the 'Great White Way' for nothing."

Although there is some evidence that the term had its roots in electrical advertising signs that appeared in New York's Madison Square in the 1890s, the earliest printed usage was apparently in a 1902 *Evening Telegram* headline. A slightly later reference to the "Great White Way" as synonym for Broadway and the Theater District appeared in the *Washington Post* in October 1903:

> The fascination of the so-called "Great White Way"—referring, of course, to the myriad of electric lights of theaters, hotels and bazaars—for the man of wit and humor is irresistible.

The term was clearly in popular usage by the time of its appearance in the *Post*, and it may have been first appropriated from the eponymous title of

A.B. Paine's 1901 book about an expedition to the South Pole—a different sort of "great white way." Whatever its genesis, the term certainly was meant to refer to the bright electric lights of Broadway that seemed to turn night to day. Over the past several decades, however, theater writers have taken note of rising African-American contributions to the national landscape by at times referring to the "Great Black Way." It was Douglas Turner Ward, then artistic director of the Negro Ensemble Company, who appears to have first used the term in 1974 to describe growing prominence of African-American artists on our stages.

According to a 1976 article in the *New York Times* by Mel Gussow, a long-time essayist for *Best Plays*:

> Broadway is burgeoning with black theater. There is so much black talent working there—actors, singers, writers, directors—and such a lively black audience that the theater district could almost be retagged the Great Black Way. At the same time, white audiences are discovering black theater. This is not an insular variety of entertainment, but very much a part of the mainstream.

For a time in the mid-1970s, Gussow's 1976 assertion rang true. A few weeks after Gussow's piece in the *Times*, the weekly newsmagazine *Time* reported that a quarter of all Broadway shows were "black." These included *Porgy and Bess*, an African-American cast in a revival of *Guys and Dolls*, *The Wiz, Bubbling Brown Sugar* and *for colored girls who have considered suicide / when the rainbow is enuf*. Gussow also noted that "more black actors are working on Broadway than ever before." By the end of the 1970s, the catchiness of the "Great Black Way" phrase had worn thin (although R.J. Smith employed it in the title of a 2006 book on Los Angeles's African-American culture in the 1940s). It was during the 1960s and 1970s, however, that the burst of creativity from the Black Arts Movement gave rise to important theater artists such as Amiri Baraka, Ed Bullins, Leslie Lee, Ntozake Shange, Richard Wesley and August Wilson.

As noted in the 2006–07 *Best Plays*, Wilson was a strong proponent of theater written, directed and performed by African Americans, but he was as forcefully opposed to colorblind and nontraditional casting. His concerns were elucidated in a 1996 speech before a Theatre Communications Group conference, quoted in part here:

> To mount an all-black production of *Death of a Salesman* or any other play conceived for white actors as an investigation of the human condition through the specifics of white culture is to deny us our own humanity, our own history and the need to make our own

investigations from the cultural ground on which we stand as black Americans.

For Wilson, African-American actors who performed "white" roles, such as Shakespearean kings, were complicit in their own cultural erasure. This topic arose in last season's edition because on subsequent nights in 2007, the opening of Wilson's final play, *Radio Golf*, was followed by a revival of *110 in the Shade* with the exquisite Audra McDonald as Lizzie in an interracial family. In the musical, set in Texas during the Great Depression, there was no notice taken of racial difference and characters mixed freely among

How did issues of race play on the Great 'White' Way this season?

themselves. It may be pointless to argue that verisimilitude was out the window when it came to *110 in the Shade*. After all, how many folks burst into spontaneous song-and-dance on 1936 Texas farms? Are we simply to pretend the "difference" does not exist? Why not use that difference in dramatic fashion to provoke new, deeper levels of understanding?

In the 2007–08 season, issues of race blew across the Broadway landscape as if they were tumbleweeds on Lizzie's dust bowl farm: touching here, rolling there, sweeping past. In 1994, Stephen C. Byrd told *Variety* that he "wanted to go after classic projects" for African-American actors and "among them were works of Tennessee Williams." Byrd's plan was to present a Broadway production of *Cat on a Hot Tin Roof* in January 1995 with Lloyd Richards directing and James Earl Jones as Big Daddy. By the time the production was ready for rehearsals more than decade later, Richards had retired and later died. Along the way, Laurence Fishburne was mentioned as a possible Brick to play opposite Jones. But works by Williams are fraught with an inherent racism that plays out against the backdrop of the author's trademark Southern gentility with a gothic twist. It is tempting to think that as Byrd worked to move his production forward, debates over race and casting may have held him back. Indeed, these emotionally charged conversations were ongoing long before Wilson's influential (and highly controversial) speech at the 1996 TCG conference.

It was James Earl Jones's desire for many years to play Big Daddy and, to some extent, the notion of it became a central part of the nontraditional-casting discussion. In 1980, Jones told the *New York Times* that he wanted to play the role but, "I wouldn't do it as a black; with makeup I would convert myself into a Caucasian." Several years later, in 1986, Jones participated in a national symposium on nontraditional casting in New York that featured a reading with Big Daddy as black and his son, Brick, as white. A year later, while playing Troy Maxson in August Wilson's *Fences* on Broadway, Jones was quoted by the *Washington Post* as saying that "part of the truth of [Big Daddy's] character is that he's white. I'd do everything I can to make people think I am an upwardly mobile cracker." Cast in a revival of *Cat* with Kathleen Turner that came to Broadway in 1990, Jones withdrew long before opening. Ward, the Negro Ensemble Company's artistic director, had come to question certain aspects of nontraditional casting by 1989. He said to Daniel Patrick Stearns in *USA Today*, "What interpretative value does it have? . . . The worst aspect of it is that black actors think they have to legitimize themselves by playing the icons of the majority culture."

Wilson himself told Patty Hartigan, writing for the *Boston Globe* in 1990, that he was

> violently opposed to nontraditional casting. . . . You can't ignore race. You go to see a play and you got a black guy playing Big Daddy. The first thing you say is, "That's a black guy up there. You got a black guy playing a white guy." Yeah, he's a good actor, but he's saying words that a black American would not say. So he is denying his humanity in order to assume someone else's humanity.

When Wilson delivered his larger polemic six years later at the TCG conference, he had carefully worked through his feelings about nontraditional casting. While many appreciated his forthright stand on behalf of African-American culture, others worried that it led to a separatist worldview, which undermined the possibility of bridging cultural divides. At the very least, however, Wilson's concerns echoed those of Arena Stage's Zelda Fichandler who told *USA Today*'s Stearns that colorblind casting was "not everybody's dream. . . . I've heard black actors say, 'Why should anybody in the audience pretend I'm not (black)?'"

Amid the conversations on cultural verisimilitude and potential erasure of identity, a 2003 Broadway production of *Cat* opened with screen beauty Ashley Judd as Maggie, Jason Patric as Brick and Ned Beatty as Big Daddy under the direction of Anthony Page—even though Byrd had secured the Broadway rights nine years earlier to do his African-American production from Williams's executor Maria St. Just. The 2003 production elicited a critical yawn due to Judd's and Patric's subdued performances. Beatty's Big Daddy, however, provided fireworks onstage and off: The veteran actor told a *New York Times* reporter that his co-stars lacked proper stage technique. Beatty's comments became the big story, which said more about the production than his intemperate remarks. By the time producer Byrd finally saw his dream realized in the season under review, he had contracted with Debbie Allen to direct and stocked his cast with Anika Noni Rose as Maggie, film star Terrence Howard as Brick, Jones as Big Daddy and Phylicia Rashad—the director's Tony Award-winning sister—as Big Mama.

Despite the Broadway-star wattage, when the production opened March 6 (100 performances as of May 31) critics faulted Allen's quirky direction for undermining the work's potential power. Joe Dziemianowicz of the *Daily News* called the production "uneven," though he said about Jones that his was "such a thundering and throbbing performance as dying Big Daddy that you feel it in your bones." Ben Brantley of the *New York Times* described the production as "flabby," noting that Rose's Maggie "pretty much runs the show whenever she's onstage, and when she's not, the show misses her management." The *Times*man also took Allen to task for allowing the production to acquire a "haze of sentimentality that makes it soft when it should be sharp." In *USA Today*, Elysa Gardner wrote that even though the production featured "an all-black cast, race is less of an issue than gender." To illustrate her point, Gardner used the pop-psychology paradigm of Venus and Mars in reviewing the performances: "it seems to take place on two different planets," she wrote. "Let's call them Venus and Mars. On Venus, we have a trio of hysterical females" (Rose, Rashad and Lisa Arrindell Anderson as Gooper's wife, Mae). On "Mars," Gardner found the counterweight of Jones whose performance was "richly nuanced and delightfully, hauntingly real." Most of the critics, including *Variety*'s David Rooney, found that Allen's "inexperience as a director shows in pedestrian physical staging with a tendency toward heavy-handedness." Hilton Als of the *New Yorker*, harking back to Gardner's comments about gender, called Allen's work "eager-to-please," though he found the women were "either caricatures or shrill harridans." Allen's direction made more than a few audience members wonder what the superb cast might have achieved with a firmer hand at the helm. Nevertheless, the production did excellent business except for a slight dip during three of the six weeks Howard was away due to a film commitment. It also attracted a large—generally elusive for Broadway producers—African-American audience.

Many audience members were shocked by earthy language in *Cat* and some wondered if it had been added or improvised, but the peppering of four-letter words issuing from Big Daddy were the work of the author from a 1974 revision. Had Williams rewritten his work to update it? By most accounts, he was returning to language that had been excised in preparation for the 1955 Broadway premiere. The production of *Cat* this season—a certifiable financial hit, even if the critics did not lavish praise—relied on the 1974 script with "some minor, estate-approved revisions to lines that wouldn't make sense for a family of black Mississippians," according to Campbell Robertson in the *New York Times*. Robertson suggested that it was jarring to hear the iconic voice of Darth Vader and CNN filling the air with words polite company often finds profane. But, as Jones mischievously said to Leslie Bennetts in *Vanity Fair*, "you couldn't say the word 'fuck' onstage"—when the play premiered in 1955—"I love saying the word 'fuck' onstage." And so he did, with gusto.

Blurring Lines

FOR A TIME near the end of this season, one could stand in the middle of 44th Street at Sixth Avenue or Eighth Avenue, look toward Times Square and see marquees lining the way that advertised three productions featuring superlative performances by African-American actors. This happened, of course, at the same time as an African-American senator was in pursuit of the US presidency. When these productions were running, however, it was unclear what kind of history Americans were about to make: we would elect either the first African American, the first woman or the oldest man to assume the job. In addition to Jones in *Cat* at the Broadhurst Theatre, Laurence Fishburne brought gravitas to the stage of the Booth as Thurgood Marshall in *Thurgood* (April 30; 37 performances as of May 31) and Stew electrified the Belasco in *Passing Strange* (February 28; 108 performances as of May 31).

Fishburne's one-man show—in which Marshall describes his participation in numerous hallmarks of the civil rights movement—was originally presented at the Westport Country Playhouse in 2006 with Jones in the role. After a later presentation in Washington, DC, author George Stevens Jr. was quoted in the *Washington Times* as saying that Jones was his "first and second choice" to do the piece on Broadway but he mentioned that "Morgan Freeman and Laurence Fishburne also would do nicely in the role." With Jones and Freeman otherwise engaged on Broadway, Fishburne, a 1992 Tony Award-winner for *Two Trains Running*, was certainly up to the task. Of the three men Stevens considered for *Thurgood*, Fishburne was the one whose work received a Tony nomination this season. Stew, book writer, lyricist, co-composer and star of *Passing Strange*, received four Tony nominations for his work on the breakthrough musical—a 2006–07 Best Play—receiving one Tony for his book. A critical darling for its narrative and musical innovation, *Passing Strange* received seven Tony nominations in total, but only Stew's book snared the award. The musical, a semi-autobiographical journey through a young African-American musician's life, earned top honors for excellence from both the New York Drama Critics' Circle and the New York Drama Desk.

Elsewhere on Broadway, the so-called "color line" was blurred in productions of two classic American plays. In each case, an African-American actor was cast in a starring role with a white actor as spouse. William Inge's *Come Back, Little Sheba*—a 1949–50 Best Play—featured S. Epatha Merkerson, a stage veteran best known for her work on television's *Law and Order* series, as the disconsolate Lola (January 24; 58 performances). Locked in a marriage of necessity to Doc (Kevin Anderson), a disappointed chiropractor and alcoholic trying desperately to stay sober, the pair married young because she was pregnant, causing Doc to forgo his dream of medical school and upper middle class respectability. At the heart of the play is a class conflict between Lola, a faded beauty who likes "peppy music" and has romantic fantasies about lost opportunity, and Doc, whose savage breast is soothed by Schubert's "Ave Maria" and who insists his wife avoid speaking in vulgarities.

Robert Brustein argued persuasively in a 1958 *Harper's* article that a "castration motif" plays out in a dream of Lola's and that she "reverts to her wifely role" through Doc's "declaration of dependence on her." Analysis of symbolic javelins and the appearance (and displacement) of well-muscled young men, however, are somewhat beside the point in *Sheba*. Here were two characters "forced" into marriage around the time of the Great Depression, when marriage and divorce rates both declined. These lives were irrevocably altered by a surprise pregnancy, which was lost under murky circumstances. A medical procedure by a woman who did not know "her business" rendered Lola permanently infertile. Far from "taming" her drunken husband of middle age and few prospects, Lola is locked in a marital cycle of hope and disappointment similar to millions of other couples in midlife.

When this "new perspective" production—as it was referred to in the Broadway playbill—was announced by Los Angeles's Center Theatre Group for its summer 2007 run, director Michael Pressman told *Variety* that he believed his production to be the "first time in which a white man and

OFF BROADWAY SEASON 2007–2008

Productions in a continuing run on May 31, 2008 in bold
Productions honored as Best Plays selections in italics
Best Plays from prior seasons are noted with a volume date in italics

NEW PLAYS (30)
Crazy Mary (Playwrights Horizons)
Intimate Exchanges
   (Brits Off Broadway)
eurydice (Second Stage Theatre)
Elvis People
The Black Eyed
   (New York Theatre Workshop)
100 Saints You Should Know
   (Playwrights)
The Rise of Dorothy Hale
A Feminine Ending (Playwrights)
A View From 151st Street
   (Labyrinth Theater Company)
Die Mommie Die!
The Overwhelming
   (Roundabout Theatre Company)
The Receptionist
   (Manhattan Theatre Club)
The Brothers Size (Public Theater)
Peter and Jerry (Second Stage)
   Special Citation
Pumpgirl (Manhattan)
Yellow Face
   (Public/Center Theatre Group)
Doris to Darlene, a Cautionary
   Valentine (Playwrights)
Unconditional (Labyrinth)
Dead Man's Cell Phone (Playwrights)
Beebo Brinker Chronicles
Secrets of a Soccer Mom
Conversations in Tusculum (Public)
Drunk Enough to Say I Love You?
   (Public)
The Four of Us (Manhattan)
The Drunken City (Playwrights)
The Little Flower of East Orange
   (Public/Labyrinth)
The New Century
   (Lincoln Center Theater)
From Up Here (Manhattan)

NEW PLAYS *(cont'd)*
Damascus (Brits/Traverse Theatre)
Good Boys and True
   (Second Stage)

PLAY REVIVALS (12)
Romeo and Juliet (Public)
A Midsummer Night's Dream
   (Public)
King Lear (BAM/RSC)
The Seagull (BAM/RSC)
The Misanthrope (NYTW)
Electra (National Theatre of Greece)
Beckett Shorts (NYTW)
Happy Days (BAM/National)
Macbeth (BAM/Chichester Festival)
Crimes of the Heart (Roundabout)
Sizwe Banzi Is Dead
   (BAM/Baxter Theatre)
Endgame (BAM)

NEW MUSICALS (8)
Walmartopia
Celia: The Life and Music of
   Celia Cruz
Greetings From Yorkville
Frankenstein
The Glorious Ones
   (Lincoln Center Theater)
Jerry Springer: The Opera
Next to Normal (Second Stage)
Adding Machine

MUSICAL REVIVALS (5)
Black Nativity
   (Classical Theatre of Harlem)
Princess Ida (G&S Players)
The Pirates of Penzance
   (G&S Players)
Trial by Jury (G&S Players)
The Mikado (G&S Players)

SOLO (10)
Beyond Glory (Roundabout)
Tom Crean: Antarctic Explorer
  (Irish Repertory Theatre)
The All-American Sport of
  Bipartisan Bashing
Runt of the Litter
Straight Up With a Twist
Fabulous Divas of Broadway
Liberty City (NYTW)
Tim Minchin
Jackie Mason: The Ultimate Jew
John Lithgow: Stories by Heart
  (Lincoln)

REVUES (3)
Three Mo' Tenors
Forbidden Broadway:
  Rude Awakening

REVUES *(cont'd)*
Make Me a Song: The Music of
  William Finn

SPECIALTIES (10)
Horizon (NYTW)
Gypsy (Encores!)
Hair: The American Tribal
  Love-Rock Musical (Public)
Jump
Fuerzabruta
G and S a la Carte (G&S Players)
Applause 69–70 (Encores!)
Juno (Encores!)
Camelot (New York Philharmonic)
No, No, Nanette (Encores!)

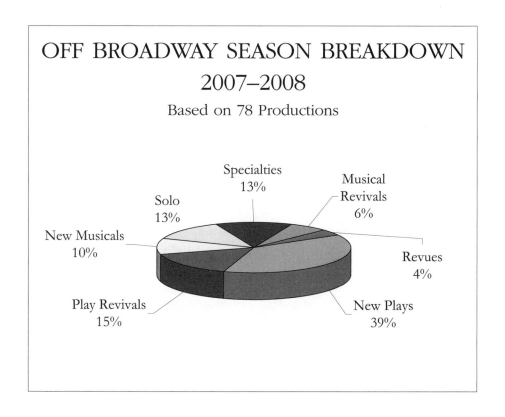

OFF BROADWAY SEASON BREAKDOWN
2007–2008
Based on 78 Productions

Specialties 13%
Musical Revivals 6%
Solo 13%
New Musicals 10%
Revues 4%
Play Revivals 15%
New Plays 39%

black woman have been cast in the lead roles"—Merkerson also played Lola in LA (Bruce Davison was originally cast as Doc but was replaced by Alan Rosenberg "due to a scheduling conflict"). But Pressman also said that the interracial "casting doesn't change the play; in fact, it makes it more universal, more timely." In the *New Yorker*, Hilton Als wrote that Pressman's casting of Merkerson was a "wonderful bit of colorblind casting"—a term that Merkerson herself disclaimed in the *New York Times* as insinuating "I'm not there." As Joe Dziemianowicz wrote in the *Daily News*, however, "the fact that Merkerson is black and Anderson is white adds dimension to this Manhattan Theatre Club presentation and suggests why Doc and Lola are so isolated." The *Times*'s Ben Brantley agreed,

> that Ms. Merkerson is an African American in a predominantly white cast only underscores the sense of Lola's enforced passivity. For a white man to marry a black woman in the Midwest of the 1950s would truly have squelched any chances for conventional success. And every time Doc looks at Lola, you can feel him assessing everything he's given up.

After *Sheba* opened at the Biltmore Theatre, Robert Simonson wrote in the *Times* that Pressman came to a realization after Merkerson had been cast. "We came around to the idea that Doc should be Caucasian," Pressman said. "When I finally realized that, the casting had the strongest resonance for me. It became an interracial couple, and it was not colorblind casting." Jackson R. Bryer, a professor emeritus of English at the University of Maryland who leads a scholarly program at the William Inge Theatre Festival in Kansas, told Simonson:

> I think when you set the play in the Deep South [as in *Cat*] or Midwest [in *Sheba*] in the 1950s, you give the audience a certain set of assumptions. . . . To suggest that an interracial couple in a small town in the Midwest in the 1950s would have ever gotten married is to stretch credibility.

Bryer added, however, "I'm more troubled by Michael Pressman saying Lola's black [in *Sheba*] than I am by Debbie Allen saying I'm supposed to forget race [in *Cat*]."

In a fascinating turn, director Mike Nichols and company chose to reverse the interracial casting in *The Country Girl* (April 27; 40 performances as of May 31). For this revival of Clifford Odets's 1950–51 Best Play, Morgan Freeman was cast as the alcoholic old actor opposite Frances McDormand, as his ambivalent wife, the "country girl" of the title. With three Academy Award-winners—Nichols, Freeman and McDormand—leading the

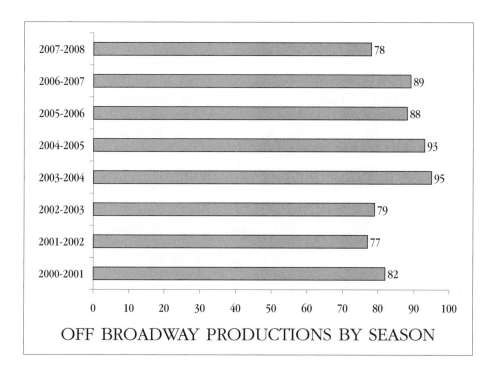

Season	Productions
2007-2008	78
2006-2007	89
2005-2006	88
2004-2005	93
2003-2004	95
2002-2003	79
2001-2002	77
2000-2001	82

OFF BROADWAY PRODUCTIONS BY SEASON

production, industry observers expected a startling new take on the backstage story of addiction and psychopathology. As the last of three 1950s plays this season to toy with cultural notions surrounding race—which never could have been attempted or addressed in the originals—*Country Girl* saw these potential flashpoints fade completely into the background due to a shaky production that had audiences unnerved for the wrong reasons.

Early reports from the production—insider gossip—reported in the *New York Post* by Michael Riedel told of a star (Freeman) who could not keep his lines straight. The cruel irony, of course, was that Freeman was playing a drunken pathological liar who has a bad case of nerves and cannot remember his lines. The situation created a metadrama that kept some theatergoers wondering who was the lost soul onstage: The character or the actor? Riedel also criticized the production's "script doctor," Jon Robin Baitz, for cutting too much from the play. In Baitz's defense, all of this controversy occurred when the show was still in previews and different things were being tried; many of the cuts were restored by opening. (Baitz once said, "People who attend first previews are sadists.")

In *USA Today*, Elysa Gardner wrote that Freeman's Frank Elgin was "intriguing" but not "fully realized," giving "little more than a glimpse of the bitter demons haunting this man." It was McDormand, however, who most undermined the production, according to Gardner. She "manages little chemistry with either of her co-stars," Gardner continued, "her cold, hard presence makes it difficult to fathom why Frank" is so dependent on her. The *Daily News*'s Dziemianowicz agreed that Freeman was not "fully convincing" and McDormand's performance was "flat" and lacked "spontaneity." Brantley, in the *Times*, took pains to note that Freeman's reported rocky relationship with the text "was undetectable in the performance I saw," but he also bemoaned the actors' inability to "make you care, for a single second" about what is at stake in the drama. *Variety*'s David Rooney saw the production (and performances) differently, noting a "thoughtfulness evident in [McDormand's] performance that lends increasing poignancy to her [character's] sacrifice." He also extolled Freeman's work as "bracing" and praised it for swinging "like a pendulum between authority and pathetic frailty in a magnetic turn." At a Wednesday matinee more than two weeks after opening, there appeared to be a performative disconnect among the three leading characters—Peter Gallagher infused much-needed energy into the proceedings as the theater director who would rescue Frank's career. It was as if there were three distinct acting styles in play—which kept audience members holding their breath and hoping for the best.

Race Matters

BEYOND THE FIVE productions, examined above, which featured African-American artists in starring roles, another seven productions also featured artists of color in significant or leading roles—all of which are addressed, in brief, below. In Mark Lamos's typically sharp revival of William Shakespeare's sprawling *Cymbeline* at Lincoln Center Theater (December 2; 40 performances), Phylicia Rashad exercised her creative muscles as the scheming queen before her collaboration with sister Debbie Allen in *Cat*. Rashad played opposite theatrical treasure John Cullum in the title role. Martha Plimpton, Michael Cerveris, John Pankow and Jonathan Cake also continued to grow in the esteem of New York audiences. Earlier in the season, Rosie Perez brought her natural ebullience to the role of Googie Gomez in a revival of Terrence McNally's *The Ritz* at Roundabout Theatre Company's Studio 54 (October 11; 69 performances). Starring Kevin Chamberlin as hapless Gaetano Proclo, who tries to hide from gangster assassins in a gay bathhouse, the production's pre-AIDS sensibility kept the comedy's farcical elements from soaring. Chamberlin, Perez, Patrick Kerr and Brooks Ashmanskas, however, provided more than a few good laughs.

Unlike the 1983 revival at Xenon (formerly Henry Miller's Theatre), which lasted but one performance, the Joe Mantello production managed an average attendance of a little more than 75 percent for the run. (That 1983 production featured Holly Woodlawn—said to be the inspiration for the first lines of Lou Reed's "Walk on the Wild Side"—as Googie).

Elsewhere on Broadway, Daniel Sunjata played handsome-but-shallow Christian opposite Kevin Kline in the title role of *Cyrano de Bergerac* (November 1; 56 performances). Binding these characters in the classic love triangle was television and film star Jennifer Garner as the much-desired Roxane. As Peter Marks wrote in the *Washington Post*, "You walk in a skeptic. You come out a believer." Garner, he continued, was a "poised, vivacious and plucky Roxane—just the sort of woman to whom a lovesick poet might scribble quatrains." John Lahr concurred in the *New Yorker* that Garner was "every inch an object of desire" whose "charismatic looks exist as an ironic contrast to the misfortune of Cyrano's." Lahr also pronounced Kline "sensational" for his facility with Edmond Rostand's poetry (as translated by Anthony Burgess), and for humor that is "more of the head than the belly." In an appraisal of Kline's work near the end of the run, the *Times*'s Charles Isherwood celebrated his Cyrano for the "quiet delicacy" that "graces it with a fine sense of psychological truth."

Dziemianowicz of the *Daily News* demurred, however, writing that the production was "emotionally stillborn," "listless" and "disappointing." *Variety*'s Rooney concurred with the *News*man noting that *Cyrano* failed "to massage the heart" due to director David Leveaux's imposition of a "modern, naturalistic feel on a play that should thrum with melodramatic grandness and hyperbole." Kline's subtle performance and the novelty of Garner's celebrity helped power the revival to nearly sellout status for the entire run. Sunjata, who received high marks as a gay baseball player in Richard Greenberg's *Take Me Out* (a 2002–03 Best Play), won only mixed notices for *Cyrano*. Playbill.com reported that the limited-run production "broke the record for highest-grossing performance of a play at the Richard Rodgers during its first week of previews" and that it kept powering through until it owned the record for highest gross for a performance of any play or musical at that theater. At $120 for the top ticket, it is also among the most expensive plays or musicals ever housed in that theater. Although the 19-performance stagehand's strike cut into revenues, a two-week extension at the end of the run aided the bottom line.

With the opening of *Cry-Baby* at the Marquis Theatre (April 24; 43 performance performances as of May 31), the twisted sensibility of John

Waters—inspired by a youth misspent in Baltimore—made a second appearance on Broadway in a musical version of one of his films. Unlike his earlier film-to-stage conversion, *Hairspray* (2,392 performances as of May 31), *Cry-Baby* did not encourage the critical hosannas of the earlier work. Elysa Gardner of *USA Today* called it a "comedy with music," as opposed to a musical comedy, noting that the show was "goodhearted" and "less snarky" than other irony-laced contemporary musicals. Where *Hairspray*—in the original film—is a celebration of changing times in race relations and the democratizing possibilities of popular music in the 1960s, *Cry-Baby* is a spoof of class-consciousness in the 1950s (and of smarmy teen-rebel movies). Ben Brantley at the *Times* told his readers that the musical was "tasteless," but not in the way expected by fans of Waters's "vulgar, trashy, tacky, freakish and seriously offensive" works. Leads Elizabeth Stanley and James Synder were found generally by the critics to be miscast or underequipped, as was Mark Brokaw's direction, which, as Brantley noted, lacked a "cohesive sensibility." *Variety*'s man on the scene, Rooney, wrote "most of the electricity onstage comes courtesy of Rob Ashford's raunchy choreography" and that Chester Gregory II as Dupree, the "coyote-voiced crooner who's Little Richard, Chubby Checker and Cab Calloway rolled into one dynamite package," was the "standout" in the show. Dziemianowicz at the *Daily News* agreed that Gregory (along with Carly Jibson) brought "big talent and oddball originality to the stage." (Gregory and Jibson had each served as replacements for leads in *Hairspray*.)

Jennifer Ikeda made her Broadway debut, except for an understudy stint in the 2005–06 revival of *Seascape*, in the Manhattan Theatre Club production of *Top Girls* by Caryl Churchill (May 7; 30 performances as of May 31). Although the play's US premiere was given Off Broadway at the Public Theater in 1982, the production this season was the first time the work appeared on Broadway. Critics were pleased with this final production of the Broadway season and felt the play was overdue to appear in such a venue. Rooney noted the "spiky brilliance" of the work and that it is still a "bracing challenge." One scene is a kind of fantasy sequence in which a group of women from different eras and cultures dine together, sharing stories of how they negotiate their lives. Rooney called it a "History channel version of *The View*," while the *Times*'s Brantley asserted that Churchill had "saved her best for first," with the drama declining in ways reminiscent of "old-fashioned weepies." *USA Today*'s Gardner, however, found continuing power in Churchill's evocation of "the enduring struggles faced by females who want it all, or at least their fair share."

Marlene (Elizabeth Marvel) is a woman promoted to run an employment agency who gathers the historical women for a meal to celebrate. As the play unfolds, however, Marlene's swagger as a powerful woman unravels when she encounters the needs of other modern women and she recognizes the hard road ahead for her female relatives. Marisa Tomei and Martha Plimpton portrayed women at the dinner, explorer Isabella Bird and "Pope Joan," as well as Marlene's sister and young daughter. As the scene shifts from the historical dinner to scenes from Marlene's present existence, the audience is confronted with how little has changed across time. Ikeda played Lady Nijo, a consort to the Japanese emperor who later became a Buddhist nun; she also appeared as a colleague of the hard-driving Marlene at the employment agency. It was the latest in a long string of notable efforts by Ikeda who has been building her work in New York productions of plays modern and classic since at least 2001.

Musical Interlude

THE BROADWAY SEASON also brought race to the fore in two musicals that combined to receive most honors in the musical categories at the Tony Awards. As mentioned above, the first Broadway revival of Rodgers and Hammerstein's *South Pacific* (April 3; 68 performances as of May 31) received seven Tonys—in the musical categories of revival, director, actor, scenery, costumes, lighting and sound design—while setting a record for musical revivals. At least one Tony voter said, privately, that she was not sure how to judge the new category of sound design, but the opening strains of *South Pacific*'s overture made a powerful case for its acoustic manipulation. After the houselights dimmed, with the stage bathed in an aquatic glow, the thrust stage of the Vivian Beaumont Theater receded silently from above the heads of the orchestra as Robert Russell Bennett's lush 1949 orchestrations made its audience's heads swim. After the thrust was restored so the action could begin, however, the music continued to pour forth in harmonious balance. Director Bartlett Sher and his designers demonstrated once again why they are at the top of their creative game in manufacturing theatrical magic. For some audience members, however, the overture provided a too-tempting invitation to hum or sing along with the music, as if at karaoke night in a local bar. (Coincidentally, the film version received its sole Academy Award for sound design in 1958, perhaps in part because so many of the leads had their voices dubbed.)

As the first Broadway production since the original—there was a 15-performance revival by the New York City Center Light Opera Company in 1955, a little more than a year after the original ended its nearly five-year run of 1,925 performances—Sher's production was the first top-flight version available in more than 50 years. While the score sticks in the mind for its pleasing music and lyrics, the story comes as something of a jolt to those who recall only the film's gauzy—and lengthy—romanticism. Nellie Forbush's distaste when she realizes that Emile de Becque is the father of mixed-race children may have a more powerful impact today than in the 1949 original, with 2008 audiences likely to be less sympathetic to her initial racist shock, which she eventually overcomes. It is, however, Lt. Cable's instant love affair with the childlike Liat that may give current audiences the greatest discomfort.

When the production prepared in Boston for its 1949 Broadway opening, critic Elliot Norton attempted to get the creative team to downplay Cable's Act II condemnation of racial bigotry in "You've Got to Be Carefully Taught," about which Norton later said he was wrong. (See pages viii and ix in the Introduction to this volume for more on the story.) For sentient beings in today's audience, however, the stridence of that song is not at issue. It is the fact that Liat's own mother, Bloody Mary, treats her very young daughter as a virtual commodity, pushing her into the arms of the handsome Cable. For anyone paying attention to the news since the Vietnam War, the scenes between Cable, Liat and Mary are redolent of child prostitution or, at the very least, sexual tourism.

Cable, of course, dies on a crucial reconnaissance mission, which the production makes clear will lead to American victory. Nellie's Emile returns from that same mission to find her caring for his mixed-race children and they proceed to live happily ever after. The daring of *South Pacific*'s racial thematics was truly pathbreaking, especially when one considers that, a little more than eight years after the production's opening, Nellie's "hometown" of Little Rock would be the focal point for Federal troops protecting nine African-American students who integrated Central High School. For all of the musical's artistic risk, however, it is worth noting that there is no happy ending for interracial couples at the end of the musical. Emile and Nellie's is a Franco-American alliance, the once-virginal Liat is left to mourn her lost love alone. (While much of the historical detail of Sher's production is scrupulous, the proximity of servicemen of color to white servicemen and women would have been unlikely in those years before the Truman desegregation of 1948.) That Sher and company negotiate the rocky shoals of these cultural waters, presenting Oscar Hammerstein II and Joshua Logan's at times unnerving book, and Richard Rodgers's voluptuous music to such grand effect, marks a crossgenerational synergy of talent that is unusual in Broadway theater.

When *In the Heights* opened Off Broadway at 37 Arts during the 2006–07 season (February 8, 2007; 181 performances), the dream of a Broadway stand was a wakeful fantasy. Charles Isherwood of the *Times* noted that the show suggested "an uptown *Rent*, plus some salsa fresca and without the sex, drugs and disease." *Variety*'s Rooney saw "a dynamic new talent in Lin-Manuel Miranda," who was a triple-threat as composer, lyricist and star. Dziemianowicz agreed that Miranda was "an exciting young talent whose Latin melodies make you wriggle in your seat," though the *Daily News* critic felt that "too many lyrics are heavy-handed exposition, delivering information instead of firing emotions." The company was buoyed by the generally warm comments, and observers believed that producers Kevin McCollum, Jeffrey Seller and Jill Furman were considering a move to Broadway. (The production cost a reported $2.5 million to get to the first performance, a very large expenditure for Off Broadway.) A month after the show opened, however, Seller told Gordon Cox of *Variety*, "A show like this can break even at about $115,000 a week, and you can gross, realistically, $250,000" Off Broadway. By late May 2007, the producers announced a July 15 closing at 37 Arts so that the creative team could revise the work in preparation for a Broadway run.

Just as spring was about to arrive this season, *In the Heights* opened at the Richard Rodgers Theatre (March 9; 94 performances as of May 31), where it rode a crest of good feelings to four Tony Awards—new musical, score, orchestrations and choreography. The tale of an uptown Latino bodega owner who sees the lives of his Latino (and Latina) neighbors change as gentrification comes to Washington Heights—sung and danced to the musical rhythms of salsa, merengue, hiphop and jazz—created, as Isherwood wrote of the Broadway production, "a vivid but somewhat airbrushed mural of urban life." Gardner of *USA Today* thought it was "not a great musical," but added, "it's about as impossible to dislike as an adorable puppy." Rooney of *Variety*, took note in his Broadway review of complaints about the Off Broadway version:

> The chief criticism leveled at the show in its previous incarnation was Quiara Alegría Hudes's sentimental book, which takes a sanitized view of a close-knit group of folks in Washington Heights, their struggle to scrape by, to trade up or to find love unmarred by the usual barrio staples of drugs, crime, violence, despair or real poverty. But that idealized perspective can be as endearing as it is limiting. It's a musical, after all, not a ghetto angstfest.

Tony Award voters, who gave top honors to a Teutonic "angstfest" in the previous season (*Spring Awakening*), apparently agreed.

New Plays on Broadway

THE FIRST NEW play of this season on Broadway, Theresa Rebeck's *Mauritius* at Manhattan Theatre Club's Biltmore Theatre, did not open until the fall was well underway (October 4; 61 performances). In this latest product from the prolific mind of the talented Rebeck, an intrafamily war erupts over objects inherited—one of which is an extremely valuable stamp from the titular country. The stellar cast of F. Murray Abraham, Dylan Baker, Bobby Cannavale, Katie Finneran and Alison Pill kept the tension rising under Doug Hughes's steady directorial hand. Unfortunately for Rebeck, however, David Mamet apparently controls dramatic license to all stories regarding people trying to make shady deals while grabbing for the proverbial brass ring. Ben Brantley, David Rooney and John Lahr all referenced *American Buffalo* in their reviews with comments such as: "Rebeck has added estrogen to a testosterone base" (Brantley, *Times*), "underlining the echoes of David Mamet" (Rooney, *Variety*) and "David Mamet for girls" (Lahr, *New Yorker*). In truth, *Mauritius* did bring to mind Mamet's iconic early work in some ways. In focusing on the play as a gender breakthrough into Mametian territory, as did some writers, the dramatic value of Rebeck's narrative and her artful, three-dimensional characters were undermined.

The next four new plays to open on Broadway—*Rock 'n' Roll* (November 4; 123 performances), *The Farnsworth Invention* (December 3; 104 performances), *August: Osage County* (December 4; 199 performances as of May 31) and *The Seafarer* (December 6; 133 performances)—were chosen as Best Plays. As such, they have been addressed in the Introduction to this volume and in essays that follow this section. Tom Stoppard's play had a tough slog, given that it opened just days before the stagehands' strike ground most of Broadway to a halt—nonprofit Broadway entities, Disney and other independent producers were not struck, which accounted for eight shows continuing—and may have kept *Rock 'n' Roll* from finding an audience. Given Stoppard's intense intellectual and polemical proclivities, it is notable that one living legend of the musical theater was overheard saying to a friend, Stoppard's "assuming an awful lot on the part of this audience; it's awfully dense."

It is difficult to measure fully the impact of the stagehands' strike, which stopped previews of *Farnsworth*, *August* and *Seafarer*. Of those three, only *August*, the Pulitzer Prize and Tony Award-winner, would continue to run at season's end—although another new play, David Mamet's joke-a-minute political comedy, *November* (January 17; 156 performances as of May 31), also ran into the next season. When Broadway business essentially stops dead, as it did during the strike, playgoing—as distinct from musicals—drops from the radar and audiences are distracted by other entertainments. *Farnsworth* also had to deal with a controversy over author Aaron Sorkin's refusal to hew slavishly to Philo T. Farnsworth's biography in a play that was more concerned with the destabilized nature of narrative—historical and anecdotal—than with lionizing the inventor. Despite the negative stories, Sorkin's play made for a crackling, clever evening (or afternoon) at the theater. But the highpoint for *Farnsworth*'s business was the week before the strike (70 percent), and the show barely broke 60 percent capacity in two other weeks during its run. *August* ran well into the next season and beyond, extremely unusual for a nonmusical play. Even with the Pulitzer in tow after April 7, however, the play could not crack 90 percent of capacity this season. Put into perspective, three weeks after *August* received the Pulitzer, musicals such as *Wicked, The Phantom of the Opera, The Lion King, South Pacific* and *Jersey Boys* all operated at more than 98 percent of capacity, with the newly minted Pulitzer honoree at just under 76 percent. Musicals long have been much bigger draws than nonmusical plays, which partly accounts for *August*'s move from the Imperial Theatre (more than 1,400 seats) to the smaller Music Box (more than 1,000) two weeks after the Pulitzer announcement. *Seafarer*'s extraordinary ensemble cast—much beloved by the critics—faced houses that did not get to 80 percent of capacity until the final week at the end of March.

A resurrection of Mark Twain's *Is He Dead?* was performed by scholar Shelley Fisher Fishkin after she discovered a manuscript among Twain's papers at the University of California, Berkeley (December 9; 105 performances). Adapted by David Ives, the play is a spoof of the starving-artist cliché—set in mid-19th century Paris—in which an artist fakes his own death to increase the value of his works. Norbert Leo Butz's manic comic energy drove the action of Michael Blakemore's production, which Dziemianowicz of the *Daily News* wrote, "turned an old-fashioned, sometimes wobbly piece of material into a delightfully silly and entertaining evening." In Butz's hands, the *Times*'s Brantley noted, "Jokes you would swear you would never laugh at suddenly seem funny." The final new Broadway play of the season, *November* by David Mamet, opened as the presidential-election year was getting underway. Starring Nathan Lane as a double-dealing politician—is that term a redundancy?—Mamet's latest attempt at comedy was about four years behind the curve. By the beginning of 2008, the incumbent President, George W. Bush, had or was near historic lows in approval ratings and Americans were in fear for the longterm health of their country. Yet there audiences sat, in the Ethel Barrymore Theatre, laughing themselves silly at lines such as: "What is it about me that people don't like?" To which the President's counsel replied, "That you're still here." Most of the pleasure, sitcom antics aside, lay in the comic perfection that is Lane operating at full tilt with superb support from Dylan Baker and Laurie Metcalf.

Mamet stirred the political pot—and may have improved ticket sales a bit—with an essay for the *Village Voice* titled "Why I Am No Longer a 'Brain-Dead Liberal.'" In the article, the playwright noted that he now questioned his earlier "article of faith that government is corrupt, that business is exploitative, and that people are generally good at heart." He went on to detail the years he had referred to himself as a "brain-dead liberal" and thought of National Public Radio as "National Palestinian Radio" (apparently for a perceived anti-Israel stance). For more than a few persons who have experience reading plays and seeing productions, the first thought must have been, "Really?" The second: "Has he ever read (or seen) one of his plays?" Beyond the solid proof of Mamet's misanthropy in his plays (and some screenplays), which made for startlingly powerful drama in the first couple of decades of his writing career, the author's nonfiction tends to be simplistic. While liberals may have been *shocked* that a man made rich by Hollywood now finds corporations more benevolent, a close reading of his *Voice* essay shows that Mamet describes only his own ill-informed experience, not the belief structure of everyone who espouses what might be termed liberal ideology. All who care for the future of the Republic (and its drama) should rejoice that Mamet's brain has now come to life—and ponder the theatrical possibilities.

Sounds of Musicals

THE SUMMER SEASON was barely underway when the first musical of the season, *Xanadu* (July 10; 375 performances as of May 31), rolled into the Helen Hayes Theatre. Based on the 1980 film starring Olivia Newton-John that became a minor camp classic, the new version sported a book by Douglas Carter Beane, the gifted wit who wrote *Why Bees in Honey Drown* and *The Little Dog Laughed*. Dripping with irony and replete with theater in-jokes, the silly retread compared favorably to its forerunner with a delightful performance by Kerry Butler in the Newton-John role, Cheyenne

Jackson as an airheaded boy inspired to create a roller disco in Southern California, Tony Roberts as a businessman who rediscovers his inner artist, and Mary Testa and Jackie Hoffman as a pair of over-the-top "goddesses." As the summer turned to fall, Tony Award voters received an invitation from Beane, sent by the Sprecher Organization, to attend the production. In his tongue-in-cheek letter, Beane stated that the "high point" of his theatrical career was receiving a Tony Award nomination for the previous season's *Little Dog Laughed* and wondered if he might have named his daughter "Antoinette"—as in Antoinette Perry, whose memory the awards honor—had he won. "Who can say?," he continued, "But I have noticed that last year's Tony winner, Tom Stoppard, has four sons and none of them are named Tony." Alas, for Beane—but fortunately, perhaps, for his daughter—he was again nominated (for book of a musical), and again did not win. The *Xanadu* producers employed a similarly jokey tone in a series of online videos—released as a DVD to benefit Broadway Cares/Equity Fights AIDS before this volume went to press—as part of a "campaign" to win Tony Awards. The group created a character named Cubby Bernstein (child actor Adam Reigler) who is converted to the *Xanadu* cause and does all he can to help the production win the coveted trophy—but "Cubby" struck out. (The producers of *Cry-Baby* also tried an amusing letter before the ballot deadline that alluded to a "stealth marketing campaign." Similarly clever, it was likewise unsuccessful.)

Young Frankenstein lumbered into the huge theatrical cavern known as the Hilton Theatre (November 8; 236 performances as of May 31), where it received much less positive notices than its earlier Broadway sibling, *The Producers*. Mel Brooks's latest film-to-stage adaptation lacked the verve of the earlier conversion. Although the musical was not without its charms, a number of missteps by the producing team of Brooks and Robert F.X. Sillerman—which included a fiasco regarding so-called "premium tickets"—led to bad feelings in an increasingly bad economy. Disney's transfer of *The Little Mermaid* to the Broadway stage, led by opera director Francesca Zambello, met with a similar lack of enthusiasm when it moved into the Lunt-Fontanne Theatre (January 10; 164 performances as of May 31). As Peter Marks wrote in the *Washington Post* of *Little Mermaid*, all of the "warmth and charm of the film manages to get away." Marks, in fact, could have been writing about Brooks's *Young Frankenstein* as well.

Passing Strange and *In the Heights*, both discussed above, were next among the new musicals on the Main Stem. Trailing in their wake was *A Catered Affair* at the Walter Kerr Theatre (April 17; 51 performances as of

May 31). Yet another work based on a narrative from other media—film and television—*Catered Affair* is a poignant musical drama in 90 intermissionless minutes with a book by theatrical polymath Harvey Fierstein (who also starred as a closeted gay uncle in the 1950s tale). Faith Prince and Tom Wopat played working-class New Yorkers whose lives of quiet desperation become more noisy when their daughter (Leslie Kritzer) says she is about to marry and move to California. A dark tale of the permanent underclass in America, the production had a difficult road ahead when more breezy shows were filling houses.

The conversion of John Waters's *Cry-Baby* from film to stage, mentioned in a section above, followed *A Catered Affair* as the next new Broadway musical. The last new musical to open on Broadway was not—as have been these last few—a film turned to other purposes. *Glory Days*, however, which opened at Circle in the Square and closed the same night (May 6; 1 performance), seemed an ill-starred attempt to exploit a perceived "youth movement" on Broadway. With a book by James Gardiner and music and lyrics by Nick Blaemire, the show was a celebration of reminiscence by a group of four young men not long out of high school. A last-minute entry to the Broadway season, *Glory Days*'s producer Ricky Stevens told *Variety*'s Mark Blankenship, "We looked at it as a regional vehicle, as a touring vehicle, and an Off Broadway vehicle, and we couldn't make any of the business models work. . . . But once I did the business model for Broadway, we said, 'It could work here.'" Stevens's producing partner, John O'Boyle, added, "It's not just a question of being on Broadway. It's a question of being in the right space." When producers spend too much time on business models, such elements as quality control sometimes get overlooked. Peter Marks of the *Washington Post*, reviewed the production at the Signature Theatre in Arlington, Virginia, and gave it an encouraging review with caveats about inadequacies in its storytelling and emotional transitions. When Marks revisited the production in New York he was as disappointed as other critics: "It's unfortunate that an interim development phase has been skipped, because as an entrant in Broadway's intense seasonal bake-off, the *Glory Days* that opened last night at Circle in the Square feels a bit undercooked." Dziemianowicz of the *Daily News* called it "clichéd" and *Times*man Brantley complained that the producers had "done this little, hopeful show no favors by dragging it into a spotlight that invites close and unforgiving inspection." As a season-ending gesture among new musicals, the *Glory Days* title could not have been more ironic.

Museum of Broadway Art?

THE TRIP TO the theatrical museum known as the Broadway revival met with typically mixed results this season. On occasion these productions can recall for us a moment in time that has passed and tell us something about ourselves in the present. More often revivals are treated as possible ATMs that producers hope will fill their pockets with cash and their arms with Tony Awards. A glance down the list of play revivals (see page 4) reveals casts led by stars of screens large and small with a few stage stars added for good measure. In fairness, though, it is worth noting that most of the play revivals were produced by nonprofit theater companies, while a little less than half of musical revivals were so funded. Roundabout Theatre Company brought Margaret Colin and Harriet Harris together for Michael Wilson's production of *Old Acquaintance* at its American Airlines Theatre (June 28; 61 performances). Although it is difficult to discern the significance of John Van Druten's 1940 tale of mature, fiction-writing career gals to a 2007 audience, there was guilty pleasure to be had in watching Colin and Harris's characters continue competition that began when they were girls. Less than two months passed before the next revival, *Grease*, returned to Broadway after an absence of less than 10 years (August 19; 306 performances as of May 31). This production was driven by a reality television program that sought stars for the latest Broadway revival. Even the presence of the terrific director-choreographer Kathleen Marshall at the helm of this 1971 trip into 1950s nostalgia could not energize the critics. Brantley wrote, "no one in the young cast of this revival . . . is flat-out terrible." *Variety*'s Rooney found it "low-wattage" and "unprepossessingly innocuous." And yet, it ran well into the following season.

Roundabout opened two revivals in October, *The Ritz* at Studio 54 (see above) and George Bernard Shaw's *Pygmalion* at the American Airlines Theatre (October 18; 69 performances). Shaw's play featured film and television star Claire Danes as Eliza Doolittle with Jefferson Mays as her sometime tormentor, Henry Higgins. According to the *Daily News*'s Dziemianowicz, the production was "always compelling and often delicious." Brantley of the *Times* thought the "stiffness" of the production focused a "glaring light on the weaknesses" of Shaw's play. Mays's prissy portrayal of Higgins was called "daring" by Dziemianowicz, but Brantley highlighted a possible homosexual subtext before dismissing the characterization as "presexual." Danes's Broadway debut was nearly drowned in her opening scene by a rainstorm special-effect that made dialogue difficult to hear. Although *Variety*'s Rooney found the production "serviceably mounted and handsomely costumed," Mays's Higgins was to him a "grating central characterization."

Chazz Palminteri's *A Bronx Tale* fits more properly into the solo-performance rubric, but it too was a revival (October 25; 111 performances). Starting Off Off Broadway at Playhouse 91 in 1989, the piece was later made into a 1993 feature film starring the author and directed by Robert De Niro. It was a work that launched a successful Hollywood career for Palminteri, and may have been a boost to the star fantasies of many a solo theater performer of the past two decades. An autobiographical tale of Palminteri's youth among wise guys and average citizens in the Bronx, the *Times*'s Isherwood called it a "rejuvenating act of faith in the complementary powers of acting and storytelling." Not everyone found the narrative so compelling: Rooney was less enthusiastic in *Variety* and called it "mildly entertaining and impressively acted" work that "never quite takes the leap from nostalgia to evocative narrative."

The first production to experience the stagehands' strike was the holiday-season revival of *Dr. Seuss's How the Grinch Stole Christmas!* (November 9; 96 performances). Although it played beautifully for the media that such a grinch-like thing could happen, it was a scheduling coincidence because *Grinch* was struck first due to an early performance on the first day of the strike. By later that day the strike against members of the League of American Theatres and Producers—which changed its name to the Broadway League a month later—was in full bloom and Theater District sidewalks were clogged with unhappy families. *Grinch* producers went to court for relief: Theirs was an extremely seasonal show on a limited engagement. As Campbell Robertson reported in the *Times*, "from a public relations perspective . . . the timing [of the first struck show] was rather unfortunate for the union." Helen E. Freedman, a judge of the New York State Supreme Court in Manhattan, granted an injunction saying, "I think one Grinch in this town is enough" and that "the show must go on." *Grinch* opened about a week before the strike was ended by negotiations.

The final revival of 2007 was the second Broadway stand for Harold Pinter's *The Homecoming*, which played at the Cort Theatre (December 16; 137 performances). With a cast led by Ian McShane, Raúl Esparza, Michael McKean and Eve Best, director Daniel Sullivan's production crackled with the subterranean terror and biting humor that helped the playwright win the 2005 Nobel Prize in Literature. Roundabout Theatre Company opened its next revival at Studio 54 with the transfer from London of James Lapine and Stephen Sondheim's *Sunday in the Park With George* (February 21; 116

performances as of May 31). The Menier Chocolate Factory production, directed by Sam Buntrock, featured a cast of British and American actors that included Daniel Evans, Jenna Russell and Michael Cumpsty in a fine ensemble effort. Perhaps most noteworthy was the inventive use of projections to bring the artists' paintings to stunning life.

One of the best stories of the season belonged to the Arthur Laurents-directed production of *Gypsy* at the St. James Theatre (March 27; 75 performances as of May 31). Laurents, who turned 90 a few months after the opening, had been famously dissatisfied with a 2003 production directed by Sam Mendes with Bernadette Peters as Mama Rose. After staging a concert version in the summer of 2007 for New York City Center Encores!, with Patti LuPone as Rose—see the Plays Produced Off Broadway section for more information—Laurents brought the production to Broadway. One theatergoer, who had seen three of the previous four Broadway productions (including the original), said she felt that the chemistry between Rose, Louise and Herbie was so exciting that it was as if she had never seen the show before. Ultimately, the production relied on LuPone's disciplined approach to her role in ways that made her character "arc" seem as if it were one thrilling aria of acting—which, of course, culminated in the sung aria that is "Rose's Turn." When LuPone and co-stars Laura Benanti and Boyd Gaines all received Tony Awards for their repective performances, Laurents must have felt some vindication for his vision. It was surprising that Laurents was not even nominated for a directing award by the New York Drama Desk, and somewhat disappointing that he left the Tony Awards empty-handed.

Patrick Stewart came back to Broadway with an electrifying *Macbeth* at the Lyceum Theatre (April 8; 52 performances). The production first took wing at the Chichester Festival Theatre in 2007 before runs in London's West End and at the Brooklyn Academy of Music. Anthony Ward's austere kitchen set was enhanced by Lorna Heavey's Big Brother-ish (as in Orwell, not reality television) projections and Adam Cork's overpowering sound score. Director Rupert Goold wound the elements together in a tightly focused production of this (relatively) brief Shakespeare play, and spiced the mix by casting the extraordinary Kate Fleetwood as the Scottish usurper's much younger lady. Stewart and Fleetwood drove the play with a *frisson* of sexual undercurrent that seemed to raise the stakes throughout the performance.

The two final revivals of the season opened in the first days of May: *Les Liaisons Dangereuses* at the Roundabout's American Airlines Theatre (May 1; 36 performances as of May 31) and *Boeing-Boeing* in a commercial production at the Longacre Theatre (May 4; 32 performances as of May 31). Returning to Broadway after little more than 20 years, *Liaisons Dangereuses* featured Laura Linney as the sexually scheming Marquise de Merteuil with Ben Daniels as the libidinous Valmont in pre-Revolutionary France. As staged by Rufus Norris on Scott Pask's smoky mirrored set with plush curtains hinting at what might lie beyond, the production disappointed with its cool attitude and disjointed acting styles among Linney, Daniels, Mamie Gummer and Kristine Nielsen. Christopher Hampton's 1985 adaptation of the Laclos novel lasted only 149 performances in its 1987 Broadway debut, the revival seemed likely to fare much worse.

On the other hand, Marc Camoletti's more modern tale of love and sex in France, *Boeing-Boeing*, was a surprising jolt to the funny bone. The farce, which ran for nearly two decades in Paris and for nearly five years in London, managed to eke out only 23 performances in its 1965 New York premiere. Long held to be inaccessible to the American sense of humor, a 2007 London revival directed by Matthew Warchus transferred with only Mark Rylance from the original cast. The premise of a swinging bachelor who juggles three international flight attendants—"air hostesses" in the play's parlance—in his Paris pad seemed sure to meet resistance on politically correct Broadway, raising the hackles of every feminist in sight (including this one). In fact, however, director Warchus unearthed perfect comic rhythms from a cast that also included Bradley Whitford, Christine Baranski, Mary McCormack, Gina Gershon and Kathryn Hahn. Despite grumbling from some who detested the deployment of female objectification and international stereotypes, the production received Tony Awards for best revival and actor in a play. When accepting his award, Rylance recited "The Back Country" by prose poet Louis Jenkins instead of the usual litany of thanks to agents, parents and co-workers. It was an inspired bit of lunacy, delivered in the same hilarious deadpan he employed in *Boeing-Boeing*.

Before reviewing trends in the Off Broadway theater of this season, it is important to take note of one final Broadway production that does not fit neatly into our other categories. Although *The 39 Steps* was nominated by the Tony Award committee for the best play honor, *Best Plays* has located the production in the specialties form. An amalgam of sound effects, quick changes (of costumes and characters) and inventive theatrical tricks, the Broadway production of *The 39 Steps* was more akin to variety acts in the old English music hall tradition than to a play. Its twisting path to Broadway and the various parents who gave it life are similarly mixed. Advertisements for the production show a pipe-smoking character clinging to the side of a moving train as a cocktail is offered through the window, which accurately depicts the whirlwind action of the piece. Above the image, however, appear the words *Alfred Hitchcock's The 39 Steps*, which also appears on a title-page image in the Roundabout Theatre Company's playbill (January 15; 115 performances as of May 31). Hitchcock, however, only directed the film version, which was based on the book by John Buchan. It was Simon Corble and Nobby Dimon who created the original theater version in 1996, which underwent several provincial tours in the UK before a textual overhaul by Patrick Barlow. The New York Drama Desk made the wise decision to honor the production as a unique theatrical experience, but perhaps the Tony nominators could not find another play to recommend. Whatever the case, the production transferred from the American Airlines Theatre to the Cort during the season.

Off Broadway: Ars Gratia Artis?

WITH THE RISING power of nonprofit entities on Broadway has come an increasing dominance of those companies Off Broadway. Although Off Broadway production for the 2007–08 season was down 12 percent overall, falling to a production total near the post-September 11 seasons of 2001–02 and 2002–03 (see chart on page 17), nonprofit companies accounted for a larger percentage of the total this season. In fact, commercial production Off Broadway has declined over the past three seasons from 48 percent of the total (2005–06) to 30 percent (2006–07) to 28 percent (2007–08). (Even though nonprofits accounted for a larger—and increasing—percentage of the total, both commercial and nonprofit production were down from the previous season.) New plays, a prime concern to this publication, were of heightened interest for the 2007–08 season due to a decline in the level of new-play production not seen since 2002–03 (see pages 14 and 15). Most of that drop was caused by reduced commercial production of new plays, which declined by nearly half this season.

Before we overemphasize the nonprofit companies as daring leaders of a New World Order in theater, it is worth mentioning that these public trusts also accounted for all of the revivals of plays and musicals Off Broadway—with many of the plays employing the time-tested technique of casting stars in key roles. Virtually all of the play revivals were classics of one sort or another. Four were plays by William Shakespeare (including the pre-Broadway *Macbeth* mentioned above), one Chekhov, one Molière, one Sophocles, three Becketts, plus *Crimes of the Heart* and *Sizwe Banzi Is Dead*. Musical revivals are so neglected Off Broadway that four of this season's five—a growing trend—were productions of the New York Gilbert and Sullivan Players, a company that also presented one of this season's specialty productions. (See the Plays Produced Off Broadway section for production details and history.) The fifth musical revival Off Broadway was a heavily adapted version of Langston Hughes's *Black Nativity*, produced by Classical Theatre of Harlem.

After nearly 40 years, *Romeo and Juliet* returned to the Delacorte Theater to begin the season's revivals in a production by the Public Theater (June 24; 12 performances). Featuring Lauren Ambrose as a Juliet "truly to die for," in the words of Brantley, the production earned generally positive notices for director Michael Greif. Martha Plimpton, Mireille Enos, Jay O. Sanders, George Morfogen, Keith David and Laila Robins followed in Central Park with *A Midsummer Night's Dream* (August 23; 16 performances). Daniel Sullivan once again worked his theatrical magic by providing "plenty to please the eye and tickle the fancy," as the *Times*'s Brantley wrote. (The Public also produced a three-performance concert version of the musical *Hair* at the Delacorte in September, but it was not available for review.)

Ian McKellen and the Royal Shakespeare Company were in residence at the Brooklyn Academy of Music's Harvey Theater for productions of *King Lear* (September 11; 14 performances) and *The Seagull* (September 12; 9 performances). McKellen took the role of the king who tragically destroys civil society through his reckless acts in *Lear* and alternated with William Gaunt as Sorin in *Seagull*. In typical BAM fashion, these Trevor Nunn-directed productions became must-see events for the cognoscenti—Brantley wrote that tickets were "pretty much unobtainable, at least by those who shun black markets and blackmail" (one ticket-reselling website had tickets available for upwards of $1,000). McKellen did not disappoint audiences as his Lear was stripped literally bare by the end of the wrenching play. Nunn's tweaking of the Chekhov text gave what might be called a "sitcom twist" to *Seagull*. The second play, however, may have been mere ballast for the *Lear* tour, which gave McKellen time to recuperate between performances of the demanding role. Brooklyn Academy of Music also presented a trio of other high-profile revivals in Samuel Beckett's *Happy Days* (January 9; 27 performances) and *Endgame* (April 30; 20 performances), which bookended Patrick Stewart's *Macbeth* (see above or in Plays Produced Off Broadway section) and the return of *Sizwe Banzi Is Dead* (April 8; 10 performances) by Athol Fugard, John Kani and Winston Ntshona. *Happy Days* featured Fiona Shaw directed by her frequent collaborator, Deborah Warner, and the actor was judged "magnificent," "dynamic" and the inevitable "brilliant." BAM's *Endgame* was directed by Andrei Belgrader with an noteworthy American cast of Max Casella, Alvin Epstein, John Turturro and Elaine Stritch. Epstein, who played Clov in the original 1958 New York production, was deemed by John Lahr to be "expert" in his portrayal of Nagg in this production. In *Variety*, Marilyn Stasio declared that if Epstein's work was not "definitive," then "the world is flat"—she also found Turturro's Hamm a "bravura performance." Charles Isherwood of the *Times* thought that Epstein and Stritch (as Nell) found a "perfectly calibrated, tragicomic rapport." *Sizwe Banzi* was a joint presentation of BAM and South Africa's Baxter Theatre Centre in a touring production that featured authors Kani and Ntshona in roles they have played for more than 30 years.

Ivo van Hove's typically iconoclastic version of *The Misanthrope* at New York Theatre Workshop (September 24; 55 performances) featured Bill Camp, Joan MacIntosh and Thomas Jay Ryan in an exploration of the isolation we experience due to the intrusions of technology. A few months later at NYTW, JoAnne Akalaitis directed a collection of four one-act plays by Samuel Beckett titled *Beckett Shorts* (December 16; 41 performances). Mikhail Baryshnikov, the great former ballet dancer, deployed his considerable movement skills in each of the four pieces. In the first, *Act Without Words I*, he appeared alone, but in the subsequent pieces he was joined by one other performer: David Neumann, Bill Camp and Karen Kandel, respectively. The National Theatre of Greece returned to City Center with Sophocles's *Electra* (October 10; 6 performances), spoken in modern Greek.

Powerhouses of Production

THE POWERHOUSES OF new-play production were the usual suspects: Playwrights Horizons, Second Stage Theatre, Labyrinth Theater Company, Roundabout Theatre Company, Manhattan Theatre Club and the Public Theater. Playwrights got the new season rolling with A.R. Gurney's *Crazy Mary* on its mainstage (June 3; 27 performances). Sigourney Weaver and Kristine Nielsen headlined Jim Simpson's production of Gurney's gentle allegory on the decline of WASP culture into a state of psychological (and financial) impoverishment. Kate Fodor's Best Play, *100 Saints You Should Know*, was next at Playwrights (September 18; 16 performances). See the Introduction to this volume or John Istel's essay in the following section. *A Feminine Ending* by Sarah Treem, directed by Blair Brown, did not receive critical support it deserved for its examination of the impact gender relationships (familial, romantic) have on art and artists (October 17; 31 performances). Brown skillfully guided her cast, which included Gillian

Jacobs, Marsha Mason and David Masur through the marshy undergrowth that vexes aspiration and fulfillment. (It is an old story: productions often do not get their footing until after the critics have come and gone.) The inventive Les Waters directed Jordan Harrison's *Doris to Darlene, a Cautionary Valentine*, which focused on a young woman's transformation from singer to pop icon (December 11; 16 performances). In the course of the play, the sources of musical inspiration—and their eventual commodification—are explored to little consequence. Mary-Louise Parker and Anne Bogart joined forces for Sarah Ruhl's dark comedy, *Dead Man's Cell Phone* (March 4; 32 performances). In Ruhl's meditation on "here today, gone today," a quirky woman answers the cellphone of a man who has died in a café, setting the story in motion. The production had a bumpy ride when Parker's rehearsal behavior caused tabloid news. In the days after opening, her performance still seemed tentative. The final new play this season at Playwrights was Adam Bock's *The Drunken City* (March 26; 31 performances). In a comic departure from *The Receptionist* (a Best Play this season) and *The Thugs*, Bock probes the forced jollity of young brides-to-be and the men who love them—or would had they the chance. Trip Cullman's production was noteworthy in part due to David Korins's tilting floor, which made the women's revelry even more palpable.

At Second Stage Theatre, Sarah Ruhl's *eurydice* got the season started on a promising, if haunting note (June 18; 80 performances). A Best Play for this season, it is covered in the Introduction and in Celia Wren's essay in the next section. Edward Albee's rethinking of *The Zoo Story*, to which he added a first act and made the character of Peter more three-dimensional in *Peter and Jerry*, received a Special Citation from *Best Plays* for this season. The play was later retitled *At Home at the Zoo*, but it is honored in this volume under the *Peter and Jerry* title in use for this season. Michael Sommers analyzes this fascinating development in Albee's career. Brian Yorkey and Tom Kitt's new musical, *Next to Normal*, created a stir as it announced bright new talents in the musical theater (February 13; 38 performances). Centering on the madness of Diana (Alice Ripley), a mother whose son died as an infant, the musical employed the clever twist of including the son as teenage figment of Diana's tormented psyche. While much of the drama rang true, its denouement, in which Diana seems to will herself better after receiving electroconvulsive therapy, seemed a contrivance of unhappy-happy ending. A virtually sung-through narrative, superbly delivered by Ripley, Brian d'Arcy James, Jennifer Damiano and Aaron Tveit, finally felt somewhat underdeveloped—especially in the one-dimensional husband character, which James enhanced in performance. The creative team, however, had plans to continue working on the piece. Michael Greif's staging style was aided by Mark Wendland's multilevel set, which provided a variety of pictorial (and dramatic) possibilities. The Second Stage season ended with Roberto Aguirre-Sacasa's *Good Boys and True* (May 19; 15 performances as of May 31). J. Smith-Cameron starred as the mother of an overprivileged son whose brutish, possibly criminal behavior makes him unrecognizable to her.

Labyrinth Theater Company, which is in residence at the Public Theater and often collaborates with that august institution, offered three productions Off Broadway this season. Bob Glaudini's *A View From 151st Street* got the season rolling in the fall in the Public's LuEsther Hall (October 18; 22 performances). Glaudini's characters, living on and among the mean streets of Upper Manhattan, attempt to make sense of a world gone crazy with drugs and violence. *View*, directed by Peter DuBois, is of a piece with the overall Labyrinth aesthetic, which plumbs the depths of marginalized. This outlook played again in Brett C. Leonard's *Unconditional*, which featured a fine ensemble that included such worthy veterans as Saidah Arrika Ekulona, Kevin Geer, John Doman and Isiah Whitlock Jr. (February 18; 24 performances). In Leonard's play, the grind of daily life and the disappointments of love cannot keep down a group of disparate New Yorkers—but it is a dark worldview, nonetheless. The final Labyrinth entry was a co-production with the Public, *The Little Flower of East Orange* by Stephen Adly Guirgis, in Martinson Hall (April 6; 33 performances). Starring Ellen Burstyn as the dying mother of a tortured writer who seeks solace at her bedside, Philip Seymour Hoffman's production received respectful notices from the critics for what they deemed an autobiographical play by Guirgis.

The season at the Laura Pels Theatre in the Harold and Miriam Steinberg Center for Theatre, home to the Roundabout Theatre Company's Off and Off Off Broadway work, began not with a new play. Stephen Lang brought his solo-performance adaptation of Larry Smith's book, *Beyond Glory*, to Off Broadway (June 21; 69 performances). Directed by Robert Falls, the monodrama told the stories of a diverse group of Medal of Honor recipients in an emotionally powerful fashion. The first new play of the Roundabout season was J.T. Rogers's *The Overwhelming* (October 23; 72 performances). Directed by Max Stafford-Clark, a longtime collaborator with Caryl Churchill, Howard Brenton and David Hare, Rogers's play tells the story of a mixed-race American family stuck in 1994 Rwanda amid deadly political quarrels and genocide. James Rebhorn, Sam Robards, Ron Cephas Jones and Linda Powell headed the cast of this taut piece of dramatic writing. The final entry to Roundabout's Off Broadway season was a high-profile revival of Beth Henley's *Crimes of the Heart* (February 14; 77 performances). A 1981 Pulitzer Prize honoree and 1980–81 Best Play, this season's production was directed by Kathleen Turner with Jennifer Dundas, Sarah Paulson and Lily Rabe as the prickly Magrath sisters. Isherwood at the *Times* called Turner's work a "confident debut," Dziemianowicz of the *Daily News* lauded it for being "assured and easygoing" and Gardner of *USA Today* remarked on the way she culled "beautifully nuanced performances" from her "splendid cast."

Lynne Meadow, the dynamic artistic director of Manhattan Theatre Club, took a sabbatical this season and was replaced by frequent artistic collaborator, Daniel Sullivan. The Off Broadway season started promisingly with Adam Bock's *The Receptionist* in the larger of MTC's two Off Broadway spaces (October 30; 72 performances). A dark journey into the American psyche in a time of unknown threats, this Best Play is studied in David Cote's essay in the following section. Abbie Spallen's *Pumpgirl* opened a few weeks later in the smaller space (December 4; 48 performances). Directed by Carolyn Cantor (and beautifully designed by her husband, David Korins), the production was a pitch-perfect evocation of desperate lives—a lot of that on stages this past decade—in a Northern Ireland border town. Told in monologues by three characters, the "pumpgirl" of the title is a gas-station attendant who wants to be one of the guys but is tolerated only, and later abused sexually. Itamar Moses's *The Four of Us* followed *Pumpgirl* into Stage II (March 25; 64 performances). Directed by Pam MacKinnon, the story of two writers whose friendship is torn by the phenomenal success of one (and the growing resentment of the other) had much in common with Van Druten's *Old Acquaintance* on Broadway. In Moses's play, however, the distance between the two men finally seems as though it may never be bridged. After development at Ars Nova, Liz Flahive's *From Up Here* opened on Stage I (April 16; 54 performances as of May 31). The extraordinary Julie White played the mother of a son who has committed some sort of potentially violent act for which everyone in the family must pay a price: embarrassment, social ostracism, etc. Directed by Leigh Silverman, the talented ensemble also included Arija Bareikis, Aya Cash, Brian Hutchison, Will Rogers and Tobias Segal.

The Public Theater's season of new work began with a piece that had been developed through the company's 2007 Under the Radar Festival. Tarell Alvin McCraney's *The Brothers Size* was a blend of African myth and modern urban circumstance in the production directed by Tea Alagic in the Shiva Theater (November 6; 56 performances). David Henry Hwang's superb satire on art, politics and identity, *Yellow Face*, was directed by Leigh

Silverman in Martinson Hall (December 10; 39 performances). A 2007–08 Best Play, Dan Bacalzo examines the piece in the next section of this volume. Richard Nelson had a difficult path before him in preparing *Conversations in Tusculum*, which he also directed (March 11; 24 performances). Set in the time not long before Julius Caesar's assassination by senators in ancient Rome—and staged in the Anspacher Theater—Nelson's play drew clear parallels between Caesar's imperial designs and those of President George W. Bush. By the time the play opened, however, Bush had been a lame-duck leader for more than a year. As a result, the play—much the same as Mamet's *November* (see above)—was somewhat past its expiration date as a piece of timely political theater. That said, Nelson's rich authorial voice had been missing from New York stages for too long and it was good to have him back. Politics continued to roam the halls of the Public with Caryl Churchill's *Drunk Enough to Say I Love You?* in the Newman Theater (March 16; 25 performances). Directed by James Macdonald, who also staged the revival of Churchill's *Top Girls* on Broadway (see above), the two-hander was an allegory on the "special relationship" between the US and the UK—in the form of a pair of male lovers—with Britain portrayed as extraordinarily needy.

Lincoln Center Theater mixed its Off Broadway offerings of new works this season to include a musical, a play and a solo show. *The Glorious Ones* by Lynn Ahrens and Stephen Flaherty started the LCT season in the Newhouse Theater (November 5; 72 performances). Centered on a traveling troupe of Italian performers in the late 16th century, the delightful, intermissionless piece imagines the lives of a *commedia dell'arte* company as they develop their style of work. Marc Kudisch led the cast of David Patrick Kelly, Natalie Venetia Belcon, Julyana Soelistyo, John Kassir, Erin Davie and Jeremy Webb. Paul Rudnick's collection of short comedies, *The New Century*, considered some of the many ways that homosexual experience has become more mainstream in today's America (April 14; 55 performances as of May 31). John Lithgow recited favorite tales from his family's past and present in *John Lithgow: Stories by Heart* (May 12; 5 performances as of May 31), which was presented on nights that *New Century* was dark.

In addition to New York Theatre Workshop's revivals there were three new works given Off Broadway premieres. (*The Sound and the Fury* is considered in our Off Off Broadway section, due to its number of performances per week.) Rinde Eckert's *Horizon*, a performance piece based on the writings of Reinhold Niebuhr, started the 2007–08 season with a meditation on the nature faith, intellect and conscience (June 5; 31 performances). It is something of a stretch to call Betty Shamieh's *The Black*

Eyed a new work given the number of workshops and readings the play had in New York before its opening at NYTW (July 31; 23 performances). The world premiere production, in fact, was staged in May 2005 at the Magic Theatre in San Francisco. In the play, a group of Arab women debate the morality and social impact of terrorist attacks. After the debacle over the purported censorship of *My Name Is Rachel Corrie* by NYTW when it was cancelled in the middle of an earlier season—the one-woman *Rachel Corrie* took a strong pro-Palestinian perspective; NYTW's producing partners accused the company of cowardice—there was some small bit of irony in the programming choice of *The Black Eyed*. (The production of *Rachel Corrie* eventually occurred in a truncated commercial run that showed the monodrama to be much less than incendiary.) The final new piece Off Broadway at NYTW was Jessica Blank and April Yvette Thompson's *Liberty City* (March 4; 16 performances). Blank, who was a co-author of the successful documentary drama *The Exonerated*, collaborated with Thompson on developing a story based on the latter's family roots in America. While on the topic of solo shows, there was one final monodrama presented by a nonprofit entity. Irish Repertory Theatre presented *Tom Crean: Antarctic Explorer* (July 22; 50 performances). Based on the life of a member of three expeditions that attempted to reach the South Pole, *Tom Crean* tells stories of hardship and courage in the face of danger.

Other significant nonprofit productions of new plays Off Broadway included Brits Off Broadway—a project of 59E59 Theaters and the Elysabeth Kleinhans Theatrical Foundation—as the 2007–08 season got underway. Alan Ayckbourn's *Intimate Exchanges* opened in Theater A under the direction of Ayckbourn and Tim Luscombe (June 14; 22 performances). The 1982 work is another of the playwright's intricate dramaturgical devices in which eight interrelated plays on love and life are played by one pair of actors who perform all roles. Near season's end a new play by David Greig, *Damascus*, was presented by Brits Off Broadway in association with Traverse Theatre Company (May 11; 23 performances as of May 31). In the Greig play, a traveling salesman who finds himself in Syria tries to overcome cultural differences he does not fully understand.

Off Broadway Commerce

IT HAS TAKEN a long way around the nonprofit companies in order to return to commercial productions. These days commercial production of new plays Off Broadway almost seems a quaint throwback to another time. Of the 30 new plays Off Broadway this season, only five were presented as commercial projects. Things are not quite so dark for new musicals, where commercial entities often dominate—as they did this season. Two of the eight new musicals Off Broadway in 2007–08 were the nonprofit-produced *The Glorious Ones* and *Next to Normal* (see above). *Walmartopia* (September 3; 136 performances), a satire on the growing dominance of a discount retail chain, took a circuitous route to the Minetta Lane Theatre that began in Wisconsin and progressed to the 2006 New York International Fringe Festival, where it received encouragement. The transferred production—despite the presence of Cheryl Freeman and Nikki M. James among the overhauled cast and creative team—did not meet its advance hyperbole. Tragedy struck when cast member Brennen Leath died of complications from diabetes following the September 22 performance. DeMond B. Nason joined the cast as a permanent replacement on October 10. *Celia: The Life and Music of Celia Cruz* (September 26; 269 performances), which celebrated the "Queen of Salsa," offered six performances a week in Spanish, two in English. The marketing technique worked well enough to keep the show running for eight months at New World Stages 2. *Greetings From Yorkville* at the Soho Playhouse told the autobiographical tale of a songwriting team—Anya Turner and Robert Grusecki—trying to make it in show business (October 4; 35 performances).

Opening a week ahead of the new Mel Brooks musical with a similar title did not help *Frankenstein*, which played at 37 Arts (November 1; 45 performances). The creative team and producers, all of whom were first-timers to New York theater, could not overcome the widely held belief that the production was, as Isherwood wrote in the *Times*, a "drably earnest two hours of throaty *Sturm und Drang*." The concert version of *Jerry Springer: The Opera*, which played at Carnegie Hall, seemed to be a brief tryout for a berth in a Broadway house (January 29; 2 performances). Nearly five years after its West End opening—it had been in development for more than two years by then—critics were wondering when the satire of the American lust for fame-at-any-price might grace a Main Stem stage. Never, is the probable answer, even if the critics would love to see it in a longer run. According to Rooney in *Variety*, Christian protesters thrust petitions at theatergoers urging them to, "'Sign up to defend Jesus and Mary' from the musical recital about to take place inside." Broadway producers love to see their names in the paper, but not for defiling Christian icons. The gem among Off Broadway musicals was the last to open this season. *Adding Machine*, an adaptation of Elmer Rice's play *The Adding Machine*, first opened in 2007 at Next Theatre Company near Chicago. The Off Broadway version of Jason Loewith and Joshua Schmidt's musical played at the Minetta Lane Theatre (February

25; 97 performances as of May 31). A 2007–08 Best Play, Jeffrey Sweet's essay on the piece appears in the next section of this volume.

Commercial producers were responsible for all three of the revues presented Off Broadway this season: *Three Mo' Tenors* (September 27; 142 performances at the Little Shubert), an African-American version of the concerts by classical tenors José Carreras, Placido Domingo and Luciano Pavarotti; *Forbidden Broadway: Rude Awakening* (October 2; 200 performances at the 47th Street Theatre), the latest installment of the Broadway-spoof franchise; and *Make Me a Song: The Music of William Finn* (November 12; 55 performances), a loosely arranged narrative of the composer's work. Solo performance is another area where commercial producers are prevalent, in part because the overhead is reduced (one performer, no scenery, simple lighting, etc.) and the return can be reasonable (tickets for solo shows often are the same price as productions with more expensive casts and production values). This season the commercial solo shows included modified standup comedy in Will Durst's *The All-American Sport of Bipartisan Bashing* (August 15; 49 performances), Tim Minchin's eponymous *Tim Minchin* (March 5; 34 performances) and *Jackie Mason: The Ultimate Jew* (March 18; 78 performances as of May 31). There were autobiographical shows such as Bo Eason's sports-oriented *Runt of the Litter* (December 9; 76 performances) and Paul Stroili's "I'm-not-gay" confessional, *Straight Up With a Twist* (January 24; 90 performances). And Alan Palmer arrived from California with *Fabulous Divas of Broadway*, in which he portrayed 32 women in 20 songs at St. Luke's Theatre (February 27; 61 performances). In the realm of specialty productions, those shows that do not easily fit into other categories, commercial producers opened only two of the 10 productions. (Because Encores! concerts and the New York Philharmonic presentation of *Camelot* are classified as specialities, it might be argued that *Jerry Springer* could have fit into the specialty group, except for its enhanced production values. See the Plays Produced Off Broadway section for details.) The first commercial specialty to open was *Jump*, at Union Square Theatre, a Korean martial arts, acrobatics and slapstick comedy spectacle in a loose narrative structure (October 7; 269 performances as of May 31). *Fuerzabruta* by Diqui James, at the Daryl Roth Theatre, is another work by the people who created the long-running *De La Guarda* and it too is a whirl of sensory stimulation that encourages—or requires—audience members to be swept along in the spectacle (October 24; 254 performances as of May 31).

The new plays in commercial runs this season were a mixed bag, with none of them managing to run even four full months. When one compares that statistic to the commercial specialties in the previous paragraph—which had run more than seven months by season's end and continued into the next—an anxiety-provoking picture of commercial Off Broadway emerges. Doug Grissom's *Elvis People* announced its closing at New World Stages before the show had opened (June 21; 4 performances). An homage to Elvis Presley's hold on American consciousness, producer Robert A. Rush pulled the plug due to weak demand for tickets. *The Rise of Dorothy Hale*, by Myra Bairstow, enjoyed the longest run of the commercial new plays in its stand at St. Luke's Theatre (October 4; 137 performances). Inspired by Frida Kahlo's disturbing 1939 painting titled *The Suicide of Dorothy Hale*, the play probed relationships among historical figures such as Hale, Harry Hopkins and Clare Boothe Luce, who commissioned the painting but was upset with its violence. Michael Badalucco, Sarita Choudhury and Laura Koffman led the talented cast.

Charles Busch put on a dress to revisit *Die Mommie Die!*, based on his film and earlier play (October 21; 97 performances). With superb support from Kristine Nielsen, Ashley Morris and Van Hansis, Busch chewed the scenery for 90 minutes and still managed to make a poignant point about how powerful women are easily marginalized by men. After an initial Off Off Broadway run at the Fourth Street Theatre in October, *Beebo Brinker Chronicles* moved to Off Broadway's 37 Arts (March 5; 63 performances). Bankrolled by lead producers Lily Tomlin and Jane Wagner, the Kate Moira Ryan and Linda S. Chapman adaptation lampooned Ann Bannon's popular 1950s and 1960s pulp novels about lesbians in Greenwich Village while taking seriously some of the issues raised. Kathleen Clark's *Secrets of a Soccer Mom* was the final entry among commercial new plays (March 5; 69 performances). Judith Ivey expanded her creative portfolio in directing this tale of mothers confronting certain demons as they engage in a soccer match against their children.

It is relatively easy to see through these brief synopses that there is a missing heft—which may or may not be a bad thing—at the core of commercially produced new plays. Commercial producers Off Broadway clearly have ceded the territory of more serious new works to the nonprofit enterprises. It is hard to blame the producers, though, in a time of economic difficulty. Even these lighter-weight productions of the 2007–08 season failed, except in once case, to make it as far as 100 performances—it is not likely that much profit is possible in that production model. Can commercial producers find their way back into the Off Broadway arena as impresarios of new plays? Wait 'til next year.

THE BEST PLAYS
OF 2007–2008

2007–2008 Best Play

ADDING MACHINE

By Jason Loewith and Joshua Schmidt

○ ○ ○ ○ ○

Essay by Jeffrey Sweet

ENSEMBLE: In numbers
The mysteries of life can be revealed
In numbers.

AS THE RAFT of uninspired adaptations of movies in recent years attests, it is not enough that a property *can* work as a musical. (On these purely functional terms, *Legally Blonde* is deemed by some to be a success.) Those who aim for something higher know they must do more than just whittle the original text and shoehorn songs in place of what has been excised. If re-conceiving a play or a film as a musical theater piece does not create a new or deeper experience, what's the point?

The classic example is the transformation of *Pygmalion* to *My Fair Lady*. Shaw wrote the story of a young woman who comes under the influence of two middle-age men who behave like adolescents. She absorbs what they have to teach, and then outgrows them by becoming an adult. The musical Alan Jay Lerner and Frederick Loewe fashioned from it has her fall in love with one of them and stay in spite of the lack of a serious prospect that he will evolve. What remains are two works with the same characters, much of the same dialogue, but distinct in intention and effect.

The musical fashioned from Elmer Rice's 1923 play *The Adding Machine* does not represent quite so radical a re-orientation, but Joshua Schmidt and Jason Loewith invest the old anthology-stuffer—and its caricatured figures—with something like humanity in *Adding Machine* (from which they trimmed the play's running time and an article from the title). The shift in approach is apparent in the show's opening number. In Rice's original, we are introduced to Mrs. Zero, a middle-age woman who harangues her middle-age husband as he lies motionless in bed. In her monologue she expresses her disdain for Westerns, talks of the other housewives' tastes in movies, observes that Mr. Zero is too cheap to take her downtown to see new films, peers to see if a female neighbor is back from a six-month jail term and loudly regrets her marriage.

Adding machines: Roger E. DeWitt, Daniel Marcus, Joel Hatch, Adinah Alexander, Niffer Clarke, Amy Warren in Adding Machine. *Photo: Carol Rosegg*

In *Adding Machine*, after the short sung prologue from the chorus quoted above, Mrs. Zero sings while "lying" in bed next to her husband. (The actors are oriented vertically onstage in a "bed" that gives the audience the illusion of a view from overhead.)

> MRS. ZERO: [. . .] Mrs. Eight
> Mrs. Eight was sayin' to me,
> "Mrs. Zero!"
> Mrs. Eight was sayin' to me,
> Only yesterday.
> "Mrs. Zero!"
> Says she.
> She says
> "*A Mother's Tears* is the best picture ever made—
> So sweet and wholesome!"
> Mrs. Eight was sayin' to me,
> "Don't miss it!"
>
> "An' they got that *big star*,
> Grace Darling—
> So sweet and wholesome,
> Starrin' in that picture show."

She says
"*A Mother's Tears* is the best picture ever made—
So sweet and wholesome!
Grace Darling!
Don't miss it!"
[. . .]

WITH THIS SONG—an aria, really—composer Joshua Schmidt and his
co-librettist Jason Loewith swiftly establish conventions they will employ
throughout their score. For the most part, rather than write in standard song
forms, they engage in modular construction. Take the words "sweet and

The ensemble makes its full presence known in a tour-de-force number.

wholesome," which are set to a distinct musical phrase. Whenever these
words return, so too does a version of the associated musical phrase.
Throughout, Schmidt and Loewith establish similar distinct phrases to be
mixed, matched and re-ordered as needed.

In the original text by Rice, Mrs. Zero's speech is straightforward,
abrasive yammer. When turned into song, however, a phrase such as, "What
I like is them love stories," sits on music that is full of yearning. Mrs. Zero
may be crass and off-putting, but the music suggests that there are
unexpressed reservoirs of longing within her unlovely shell, including dismay
that her life with Mr. Zero can't be counted "one of them love stories." All
the while, here and throughout the score, Schmidt and Loewith add
comments and echoes of phrases from the rest of the ensemble.

The ensemble makes its full presence known in a tour-de-force number
that begins the second scene. Three middle-age male-female pairs sit in the
dimly-lit accounting room of a large department store. As the women read
(at varying speeds) a series of figures, the men make calculations on pads.
Gradually, the private thoughts of two of the men enter the mix—one
betraying his obsession with women, the other fixed on beer. The number
evolves until the six become one synchronized, efficient aural machine.
The focus gradually shifts to one of these pairs—Mr. Zero and Daisy. He is
unhappy with the speed at which she reads the numbers, she keeps muttering
about wanting a transfer to get away from his crabbiness. We're privy, too,
to their internal thoughts. Zero claims to be disgusted by women, and he is

particularly worried about a woman he reported to the police—the one who used to parade undressed so he could see her through his apartment window. She got a sentence of six months and is due to be released. He is afraid that if she returns to the building she could cause him problems with Mrs. Zero.

Daisy, meanwhile, speculates about different methods of suicide and remembers when Zero used to be pleasant and attentive. At two points, their reveries intersect—when they dream of Mrs. Zero dying, and they imagine that they would then be free to marry. They simultaneously, though separately, remember a company picnic:

> DAISY: Remember the picnic?
> That time, the store picnic?
> The year that your wife couldn't come?
> You touched my hand—
> You brushed my knee—
>
> ZERO: Remember that time?
> When the wife didn't go?
> We sat all day
> Under them trees—

TODAY MARKS THE twenty-fifth anniversary of Zero's employment in his job. He hopes and expects that the company will reward him by promoting him to the front office and giving him a raise. At the end of the sequence, Daisy exits and Zero approaches the boss. It doesn't go as planned. The boss does not recognize him, and, after giving *pro forma* acknowledgment to the time Zero has devoted to the business, informs him that management has acquired adding machines so Zero's services will no longer be required. Nothing personal, of course, but the rules of business create their own imperatives. We leave Zero, mid-scene, struggling with the news.

At this point, Schmidt and Loewith depart from the original by focusing on Daisy; she sings a pastiche of a 1920s ballad called "I'd Rather Watch You" in which she claims that movie stars such as Douglas Fairbanks pale in comparison to the life she imagines with Zero. The lyrics are naïve and the tuneful music as conventional as the words they support, but the modest sentiments Daisy expresses are genuinely touching.

In the next scene, Zero arrives home late from the office. Mrs. Zero is distracted by the inconvenience of him arriving unprepared for the party she is throwing for other couples tonight, and she doesn't notice that he is walking in a daze. The couples, the Ones and Twos, arrive and what follows is a scene set mostly as a demented waltz showcasing the banality and

Pretty in pastiche: Amy Warren and Joe Farrell in Adding Machine. *Photo: Carol Rosegg*

mean-spiritedness of the couples' conversation—weather, fashion, the failings and betrayals of others, the hostility toward (and fear of) foreigners and ethnics. Zero plays no active part in this, mechanically fulfilling the function of host, handing out drinks. Then: a heavy knock at the door. Zero anticipates the identity of the new arrivals—the police. They have come for him. He killed the boss today.

The setting instantly shifts to a courtroom where Zero confesses his crime. He confesses other things, too—how "a nigger" once stepped on his foot in the subway and lucky for him Zero didn't have a gun handy, how he tossed a pop bottle while in a crowd shouting, "Kill the umpire," and how he called the police on his scantily clad neighbor because his wife was mad that he looked at her. As for killing the boss, the guy kept going through the motions, saying how sorry he was to lose Zero as a valued employee. The mealy-mouthed attitude was too much provocation. "I'm like anyone else," he sings, "What would you do?"

The next scene is set on death row, the night before Zero is to be executed. Mrs. Zero comes to say goodbye. Given what we've seen of them together before, their greeting is surprisingly tender. Zero is propelled into ecstasy when he sees what she's brought him: ham and eggs. His song about them contain the first joyful notes he utters. He tries to comfort his wife with the hope that soon she will find another to cook for. Reprising elements from her opening number, she sings of the comfort someone else tried to offer her:

> MRS. ZERO: Mrs. Seven.
> Mrs. Seven was sayin' to me,
> "Mrs. Zero," says she.
> "Wearing black is so slimming, darling."
> Says she!
> "And I'll find you a veil to wear with that pretty black dress."
> So sweet and wholesome . . .
> So sweet and wholesome . . .
> So sweet and . . ."
> (*she breaks off in tears*)
> So lonely!

In a wistful number called "Didn't We?," they sing a duet of the occasional (and questionable) good times they had—though he doesn't remember her claim that he took her to the opera. He raises the subject of

Idiots' delight: Roger E. DeWitt, Joel Hatch and Daniel Marcus in Adding Machine. *Photo: Carol Rosegg*

the scrapbook she has kept to chronicle his life. It will come to an end with the newspaper's report of his execution. She'll leave it "on the parlor table, right where everyone can see it." Zero, however, makes the mistake of suggesting that, if something happens to her, she see to it the book to be given to Daisy Devore, his work partner down at the store. Mrs. Zero flares up in jealousy:

> MRS. ZERO: What's between you,
> Between you and Miss Devore?
>
> ZERO: (*spoken*) I shoulda given it to her in the first place! That's what I shoulda done!
>
> MRS. ZERO: I was a fool
> A fool for marryin' you . . .
> And after all I've done for you!
> I won't stand for it!
>
> MR. ZERO: I'd a married her if I met her first!
>
> MRS. ZERO: I won't stand for it!
> Now we're through!

Zero now meets another death row inmate, Shrdlu. He, too, is a killer, but he insists his murder is worse than Zero's crime: in a sudden outburst, he cut his mother's throat at the dinner table. (Reading between the lines of the story he tells, the audience gleans that the mother was an oppressive, moralistic figure who squelched Shrdlu's every healthy impulse as sinful.) Shrdlu looks forward to execution and to freedom in the flames of damnation he sings about in a gospel-flavored number. A character called the Fixer arrives to escort Zero to his execution. Zero pleads for another chance. The Fixer hesitates:

> FIXER: What would you do, Zero? Imagine what would happen if I *could* give you another chance . . . what would you do?
>
> ZERO: I . . . I'd make up with the wife. Go out and look for a job I guess.
>
> FIXER: Adding figures?
>
> ZERO: Well I ain't young enough to take up somethin' new!
>
> FIXER: (*brief consideration, followed by the snap of his fingers*) Put the skids under him, and make it snappy!

And the condemned is dispatched.

ZERO SUDDENLY FINDS himself in the Elysian Fields. In contrast to what we have seen before, this is a place of color and light. The chorus tells him that he's reached a world where "the burdens of life lie behind you." And he encounters someone he knows—a dismayed Shrdlu. This is not the afterlife of pain and torment Shrdlu had expected. He couldn't even find his mother to apologize to her. Not being in a place where he will be punished is agonizing.

Shrdlu disappears, and another face from the past comes into view: Daisy. Zero is startled to see her. She reveals that she accidentally blew the light out on the gas in her apartment. She's pleased to be in the Elysian Fields. It reminds her of the country where she and Zero once spent a day together during the company picnic. Now, reprising their earlier separate reveries, they reveal to each other how important that day was. She remembers that day when his knee touched hers. He confesses that touch was "accidental on purpose."

> DAISY: (*spoken*) Do you mean it?
>
> ZERO: (*spoken*) Sure I mean it . . .
> You mean you didn't know?
>
> [. . .]

> ZERO: I felt like kissin' you
> But I didn't have the nerve, the nerve—
> I thought of kissin' you—
>
> DAISY: Wishin' 'bout nobody else but you . . .
> Wishin' 'bout nobody else but you . . .
>
> Wishin' 'bout nobody else but you . . .
>
> [. . .]
>
> ZERO: Oh Daisy!
> If I only knew . . .
> (*spoken*)
> An' me bawlin' you out
>
> DAISY: (*spoken*) Them was the times I . . . I'd think I didn't wanna go on livin'. . .
>
> ZERO: Daisy—
> There's something else
> I wanted to ask you.
>
> DAISY: (*spoken*) What?
>
> ZERO: Well—
> When you told me—
> Told me you blew out the gas
> Was it just kinda accidental?
>
> DAISY: Accidental on purpose!

They are free now to confess their attraction, which they do with an abandon we've not seen before. They kiss passionately, then dance to a lush arrangement of Daisy's earlier song, "I'd Rather Watch You."

But Zero isn't good at coordinating dancing, kissing and stuff like that. He is also confused. How could it be that a murderer and a suicide would be rewarded in the afterlife with happiness? Shrdlu returns with what he's learned: in this place nobody cares what they did before they came here. All are free to pursue their hearts' content. Zero responds, "You mean, like . . . whores? And suicides? And . . . murderers? [. . .] What kinda dump is this anyway?" Zero decides he does not want to stay in a place with people who are not respectable. He apologizes to Daisy, but he can't stay here with her. He exits. In despair, she cries, "I might as well be alive!"

The stage plunges into darkness. When we can see again, it is Zero sitting at an adding machine, adding columns of numbers and singing of the joy he has found in this corner of the afterlife. No bosses to complicate matters, just the blissful certainty of adding up unambiguous numbers: His kind of freedom. The Fixer (now referred to as Charles in the script) interrupts his bliss with the unwelcome information that it is time for Zero to go back. "Do you think they're going to all the trouble of making a soul just to use it once? Why man, they use a soul over and over again—over and over until it's worn out."

> ZERO: (*pause, he considers this*) Nobody ever told me that. How was I to know?
>
> CHARLES: Use your brains! Where would we put them all? We're crowded enough as it is. Why, this place is nothing but a kind of repair and service station—a cosmic laundry you might say. [. . .] That's what we've been doing all this time while you've been at that machine—wash, rinse, dry, scrub, wash, rinse, dry . . . your soul was an awful mess!
>
> [. . .]
>
> ZERO: Wait. If it's all been downhill, what was I when I started? A king or somethin'?
>
> CHARLES: You were a monkey. A hairy, chattering, long-tailed monkey. But you weren't so bad then—same as everyone else. And you did just what all the other monkeys did, but at least you got some exercise. And there was this one little red-headed chimp—well, never mind. Yes sir, you weren't so bad, but even on that first go-round there was a bigger, smarter monkey you kowtowed to . . . the mark of the slave was on you from the very start.
>
> ZERO: You ain't very particular about what you call people, are you?

Charles now reveals a machine that drawfs the adding machine on which Zero has been playing—the recycling machine that sends refurbished souls out into the world to be reborn. Zero protests, but Charles orders him to the conveyer belt, secure in the sad knowledge that Zero will come to grief again in the same old dumb way. "You chose the machine, Zero! Every time! So it chose you!"

Now Zero sees another soul on the belt: Daisy. He calls out and runs to her, embraces and kisses her just before they are shoved back into the world. All action and sound stop for a second, and Charles says, "I'll tell the world this is a lousy job." The end. Note that Charles's last line suggests that he, like Zero, is condemned to fulfill a function in the cosmic machine.

AS WITH *AUGUST: OSAGE COUNTY, Adding Machine* arrived in New York via the Chicago Off Loop theater scene (and, like Tracy Letts's play, it received the Joseph Jefferson Award as best new work in its category). Director David Cromer's work made an impressive splash in New York. The cast of the Off Broadway production was likely the lumpiest company of players seen in New York in recent memory. Joel Hatch's Mr. Zero was a near-zombie, benumbed by routine, his voice strangled to a faintly-protesting nasality. His wife, similarly doughy of figure, was played by Cyrilla Baer, who managed to make a big impression playing small-mindedness. Amy Warren found a touching delicacy in Mr. Zero's sentimental co-worker, Daisy, the most sympathetic (and pathetic) figure in the piece.

Rice's original text is probably a bit heavy-handed for today's tastes. Few contemporary playwrights would dare to give characters names so overtly symbolic as Mr. and Mrs. Zero and their numbered set. Part of the wonder of what Schmidt and Loewith have accomplished is to remain faithful to Rice's play without succumbing to the temptation to overlay irony in order to distance themselves from it. By embracing Rice's seeming weaknesses, they reveal and heighten the strengths. This is one of the rare instances in which a musical adaptation improves on the original.

2007–2008 Best Play

AUGUST: OSAGE COUNTY

By Tracy Letts

○ ○ ○ ○ ○

Essay by Chris Jones

BEVERLY: My wife takes pills and I drink. That's the bargain we've struck . . . *one* of the bargains, just one paragraph of our marriage contract . . . cruel covenant. She takes pills and I drink. I don't drink *because* she takes pills.

As to whether she takes pills because I drink . . . I learned long ago not to speak for my wife.

WHEN TRACY LETTS'S *August: Osage County* opened at the Steppenwolf Theatre in July 2007, it was a theatrical tornado that seemed to have been blown across the plains, sweeping along a howlingly dysfunctional family from Oklahoma. The production was deposited in the Windy City, aptly, at the home of the consummate all-American acting ensemble, where domestic strife has been the stock-in-trade since Gary Sinise and John Malkovich sparred in *True West*. Here was a new, loud, American play of uncommon ambition: a three-act, three-and-a-half hour, large-cast screech offering no sop whatsoever to subtlety, nuance or pre-existing expectation. It was a wide-open epic unconcerned with the usual mealy-mouthed denizens of the Upper East Side or shallow Hollywood power-players. *August: Osage County* took on the sprawling, anonymous hinterland and myriad contradictions of middle-class life in arid flyover country.

Anna D. Shapiro's career-making production would become a colossal success in Chicago and New York. It would remind the theater world of Steppenwolf's ensemble-driven aesthetic and help the company introduce its new generation of artists. On Broadway, it would become far and away the most successful nonmusical of the 2007–2008 season, surviving a potentially devastating stagehands' strike, handling a costly move from the Imperial to the Music Box Theatre—to make way for *Billy Elliot*—and greatly outlasting its planned limited-run. According to *Variety*, this 210-minute drama outgrossed half of the musicals on the Great White Way for many weeks of the season under review.

Bad news: Madeleine Martin, Kimberly Guerrero, Amy Morton, Jeff Perry and Troy West in August: Osage County. *Photo: Joan Marcus*

Shapiro, Letts and Steppenwolf actors Deanna Dunagan (the original Violet Weston and a virtual unknown in New York) and Rondi Reed (the original Mattie Fae) would all win 2008 Tony Awards. Amy Morton (Barbara) would receive a Tony nomination and widespread acclaim for her emotionally intense performance. The script would become the fasting selling title in the history of its publisher, Theatre Communications Group, according to TCG's director of publications, Terence Nemeth. And *August: Osage County* would win the Pulitzer Prize for Drama. On that warm summer weekend in Chicago, however, no one expected anything of the sort.

BEFORE *AUGUST: OSAGE COUNTY,* the Chicago-based Letts was known primarily as a hip ironist for the post-Tarantino world, a shrewd author of noir potboilers such as *Killer Joe* and *Bug*—an arch, elusive formalist drawn to write plays suffused with sex, horror, violence and trailer-park eccentrics. His earlier plays had mostly been quirky, 90-minute, Off Broadway entertainments: racy in theme, droll in language, sophisticated in awareness of familial hypocrisy and shrewdly self-aware to boot. But Letts's dramas were not known for emotional weight or main-course dramatic substance.

This new play, however, which left wholly unprepared Chicago audiences gasping in their seats, was something else entirely. To Chicago audiences, it was immediately obvious that Letts, an actor as well as a playwright, had created *August: Osage County* specifically for this particular group of Steppenwolf actors, many of whom he knew in the most intimate of ways. Clearly, he was borrowing from his actors' lives as much as from his own family. Remarkably, however, a member of Letts's own family was also acting in the play.

This new play left Chicago audiences gasping in their seats.

Tracy Letts's father, Dennis Letts, a former college professor in the family's home state of Oklahoma and a late-in-life actor, appeared in the original Steppenwolf cast in the role of patriarch Beverly Weston. This seemed, all at once, a cryptic acknowledgement of the play's autobiographical roots, a simple coincidence, a caustic in-joke, and a son's warm gesture to his beloved father. The last interpretation came into sharper focus after the Broadway transfer, when it was revealed that the elder Letts was suffering from an advanced form of cancer. Shortly after opening the play on Broadway, he died, lending the subsequent success of his son's play a bittersweet aura for all involved. The strange personal intensity of this Steppenwolf production, however, was not limited to the relationship between a father and his complicated son.

Many in the Steppenwolf ensemble had arrived in Chicago if not from the rural Oklahoma setting of *August*, then from comparable small towns in Iowa or downstate Illinois. They understood the landscape that Letts was painting. Moreover, Letts had focused his play almost entirely on outspoken, middle-age (or older) characters, providing a set of impossibly juicy roles for the demographic in which the Steppenwolf acting ensemble was most generously represented. There had never been a show at Steppenwolf that fit its actors so glove-like: the usual gap between performer and material seemed almost to have disappeared.

Letts had also thrown a gauntlet by challenging one of the most sacred traditions in the American theater: the ambitious epic on the horror of life in a family racked by substance abuse, alcoholism, failure, adultery and shame. *August: Osage County* seemed to be a semiconscious attempt to update characters and themes familiar from such semi-autobiographical Eugene O'Neill works as *Long Day's Journey Into Night* for a new theatergoing generation. In Chicago and New York, almost every critic agreed that *August* was a riveting, brilliantly acted piece of theater and a vicarious good time. But when it came to the question of whether or not this was a truly great American play—an heir to, if not a peer of, the O'Neill model—a split emerged. The nuance and verbiage of the arguments varied, but the gist of the debate was easy to discern and understand. Some critics thought the play was the first great American drama of the 21st century. Others thought it was an enjoyable but terribly overpraised melodrama in the Lillian Hellman, rather than the O'Neill, tradition.

The side where one landed depended on whether one saw the characters bearing sufficient magnitude with the narrative carrying appropriate thematic heft. It also depended on whether one thought the great American play could—or even should—be updated for an era when

Meal or melee? (clockwise from left) Francis Guinan, Ian Barford, Rondi Reed, Deanna Dunagan, Sally Murphy, Amy Morton, Mariann Mayberry, Brian Kerwin, Jeff Perry in August: Osage County. *Photo: Joan Marcus*

audiences require a little more free-flowing, self-aware juice with their traditional American steak. One could argue, with foundation, that *August: Osage County* cheapened the form. Or one could argue—with even firmer foundation—that it revitalized drama as no other in decades. Either way, audiences flocked to see the play in Chicago and New York.

IN THE PROLOGUE to *August: Osage County*, we see an aging English professor (and sometime poet) named Beverly Weston sitting in the office of his three-story home in Pawhuska, Oklahoma. He has hired a young, calm, Native-American woman named Johnna to care for his wife, Violet—a drug addict who suffers from "a touch of cancer"—and the home the two of them share.

"Life is very long," is the first line Beverly Weston speaks in this very-long play, hinting at both the character's weariness and the self-awareness that marks the entire enterprise. Beverly talks to this quiet young woman of books, T.S. Eliot, quiet refuges and his marriage. "My wife takes pills and I drink," he tells his new domestic employee. "That's the bargain we have struck." By the beginning of Act I proper, Beverly Weston has disappeared and the Weston clan begins to gather in the heat.

We first meet the brassy Mattie Fae (Violet Weston's sister), her long-suffering husband Charlie and the mousy, insecure Ivy, the middle of Beverly and Violet's three grown daughters and the only one to still live in the area. Between popping pills, Violet tells her relatives that she has no idea what has happened to her husband, who may have gone fishing, or drinking or even writing poetry after years of writers' block. Before long, the eldest Weston sister, Barbara, arrives from Colorado with her estranged husband Bill—an academic in the midst of an affair with one of his students—and their precocious but troubled teenage daughter, Jean. Barbara, who suffers from the hot flashes of approaching menopause, is none too pleased to be back in rural Oklahoma:

> BARBARA: The jokers who settled this place. The Germans and the Dutch and the Irish. Who was the asshole who saw this flat, hot nothing and planted his flag? I mean, we fucked the Indians for *this*?

This godforsaken place is not the Midwest, she asserts:

> BARBARA: [. . .] *Michigan* is the Midwest, God knows why. This is the Plains: a state of mind, right, some spiritual affliction, like the Blues.

As Violet's pills kick in, Violet and Barbara begin to argue.

Later this day, Violet tells her daughter more about her arrangement with Beverly that, if one of them disappeared, the other would open a safe-deposit box. She has done so, but found no clues. She blames Barbara, however—who has moved away—for her husband's malaise. As the dope-smoking Jean, a teenage girl, complains about her parent's lousy marriage to the assiduously neutral Johnna, Barbara tries to assure her mother that Beverly will be back. But, angrily sharing a couch with the husband who no longer loves her, Barbara tells Bill that she thinks her father is dead.

The arrival of Sheriff Gilbeau—ironically, an old flame of Barbara's—confirms Barbara's suspicions. The Sheriff reports that Beverly's body has been hooked on the fishing lines of two good old boys at a nearby lake, and his boat has washed up on a sandbar. He appears to have killed himself. Stoned and in shock, Violet does a weird little dance at the first-act curtain falls.

The second act takes place on the afternoon of Beverly's funeral. The third Weston sister, the needy Karen, has now arrived from Florida, with her sleazy boyfriend Steve in tow. As the assembled group talks and goes through family memorabilia, it becomes clear that Violet and Mattie Fae still treat Ivy as a child; still regard Karen as a shallow profligate; and look toward Barbara with a mixture of deference and distrust.

Meanwhile, Steve, a blown-dry businessman of middle age, pays attention to 15-year-old Jean, chatting conspiratorially with the girl about smoking pot. In a fluster, the child-like Little Charles (Mattie Fae and Charles's adult son) arrives, having overslept his uncle's funeral—the kind of mistake his mother always expects him to make. As the household splits into numerous conversations on different levels of the house, however, we learn that Ivy and Little Charles (cousins, it appears) are romantically involved.

Act II climaxes with the part of the play that has received the most attention and acclaim: a funeral family dinner party from hell. As the Weston family gathers for a meal, Violet unleashes a series of violent, semi-comic personal attacks on all three of her daughters and their partners. As the meal progresses, Violet gets more and more out of control:

CHARLIE: You're in rare form today, Vi.
[. . .]

VIOLET: I'm just truth-telling.
(*Cutting her eyes to Barbara.*)
Some people get antagonized by the truth.

CHARLIE: Everyone here loves you, dear.

VIOLET: You think you can *shame* me, Charlie? Blow it out your ass.

True love: Rondi Reed, Sally Murphy and Deanna Dunagan in August: Osage County. *Phopto: Joan Marcus*

The fight between Barbara and her mother continues to escalate, with an increasingly agitated and aggressive Barbara fighting back and attacking her mother's addiction. Act II ends with Barbara towering over her mother and screaming in her face:

BARBARA: I'M RUNNING THINGS NOW!

AT THE TOP of the third act, the Weston sisters share a quiet, intimate moment in their late father's office, discussing their problematic mother. Even though her sisters disapprove, Ivy is determined to pursue her relationship with Little Charles, and move with him to New York. Each of the sisters realizes that they've remained isolated from others' lives, and they spar over whose responsibility it is to care for their addict of a mother.

Violet then makes an appearance, and tells dark stories of her own childhood, suggesting that her own caustic meanness is rooted in her own lack of a decent childhood. "My momma was a nasty, mean old lady," Violet says. "I suppose that's where I got it from." For a few moments, it seems that there is rapprochement in Osage County. But after this brief respite, a series of revelations shows that the Weston sisters' world is in the throes of utter destruction.

First, the hitherto compliant Charles confronts his wife Mattie Fae, prodding her to find a more generous place in her heart for own son. But Barbara soon learns why Mattie Fae is tough on Little Charles and vehemently opposed to the relationship with his first cousin. Mattie Fae has a confession to make:

> MATTIE FAE: Little Charles is not your cousin. He's your brother. He's your blood brother. Half-brother. He's your father's child. Which means that he is Ivy's brother. Do you see? Little Charles and Ivy are brother and sister.

Mattie Fae and Beverly, it is thus revealed, were lovers. Violet knew all about the brief affair, even if it was never openly discussed.

Next, Steve makes a sexual pass at teenage Jean—but his late-night groping is interrupted by Johnna, who bangs him on the head with a kitchen pan. The commotion wakes the house and Barbara's life continues to implode. To her mother's horror, Jean points out that her outraged father is not so different from Steve and is currently sleeping with a woman only a few years older than Jean herself. Although in shock, Karen stands by her errant lover as she follows him out of this house of horrors. She appears to think she has no other choice:

> KAREN: I'm not defending him. He's not perfect. Just like all the rest of us, down here, in the muck. I'm no angel myself. I've done some things I'm not proud of. Things you'll never know about. Know what? I may even have to do some things I'm not proud of *again*. Cause sometimes life puts you in a corner that way. And I am a human being after all.
> [. . .]
> And anyway, you have your own hash to settle. Before you start making speeches to the rest of us.

In the next scene, Johnna tells Barbara that she will stay on. She needs the work and seems strangely unaffected by all the Weston bile, and the Sheriff reappears, seemingly interested in rekindling his old friendship with Barbara. But he also has new information to impart—Beverly, it appears, spent the two nights before his death in the Country Squire Motel.

Ivy later summons the courage and tells Violet about her relationship with Little Charles. With callous disregard for her horrified daughter's feelings, Violet reveals the truth about where Little Charles came from. "Why did you tell me? Why in God's name did you tell me this?," screams the hysterical

Ivy before running out of the house, perhaps into the arms of her brother—and perhaps forever. "You will never see me again," she screams to her shellshocked sister.

Reeling from that encounter, Barbara then learns that Violet actually knew Beverly was at the motel. He had left him a note, it turns out. But she didn't call for two days—and he was already checked out. This revelation that her mother could have saved her father nearly pushes Barbara over the edge and she walks out of the house. As the curtain falls, Violet is alone in the house—except for Johnna. Violet slowly, painfully climbs the stairs to the attic and puts her head in Johnna's lap, as if she were the most malevolent baby imaginable.

LETTS MADE SLIGHT changes in the script between Chicago and Broadway, though Shapiro's production otherwise remained much the same. The third-act revelations were spaced in less overwhelming fashion, and the order of the characters' final exits in Act III was changed. By letting Barbara be the last character to leave the house, Letts better focused the play on the iconic mother-daughter battle. In New York, *August* more obviously became Barbara's play (even if the Tony Award went to the relentless Dunagan) and Morton's emotional torrent of a performance developed even greater importance. On the other hand, the Broadway production used electronic amplification, which may have reduced the physical strain and strife that was such a feature of the acoustic production in the intimate Steppenwolf theater.

In some ways, *August: Osage County* is a play without obvious basis in reality. Its characters are extreme, its revelations overwhelming, its traumas eye-popping. But for small-town academics, at least, the piece rings uncommonly true. Beverly Weston—a formalist poet stuck in the Plains—has passed on a toxic mix of education, sophistication, isolation and alienation to his children. If Edward Albee's *Who's Afraid of Virginia Woolf?* nails the impotence of life on a milquetoast East Coast campus, *August* points to the cultural disconnect of a humanities professor forced—for the rare job—to rear his family in a rural, arid setting where artists and writers mostly look ridiculous. It is a place that seems a million miles from tweedy campuses of falling leaves.

The play asks: Whither a poet in Oklahoma? Can one really spout Eliot to the sons and daughters of oil men and be happy? Can one do so without drinking or doping oneself? And, if one can, what in the hell are the children to do? And their children? Therein lies another major theme of this play: the inability of its characters to come to terms with their environment. In many ways, the placid character of Johnna—a Native American who literally lives in the attic and descends to cook, clean and handhold for the white people—is the most interesting (and underexplored) figure in the play. Her presence comforts and helps the Westons, yet it also reminds us of their hapless illegitimacy. The land, after all, belongs to Native Americans. Johnna, whose family was loving and functional—or so we are told—is demonstrably at ease there. She is also at ease with her loss. Nothing the Westons do can faze her.

White settlers may think they had tamed it long ago, but *August* suggests that the space, heat and isolation of the Plains provokes dysfunction as one of the inevitable prices paid. One need only ponder the example of Dick Cheney, George W. Bush's vice president, who was, arguably, formed by the mores of his home state of Wyoming into a dangerous mix of stubbornness, resilience and bitterness. "This country was always a whorehouse," declares the mad-as-hell Barbara, in an apparent reference to the Bush-Cheney administration sparked by the dog-eat-dog Plains, "but at least it used to have some promise." In many ways, *August* explores the slow death of the atrophied, exurban American family.

SO WAS THIS the first great American play of the 21st century? It is probably too early to say. But *August* surely updated the all-too-familiar memoir about maturing amid parental crazies. It surely caught the popular imagination. It surely had the audience's eyes popping out on stalks. In New York, it felt as tough the audience suddenly had a terrifying encounter with the very kinds of friends and relatives they moved to the city—and vacationed in Europe—to ignore. Thanks to Steppenwolf, they were suddenly b-a-a-c-k. And you only had to look around the orchestra to see the shock.

Letts is hardly the first dramatist to observe that we all turn into our parents. But amid all of its genre-driven games and Gothic revelations, this was a play that dispensed terrifying truths. When Amy Morton's Barbara collapsed in agony on the stairs after hearing of her beloved father's demise, we instantly recognized the moment as one of horror that awaits us all. When Sally Murphy's Ivy made her pathetic play for happiness with her cousin—or, rather, her brother—we understood and wished her well. When Mariann Mayberry's Karen could not dump her louse of a boyfriend, we made allowances. Like her, we have come to know that "everything lives in the middle."

And many of us could even understand the marriage of Violet and Beverly, founded on mutual personal unhappiness, amplified by lives of promise and regret, focused on the joys and disappointments of children and always lived smack in the middle of absolutely nowhere.

2007–2008 Best Play

DIVIDING THE ESTATE

By Horton Foote

○ ○ ○ ○ ○

Essay by Garrett Eisler

LUCILLE: Who wrote *The Grapes of Wrath*?

PAULINE: John Steinbeck.

LUCILLE: Oh, yes. I think I read that. What is it about?

MARY JO: Didn't you hear her? The dust bowl.

PAULINE: And the Okies.

LUCILLE: Oh, yes, I think I do remember that.

HORTON FOOTE MAY have written *Dividing the Estate* in 1989, but by the time it finally opened in New York eighteen years later, it could not have seemed more current. The day the *New York Times* ran a rave review of the Primary Stages production, the paper also reported that home prices had just experienced "the steepest monthly price drop since December 1970." By year's end home foreclosures rose more than 75 percent over 2006 rates and housing sales plummeted 25 percent. The subprime mortgage crisis of 2007 was well underway and Foote's play about a Texas family's dependence on their overvalued property found its moment.

Across seven decades, Foote has not only been impressively prolific (more than 60 plays, screenplays and teleplays) but a consistently insightful chronicler of American life across the 20th century. Because so many of his characters hail from rural and smalltown Texas, he has long been marginalized by critics as a "regional writer." Among his most prominent titles are the modern classic *The Trip to Bountiful* (written first for television in 1953, then for the stage and later for a successful 1985 feature film); the screen adaptation of Harper Lee's *To Kill a Mockingbird* (1962) and his own original screenplay *Tender Mercies* (1984), both Academy Award-winners; and the epic nine-play cycle *Orphans' Home*, chronicling 25 years in the life a single Texas family in and around a single Texas town—the fictional Harrison, Texas, modeled on his hometown of Wharton and the setting of *Dividing the Estate*.

Good son: Devon Abner and Penny Fuller in Dividing the Estate. *Photo: James Leynse*

During the past decade or so, New York has enjoyed something of a Foote renaissance. The Signature Theatre Company devoted its 1994–95 season to Foote and premiered *The Young Man From Atlanta*, which received the 1995 Pulitzer Prize, a Best Play honor from this series and later ran on Broadway for 84 performances (1997). Since 1998, director Michael Wilson—who staged this production—has vigorously championed Foote's work at Hartford Stage Company, leading to Off Broadway transfers, including *The Day Emily Married* at Primary Stages in 2004. Signature revisited Foote in 2005 with a soldout revival of *The Trip to Bountiful*, which later had a successful run at Chicago's Goodman Theatre, where artistic director Robert Falls has also been a Foote advocate. President Bill Clinton is apparently a fan as well, awarding Foote a 2000 National Medal of Arts.

When the first version of *Dividing the Estate* premiered at Princeton's McCarter Theatre Center—March 31, 1989—it was dismissed by a visiting *New York Times* critic as "outlandishly overwritten" like "an early, rough draft," forestalling a New York transfer at the time. But with his star rising once again at the onset of a new century (as he himself entered his tenth decade), Foote was able to resuscitate the project at last. Ever a perfectionist, Foote revisited the text with an eye to streamlining. "He did a lot of work on it. He reconceived," said Casey Childs, executive producer of Primary Stages. "We consider it a new play." The question of how "new" the play was in 2007, however, became thorny once it proved successful. When nomination season arrived the following spring, Foote was adamant that the Lucille Lortel Awards consider it a new work. The Lortel committee eventually overruled Foote's appeal, nominating the Primary Stages production for best revival. (As with *Young Man*'s Tony Award nomination for best play 10 years earlier, Foote did not win.)

Foote exhibits a dry wit and a taste for eccentric characters.

GIVEN FOOTE'S REPUTATION for quiet contemplative plays set to the slow tempo of rural life in earlier times (earning him the moniker "Chekhov of the South"), *Dividing the Estate* is by comparison quite raucous. In place of quiet desperation, the combative members of the Gordon clan offer rude indignation. Foote has always exhibited a dry wit and a taste for eccentric characters, but *Estate* is uncharacteristically comic in conception, and dark at that. Chekhov may still hover over this tale of petty former aristocrats letting their property slip away, but if it is part *Cherry Orchard* it is also akin to Lillian Hellman's *The Little Foxes*.

The play's central figure—though there are no starring roles in such a true ensemble piece—is Stella Gordon, the octogenarian matriarch of this once-upstanding Harrison, Texas, family. Still living in the house where she was born, Stella is the last remaining link to the days of King Cotton, formerly the chief income of this 5,000-acre estate. Faded glory figures prominently in the play, in numerous anecdotes Foote scatters throughout the dialogue. While such discursive trips down memory lane are perhaps an acquired taste, the drifting quality of Stella's memories are especially haunting. When she chats, for instance, with Doug, an aged servant to the family her entire life, the amnesia of both characters is as affecting as it is telling about their social irrelevancy:

> STELLA: When did you come to work here?
>
> DOUG: When I was five years old. Your papa brought my mama in from the farm after my daddy was killed by one of the bulls, and she cooked for you all.

STELLA: Henrietta?

DOUG: Yes'um. I remember the day you was born and the day you got married, and the day your husband, Mister Charles, died.

STELLA: Charlie wasn't my husband, Doug. He was Lucille's husband—Donald was my husband.

DOUG: Yes'um that's how it was. I remember all of it.

Stella's 40-year marriage to the late Donald, produced three children: Lucille, Lewis and Mary Jo. After Donald's death Lucille's husband Charlie took over the duties of managing the estate until he "died an early death" in the blistering heat of the fields. Lucille's son—called "Son" by everyone—quit college, being the only man in the family capable of saving the estate from total financial ruin. Or at least postponing it.

Of Stella's children, only Mary Jo has left the nest to start a family of her own. Lewis (called "Brother") and Lucille both remain unemployed and dependent upon the estate for subsistence, even well into their 50s. Lewis's disintegration into alcoholism, gambling debt and underage skirt-chasing sounds a note of pathetic underachievement at the very outset of the play, as he begs Son to loan him $10,000 to appease the angry father of his latest female companion. Lewis already has a debt of $200,000—which he considers simply an "advance" on his inheritance. Entrusted with policing his own elders, Son barely has space for a life of his own. After an earlier marriage fell apart when the family's antics drove his wife to the brink, he now hopes to start over with Pauline, a local schoolteacher to whom he has just proposed.

In revising the play Foote has not updated it. The time is still 1987, the era in which it was written. What was at first a contemporary play thus now plays as a modern period piece; while the period may be recent, it is a moment that stands as pivotal in American history. The year of one of the nation's worst recent recessions, it marked the transition from Reagan-era optimism and expansionism into the uncertainty of globalization and rapid technological advancement. Thus, Mary Jo's husband, Bob, can admit that Houston is suffering a "depression" yet moments later assert "there is still a lot of money" there.

In downtown Harrison, we're told, despite an effort at urban renewal and a tourist-friendly "restoration" of historical buildings, most of the storefronts lie empty and housing values have declined by half. Local factories and natural resources have been bought out by foreign companies and movie theatres have closed thanks to video-cassette machines. In their insular fashion, the Gordons still cannot get a handle on how the landscape

Little foxes? Penny Fuller, Hallie Foote and Elizabeth Ashley in Dividing the Estate. *Photo: James Leynse*

of America is changing. Thanks to new waves of immigration and porous trade borders, the world has come to Harrison, Texas—a town where everyone used to know everyone else by name.

> LUCILLE: We have a plastic factory here now, you know. [. . .] We had a mattress factory about six years ago, but it didn't seem to prosper.
>
> MARY JO: Who owns the plastic factory? Anyone we know?
>
> LUCILLE: No, it's owned by a man from Taiwan.
>
> MARY JO: Taiwan? My God, how did he ever get here?
>
> LUCILLE: I don't know. They're all over the coast fishing.
>
> MARY JO: They're not from Taiwan, Sister—they're from Vietnam.

WELCOME TO TEXAS, 1987. Not all businessmen are white and the French own the sulphur mines, into which they dump toxic waste. One of Foote's many ironies in the play, however, is that the Gordons were far from true plantation aristocracy themselves: the founder of the dynasty was an ex-Union soldier who came to Harrison during Reconstruction to buy cheap land and fleece the locals. (His legacy is recounted in Foote's 2001 play *The*

Carpetbaggers' Children.) The play's perspective on its characters and their history has been enriched by time. Foote's characteristic elegies of the vanishing past play less as nostalgia than as autopsy. In his investigation of the family's demise, the playwright asks not only what happened to the Gordons, but also what happened to Harrison—and by extension, America—at the close of the 20th century.

The family reunion that begins the play—Mary Jo, Bob and their two daughters are driving in for dinner from Houston—quickly turns into an estate-planning seminar. While Stella has always assumed the family home and property would be handed down in perpetuity, her children have less interest in preserving a dynasty that no longer profits them. Lewis sets the plot in motion by calling for Stella to divide the estate: give each of the three children his or her share and *now*. Mary Jo and Bob also press for immediate financial gratification; Bob hasn't made a real estate sale in recession-era Houston for four months and one of their daughters is getting married. Only Lucille, whose modest needs are provided for by her son and mother, is content to live within her means.

Deathwatch: Jenny Dare Paulin, Nicole Lowrance, Hallie Foote and James DeMarse in Dividing the Estate. *Photo: James Leynse*

The drive to divide may seem heartless and crass, but Stella's stubborn insistence on a family unity that no longer exists emerges as equally short sighted, if more sympathetic. She cannot bring herself to dissolve the family heritage she identifies with the property itself. Stella even threatens to bypass her children entirely when it comes to the ownership of the house, which she is determined to keep out of their hands and bequeath to Son on the condition that he never sell it and passes it down to *his* children, ensuring at least a few more generations of Gordons on this land.

The estate's history is most effectively embodied onstage not by any Gordon, but by the 92-year-old Doug, the last of a long line of African-American sharecroppers who once tilled the Gordon fields and whom Stella has known all her life. Stella taught him to read and write when she was just a girl, while he and his mother Henrietta worked in the family's kitchen. Though Doug is of little use now, Stella's loyalty to him is unconditional. Doug's sudden death, which ends the first act of *Dividing the Estate*, eloquently eulogizes the complex relationships these people once had to this land and to each other.

AFTER DOUG'S PASSING, Stella's seems not long to follow. As Act II begins, her resistance to Mary Jo and Bob's incessant financial planning turns to resignation. Bob is preoccupied with the threat of a heavy estate tax that could be levied on any inheritance they receive from Stella—so he urges her to dole all of it out now in little pieces, under the radar of the government. Stella is unconcerned about that, but compromises on allowing the family to entertain offers from oil and gas companies for drilling leases. Son echoes his grandmother's sense of history when he muses how "sad" that might be, however lucrative, since "it means we no longer know how to make a living out of our own land unless we find oil and gas there."

Stella retires upstairs, expiring peacefully offstage, much to the family's surprise. Mary Jo and her husband make no effort to conceal their utterly practical assessment of what, to most, would be inconsolable loss.

> BOB: What is it, honey?
>
> MARY JO: Mama has left us, Bob.
>
> BOB: My God!
>
> MARY JO: She has gone to her rest.
>
> BOB: My God Almighty! (*A pause.*) Well, the estate is going to be divided now, after all these years. [. . .]
>
> MARY JO: Will you go call the funeral parlour, Bob? Ask them please to come get Mama?

BOB: I will. And then I'm going to call the bank and tell them we will have some money soon. I'm sure tomorrow or the next day I can borrow on our share of the estate.

MARY JO: I'm sure you can.

(*BOB starts out.*)

MARY JO: Bob, how much do you think our share will be?

BOB: Oh, I'd just be guessing until I see some actual figures. But enough. And it's come just in time let me tell you.

The moment might appear crude or clichéd were it not for the matter-of-factness with which the two alternate between obligatory grieving and irrepressible fulfillment. Neither they nor Foote have time for sentimentality when the stakes are this high. "Now, now. It's going to be all right," Bob consoles Mary Jo, adding without a trace of irony: "But I was scared to death for awhile." "I know you were," Mary Jo replies. "I was, too." No Lord and Lady Macbeth here—just a couple of scared Houston suburbanites who are overextended.

A week later, the Gordon siblings are dividing furnishings and hiring lawyers. "Oh, I think it is a shame for brothers and sisters to need lawyers," protests Lucille—before retaining an attorney herself. When Bob, Lewis and Son go downtown to meet with Stella's lawyer, however, Foote has one more twist in store for his hapless heirs. The estate, for all practical purposes, turns out to be worthless. As the men explain upon their return to a shellshocked room, more than a fifth of whatever value the government estimates as the estate's worth must go to taxes, plus another 10 percent to the lawyer just for officiating the transactions. Any legal appeal to lessen the taxes would, of course, be costly in itself—and could delay any actual payouts for years.

In yet another of Foote's mischievous ironies, this means the Gordons will have to raise money in order to inherit relatively little. With all of the advances that Lewis and Mary Jo have taken over the years, there is not enough on hand now to pay the taxes, fees and various cash bequests called for by Stella's will. They have no choice now but to sell the estate. In better times, the house itself would fetch a handsome price, but in the current housing slump the family will be lucky to get anything. The House of Gordon has truly fallen. With the will in probate, no funds may be released or even borrowed against for the foreseeable future without permission of the executor, who is the lawyer.

This grand climactic accounting plays as both a cruel joke of fate and a comeuppance, with Mary Jo and Bob, no doubt, the most deserving. It is a masterly scene with its flurry of figures and balance-sheet calculations, but Foote never lets us forget the more wounding emotional costs. The two remaining servants, for instance, are elated to hear Stella left them each $5,000 in the will—before they are told they will not receive it until the litigation ends, *and* that they are dismissed from their jobs because the Gordons can no longer pay them. Adding insult to injury, Bob also tells Mary Jo that their Houston home has just been foreclosed. He was so confident the inheritance would save the day, he had deemed it unnecessary to mention.

By dividing, the Gordons have ended up conquering only themselves. The only solution, as Son insists, is to finally live and work together as a family unit. With his less individualistic and clearly more sensible work ethic, Son proposes a model of collectivism, quite a radical idea to this house full of once-rich Texans. With each contributing according to his or her abilities even Lucille and Mary Jo, who have never worked a day in their lives, will have to earn their daily bread. Son's fiancée, the schoolteacher Pauline, comes to the fore in the play's closing moments, as the messenger of a new age. Having annoyed the family for much of the play with her frequent tributes to the increasingly multicultural diversity of Texas, fate now seems to vindicate her, much to Mary Jo's chagrin.

> PAULINE: I think it can be exciting, and a real challenge to us all. We can be like the Korean and Vietnamese families moving into Houston, and all over the coast—they live together, they work together.
>
> MARY JO: Well, I'm neither Korean or Taiwanese, thank you.

Mary Jo fights the humiliation of this mighty fall to the end, but it has taken a crisis of this magnitude to force the Gordons to finally break out of their bubble and acknowledge the world around them—even if that means getting a job. Appropriately, Foote includes among Pauline's digressions a reference to *The Grapes of Wrath*. With no jobs, no cash or credit, and in some cases no home, the Gordons just may be the new "Okies" of the dispossessed Texas aristocracy. For good measure, before the final curtain Foote adds to the mix a new member of the family—Lewis's teenage girlfriend Irene, cashier at the local "Whataburger" chain. Rich and poor, young and old, carpetbagger and native, everyone is truly equal now.

WHILE GENERALLY APPRECIATIVE of the play on its own merits, some reviewers could not resist comparisons to other southern dysfunctional-family inheritance plays—especially *Cat on a Hot Tin Roof*. The *New York Post*'s Frank Scheck called it "a more polite variation" on *Cat*, "minus the sex."

Also frequently invoked was the season's reigning new hit play, Tracy Letts's *August: Osage County*, whose intoxicated frenzies certainly offered more emotional fireworks. But others saw a more satiric streak to *Dividing* that distinguished it from that genre; *The New York Sun*'s Eric Grode deemed it a "mildly dark comedy—or perhaps a chipper tragedy." *The New York Times*'s Ben Brantley could not conceal a personal delight in the Gordons' idiosyncratic idioms, "As always with Mr. Foote, even big events are folded into a conversational style that meanders like a lazy river, giving as much emphasis to the mundane as the monumental." Such notices gave the small, nonprofit Primary Stages a great success, but due to the constraints of the company's season schedule and the heavily booked 59E59 space, the production was unable to extend past the slated four-week run, closing October 27. However, Primary Stages and Lincoln Center Theater soon announced a joint venture to transfer the Michael Wilson production to Broadway in November 2008.

It was the lively cast that generated enthusiasm for this production. While the character of Stella dies well before the play's end, it was hard to eclipse Elizabeth Ashley as the perceived star of the show—especially given her long association with the work of Tennessee Williams. For some, the most notable performance was that by Foote's frequent and important collaborator, his daughter Hallie. The hardhearted Mary Jo is a role that could easily come off as shrewish in lesser hands, but the younger Foote clearly shares her father's deep empathy for his characters. Now 57 and a veteran of nearly all of her father's plays, Hallie Foote's willful and sharp performances have become a regular attraction of both premieres and revivals of her father's work. With both Horton and Hallie Foote receiving their due in the New York theatre—and with Hallie's real-life husband Devon Abner playing Son, to boot—*Dividing the Estate* became not just an affecting play, but a moving theatrical event.

2007–2008 Best Play

EURYDICE

By Sarah Ruhl

○ ○ ○ ○ ○

Essay by Celia Wren

ORPHEUS: I'm going to make each strand of your hair into an instrument. Your hair will stand on end as it plays my music and become a hair orchestra. It will fly you up into the sky.

EURYDICE: I don't know if I want to be an instrument.

ORPHEUS: Why?

EURYDICE: Won't I fall down when the song ends?

ORPHEUS: That's true. But the clouds will be so moved by your music that they will fill up with water until they become heavy and you'll sit on one and fall gently down to earth.

T HE RIVER LETHE could hardly have expected the extreme makeover it gets in *eurydice*, Sarah Ruhl's achingly wistful, myth-transmuting play. The dramatist channels the legendary Hadean stream into a range of eerie liquid phenomena: ghostly dripping sounds; a mysterious water pump; a daydream of weeping clouds; an elevator in which it is always raining. The aquatic imagery—which might, in another context, give a professional plumber the heebie-jeebies—shimmers at the heart of *eurydice*, helping the play muse eloquently on the subjects of memory and grief. Tears, after all, are another liquid variant—not that Ruhl's play overtly depicts or demands them: *eurydice* grapples with wrenching emotion without ever straying into sentimentality.

That there is more to this 90-minute drama than water metaphors goes without saying, given that Ruhl is arguably the current moment's most acclaimed young dramatist. Just nine months before *eurydice*'s 2007 opening at New York's Second Stage Theatre, she pocketed one of the prestigious MacArthur Fellowships (popularly termed "genius grants") for her plays, which tend to share a trademark steely poetry, a metaphysical adventurousness and an enigmatic whimsy that can mask a pronounced sadness.

Water wonder: Maria Dizzia in eurydice. *Photo: Joan Marcus*

Written after the death of Ruhl's father—and dedicated to him—*eurydice* brims with those qualities, not least the deadpan humor. In Ruhl's hands, the god Pluto becomes a tricycle-riding brat; the Underworld's residents include a chorus of obnoxious talking stones; and a dead man, offering his daughter wisdom from the far side of the grave, solemnly tells her that "toasting bread without burning requires singleness of purpose, vigilance and steadfast watching." In overhauling the Orpheus legend, Ruhl may be trekking in the wake of Jean Cocteau, Jean Anouilh and Tennessee Williams, but she also owes a debt to Lewis Carroll. She acknowledges that influence in the script's introductory notes, which state that "the Underworld should resemble the world of *Alice in Wonderland* more than it resembles Hades." Still, even the play's flashes of zaniness illuminate its chief concerns: Loss and bereavement, Ruhl seems to suggest, are as disorienting as any down-the-rabbit-hole freefall.

Holding its curiouser-and-curiouser trappings in reserve, *eurydice*—which had its 2003 world premiere at Madison Repertory Theatre in Wisconsin—opens with intimations of calm, expansiveness and water. That vision received an apt physical embodiment, at Second Stage Theatre, in designer Scott Bradley's blue-green tile set, which stayed in place throughout the production. The young lovers Orpheus and Eurydice are basking in each other's presence at the beach, wearing, as specified in the stage directions, "swimming outfits from the 1950s." The retro costuming adds an element of nostalgia, subtly establishing the motifs of change and bygone time.

Some young beaux may do their courting with Tiffany baubles—nothing so vulgar or trifling for this Orpheus guy! Through silent gestures, in the play's initial moments, the musician purports to give Eurydice the sea, the sky and the stars. "That's very generous," she responds, playing along.

The play opens with intimations of calm and expansiveness.

Orpheus's caprice points to the sense of power and invincibility people tend to experience in the throes of new love—a euphoria that will prove all too short-lived once death enters the picture.

While head-over-heels in love, Orpheus and Eurydice are not actually on the same wavelength, their dialogue reveals. He is obsessed with music, contemplating—in the eccentric exchange cited atop this essay—turning his beloved into a one-woman orchestra pit. By contrast, she volunteers, "I'm bad at remembering melodies," and she flubs the rhythm of a tune he tries to teach her. Her own preferred pastime is reading—especially when it is a volume that is as "interesting" as the unnamed one she claims to have just perused.

Throughout the couple's oddly vague chat about books, music and memory—a conversation that concludes with their blissful agreement to marry—the word "interesting" keeps appearing. Speaking of the song he has just composed for Eurydice, Orpheus announces that "It's not *interesting* or *not interesting*. It just—is." Each time the term "interesting" crops up, it seems more banal and meaningless, providing a first taste of one of the play's salient themes: the fallibility of language in the face of love and death.

That concept tinges the following scene—one of many in the play that emphasize loneliness, depicting a character stranded on the wrong side of mortality, pining for a loved one. Eurydice's deceased Father, writing her a letter on the occasion of her marriage, advises her on toast preparation and other topics, and describes the creepy environment of the afterlife, which echoes with "strange high-pitched noises—like a tea kettle always boiling over." Language is none too potent here: Unlike the Father, most dead people have forgotten how to read and write.

In the land of the living, a thirsty Eurydice, fetching water from an outside pump, during her wedding festivities, encounters the Nasty Interesting Man, who invites her to a party full of "interesting" people. Now the term "interesting" acquires a new overtone, implying a flashy novelty that tempts the susceptible away from the loved, trusted and familiar. Ruhl's play is full of such evolving, eddying verbal and pictorial resonances, refracting like waves in a troubled pond, or motifs in a symphony. The published script even divides the drama into three "movements," as if taking a cue from Orpheus.

The Man discovers the Father's letter and—after brief scenes of the newlyweds dancing and the Father dancing empathetically, alone—lures Eurydice to his high-rise apartment on the pretext of giving her the epistle. When he attempts to seduce her (she needs a man with "big stupid hands like potatoes" he tells her, in one of the script's characteristic flashes of sphinx-like lyricism), she flees and falls to her death—a tragedy that Ruhl

Private journey: Maria Dizzia and Joseph Parks in eurydice. *Photo: Joan Marcus*

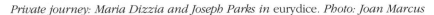

chronicles via a haunting sound montage: "xylophones, brass bands, sounds of falling, sounds of vertigo."

"THERE IS NO set change," Ruhl notes in the script as the action moves more fully into the stygian region. Dripping sounds signal the new location, as does the appearance of three bizarre personages who announce themselves to be Stones. The raining elevator opens its doors, discharging Eurydice, who is dressed in a 1930s suit—again that tinge of nostalgia. Death has stripped her of verbal skills. Efforts to speak yield only "a great humming noise," a phenomenon explained by the talking rocks:

> THE STONES: Eurydice wants to speak to you.
> But she can't speak your language anymore.
> She talks in the language of dead people now.
>
> LITTLE STONE: It's a very quiet language.
>
> LOUD STONE: Like if the pores in your face
> opened up and talked.

If this trio is unfeeling, Eurydice does have a friend in Hades: her father. The newly Lethe-immersed heroine doesn't recognize her parent—she takes him for a hotel porter—and she doesn't initially comprehend his speech. "When you were alive, I was your tree," he tells her, in a line that drives home the play's message about the quicksand nature of language. The metaphor hits its target. "My tree!" she responds, understanding. "Yes, the tall one in the backyard! I used to sit all day in its shade!"

The searingly tender scenes that follow chronicle the thawing of the father-daughter relationship. When the weary Eurydice requests a room, her parent makes one for her out of string. There are, apparently, no more substantial chambers in the Underworld. He shares family memories, teaches her words ("Defunct. [. . .] It means dead in a very abrupt way. Not the way I died, which was slowly. But all at once, in cowboy boots."), and sings the tune "I Got Rhythm," which harkens back to Eurydice's difficulty with rhythm in the play's opening sequence.

Peppered between the family intimacies, brief monologue snippets capture the grieving Orpheus. He fails to reach his wife by telephone, but writes her letters and sends her the collected works of William Shakespeare. The book and missives reach her, but she has forgotten how to read and tries to decipher a letter by standing on it. Patiently, her father teaches her. Audiences will appreciate the heart-rending irony in his choice of instruction text: the *King Lear* speech in which the monarch reconciles with the soon-to-be-dead Cordelia, imagining living with her "like birds i' the cage."

The fact that a "cage" is structurally similar to a room made of string makes this literary echo all the more affecting.

Such cozy domesticity is too good to last. One day, while the Father is out, the Lord of the Underworld zooms up on his tricycle, heralded by heavy-metal music. Bearing a distinct similarity to the Nasty Interesting Man—he is played by the same actor—the kid is simultaneously cute and chilling:

> CHILD: I am Lord of the Underworld.
>
> EURYDICE: Very funny.
>
> CHILD: I am.
>
> EURYDICE: Prove it.
>
> CHILD: I can do chin-ups inside your bones. Close your eyes.
>
> (*She closes her eyes.*)
>
> EURYDICE: Ow.
>
> CHILD: See?

This pint-sized infernal tyrant, who seems smitten with Eurydice, threatens to re-submerge her in the River Lethe, so that she forgets about her father and the desirability of rooms. "You need a lover. I'll be back," he tells her, riding off with a "hysterical laugh."

MEANWHILE, ORPHEUS BRAINSTORMS strategies for liberating his wife. In one of the most beautiful of his solo scenes, he stands shouting in a storm and imagines hitching a ride with a raindrop:

> ORPHEUS: If a drop of water enters the soil
> At a particular angle, with a particular pitch,
> What's to say a man can't ride one note
> Into the earth like a fireman's pole?
>
> (*He puts a bucket on the ground to catch rain falling.*
> *He looks at the rain falling into the bucket.*
> *He tunes his guitar, trying to make the pitch of each note*
> *correspond with the pitch of each water drop.* [. . .])

The resourceful husband makes it to Hades, and—as in the traditional Greek myth—receives permission to lead Eurydice out, provided he does not glance back at her during their journey. Though obviously emotionally devastated, the Father urges her to follow her spouse, because, "you should love your family until the grapes grow dust on their purple faces."

But Eurydice loses her nerve as she walks. She wishes she could return to her father—and finally, fatally, calls Orpheus's name, prompting

Father's words: Maria Dizzia and Charles Shaw Robinson in eurydice. *Photo: Joan Marcus*

him to look back. Ever conscious of this play's sound dimension, Ruhl stipulates that a "ping" should resound as supernatural forces—or psychological ones, depending on interpretation—drive the couple apart. As so often in *eurydice*, it is the juxtaposition between the vividly specific and the overwhelmingly mystical that gives the moment its unsettling power. The aftermath of the rescue attempt unfurls almost as a melancholy coda. Deserted and desperately lonely, the Father dips himself in the river of forgetting. Another ping sounds with this development, which may remind English majors of Tennyson's rest-in-oblivion poem "The Lotus-Eaters," a borrowing from Greek mythology, as with Ruhl's play.

Arriving at their former stomping grounds, Eurydice finds that she is too late to resume her beatific afterlife-with-father. She attempts to rouse him, but cannot. "Didn't you already mourn for your father, young Lady?" the obstreperous Loud Stone inquires. Eurydice's rage at the unsympathetic Stones summons the Lord of the Underworld, who—as if he has downed a *Wonderland* "Drink Me" potion—has mysteriously grown tall. In a macabre counterpoint to Orpheus's proposal, the Lord threatens to marry Eurydice: "The wedding songs are already being written," he ghoulishly informs her. "A song is two dead bodies rubbing under the covers to keep warm."

After composing a loving letter to Orpheus, the play's protagonist douses herself in the Lethe (ping) and falls asleep. Just after she does so—in yet another instance of tragically bad timing—Orpheus himself arrives in the raining elevator. He discovers her letter, but has forgotten how to read it. The two spouses never could synchronize their rhythms.

LES WATERS'S STAGING of *eurydice*—which ran at Yale Repertory Theatre in the fall of 2006, and landed at Second Stage in June 2007 (the director, designers and several of the actors had also been with a 2004 version at Berkeley Repertory Theatre)—reveled both in the play's poignancy and in its through-the-lookingglass oddness. For instance, Maria Dizzia's and Joseph Parks's Eurydice and Orpheus seemed almost childlike, emphasizing the tug-at-the-heartstrings factor, while Mark Zeisler's ghoulishly cranky and gleeful Lord of the Underworld broadcast Mad Hatter outlandishness. (Charles Shaw Robinson played the vulnerable Father.)

The production's design was equally sophisticated. Although the set's turquoise tiles evoked streams and pools, any Monet-style serenity was offset by the tilted trim and apertures along the rear wall, the marks of a universe off-kilter. Furthering this topsy-turvy quality, upside-down chandeliers rose from the floor when Eurydice traveled to the Underworld. (In a production notebook published in the December 2006 edition of *American Theatre*, designer Bradley confided that this image had come to him in a dream shortly after the death of his partner.)

Admittedly, it was the raining elevator—whose angles were also askew—that provided the principal *coup de théâtre*: When the doors opened, Russell H. Champa's dramatic lighting illuminated figures drenched in falling torrents, and water gushed from the contraption's floor onto the main part of the stage—a hallucinatory, pulse-quickening tableau, as if Salvador Dalí were working for the Weather Channel.

In the show's other sequences, Champa's lighting shifted between luminous and—for the Lord of the Underworld's cameos—rock-concert lurid, while Bray Poor's sound design waxed elegiac and spooky, by turns. Meg Neville's costumes kept pace with this intensity: Her eye-catching sherbet-pink 1930s suit, for Eurydice's afterlife sequences, underscored the incongruity of the heroine's Hadean sojourn. And then there were the splendidly ragged brown costumes for the Stones (Gian-Murray Gianino as the Loud Stone; Carla Harting as the Little Stone; Ramiz Monsef as the Big Stone), whom Neville and director Waters turned into a seedy Victorian music-hall trio, with whitened faces and dark circles under their eyes. The aura of Dickensian grotesque created by the costumes, together with the actors' suitably shrill, grouchy delivery of their lines—Ruhl's script urges that the Stones be rendered as "nasty children at a birthday party"—gave their scenes a touch of gallows humor.

Drolly freakish as they are, the Stones contribute to the play's overarching preoccupation with grief. A mourning or spiritually afflicted person is sometimes said to be "heavy-hearted" and Ruhl hints at that heaviness of spirit with the imagery of stones. Just as the adjective "stonyhearted" signifies pitilessness, so the Stones imply the inexorability of death and time. "You'll break your hand," the Big Stone gloats when a frustrated Eurydice tries to hit him and his buddies, in the play's final scene.

The play's water imagery conveys emotion in a similarly indirect way. We don't see Eurydice, Orpheus and the Father crying. Rather, the raining elevator, the water pump, and those ubiquitous dripping sounds serve as powerful objective correlatives for sorrow, while wholly avoiding mawkishness. It is almost as if, in *eurydice*, the entire universe were weeping over death, chronology and the pain of lost love. For our skeptical, self-conscious, post-postmodern age, a *King Lear*-variety storm might be hard to swallow—but cosmic desolation that resembles a leaky faucet? That seems about right.

IT IS PERHAPS because of *eurydice*'s subtly tragic ethos that the play has struck such a chord (the *New Yorker*'s John Lahr dubbed the drama "luminous" and "exhilarating"; the *New York Times*'s Charles Isherwood called it "devastatingly lovely"; and, just as tellingly, in the 2008-09 season, the drama is to receive productions around the country). We live in a world where many frustrating boundaries have been erased. Technological innovations such as cell phones, blogs, YouTube, and Twitter extend the borders of the self—people can share their activities and musings not only with loved ones but with the entire planet, should they so choose—while virtual-reality computer games permit one existence to blur into another.

By contrast, Ruhl's Orpheus riff is full of limits and boundaries: the string room; the aerobically strenuous staircase leading to the Nasty Man's apartment; the division between the loved and the "interesting"; the communication barrier between the cognizant and the Lethe-dunked; the gap between the Underworld and life. The play acknowledges and comes to terms with mortality and ticking clocks—obstacles that continue to stonewall our cyber-savvy era. After all the sad plot twists and Cheshire Cat-style antics have subsided, *eurydice*'s tone is one of incantatory resignation—a mood very like the eponymous heroine's, when she speaks of her beloved yet strangely alien husband:

> EURYDICE: [. . .] This is what it is to love an artist: The moon is always rising above your house. [. . .] But he is always going away from you. Inside his head there is always something more beautiful.

2007–2008 Best Play

THE FARNSWORTH INVENTION

By Aaron Sorkin

○ ○ ○ ○ ○

Essay by Christopher Rawson

SARNOFF: [. . .] And by the way the ends do justify the means, *that's what the means are for.* [. . .]

THUS DAVID SARNOFF, immigrant, American original and captain of industry, in his opening monologue as chief narrator of *The Farnsworth Invention*. Aaron Sorkin's skillful, entertaining modern history play is about the invention of television and the ultimately more important battle over patent rights, recognition, commercial ownership and the judgment of posterity. That this play is itself a late skirmish in that battle and has stirred a vehement historical controversy is nearly as interesting as the play itself.

As to Sarnoff's aphorism about ends and means, it is clearly bogus, or at best a tautology. The means that lead to a certain end are without doubt instrumental to that end, but that doesn't mean that either means or ends are necessarily justified. To say so is pure Panglossian illogic: that whatever is must be for the best. Only a rhetorical bully or someone as supremely—or defensively—certain as Sarnoff of the rightness of his own ends would say this as though it were some kind of justification. This is really an early instance of the slipperiness of Sarnoff as narrator. And it is as narrator that he begins the play, not quite in his own character, but as stage manager of his and Farnsworth's story, which means he assumes knowledge of things Sarnoff, as character, could never know.

SARNOFF: Good evening, I'm David Sarnoff. There's a rule in storytelling that says you never tell your audience something they already know but I'm going to chance it anyway by starting like this: The only reason you can see me right now is because light is reflecting off of me. Light bounces and I wanted to make sure everyone knew that or 20 minutes in you're going to be thinking what in hell is happening? Can we show everyone else?

Pools of light then flood the other actors (on Broadway, there were 19, playing 36 named roles plus others), all "placed variously around the stage,"

Ever happen? Jimmi Simpson and Hank Azaria in The Farnsworth Invention. *Photo: Joan Marcus*

as the stage direction has it—a general-science version of the higher physics of light to come.

Sarnoff as narrator then shows us his first scene, which is of Farnsworth visiting his ninth grade science teacher, a telling encounter because the initial concept of television is already forming in his precocious mind. But then we meet the other narrator, the adult Farnsworth, who alternates that function with Sarnoff. And the first scene Farnsworth, as narrator, shows is of the 10-year-old Sarnoff, cursing a Cossack who is torching his native village near Minsk. "There's a lot about his history that's a little cloudy to me," Farnsworth as narrator admits, and then he calls on the elder Sarnoff to translate the ballsy curses of his 10-year-old self—an equally telling encounter, given the buccaneer of capitalism Sarnoff becomes.

Farnsworth is essentially a conventional docudrama given fresh personality and immediacy by this use of split narrators who are also the central antagonists. The substance of the play seems to lie in its recovery of lost history, but it does not really care about "history" very much, hence its willingness—as a resulting controversy has insisted—to reshape the facts. The play is truly about its own telling. That the narrators, especially Sarnoff, are allowed to misremember, twist, exaggerate and even fabricate adds a dimension of ironic modern indeterminacy in which the tellers—who in their non-narrative selves are the true subject of the play as docudrama—create their own larger metadrama. The apparent engine of the play—the recovery of who invented television and how credit for that accomplishment was or was not stolen—is subsumed in the larger story of how the story has been (and continues to be, in this play) understood and

It is no accident that the play's title sounds like a chess gambit.

dramatized.

SORKIN STACKS THE deck for Sarnoff by making him the major teller of the tale. Oh, Farnsworth gets to tell the tale, too, but in the cleverest choice by this very clever playwright, Farnsworth mainly narrates Sarnoff's story, while Sarnoff mainly narrates Farnsworth's. And of course Farnsworth's is the tale most at issue, the tale that most needs telling, the tale advertised in the play's title. Here the story is told by his antagonist, who frames and interprets what his subject enacts. Farnsworth as narrator gets to do the same for (or to) his subject, Sarnoff, but the focus is not equal: Sarnoff as narrator begins and ends the play. That seems to give Farnsworth's story pride of place, but not really, since Sarnoff is in charge.

It is no accident that the play's title sounds like a chess gambit, because the battle between the Farnsworth and Sarnoff narrators is presented very much as a chess match, albeit one in which Farnsworth plays with few pieces and Sarnoff hides effectively behind many. Granted, what is real and what invented, whether covertly by the playwright or quite openly by the competing narrators, is continually complicated by many a disclaimer and metanarrative twist and evasion. In the end, however, the true chess master is—as you might expect in advance—the native Russian, not the bumpkin from Utah. Although the story proceeds chronologically, the interwoven presence of the two narrators continually invokes a broader consciousness. Initially, we like both men equally, since both arose from dirt and each seems to take pleasure in the other's exploits. We catch glimpses of the battle to come, though, when Sarnoff chillingly says of Farnsworth's ninth grade science teacher, "a decent enough guy but he'll be easy to destroy during despositions."

Sarnoff's early success centered on his skill with telegraphy and knowing how to milk a sudden opportunity (much the same as Andrew Carnegie's early success, in fact). At age 22 Sarnoff was a manager with RCA and surer than his colleagues of the potential of this new thing—radio—through which one person could speak to millions. At roughly the same time, as the alternating narrators tell it, Farnsworth was trying to raise a stake to build a lab and turn his concept of television into technical reality. But even early in the play, playwright Sorkin has the hayseed savant and immigrant manipulator interrogate the factual authority of their own stories.

This interplay between narrators—and the stories they simultaneously tell and see enacted—prevents any sense that we are witnessing, in the familiar documentary mode, a lecture. And the quick alternation of narrative passages and dramatic scenes allows the parallel stories to move quickly. Sarnoff as narrator can be impatient, but that edginess colors the Sarnoff character, too, making him more engaging.

> SARNOFF: I'd like you to set up lunch with Walter Gifford.
>
> BETTY: Yes sir, at his earliest convenience?
>
> SARNOFF: No, I don't care if it's convenient.

Still, in a struggle between a scientific innovator and a financial entrepreneur, it is obvious whom we will favor. Sarnoff is a capitalist bully: "if television

Light box: Company members of The Farnsworth Invention. *Photo: Joan Marcus*

gets invented," he says, "it's not gonna get invented by a guy at Westinghouse, it's gonna get invented by RCA."

In the hunt for the needed technological breakthrough, Farnsworth makes progress only when he finally sees the California financier, William Crocker. One of Crocker's men advises caution:

> ATKINS: [. . .] What do you imagine the practical application being? To say nothing of the marketable one?
>
> CROCKER: The practical and marketable applications of owning the patent on a device that would allow anyone access to all visual information in the world? I'm sure we'll think of something.

This dry sarcasm is characteristic of Sorkin's snappy dialogue, which is especially strong in its caustic mode. Sarnoff uses it too: the master of radio, itself a new technology but already profitable, he sees the potential of television right from the start:

> WACHTEL: David, can I say something please, before we start doing things that might make us look foolish in the eyes of, at the very least, our shareholders? It's a gadget, it's a parlor trick for a couple of rich people. It's something you show at the World's Fair.
>
> SARNOFF: You're wrong.
>
> WACHTEL: The thing's a monstrosity, David. It's huge and unsightly. Think of a person's home, where the hell are they gonna put it?
>
> SARNOFF: Where they used to put their radio.

While Farnsworth's essential breakthroughs are scientific, Sarnoff's are commercial. He thunders: "we have to control the patents and we shouldn't be paying royalties, we should be collecting them." But he is big enough for idealism, too. His initial battles over radio, precursor to those over television, focus on his attempt to keep it commercial-free. The profit would be in selling the hardware; broadcasts would be a public service.

> GIFFORD: You think if radio's bad once in a while that people won't start listening, that's your nightmare?
>
> SARNOFF: I don't know which is my nightmare. That radio's bad and people don't start listening or that radio's bad and they do.

Sarnoff loses that battle over the full commercial exploitation of radio, and he loses it over television, too, as Farnsworth stresses with full irony:

> PHILO: Damn. If only there was a powerful person in broadcasting with the courage of his convictions who could do something about this.
>
> SARNOFF: (*To Philo*) Well I assume that was meant for me there, Billy-Bob, so I'll just say that I've spent more time and effort than anyone ever trying to make television and radio informative,

entertaining and sophisticated.
PHILO: Job well done.

IT IS SARNOFF the narrator who first introduces Farnsworth's fondness for the bottle—much disputed in the controversy after the play appeared. This is part of the play's structural imbalance, letting Sarnoff talk about Farnsworth's personal life while Farnsworth the narrator does not get to talk about Sarnoff's. Indeed, Sarnoff's story is inhabited mainly by business rivals and associates, while Farnsworth's is full of relatives and friends—who are also his colleagues, since he lives and works on a shoestring. The play gets closer to Farnsworth the man, as suggested by the small detail that Sorkin's script calls the one character "Sarnoff," not "David," and the other "Philo," not "Farnsworth." This seems condescending. One result is that when the play needs to get close to Sarnoff, the only available vehicle is his French wife, who out of nowhere has a scene in which she questions his business dealings and says, "I think you just stole television." Sorkin needs someone to say it, so he arbitrarily drafts her.

Along with the scope of its subject, the size of its means—all those actors—and the romance of seeing real people behind iconic names, *Farnsworth* offers Sorkin's crisp dialogue, his ear honed in many years of high-profile television writing. Aphorisms come easily to him: "Showing off for women is a powerful incentive." He manages parallel stories with skill, alternating narration and brief scenes to move his story quicker. And you can see him give fresh life to the techniques of documentary, especially in insisting on the radical relativity of documentary "truth," making the slipperiness of fact a frank subject.

Still, the play sometimes seems captive to its need to fill in the rush of history. One moment RCA stock shoots so high that a $10,000 investment is worth more than a million dollars, then the market crashes. In Act II, the battle is fully drawn, complete with industrial espionage (including pretty women), a race to the technological finish line, a threat to the life of Farnsworth's son and a climactic showdown in court—the latter, raw meat to Sorkin, who at age 26 wrote *A Few Good Men*, with its own crackling courtroom scenes. Here, Sorkin is particularly free with the historical record, according to the subsequent controversy. Then, at the climactic ruling in the patent case between the two men, the judge finds for Sarnoff.

But in fact, he found for Farnsworth. Sorkin immediately has Sarnoff fudge the issue: "I may be wrong, he may have won that first one and lost on appeal. Or lost and then won and lost again. [. . .] It didn't matter." But of course it does matter, if history matters. As Sarnoff himself says, the issue

Boy wonder: Jimmi Simpson in The Farnsworth Invention. *Photo: Joan Marcus*

is, who invented television? The play answers that question upfront, in its title. Why then do we not all know the Farnsworth name? That is the interesting story, but it would not be as easily told, depending as it does on a series of lawsuits, varied settlements and the power of a great corporation extended relentlessly in time. At one point, RCA paid Farnsworth $1 million, though you would not know it from *The Farnsworth Invention*.

Compared to this re-writing of history, it is small potatoes that Sorkin then invents a meeting for Sarnoff and Farnsworth, a meeting we have long been prepared for in ersatz encounters between the two in their narrator personas. Schiller to the contrary, Mary Stuart and Elizabeth I never actually met; we don't actually know that Antonio Salieri poisoned Mozart; and as to the historic character of Richard III, there might be a successful—and extremely profitable—suit against Shakespeare in some universal court of slander. But none of this gainsays the success of *Mary Stuart*, *Amadeus* or *Richard III* on the stage, where the focus of *Best Plays* lies. Playwrights are not sworn before the bar of history. Whatever license Sorkin takes to rearrange facts, he is true to the general theme of shenanigans behind the scenes. Indeed, he recapitulates those shenanigans himself in telling his tale. And he is crystal clear on the final moral of public service versus commercial advantage:

PHILO: We both blew it huge, but the difference is, I didn't know the answer to my light dissipation problems. You knew that once there was a financial incentive for a news broadcast to be popular it would be making a mockery out of both of our lives, to say nothing of a society being informed enough to participate in its own democracy.

SARNOFF: Yes.

PHILO: Yes?

SARNOFF: I made one single miscalculation in my life and that was I had no idea how successful the thing was gonna be at delivering consumers to advertisers. And my friend, once you're good at that you're gonna have a hard time being good at anything else.

Sorkin does allow Sarnoff to express some regret, though he cloaks it in his pride at having assisted mankind in taking its latest step toward the stars:

SARNOFF: [. . .] We came out of the cave, went over the hill, crossed the ocean, pioneered a continent and took to the heavens. We were meant to be explorers. Explorers, builders and protectors. I don't think I stole television—if I did, I did it fair and square. But he deserved better in my hands. He was gonna do a lot more, but I burned his house down so he wouldn't burn mine down first.

FARNSWORTH CERTAINLY HELPS to resurrect a largely forgotten American original, an individual genius buried in semi-oblivion by America's competing genius for corporate power. American myth claims to exalt its inventors, but American history belongs more to those who know how to package and merchandise. Even great innovators such as Westinghouse and Edison are better known because of their success as entrepreneurs. Having exhumed Philo T. Farnsworth, the play then consigns him back into reaffirmed obscurity.

Except, of course, that he lives onstage. On Broadway, he did so for only 34 previews and 104 performances, not bad for a serious play but certainly a disappointment for such an entertaining show with a knowing consortium of producers, led by the Dodgers and Steven Spielberg, the commanding director Des McAnuff and especially the savvy playwright Sorkin, wizard of *The West Wing*. The timing for the production may have had something to do with its brief run. The opening came not long after the November 2007 Broadway strike, and the run fit entirely into those dark days of winter. But how much do theatergoers care about the history of innovation and capitalism, anyway?

Perhaps it is David Sarnoff who is the tragic success worthy of a play—a driven man with the ruthlessness of a Cossack. He knew business was no simple sporting event where the winner and loser can be clearly identified, but was (and is) an ongoing story. Playing Sarnoff with edge and authority was Hank Azaria, whose only previous Broadway turn was in *Spamalot* (another foray into history and myth). Jimmi Simpson made his Broadway debut as Farnsworth and was rewarded with a Theatre World Award. The cast was strengthened by such veterans as Michael Mulheren. But there were no other awards. If the final verdict is still to be rendered on Sarnoff versus Farnsworth, so too on *The Farnsworth Invention*.

2007–2008 Best Play

100 SAINTS YOU SHOULD KNOW

By Kate Fodor

○ ○ ○ ○ ○

Essay by John Istel

THERESA: A surge of the heart. A cry of recognition and love.

ABBY: What does that mean?

THERESA: I don't know. It has to do with God. Or maybe just some kind of spirit or—connectedness or something.

KATE FODOR'S PLAY *100 Saints You Should Know* deals with heavy, ineffable questions about faith in God, spirituality and organized religion with a light touch that is ethereal, not earthy. Although the setting, characters and dialogue remain rooted in the realistic contemporary dramatic tradition, the five-character play—peppered with witty dialogue and humor—shows how ordinary people strive for a taste of the extraordinary, often in silly, stumbling efforts.

Plays grappling with such substantial religious or moral dilemmas of faith in a secular society usually tend to be epic and historical (think *Angels in America*, *A Man for All Seasons*, or *Saint Joan*), overblown and melodramatic such as *Agnes of God*, or absurdist as in *Waiting for Godot* and Christopher Durang's *Miss Witherspoon*. Fodor's *100 Saints* is one of this season's Best Plays because the playwright adroitly juggles the mundane and the miraculous, the everyday and the effervescent. This easygoing, natural tone belies the play's craft, which is partly due to the lack of authorial agenda. Fodor prefers to pose bright questions and then let them fizz unanswered.

The lights rise on Theresa (Janel Moloney), a middle-age housecleaner for Magic Maids cleaning service, scrubbing a toilet. It is not just any toilet, however; it is the private bathroom of Saint Dominic's Rectory, where Father Matthew McNally (Jeremy Shamos), a Roman Catholic priest, resides. He absent-mindedly walks in on her labor, needing to use the facilities. Theresa suggests that she go clean the kitchen so he may take care of his business. Matthew demurs at first, stammering, timid as a deer. She insists. He accepts. She leaves as the lights fade.

Meet cute? Jeremy Shamos and Janel Moloney in 100 Saints You Should Know. *Photo: Joan Marcus*

In this seemingly innocuous opening scene, Fodor has not only introduced us to the two main characters, she implicitly reveals longings that will occupy centerstage. Theresa, the downtrodden, single mom, literally looks up to Father McNally, and inwardly craves some spiritual awakening. Matthew, meanwhile, is spiraling down, questioning a career that requires him to ignore his need for physical contact, for intimacy.

After the fleeting opening between these two moths flitting about the lantern of faith, they separate and we see alternating views of their home lives in an unnamed working-class suburb. Each character struggles with a single dominant family relationship: Theresa with her pugnacious and precocious teenager, Abby; Matthew with his overbearing, rigid mother Colleen. Add a pivotal fifth character, and by the end of the two acts the quintet intersects in ways that may at times seem contrived but still manage to reveal each to be a modern-day Jacob, wrestling with some mysterious, untended but vengeful angel constricting their souls.

The second scene reveals Theresa's tortured turn as an unwed mother, with little money. Her bright teenage daughter (Zoe Kazan, in a masterly performance) spends time with a friend on the verge of dropping out of high school. We also learn that Abby cannot stand her mom's boyfriend, that she dabbles with sex and drugs, and possesses a typical teenager's acerbic skill at skewering pretense. Fodor's sense of humor and pathos floods these mother-daughter scenes. Here is Abby answering her mother's question about why her friend would quit school:

> ABBY: Well, let's see. You have two choices. You could ride a bus that smells like a barfed-up boloney sandwich to the worst high school in the state where some dumb-ass security guard searches your backpack and gets off on touching your tampons and then you

There are many ways to read these intersecting journeys of faith.

> could sit through some class where the teacher puts on a movie and falls asleep at his desk and it's a federal case if you ask to go to the bathroom because they assume you're going in there to shoot up or something and some guy writes "Nice Tits" on your locker in permanent marker and all the girls think you're a loser because you're not on the fucking cheerleading team. Or you could, you know, not go.

Theresa can't bear to hear all Abby's complaints, many of which are leveled at her: for being a maid, for not leaving food in the fridge, for not providing Abby with a father, for having a loser boyfriend, for having the audacity to try to give her daughter advice. Such efforts are not met with gratitude.

> ABBY: Oh my god, shut up, shut up! You act like such a fucking know-it-all!
>
> THERESA: I know more than I did when I was 16.
>
> ABBY: I hope so because if you end up having some ugly little pig baby with that hog man you bring here, you will never see me again. I will run *so* far away. Do you understand that?
>
> THERESA: You want Doug to stop coming over? Is that why you're so mad at me all the time?
>
> ABBY: I'm not mad at you. I hate you. Those are two different things.

It is little wonder that a woman in Theresa's position might start watching TV preachers, harboring a longing for some kind of religious certainty about the mysterious complexities of modern human life. To describe the inner absence, she turns to her namesake, Saint Teresa of Avila, an ecstatic mystic, who she read about in the book whose title lends the play its name and was a gift from her grandmother. Maybe Abby's right and her boyfriend is a loser because Theresa quotes her Saint later in the play to explain her longing: it's for that "surge of the heart. A cry of recognition and love."

IT IS MATTHEW'S turn in the next scene. We meet his foil: his Irish Catholic mother Colleen (beautifully played by Lois Smith), who turns out to be just as funny as Abby. At first, neither she nor the audience know why "Mattie" has returned suddenly to his boyhood home. We meet Colleen in her modest living room as she calls for a food order from Frank, her local grocer, in order to supply her pride and joy with sustenance. The mother and son then turn to a game of Scrabble, which is a traditional way for the two to spend time. Perhaps not since *The Gin Game* has a parlor activity been so adeptly written and staged. The game strips the characters to their primal concerns. For instance, we find out as she plays that the fretful widow Colleen has a fear of the power of words. Or at least some of them.

Not "bad": Janel Moloney and Zoe Kazan in 100 Saints You Should Know. *Photo: Joan Marcus*

COLLEEN: All right, all right. Let's see. I could do "cats" and get six points off of your C there, but then we'd have "juiced" and "cats," which gives me the picture of a man trying to wring the juice out of some poor, unfortunate cats! We wouldn't want that sitting on the board the whole time, would we? "Juiced" and "cats"?

Colleen's squeamishness suggests her general fear of any kind of deep contact. Hers is a reticent, old-school love, even for her son. We realize it is little wonder Mattie chose the ministry as a profession, forsaking such companionship. As the game goes on, Colleen chatters away about her sister in Ireland and her love of Scrabble, even though she always loses. Mattie suggests that Colleen's poor form at the game is because she was educated "by semi-literate nuns in a one-room schoolhouse in Galway." She explains she loses on purpose—Scrabble is a way to "keep the conversation going." She always tries to place her tiles in the most accommodating board position to allow a lot of connections. Then she tries a word that her son has been reflecting deeply about.

COLLEEN: Yes, all right. (*She looks at the wooden tiles on her holder, then puts a few on the board.*) There's "soul." As in the thing the Lord sees into, isn't that right, Mattie?

MATTHEW: The thing the Lord sees into is your S-O-U-L, Ma, not your S-O-L-E. That's fish.

COLLEEN: I sent you to Harvard. You went there, but I sent you there, do you understand? I filled out the scholarship forms and got you the money from Saint Agnes and worked at the Hallmark shop with the colored women. So you were the one to get the education, but I was the one to give it.

MATTHEW: You think I learned how to spell the word soul at Harvard?

COLLEEN: I think you learned to talk to your mother like this at Harvard. I think at Harvard they taught you to be rude.

This exchange provokes talk of Saint John of the Cross, whose book *The Dark Night of the Soul* Matthew has been reading every night in bed, wondering whether the 16th century mystic's description of an "ecstatic union" with God really describes physical human love. His mother certainly thinks so for she cringes when Matthew recites some of the more purplish prose:

And the fanning of the cedars made a breeze.
The breeze blew from the turret as I parted his locks;
With his gentle hand, he wounded my neck
And caused all my senses to be suspended.

This causes Colleen to shout, "Stop it" and the audience to wonder if Mattie is ripe for a love affair, or certainly to guess that he may have already compromised his vow.

Fodor introduces us to the fifth and final character next. He is Garrett (Will Rogers) the teenage son of Frank the grocer. He meets Matthew in the driveway as they are both carrying boxes. Garrett has Colleen's groceries; Mattie's throwing out a box of his father's old shoes, 17 identical pairs in brown suede. Fodor's mirroring again subtly underscores what on the surface is an everyday encounter: Garrett carries what feeds the body; Matthew has a carton full of old "soles." Garrett is gawky and awkward, and reveals that his father has warned him to stay away from the priest. He wants to ask Matthew some questions, which we later discover are because the young man questions his sexuality. At first a seemingly arbitrary character, Garrett becomes the string that laces all of the characters together.

Theresa knocks on Colleen's door looking for Father McNally because she found his leather-bound copy of *The Dark Night of the Soul* under his bed, as she was cleaning the rectory. She uses the attempt to return the Saint John of the Cross volume as a pretext to seek out his guidance about her own awakening. Even though it is around nine in the evening, Colleen insists she stay and have some dinner, though Matthew does not seem keen for her to be there. Fodor then reveals that Matthew has not been honest with his mother about why he is really home: he has been given a three-month sabbatical because the church secretary found nude photographs of men. Theresa promises to keep his secret and then reveals her latest passion: "I've been thinking, and I guess I have some questions. About God. And how you—how a person—you know, how you're supposed to—I mean, I guess I have some questions about God and maybe prayer." He coolly suggests she speak to the visiting priest who is covering for him.

The playwright then cuts to the next scene, which takes place outside the house where Abby—who has been dragged along by her mother—entertains herself with Garrett who has returned to ask his own questions of Father McNally. Garrett discovers Abby pissing by a tree. Garrett doesn't understand why she doesn't go inside to use a toilet.

> ABBY: I would not set foot in that crappy little house if I hadn't peed in six months. I'd rather piss in a pot of poisonous snakes.
>
> GARRETT: Um. OK.
>
> ABBY: Also? I'm just bad.
>
> GARRETT: On purpose?
>
> ABBY: Yeah, I'm bad on purpose.

Tempting fate: Zoe Kazan and Will Rogers in 100 Saints You Should Know. Photo: Joan Marcus

It turns out both teenagers feel they are "bad": Garrett because he is from a firmly Catholic, God-fearing family and he likes to look at gay porn on the internet. He is sure that he is doomed to eternal fire. Abby's "badness" is just being conventionally unconventional, rebelling by drinking and being a smartass. They share Garrett's flask of booze that he carries around to ward off his own depression and loneliness.

Back inside, Matthew excuses himself to bed and the two moms, a generation apart, have a little chat. In a typically Fodor-esque comic retort, Theresa mollifies Colleen's concern that she has left a child in the car: "She's got a Walkman and a video game. You can leave her like that for hours, like a brain in a jar." The scene ends with Colleen assuring her visitor that her "son belongs to God" and she shouldn't harbor any romantic ideas. Cutting back outside, we find the two teens increasingly sloshed. When Garrett reveals to Abby that he came to find out whether he is really "a fag in the eyes of the Lord," she offers absolution through an improvised ritual that concludes with climbing a tree. This is how it begins:

> GARRETT: I don't want to be gay as a big fruit salad. I want to meet a nice wife someday.

> ABBY: Then repent! Put your underwear on your head and say eleven Hail Marys! (*Waving her hands like a TV preacher.*) Holy moly, holy moly, little baby Jesus!

Then Abby makes him take five shots and get undressed.

Fodor, a relatively new playwright—this is her second major production, the first was *Hannah and Martin*—then resorts to the playwriting ritual known as the "confessional monologue." Father McNally stands before us and explains his crisis of faith. It began with Saint John of the Cross's florid descriptions of God's nocturnal visits and then was exacerbated when he found a book of George Platt Lynes photographs. The famous mid-20th century photographer's male nudes astounded him. The result has been a break from faith. Fodor's monologue, perhaps structurally and dramaturgically lacking polish, shows her facility with coupling language to ideas:

> MATTHEW: When God called me to service, he called me through beauty. In the church, there was incense and quiet. Dark wood. Masses and requiems. I went to talk to Father Michaels, and his study smelled of books, and bits of colored light from the stained glass windows were thrown across the floor like someone had spilled a handful of rubies, and I thought, "For wisdom is better than rubies, and all the things that may be desired are not to be compared to it," and those words were my calling. So one can be called to God by beauty. But I know, also, now, that one can be called away from God by beauty.

The first act ends in the next scene when Abby and Garrett stumble into the living room to interrupt the two mothers. The boy has fallen out of the tree and bashed his head. He is barely conscious at first but then slumps and blacks out, as do the lights before intermission.

THE SECOND ACT begins in a hospital waiting room. Matthew and Theresa wait for news about Garrett because his parents are away in Minnesota. The scene seems overly long, perhaps because Fodor uses the characters' need to kill time as a way of offering up exposition that most playwrights would have dished out earlier. We learn about Theresa's life as a free-and-easy, acid-dropping follower of the Grateful Dead and how one of Matthew's homilies jumpstarted her on her spiritual journey. Thinking back on her life, she says, "I was looking for something enormous and expansive, but somehow I ended up with this little scrap of a life. I mean, this little nothing thing. You could just vacuum it up with the Dustbuster and it'd be gone."

When it is Matthew's turn he confesses that he is tired of the complete lack of physical contact he must endure as a priest. "There's not a lot of touching in this kind of life. I don't really touch anyone, and no one touches me, which is OK, because I'm not very comfortable with being touched." Theresa offers to touch him and she massages his head. It is not sexual, according to the stage directions, but "it is intimate." It may also have cemented his fall.

Back at his house, Matthew informs his mother matter-of-factly that Garrett has died. He admits that he did not administer Last Rites. She asks what he did do. Matthew says that he just held the boy's hand. Physical contact has become his new avenue to God. They then discuss his break from the Church.

> MATTHEW: I don't know if I love God properly anymore.
>
> COLLEEN: All men of faith have doubts, Mattie. Pray on it.
>
> MATTHEW: I'm not finding prayer very useful.
>
> COLLEEN: What do you need, then?
>
> MATTHEW: Love.
>
> COLLEEN: God loves you.
>
> MATTHEW: Sex.
>
> COLLEEN: Don't you dare say that word to me like that!

It turns out that God's love isn't enough for Matthew anymore. Similarly, Theresa's lifelong belief that religion was only a fairytale, "like Babar" she told Abby, isn't enough for her. Deep in their souls, both crave more.

Of course, Colleen doesn't understand any of this. She has been removed from physical love and intimacy for too long. She and her son's conflicting views of ultimate fulfillment come to a climax.

> COLLEEN: You tell me you don't love God, you don't love the Church. You don't want to do the work that God called you to do and that I raised you to do. And you want me to stand here and pour out love for you? In return for what? What should I love you *for*?
>
> MATTHEW: For nothing, Ma! For nothing! That's what you're supposed to love me for. If you find me drunk in a ditch, you're supposed to lean down and wipe the spit off my chin and tell me you love me because I'm your son.

Colleen thinks he's being selfish and goes off to bed, admonishing her son to pray.

The scene shifts to Theresa putting Abby to bed. The teen is anguished over Garrett's death. She blames herself and doesn't understand why she acts so mean and wonders again if it is just because she is a "bad person." The play ends at the McNally household when Colleen awakens from a nightmare and comes to the living room. She and her son kneel and offer the Prayer of Commendation for Garrett's soul. When Matthew is done, Colleen says amen, and the lights black out.

THERE ARE MANY ways to read Mattie and Theresa's intersecting journeys of faith and the tragedy that occurs when they cross paths. Some might say that Garrett's naked fall from a tree makes him a Jesus figure of sorts. He must die for all of our—and all of the characters'—sins, some of which are on display: homophobia, selfishness, frigidity. Certainly each of the four survivors has confronted his or her "brokenness" or failing by the end of the play and each explicitly or implicitly vows to change. (One of the production's pitch-perfect touches was the use of Leonard Cohen's "Hallelujah Song" between scenes, itself a "cry for recognition and love"). For Matthew and Theresa, these changes mean that they are traveling toward "truth" in opposite directions. The strength of Fodor's play is that each character not only has an exculpatory moment, but each point of view radiates its own profoundly human value and worth.

In a program note, the playwright admits she does not hold any particular set of religious beliefs. She writes that she does believe in "things that can't be seen or properly measured: the power of art, of words, of touch, of truth, of simple human goodness." *100 Saints You Should Know* makes these everyday miracles manifest through the ordinary nature of her characters and their travails. Fodor's writing has a warm, generous, embracing spirit that hovers over every scene in the play, allowing us to forgive its trespasses and admire its power.

2007–2008 Best Play

THE RECEPTIONIST

By Adam Bock

○ ○ ○ ○ ○

Essay by David Cote

BEVERLY: [. . .] I like the people but the office. This chair is terrible. It's. But don't dare ask for a new one. I should have asked Steve but they reassigned him before I. And I don't dare ask the new person. Randy I think? Because I don't want to be a person who makes a fuss. [. . .]

ADAM BOCK'S SLY, disturbing study in complicity and systematic dehumanization, *The Receptionist*, takes place in an America where cheerful office workers briskly torture prisoners for information, but their real concerns are gossip, guarding office supplies and finding a nice boyfriend. Bock reveals vicious cruelty beneath workplace banalities with almost sadistic deliberation.

The first scene is a casual, folksy monologue delivered by Mr. Raymond (Robert Foxworth), a plain-suited, mustachioed middle-management type. In a generic office setting, Mr. Raymond points a video camera at the audience. While doing so, he addresses an unseen visitor facing the camera. His tone is warm and intimate as he talks about rabbit hunting. "I didn't like it," he recalls. "We'd be out in the woods and I'd spot one. I wouldn't want him to notice it. He used a bow and arrow. They scream." He then tells his guest that what he really likes is fly-fishing. He savors the relaxation and calm of waiting for the fish to tug at your line. He shares his fishing philosophy: If you catch a healthy one, let it go. If, however, your catch is damaged—hook tearing gill or eyeball—you should kill it out of kindness. With exceeding simplicity, Mr. Raymond describes how he bleeds a fish slowly, so death is as painless as possible. As a whiff of menace fills the air, Mr. Raymond alludes to more concrete, worldly matters. His wife does not fish, Mr. Raymond confides:

MR. RAYMOND: She spends her time thinking about the
Which I understand. She sees pictures of the people over there and
what we're doing to them and she cries. I keep telling her "Don't
look at those pictures."

Having fun: Kendra Kassebaum and Jayne Houdyshell in The Receptionist. *Photo: Joan Marcus*

We have friends whose kids are over there. We gotta believe we're
doing the right thing.
But she
I don't like thinking about it. It makes me sad. It's like we're all
trapped in a

When things are hard I think about fly fishing.

Here, in concentrated form, Bock foreshadows the moral urgency and global
scale of his play in fragmented, vaguely ominous language. How does the
hunter minimize pain inflicted on his prey? If you see atrocities being
committed, do you act or avert your eyes? Mr. Raymond doesn't get to the
end of his sentences, as if going through that door will expose an unwanted
horror. We still don't know what Mr. Raymond was about to do to his guest.
That is for later.

PART TWO BRINGS us to the Northeast Office where Beverly Wilkins
(Jayne Houdyshell) works as the front-desk receptionist. As executed by
scene designer David Korins, her desk is a large circular mass, floating in a

dark-colored office space with doors leading offstage and many shelving units upstage. These shelves, filled with files, will become important in the final moments of the play. The desk, equipped with telephone, computer, Rolodex, pens and other clutter is—as Bock's stage direction coyly puts it—"nothing special."

Beverly is on the phone with her girlfriend, Cheryl Lynn, who had an exciting weekend at a casino down at the shore. Cheryl Lynn met a married man from Flom, Minnesota who was betting at the blackjack tables. We

As he expertly balances banality and horror, Bock gives the audience clues.

don't hear Cheryl Lynn's side of the conversation but we infer—from the way Beverly clucks and gasps—that the naughty friend had a good time. The way Bock crafts Beverly's lines in this opening section, there are no stage directions regarding incoming calls, but the unadorned, poetically structured language conveys the staccato, mechanical flow of Beverly's discourse, a series of stops and starts:

> BEVERLY: [. . .] It's ok for
> Just give me a second. I have a call.
> Northeast office.
> Oh hey Sandra! How are you? No, he's not in at the moment, can I
> put you into his voicemail? Ok. Here you go.
> Cheryl Lynn? I'm back. Listen.
>
> No really it's ok for
> Awch. Give me another second I have a call. I know, right?
> Northeast office. [. . .]

Beverly is a theatrical cousin of Samuel Beckett's Winnie, another stiff-upper-lip matron who maintains a positive attitude in the midst of trying circumstances. Bock draws the Winnie parallel even closer with his early stage direction: "The reception area of an office. The receptionist's desk has a tall front. Perhaps we can only see her shoulders and her head when she sits down?" Perhaps, indeed. As with the *Happy Days* heroine buried in a mound of earth up to her waist (and later her neck), Beverly is physically enmeshed. She is trapped, but avoids despair by hewing to her rituals. If our title character had power, you might characterize her as a spider at the center of its web.

And yet, Beverly does have power, at least over the lines of communication in the office, as well as emotional pull with her friends and coworkers. She chides Cheryl Lynn for dallying with a married man and, on cue, Lorraine (Kendra Kassebaum) enters. Lorraine is a younger woman with more than her share of romantic troubles. Chronically late to work, always protesting that she missed her bus, Lorraine appears to be the Northeast office's flakiest employee. (About ten minutes into the play, we have no idea what the business is or if other employees work here.)

Lorraine reports to Beverly that, per her advice, she went out to a nightclub, to help her forget about an ex-boyfriend, Glen. She went with her friend, Brenda, who drove, so Lorraine was stuck at the club as Brenda flirted with a guy named Tony who owns a pool-cleaning company. Tony, Lorraine tells Beverly, has a tattoo of a rhinoceros on his shoulder. Except for the possible faint echo of Eugene Ionesco's *Rhinoceros*—that absurdist fable of fascistic conformity—this water cooler chatter is banal stuff, and pointedly so. Brenda has a tattoo of an anarchist symbol, which she showed to Tony. The juxtaposition of conformity (rhinoceros) and rebellion (anarchy) is provocative, if ultimately superficial—and no one remarks on it. Beverly, motherly dispenser of advice, comforts the depressed, lovelorn Lorraine and assures her that she can do better than egotistical jerks such as Glen.

Present menace: Kendra Kassebaum, Jayne Houdyshell, Josh Charles and Robert Foxworth in The Receptionist. *Photo: Joan Marcus*

Our capable telephone jockey is gatekeeper, servant and den mother in one package.

Beverly next tells Lorraine about Cheryl Lynn's escapades at the casino with the married man, and the meandering banter alternates between the oddness of the married man's hometown ("Who'd name a town that? Flom.") and the possibility that Lorraine's ex, Glen, might be a narcissist. Beverly helpfully recommends a book that another girlfriend was reading: *HELP! I'm in Love with a Narcissist!* Over the next couple of minutes, Lorraine, apparently not the most industrious worker in this office, wanders back and forth from her office, chatting with Beverly, leafing through magazines on the desk and generally avoiding whatever it is that she does. Soon, a short but noticeable whistle brings us to attention. There is a lull in Beverly and Lorraine's chit-chat, until the receptionist notes:

> BEVERLY: [. . .] Something went wrong yesterday. With a client. Mr. Raymond came back to the office very upset. He said something about letting a fish go. And he
>
> You were out.
>
> LORRAINE: Oh.
> Ok. So I better.
>
> (*LORRAINE exits into her office. Beverly sits and stares off.*)

The "something" that went wrong could be anything: misunderstanding over a contract, disagreement over procedure, lack of satisfaction with the company's services. Whatever it is, it is probably related to the fact that Mr. Raymond is not in the office at his usual time. Beverly straightens magazines on a coffee table. Lorraine re-enters and resumes her inane conversation about her ex-boyfriend ("Glen was wearing a pair of glasses I helped him pick out") as if nothing happened. Bock repeats this trick of raising red flags, only to let his characters deflect or ignore them. Beverly tells Lorraine she is working; Lorraine again retreats to her office; Beverly orders a birthday cake over the phone; she then takes a birthday card to Lorraine's office to sign. They chuckle over the funny illustration on the card: a pony smoking a pipe. "People are crazy!" Beverly cackles insipidly.

WITH THE ENTRANCE of Martin Dart (Josh Charles), the plot—such as it is—thickens. A charming yet focused young executive, Mr. Dart is from the central office and he is here to see Mr. Raymond. He says he will wait until Mr. Raymond gets back. Beverly takes a call from her daughter, Janey, who is distraught about something at school. This leads to some bonding talk with Mr. Dart, whose four-year-old apparently eats paste in kindergarten.

The teacher, Mr. Dart says, is worried. "Tell her to stop scaring you," says Beverly, always ready with advice. "He's four! Everyone eats paste." Mr. Dart asks if he could borrow one of Beverly's pens, and she begrudgingly lends him a superfine point Flexor. "Make sure you give that back to me," she says with dead seriousness. "People keep stealing my pens. And my highlighters."

Lorraine, with nothing better to do, makes one of her periodic peregrinations into the reception area, and catches sight of an attractive stranger waiting. After some comical coming and going, Lorraine asks for a couple of "those good pens," prompting another flash of office-supply covetousness from Beverly. They quibble over whether or not Beverly gave Lorraine a box of Flexors last week, until Mr. Dart gallantly lends Lorraine his pen. "He's handsome," she whispers to Beverly. "Find out if he's married."

Next comes some harmless flirting between Mr. Dart and Lorraine, while Beverly goes downstairs to pick up the mail. Lorraine, eager to spend more time with Mr. Dart, is happy to handle the switchboard for a few minutes. Left alone, Lorraine and Mr. Dart chat and flirt. They laugh over how they would both go crazy if they had to answer phones all day like Beverly. Lorraine says she would "snap" and they would fire her.

> MR. DART: They'd never fire you.
>
> LORRAINE: I'd be out.
>
> MR. DART: You're too pretty.
>
> LORRAINE: Shut up.
>
> MR. DART: You are. You are.
>
> LORRAINE: Shut up.
>
> MR. DART: You're a very attractive woman.
>
> LORRAINE: Mr. Dart.
>
> MR. DART: Martin.

The flirting grows more intense, until it starts to worry Lorraine. Flirting in the workplace can be fun, she concedes, but it can get people into trouble. Beverly returns, Lorraine exits, and Beverly takes a call from her husband, Bob. We learn that Bob and Beverly share a hobby: collecting teacups. Mr. Raymond calls. Beverly forgets to put Mr. Dart on the line (or tell Mr. Raymond that Mr. Dart has been waiting for him), but she informs Mr. Dart that Mr. Raymond will be in soon. Mr. Dart, perhaps a touch annoyed, goes out to get a paper—he will be back.

Innocent's end: Jayne Houdyshell and Josh Charles in The Receptionist. *Photo: Joan Marcus*

Beverly chastises Lorraine for being such a flirt with a married man, which nearly brings neurotic Lorraine to tears. She looks at a model on the cover of a magazine and bemoans not being perfect, not having the perfect boyfriend, being stupid. "Bob spent all the money for our phone bill on a teacup," Beverly says, by way of commiseration. "The world's a mess," Lorraine says, in a burst of solipsistic hyperbole—even if the basic sentiment is valid. On that line, Mr. Raymond finally arrives. Clearly preoccupied, he mutters:

> MR. RAYMOND: I had an unfortunate afternoon. Yesterday.
> I broke his little finger. I thought that would do it. But
>
> (*He exits into his office.*)

IF THE PLAYGOER were not paying close attention, this major revelation might be lost. Expertly balancing banality and horror, Bock give the audience clues: This is a privatized torture facility, part of a network of offices where suspected terrorists are brought to undergo torture or, as Dick Cheney might say, "enhanced interrogation techniques." Mr. Raymond huddles with Lorraine and explains the situation:

> MR. RAYMOND: I got him set up. He'd been prepped. He hadn't slept in eleven days. The last three days he'd been on the box.
>
> LORRAINE: Uh huh.
>
> MR. RAYMOND: And that was after his feet'd been worked over.
>
> LORRAINE: Right.
>
> MR. RAYMOND: So I sized him up and I thought "This one's gonna be"
>
> LORRAINE: Sure.
>
> MR. RAYMOND: And I broke his little finger.
>
> LORRAINE: On his right hand?
>
> MR. RAYMOND: Yeah.

The prisoner did not talk, Mr. Raymond reports, so he applied "the wire to his eye," but still nothing. "I saw something," he says, meaning some glint of innocence in his eye. There is a pause, which Beverly fills with "Bob bought another teacup," an on-the-nose juxtaposition of the banal and the brutal. Mr. Raymond says he tortured the prisoner's wife in front of him. Still no response. And now, this morning he discovered that he hanged himself with his shoelaces.

Mr. Dart returns, taking Mr. Raymond by surprise. Beverly thought she had told her boss that a gentleman from central office was here to see him, but Mr. Raymond was not expecting him. Trying to conceal his agitation, Mr. Raymond makes small talk with Mr. Dart, then asks him to wait a moment as he gets ready for a meeting. They enter Mr. Raymond's office, still pleasant and professional, but within seconds shouting is heard from behind the door. Mr. Raymond runs into the reception area, as if escaping, but Mr. Dart follows, calming him down and insisting he put on his jacket and accompany him. "Please call my wife," the helpless, cornered Mr. Raymond asks Beverly.

Part Three takes place the next morning. Beverly arrives, business as usual, except that she finds Lorraine at work—early!—with her coat still on. Lorraine laughingly explains that, for once, she caught her bus. She's even at work before Mr. Raymond. There is more news about Lorraine's drama with Glen: He stopped by to show off a new car and tried to kiss her. She resisted—a sign of improvement. Beverly checks the office voicemail and is startled to find several worried messages from Mrs. Raymond's wife. Apparently, her husband did not come home last night. Beverly wants to call the central office to see what happened, but Lorraine warns her against it. Mr. Raymond was taken there; he is not coming back. Lorraine suggests that maybe Mr. Raymond was right about the client who he said knew nothing. Beverly cannot believe her ears and takes a scolding tone with Lorraine:

> BEVERLY: Terrible things happen when we're too trusting.
>
> LORRAINE: (*Very quiet.*) I know. I know.
>
> BEVERLY: Terrible things.
>
> LORRAINE: It's just
> If you can't trust anyone, how can you trust anyone?
>
> BEVERLY: People can get hurt. We know that. And our job is to make sure that doesn't happen. Your job.

Beverly, who never stains her fingers with the blood of the accused, is absolute in her conviction that the violence taking place in her office is nothing compared to the violence that might take place outside it.

The remaining 10 minutes or so of the play tumble in a sickening flash. Lorraine extricates herself from the office on the pretext of getting a croissant. She offers to get Beverly a sesame bagel with "only a smush." Soon after her exit, the cheerfully sinister Mr. Dart enters. After discovering that Lorraine has made a dash for it, he turns his sights on Beverly. He asks her to come down to the central office with him to answer some questions. Beginning to panic, Beverly nervously resists, but he is firm:

> MR. DART: We need you to tell us what you know about Mr. Raymond and his activities. And about Miss Taylor.
>
> BEVERLY: No. Mr. Dart. No. No. Martin. (*Laughs.*)
> No.
>
> MR. DART: We all have to do our part.
>
> BEVERLY: No.
>
> MR. DART: Mrs. Wilkins.
>
> BEVERLY: Beverly.
>
> MR. DART: Mr. Wilkins.
>
> BEVERLY: No. Martin. Mr. Dart. No.
>
> MR. DART: (*Looks away.*)

Eventually, Beverly acquiesces, but not before leaving an outgoing message on the main switchboard, sending any future callers directly into voicemail.

Part Four is a final, disturbing tableau in which Beverly finds herself surrounded by a moving mass of shelves. They are the shelves from the office, which held hundreds of files—no doubt of clients who had passed through the Northeast office. This ending departs from Bock's written description of the wordless Part Four, in which Beverly sits in a chair, similar to Mr. Raymond in Part One. A phone rings, and she jumps. The new, quietly spectacular ending was devised by director Joe Mantello and designer Korins.

MANTELLO'S PRODUCTION FOR Manhattan Theatre Club served the play well, with a first-rate cast and a blandly efficient tone. The fine ensemble meshed well together, anchored by Jayne Houdyshell, an ample, motherly figure with a fluting voice and natural comic timing. Houdyshell made Beverly's willful ignorance of her moral culpability coldly convincing. The character could have become a cheap joke or a shrill commentary on American complacency, but Beverly seemed a persuasive Everywoman who finds herself caught in the gears she helped to grease. Houdyshell specializes in self-deluded older women (Bruce Norris's *The Pain and the Itch* and Lisa Kron's *Well*, both recent Best Plays); perhaps one day we will see her Winnie.

For those following Bock, *The Receptionist* was seen as a companion piece to his 2006 drama, *The Thugs,* which played at Soho Rep in October 2006. Also brief (50 minutes) and set in a corporate environment, *The Thugs* concerns a group of squabbling, craven office temps who fear that something dreadful is happening on the fourth floor. A shrewd producer would pair *The Thugs* with *The Receptionist* for a darkly funny evening of post-September 11 paranoia. Both are Orwellian workplace tragicomedies in a minor key, and resonate long after their modest running times.

Of particular note is Bock's idiosyncratic language. His exquisite arabesques of indecision may have their origin in the absurdists (Ionesco) and British postwar experimenters (Harold Pinter, Caryl Churchill), but it is also very much a modern tongue. One might call it the music of a multitasked mind filled with trivia, halting midsentence as if surfing to another channel. Reading a script or attending a performance, one is aware of the stylization—as one is in Pinter or David Mamet—but there is also faithfulness to the oddity of everyday speech. Elliptical, demotic, flat and quirky, Bock's dialogue flirts with the danger of becoming meaningless noise, filler, distraction—as so many collected teacups in Beverly's home, or files on shelves looming around the receptionist's desk.

2007–2008 Best Play

ROCK 'N' ROLL

By Tom Stoppard

○ ○ ○ ○ ○

Essay by Charles Wright

LENKA: "Make love not war" was more important than "Workers of the world, unite."

TOM STOPPARD HAD been absent from Broadway only five months in October, when *Rock 'n' Roll* commenced previews at the Bernard B. Jacobs Theatre. During the 2006-07 season, *The Coast of Utopia*—Stoppard's Best Play about 19th century intellectuals who supplied the ideological underpinnings for the Bolshevik Revolution—elicited critical huzzahs, jubilant word of mouth and enough contrarian press to whet appetites of even the most reluctant theatergoers. The production consolidated Lincoln Center Theater's reputation as one of the world's great companies, captured more Tony Awards than any previous nonmusical and attracted hordes of highbrow tourists for each of the nine "marathons" in which all three dramas could be seen in a day. Due to its starry cast's other obligations, *Coast* closed in May—after a nine-week extension—with tickets still in demand. During the trilogy's run, New Yorkers visiting London had raved about another Stoppard drama, directed by Trevor Nunn, which premiered at the nonprofit Royal Court and moved into a commercial engagement at the Duke of York's. In the wake of *Coast*'s triumph, LCT judged the moment ripe to transport that London production of *Rock 'n' Roll* from the West End to Broadway.

Shortly before the New York opening, Stoppard wrote an article for the November 2007 issue of *Vanity Fair* in which he remarked that *Rock 'n' Roll* is "partly about Communism, partly about consciousness, slightly about Sappho and mainly about Czechoslovakia between 1968 and 1990." That précis reflects the trademark insouciance, presumably tongue-in-cheek, of the playwright's public persona. Indeed those topics, plus a generous amount of rock music, figure in this new play; but, what is more important, *Rock 'n' Roll* is the latest volley in Stoppard's assault on communism and, in light of the timing, it is a de facto epilogue to last season's trilogy. *Rock 'n' Roll* dramatizes Alexander Herzen's parting cry in *Salvage*: "[U]ntil we stop killing our way toward [utopia], we won't be grown up as human beings."

119

Vinyl person: Stephen Kunken and Rufus Sewell in Rock 'n' Roll. *Photo: Joan Marcus*

The action begins in a "leafy suburb" on an English summer evening in 1968. Stage designer Robert Jones established the location with an exquisite backdrop of lacy stonework atop distant buildings in one of the Cambridge colleges. A teenager in hippie garb (played by Alice Eve), possibly tripping on an illicit substance, listens raptly as a young man, crouching on a backyard wall, sings and plays a "single reed like a penny whistle." The song, derived from a James Joyce poem, indicates that the piper is 22-year-old Syd Barrett, newly separated from the band Pink Floyd.

> THE PIPER: "Lean out your window,
> Golden Hair,
> I heard you singing
> In the midnight air. [. . .]"

Barrett is among a handful of real personages whom Stoppard employs as offstage characters to advance the story and adumbrate its themes. Others include playwright Václav Havel and Ivan Martin Jirous, artistic director of the Plastic People of the Universe, a Czech rock band whose name alludes to a Frank Zappa song. The Plastics' arrest in March 1976 was a landmark in the development of Czech dissent and is a turning point in Stoppard's narrative. Charter 77 (which was drafted in response to the Plastics' trial and set the agenda for the Velvet Revolution) is essential to the story of *Rock 'n' Roll*'s Jan and Max.

Since *Rock 'n' Roll* concerns two decades of the century that Marxist historian Eric Hobsbawm calls, perhaps hyperbolically, "the most murderous as well as the most revolutionary era in history," Stoppard's pastoral opening—with a 1960s flower-child mesmerized by a facsimile of the Greek god Pan—is ironic. It is a contrast to the play's sociopolitical background of

---

The likely model for Max is Marxist historian Eric Hobsbawm.

---

cold war, East Asian conflict and civil disobedience around the globe; it evokes the moral aspirations of the epoch's peace, civil-rights and self-actualization movements, and the spiritual fervor of the artistic revolution whereby Abbey Road vanquished Tin Pan Alley.

What follows is a complicated skein of narratives taking place on both sides of the Iron Curtain, in Cambridge and Prague. At the beginning of Act I, Alexander Dubcek—who espoused a gentler version of Marxist socialism than the prevailing Soviet model—has been elected Secretary of Czechoslovakia's Communist Party. A democratizing zeal among intellectuals is effecting the cultural thaw that will come to be known as Prague Spring. The Kremlin, displeased with assertions of Czech independence, has dispatched troops, supported by other Warsaw Pact nations, to curtail the liberalizing trend. By curtain call, Soviet communism has collapsed; English voters have affirmed what one character calls "the most reactionary Tory government of modern times"; and the Velvet Revolution is ushering forward a new Czech Republic, with Havel as president.

THE PROTAGONISTS OF *Rock 'n' Roll*—Jan (Rufus Sewell) and Max (Brian Cox)—are men of different generations who yearn for a humane implementation of Marxist socialism. Stoppard poses them in Shavian opposition to each other (at least until the denouement, when they effect a rapprochement). Jan, the younger, is an intellectual of Havel's generation and a contemporary of Stoppard, who was born in Czechoslovakia in 1937. Max, an Englishman—two decades Jan's senior and his mentor—is a Cambridge don whose field is philosophy. Because they can meet only when Max visits Prague for academic conferences, the two grapple separately with the intellectual incongruities of Marxism-in-practice and with intrusions of the secret police. In Milan Kundera's *The Unbearable Lightness of Being*, a character remarks that the secret police "need to trap people, . . . to force them to collaborate and set other traps for other people, so that gradually they can turn the whole nation into a single organization of informers." At the end of the play, with Communist rule abolished, Jan recalls the dynamic between informers and the police:

> JAN: [The secret police] think they're using you, but really you're using them. But finally, in '76, they reminded me who was using who. They smashed up my records. Because, in the end, there are two realities, yours and theirs.

Rock 'n' Roll is dedicated to Havel who, in addition to being an offstage character and fellow dramatist, is reportedly Stoppard's friend. In an introduction to the revised script (Grove Press, 2007), Stoppard acknowledges that Havel's essays and published letters influenced his imagination as he fleshed out Jan and his Czech environment. The likely model for Max is Hobsbawm, president and professor emeritus of history at Birkbeck, University of London, who (like Max) was born in 1917 but was never

Live now: Alice Eve and Sinead Cusack in Rock 'n' Roll. *Photo: Joan Marcus*

associated with Cambridge or Oxford. The notion of an Oxbridge philosopher committed to dialectical materialism immediately after World War II is an ahistorical fancy, but it permits Stoppard to draw an analogy between the intellectual tension inherent in Max's abiding Marxism and the mind-body problem, as articulated in recent Anglo-American philosophy.

Similar to Stoppard, Jan is a Jew who fled the Nazis with his parents and spent formative years as a schoolboy in England. Unlike Stoppard, Jan returned to Czechoslovakia and was educated under the communist dictatorship that developed after World War II. At the drama's outset, Jan has been a postdoctoral student at Cambridge University for two years. His experience in Britain has convinced him that freedom of expression is an essential value. He is returning to Czechoslovakia after the Soviet invasion to confirm his mother's welfare and because, as a Marxist, he wants to experience the Prague Spring's mix of liberalized communism and renewed nationalism. Believing he will be permitted to complete his studies in England, Jan leaves his personal effects with Max and travels with only vinyl recordings—his treasured "rock 'n' roll." Later, when a man with a Czech accent—eventually revealed to be associated with the secret police—claims Jan's possessions, it is clear that the Prague sojourn will not be the brief sabbatical Jan has envisioned.

On first inspection, Jan concludes that "Czechoslovakia [. . .] is showing the way—a Communist society with proper trade unions, legal system, no censorship—progressive rock." Confident that "socialism with a human face" is being unveiled, he extends his stay.

> JAN: For once this country found the best in itself. We've been done over by big powerful nations for hundreds of years but this time we refused our destiny.

As officials tighten restrictions on speech, Jan is unable to get a teaching job; he and his fellow intellectuals must resort to *samizdat* and other covert forms of communication. The government shuts down the newspaper for which he writes and, when it reopens, Jan is demoted to kitchen porter.

At an "amateur rock competition," Jan encounters the Plastics and concludes that, if they are openly performing anti-establishment songs by the Velvet Underground and defying the social anathema on long hair, then everything is "basically okay." Despite the content of the western songs they cover, the Plastics are apolitical; yet they have political significance thrust upon them by a government that brands their music "socially negative." The standing of rock music becomes Jan's bellwether for the status of human rights in his homeland. As Jan observes the suppression of pop music and finds himself jailed for association with the Plastics, the scales fall from his eyes. Seeing remnants of his vinyl records smashed by the secret police, Jan recognizes that, in Communist society, there is no escaping political entanglement. "Everything's dissident," he says, "except shutting up and eating shit."

"EXACTLY AS OLD as the October Revolution," Max has "[grown] up with the fight against Fascism." He characterizes himself as "half-famous for not leaving the Communist Party." (His peers, by contrast, resigned in outrage when the Soviets invaded Hungary in 1956.) Max has observed Communism from a cozy vantage point inside liberal democracy and assessed activities beyond the Iron Curtain based on fragmentary information (comparable, the play suggests, to the literary fragments that his wife studies).

Max's loyalty to the Party is mirrored by his husbandly devotion to Eleanor (Sinead Cusack), a Cambridge classicist who is treated for cancer in the course of the play. Eleanor's field is Greek literature and, specifically, Sappho, the 7th century BC poet. Most of Sappho's *oeuvre* was lost for centuries; but, over the past 120 years, archeologists have located partial texts of her poems. While oncologists and surgeons have been dismantling Eleanor's body in an effort to impede rogue cells, she has been re-assembling Sappho's words and thoughts from the time-mutilated documents. It would be didactic to read too much into the fact that Sappho and "consciousness" are Eleanor and Max's topics of research, respectively—but it is impossible to ignore Stoppard's choice.

Situated at a comfortable remove from totalitarian society, Max retains faith that Karl Marx's utopian ideal can become a political reality despite the atrocities of modern history.

> MAX: When the revolution was young [. . . t]he struggle was for socialism through organized labour, and that was that. What remains of those bright days of certainty? [. . .] The Party is losing confidence in its creed. Why do people go on as if there's a danger we might forget communism's crimes, when the danger is we'll forget its achievements?

As a philosopher steeped in materialism and analytic methodology, Max rejects notions of "consciousness," "mind," or "soul" as separable from physiology. Yet he supports totalitarian governments that embody mere fragments of Marx's vision. At the same time, Eleanor is consumed with doubt that Max can believe that her essential nature, value and appeal are unchanged by illness and surgery. In what reads as heavyhanded apart

Cambridge autumn: Nicole Ansari, Brian Avers, Alexandra Neil, Quentin Maré, Rufus Sewell and Brian Cox in Rock 'n' Roll. *Photo: Joan Marcus*

from its context but proves powerful in performance—especially in the Cusack's intelligent portrayal on Broadway—Stoppard contrasts Marxism-in-practice to Eleanor's beleaguered physiology. When Eleanor laments that "they've cut, cauterized and zapped away my breasts, my ovaries, my womb, half my bowel, and a nutmeg out of my brain," the distinction is clear: A human being retains her identity, despite constituent parts being scooped out and lopped off. Thanks to medical intervention and despite catastrophic illness, she may even flourish, both physically and intellectually (as Eleanor has for a number of years). A political philosophy, such as Marxism, on the other hand, cannot undergo radical surgery without being transformed.

Although Max and Jan travel different routes, both resolve that the welfare of the many cannot be served by injustice or enforced suffering that benefits a few: There can be no common good apart from the well-being of individuals.

> MAX: "From each according to his abilities, to each according to his needs." It was the right idea in the wrong conditions for fifty years and counting. [. . .]

Utopianism, they conclude, is irreconcilable with human psychology.

JAN: [. . .] Perhaps we aren't good enough for this beautiful idea. [. . .] Marx knew we couldn't be trusted. First the dictatorship, till we learned to be good, then the utopia where a man can be a baker in the morning, a lawmaker in the afternoon and a poet in the evening. But we never learned to be good, so look at us.

MATCHING STOPPARD'S CHARACTERS to particular ideologies, political movements and historical figures is a critics' game that suggests *Rock 'n' Roll* is more schematic than it happens to be in performance. As Ben Brantley of the *New York Times* observed in his adulatory review, *Rock 'n' Roll* is not a "clear-cut debate play," and its characters "can't be boiled down to single, consistent positions, though that would make life much simpler for them." Stoppard surrounds Jan and Max with figures who, though less intricately drawn, are nonetheless superbly shaded. In Prague, there are Jan's friends Ferdinand (Stephen Kunken) and Magda (Mary Bacon), and a member of the secret police (Ken Marks), who is more bureaucratic than villainous—though nonetheless despicable. The Cambridge part of the story includes three generations of Max's family—Eleanor, daughter Esme (Alice Eve in Act I, Sinead Cusack in Act II), and granddaughter Alice (Eve); as well as Esme's ex-husband (Quentin Maré), his new bride (Alexandra Neil), Alice's beau (Brian Avers) and Jan's former girlfriend (Nicole Ansari), who has been Eleanor's pupil and, in middle age, is Max's once and future lover.

Rock 'n' Roll features witty, tendentious dialogue—as one expects—but its characters exhibit an impressive degree of emotional verisimilitude with the intensity of feeling increasing as the play unfolds. Critics earlier faulted Stoppard for the chilliness and excessive intellectuality of his plays. In recent years, however, his work has been marked by increasing poignance and variety of emotion. "As in *Utopia*," Brantley wrote of *Rock 'n' Roll*, "the waywardness of life and of human nature keeps subverting doctrinaire systems of thought, whether their symbols be a hammer and sickle or a peace sign." Near the play's end, Stoppard shifts dramaturgical gears definitvely, transforming his political drama into a romance. When Jan is free to travel—courtesy of the Velvet Revolution—he returns to England, where he renews acquaintance with Esme, the flower-child of the opening scene. In a result only lightly foreshadowed, the two live together in the emerging Czech Republic and the drama ends, in 1990 Prague, with the couple engaging in activities unthinkable under the old regime: open displays of affection, a buoyant response to the Rolling Stones's Prague debut in Strahov Stadium, "where the Communists had their big shows." After an evening of theater freighted with themes of mutability, loss and missed opportunity, Stoppard brings the curtain down on events that illustrate Jan's post-Communist declaration: "Life has become amazing."

It is a safe bet that most writers, grappling with such sweeping material, would choose a literary form that encourages expansiveness, rather than submitting to the abridgement and condensation demanded by the stage. It is tempting to think of Stoppard as a novelist in playwright's clothing; yet there are scenes in this play, such as the luncheon party in Act II and the brief final episode at Strahov Stadium, that are so intensely theatrical one cannot imagine them rendered effectively in prose. At the outset of his career, under commission from a London publisher, Stoppard tried his hand at the novel; but success with *Rosencrantz and Guildenstern Are Dead* seemed to seal his literary fate. Instead of experimenting in other forms, he has consistently shattered the commandments of contemporary writing primers, stretching the stage-play to accommodate numerous characters, long chronologies and unruly narratives; using it to exercise the intellectual friskiness that brought him fame initially and the moral conviction that makes him a noteworthy foe of political cant—plus the tenderness that marks much of his work, at least since *The Real Thing*.

At three-score years and ten, Stoppard is in peerless command of theatrical technique. He has infused *Rock 'n' Roll* with all of the energy and conviction associated with the proletarian art form of its title. On Broadway, the entr'acte blackouts throbbed with pop songs familiar and obscure; but the playwright's dialogue was, at all times, comparably dynamic. Rock—with its improvisational riffs, powerful bass and indifference to fine points of music theory—is an ideal symbol of what was lost or destroyed under Communist dictatorships and reclaimed, in the case of Czechoslovakia, by the Velvet Revolution. The final beats of *Rock 'n' Roll*, with Jan and Esme bouncing to strains of the Stones in Prague, are likely to recall—for any true Stoppardian—Alexander Herzen's reflection in *Salvage*: "Our meaning is in how we live in an imperfect world, in our time. We have no other."

2007–2008 Best Play

THE SEAFARER

By Conor McPherson

○ ○ ○ ○ ○

Essay by Charles McNulty

RICHARD: Mr. Lockhart, take it from me: Sharky will never kill all that pain. He'd have to drink Lough Derg dry, God help him!

THE BUILDING BLOCKS of Conor McPherson's *The Seafarer* do not make an especially strong case for the play's originality. This reworking of the Faust myth—set on Christmas Eve in a living room that would not be out of place in a classic television sitcom—gathers together what appears to be a motley crew of modern-day stage Irishman. Booze is consumed, recriminations are slung and that bludgeoning Gaelic wit—which Martin McDonagh has fiendishly popularized for contemporary audiences—runs riot. If that were not enough, the drama reaches its climax via one of the creakier devices of contemporary dramaturgy—an everything-on-the-line poker game.

When the play opened at the Booth Theatre on Broadway in December 2007, after a successful world premiere at London's National Theatre the previous year, much of the praise was focused on the tightly knit ensemble. Directed by McPherson and featuring two actors from the London cast, Jim Norton and Conleth Hill, the New York production was so seamlessly wrought that critics spent more time extolling the company than appreciating (never mind analyzing) the play. This underselling of *The Seafarer* did not just occur on the American side of the pond. In his *Daily Telegraph* review, Charles Spencer reduced the play to a kind of biographical exorcism, calling the work "McPherson's own personal thanksgiving for escaping alcoholism," and advising the playwright that it was time for him to offer "more than a view through a glass, darkly." Less ad hominem in his criticism, Benedict Nightingale of *The Times* confessed that while he admired the "fine writing," he was plagued by "doubts" over dramatic choices that cried for more depth and clarity.

Of course there was a reason for the New York reviewers' disproportionate attention to the quality of the acting: David Morse, Sean

Christmas cheer: Jim Norton and Sean Mahon in The Seafarer. *Photo: Joan Marcus*

Mahon and Ciarán Hinds melded with Norton and Hill into one of most estimable Broadway ensembles of the season. Yet it seemed odd that actors would receive such encomiums in a work that was variously dismissed as "basically one long drunk scene" or "standard issue Irish-playwright whiskey-sodden banter." Surely the performers could not be this good without having something more meaningful to play? Loving the production but not the play, the *New York Times*'s Charles Isherwood chalked up the brilliance of the cast to the giddy pleasures of portraying inebriated souls. "Such material is catnip to actors, of course, who get to astonish us by the crispness of their control in depicting people who are losing it," he wrote. Isherwood appreciated the way the performers went "beyond mere technical aplomb to turn the play into a sustained meditation on the dangerous allure of killing the lonely nights by diving into a bottle." But he confessed to having "hangover" reservations about the "hokey" dramaturgy the next morning. Ben Brantley, Isherwood's colleague who reviewed *The Seafarer* for the *New York Times* in London and New York, however, was more taken with the drama, which he described as "a thinking-person's alternative to *It's a Wonderful Life*." In Brantley's estimation, "McPherson is considering the impenetrable, scary mystery that is being alive and the blundering ways that poor humans deal with it. *The Seafarer* portrays the forms of amnesia and anesthesia that allow people to wake up with themselves."

Although Brantley does not elaborate his existentialist interpretation, the words "amnesia" and "anesthesia" provide clues into how the play manages to transcend its inebriated surface clichés to become a vehicle of revelatory character acting. Drinking, the dominant preoccupation of McPherson's characters, is a means not just of killing the pain but of temporarily blotting out memory itself. What can seem like yet another Irish play about garrulous lushes in tragicomic search of a 12-step program is actually about something far deeper than an individual's quest for "recovery"—namely, the universal struggle to cope with inexpiable guilt and the horrific fallibility of living.

McPherson once again injects the occult into the quotidian details of life.

THE EASILY OVERLOOKED brilliance of *The Seafarer* lies not in its conventional plot but in the unconventionally roomy interstices of what characters can remember and feel. Recourse to the bottle, rather than being an occupation in and of itself, is a self-deadening means of contending with the mucky parallel realm of one's unseen past, which is always threatening to sink the visible order into complete chaos. In McPherson's adroit hands, this rather prosaic subject of drunks on a holiday bender stealthily assumes a mythic reach, with nary a false psychological note.

As with many of the author's works, the occult is injected into the quotidian as a way of manifesting the dark shadows hovering behind workaday facades. In *The Weir*, the play in which McPherson made his Broadway debut in 1999, ghost stories—lyrical but not less hair-raising for being so—served as a communal outlet for very real grief. And in his 2005–06 Best Play, *Shining City*, which had an acclaimed run at Manhattan Theatre Club's Biltmore Theatre, paranormal incidents—including an ending that had audiences trembling in their seats—subvert the illusion that all is calm and rationally explicable. In *The Seafarer*, the devil himself, disguised as suave business executive, arrives at the home of two brothers, one of whom has a Faustian debt he would rather forget. Morse, the terrific American actor who became one with his Gaelic cast members, took the role of Sharky, the abstemious (for the time being) alcoholic with burdensome secrets. Sharky has returned to care for his older brother, Richard—Norton, in a performance justly rewarded with a Tony Award—a cantankerous, blind invalid with a liquor-fueled tongue who will not let sleeping dogs lie. Reunited in their childhood home, the two are bound as if they were a Beckettian duo who find the idea of staying together as insufferable as the alternative.

Set in a ratty North Dublin residence conspicuously missing "a woman's touch," as the stage directions note, the locale has a hellish ambience that aspires to seem banal. As McPherson specifies, "the main entrance is down a flight of stairs from the ground floor, giving a basement feel to the room." Outside, winos leave filth requiring regular buckets of hot water and soap. Inside, the décor, smacking of a Salvation Army thrift store, includes artifacts from pubs, such as "a big mirror advertising whisky, ashtrays, beer mats, a bar stool or two somewhere." The holidays are in evidence by a scrawny artificial Christmas tree, which pitifully occupies a forlorn corner of the living room, and a picture of the Sacred Heart with a faulty red light that needs to be tapped to stay illuminated. In short, not only is squalor general, but even the Christmas magic is on the fritz.

An old friend of the brothers, Ivan (Hill), has stayed the night, having been in no condition to make it home on his own. In his drunkenness, he

In the details: Ciarán Hinds in The Seafarer. Photo: Joan Marcus

mislaid his glasses, a crucial plot point that ties to the play's thematic preoccupation with vision and its loss. Characters either literally cannot see, as in the case of Richard whose eyesight left him on Halloween after falling into a dumpster, head first, while trying—in his own account—to seize a few discarded rolls of wallpaper. Or they are metaphorically myopic, as in the case of Sharky, whose moral failures have induced a kind of self-protective blackout.

Sharky is one of the walking wounded with bandages on his face and hands from his latest drunken brawl. At first glance, he seems the innocent victim, the butt not just of his brother's derision but also of the world's violent abuse. He reports that he was jumped by a group of men for idly telling them to get off the hood of a car as he was leaving a pub. Yet something seems missing from his account, which he offers only reluctantly, albeit with a vivid description of the blood "pumping" out of his nose. A lonely, itinerant figure who has been scraping by with odd jobs across Ireland, Sharky is imprisoned in a reticent solitude that renders him distressingly sympathetic. We see him cleaning for his brother, who taunts him with insults and wisecracks. Amid all the dissolute chaos, Sharky's vulnerability calls to us. It is only over time that we learn of the enormous guilt he has been shouldering, and begin to see that his penance—almost to the point of martyrdom—has not been for imaginary sins.

Sharky's victimization is raised to a comic-pathetic level when it is announced that Nicky (Mahon) will be paying a holiday call. A friend of Richard's, Nicky is not only living with Sharky's ex-wife and helping out with her kids but he is now driving Sharky's old car—yet things are never exactly as they seem. McPherson continually demands that we readjust our impressions. Nicky, who is treated more or less as an affable mooch, will turn out to have more substance than Sharky is prepared to acknowledge. Moreover, Sharky's resentment comes from such a murky place that one cannot help suspecting that a good deal of his rage is self-directed. A sociable boozer, Richard insists that Sharky get his guest's customary beer:

> RICHARD: Nicky drinks Miller, Sharky. We all understand that you have issues with life and it's a struggle for you to grasp human relationships, but Nicky is a friend of mine. And a friend of Ivan's . . . and . . .
>
> IVAN: Ah, he can be very messy, Richard.
>
> RICHARD: (*With finality*) The man is welcome here!

Richard wants them all to get "nice and Christmassy," which means a few token mince pies and many bottles of booze. One of the play's keen sources of humor, acidulously delivered by Norton, is the careening tone of his speech. One minute he is berating Sharky—sometimes with profanity, sometimes with literary quotation—the next he is perversely demanding that sentimental tradition be upheld.

ONE COULD HARDLY describe the characters of *The Seafarer* as integrated, yet they are fully observed in their personal disorder and disarray. McPherson captures their fragmented psyches with a trenchant wit that incrementally adds to our psychological understanding. Truth is momentarily snagged by laughter, reality seized by an accrual of behavioral quirks. The process, advancing in large part through implication and induction, is an unfolding revelation of what has been habitually deflected. To put it another way, McPherson opens the sutures that conceal an ulcerated wound.

The accelerating agent of this exposure is a stranger from another realm. Mr. Lockhart (a sinisterly perfect Hinds) arrives with Nicky, and is immediately welcomed by Richard, who is clearly impressed by his elegance—which signals deep pockets for poker-game fleecing. Sharky has no recollection of having met this well-dressed gentleman, though Lockhart reminds him at the first private opportunity that they were once locked in the same cell.

> SHARKY: You've a good memory.
>
> LOCKHART: Old as the hills, Sharky. You know I was sure I'd run into you today. (*Laughs*) But you're off the drink! Now that completely threw me, I have to say! Do you know how many pubs I was in?
>
> SHARKY: Were you looking for me?

From Marlowe to Milton to Goethe, devils have cropped up in blue-chip literature and invariably stolen the show. The originality of McPherson's contribution lies in how assuredly his dashing fiend is ushered into a modern-day comic setting. In truth, there is an almost suburban aspect to this menacing Lockhart. He is the type of good listener to whom one could imagine spilling one's secret at a tavern after a trying day's work—which is apparently the way Nicky has come to keep such pernicious company.

The nature of Lockhart's conversation with Sharky, however, is far from innocent. He is there to claim the debt of his soul, which was contracted in jail, though the details conveniently escape Sharky.

> LOCKHART: No, hold on. Are you seriously trying to tell me . . . ? You're seriously standing there telling me that it's never struck you as odd? Down all these years that you just walked out of jail? After what you did? Ah, that's brilliant!

Soul survivor: Jim Norton, Sean Mahon, Conleth Hill, David Morse and Ciarán Hinds in The Seafarer. *Photo: Joan Marcus*

The audience struggles to descry these long ago events, and McPherson increases the suspense by unveiling them as kind of memory strip-tease. Sharky claims he was in prison for an inconsequential "fight with some wino."

> LOCKHART: Well no, not quite. His name was Laurence Joyce. He was sixty-one. He was a vagrant. He said he was trying to get to Cardiff? . . . Said he had some family there? Said his wife was once the Cardiff Rose? You beat him up in the back of O'Dowd's public house in the early hours of the twenty-fourth of December 1981. You killed him. (*Short pause*) I let you out. I set you free.

Could there be anything more terrifying than the realization that you are the culprit in a long-repressed nightmare that is quickly coming back to life? The plot is as familiar as *Damn Yankees*, and there is a contrivance in how the devil insists on "playing" cards for Sharky's soul. But the way the banished past returns to claim its due is genuinely scary. (Note the humanizing detail of the "Cardiff Rose.") McPherson focuses this retrospective ambush on Sharky, though not exclusively. All of the characters are fugitives of mistakes and misdeeds that refuse to die a quiet death. Even Ivan, the hapless drunken dupe, has a treacherous secret that Lockhart draws out, a piece of "ancient history" involving a hotel fire and a fatal bet over Ivan's culpability in the matter.

FREUD HAS A phrase to summarize McPherson's undertaking—"the return of the repressed." This psychology has for decades informed the content of scores of plays, but what is impressive in *The Seafarer* is the way it influences the manner in which the drama unfolds. The plotting of this modern tale of horror is as much a function of Sharky's internal despair as it is of diabolical intervention. In this respect alone, McPherson's play can be compared to *Macbeth*, whose protagonist is similarly abetted by occult forces that work on what already resides in a susceptible heart. More intertextually resonant, perhaps, is Milton's "Which way I fly is Hell, myself am Hell" sentiment. To define the storied torments of the underworld, Lockhart offers a succession of prose snapshots from Sharky's alienated life:

> LOCKHART: What's hell? (*Gives a little laugh*) Hell is . . . (*Stares gloomily*) Well, you know, Sharky, when you're walking round and round the city and the streetlights have all come on and it's cold. Or you're standing outside a shop where you were hanging around reading the magazines, pretending to buy one 'cause you've no money and nowhere to go and your feet are like blocks of ice in those stupid little slip-on shoes you bought for chauffeuring. And you see all the little people who seem to live in another world all snuggled up together in the warmth of a tavern or a cozy little house, and you just walk and walk and walk and you're on your own and nobody knows who you are. [. . .]

Hell, it turns out, is not other people, as Sartre has it. It is the complete lack of attachment to anyone else, the decoupling of the individual from his community.

> LOCKHART: And you don't know anyone and you're trying not to hassle people or beg, because you're trying not to drink, and you're hoping you *won't* meet anyone you know because of the blistering shame that rises up in your face and you have to turn away because you know you can't even deal with the thought that someone might love you, because of all the pain you cause. [. . .]

Nicky knows the pain Sharky inflicted on Eileen with his erratic alcoholic behavior. In defending himself as a more suitable partner, he reveals the traumatic reality of his predecessor's mental state:

> NICKY: At least I don't be getting into mills all the time and getting barred out of pubs all over the place! At least I don't be waking up screaming and roaring at all hours of the night having bad dreams and freaking the kids out and waking the whole place up!

Yet for all of the play's shellshock and horror, *The Seafarer* is finally an unapologetically redemptive drama. If emptiness and desolation are the devil's feeding ground, then connection and fellowship are what can drive evil away. Richard's open door (and open bar) policy to his guests, his tolerant embrace of their shortcomings and their reciprocal abidance of his more unsavory qualities provide a bulwark against Lockhart's plans for slipping Sharky through a nefarious hole in the wall. As Richard says to his brother on Christmas morning, just after Lockhart has slithered off empty-handed:

> RICHARD: Ah, buck up will you, Sharky! I don't want the whole, (*A mocking, unfair impression of Sharky*) "Aw, life is too hard and I can't take it!" off you today now, right? Do you hear me? We all know you're an alcoholic and your life is in tatters and you're an awful fucking gobshite. We all know that. But you know what? You're alive, aren't you? (*Beat*) Aren't you?

The queasily hopeful message of McPherson's vision is that though we may feel condemned by our sins, it is our virtues, accidental or not, that ultimately have the power to save us.

2007–2008 Best Play

YELLOW FACE

By David Henry Hwang

○ ○ ○ ○ ○

Essay by Dan Bacalzo

> DHH: Years ago, I discovered a face—one I could live better and more fully than anything I'd ever tried. But as the years went by, my face became my mask. And I became just another actor—running around in yellow face.

FOLLOWING THE SUCCESS of his play *M. Butterfly*, a 1987–88 Best Play and Tony Award-winner, David Henry Hwang became a prominent representative for Asian Americans in the theater. This became apparent during the 1990 protests surrounding the US premiere of *Miss Saigon*. After a successful run in London, producer Cameron Mackintosh sought to bring the musical to Broadway. He initially faced resistance from the Actors' Equity union, because the part of a Eurasian character named The Engineer would not be cast with an Asian-American actor. It would instead be played by the show's original star, Jonathan Pryce. It appeared to be yet another example of "yellow face" casting, in which a Caucasian actor would play an Asian.

This practice, similar to the use of "blackface" by white minstrels, stretches back to the 1800s. Not only did it limit the opportunities for actors of Asian descent, it also tended to perpetuate numerous stereotypes. Some of the more notable 20th-century examples of yellow face include Warner Oland as the 1930s Chinese detective Charlie Chan in as many as 16 films, Luise Rainer as Chinese peasant O-Lan in *The Good Earth* (1937), and Mickey Rooney as the offensively caricatured Mr. Yunioshi in *Breakfast at Tiffany's* (1961).

The *Miss Saigon* controversy proved that such casting practices were not a thing of the past. In London, Pryce even used prosthetic makeup to make his eyes appear slanted (due to the protests, this makeup design was not repeated on Broadway). Hwang was one of the more vocal opponents of the *Miss Saigon* casting, writing a letter to Actors' Equity that was quoted in the *New York Times*, and even meeting with Mackintosh to discuss the

Dad, please! Hoon Lee and Francis Jue in Yellow Face. *Photo: Joan Marcus*

matter. He later wrote a play called *Face Value* (1993), a farce on racial identity inspired by the *Miss Saigon* controversy; it was widely panned in its out-of-town tryout in Boston and closed prior to its Broadway opening after only eight previews.

These well-publicized events provide the starting points for Hwang's *Yellow Face*, a bold mixture of fact and fiction that premiered in Los Angeles at the Mark Taper Forum in a 2007 co-production with the Public Theater, which staged the show Off Broadway (all actors' names are from the New York production). The central character—who is called David Henry Hwang within the script, but is referenced in the text and the play's program as "DHH"—is a fictionalized version of the playwright. DHH was portrayed on stage by actor Hoon Lee, who does not bear much physical resemblance to Hwang. The Leigh Silverman production did not make an attempt at mimicry, and the majority of the supporting players inhabited multiple roles, frequently crossing racial (and sometimes gender) lines. This underscored the fluidity of identity that is one of the play's primary themes.

While many authors have used their own autobiographies to provide inspiration for their works, Hwang takes the conceit further than most. In interviews about the play, he was reluctant to say just how much of it was "true" and how much fiction. Certain aspects are well documented, and the play even incorporates verbatim news headlines and excerpts from articles. There are also a large number of real personalities that appear in the script under their actual names, ranging from actors Jane Krakowski, Mark Linn-Baker, and B.D. Wong to politicians John Kerry, Tom DeLay, and Fred Thompson. While Hwang playfully satirizes some of these figures, he reserves the harshest criticism for the character of DHH, who is presented as a somewhat shallow, vain and needy man overly concerned with what others think of him. Of course, this also allows the playwright to show the character's growth as the play unfolds.

Many use autobiography as inspiration, Hwang takes it further than most.

Adding to the self-referential nature of the production was the fact that Hwang's real-life wife, actress Kathryn Layng, was a member of the ensemble, although there was no stage equivalent of her within the play. Instead, DHH is presented as a single man with a penchant for porn and chatting with girls online. While Hwang eventually discloses some of the play's major falsehoods by the end of *Yellow Face*, his primary interest seems to be in showing how ideas of "truth" are constructed in life, the media and art.

YELLOW FACE BEGINS with a capsule history of the *Miss Saigon* protests. DHH is drawn into the battle against the musical blockbuster, but then has second thoughts as the controversy escalates. He does not want to be seen as promoting censorship or shutting down the production. In fact, DHH seems a little embarrassed that his name and reputation are being used to give weight to the dispute and worries that the whole brouhaha is making him and the other Asian-American protestors "look bad."

The play's action kicks into high gear once DHH hires an actor named Marcus G. Dahlman (Noah Bean) to play the lead role in *Face Value*, under the mistaken impression that he is Asian American. Actors' Equity rules forbid asking about race in an audition, leading to a heated discussion between DHH and producer Stuart Ostrow (Lucas Caleb Rooney):

> STUART: Does he look Asian to you?
>
> DHH: What do you mean, "look Asian"?
>
> STUART: Well, he doesn't seem to possess—any Asian features . . . at all.

> DHH: And what exactly are "Asian features"?
>
> STUART: He's got dark hair, but—
>
> DHH: Short, high cheekbones, slanty eyes?
>
> STUART: David—
>
> DHH: I gotta say, I find your question sort of offensive. Asian faces come in a variety of shapes and sizes—just like any other human beings. Which we are, you know.

DHH soon finds out, however, that Marcus is, in fact, Caucasian. Since Equity also doesn't allow actors to be fired on the basis of race, DHH tries to help pass Marcus off as Asian American, enjoining him to shorten his name to Marcus Gee and creating an elaborate back story about his being descended from Russian-Siberian-Asian Jews.

After DHH finds another excuse to fire Marcus and *Face Value* bombs, he thinks that is the end of it. However, Marcus discovers he likes being Asian American and because his status as such was validated by DHH, he is able to become an activist for Asian-American causes, is recognized and lauded within the Asian-American community, and even starts dating Leah (Julienne Hanzelka Kim), an Asian-American woman who was formerly romantically involved with DHH. After hearing about what Marcus is doing, DHH reacts with a combination of disbelief, outrage and jealousy.

Seriously? Hoon Lee and Julienne Hanzelka Kim in Yellow Face. Photo: Joan Marcus

Bean's performance emphasized Marcus's charm and well-meaning enthusiasm, which made the frustrated DHH an even more comic figure, especially as portrayed by Lee. In one of the play's funniest scenes, Marcus gently chastises DHH for not being more active in the community:

> MARCUS: They're honoring me next week in DC. We could really use your support.
>
> DHH: I was an Asian-American role model back when you were still a Caucasian!
>
> MARCUS: David, c'mon—is this a popularity contest?
>
> DHH: No, I am not in a popularity contest with you.
>
> MARCUS: This is about collective empowerment, agreed?
>
> DHH: Fuck. That's so easy for you to say.
>
> MARCUS: What?
>
> DHH: You come in here with that, that face of yours. Call yourself Asian. Everyone falls at your feet. But you don't have to live as an Asian—every day of your life. No, you can just skim the cream, you, you, you ethnic tourist!

The two characters discuss the Chinese concept of "face," which Marcus says means that, "the face we choose to show the world—reveals who we really are." Identity, he seems to be saying, cannot only be "performed," but the performance can become the reality. By standing up for racial justice as an Asian American, Marcus has found a sense of purpose in his life; this is the "face" he embraces. And yet, is it possible to perform race in this manner? A number of gender and queer theorists, such as Judith Butler and Jose Muñoz, have written about the performativity of identity, which can be easily applied to Marcus's situation. These theorists argue that conceptions of race and gender are determined by external social forces, rather than some sort of essential identity that comes with membership in a particular demographic group. This does not mean, however, that these socially constructed categories have no power, nor does it mean one can alter one's identity so easily. Marcus may think he can determine for himself the identity he wishes to inhabit, but can he continue to say and do all of the "right" things, while refusing to acknowledge the pre-existing societal category he once inhabited? DHH thinks not, and is determined to prove Marcus a fraud.

A secondary plot thread concerns the relationship between DHH and his father—referred to in the script as HYH (Francis Jue), which are the initials of Hwang's actual father, Henry Yuan Hwang. HYH was the founder and CEO of Far East National Bank, and is depicted in the play as the quintessential self-made man. He is fond of comparing himself to Frank Sinatra, insisting that he gets to do things "My Way." Jue's performance—which earned a Lucille Lortel Award, an Obie Award, and a Drama Desk Award nomination—was full of humor and charisma. HYH is shown as a dynamic and sometimes dominating force within DHH's life, as evidenced in the following scene where the elder Hwang convinces his son to join the board of directors of his bank:

> DHH: But I don't know the first thing about banking.
>
> HYH: You used to work in the bank! Back in college, during the summers, remember?
>
> DHH: As a teller!
>
> HYH: And you were a good teller too. Every night, your drawer balanced.
>
> DHH: And what's my title gong to be? "Director of Nepotism"?
>
> HYH: If that's the title you want, fine, you can have it.
>
> DHH: Dad, I'm not in the least qualified.
>
> HYH: What do you mean, you're not qualified? You're my son, aren't you?

HYH puzzles over his son's obsession with identity politics, and fervently believes in the American Dream: the idea that anyone can become what he or she wants to be, regardless of race or background. Everything changes when HYH is caught in a government probe alleging that Far East National was helping to launder money for the Central Bank of China. (This financial scandal is also historically verifiable.) While he at first relishes the opportunity to fight the false allegations, HYH gradually becomes disillusioned by his unfair treatment.

WITHIN THE PLAY, Hwang links his father's troubles to a resurgence of anti-Asian sentiments that called to mind the "Yellow Peril" fears of the late 19th and early 20th centuries. During this period in American history, there was a strong backlash against Asian immigrants who were perceived as a threat to the nation rather than as part of it. They were often described as an invading horde, and seen as unassimilable. In *Yellow Face*, Hwang works into the plot the false espionage accusations against nuclear physicist Wen Ho Lee, as well as the campaign finance scandals of the late 1990s that had a decidedly anti-Asian bias. The playwright contends that these were not isolated incidents, but that they formed an overall pattern with racist overtones.

J'accuse! Hoon Lee and Noah Bean in Yellow Face. *Photo: Joan Marcus*

In a pivotal Act II scene, DHH meets up with a *New York Times* reporter (Anthony Torn) referred to in the script as "Name Withheld on Advice of Counsel" or NWOAOC for short. The reporter wants to question DHH about his involvement with Far East National, because he was on the bank's board during the time of the alleged financial irregularities.[1] During the course of their interview, NWOAOC claims to have no political agenda, and yet the questions he asks and the way that he asks them suggest bias. DHH says that NWOAOC will make "a fascinating character," and that their conversation has provided him with something new to write about:

> DHH: I already have everything I need to write my play.
>
> NWOAOC: As if that's so difficult? Anything missing from your story—hell, you just go make it up.

---

[1] Editor's note: A lengthy, front-page investigative article by Tim Golden and Jeff Gerth titled "China Sent Cash to US Bank, With Suspicions Slow to Rise" appeared May 12, 1999, in the *New York Times*. In it David Henry Hwang's playwriting success and former bank directorship are mentioned. The article appeared alongside two other page-one pieces that detail campaign contributions made by Chinese nationals and chart rising nationalism among the Chinese young. It is unknown if Golden's and Gerth's were the names "withheld" from *Yellow Face*.

DHH: Isn't that what all writers do?

NWOAOC: I search for a story to fit the facts, not the other way around.

DHH: But you arrange the facts, decide what's important and what's not—until you find a story that makes sense to your mind.

Hwang's point is that all writers have a perspective that determines what and how they write, whether one is a playwright who deals primarily in the realm of fiction or a reporter who is supposedly neutral. However, the latter can be more damaging because it makes a claim of objectivity which does not, in fact, exist. Torn was both riveting and creepy as NWOAOC, exuding a self-satisfied confidence that gives way to a barely suppressed anger by the end of the scene as DHH turns the tables on him.

Ironically, Marcus also comes under investigation because he used his stage name when making a contribution to a political campaign. Since these government probes were targeting donors with Asian-sounding last names, DHH convinces Marcus that the only way to blow the lid on the absurdity of this racial bias is for them to publicly come clean about Marcus's actual ethnicity—even if it means that both of them will "lose face." By showing the world that these racially profiled investigations accidentally targeted a white man, the whole enterprise becomes ripe for ridicule. DHH tells the audience that this "marked the turning point in the Chinese espionage scandals of the late 1990s." This action, however, also alienates Marcus from the Asian-American community he had come to love—specifically from Leah, who is unable to look past his deception.

It also comes too late for HYH. Although the investigation into his bank comes to naught, HYH's health deteriorates and by the end of the play he is dead. At his father's funeral, DHH and Marcus have one last scene together, in which it is revealed that Marcus is actually a completely fictional character that was created for this play. DHH explains why he needed Marcus in one of the show's more poignant speeches:

DHH: That's where you came in. To take words like "Asian" and "American," like "race" and "nation," mess them up so bad no one has any idea what they even mean anymore. Cuz that was Dad's dream: a world where he could be Jimmy Stewart. And a white guy—can even be an Asian. (*pause*) That's what you do after your father dies. You start making his dream your own.

IN BOTH THE structure and content of his play, Hwang explodes notions of truth and authenticity. He exposes these concepts as subjective and prone to manipulation. At the same time, he does not deny their power. There are real effects produced by truth claims, even if their verity is suspect. A play, however, also allows Hwang to do just that: "play" with versions of the truth. By presenting *Yellow Face* as a theatrical "mockumentary," Hwang is able to poke fun at some of the more extreme aspects of identity politics, while still showing that racism is ever present, and affecting our everyday lives.

In the production at the Public Theater, the action was staged simply and fluidly on a large square platform designed by David Korins (a more complex set was utilized for the Los Angeles production, but was scrapped for the New York staging). Microphones hung from the ceiling, and helped to establish a presentational quality to the proceedings, reinforced by the fact that when not "on," the actors sat in chairs around the central square, still in complete view of the audience. Donald Holder's lighting design helped to mark the many transitions of time, location, and character.

Yellow Face won an Obie Award for Hwang's playwriting, and it was a finalist for the Pulitzer Prize in Drama. It received a few rave reviews, from writers such as *Newsday*'s Linda Winer, who called it a "smart and delightful and scary new quasi-mock-autobiographical docudrama." *Variety*'s Marilyn Stasio declared it "a delicious comedy of errors." These good notices contributed to the play's success, and its run at the Public was extended twice. Many critics, however, gave the show more mixed reviews. Ben Brantley, in the *New York Times*, called it a "lively, messy and provocative cultural self-portrait of a play" while also writing that it "takes such a radical twist in tone that it leaves you with whiplash." Although he acknowledged the play's ambition, he criticized how the farcical structure of Act I gives way to a more serious, dramatic story following the intermission. The satirical first act, he felt, was more successful, while the second act was too fragmented and the entirety of the play was a "scattershot personal venting of painful emotions." Although Brantley was quick to dismiss the work as the playwright's version of therapy, this is an unfair assessment that is leveled against a number of autobiographically inspired plays and ignores the artistry involved in the crafting of the tale.

Yellow Face lures the audience in with a comic treatment of the issues, lampooning a number of perspectives and people—not the least of whom is David Henry Hwang himself. Even from the beginning, however, the playwright signals his more serious intents. The turn to darker, more dramatic material as the play progresses creates a satisfying narrative arc that demonstrates the complexity of issues Hwang evokes in order to tell the story of a father and a son—as well as the twisting cultural landscape wherein racial identity still affects the way others see you, and the way you see yourself.

2007–2008 Special Citation

PETER AND JERRY

By Edward Albee

○ ○ ○ ○ ○

Essay by Michael Sommers

EDITOR'S NOTE: As this volume was in preparation for publication, Edward Albee told us that Peter and Jerry *had been renamed* At Home at the Zoo—*a typically artful rendering. We note this here, but in the interest of historical accuracy we have retained the title within this essay under which the play was considered during the 2007–2008 season. We have, however, indexed the play under both titles for ease of future reference.*

> ANN: Then that must be what I wanted—a little . . . . disorder around here, a little . . . . chaos.
>
> PETER: And we don't have that.
>
> ANN: No. A little madness. Wouldn't that be good?

PLAYWRIGHTS RANGING FROM William Shakespeare to Neil Simon have returned to some of their finest works in sequels, prequels and drastically revised versions. In most cases, the results have not yielded enduring theatre. But that knowledge did not deter Edward Albee from expanding *The Zoo Story* into *Peter and Jerry.*

Among the most famous and frequently performed American plays of the past 50 years, *The Zoo Story* scarcely needs an introduction. This great one-act, regarding the fatal Central Park encounter between mild-mannered Peter and excitable Jerry, often is the first Albee play students tackle in the classroom. Over the years, countless critics have analyzed Albee's indelible evocation of mid-20th-century alienation. Notwithstanding the distinguished achievement of *Who's Afraid of Virginia Woolf?*, *Three Tall Women* and 30 other works, the immediacy and emotional impact of *The Zoo Story* make this one-act an especially powerful drama.

There is no arguing that *The Zoo Story* has long been regarded as a global classic. Written by Albee in the three weeks leading up to his 30th birthday, it was first produced at the Berlin Art Festival in September 1959

East Side Story: Bill Pullman and Johanna Day in Homelife, *the first act of* Peter and Jerry *(now* At Home at the Zoo*). Photo: Joan Marcus*

before its New York premiere at the Provincetown Playhouse in January 1960. *The Zoo Story* put its newcomer author on the theatrical map, even though the drama received short shrift from *Best Plays* back then. This is not to say that *Best Plays* was not doing its best to keep current with changing theatrical times. In order to recognize the growing importance of the burgeoning Off Broadway scene, the *Best Plays* volume covering the 1959-1960 season augmented its usual collection of ten Broadway works with a new feature: An excerpt from a significant Off Broadway text. Jack Gelber's jazzy saga about hipster junkies waiting for their next fix, *The Connection*, was designated as the most noteworthy premiere and commanded five pages of summary and excerpts. Henry Hewes's commentary on the Off Broadway season placed Gelber's name at the top of a list of worthy new writers but immediately added that Albee was "of equal promise" and devoted two paragraphs to *The Zoo Story* and its circuitous route to New York via the German-language production in Berlin.

Originally sharing a bill with Samuel Beckett's *Krapp's Last Tape*, *The Zoo Story* has been since paired with other plays including Albee's *The Death of Bessie Smith* and *The American Dream*. But in a conversation with me shortly before *Peter and Jerry* opened at Second Stage Theatre in

November 2007, the playwright declared he never felt his own works or any others made ideal companion pieces. Albee was vague on the time he thought of it, but perhaps as long as 10 years ago he decided to augment *The Zoo Story* with another work centering on the figure of Peter. "The balance is a little off," says Albee about *The Zoo Story*. "Jerry talks all the time and Peter doesn't have much to say. I wish I knew more about Peter."

Albee does not believe playwrights should significantly revise their earlier works. "You can't do that because you are not the same person you were when you wrote the play," says Albee. So he did not alter *The Zoo*

Albee has written a "first act" for his classic play, *The Zoo Story*.

Story appreciably, but instead composed *Homelife*, which Albee insists is not intended to be a prequel ("a term I loathe"), but rather "the first act of the entire play." Albee even says he conceived his visit with Peter and his wife, Ann, in their living room back when he first envisioned *The Zoo Story* in the late 1950s. "It's just that I didn't bother to write it down."

The playwright noted how he immediately reconnected with his original creative impulse. "*Homelife* practically wrote itself," says Albee, admitting to some surprise how easily he realized the character of Ann. "I knew exactly who she was because I knew who Peter would have for a wife," he figures. "I revealed to myself infinitely more than I had consciously known about their relationship." A seriocomic study in banal civilization, *Homelife* presents a revealing conversation between a reasonably comfortable American married couple of today. Described by Albee as a bland and tidy gentleman in his mid-40s, Peter and the "unexceptional" Ann are viewed in the "Danish-modernish" living room of their duplex in Manhattan's smart East 70s, located a few blocks from Central Park. On this early Sunday afternoon, the couple's unseen two daughters are upstairs and Peter is reading what he soon describes as the most important and boring textbook his firm has ever published.

AS THE PLAY begins, Ann emerges from the kitchen and casually announces, "We should talk." Immersed in his book, Peter scarcely registers Ann's remark. When he does, their chat is domestic: Andirons, kids, microwaves, cats, parakeets. "We have two of everything," observes Ann. When their inconsequential talk drifts into their sleeping habits and Ann's tendency to predawn wanderings, she reveals to the nonplused Peter some vague thoughts about having her breasts cut off as some sort of preventative measure against cancer. Relatively glib exchanges between the couple ensue regarding mortality, love affairs, crazy people and the glimmering notion of "*thinking* about thinking about something."

Emboldened by Ann's candor, Peter then cautiously confides a perception that his penis is growing smaller. "Retreating," he describes it. Ann stifles her amusement and tries to be sympathetic, especially since she is well aware that sex and talk of it are not Peter's strongest suits. "Mr. Circumspection," Ann calls him. Cool, even bantering, discussion of circumcision and genital mutilation somehow circles back to Ann's opening statement about them needing to talk, although now she cannot remember why. Talk they do, however, and their conversation leads them to entertain the notion of some terrible unknown suddenly threatening their placid existence. In doing so, Peter and Ann recognize they do not confide their deepest fears to each other.

> ANN: Why bother? If there's nothing to be done . . . . why bother? If there's no help . . . . why bother?

No satisfaction: Johanna Day in Homelife, *the first act of* Peter and Jerry *(now* At Home at the Zoo*). Photo: Joan Marcus*

PETER: (*Shy*) To . . . . share?

ANN: Be helpless together? Cling like marmosets?

PETER: People need that sometimes.

While appreciating their mutual affection, Ann is concerned.

ANN: That nothing is . . . . ultimately . . . . sufficient—not you, not us, not . . . . me? And I know you're probably going through this, too. Or—worse—that maybe you're *not*, that maybe none of it's ever occurred to you—that you . . . . don't have it *in* you?"

A few moments later, Peter quietly responds:

PETER: (*Engaged, but rational*) I thought we both made a decision—when we decided to be together, or even before we knew each other—I thought we made a decision, *must* have made one, that what we wanted was a smooth voyage on a safe ship, a view of porpoises now and then, a gentle swell, bright clouds way off, a sense that it was a . . . . familiar voyage, though we'd never taken it before—a pleasant journey, all the way through. And that's what we're having . . . . (*slight doubt*) isn't it?

[. . .]

ANN: No; *yes*. That's what we've both wanted: stay away from icebergs; avoid the Bermuda Triangle; remember where the lifeboats are, knowing, of course, that most of them don't work—no need. Yes; that's what we've wanted . . . . and that's what we've had—for the most part. And isn't it frightening.

Drifting deeper into talk regarding sexual intimacy, Ann observes how other longterm couples can still become like animals in their lust for each other. She regrets the lack of passion in their otherwise pleasurable lovemaking.

ANN: [. . .] But where's the . . . . the rage, the . . . . animal? We're animals! Why don't we behave like that . . . . like beasts? Is it that we love each other too safely, maybe? That we're secure? That we're too . . . . civilized? Don't we ever *hate* one another?

Then Peter reveals at length and in graphic detail a brutal sexual encounter during his college days when he and a strange sorority girl drunkenly coupled. It was raw, atavistic sex ending in pain, blood and shame, and that is why Peter has taken care never to hurt anyone again.

In the aftermath of Peter's confession, Ann signals her rueful acceptance of the lack of surprise in their relationship by sharply slapping his face. Immediately kissing Peter, Ann explains she simply wanted to astonish him with something unexpected. Falling into laughter, they wishfully riff together upon some unforeseen chaotic event—a tornado, perhaps—sweeping away the contents of their orderly home life. When their mirth subsides, Ann returns to the kitchen where she is making a spinach dish and Peter departs for the park, his dull book in hand. "I love you," they both say in parting.

THE ZOO STORY comprises the second act of Peter and Jerry. While Albee claims that he does not later revise his plays, he does admit to making "little snips here and there" to eliminate what he sees as overwritten passages. Since the original publication of The Zoo Story, Albee has whittled away both at Jerry's lengthy "dog story" monologue at the drama's center as well as that character's dying aria at the conclusion. Other than an additional trim of 10 lines or so, the text here otherwise remains the same as Albee's 1999 version of his play. Because The Zoo Story is so well known, it is unnecessary to summarize the work at length here.

Set in Central Park later during the same sun-drenched afternoon as Homelife, Peter is discovered on a bench, reading his book, as Jerry comes into view and loudly announces he has just been to the zoo. A carelessly dressed man in his late 30s, Jerry is a weary yet excitable fellow who insists on talking to Peter. Too polite to walk away, Peter responds amiably to Jerry's probing inquiries about his life. Jerry then describes his own empty, threadbare existence spent in a small room at the top of a shabby brownstone on the Upper West Side. He has no family and apparently no friends. Jerry's candid remarks about his briefly homosexual ways as an adolescent and his current frequenting of prostitutes make Peter obviously uncomfortable. Is this leading to something sordid in the park?

But soon Jerry launches into an extended tale about his disgusting landlady and, more specifically, his relationship with her "black monster" of a dog. In brief, Jerry's story relates how he first attempted to make friends with the ugly, hostile creature. When hamburgers did not soothe the beast, Jerry decided to kill him with poison. But the dog recovered and finally the two of them settled into mutual indifference. Jerry's bleak awareness of his failure to communicate with an animal—let alone a human being—concludes in total despair.

> JERRY: [. . .] I have learned that neither kindness nor cruelty by themselves, independent of each other, creates any effect beyond themselves; and I have learned that the two combined, together, at the same time, are the teaching emotion. [. . .] The dog and I have attained a compromise; more of a bargain, really. We neither love nor hurt because we do not try to reach each other. And, *was* trying to feed the dog an act of love? And, perhaps, was the dog's attempt

Making contact: Bill Pullman and Dallas Roberts in The Zoo Story, *the second act of* Peter and Jerry *(now* At Home at the Zoo*). Photo: Joan Marcus*

> to bite me *not* an act of love? If we can so misunderstand, well then, why have we invented the word love in the first place? [. . .]

Thanks to the preceding *Homelife* episode, of course, Jerry's increasingly frenzied monologue on the loneliness of the human condition now can be seen as a warped but meaningful reflection of the hollow relationship between Peter and Ann. Peter realizes it, too, and his angry response kicks the play into its final passages, as a tussle over a park bench escalates into suicide-murder. In a deliberate act of martyrdom, Jerry impales himself upon his own knife, which Peter defensively holds out. All but blessing Peter and confirming his animal nature, Jerry sends the howling man on his way and dies.

Leaving aside the psychosexual, religious and social themes of the play, which have been endlessly addressed elsewhere, *The Zoo Story* essentially concerns itself with the terror of human isolation and alienation. A complimentary work, *Homelife* considers how the same issues can fester even within a seemingly contented marriage. (Given how successfully they have explored this dark theme during their long careers, it is a pity that Albee and his eminent contemporary, Stephen Sondheim, never collaborated on a musical.) In providing this glimpse into Peter's existence and conjuring the character of his coolly empathetic partner, Ann, the playwright also gives viewers a likely notion of what happens in the immediate wake of the two-act story. Fleeing the park, Peter probably will head like a wounded animal right back home, where Ann will try to comfort him and, no doubt, stick by his side as their cool, predictable world falls apart in the devastating aftermath of Peter's encounter with Jerry. The couple's vague, wishful fantasies about the coming of some terrible event to shake up their symmetrical existence strikes home with a vengeance.

CONSECUTIVELY NUMBERING THE new and old works into one text—and retitling the post-Second Stage version as *At Home at the Zoo*—Albee insists that the two parts comprise an entire piece. "It is the whole play," he declares. "Things have happened to Peter in the first act that are going to be important to his reactions to Jerry in the second act. This is a fuller experience by far than just *Zoo Story*."

It is true that the new piece offers deeper insights to Peter's buttoned-down character and also gives viewers an extra punch derived from how a couple's worst fears can come true in a way they never anticipated. Yet to spectators who grew up with *The Zoo Story*, *Peter and Jerry* may register more as two connected but separate plays. That is not a bad thing. The contrast between the emotional ice of the new work and the emotional savagery of the classic is striking indeed. Time alone will tell whether this two-act version proves to be as enduring an entity as *The Zoo Story*. Speaking of time, anachronistic references to microwaves and Stephen King remove *Peter and Jerry* from the 1950s circumstances of the original piece to situate the drama somewhere indefinitely in the later 20th century; meant perhaps to point up the timelessness of emotional estrangement.

As a standalone work, the pensive *Homelife* is characteristic of Albee's studies in wintry, upper-middle-class relationships such as *Marriage Play* (1987) and *The Goat, or Who Is Sylvia?* (2002). The characters are mature, urbane individuals who, at least in each play's beginning, have achieved some sort of equilibrium between their worst urges and better natures. Yet they express longings that jeopardize their carefully constructed worlds. Edged in sardonic humor, the language tends to be a bit formal, even mannered. The dialogue is structured as a series of interrupted thoughts, repetitions and, toward the conclusion, longer speeches. Not unlike a composer, Albee annotates his carefully punctuated wordplay with specific stresses upon certain words and even syllables as well as with many parenthetical notations of emotional intent, e.g., (*sincere*), (*calm*), (*not accusatory*), (*a little embarrassed*).

Elegantly stylized in its heightened conversations, *Peter and Jerry* unfolds in a mildly surreal manner that suggests the action occurs behind a glass wall. Director Pam MacKinnon's keen Second Stage production underscored the play's slightly—and ironically—detached tone with stark settings by designer Neil Patel featuring a glossy floor and an unearthly green backdrop. Exceptional performances successfully navigated the subtleties of Albee's insinuating text. As the gentlemanly Peter, Bill Pullman lent a tight-lipped quality to his character's passive ways that hinted at the strain of being a nice guy in a cruel world. A bearded, melancholy Dallas Roberts told Jerry's shaggy-dog stories with increasing frustration and rage. Johanna Day crisply portrayed Ann with a knowing yet always compassionate nature.

Celebrating his 80th birthday during the 2007–08 theater season, Albee was represented by three more major productions in the metropolitan area. January saw director Emily Mann's world premiere of his sardonic comedy *Me, Myself and I* at McCarter Theatre Center in Princeton, where Tyne Daly genially depicted the befuddled mother of 28-year-old identical twin sons plagued by personal-identity issues. In April, Albee himself staged a lightly cartoonish revival of *The American Dream* and *The Sandbox* at the Cherry Lane Theatre with Judith Ivey and George Bartenieff playing Mommy and Daddy in both satirical works. In June, after the 2007–08 *Best Plays* season had closed, Mercedes Ruehl was scheduled to portray sculptor Louise Nevelson in *Occupant*, directed by MacKinnon for Signature Theatre Company. (Slated for a 2002 staging by Signature, the original production never officially opened when Anne Bancroft took ill during previews.)

At last word, Albee said he had at least two more plays mulling in his head. Since Albee usually evolves his creations slowly, it may be some time before they finally materialize on stage, but chances are that the great American author—whose plays have been honored nine times in these annual records—will once again have a notable work cited by *Best Plays*.

PLAYS PRODUCED IN
NEW YORK

PLAYS PRODUCED ON BROADWAY

○ ○ ○ ○ ○

FIGURES IN PARENTHESES following a play's title give the number of performances from the press-opening date. These figures do not include previews or extra nonprofit performances. In the case of a transfer, the prior run is noted but not added to the figure in parentheses.

Plays marked with an asterisk (*) were still in a projected run June 1, 2008. Their number of performances is figured through May 31, 2008.

In a listing of a show's numbers—dances, sketches, musical scenes, etc.—the titles of songs are identified wherever possible by their appearance in quotation marks (").

HOLDOVERS FROM PREVIOUS SEASONS

BROADWAY SHOWS THAT were running on June 1, 2007 are listed below. More detailed information about them appears in previous *Best Plays* volumes of the years in which they opened. Important cast changes since opening night are recorded in the Cast Replacements section in this volume.

*The Phantom of the Opera (8,643). Musical with book by Richard Stilgoe and Andrew Lloyd Webber; music by Andrew Lloyd Webber; lyrics by Charles Hart; additional lyrics by Richard Stilgoe; adapted from the novel by Gaston Leroux. Opened January 26, 1988.

Beauty and the Beast (5,461). Musical with book by Linda Woolverton; music by Alan Menken; lyrics by Howard Ashman and Tim Rice. Opened April 18, 1994. Production hiatus September 6, 1999 through November 15, 1999 during change of theater. (Closed July 29, 2007)

*Rent (5,009). Transfer from Off Broadway of the musical with book, music and lyrics by Jonathan Larson. Opened Off Off Broadway January 26, 1996 and Off Broadway February 13, 1996 where it played 56 performances through March 31, 1996; transferred to Broadway April 29, 1996.

*Chicago (4,786). Revival of the musical based on the play by Maurine Dallas Watkins; book by Fred Ebb and Bob Fosse; music by John Kander; lyrics by Fred Ebb; original production directed and choreographed by Bob Fosse. Opened November 14, 1996.

*The Lion King (4,371). Musical adapted from the screenplay by Irene Mecchi, Jonathan Roberts and Linda Woolverton; book by Roger Allers and Irene Mecchi; music by Elton John; lyrics by Tim Rice; additional music and lyrics by Lebo M, Mark Mancina, Jay Rifkin, Julie Taymor and Hans Zimmer. Opened November 13, 1997.

*Mamma Mia! (2,734). Musical with book by Catherine Johnson; music and lyrics by Benny Andersson and Björn Ulvaeus, some songs with Stig Anderson. Opened October 18, 2001.

*Hairspray (2,393). Musical with book by Mark O'Donnell and Thomas Meehan; music by Marc Shaiman; lyrics by Marc Shaiman and Scott Wittman; based on the film by John Waters. Opened August 15, 2002.

*Avenue Q (1,996). Transfer from Off Off Broadway of the musical with book by Jeff Whitty; music and lyrics by Robert Lopez and Jeff Marx. Opened July 31, 2003.

*Wicked (1,893). Musical with book by Winnie Holzman; music and lyrics by Stephen Schwartz; based on a novel by Gregory Maguire. Opened October 30, 2003.

*Spamalot (1,317). Musical with book and lyrics by Eric Idle; music by John Du Prez and Mr. Idle; based on the motion picture *Monty Python and the Holy Grail.* Opened March 17, 2005.

The 25th Annual Putnam County Spelling Bee (1,136). Transfer from Off Broadway of the musical with book by Rachel Sheinkin; music and lyrics by William Finn; conceived by Rebecca Feldman; additional material by Jay Reiss. Opened May 2, 2005. (Closed January 20, 2008)

*Jersey Boys: The Story of Frankie Valli and the Four Seasons (1,050). Musical with book by Marshall Brickman and Rick Elice; music by Bob Gaudio; lyrics by Bob Crewe. Opened November 6, 2005.

The Color Purple (910). Musical with book by Marsha Norman; music and lyrics by Brenda Russell, Allee Willis, Stephen Bray; adapted from the novel by Alice Walker and the Warner Bros./Amblin Entertainment film. Opened December 1, 2005. (Closed February 24, 2008)

The Drowsy Chaperone (674). Musical with book by Bob Martin and Don McKellar; music and lyrics by Lisa Lambert and Greg Morrison. Opened May 1, 2006. (Closed December 30, 2007)

Tarzan (486). Musical with book by David Henry Hwang; music and lyrics by Phil Collins; based on *Tarzan of the Apes* by Edgar Rice Burroughs and the Disney film *Tarzan.* Opened May 10, 2006. (Closed July 8, 2007)

*A Chorus Line (670). Revival of the musical with book by James Kirkwood and Nicholas Dante; music by Marvin Hamlisch; lyrics by Edward Kleban. Opened October 5, 2006.

Grey Gardens (308). Transfer from Off Broadway of the musical with book by Doug Wright; music by Scott Frankel; lyrics by Michael Korie; based on the film *Grey Gardens* by David Maysles, Albert Maysles, Ellen Hovde, Muffie Meyer and Susan Froemke. Opened November 2, 2006. (Closed July 29, 2007)

Les Misérables (463). Revival of the musical with book by Alain Boublil and Claude-Michel Schönberg; music by Mr. Schönberg; lyrics by Herbert Kretzmer; based on the novel by Victor Hugo; French text by Mr. Boublil and Jean-Marc Natel; additional material by James Fenton; adapted by John Caird and Trevor Nunn. Opened November 9, 2006. (Closed January 6, 2008)

*Mary Poppins (643). Musical with book by Julian Fellowes; music and lyrics by Richard M. Sherman and Robert B. Sherman; additional music and lyrics by George Stiles and Anthony Drewe; based on the stories of P.L. Travers and the film by Walt Disney Productions. Opened November 16, 2006.

Company (246). Revival of the musical with book by George Furth; music and lyrics by Stephen Sondheim. Opened November 29, 2006. (Closed July 1, 2007)

*Spring Awakening (595). Transfer from Off Off Broadway of the musical with book and lyrics by Steven Sater, music by Duncan Sheik; based on the play by Frank Wedekind. Opened December 10, 2006.

Journey's End (125). Revival of the play by R.C. Sherriff. Opened February 22, 2007. (Closed June 10, 2007)

Talk Radio (121). Revival of the play by Eric Bogosian; created for the stage with Tad Savinar. Opened March 11, 2007. (Closed June 24, 2007)

*Curtains (478). Musical with book by Rupert Holmes and Peter Stone; music by John Kander; lyrics by Fred Ebb, Mr. Kander and Mr. Holmes. Opened March 22, 2007.

The Year of Magical Thinking (144). Solo performance piece by Joan Didion; based on her memoir. Opened March 29, 2007. (Closed August 25, 2007)

The Pirate Queen (85). Musical with book by Alain Boublil, Claude-Michel Schönberg, Richard Maltby Jr.; music by Mr. Schönberg; lyrics by Messrs. Boublil, Maltby Jr. and John Dempsey; based on the novel *Grania: She-King of the Irish Seas* by Morgan Llywelyn. Opened April 5, 2007. (Closed June 17, 2007)

A Moon for the Misbegotten (71). Revival of the play by Eugene O'Neill. Opened April 9, 2007. (Closed June 10, 2007)

Inherit the Wind (100). Revival of the play by Jerome Lawrence and Robert E. Lee. Opened April 12, 2007. (Closed July 8, 2007)

Frost/Nixon (137). By Peter Morgan. Opened April 22, 2007. (Closed August 19, 2007)

*Legally Blonde (433). Musical with book by Heather Hach; music and lyrics by Laurence O'Keefe and Nell Benjamin; based on the novel by Amanda Brown and the MGM film. Opened April 29, 2007.

Manhattan Theatre Club production of **LoveMusik** (60). Musical with book by Alfred Uhry; music by Kurt Weill; lyrics by Maxwell Anderson, Bertolt Brecht, Howard Dietz, Roger Fernay, Ira Gershwin, Oscar Hammerstein II, Langston Hughes, Alan Jay Lerner, Maurice Magre, Ogden Nash, Elmer Rice, Mr. Weill; based on the letters of Mr. Weill and Lotte Lenya. Opened May 3, 2007. (Closed June 24, 2007)

Deuce (121). By Terrence McNally. Opened May 6, 2007. (Closed August 19, 2007)

Radio Golf (64). By August Wilson. Opened May 8, 2007. (Closed July 1, 2007)

Roundabout Theatre Company production **110 in the Shade** (94). Revival of the musical with book by N. Richard Nash; music by Harvey Schmidt; lyrics by Tom Jones; based on a play by N. Richard Nash. Opened May 9, 2007. (Closed July 29, 2007)

PLAYS PRODUCED JUNE 1, 2007–MAY 31, 2008

Roundabout Theatre Company production of **Old Acquaintance** (61). Revival of the play by John Van Druten. Todd Haimes artistic director, Harold Wolpert managing director, Julia C. Levy executive director, at the American Airlines Theatre. Opened June 28, 2007. (Closed August 19, 2007)

Katherine Markham .... Margaret Colin	Deirdre Drake .... Diane Davis
Rudd Kendall .... Corey Stoll	Karina .... Gordana Rashovich

Gal pals: Harriet Harris and Margaret Colin in Old Acquaintance. *Photo: Joan Marcus*

Mildred Watson Drake ....Harriet Harris   Preston Drake ....Stephen Bogardus
Susan ....Cynthia Darlow

Understudies: Ms. Colin—Gordana Rashovich; Ms. Harris—Cynthia Darlow; Messrs. Bogardus, Stoll—Tony Carlin; Mses. Davis, Rashovich, Darlow—Virginia Kull.

Direction, Michael Wilson; scenery, Alexander Dodge; costumes, David C. Woolard; lighting, Rui Rita; sound and music, John Gromada; wigs and hair, Paul Huntley; casting, Jim Carnahan; stage management, Roy Harris; press, Boneau/Bryan-Brown, Adrian Bryan-Brown, Matt Polk, Jessica Johnson, Amy Kass.

Time: November–December 1940. Place: New York City. Presented in three parts.

Two female writers of a certain age—one popular, the other "literary"—are friendly rivals in matters of work, family and love. First presentation of record was given at Boston's Plymouth Theatre (12/9–21/1940; 16 performances), before a Broadway opening at the Morosco Theatre and a transfer to the Broadhurst for its final six weeks (12/23/1940–5/17/1941; 170 performances). Jane Cowl and Peggy Wood played Katherine and Mildred.

*Xanadu (375). Musical with book by Douglas Carter Beane; music and lyrics by Jeff Lynne and John Farrar; based on the Universal Pictures film *Xanadu* by Richard Danus and Marc Rubel. Produced by Robert Ahrens, Dan Vickery, Tara Smith, B. Swibel, Sarah Murchison, Dale Smith at the Helen Hayes Theatre. Opened July 10, 2007.

Sonny ....Cheyenne Jackson   Calliope; Aphrodite ....Jackie Hoffman
Thalia; others...........................Curtis Holbrook   Terpsicore; others ....André Ward
Euterpe; others.............................Anika Larsen   Clio; Kira ....Kerry Butler
Erato; others ....Kenita R. Miller   Danny Maguire; Zeus ....Tony Roberts
Melpomene; Medusa ....Mary Testa   Featured Skater ....Marty Thomas

Musicians: Chris Biesterfeldt guitar; Eric Stern, Karl Mansfield synthesizer; Eric Halvorson drums.

Understudies: Ms. Butler—Anika Larsen, Kenita R. Miller, Patti Murin; Mr. Jackson—Curtis Holbrook, André Ward; Mr. Roberts—Peter Samuel; Ms. Testa—Annie Golden, André Ward; Ms. Hoffman—Annie Golden.

Swings: Marty Thomas, Patti Murin

Direction, Christopher Ashley; choreography, Dan Knechtges; scenery, David Gallo; costumes, David Zinn; lighting, Howell Binkley; sound, T. Richard Fitzgerald and Carl Casella; projections, Zachary Borovay; wigs and hair, Charles G. LaPointe; music direction and arrangements, Eric Stern; music coordination, John Miller; associate producers, Cari Smulyan, Allicat Productions, Marc Rubel, Christopher R. Webster III and Maggie Fine, Udanax LLC; casting, Cindy Tolan; stage management, Arturo E. Porazzi; press, Fifteen Minutes Public Relations, Pete Sanders, Andrew Snyder.

Time: 1980. Place: Los Angeles and Mount Olympus. Presented without intermission.

Spoof of a 1980 film that celebrated the many divine possibilities of wedding disco music to roller skating.

MUSICAL NUMBERS

Scene 1: Venice Beach
"I'm Alive" .... Muses, Clio; Kira
Scene 2: Santa Monica Pier
"Magic" .... Sonny, Kira, Muses
"Evil Woman" .... Melpomene, Calliope, Sirens
Scene 3: Outside the Auditorium
"Suddenly" .... Sunny, Kira
Scene 4: Danny Maguire's Office
"Whenever You're Away From Me" .... Danny, Kira, Young Danny

Strange magic: Mary Testa, Kerry Butler and Jackie Hoffman (all facing camera) in Xanadu. *Photo: Paul Kolnik*

Scene 5: Inside Auditorium
"Dancin'" .... '40s and '80s Singers, Kira, Sonny, Danny
"Strange Magic" .... Sunny, Kira, Melpomene, Calliope, Eros
"All Over the World" .... Company
"Don't Walk Away" .... Sonny, Kira, Muses
Scene 6: Venice Beach
"Fool" .... Kira, Melpomene, Calliope
"The Fall" .... Sonny, Muses
"Suspended in Time" .... Kira, Sonny
Scene 8: Mount Olympus
"Have You Never Been Mellow?" .... Zeus, Hera, Aphrodite, Thetis,
Cyclops, Medusa, Centaur

Scene 8: Club Xanadu
"Xanadu" .... Company

Grease (306). Revival of the musical with book, music and lyrics by Jim Jacobs and Warren Casey; additional songs by Barry Gibb, John Farrar, Louis St. Louis, Scott Simon. Produced by Paul Nicholas and David Ian, Nederlander Presentations Inc., Terry Allen Kramer, in association with Robert Stigwood, at the Brooks Atkinson Theatre. Opened August 19, 2007.

Danny Zuko	Max Crumm	Cha-Cha Di Gregorio	Natalie Hill
Sandy Dumbrowski	Laura Osnes	Marty	Robyn Hurder
Doody	Ryan Patrick Binder	Jan	Lindsay Mendez
Miss Lynch	Susan Blommaert	Betty Rizzo	Jenny Powers
Vince Fontaine	Jeb Brown	Sonny LaTierri	José Restrepo
Teen Angel	Stephen R. Buntrock	Kenickie	Matthew Saldivar
Roger	Daniel Everidge	Eugene Florczyk	Jamison Scott
Patty Simcox	Allison Fischer	Frenchy	Kirsten Wyatt

Ensemble: Josh Franklin, Cody Green, Natalie Hill, Emily Padgett, Keven Quillon, Brian Sears, Christina Sivrich, Anna Aimee White.

Musicians: Kimberly Grigsby conductor, synthesizer; Chris Fenwick associate conductor, piano, synthesizer; Michael Blanco bass; Michael Aarons, Jim Hershman guitar; John Scarpulla tenor saxophone, woodwinds; Jack Bashkow woodwinds; John Clancy drums.

Understudies: Messrs. Crumm, Brown—Josh Franklin; Messrs. Saldivar, Restrepo—Cody Green; Mses. Powers, Hurder—Natalie Hill; Messrs. Crumm, Buntrock—Matthew Hydzik; Mses. Fischer, Osnes—Emily Padgett; Messrs. Everidge, Restrepo—Keven Quillon; Messrs. Binder, Scott—Brian Sears; Mses. Wyatt, Mendez, Blommaert—Christina Sivrich; Mses. Hill, Wyatt, Mendez—Amber Stone; Mses. Hurder, Fischer, Osnes—Anna Aimee White.

Swings: Matthew Hydzik, Amber Stone.

Direction and choreography, Kathleen Marshall; scenery, Derek McLane; costumes, Martin Pakledinaz; lighting, Kenneth Posner; sound, Brian Ronan; wigs and hair, Paul Huntley; orchestrations, Christopher Jahnke; music coordination, Howard Joines; executive producer, Max Finbow; casting, Jay Binder, Jack Bowdan, Megan Larche; stage management, David John O'Brien; press, Barlow-Hartman, John Barlow, Michael Hartman, Ryan Ratelle, Melissa Bixler.

Time: 1959. Place: Rydell High School and other teen environs. Presented in two parts.

Parody of 1950s mores and music. First presentation of record was given at Kingston Mines Theater in Chicago (2/5–9/5/1971), before a production opened at the Eden Theatre (2/14–6/4/1972; 128 performances)—which earlier had been home to the Phoenix Theatre. Numerous sources note the Eden run as an Off Broadway production. In the 1971–72 edition of *Best Plays*, however, editor Otis L. Guernsey Jr. wrote that the Eden Theatre production operated under "first-class Broadway contracts" and the show was made eligible for the 1972 Tony Awards—it won none. In its end-of-season statistics by Clara Rotter, the *New York Times* classified the production as having closed Off Broadway after 128 performances and noted a move to Broadway. After mixed reviews and its difficult 16-week run at the Eden—during which time the producers sued *Variety* for making the production appear "less of a hit than it really was"—the production

It's the word: Jenny Powers and Matthew Saldivar in Grease. *Photo: Joan Marcus*

moved to the Broadhurst Theatre (6/7–11/18/1972) before runs at the Royale (11/21/1972–1/27/1980) and the Majestic (1/29–4/13/1980). The generally reported number of performances—3,388—includes the Eden run of 128 performances. The 2007–08 version, which also spawned a reality television program that chose performers for the production, was the second Broadway revival. The first revival played at the Eugene O'Neill Theatre (5/11/1994–1/25/1998; 1,505 performances, with a hiatus 2/23–4/7/1997).

ACT I

Prologue
Scene 1: Rydell High, 1959
  "Grease" .... Company
(Barry Gibb)
Scene 2: Cafeteria; School Steps
  "Summer Nights" .... Danny, Sandy, Company
Scene 3: Locker Room
  "Those Magic Changes" .... Doody, Company
Scene 4: Marty's Bedroom
  "Freddy, My Love" .... Marty, Pink Ladies
Scene 5: Street Corner
  "Greased Lightnin'" .... Kenickie, Guys
Scene 6: Rydell High
  "Rydell Fight Song" .... Sandy, Patty
Scene 7: Bleachers
  "Mooning" .... Roger, Jan
  "Look at Me, I'm Sandra Dee" .... Rizzo
  "We Go Together" .... T-Birds, Pink Ladies

ACT II

Scene 1: School Gym; Sandy's Room
"Shakin' at the High School Hop" .... Company
"It's Raining on Prom Night" .... Jan, Sandy
"Born to Hand-Jive" .... Vince, Company
Scene 2: School Steps
"Hopelessly Devoted to You" .... Sandy
(John Farrar)
Scene 3: Outside Burger Palace
"Beauty School Dropout" .... Teen Angel, Girls
Scene 4: Drive-In Movie
"Sandy" .... Danny
(Scott Simon and Louis St. Louis)
Scene 5: Jan's Rec Room
"Rock 'n' Roll Party Queen" .... Doody, Roger
"There Are Worse Things I Could Do" .... Rizzo
"Look at Me, I'm Sandra Dee" (Reprise) .... Sandy
Scene 6: Inside Burger Palace
"You're the One That I Want" .... Danny, Sandy, Company
(John Farrar)
"We Go Together" (Reprise) .... Company

Manhattan Theatre Club production of **Mauritius** (61). By Theresa Rebeck. Lynne Meadow artistic director, Daniel Sullivan acting artistic director, Barry Grove executive producer, in association with the Huntington Theatre Company (Nicholas Martin artistic director, Michael Maso managing director), at the Biltmore Theatre. Opened October 4, 2007. (Closed November 25, 2007)

Jackie	Alison Pill	Sterling	F. Murray Abraham
Philip	Dylan Baker	Mary	Katie Finneran
Dennis	Bobby Cannavale		

Understudies: Mr. Cannavale—Rod Brogan; Mses. Pill, Finneran—Katya Campbell; Messrs. Baker, Abraham—Robert Emmet Lunney.

Direction, Doug Hughes; scenery, John Lee Beatty; costumes, Catherine Zuber; lighting, Paul Gallo; sound and music, David Van Tieghem; fight direction, Rick Sordelet; casting, David Caparelliotis; stage management, Charles Means; press, Boneau/Bryan-Brown, Chris Boneau, Aaron Meier, Steven Padla, Heath Schwartz, Christine Olver.

Time: The present. Presented in two parts.

Two sisters become enmeshed in a rising-stakes battle over a rare, valuable stamp left by a dead parent. First presentation of record was given by Boston's Huntington Theatre Company (10/18–11/12/2006).

Roundabout Theatre Company production of **The Ritz** (69). Revival of the play by Terrence McNally. Todd Haimes artistic director, Harold Wolpert managing director, Julia C. Levy executive director, at Studio 54. Opened October 11, 2007. (Closed December 9, 2007)

Old Man Vespucci	Teddy Coluca	Michael Brick	Terrence Riordan
Carmine Vespucci	Lenny Venito	Googie Gomez	Rosie Perez
Vivian Proclo	Ashlie Atkinson	Tiger	Lucas Near-Verbrugghe
Aunt Verap;		Duff	David Turner
Maurine	Angela Pietropinto	Patron in Chaps	Matthew Montelongo
Abe	Adam Sietz	Crisco Patron	Ryan Idol
Claude Perkins	Patrick Kerr	Chuck	Teddy Coluca
Gaetano Proclo	Kevin Chamberlin	Snooty Patron	Jeffrey Evan Thomas
Chris	Brooks Ashmanskas	Sheldon Farenthold	Seth Rudetsky

Stamp act: F. Murray Abraham, Bobby Cannavale, Alison Pill, Dylan Baker and Katie Finneran in Mauritius. *Photo: Joan Marcus*

Chubby chased: Kevin Chamberlin and Matthew Montelongo in The Ritz. *Photo: Joan Marcus*

Other Patrons: Josh Breckenridge, Justin Clynes, Andrew R. Cooksey, Mark Leydorf, Billy Magnussen, Nick Mayo, Dillon Porter.

Standbys: Ms. Perez—Andréa Burns.

Understudies: Messrs. Chamberlin, Venito, Coluca—Kevin Carolan; Mr. Ashmanskas—Seth Rudetsky; Mr. Kerr—Lucas Near-Verbrugghe; Ms. Atkinson—Angela Pietropinto; Messrs. Riordan, Near-Verbrugghe, Turner—Billy Magnussen; Mr. Sietz—Teddy Coluca; Mr. Rudetsky and Patrons—Mark Leydorf.

Direction, Joe Mantello; choreography, Christopher Gattelli; scenery, Scott Pask; costumes, William Ivey Long; lighting, Jules Fisher and Peggy Eisenhauer; sound, Tony Meola; wigs and hair, Paul Huntley; casting, Jim Carnahan; stage management, Tripp Phillips, press, Boneau/Bryan-Brown, Adrian Bryan-Brown, Matt Polk, Jessica Johnson, Amy Kass.

Time: 1970s. Place: A gay bathhouse in New York City. Presented in two parts.

A heterosexual man hides in a gay bathhouse from his murderous in-laws in a farce from the pre-AIDS era of the sexual revolution. First presentation of record was given at Yale Repertory Theatre as *The Tubs* (1/5/1974; 35 performances). A 1974–75 *Best Plays* choice, the original Broadway production opened at the Longacre Theatre (1/20/1975–1/4/1976; 400 performances). Rita Moreno received the 1975 Tony Award for best featured actress for her portrayal of Googie Gomez. A revival at the disco Xenon, formerly Henry Miller's Theatre, played for one performance May 2, 1983, and closed the same evening.

Roundabout Theatre Company production of **Pygmalion** (69). Revival of the play by George Bernard Shaw. Todd Haimes artistic director, Harold Wolpert, managing director, Julia C. Levy executive director, at the American Airlines Theatre. Opened October 18, 2007. (Closed December 16, 2007)

Miss Eynsford Hill .... Kerry Bishé	Freddy Eynsford Hill .... Kieran Campion
Mrs. Eynsford Hill .... Sandra Shipley	Liza Doolittle .... Claire Danes
Bystander; Taxi Driver .... Doug Stender	Colonel Pickering .... Boyd Gaines

Over there: Chazz Palminteri in A Bronx Tale. *Photo: Joan Marcus*

Henry Higgins .... Jefferson Mays
Sarcastic Bystander .... Tony Carlin
Mrs. Pearce .... Brenda Wehle
Alfred Doolittle .... Jay O. Sanders
Mrs. Higgins .... Helen Carey
Parlor Maid .... Karen Walsh

Other bystanders: Jonathan Fielding, Robin Moseley, Jennifer Armour, Brad Heikes, Curtis Shumaker.

Understudies: Mses. Danes, Bishé—Karen Walsh; Messrs. Mays, Gaines—Tony Carlin; Mses. Shipley, Wehle, Walsh—Robin Moseley; Ms. Carey—Sandra Shipley; Messrs. Campion, Stender, Carlin—Jonathan Fielding; Mr. Sanders—Doug Stender.

Direction, David Grindley; scenery and costumes, Jonathan Fensom; lighting, Jason Taylor; sound, Gregory Clarke; wigs and hair, Richard Orton; casting, Jim Carnahan; stage management, Arthur Gaffin, press, Boneau/Bryan-Brown, Adrian Bryan-Brown, Matt Polk, Jessica Johnson, Amy Kass.

Time: 1913. Place: London. Presented in two parts.

A pedant resolves to prove his theory that anyone can be taught to overcome class difference through careful tutelage. First presentation of record was given in German at the Hofburg Theatre in Vienna (10/16/1913), before a run at the Lessing Theatre in Berlin. First US presentation of record was given by the German stock company of the Irving Place Theatre (3/18/1914). First presentation of record in English was given at His Majesty's Theatre in London (4/11/1914), with Mrs. Patrick Campbell as Eliza Doolittle, Herbert Beerbohm Tree as Higgins and Philip Merivale as Pickering. First US presentation of record was given at the Park Theatre (10/12–11/7/1914; 32 performances), before the production moved to the Liberty (11/9–11/21/1914; 16 performances) and Wallack's (11/23–12/12/1914; 24 performances). Campbell reprised Eliza and Merivale assumed the Higgins role for those 72 performances in New York. The 2007–08 production was the fifth Broadway revival.

A Bronx Tale (111). Revival of the solo performance piece by Chazz Palminteri. Produced by Go Productions, John Gaughan, Trent Othick, Matt Othick, Neighborhood Films, in association with Jujamcyn Theaters, at the Walter Kerr Theatre. Opened October 25, 2007. (Closed February 24, 2008)

Performed by Mr. Palminteri.

Direction, Jerry Zaks; scenery, James Noone; costumes, Isaia; lighting, Paul Gallo; sound and music, John Gromada; executive producer, Nicole Kastrinos; associate producers, Robert M. Moretti, Richard Carrigan; stage management, James Harker; press, Boneau/Bryan-Brown, Adrian Bryan-Brown, Jackie Green, Matt Ross.

Presented without intermission.

A Bronx native reminisces about the drama of wise guys and average citizens co-existing in a tough New York neighborhood. First presentation of record was given Off Off Broadway at Playhouse 91 (10/18–12/24/1989). The piece was expanded into a 1993 film written by Palmintieri and directed by Robert De Niro.

Cyrano de Bergerac (56). Revival of the play by Edmond Rostand; translated and adapted by Anthony Burgess. Produced by Susan Bristow LLC, James L. Nederlander, Terry Allen Kramer, Stewart F. Lane, Bonnie Comley, Barbara Manocherian, Stephanie P. McClelland, Jon B. Platt at the Richard Rodgers Theatre. Opened November 1, 2007. (Closed January 6, 2008)

Cyrano de Bergerac .... Kevin Kline
Roxane .... Jennifer Garner
Christian de Neuvillette .... Daniel Sunjata
Comte de Guiche .... Chris Sarandon
Ragueneau .... Max Baker
Le Bret .... John Douglas Thompson
Roxane's Duenna;
  Sister Marthe .... Concetta Tomei
Ligniere;
  Theophraste Renaudot .... Euan Morton
Castel-Jaloux .... Peter Jay Fernandez
Jodelet; others .... MacIntyre Dixon
Valvert; Cadet .... Carman Lacivita
Montfleury; others .... Tom Bloom
Cuigy; Cadet .... Baylen Thomas
Brissaille; Cadet .... Piter Marek
Musketeer;
  Cadet .... Daniel Stewart Sherman
Lise;
  Mother Marguerite .... Nance Williamson

Toastmaster: Kevin Kline and company in Cyrano de Bergerac. *Photo: Carol Rosegg*

Poet; Cadet .... Fred Rose
Theatregoer; others .... Thomas Schall
Page; others .... Lucas Papaelias
Page; others .... Alexander Sovronsky
Foodseller; Nun .... Kate Guyton
Actress; Sister Claire .... Ginifer King

Theatregoer's Son;
  Cadet .... Davis Duffield
Guard; others .... Keith Eric Chappelle
Lady; others .... Leenya Rideout
Cadet .... Stephen Balantzian
Cadet .... Amefika El-Amin

Understudies: Mr. Kline—Thomas Schall; Ms. Garner—Ginifer King; Mr. Sunjata—Baylen Thomas; Mr. Sarandon—Stephen Balantzian; Mr. Baker—Daniel Sherman; Mr. Thompson—Stephen Balantzian; Ms. Tomei—Kate Guyton; Mr. Fernandez—Keith Eric Chappelle; Mr. Dixon—Thomas Schall; Mr. Lacivita—Keith Eric Chappelle; Mr. Bloom—Daniel Stewart Sherman; Ms. Williamson—Kate Guyton.

Direction, David Leveaux; scenery, Tom Pye; costumes, Gregory Gale; lighting, Donald Holder; sound, David Van Tieghem; music; Messrs. Papaelias and Sovronsky; wigs and hair, Tom Watson; music arrangements, Messrs. Papaelias, Sovronsky and Rose; vocal arrangements, Ms. Rideout; casting, JV Mercanti; stage management, Marybeth Abel; press, Barlow-Hartman, John Barlow, Michael Hartman, Leslie Baden, Devin Robak.

Time: 1640–55. Place: Various locations in France. Presented in two parts.

Swashbuckling poet with an overdeveloped olfactory organ assists, against his own interest, a handsome dolt who pursues a beautiful woman. First presentation of record was given at Paris's Porte St. Martin Theatre (12/28/1897), with Constant Coquelin in the title role. First presentation of record in English was given in New York at the Garden Theatre (10/3–11/26/1898), with Richard Mansfield in the title role and Margaret Anglin as Roxane. José Ferrer received the first Tony Award as best dramatic actor in 1947 for his portrayal of the title character in the 1946–47 production of *Cyrano*, which ran a combined 193 performances at the Alvin Theatre and the Ethel Barrymore Theatre. (Fredric March was Ferrer's co-honoree that first year for *Years Ago* by Ruth Gordon, which ran 206 performances at the Mansfield Theatre.)

Rock 'n' Roll (123). By Tom Stoppard. Produced by Bob Boyett and Sonia Friedman Productions, Ostar Productions, Roger Berlind, Tulchin/Bartner, Douglas G. Smith, Dancap Productions, Jam Theatricals, the Weinstein Company, in association with Lincoln Center Theater (André Bishop artistic director, Bernard Gersten executive producer) and the Royal Court Theatre, at the Bernard B. Jacobs Theatre. Opened November 4, 2007. (Closed March 9, 2008)

Piper; Policeman	Seth Fisher	Ferdinand	Stephen Kunken
Esme (young); Alice	Alice Eve	Milan; Waiter	Ken Marks
Jan	Rufus Sewell	Lenka	Nicole Ansari
Max	Brian Cox	Stephen	Brian Avers
Eleanor; Esme (older)	Sinead Cusack	Candida	Alexandra Neil
Gillian; Magda	Mary Bacon	Pupil	Anna O'Donoghue
Interrogator; Nigel	Quentin Maré		

Understudies: Mr. Fisher—Brian Avers, Joseph Collins; Ms. Eve—Anna O'Donoghue; Mr. Sewell—Brian Avers, Joseph Collins; Mr. Cox—Ken Marks, Joe Vincent; Ms. Cusack—Alexandra Neil, Angela Reed; Ms. Bacon—Anna O'Donoghue, Angela Reed; Mr. Maré —Joseph Collins, Joe Vincent; Mr. Kunken—Joseph Collins, Seth Fisher; Mr. Marks—Joe Vincent; Ms. Ansari—Mary Bacon, Angela Reed; Mr. Avers—Joseph Collins, Seth Fisher; Ms. Neil—Mary Bacon, Angela Reed; Ms. O'Donoghue—Seth Fisher, Angela Reed.

Direction, Trevor Nunn; scenery, Robert Jones; costumes, Emma Ryott; lighting, Howard Harrison; sound, Ian Dickinson; casting, Tara Rubin Casting (US), Lisa Makin (UK); associate producer, Tim Levy; stage management, Rick Steiger; press, Boneau/Bryan-Brown, Adrian Bryan-Brown, Jim Byk, Matt Ross.

Songs included: "Wish You Were Here" (Roger Waters and David Gilmour, 1975), "Welcome to the Machine" (Roger Waters, 1975), "Vera" (Roger Waters, 1976), "Bring it on Home to Me" (Sam Cooke, 1962), "It's All Over Now" (Bobby Womack and Shirley Womack, 1964), "The Last

True believer: Rufus Sewell in Rock 'n' Roll. *Photo: Joan Marcus*

Touching moment? Roger Bart, Megan Mullally and Sutton Foster in Young Frankenstein.
Photo: Paul Kolnik

Time" (Mick Jagger and Keith Richards, 1965), "Street Fighting Man" (Mick Jagger and Keith Richards, 1968), "Break on Through (to the Other Side)" (Jim Morrison, John Densmore, Ray Manzarek and Robby Krieger, 1966), "I'll Be Your Baby Tonight" (Bob Dylan, 1968), "I Still Haven't Found What I'm Looking For" (music by U2; lyrics by Bono and the Edge, 1987), "Give Peace a Chance" (John Lennon, 1969), "A Hard Day's Night" (John Lennon and Paul McCartney, 1964), "Wouldn't It Be Nice" (Tony Asher, Mike Love and Brian Wilson, 1966), "Milk Cow Blues" (John Adam Estes, 1930).

Time: 1968–90. Place: Prague and Cambridge. Presented in two parts.

Polemic on radicals in the former Czechoslovakia who pine for a world in which rock 'n' roll's revolutionary thematics can create change and freedom. First presentation of record was given at the Royal Court Theatre (6/3–7/15/2006) before a West End run at the Duke of York's Theatre (7/22/2006–2/25/2007). A 2007–08 *Best Plays* choice (see essay by Charles Wright in this volume).

*Young Frankenstein (236). Musical with book by Mel Brooks and Thomas Meehan; music and lyrics, Mr. Brooks; based on the story and screenplay by Gene Wilder and Mel Brooks for the 20th Century Fox film. Produced by Robert F.X. Sillerman and Mel Brooks, in association with the R/F/B/V Group, at the Hilton Theatre. Opened November 8, 2007.

Herald .... Paul Castree	Igor .... Christopher Fitzgerald
Ziggy ....Jim Borstelmann	Equines .... Eric Jackson,
Inspector Kemp ....Fred Applegate	Justin Patterson
Frederick Frankenstein ....Roger Bart	Inga... Sutton Foster
Mr. Hilltop .... Jack Doyle	Lawrence ....Jim Borstelmann
Telegraph Boy ....Brian Shepard	Frau Blucher .... Andrea Martin
Elizabeth .... Megan Mullally	Victor .... Kevin Ligon
Shoeshine Man ....Jim Borstelmann	Monster .... Shuler Hensley

Hermit	Fred Applegate	Tasha	Linda Mugleston
Sasha	Eric Jackson	Bob	Paul Castree
Masha	Heather Ayers	Ritz Specialty	Eric Jackson
Basha	Christina Marie Norrup	Count	Matthew LaBanca

Medical Students: Justin Patterson, Matthew LaBanca, Kevin Ligon.

Transylvania Quartet: Paul Castree, Jack Doyle, Kevin Ligon, Brian Shepard.

Ensemble: Heather Ayers, Jim Borstelmann, Paul Castree, Jennifer Lee Crowl, Jack Doyle, Renée Feder, Amy Heggins, Eric Jackson, Matthew LaBanca, Kevin Ligon, Barrett Martin, Linda Mugleston, Christina Marie Norrup, Justin Patterson, Brian Shepard, Sarrah Strimel.

Orchestra: Patrick S. Brady conductor, keyboard 3; Gregory J. Dlugos associate conductor, keyboard 1; David Gursky assistant conductor, keyboard 2; Rick Dolan concertmaster; Ashley D. Horne; Helen H. Kim violin; Maxine Roach, Deborah Shufelt-Dine viola; Laura Bontrager, Chungsun Kim cello; Bob Renino string bass; Vincent DellaRocca, Steven J. Greenfield, Charles Pillow, Frank Santagata woodwinds; Don Downs, Glenn Drewes, Scott Harrell trumpet; Timothy Sessions tenor trombone; Mike Christianson bass trombone; Patrick Pridemore, Judy Yin-Chi Lee, French horn; Charlie Descarfino percussion; Perry Cavari drums.

Understudies: Mr. Applegate—Jim Borstelmann, Kevin Ligon; Mr. Bart—Paul Castree, Matthew LaBanca; Ms. Mullally—Heather Ayers, Linda Mugleston; Mr. Fitzgerald—James Gray, Brian Shepard; Ms. Sutton—Renée Feder, Christina Marie Norrup; Ms. Martin—Heather Ayers, Linda Mugleston; Mr. Hensley—Jim Borstelmann, Justin Patterson.

Swings: James Gray, Kristin Marie Johnson, Craig Waletzko, Courtney Young.

Direction and choreography, Susan Stroman; scenery, Robin Wagner; costumes, William Ivey Long; lighting, Peter Kaczorowski; sound, Jonathan Deans; special effects, Marc Brickman; wigs and hair, Paul Huntley; orchestrations, Doug Besterman; musical arrangements and supervision, Glen Kelly; music direction and vocal arrangements, Mr. Brady; music coordination, John Miller; associate producer, One Viking Productions, Carl Pasbjerg; casting, Tara Rubin Casting; stage management, Steven Zweigbaum; press, Barlow-Hartman, John Barlow, Michael Hartman, Dennis Crowley, Michelle Bergmann.

Time: 1934. Place: Transylvania and New York. Presented in two parts.

Theater version of the 1974 film spoof of Mary Shelley's Frankenstein tale.

ACT I

Scene 1: A village in Transylvania, 1934
"The Happiest Town" .... Villagers
Scene 2: Medical school, New York City
"The Brain" .... Frederick, Students
Scene 3: Hudson River, Pier 57
"Please Don't Touch Me" .... Elizabeth, Voyagers
Scene 4: A railroad station in Transylvania
"Together Again" .... Frederick, Igor
Scene 5: A hay wagon
"Roll in the Hay" .... Inga, Frederick, Igor
Scene 6: Castle Frankenstein
Scene 7: The grand hall of Castle Frankenstein
"Join the Family Business" .... Victor, Frederick,
Ancestors
Scene 8: The laboratory
"He Vas My Boyfriend" .... Frau Blucher
Scene 9: The town hall
"The Law" .... Kemp, Villagers
Scene 10: The laboratory
"Life, Life" .... Frederick
Scene 11: The courtyard of Castle Frankenstein
"Welcome to Transylvania" .... Transylvania Quartet
"Transylvania Mania" .... Igor, Frederick, Inga,
Kemp, Villagers

ACT II

Scene 1: The forest
"He's Loose" .... Kemp, Villagers
Scene 2: The laboratory
"Listen to Your Heart" .... Inga
"Surprise" .... Elizabeth, Igor, Frau Blucher,
Sasha, Masha, Basha, Tasha, Bob
Scene 3: A remote cottage in the forest
"Please Send Me Someone" .... Hermit
Scene 4: The dungeon of Castle Frankenstein
"Man About Town" .... Frederick
Scene 5: A theater in Transylvania
"Puttin' on the Ritz" (Irving Berlin) .... Frederick, Monster, Inga,
Igor, Frau Blucher, Ensemble
Scene 6: A cave in the forest
"Deep Love" .... Elizabeth
Scene 7: The laboratory
Scene 8: The village square
Frederick's Soliloquy .... Frederick
"Deep Love" (Reprise) .... Monster
Finale Ultimo .... Company

Dr. Seuss's How the Grinch Stole Christmas! (96). Revival of the musical with book
and lyrics by Timothy Mason; music by Mel Marvin; additional music and lyrics by
Albert Hague and Theodor Seuss Geisel (Dr. Seuss); based on the book *How the Grinch
Stole Christmas* by Dr. Seuss. Produced by Running Subway, EMI Music Publishing,
Michael Speyer, Allen Spivak, Janet Pailet, Amy Jen Sharyn and Maximum Entertainment,
in association with Citi, at the St. James Theatre. Opened November 9, 2007. (Closed
January 6, 2008)

Old Max .... Ed Dixon
Cindy-Lou Who .... Caroline London (alt.);
Athena Ripka (alt.)
Papa Who .... Aaron Galligan-Stierle
Mama Who .... Tari Kelly
Grandpa Who .... Darin De Paul
Grandma Who .... Jan Neuberger
Boo Who .... Jordan Samuels (alt.);
Johnny Schaffer (alt.)

Annie Who .... Katie Micha (alt.);
Sami Gayle (alt.)
Danny Who .... Sky Flaherty (alt.);
Andy Richardson (alt.)
Betty-Lou Who .... Janelle Viscomi (alt.);
Jahaan Amin (alt.)
Young Max .... Rusty Ross
The Grinch .... Patrick Page

Citizens of Whoville: Hunter Bell, Janet Dickinson, Carly Hughes, Josephine Rose Roberts,
William Ryall, Jeff Skowron.
Little Whos: Brianna Gentilella, Michael Hoey, Marina Micalizzi, Simon Pincus, Tianna Jane
Stevens (red cast); Juliette Allen Angelo, Caitlin Belcik, Joseph Harrington, Jillian Mueller, Jacob
Pincus (white cast).
Orchestra: Joshua Rosenblum conductor; Sue Anschutz associate conductor, keyboard; Mark
C. Mitchell assistant conductor, keyboard; Louis Bruno bass; Steven Kenyon, Robert DeBellis,
Terrence Cook, John Winder woodwinds; Christian Jaudes, Philip Granger, Wayne J. Du Maine
trumpet; Wayne Goodman, Robert Fournier trombone; David Roth percussion; Gregory Landes
drums.
Understudies: Mr. Page—William Ryall, Jeff Skowron; Mr. Dixon—Darin De Paul, William
Ryall; Messrs. Ross, Galligan-Stierle—Hunter Bell, Kurt Kelly; Mr. Galligan-Stierle—Hunter Bell;
Mr. De Paul—Jeff Skowron; Ms. Kelly—Carly Hughes; Ms. Neuberger—Janet Dickinson; Mses.
London and Ripka—Juliette Allen Angelo, Tianna Jane Stevens.
Swings: Eamon Foley, Amy Griffin, Liesl Jaye, Kurt Kelly, Jess Le Protto, Heather Tepe.
Direction, Jack O'Brien and Matt August; choreography, John DeLuca and Bob Richard; scenery,
John Lee Beatty; costumes, Robert Morgan; lighting, Pat Collins; sound, Acme Sound Partners;

special effects, Gregory Meeh; wigs and hair, Thomas Augustine; orchestrations, Michael Starobin; vocal arrangements and music direction; Mr. Rosenblum; dance music arrangements, David Krane; music coordination, Seymour Red Press; executive producer, James Sanna; producer, Mr. Rosenblum; associate producer, Audrey Geisel; casting, Telsey and Company; stage management, Daniel S. Rosokoff; press, Alison Brod Public Relations, Alison Brod, Jodi Hassan, Jen Roche, Annabelle Abouab.

Time: Christmas. Place: Whoville. Presented without intermission.

Musical based on the popular children's book about the true gifts of Christmas. First presentation of this production, as created and directed by Jack O'Brien, was given at the Old Globe in San Diego (1998). An earlier version was produced in 1994 by the Children's Theatre Company, Minneapolis. First Broadway presentation of Mr. O'Brien's production was given at the Hilton Theatre (11/8/2006–1/7/2007; 107 performances).

MUSICAL NUMBERS

"Who Likes Christmas?" .... Whoville Citizens
"This Time of Year" .... Old Max, Young Max
"I Hate Christmas Eve" .... Grinch, Young Max, Papa Who,
Mama Who, Grandma Who, Grandpa Who,
Cindy-Lou Who, Betty-Lou Who,
Danny Who, Annie Who, Boo Who
"Whatchama Who" .... Grinch, Little Whos
"Welcome, Christmas" .... Whoville Citizens
(music by Albert Hague, lyrics by Dr. Seuss)
"I Hate Christmas Eve" (Reprise) .... The Grinch
"It's the Thought That Counts" .... Mama Who, Papa Who, Grandma Who,
Grandpa Who, Whoville Citizens, Little Whos
"One of a Kind" .... Grinch
"Now's the Time" .... Papa Who, Mama Who,
Grandma Who, Grandpa Who
"You're a Mean One, Mr. Grinch" .... Old Max, Young Max, Grinch
(music by Albert Hague, lyrics by Dr. Seuss)
"Santa for a Day" .... Cindy-Lou Who, Grinch
"You're a Mean One, Mr. Grinch" (Reprise) .... Old Max
(music by Albert Hague, lyrics by Dr. Seuss)
"Who Likes Christmas?" (Reprise) .... Whoville Citizens
"One of a Kind" (Reprise) .... Young Max, Grinch, Cindy-Lou Who
"This Time of Year" (Reprise) .... Old Max
"Welcome, Christmas" (Reprise) .... Whoville Citizens
(music by Albert Hague, lyrics by Dr. Seuss)
"Santa for a Day" (Reprise) .... Cindy-Lou Who, Grinch, Whoville Citizens
"Who Likes Christmas?" (Reprise) .... Grinch, Young Max,
Old Max, Whos Everywhere

Lincoln Center Theater production of **Cymbeline** (40). Revival of the play by William Shakespeare. André Bishop artistic director, Bernard Gersten executive producer, in the Vivian Beaumont Theater. Opened December 2, 2007. (Closed January 6, 2008)

In Britain (During the Roman Empire)
Cymbeline .... John Cullum
Princess Imogen .... Martha Plimpton
Helen .... Gordana Rashovich
Queen .... Phylicia Rashad
Lord Cloten .... Adam Dannheisser
Posthumus Leonatus .... Michael Cerveris
Pisanio .... John Pankow
Cornelius .... Herb Foster
Two Gentlemen .... Richard Topol,
Daniel Breaker

In Italy
Philario .... Daniel Oreskes
Iachimo .... Jonathan Cake
Frenchman .... Anthony Cochrane
Dutchman .... Jeff Woodman
Spaniard .... Noshir Dalal

Romans in Britain
Caius Lucius .... Ezra Knight
Roman Captain .... Anthony Cochrane
Philarmonus .... Michael W. Howell

Lost and found: John Cullum, Michael Cerveris and Martha Plimpton in Cymbeline.
Photo: Paul Kolnik

In Wales (Living as Outcasts)
Belarius .... Paul O'Brien
Guiderius .... David Furr
Arviragus .... Gregory Wooddell
    Apparitions
Ghost of Sicilius Leonatus .... Herb Foster

Ghost of Posthumus's
    mother .... Gordana Rashovich
Ghosts of Brothers .... Noshir Dalal,
                                                            Adam Greer
Jupiter .... Daniel Oreskes

Ensemble: Jeffrey M. Bender, Jordan Dean, LeRoy McClain, Nancy Rodriguez, Michael Rossmy.

Understudies: Mr. Dannheisser—Jeffrey M. Bender; Messrs. Knight, Oreskes—Anthony Cochrane; Mr. Greer—Noshir Dalal; Mr. Furr—Jordan Dean; Mr. Cullum—Herb Foster; Mr. Cerveris—David Furr; Messrs. Wooddell, Topol, Breaker, Dalal—Adam Greer; Mr. Pankow—Ezra Knight; Mr. Cochrane—LeRoy McClain; Mr. O'Brien—Daniel Oreskes; Ms. Rashad—Gordana Rashovich; Mses. Rashovich, Plimpton—Nancy Rodriguez; Messrs. Woodman, Dalal—Michael Rossmy; Mr. Cake—Gregory Wooddell; Messrs. Foster, Topol, Breaker, Howell—Jeff Woodman.

Direction, Mark Lamos; choreography, Seán Curran; scenery, Michael Yeargan; costumes, Jess Goldstein; lighting, Brian MacDevitt; sound, Tony Smolenski IV and Walter Trarbach; music, Mel Marvin; fight direction, Rick Sordelet; casting, Daniel Swee; stage management, Michael McGoff; press, Philip Rinaldi, Barbara Carroll.

Presented in two parts.

Romance that demonstrates humanity's reliance on happenstance (with a bit of help from the great beyond). Earliest known performance was at the Globe Theatre in 1611. The first New York presentation of record was 12/28/1767 by the American Company (David Douglass played Iachimo, Lewis Hallam II played Posthumus) at the John Street Theatre.

The Farnsworth Invention (104). By Aaron Sorkin. Produced by Dodger Properties and Steven Spielberg for Rabbit Ears, LLC, in association with Fred Zollo and Jeffrey Sine, Dancap Productions, Latitude Link, Pelican Group, at the Music Box. Opened December 3, 2007. (Closed March 2, 2008)

David Sarnoff .... Hank Azaria	Justin Tolman .... Jim Ortlieb
Lizette Sarnoff .... Nadia Bowers	Sarnoff's Father .... Michael Pemberton
Pem's Father .... Kyle Fabel	Betty .... Katharine Powell
Atkins .... Maurice Godin	Harlan Honn .... Steve Rosen
Young Philo .... Christian M. Johansen	Philo T. Farnsworth .... Jimmi Simpson
Wilkins .... Aaron Krohn	Russian Officer .... James Sutorius
George Everson .... Bruce McKenzie	Sarnoff's Mother .... Margot White
Young Sarnoff .... Malcolm Morano	Pem Farnsworth .... Alexandra Wilson
Stan Willis .... Spencer Moses	Wachtel .... William Youmans
Leslie Gorrell .... Michael Mulheren	

Understudies: Mr. Azaria—Steve Rosen; Mr. Simpson—Spencer Moses; Messrs. Krohn, Mulheren, Ortlieb, Pemberton, Sutorius—Brian Russell; Messrs: Godin, McKenzie, Rosen—Aaron Krohn; Messrs. Fabel, Youmans—Spencer Moses; Messrs. Johansen, Morano, Moses—Javier Picayo; Mses. Bowers, Powell, White, Wilson—Kate MacCluggage.

Direction, Des McAnuff; scenery, Klara Zieglerova; costumes, David C. Woolard; lighting, Howell Binkley; sound, Walter Trarbach; music, Andrew Lippa; wigs and hair, Mark Adam Rampmeyer; fight direction, Steve Rankin; executive producer, Sally Campbell Morse; associate producer, Lauren Mitchell; casting, Tara Rubin Casting and Sharon Bialy, Sherry Thomas; stage management, Frank Hartenstein; press, Boneau/Bryan-Brown, Adrian Bryan-Brown, Susanne Tighe, Heath Schwartz.

Presented in two parts.

The invention of technology used to create a stable television picture sets powerful corporate interests against a committed visionary. Except for Messrs. Azaria and Simpson, all actors played

My way: Hank Azaria in The Farnsworth Invention. *Photo: Joan Marcus*

multiple roles in the ensemble. Commissioned by the Abbey Theatre, Dublin, the first presentation of record was given at a La Jolla Playhouse workshop (2/20–3/25/2007; 40 performances). A 2007–08 *Best Plays* choice (see essay by Christopher Rawson in this volume).

*August: Osage County (199). By Tracy Letts. Produced by Jeffrey Richards, Jean Doumanian, Steve Traxler, Jerry Frankel, Ostar Productions, Jennifer Manocherian, the Weinstein Company, Debra Black, Daryl Roth, Ronald and Marc Frankel, Barbara Freitag, Rick Steiner, Staton Bell Group, in association with the Steppenwolf Theatre Company (Martha Lavey artistic director, David Hawkanson executive director), at the Imperial Theatre. Opened December 4, 2007. Production hiatus April 21–28, 2008 for transfer to the Music Box. Re-opened April 29, 2008.

Beverly Weston .... Dennis Letts	Mattie Fae Aiken .... Rondi Reed
Violet Weston .... Deanna Dunagan	Charlie Aiken .... Francis Guinan
Barbara Fordham .... Amy Morton	Little Charles .... Ian Barford
Bill Fordham .... Jeff Perry	Johnna Monevata .... Kimberly Guerrero
Jean Fordham .... Madeleine Martin	Steve Heidebrecht .... Brian Kerwin
Ivy Weston .... Sally Murphy	Sheriff Deon Gilbeau .... Troy West
Karen Weston .... Mariann Mayberry	

Understudies: Messrs. Guinan, Letts—Munson Hicks; Mses. Dunagan, Reed—Susanne Marley; Messrs. Kerwin, Perry, West—Jay Patterson; Mses. Morton, Mayberry, Murphy—Dee Pelletier; Ms. Martin—Molly Ranson; Ms. Guerrero—Kristina Valada-Viars; Mr. Barford—Troy West.

Direction, Anna D. Shapiro; scenery, Todd Rosenthal; costumes, Ana Kuzmanic; lighting, Ann G. Wrightson; sound, Richard Woodbury; music, David Singer; fight direction, Chuck Coyl; dramaturg, Edward Sobel; casting, Erica Daniels, Stuart Howard, Amy Schecter, Paul Hardt;

Hell night: David Morse and Ciarán Hinds in
The Seafarer. *Photo: Joan Marcus*

dramaturgy, Edward Sobel; stage management, Deb Styer; press, Jeffrey Richards Associates, Irene Gandy, Judith Hansen, Elon Rutberg.

Time: The present. Place: Large home outside Pawhuska, Oklahoma. Presented in three parts.

An extended family in Oklahoma display their many dysfunctions in a time of crisis. First presentation of record was given in Chicago at Steppenwolf Theatre Company's Downstairs Theatre (6/28–8/26/2007). Letts received the 2008 Pulitzer Prize in Drama for this work. Received five 2008 Tony Awards in the areas of best play (Mr. Letts), direction (Ms. Shapiro), actress (Ms. Dunagan), featured actress (Ms. Reed) and scene design (Mr. Rosenthal). A 2007–08 *Best Plays* choice (see essay by Chris Jones in this volume).

The Seafarer (133). By Conor McPherson. Produced by Ostar Productions, Bob Boyett, Roy Furman, Lawrence Horowitz, Jam Theatricals, Bill Rollnick, Nancy Ellison Rollnick, James D'Orta, Thomas S. Murphy, Ralph Guild, Jon Avnet, Philip Geier, Keough Partners, Eric Falkenstein, Max OnStage, in association with the National Theatre (UK), at the Booth Theatre. Opened December 6, 2007. (Closed March 30, 2008)

Ivan Curry	Conleth Hill	James "Sharky" Harkin	David Morse
Mr. Lockhart	Ciarán Hinds	Richard Harkin	Jim Norton
Nicky Giblin	Sean Mahon		

Understudies: Messrs. Norton, Hinds—Peter Rogan; Messrs. Morse, Hill, Mahon—Declan Mooney.

Direction, Mr. McPherson; scenery and costumes, Rae Smith; lighting, Neil Austin; sound, Mathew Smethurst-Evans; fight direction, Thomas Schall; casting, Laura Stanczyk and Howie Cherpakov; stage management, Barclay Stiff; press, Boneau/Bryan-Brown, Adrian Bryan-Brown, Aaron Meier, Christine Olver.

Time: Christmas. Place: Baldoyle, north of Dublin. Presented in two parts.

A man with a blind, alcoholic brother and drunken friends faces his dark past when a demonic gambler comes to call. First presentation of record was given at the National Theatre's Cottesloe Theatre (9/28/2006–1/30/2007) before a UK tour. A 2007–08 *Best Plays* choice (see essay by Charles McNulty in this volume).

Is He Dead? (105). By Mark Twain; adapted by David Ives. Produced by Bob Boyett, Roger Berlind, Daryl Roth, Jane Bergère, E. Morten, P. Robbins, J. O'Boyle, Ricky Stevens, Sonia Friedman Productions, Ambassador Theatre Group, Tim Levy, in association with Shelley Fisher Fishkin, at the Lyceum Theatre. Opened December 9, 2007. (Closed March 9, 2008)

Agamemnon "Chicago"	Michael McGrath	Bastien André	Byron Jennings
Hans "Dutchy"	Tom Alan Robbins	Madame Bathilde	Patricia Conolly
Papa Leroux	John McMartin	Madame Caron	Marylouise Burke
Marie Leroux	Jenn Gambatese	Phelim O'Shaughnessy	Jeremy Bobb
Cecile Leroux	Bridget Regan	Basil Thorpe; others	David Pittu
Jean-Francois Millet	Norbert Leo Butz		

Understudies: Messrs. Butz, McGrath, Bobb, Pittu—Sheffield Chastain; Messrs. McMartin, Jennings, Robbins—Wilbur Edwin Henry; Mses. Gambatese, Regan—Liv Rooth; Mses. Conolly, Burke—Peggy J. Scott.

Direction, Michael Blakemore; choreography, Pamela Remler; scenery, Peter J. Davison; costumes, Martin Pakledinaz; lighting, Peter Kaczorowski; sound and music, David Van Tieghem; wigs and hair, Paul Huntley; associate producers, Jacki Barlia Florin, Robert G. Bartner; casting, Jay Binder, Jack Bowdan; stage management, Alexander Libby; press, Boneau/Bryan-Brown, Adrian Bryan-Brown, Steven Padla, Heath Schwartz.

Time: 1846. Place: Paris. Presented in two parts.

Farcical satire on the pretentious behavior that underpinned the world of fine art in the 19th century. First presentation of record for the 1898 play discovered by Fishkin during her 2002 research of the Mark Twain papers at the University of California, Berkeley. Fishkin published a version of the text with her foreword and notes in 2006 (University of California Press).

The Homecoming (137). Revival of the play by Harold Pinter. Produced by Jeffrey Richards, Jerry Frankel, Jam Theatricals, Ergo Entertainment, Barbara and Buddy Freitag, Michael Gardner, Herbert Goldsmith Productions, Terry E. Schnuck, Harold Thau, Michael Filerman, Lynne Peyser, Ronald Frankel, David Jaroslawicz; in association with Love Bunny Entertainment, at the Cort Theatre. Opened December 16, 2007. (Closed April 13, 2008)

Max	Ian McShane	Joey	Gareth Saxe
Lenny	Raúl Esparza	Teddy	James Frain
Sam	Michael McKean	Ruth	Eve Best

Understudies: Messrs. McShane, McKean—Jarlath Conroy; Ms. Best—Francesca Faridany; Messrs. Esparza, Frain, Saxe—Creighton James.

Direction, Daniel Sullivan; scenery, Eugene Lee; costumes, Jess Goldstein; lighting, Kenneth Posner; sound, John Gromada; fight direction, Rick Sordelet; casting, Telsey and Company; stage management, Roy Harris; press, Jeffrey Richards Associates, Irene Gandy, Judith Hansen, Elon Rutberg.

Time: Summer. Place: An old house in North London. Presented in two parts.

A family of working-class Englishmen battle for sexual primacy among themselves when the attractive American wife of one arrives for a visit. First presentation of record was given by the Royal Shakespeare Company in London's Aldwych Theatre (6/3/1965) after a provincial tour of the Peter Hall production. The RSC production transferred to Broadway's Music Box with one cast change—Michael Bryant was replaced by Michael Craig (1/5–10/14/1967; 324 performances). It was a 1966–67 *Best Plays* choice. The first Broadway production received four 1967 Tony Awards in the areas of best play (Mr. Pinter), direction (Mr. Hall), actor (Paul Rogers) and featured actor (Ian Holm). The 2007–08 production was the second Broadway revival.

*****The Little Mermaid** (164). Musical with book by Doug Wright; music by Alan Menken; lyrics by Howard Ashman and Glenn Slater; based on the story by Hans Christian Andersen and the Disney film by John Musker, Ron Clements and Mr. Ashman. Produced by Disney Theatrical Productions, under the direction of Thomas Schumacher, at the Lunt-Fontanne Theatre. Opened January 10, 2008.

Pilot	Merwin Foard	Scuttle	Eddie Korbich
Prince Eric	Sean Palmer	Ursula	Sherie Rene Scott
Grimsby	Jonathan Freeman	Flotsam	Tyler Maynard
King Triton	Norm Lewis	Jetsam	Derrick Baskin
Sebastian	Tituss Burgess	Carlotta	Heidi Blickenstaff
Ariel	Sierra Boggess	Chef Louis	John Treacy Egan
Flounder	Trevor Braun (alt.); Brian D'Addario (alt.)		

Gulls: Robert Creighton, Tim Federle, Arbender J. Robinson.

Mersisters: Cathryn Basile, Cicily Daniels, Michelle Lookadoo, Zakiya Young Mizen, Chelsea Morgan Stock, Kay Trinidad.

Ensemble: Adrian Bailey, Cathryn Basile, Heidi Blickenstaff, Robert Creighton, Cicily Daniels, Tim Federle, Merwin Foard, Ben Hartley, Michelle Lookadoo, Alan Mingo Jr., Zakiya Young Mizen, Arbender J. Robinson, Bahiyah Sayyed Gaines, Bret Shuford, Chelsea Morgan Stock, Kay Trinidad, Daniel J. Watts.

Orchestra: Michael Kosarin conductor; Greg Anthony associate conductor, keyboard 2; Suzanne Ornstein concertmaster; Mineko Yajima violin; Roger Shell cello 1; Deborah Assael-Migliore cello 2; Richard Sarpola bass; Steven Kenyon reed 1; David Young reed 2; Marc Phanuef reed 3; Nicholas Marchione lead trumpet; Frank Greene trumpet; Gary Grimaldi trombone; Jeff Caswell bass trombone, tuba; Zohar Schondorf, French horn; Aron Accurso keyboard 1; Andrew Grobengieser keyboard 3; Joe Passaro percussion; John Redsecker drums.

Understudies: Ms. Boggess—Betsy Morgan, Chelsea Morgan Stock; Ms. Scott—Heidi Blickenstaff, Cicily Daniels; Mr. Palmer—Arbender J. Robinson, Bret Shuford; Mr. Lewis—Adrian Bailey, Merwin Foard; Mr. Burgess—Derrick Baskin, Alan Mingo Jr.; Mr. Korbich—Robert Creighton,

Tim Federle; Mr. Freeman—Merwin Foard, Price Waldman; Mr. Maynard—Bret Shuford, Jason Snow, Price Waldman; Mr. Baskin—Tim Federle, Price Waldman; Mr. Egan—Robert Creighton, Merwin Foard.

Swings: James Brown III, Meredith Inglesby, Joanne Manning, Betsy Morgan, Jason Snow, Price Waldman.

Direction, Francesca Zambello; choreography, Stephen Mear; scenery, George Tsypin; costumes, Tatiana Noginova; lighting, Natasha Katz; sound, John H. Shivers; projections and video, Sven Ortel; wigs and hair, David Brian Brown; fight direction, Rick Sordelet; orchestrations, Danny Troob; vocal orchestrations and music direction, Mr. Kosarin; dance arrangements, David Chase; music coordination, Michael Keller; associate producer, Todd Lacy; casting, Tara Rubin Casting; stage management, Clifford Schwartz; press, Boneau/Bryan-Brown; Chris Boneau, Matt Polk, Juliana Hannett, Danielle Crinnion.

Interspecies love blooms by, on and in the sea. Based on the 1989 Disney film, the first presentation of record was given in the Ellie Caulkins Opera House at the Denver Center for the Performing Arts (8/23–9/9/2007).

ACT I

Overture .... Orchestra
"Fathoms Below" .... Pilot, Sailors,
Prince Eric, Grimsby
(lyrics by Howard Ashman and Glenn Slater)
"Daughters of Triton" .... Mersisters
(lyrics by Howard Ashman)
"The World Above" .... Ariel
(lyrics by Glenn Slater)
"Human Stuff" .... Scuttle, Gulls
(lyrics by Glenn Slater)
"I Want the Good Times Back" .... Ursula, Flotsam, Jetsam, Eels
(lyrics by Glenn Slater)
"Part of Your World" .... Ariel
(lyrics by Howard Ashman)
"Storm at Sea" .... Orchestra
"Part of Your World" (Reprise) .... Ariel
(lyrics by Howard Ashman)
"She's in Love" .... Mersisters, Flounder
(lyrics by Glenn Slater)
"Her Voice" .... Prince Eric
(lyrics by Glenn Slater)
"The World Above" (Reprise) .... King Triton
(lyrics by Glenn Slater)
"Under the Sea" .... Sebastian, Sea Creatures
(lyrics by Howard Ashman)
"Sweet Child" .... Flotsam, Jetsam
(lyrics by Glenn Slater)
"Poor Unfortunate Souls" .... Ursula
(lyrics by Howard Ashman)

ACT II

Entr'acte .... Orchestra
"Positoovity" .... Scuttle, Gulls
(lyrics by Glenn Slater)
"Beyond My Wildest Dreams" .... Ariel, Carlotta, Maids
(lyrics by Glenn Slater)
"Les Poissons" .... Chef Louis
(lyrics by Howard Ashman)
"Les Poissons" (Reprise) .... Chef Louis, Chefs
(lyrics by Howard Ashman)

"One Step Closer" .... Prince Eric
(lyrics by Glenn Slater)
"I Want the Good Times Back" (Reprise) .... Ursula, Flotsam, Jetsam
(lyrics by Glenn Slater)
"Kiss the Girl" .... Sebastian, Animals
(lyrics by Howard Ashman)
"Sweet Child" (Reprise) .... Flotsam, Jetsam
(lyrics by Glenn Slater)
"If Only" .... Ariel, Prince Eric,
Sebastian, King Triton
(lyrics by Glenn Slater)
"The Contest" .... Grimsby, Princesses
(lyrics by Glenn Slater)
"Poor Unfortunate Souls" (Reprise) .... Ursula
(lyrics by Howard Ashman)
"If Only" (Reprise) .... King Triton, Ariel
(lyrics by Glenn Slater)
Finale .... Prince Eric, Ariel, Company
(lyrics by Howard Ashman and Glenn Slater)

*__Roundabout Theatre Company__ presentation of __The 39 Steps__ (115). By Patrick
Barlow; adapted from the book by John Buchan; based on a concept by Simon Corble
and Nobby Dimon; inspired by the Alfred Hitchcock film. Todd Haimes artistic director,
Harold Wolpert managing director, Julia C. Levy executive director, in association with
Bob Boyett, Harriet Newman Leve, Ron Nicynski, Stewart F. Lane, Bonnie Comley,
Manocherian Golden Productions, Olympus Theatricals, Douglas Denoff, Marek J. Cantor,

Hot pursuit: Cliff Saunders and Charles Edwards in The 39 Steps. *Photo: Joan Marcus*

Pat Flicker Addiss, Huntington Theatre Company (Nicholas Martin artistic director, Michael Maso managing director) and Edward Snape for Fiery Angel Ltd., at the American Airlines Theatre. Opened January 15, 2008. Production hiatus March 30–April 28, 2008 for transfer to Cort Theatre. Re-opened May 8, 2008, after 11 previews in the new venue.

Man #1 .... Cliff Saunders   Richard Hannay .... Charles Edwards
Man #2 .... Arnie Burton   Annabella Schmidt; others .... Jennifer Ferrin

Understudies: Ms. Ferrin—Claire Brownell; Messrs. Saunders, Burton—Cameron Folmar; Mr. Edwards—Mark Shanahan.

Direction, Maria Aitken; choreography, Toby Sedgwick and Christopher Bayes; scenery and costumes, Peter McKintosh; lighting, Kevin Adams; sound, Mic Pool; associate producer, Sydney Beers; casting, Jay Binder, Jack Bowdan; stage management, Nevin Hedley; press, Boneau/Bryan-Brown, Adrian Bryan-Brown, Matt Polk, Jessica Johnson, Amy Kass.

Time: 1935. Place: A London flat. Presented in two parts.

Employing sound effects and quick changes—which are part of the performance—four actors on a nearly bare stage portray the characters and situations occurring in Alfred Hitchcock's film of the same title. First presentation of record was Messrs. Corble and Dimon's version given by the North Country Theatre Company (UK) at the Georgian Theatre Royal (5/3/1996) in Richmond, North Yorkshire, before several provincial tours in the UK. After negotiations with various rightsholders to Mr. Hitchcock's film and Mr. Buchan's novel, Mr. Barlow revised the text before another UK tour, which led to a run at London's Tricycle Theatre (8/14–9/9/2006) and a transfer to the Criterion Theatre in the West End (9/15/2006). First US presentation of record was given by the Huntington Theatre Company, Boston (9/19–10/14/2007). The 2007–08 Broadway production received Tony Awards for best lighting of a play (Mr. Adams) and sound design of a play (Mr. Pool).

*November (156). By David Mamet. Produced by Jeffrey Richards, Jerry Frankel, Jam Theatricals, Bat-Barry Productions, Michael Cohl, Ergo Entertainment, Michael Filerman, Ronald Frankel, Barbara and Buddy Freitag, James Fuld Jr., Roy Furman, JK Productions, Harold Thau, Jamie deRoy, Ted Snowdon, Wendy Federman at the Ethel Barrymore Theatre. Opened January 17, 2008.

Charles Smith .... Nathan Lane   Clarice Bernstein .... Laurie Metcalf
Archer Brown .... Dylan Baker   Dwight Grackle .... Michael Nichols
Representative of NATBPM* ..... Ethan Phillips

Standbys: Mr. Lane—Richard Kline; Ms. Metcalf—Amy Hohn; Messrs. Baker, Phillips—Greg Stuhr; Mr. Nichols—Victor Talmadge.

Direction, Joe Mantello; scenery, Scott Pask; costumes, Laura Bauer; lighting, Paul Gallo; casting, Telsey and Company; stage management, Jill Cordle; press, Jeffrey Richards Associates, Irene Gandy, Elon Rutberg.

Time: Morning; Night; Morning. Place: An office. Presented in two parts.

A US President is willing to do almost anything for money and/or votes. (*National Association of Turkey By-Products Manufacturers)

Manhattan Theatre Club production of **Come Back, Little Sheba** (58). Revival of the play by William Inge. Lynne Meadow artistic director, Daniel Sullivan acting artistic director, Barry Grove executive producer, at the Biltmore Theatre. Opened January 24, 2008. (Closed March 16, 2008)

Doc .... Kevin Anderson   Milkman .... Matthew J. Williamson
Marie .... Zoe Kazan   Messenger .... Daniel Damon Joyce
Lola .... S. Epatha Merkerson   Bruce .... Chad Hoeppner
Turk .... Brian Smith   Ed .... Keith Randolph Smith
Postman .... Lyle Kanouse   Elmo .... Joseph Adams
Mrs. Coffman .... Brenda Wehle

Understudies: Mr. Anderson—Joseph Adams; Messrs. Adams, Smith, Kanouse—Phillip Clark; Ms. Merkerson—Caroline Stefanie Clay; Mr. Joyce—Chad Hoeppner; Messrs. Smith, Williamson, Hoeppner—Daniel Damon Joyce; Ms. Wehle—Darrie Lawrence.

Direction, Michael Pressman; scenery, James Noone; costumes, Jennifer von Mayrhauser; lighting, Jane Cox; sound, Obadiah Eaves; music, Peter Golub; fight direction, J. David Brimmer; casting, David Caparelliotis, Nancy Piccione; stage management, James FitzSimmons; press, Boneau/Bryan-Brown; Chris Boneau, Aaron Meier, Heath Schwartz, Christine Olver.

Time: Spring 1950. Place: A home in a Midwestern city. Presented in two parts.

Lives filled with longing for lost youth and missed opportunity lead to unquiet desperation. First presentation of record was given by the Theatre Guild at Westport Country Playhouse in Connecticut (9/12–17/1949; 7 performances) before a pre-Broadway tour to the Playhouse in Wilmington, Delaware (1/26–28/1950) and the Colonial Theatre in Boston (1/30–2/11/1950). A 1949–50 *Best Plays* choice, the original Broadway production opened at the Booth Theatre (2/15–7/29/1950; 191 performances). The first Broadway production received 1950 Tony Awards for best actor in a play (Sidney Blackmer) and best actress in a play (Shirley Booth). First presentation of record of the 2007–08 "new perspective" on the play—in which an African American plays the role of Lola—was given at the Center Theatre Group's Kirk Douglas Theatre (6/17–7/15/2007). This season's production was the first Broadway revival of the play.

*Roundabout Theatre Company** presentation of the **Menier Chocolate Factory** production of **Sunday in the Park With George** (116). Revival of the musical with book by James Lapine; music and lyrics by Stephen Sondheim. Todd Haimes artistic director, Harold Wolpert managing director, Julia C. Levy executive director, in association with Bob Boyett, Debra Black, Jam Theatricals, Stephanie P. McClelland, Stewart F. Lane, Bonnie Comley, Barbara Manocherian, Jennifer Manocherian, Ostar Productions, Menier Chocolate Factory (David Babani artistic director), at Studio 54. Opened February 21, 2008.

ACT I

George	Daniel Evans	Celeste #2	Jessica Grové
Dot	Jenna Russell	Louis	Drew McVety
Old Lady	Mary Beth Peil	Louise	Kelsey Fowler (alt.);
Nurse	Anne L. Nathan		Alison Horowitz (alt.)
Franz	David Turner	Frieda	Stacie Morgain Lewis
Jules	Michael Cumpsty	Soldier	Santino Fontana
Yvonne	Jessica Molaskey	Mr.	Ed Dixon
Boatman	Alexander Gemignani	Mrs.	Anne L. Nathan
Celeste #1	Brynn O'Malley		

Bathers: Santino Fontana (alt.), Drew McVety (alt.), Kelsey Fowler (alt.), Alison Horowitz (alt.).

ACT II

George	Daniel Evans	Photographer	Jessica Grové
Marie	Jenna Russell	Charles Redmond	Ed Dixon
Dennis	Alexander Gemignani	Alex	Santino Fontana
Bob Greenberg	Michael Cumpsty	Betty	Stacie Morgain Lewis
Naomi Eisen	Jessica Molaskey	Lee Randolph	David Turner
Harriet Pawling	Anne L. Nathan	Blair Daniels	Mary Beth Peil
Billy Webster	Drew McVety	Elaine	Brynn O'Malley

Orchestra: Caroline Humphris conductor, piano; Thomas Murray associate conductor, keyboard; Matthew Lehmann violin; Mairi Dorman-Phaneuf cello; Todd Groves woodwinds.

Standby: Messrs. Dixon, Gemignani, Cumpsty—Andrew Varela.

Understudies: Mses. Molaskey, Nathan, Piel—Colleen Fitzpatrick; Mr. Evans—Santino Fontana; Messrs. Fontana, McVety, Turner—Jeff Kready; Ms. Russell—Brynn O'Malley; Mses. O'Malley, Grové, Lewis—Hayley Podschun.

Direction, Sam Buntrock; choreography, Christopher Gattelli; scenery and costumes, David Farley; lighting, Ken Billington; sound, Sebastian Frost; projections, Timothy Bird and the Knifedge Creative Network; wigs and hair, Tom Watson; orchestrations, Jason Carr and Michael Starobin; music direction and supervision, Ms. Humphris; music coordination, John Miller; casting, Jim Carnahan; stage management, Peter Hanson; press, Boneau/Bryan-Brown, Adrian Bryan-Brown, Matt Polk, Jessica Johnson, Amy Kass.

Time: Sundays, 1884–86; 1984. Place: A Paris park; an American art museum. Presented in two parts.

An artist focuses intensely and faithfully on his work to the exclusion of all else. First presentation of record was given in a workshop at Playwrights Horizons (7/6–30/1983; 25 performances) before a Broadway production played at the Booth Theatre (05/2/1984–10/13/1985; 604 performances). A 1984–85 *Best Plays* choice, the musical received 1984 Tony Awards for scenic design (Tony Straiges) and lighting design (Richard Nelson). In 1985, it received the Pulitzer Prize in Drama. First presentation of record of the Sam Buntrock production was given at London's Menier Chocolate Factory (11/29/2005–3/12/2006) before a transfer to Wyndham's Theatre in the West End (5/23–9/2/2006). The 2007–08 production was the first fully staged Broadway revival. There was, however, a 10th Anniversary Concert version, with many of the original Broadway cast members, which played one performance at the St. James Theatre (5/15/1994).

ACT I

"Sunday in the Park With George" .... Dot
"No Life" .... Jules, Yvonne
"Color and Light" .... Dot, George
"Gossip" .... Celeste #1, Celeste #2, Boatman, Nurse, Old Lady, Jules, Yvonne
"The Day Off" .... George, Nurse, Franz, Frieda, Boatman, Soldier, Celeste #1, Celeste #2, Yvonne, Louise, Jules, Louis
"Everybody Loves Louis" .... Dot
"Finishing the Hat" .... George
"We Do Not Belong Together" .... Dot, George
"Beautiful" .... Old Lady, George
"Sunday" .... Company

ACT II

"It's Hot Up Here" .... Company
"Chromolume #7" .... Company
"Putting It Together" .... George, Company
"Children and Art" .... Marie
"Lesson #8" .... George
"Move On" .... George, Dot
"Sunday" .... Company

Passing Strange (108). Transfer from Off Broadway of the musical with book and lyrics by Stew; music by Stew and Heidi Rodewald. Produced by the Shubert Organization, Elizabeth Ireland McCann LLC, Bill Kenwright, Chase Mishkin, Terry Allen Kramer, Barbara and Buddy Freitag, Broadway Across America, Emily Fisher Landau, Peter May, Boyett Ostar, Elie Hirschfeld, Jed Bernstein, Wendy Federman, Jacki Barlia Florin, Spring Sirkin, Ruth Hendel, Vasi Laurence, Pat Flicker Addiss, Janet Pailet, Steve Klein, in association with the Public Theater (Oskar Eustis artistic director, Mara Manus executive director) and Berkeley Repertory Theatre (Tony Taccone artistic director, Susan Medak managing director), at the Belasco Theatre. Opened February 28, 2008.

Narrator .... Stew
Bass; Vocals .... Heidi Rodewald
Keyboard; Guitar;
    Backing Vocals .... Jon Spurney
Drums .... Christian Cassan
Guitar; Keyboard;
    Backing Vocals .... Christian Gibbs

Los Angeles

Mother	Eisa Davis	Sherry	Rebecca Naomi Jones
Youth	Daniel Breaker	Franklin	Colman Domingo
Terry	Chad Goodridge	Edwina	de'Adre Aziza

Amsterdam

Renata	Rebecca Naomi Jones	Joop	Colman Domingo
Christophe	Chad Goodridge	Marianna	de'Adre Aziza

Berlin

Hugo	Chad Goodridge	Desi	Rebecca Naomi Jones
Sudabey	de'Adre Aziza	Mr. Venus	Colman Domingo

Understudies: Mr. Domingo—Billy Eugene Jones; Mses. Aziza, Jones—Kelly McCreary; Ms. Davis—Karen Pittman; Stew—David Ryan Smith; Messrs. Breaker, Goodridge—Lawrence Stallings.

Direction, Annie Dorsen; choreography, Karole Armitage; scenery, David Korins; costumes, Elizabeth Hope Clancy; lighting, Kevin Adams; sound, Tom Morse; orchestrations and music supervision, Stew and Ms. Rodewald; music coordination, Seymour Red Press; executive producer, Joey Parnes; associate producer, S.D. Wagner; casting, Jordan Thaler and Heidi Griffiths; stage management, Tripp Phillips; press, Sam Rudy Media Relations, Sam Rudy, Dale R. Heller, Robert Lasko, Charlie Siedenburg.

Presented in two parts.

An African-American musician from Los Angeles accumulates a wide range of experience as he matures in Europe. First presentation of record was given at Berkeley Repertory Theatre (10/19–12/3/2006) after development, with collaborator Ms. Dorsen, at the Sundance Theatre Lab (7/2005). A 2006–07 *Best Plays* choice, its first New York presentation of record was given Off Broadway at the Public Theater (5/14–7/1/2007; 56 performances).

Strange *trip: Stew and Rebecca Naomi Jones in* Passing Strange. *Photo: Michal Daniel*

ACT I

Prologue ("We Might Play All Night") .... Narrator, Heidi, Band
"Baptist Fashion Show" .... Narrator, Company
"Blues Revelation"; "Freight Train" .... Narrator, Company
"Arlington Hill" .... Narrator
"Sole Brother" .... Youth, Terry, Sherry
"Must've Been High" .... Narrator
"Mom Song" .... Narrator, Mother, Company
"Merci Beaucoup, M. Godard" .... Narrator, Stewardesses
"Amsterdam" .... Company
"Keys" .... Marianna, Youth, Narrator
"We Just Had Sex" .... Youth, Marianna, Renata
"Stoned" .... Youth, Narrator

ACT II

"May Day" .... Narrator, Company
"Surface" .... Mr. Venus
"Damage" .... Narrator, Desi, Youth
"Identity" .... Youth
"The Black One" .... Narrator, Company
"Come Down Now" .... Heidi, Desi
"Work the Wound" .... Youth, Narrator
"Passing Phase" .... Youth, Narrator
"Love Like That" .... Narrator, Heidi

*Cat on a Hot Tin Roof (100). Revival of the play by Tennessee Williams. Produced by Front Row Productions and Stephen C. Byrd with Alia N. Jones, in association with Clarence J. Chandran, Norm Nixon, Michael Fuchs, Anthony Lacavera, Edward J. Jones, Sheanna Pang, Jovan Vitagliano, Al Wilson, at the Broadhurst Theatre. Opened March 6, 2008.

Maggie	Anika Noni Rose	Sookey	Marja Harmon
Brick	Terrence Howard	Dixie	Alessandra Chisolm
Reverend Tooker	Lou Myers	Trixie	Marissa Chisolm
Doctor Baugh	Count Stovall	Lacey	Clark Jackson
Mae	Lisa Arrindell Anderson	Big Daddy	James Earl Jones
Sonny	Skye Jasmine Allen-McBean	Household Staff	Bethany Butler,
Big Mama	Phylicia Rashad		Robert Christopher Riley
Gooper	Giancarlo Esposito		

Understudies: Mr. Jones—Count Stovall; Messrs. Howard, Myers, Jackson—Robert Christopher Riley; Mses. Rose, Anderson—Marja Harmon, Bethany Butler; Messrs. Esposito, Stovall; Myers—Clark Jackson; Ms. Rashad—Lynda Gravátt.

Direction, Debbie Allen; scenery, Ray Klausen; costumes, Jane Greenwood; lighting, William H. Grant III; sound, John H. Shivers; music, Andrew "Tex" Allen; wigs and hair, Charles G. LaPointe; associate producers, Beatrice L. Rangel, Terrie Williams; casting, Peter Wise and Associates; stage management, Gwendolyn M. Gilliam; press, Springer Associates, Gary Springer, Joe Trentacosta, Shane Marshall Brown, D'Arcy Drollinger, Jennifer Blum, Ethnee Lea.

Time: A summer evening. Place: A plantation in Mississippi. Presented in three parts.

A family struggles over its legacy—and the meaning of "truth"—when the patriarch is ill with cancer. Plans for this all-African-American version were announced in a 1994 *Variety* interview with Mr. Byrd, who originally planned a January 1995 opening. A 1954–55 *Best Plays* choice, the original Broadway production opened at the Morosco Theatre (3/24/1955–11/17/1956; 694 performances). First titled *Cat on a Tin Roof*—the tin got warmer before rehearsals began in New York—the play was based on a Williams short story, "Three Players of a Summer Game" published in *The New Yorker* (1952). According to critic Henry Hewes, it was he who suggested the playwright adapt his story. The play received the 1955 Pulitzer Prize in Drama. The 2007–08 production was the fourth Broadway revival.

Home and heart: Andréa Burns, Robin De Jesús, Christopher Jackson, Lin-Manuel Miranda, Karen Olivo and Janet Dacal. Photo: Joan Marcus

*In the Heights (94). Transfer from Off Broadway of the musical with book by Quiara Alegría Hudes; music and lyrics by Lin-Manuel Miranda. Produced by Kevin McCollum, Jeffrey Seller, Jill Furman, Sander Jacobs, Goodman/Grossman, Peter Fine, Everett/Skipper at the Richard Rodgers Theatre. Opened March 9, 2008.

Graffiti Pete	Seth Stewart	Camila	Priscilla Lopez
Usnavi	Lin-Manuel Miranda	Sonny	Robin De Jesús
Piragua Guy	Eliseo Román	Benny	Christopher Jackson
Abuela Claudia	Olga Merediz	Vanessa	Karen Olivo
Carla	Janet Dacal	Nina	Mandy Gonzalez
Daniela	Andréa Burns	Bolero Singer	Doreen Montalvo
Kevin	Carlos Gomez		

Ensemble: Tony Chiroldes, Rosie Lani Fiedelman, Joshua Henry, Afra Hines, Nina Lafarga, Doreen Montalvo, Javier Muñoz, Krysta Rodriguez, Eliseo Román, Luis Salgado, Shaun Taylor-Corbett, Rickey Tripp.

Orchestra: Alex Lacamoire conductor, keyboard 1, Zachary Dietz associate conductor, keyboard 2; Irio O'Farrill Jr. bass; Manny Moreira guitar; Dave Richards, Kristy Norter reeds; Raul Agraz, Trevor Neumann trumpet; Joe Fiedler, Ryan Keberle trombone; Doug Hinrichs, Wilson Torres percussion; Andres Forero drums.

Understudies: Messrs. Stewart, Miranda—Michael Balderrama; Mses. Merediz, Lopez, Burns—Blanca Camacho, Doreen Montalvo; Mr. Gomez—Tony Chiroldes; Mses. Gonzalez, Olivo—Janet Dacal, Mr. Jackson—Rogelio Douglas Jr., Joshua Henry; Ms. Dacal—Stephanie Klemons; Ms. Gonzalez—Nina Lafarga; Messrs. De Jesus, Miranda—Javier Muñoz; Mses. Dacal, Gonzalez, Olivo—Krysta Rodriguez; Mr. Gomez—Eliseo Román; Messrs. De Jesus, Miranda—Shaun Taylor-Corbett; Mr. Stewart—Rickey Tripp.

Swings: Michael Balderrama, Blanca Camacho, Rogelio Douglas Jr., Stephanie Klemons.

Direction, Thomas Kail; choreography, Andy Blankenbuehler; scenery, Anna Louizos; costumes, Paul Tazewell; lighting, Howell Binkley; sound, Acme Sound Partners; orchestrations and music arrangements, Alex Lacamoire and Bill Sherman; music direction, Mr. Lacamoire; music coordination, Michael Keller; associate producers, Ruth Hendel, Harold Newman; casting, Telsey and Company; stage management, J. Philip Bassett; press, Barlow-Hartman, Michael Hartman, John Barlow, Wayne Wolfe, Melissa Bixler.

Time: Fourth of July weekend. Place: Washington Heights in New York City. Presented in two parts.

A New York bodega owner celebrates his Latino roots as he and his neighbors pursue their American dreams. First presentation of record was in a reading at the Eugene O'Neill Theater Center in Connecticut (7/23–31/2005) before an Off Broadway run at 37 Arts (2/8–7/15/2007; 181 performances). Received 2008 Tony Awards for best musical, score (Mr. Miranda), choreography (Mr. Blankenbuehler), orchestrations (Messrs. Lacamoire and Sherman).

ACT I

"In the Heights"	Usnavi, Company
"Breathe"	Nina, Company
"Benny's Dispatch"	Benny, Nina
"It Won't Be Long Now"	Vanessa, Usnavi, Sonny
"Inutil"	Kevin
"No Me Diga"	Daniela, Carla, Vanessa, Nina
"96,000"	Usnavi, Benny, Sonny, Vanessa, Daniela, Carla, Company
"Paciencia y Fe" ("Patience and Faith")	Abuela Claudia, Company
"When You're Home"	Nina, Benny, Company
"Piragua"	Piragua Guy
"Siempre" ("Always")	Camila
"The Club; Fireworks"	Company

ACT II

"Sunrise"	Nina, Benny, Company
"Hundreds of Stories"	Abuela Claudia, Usnavi
"Enough"	Camila
"Carnival del Barrio"	Daniela, Company
"Atencion"	Kevin
"Alabanza"	Usnavi, Nina, Company
"Everything I Know"	Nina
"No Me Diga" (Reprise)	Daniela, Carla, Vanessa
"Piragua" (Reprise)	Piragua Guy
"Champagne"	Vanessa, Usnavi
"When the Sun Goes Down"	Nina, Benny
Finale	Usnavi, Company

*Gypsy (75). Revival of the musical with book by Arthur Laurents; music by Jule Styne; lyrics by Stephen Sondheim; based on the memoirs of Gypsy Rose Lee. Produced by Roger Berlind, the Routh-Frankel-Baruch-Viertel Group, Roy Furman, Debra Black, Ted Hartley, Roger Horchow, David Ian, Scott Rudin, Jack Viertel at the St. James Theatre. Opened March 27, 2008.

Uncle Jocko; Pastey	Jim Bracchitta	Driver; Yonkers	Pearce Wegener
Georgie; others	Bill Bateman	Boy Scout	Andy Richardson
Vladimir; Rich Boy	Kyrian Friedenberg	Weber; Phil	Brian Reddy
Balloon Girl	Katie Micha	Herbie	Boyd Gaines
Baby June	Sami Gayle	Dainty June	Leigh Ann Larkin
Baby Louise	Emma Rowley	Louise	Laura Benanti
Charlie;		L.A.	Steve Konopelski
Tap Dancer	Matthew Lobenhofer	Tulsa	Tony Yazbeck
Hopalong	Rider Quentin Stanton	Kansas	John Scacchetti
Rose	Patti LuPone	Little Rock	Geo Seery
Pop; Cigar	Bill Raymond	East St. Louis	Matty Price

Waitress; Renée .... Jessica Rush
Miss Cratchitt;
  Mazeppa .... Lenora Nemetz
Agnes .... Nicole Mangi
Marjorie May .... Alicia Sable
Geraldine .... Mindy Dougherty

Edna Mae .... Nancy Renée Braun
Carol Ann .... Sarah Marie Hicks
Betsy Ann .... Beckley Andrews
Tessie Tura .... Alison Fraser
Electra .... Marilyn Caskey

Orchestra: Patrick Vaccariello conductor; Marilyn Reynolds, Fritz Krakowski, Eric DeGioia, Dana Ianculovici violin; Crystal Garner, Sally Shumway viola; Peter Prosser, Vivian Israel cello; Brian Cassier bass; Edward Salkin, Adam Kolker, Dennis Anderson, Ralph Olsen, John Winder woodwinds; Tony Kadleck, James Delagarza, Kamau Adilifu trumpet; Bruce Eidem, Wayne Goodman, Robert Fournier trombone; Nancy Billman, French horn; Jeffrey Harris keyboard; Thad Wheeler percussion; Paul Pizzuti drums; Susan Jolles harp.

Standbys: Ms. LuPone—Lenora Nemetz; Mr. Gaines—Jim Bracchitta; Ms. Benanti—Jessica Rush; Ms. Larkin—Mindy Dougherty; Mr. Yazbek—Pearce Wegener; Mses. Fraser, Nemetz, Caskey—Dorothy Stanley; Ms. Nemetz—Jessica Rush, Dorothy Stanley; Mr. Bateman (Georgie)—Matt Gibson; Mr. Bateman (Bougeron-Cochon)—John Scacchetti; Mr. Bracchitta (Uncle Jocko)—Andrew Boyer; Mr. Bracchitta (Pastey)—Pearce Wegener, Matt Gibson; Mses. Gayle, Rowley—Katie Micha; Mr. Raymond (Cigar)—Bill Bateman, Andrew Boyer; Messrs. Raymond (Pop), Reddy—Andrew Boyer; Mses. Micha, Mangi—Alicia Sable; Messrs. Wegener, Konopelski, Scacchetti—Matty Price, Matt Gibson; Ms. Rush—Lisa Rohinsky.

Swings: Matt Gibson, Lisa Rohinsky.

Direction, Mr. Laurents; choreography, Jerome Robbins and Bonnie Walker; scenery, James Youmans; costumes, Martin Pakledinaz; lighting, Howell Binkley; sound, Dan Moses Schreier;

Together, wherever: Boyd Gaines and Patti LuPone in Gypsy. *Photo: Paul Kolnik*

wigs and hair, Paul Huntley; orchestrations, Sid Ramin and Robert Ginzler; dance arrangements, John Kander; music direction, Mr. Vaccariello; music coordination, Seymour Red Press; casting, Jay Binder; stage management, Craig Jacobs; press, Barlow-Hartman, John Barlow, Michael Hartman, Ryan Ratelle, Melissa Bixler.

Time: Age of vaudeville. Place: Various theatrical locations. Presented in two parts.

The ultimate stage mother pushes her daughters into the limelight she would like to have for herself. First presentation of record was given in a pre-Broadway run at the Shubert Theatre in Philadelphia (4/13–5/16/1959). The original Broadway production opened at the Broadway Theatre (5/21/1959–7/9/1960) before taking a five-week hiatus and transferring to the Imperial Theatre (8/15/1960–3/25/1961; 702 total performances). The 2007–08 production was a transfer from New York City Center Encores! concert series. It was the fourth Broadway revival and received 2008 Tony Awards for best actress (Ms. LuPone), featured actor (Mr. Gaines) and featured actress (Ms. Benanti) in a musical—the biggest sweep of any *Gypsy* production on Broadway. For past productions of *Gypsy*, Tony Awards were given to Angela Lansbury (1975) and Tyne Daly (1990) for their portrayals as Rose. The 1989–90 season also saw the show receive the 1990 Tony Award for best revival (Fran and Barry Weissler, Kathy Levin, Barry Brown). Ethel Merman and Bernadette Peters are the two Broadway Roses not to be honored with Tony Awards.

ACT I

Overture .... Orchestra
Scene 1: Vaudeville theater stage, Seattle
   "May We Entertain You" .... Baby June, Baby Louise
Scene 2: Kitchen, Seattle
   "Some People" .... Rose
Scene 3: Road between Seattle and Los Angeles
   "Some People" (Reprise) .... Rose
Scene 4: Backstage of vaudeville theater, Los Angeles
   "Small World" .... Rose, Herbie
Scene 5: Stage of vaudeville theater, Los Angeles
   "Baby June and Her Newsboys" .... Baby June, Baby Louise, Newsboys
Scene 6: Hotel room, Akron
   "Have an Eggroll, Mr. Goldstone" .... Rose, Herbie, June, Mr. Goldstone, Boys
   "Little Lamb" .... Louise
Scene 7: Chinese restaurant, New York
   "You'll Never Get Away From Me" .... Rose, Herbie
Scene 8: Stage of Grantziger's Palace Theatre, New York
   "Dainty June and Her Farmboys" .... Dainty June, Farmboys
Scene 9: Mr. Grantziger's Office
   "If Momma Was Married" .... Louise, June
Scene 10: Theatre alley, Buffalo
   "All I Need Is the Girl" .... Tulsa, Louise
Scene 11: Railway station, Omaha
   "Everything's Coming Up Roses" .... Rose

ACT II

Entr'acte .... Orchestra
Scene 1: The desert, Texas
   "Madame Rose's Toreadorables" .... Louise, Hollywood Blondes
   "Together Wherever We Go" .... Rose, Herbie, Louise
Scene 2: Backstage of a burlesque house, Wichita
   "You Gotta Get a Gimmick" .... Mazeppa, Electra, Tessie Tura
Scene 3: Backstage corridor, Wichita
Scene 4: Backstage and onstage: Wichita, Detroit, Philadelphia and Minsky's Burlesque
   "The Strip" .... Louise
Scene 5: Louise's dressing room, Minsky's Burlesque ....
Scene 6: Stage
   "Rose's Turn" .... Rose

*Lincoln Center Theater production of **South Pacific** (68). Revival of the musical with book by Oscar Hammerstein II and Joshua Logan; music by Richard Rodgers; lyrics by Mr. Hammerstein; adapted from *Tales of the South Pacific* by James A. Michener. André Bishop artistic director, Bernard Gersten executive producer, in association with Bob Boyett, in the Vivian Beaumont Theater. Opened April 3, 2008.

Ens. Nellie Forbush	Kelli O'Hara	Morton Wise	Genson Blimline
Emile de Becque	Paulo Szot	Richard West	Nick Mayo
Ngana	Laurissa Romain	Johnny Noonan	Jeremy Davis
Jerome	Luka Kain	Billy Whitmore	Robert Lenzi
Henry	Helmar Augustus Cooper	Tom O'Brien	Mike Evariste
Bloody Mary	Loretta Ables Sayre	James Hayes	Jerold E. Solomon
Liat	Li Jun Li	Kenneth Johnson	Christian Carter
Luther Billis	Danny Burstein	PO Hamilton Steeves	Charlie Brady
Stewpot	Victor Hawks	Staff Sgt. Thom. Hassinger	Zachary James
Professor	Noah Weisberg	Lt. Eustis Carmichael	Andrew Samonsky
Lt. Joseph Cable	Matthew Morrison	Lt. Genevieve Marshall	Lisa Howard
Capt. George Brackett	Skipp Sudduth	Ens. Dinah Murphy	Laura Marie Duncan
Cmdr. William Harbison	Sean Cullen	Ens. Janet MacGregor	Laura Griffith
Lt. Buzz Adams	George Merrick	Ens. Connie Walewska	Margot de la Barre
Yeoman Herbert Quale	Christian Delcroix	Ens. Sue Yaeger	Garrett Long
Radio Op. Bob McCaffrey	Matt Caplan	Ens. Cora MacRae	Becca Ayers

Bloody Mary's Assistants: MaryAnn Hu, Emily Morales, Kimber Monroe.

Ensemble: Becca Ayers, Genson Blimline, Charlie Brady, Matt Caplan, Christian Carter, Helmar Augustus Cooper, Jeremy Davis, Margot de la Barre, Mike Evariste, Laura Griffith, Lisa Howard, MaryAnn Hu, Zachary James, Robert Lenzi, Garrett Long, Nick Mayo, George Merrick, Kimber Monroe, Emily Morales, Andrew Samonsky, Jerold E. Solomon.

Orchestra: Ted Sperling conductor; Fred Lassen associate conductor; Charles duChateau assistant conductor, cello; Belinda Whitney concertmaster, violin; Antoine Silverman, Karl Kawahara, Katherine Livolsi-Landau, Lisa Matricardi, James Tsao, Michael Nicholas, Rena Isbin violin; David Blinn, David Cresswell viola; Peter Sachon, Caryl Paisner cello; Lisa Stokes-Chin bass; Liz Mann flute, piccolo; Todd Palmer, Shari Hoffman clarinet; Matt Dine oboe, English horn; Damian Primis bassoon; Robert Carlisle, Chris Komer, Shelagh Abate, French horn; Dominic Derasse, Gareth Flowers, Wayne duMaine trumpet; Mark Patterson, Mike Boschen trombone; Marcus Rojas tuba; Bill Lanham percussion, drums, Grace Paradise harp.

Understudies: Ms. O'Hara—Laura Marie Duncan, Garrett Long; Mr. Szot—William Michals; Ms. Romain, Mr. Kain—Kimber Monroe; Mr. Cooper—Christian Carter, Mike Evariste; Ms. Sayers—MaryAnn Hu, Lisa Howard; Ms. Li—Wendi Bergamini, Emily Morales; Mr. Burstein—Victor Hawks, Nick Mayo; Mr. Hawks—Genson Blimline, Jeremy Davis; Mr. Morrison—Robert Lenzi, Andrew Samonsky; Mr. Sudduth—Victor Hawks, Genson Blimline; Mr. Weisberg—Matt Caplan, George Merrick; Mr. Cullen—George Merrick, Andrew Samonsky; Mr. Caplan—Grady McLeod Bowman, George Psomas; Mr. Delcroix—Grady McLeod Bowman, George Psomas; Ms. Duncan—Wendi Bergamini, Garrett Long; Mr. Samonsky—Charlie Brady, Nick Mayo; Mr. Merrick—Charlie Brady, Nick Mayo.

Swings: Wendi Bergamini, Grady McLeod Bowman, Darius Nichols, George Psomas.

Direction, Bartlett Sher; choreography, Christopher Gattelli; scenery, Michael Yeargan; costumes, Catherine Zuber; lighting, Donald Holder; sound, Scott Lehrer; orchestrations, Robert Russell Bennett; dance and music arrangements, Trude Rittmann; music direction, Mr. Sperling; music coordination, David Lai; casting, Telsey and Company; stage management, Michael Brunner; press, Philip Rinaldi, Barbara Carroll.

Time: World War II. Place: South Pacific islands. Presented in two parts.

Star-crossed lovers in a beautiful, but dangerous war zone struggle to reconcile their personal biases, patriotic duty and romantic feelings. First presentation of record was given in New Haven at the Shubert Theatre (3/7–12/1949) before a run in Boston's Shubert Theatre (3/15–4/2/1949) on the way to the Broadway opening at the Majestic Theatre (4/7/1949–5/16/1953). The Broadway production's hiatus in 1953 marked its return to Boston, where it played in the Opera House for six weeks (5/18–6/27/1953) before returning to its new venue in New York, the Broadway

Theatre (6/29/1953–1/16/1954; 1,925 total Broadway performances). The original Broadway production received nine 1950 Tony Awards in the musical categories of best musical, producer (Messrs. Logan, Hammerstein, Rodgers and Leland Hayward), direction (Mr. Logan), libretto (Messrs. Hammerstein and Logan), score (Mr. Rodgers), actor (Ezio Pinza), actress (Mary Martin), featured actor (Myron McCormick) and featured actress (Juanita Hall). In what may be considered a calendrical oddity, Jo Mielziner's 1949 Tony Award for scene design cited *South Pacific* along with *Sleepy Hollow, Summer and Smoke, Anne of the Thousand Days* and *Death of a Salesman*. It might be fairly argued, therefore, that *South Pacific* received 10 Tony Awards in total. The musical also received the 1950 Pulitzer Prize in Drama. It is worth noting that Mr. Michener's material on which the musical was based had earlier received the 1948 Pulitzer Prize in Fiction. The 2007–08 production marked the first Broadway revival and it received seven 2008 Tony Awards in the musical categories of best revival (Lincoln Center Theater, Mr. Bishop and Mr. Gersten), direction (Mr. Sher), actor (Mr. Szot), scene design (Mr. Yeargan), costume design (Ms. Zuber), lighting design (Mr. Holder) and sound design (Mr. Lehrer). Following a restoration project, Mr. Rodgers's music for this production was presented with the 30-player orchestration created for the original version.

ACT I

Overture
Scene 1: The terrace of Emile de Becque's plantation home
"Dites-moi" .... Ngana, Jerome
"A Cockeyed Optimist" .... Nellie
"Twin Soliloquies" .... Nellie, Emile
"Some Enchanted Evening" .... Emile
"Dites-moi" (Reprise) .... Ngana, Jerome, Emile
Scene 2: Another part of the island
"Bloody Mary" .... Seabees
"There Is Nothin' Like a Dame" .... Billis, Seabees
"Bali Ha'i" .... Bloody Mary
Scene 3: The company street
Scene 4: Inside the island commander's office
Scene 5: The company street
"My Girl Back Home" .... Cable, Nellie
Scene 6: The beach
"I'm Gonna Wash That Man Right Outa My Hair" .... Nellie, Nurses
"Some Enchanted Evening" (Reprise) .... Emile, Nellie
"A Wonderful Guy" .... Nellie, Nurses
Scene 7: Inside the island commander's office
Scene 8: On Bali Ha'i
"Bali Ha'i" (Reprise) .... Island Women
Scene 9: Inside a hut on Bali Ha'i
"Younger Than Springtime" .... Cable
Scene 10: Near the beach on Bali Ha'i
Scene 11: Emile's terrace
Finale .... Nellie, Emile

ACT II

Entr'acte
Scene 1: A performance of "The Thanksgiving Follies" .... Nellie, Nurses, GIs
Scene 2: Backstage at "The Thanksgiving Follies"
"Happy Talk" .... Bloody Mary, Liat
Scene 3: The stage
"Honey Bun" .... Nellie, Billis, Company
Scene 4: Backstage
"You've Got to Be Carefully Taught" .... Cable
"This Nearly Was Mine" .... Emile
Scene 5: The radio shack
Scene 6: The beach
"Some Enchanted Evening" (Reprise) .... Nellie

Scene 7: The company street
Scene 8: Emile's terrace
Finale .... Emile, Nellie, Ngana, Jerome

Macbeth (52). Transfer of the Off Broadway revival of the play by William Shakespeare. Produced by Duncan C. Weldon and Paul Elliott, Jeffrey Archer, Bill Ballard, Terri and Timothy Childs, Rodger Hess, David Mirvish, Adriana Mnuchin and Emanuel Azenberg, in association with the Brooklyn Academy of Music and the Chichester Festival Theatre, at the Lyceum Theatre. Opened April 8, 2008. (Closed May 24, 2008)

Duncan; Doctor .... Byron Jennings	Ross .... Tim Treloar
Malcolm .... Scott Handy	Angus .... Bill Nash
Sergeant; Murderer .... Hywel John	Lady Macbeth .... Kate Fleetwood
Donalbain;	Lady Macbeth's Servant .... Oliver Birch
Young Seyward .... Ben Carpenter	Fleance .... Henry Hodges (alt.),
Witch .... Sophie Hunter	Emmett White (alt.)
Witch; Gentlewoman .... Polly Frame	Seyton .... Christopher Patrick Nolan
Witch .... Niamh McGrady	Macduff .... Michael Feast
Macbeth .... Patrick Stewart	Lady Macduff .... Rachel Ticotin
Banquo .... Martin Turner	Old Seyward;
Lennox .... Mark Rawlings	Murderer .... Christopher Knott

Macduff Children: Henry Hodges, Gabrielle Piacentile, Jacob Rosenbaum, Phoebe Keeling VanDusen.

Understudies: Messrs. Treloar, Knott—Oliver Birch; Messrs. Handy, John, Nash—Ben Carpenter; Mses. Fleetwood, McGrady, Mr. Birch—Polly Frame; Mses. Hunter, Frame, McGrady—Sophie

Murderous marriage: Patrick Stewart and Kate Fleetwood in Macbeth. *Photo: Manuel Harlan*

Hunter, Rachel Ticotin; Messrs. Nolan, Carpenter—Hywel John; Messrs. Jennings, Birch—Christopher Knott; Mses. Ticotin, Frame—Niamh McGrady; Mr. Turner—Bill Nash; Mr. Rawlings—Christopher Patrick Nolan; Mr. Feast—Mark Rawlings; Mr. Stewart—Tim Treloar.

Direction, Rupert Goold; choreography, Georgina Lamb; scenery and costumes, Anthony Ward; lighting, Howard Harrison; sound and music, Adam Cork; video and projections, Lorna Heavey; fight direction, Terry King; stage management, Jane Pole; press, Barlow-Hartman, Michael Hartman, John Barlow, Tom D'Ambrosio, Michelle Bergmann.

Presented in two parts.

A Scottish thane and his lady wife are seized by a power madness that leads to murder and ruin. First presentation of record was given at the Globe Theatre (4/20/1611) with Richard Burbage in the title role. It is believed, however, to have been given earlier at Hampton Court (8/7/1606). First presentation of record in this country was given at the John Street Theatre (3/3/1768) with Lewis Hallam II in the title role. In May 1849, there were three competing productions in New York, two of which—with the Englishman William Charles Macready and the American Edwin Forrest in the title roles—helped to spark the deadly Astor Place Riots (5/7–10/1849). First presentation of record of the 2007–08 production was given in the Minerva Theatre by the Chichester Festival Theatre (5/25–9/1/2007) before a run in the West End's Gielgud Theatre (9/24–12/1/2007). The Brooklyn Academy of Music presented the production Off Broadway in its Harvey Theater (2/13–3/22/2008; 40 performances) before the Broadway stand. (See Plays Produced Off Broadway section of this volume.)

*A Catered Affair (51). Musical with book by Harvey Fierstein; music and lyrics by John Bucchino; based on the Turner Entertainment film by Gore Vidal and the teleplay by Paddy Chayefsky. Produced by Jujamcyn Theaters, Jordan Roth, Harvey Entertainment, Ron Fierstein, Richie Jackson, Daryl Roth, John O'Boyle, Ricky Stevens, Davis-Tolentino, Barbra Russell, Ron Sharpe, in association with Frankel-Baruch-Viertel-Routh Group, Broadway Across America, True Love Productions, Rick Steiner, Mayerson-Bell-Staton-Osher Group, Jan Kallish, at the Walter Kerr Theatre. Opened April 17, 2008.

Winston	Harvey Fierstein	Ralph	Matt Cavenaugh
Pasha; Mrs. Halloran	Lori Wilner	Sam; Mr. Halloran	Philip Hoffman
Myra;		Tom	Tom Wopat
Dress Saleswoman	Kristine Zbornik	Aggie	Faith Prince
Dolores; Caterer	Heather MacRae	Alice; Army Sergeant	Katie Klaus
Janey	Leslie Kritzer		

Orchestra: Constantine Kitsopoulos conductor; Ethyl Will associate conductor, piano; Dale Stuckenbruck concert master; Liz Lim-Dutton violin; Ken Burward-Hoy viola; Susannah Chapman cello; John Arbo bass; Jim Ercole, Don McGeen woodwinds; Neil Balm trumpet, flugelhorn; Dean Witten percussion.

Understudies: Ms. Prince—Jennifer Allen, Lori Wilner; Mr. Wopat—Philip Hoffman, Mark Zimmerman; Messrs. Fierstein, Hoffman—Mark Zimmerman; Ms. Kritzer—Katie Klaus, Britta Ollmann; Mr. Cavenaugh—Matthew Scott; Mses. Wilner, Zbornik, MacRae—Jennifer Allen; Ms. Klaus—Britta Ollmann.

Direction, John Doyle; scenery, David Gallo; costumes, Ann Hould-Ward; lighting, Brian MacDevitt; sound, Dan Moses Schreier; projections, Zachary Borovay; wigs and hair, David Lawrence; orchestrations, Jonathan Tunick; music direction and arrangements, Mr. Kitsopoulos; music coordination, John Miller; associate producers, Stacey Mindich, Rhoda Mayerson; casting, Telsey and Company; stage management, Adam John Hunter; press, O and M Company, Rick Miramontez, Jon Dimond, Molly Barnett, Jaron Caldwell.

Time: June 1953 and later. Place: Bronx, New York. Performed without intermission.

A hardscrabble working-class family confronts certain priorities and difficult truths when a daughter announces her engagement. First presentation of record was given at the Old Globe, San Diego (9/30–11/4/2007).

MUSICAL NUMBERS

"Partners" .... Tom, Sam, Ralph, Janey
"Ralph and Me" .... Janey

"Married" .... Aggie
"Women Chatter" .... Myra, Pasha, Dolores
"No Fuss" .... Aggie
"Your Children's Happiness" .... Mr. and Mrs. Halloran
"Immediate Family" .... Winston
"Our Only Daughter" .... Aggie
"One White Dress" .... Janey, Aggie
"Vision" .... Aggie
"Don't Ever Stop Saying 'I Love You'" .... Janey, Ralph
"I Stayed" .... Tom
"Married" (Reprise) .... Aggie
"Coney Island" .... Winston
"Don't Ever Stop Saying 'I Love You'" (Reprise) .... Ralph, Janey, Tom
"Coney Island" (Reprise) .... Winston, Company

*Cry-Baby (43). Musical with book by Mark O'Donnell and Thomas Meehan; music
and lyrics by David Javerbaum and Adam Schlesinger; based on the Universal Pictures
film by John Waters. Produced by Adam Epstein, Allan S. Gordon, Élan V. McAllister,
Brian Grazer, James P. MacGilvray, Universal Pictures Stage Productions, Anne Caruso,
Adam S. Gordon, Latitude Link, the Pelican Group, in association with Philip Morgaman,
Andrew Farber, Richard Mishaan, at the Marquis Theatre. Opened April 24, 2008.

Mrs. Vernon-Williams	Harriet Harris	Dupree	Chester Gregory II
Baldwin	Christopher J. Hanke	Cry-Baby	James Snyder
Allison	Elizabeth Stanley	Lenora	Alli Mauzey
Skippy Wagstaff	Ryan Silverman	Bailiff	Marty Lawson
Pepper	Carly Jibson	Judge Stone	Richard Poe
Wanda	Lacey Kohl	Father Officer O'Brien	Stacey Todd Holt
Mona	Tory Ross	Radio DJ	Michael Buchanan

The Whiffles: Nick Blaemire, Colin Cunliffe, Peter Matthew Smith.

Ensemble: Cameron Adams, Ashley Amber, Nick Blaemire, Michael Buchanan, Eric L. Christian,
Colin Cunliffe, Stacey Todd Holt, Laura Jordan, Marty Lawson, Spencer Liff, Mayumi Miguel, Tory
Ross, Eric Sciotto, Ryan Silverman, Peter Matthew Smith, Allison Spratt, Charlie Sutton.

Orchestra: Lynne Shankel conductor, keyboard 1; Henry Aronson associate conductor, keyboard
2, accordion; Cenovia Cummins, Maxim Moston violin, mandolin; Orlando Wells violin, viola;
Sarah Seiver cello; Steve Count bass; John Benthal, Chris Biesterfeldt guitar; Scott Kreitzer, Cliff
Lyons, Roger Rosenberg reeds; Barry Danielian trumpet; Dan Levine trombone; Joe Mowatt
percussion; Frank Pagano drums.

Understudies: Mr. Snyder—Ryan Silverman, Eric Sciotto; Ms. Stanley—Allison Spratt, Cameron
Adams; Ms. Harris—Laura Jordan, Tory Ross; Mr. Poe—Stacey Todd Holt, Peter Matthew Smith;
Mr. Hanke—Colin Cunliffe, Peter Matthew Smith; Ms. Jibson—Tory Ross, Lisa Gajda; Ms. Ross—Lisa
Gajda; Ms. Kohl—Ashley Amber, Courtney Laine Mazza; Mr. Gregory—Eric L. Christian, Michael
Buchanan; Ms. Mauzey—Allison Spratt, Courtney Laine Mazza.

Swings: Lisa Gajda, Michael D. Jablonski, Brendan King, Courtney Laine Mazza.

Direction, Mark Brokaw; choreography, Rob Ashford; scenery, Scott Pask; costumes, Catherine
Zuber; lighting, Howell Binkley; sound, Peter Hylenski; wigs and hair, Tom Watson; fight direction,
Rick Sordelet; orchestrations, Christopher Jahnke; dance music arrangements, David Chase; music
direction and arrangements, Ms. Shankel; music coordination, John Miller, casting, Telsey and
Company; stage management, Rolt Smith; press, Richard Kornberg and Associates, Richard
Kornberg, Don Summa, Alyssa Hart, Billy Zavelson.

Time: 1954. Place: Baltimore. Presented in two parts.

Bad kids and good kids clash over contemporary mores—and what the heart wants—in a
spoof of 1950s values. First presentation of record was given in the Mandell Weiss Theatre at La
Jolla Playhouse in California (11/18–12/16/2007).

ACT I

"The Anti-Polio Picnic" .... Mrs. Vernon-Williams, Allison,
Baldwin, Company

"Watch Your Ass" ....Pepper, Wanda, Mona,
Dupree, Cry-Baby, Company
"I'm Infected" .... Allison, Cry-Baby, Company
"Squeaky Clean" .... Baldwin, Whiffles
"Nobody Gets Me" .... Cry-Baby, Pepper, Wanda,
Mona, Company
"Nobody Gets Me" (Reprise) .... Allison
"Jukebox Jamboree" .... Dupree
"A Whole Lot Worse" ....Pepper, Wanda, Mona
"Screw Loose" .... Lenora
"Baby Baby Baby Baby Baby (Baby Baby)" .... Cry-Baby, Allison, Company
"Girl, Can I Kiss You . . .?" .... Cry-Baby, Allison, Company
"I'm Infected" (Reprise) .... Allison, Cry-Baby
"You Can't Beat the System" .... Company

ACT II

"Misery, Agony, Helplessness, Hopelessness, Heartache and Woe" .... Allison, Cry-Baby,
Dupree, Pepper,
Wanda, Mona,
Mrs. Vernon-Williams, Company
"All in My Head" ....Baldwin, Lenora, Company
"Jailyard Jubilee" .... Dupree, Company
"A Little Upset" .... Cry-Baby, Dupree,
Allison, Company
"I Did Something Wrong . . . Once" .... Mrs.Vernon-Williams
"Thanks for the Nifty Country!" .... Baldwin, Whiffles
"This Amazing Offer" .... Baldwin, Whiffles
"Do That Again" ....Cry-Baby, Allison
"Nothing Bad's Ever Gonna Happen Again" .... Company

The Country Girl (40). Revival of the play by Clifford Odets; revisions by Jon Robin
Baitz. Produced by Ostar Productions, Bob Boyett, the Shubert Organization, Eric
Falkenstein, Roy Furman, Lawrence Horowitz, Jam Theatricals, Stephanie P. McClelland,
Bill Rollnick, Nancy Ellison Rollnick, Daryl Roth, Debra Black, in assocation with Jon
Avnet, Ralph Guild, Michael Coppel, Jamie deRoy, Michael Filerman, Philip Geier,
Donald Keough, Max OnStage, Mary Lu Roffe, at the Bernard B. Jacobs Theatre. Opened
April 27, 2008.

Bernie Dodd	Peter Gallagher	Paul Unger	Remy Auberjonois
Larry	Lucas Caleb Rooney	Frank Elgin	Morgan Freeman
Phil Cook	Chip Zien	Georgie Elgin	Frances McDormand
Nancy Stoddard	Anna Camp	Ralph	Joe Roland

Understudies: Messrs. Gallagher, Rooney—Joe Roland; Ms. Camp—Amanda Leigh Cobb; Mr.
Freeman—Peter Ratray; Ms. McDormand—Angela Reed.

Direction, Mike Nichols; scenery, Tim Hatley; costumes, Albert Wolsky; lighting, Natasha
Katz; sound, Acme Sound Partners; wigs and hair, David Brian Brown; casting, Tara Rubin Casting;
stage management, Barclay Stiff; press, Boneau/Bryan-Brown, Adrian Bryan-Brown, Jackie Green,
Matt Ross.

Time: 1950. Place: Various locations in New York and Boston. Presented in two parts.

An alcoholic actor struggles in his attempt to mount a comeback while receiving conditional
support from his wife and his director. A 1950–51 *Best Plays* choice, the original Broadway
production opened at the Lyceum Theatre (11/10/1950–6/2/1951; 235 performances). First
presentation of record was given at Boston's Majestic Theatre (10/23–11/4/1950) in preparation
for the Broadway opening. Directed by the author, the original production received 1951 Tony
Awards in the categories of best actress (Uta Hagen) and scene design (Boris Aronson).

Thurgood (37). By George Stevens Jr. Produced by Vernon Jordan, the Shubert
Organization, Bill Rollnick, Nancy Ellison Rollnick, Matt Murphy, Daryl Roth, Debra

Black, Roy Furman, Jam Theatricals, Lawrence Horowitz, Eric Falkenstein, Max OnStage, James D'Orta, Jamie deRoy, Amy Nederlander, in association with Ostar Productions and the Westport Country Playhouse, at the Booth Theatre. Opened April 30, 2008.

Thurgood Marshall .... Laurence Fishburne

Direction, Leonard Foglia; scenery, Allen Moyer; costumes, Jane Greenwood; lighting, Brian Nason; sound, Ryan Rumery; projections, Elaine J. McCarthy; stage management, Marti McIntosh; press, Fifteen Minutes Public Relations, Pete Sanders, Corey Martin, Clifton Guterman.

Time: Various moments in Justice Marshall's life. Place: Howard University Law School. Presented without intermission.

The first African-American Justice of the Supreme Court shares his thoughts about life liberty, property and his own relation to these matters in a speech given at a historically black college. First presentation of record was given at the Westport Country Playhouse in Connecticut, with James Earl Jones in the title role (5/11–21/2006).

*Roundabout Theatre Company production of **Les Liaisons Dangereuses** (36). Revival of the play by Christopher Hampton; adapted from the novel by Choderlos de Laclos. Todd Haimes artistic director, Harold Wolpert managing director, Julia C. Levy executive director at the American Airlines Theatre. Opened May 1, 2008.

La Marquise de Merteuil .... Laura Linney	La Présidente de Tourvel .... Jessica Collins
Madame de Volanges .... Kristine Nielsen	Émilie .... Rosie Benton
Cécile Volanges .... Mamie Gummer	Le Chevalier Danceny .... Benjamin Walker
Major-domo .... Tim McGeever	Footman; Tenor .... Kevin Duda
Le Vicomte de Valmont .... Ben Daniels	Maid; Soprano .... Jane Pfitsch
Azolan .... Derek Cecil	Servants .... Delphi Harrington,
Madame de Rosemonde .... Siân Phillips	Nicole Orth-Pallavicini

Understudies: Mses. Linney, Nielsen—Nicole Orth-Pallavicini; Mses. Gummer, Benton—Jane Pfitsch; Messrs. McGeever, Walker—Kevin Duda; Messrs. Daniels, Cecil—Tim McGeever; Ms. Phillips—Delphi Harrington; Ms. Collins—Rosie Benton.

Direction, Rufus Norris; scenery, Scott Pask; costumes, Katrina Lindsay; lighting, Donald Holder; sound, Paul Arditti; wigs and hair, Paul Huntley; fight direction, Rick Sordelet; casting, Jim Carnahan and Carrie Gardner; stage management Arthur Gaffin; press, Boneau/Bryan-Brown, Adrian Bryan-Brown, Matt Polk, Jessica Johnson, Amy Kass.

Time: The 1780s. Place: Paris and the Bois de Vincennes. Presented in two parts.

Aristocratic sexual predators employ seductive techniques to counter ennui in the years before the French Revolution. Mr. Laclos's epistolary novel was first published in 1782. First presentation of record of Mr. Hampton's adaptation was given in the Other Place by the Royal Shakespeare Company at Stratford-Upon-Avon (9/25/1985) before a run in the Pit at London's Barbican Center (1/8/1986). The production later engaged a long run at the Ambassadors Theatre in the West End (10/14/1986–9/29/1990; 1,658 performances). A 1986–87 *Best Plays* choice, the original Broadway production opened at the Music Box (4/30–9/6/1987; 149 performances). The 2007–08 production was the first Broadway revival. It received a 2008 Tony Award for costume design of a play (Katrina Lindsay).

*Boeing-Boeing (32). By Marc Camoletti; translated by Beverley Cross and Francis Evans. Produced by Sonia Friedman Productions, Bob Boyett, Act Productions, Matthew Byam Shaw, Robert G. Bartner, the Weinstein Company, Susan Gallin, Mary Lu Roffe, Broadway Across America, Tulchin/Jenkins/DSM, the Araca Group at the Longacre Theatre. Opened May 4, 2008.

Gloria .... Kathryn Hahn	Robert .... Mark Rylance
Bernard .... Bradley Whitford	Gabriella .... Gina Gershon
Berthe .... Christine Baranski	Gretchen .... Mary McCormack

Understudies: Mr. Whitford—Ray Virta; Ms. Baranski—Pippa Pearthree; Mses. Gershon, Hahn, McCormack—Roxanna Hope.

Direction, Matthew Warchus; choreography, Kathleen Marshall; scenery and costumes, Rob Howell; lighting, Hugh Vanstone; sound, Simon Baker; music, Claire Van Kampen; associate producers, Tim Levy, Jill Lenhart, Douglas G. Smith; casting, Jim Carnahan; stage management, William Joseph Barnes; press, Barlow-Hartman, Michael Hartman, John Barlow, Dennis Crowley, Michelle Bergmann.

Time: Early 1960s. Place: Bernard's Paris apartment. Presented in two parts.

A hyperactive journalist juggles three attractive female flight attendants, each of whom believes that he is her fiancé. First presentation of record was given at the Comédie Caumartin in Paris (1960–61). First presentation of record in English was given at London's Apollo Theatre (2/20/1962–5/8/1965) before a transfer to the Duchess Theatre (5/10/1965–1/7/1967). First US presentation of record was given at Boston's Wilbur Theatre (1/26–30/1965) in preparation for its Broadway opening at the Cort Theatre (2/2–20/1965; 23 performances). The 2007 British revival that transferred to the US this season opened at the Comedy Theatre in London (2/15/2007–1/5/2008) before its run began at Broadway's Longacre Theatre (5/4/2008; 32 performances as of May 31). The 2007–08 production was the first Broadway revival. It received 2008 Tony Awards in the play categories of best revival (see producers above) and best actor (Mr. Rylance).

Glory Days (1). Musical with book by James Gardiner; music and lyrics by Nick Blaemire. Produced by John O'Boyle, Ricky Stevens, Richard E. Leopold, Lizzie Leopold, Max Productions and Broadway Across America, in association with the Signature Theatre (Virginia), at Circle in the Square. Opened May 6, 2008. (Closed May 6, 2008)

Will	Steven Booth	Skip	Adam Halpin
Andy	Andrew C. Call	Jack	Jesse JP Johnson

Everyman? Mark Rylance in Boeing-Boeing.
Photo: Joan Marcus

Musicians: Ethan Popp conductor, keyboard; Alec Berlin, associate conductor, guitar; Gary Bristol bass; Damien Bassman drums.

Understudies: Messrs. Booth, Johnson—Alex Brightman; Messrs. Call, Halpin—Jeremy Woodard.

Direction, Eric Schaeffer; scenery, Jim Kronzer; costumes, Sasha Ludwig-Siegel; lighting, Mark Lanks; sound, Peter Hylenski; orchestrations and music supervision, Jesse Vargas; vocal arrangements; Messrs. Blaemire and Vargas; music direction, Mr. Popp; music coordination, Mike Keller; casting, Tara Rubin Casting, stage management, Gregg Kirsopp; press, Boneau/Bryan-Brown, Adrian Bryan-Brown, Jim Byk, Adriana Douzos, Matt Ross.

Time: The present. Place: Bleachers near an athletic field. Presented without intermission.

Four friends re-unite not long after high school to reminisce about the good old days. First presentation of record was given by Signature Theatre Company in Virginia (1/20–2/17/2008).

MUSICAL NUMBERS

"My Three Best Friends" .... Will
"Are You Ready for Tonight?" .... Will, Andy, Skip, Jack
"We've Got Girls" .... Will, Andy
"Right Here" .... Will, Andy, Skip, Jack
"Open Road" ....Jack
"Things Are Different" .... Will, Andy
"Generation Apathy" .... Skip
"After All" .... Will
"The Good Old Glory Type Days" .... Will, Andy, Skip, Jack
"The Thing About Andy" .... Will, Jack
"Forget About It" .... Will, Andy, Skip, Jack
"Other Human Beings" .... Jack, Andy
"My Turn" ....Andy
"Boys" .... Will, Skip
"My Next Story" .... Will

*Manhattan Theatre Club production of **Top Girls** (30). Revival of the play by Caryl Churchill. Lynne Meadow artistic director, Daniel Sullivan acting artistic director, Barry Grove executive producer, at the Biltmore Theatre. Opened May 7, 2008.

Patient Griselda;		Marlene	Elizabeth Marvel
others ....Mary Catherine Garrison		Pope Joan; Angie	Martha Plimpton
Waitress; Louise .... Mary Beth Hurt		Dull Gret; Nell	Ana Reeder
Lady Nijo; Win ....Jennifer Ikeda		Isabella Bird; others	Marisa Tomei

Understudies: Mses. Marvel, Plimpton—Tina Benko; Mses. Garrison, Ikeda—Angela Lin; Mses. Hurt, Reeder, Tomei—Anne Torsiglieri.

Direction, James Macdonald; scenery, Tom Pye; costumes, Laura Bauer; lighting, Christopher Akerlind; sound, Darron L. West; music, Matthew Herbert; wigs and hair, Paul Huntley; casting, Nancy Piccione; stage management, Martha Donaldson; press, Boneau/Bryan-Brown, Chris Boneau, Aaron Meier, Heath Schwartz, Christine Olver.

Time: Early 1980s. Place: London and Suffolk, England. Presented in three parts.

Women from across time—famous, notorious, ordinary—interact on a variety of levels as they negotiate gender roles amid the status quo of their lives. First presentation of record was given at London's Royal Court Theatre (8/28/1982) before it transferred to Off Broadway's Public Theater (12/29/1982–1/30/1983; 40 performances). After the initial run, the production was recast with US actors and re-opened at the Public (3/15–5/29/1983; 89 performances). The 2007–08 production was the first Broadway production.

PLAYS PRODUCED OFF BROADWAY

○○○○○

FOR THE PURPOSES of *Best Plays* listing, the term "Off Broadway" signifies a show that opened for general audiences in a Manhattan theater seating 499 or fewer and 1) employed an Equity cast, 2) planned a regular schedule of eight performances per week in an open-ended run (seven per week for solo shows and some other exceptions) and 3) offered itself to public comment by critics after a designated opening performance.

Figures in parentheses following a play's title give the number of performances from the press-opening date. These numbers do not include previews or extra nonprofit performances. Performance interruptions for cast changes and other breaks have been taken into account. Performance numbers are figured in consultation with press representatives and company managements.

Plays marked with an asterisk (*) were still in a projected run on June 1, 2008. The number of performances is figured from press opening through May 31, 2008.

In a listing of a show's numbers—dances, sketches, musical scenes, etc.—the titles of songs are identified wherever possible by their appearance in quotation marks (").

HOLDOVERS FROM PREVIOUS SEASONS

OFF BROADWAY SHOWS that were running on June 1, 2007 are listed below. More detailed information about them appears in previous *Best Plays* volumes of appropriate date. Important cast changes since opening night are recorded in the Cast Replacements section in this volume.

*Perfect Crime (8,617). By Warren Manzi. Opened October 16, 1987.

*Blue Man Group (Tubes) (8,849). Performance piece by and with Blue Man Group. Opened November 17, 1991.

*Stomp (6,008). Percussion performance piece created by Luke Cresswell and Steve McNicholas. Opened February 27, 1994.

*I Love You, You're Perfect, Now Change (4,937). Musical revue with book and lyrics by Joe DiPietro; music by Jimmy Roberts. Opened August 1, 1996.

*Naked Boys Singing! (2,690). Musical revue conceived by Robert Schrock; written by various authors. Opened July 22, 1999.

*Altar Boyz (1,358). Transfer from Off Off Broadway of the musical with book by Kevin Del Aguila; music and lyrics by Gary Adler and Michael Patrick Walker; conceived by Marc Kessler and Ken Davenport. Opened March 1, 2005.

A Jew Grows in Brooklyn (350). Transfer from Off Off Broadway of the solo performance piece by Jake Ehrenreich. Opened June 7, 2006. (Closed September 17, 2006) Production hiatus due to permanent closing of theater on September 30, 2006. Re-opened October 11, 2006 at 37 Arts. (Closed June 10, 2007)

No Child . . . (301). Transfer from Off Off Broadway of the solo performance piece by Nilaja Sun. Opened July 16, 2006. (Closed June 3, 2007)

The Fantasticks (628). Revival of the musical with book by Tom Jones; music by Harvey Schmidt; lyrics by Mr. Jones; based on *Les Romanesques* by Edmond Rostand. Opened August 23, 2006. (Closed February 24, 2008)

*My Mother's Italian, My Father's Jewish, and I'm in Therapy! (649). Solo performance piece by Steve Solomon. Opened December 8, 2006.

In the Heights (181). Musical with book by Quiara Alegría Hudes; music and lyrics by Lin-Manuel Miranda. Opened February 8, 2007. (Closed July 15, 2007)

Bill W. and Dr. Bob (111). By Stephen Bergman and Janet Surrey. Opened March 5, 2007. (Closed June 10, 2007)

Spalding Gray: Stories Left to Tell (129). By Kathleen Russo and Lucy Sexton; adapted from the writing of Spalding Gray. Opened March 6, 2007. (Closed June 26, 2007)

Be (124). By Eylon Nuphar and Boaz Berman. Opened March 13, 2007. (Closed July 1, 2007)

Manhattan Theatre Club production of **Blackbird** (68). By David Harrower. Opened April 10, 2007. (Closed June 10, 2007)

The Public Theater presentation of **Passing Strange** (56). Musical with book and lyrics by Stew; music by Stew and Heidi Rodewald. Opened May 14, 2007. (Closed July 1, 2007)

Irish Repertory Theatre production of **Gaslight** (61). By Patrick Hamilton. Opened May 17, 2007. (Closed July 8, 2007)

Phallacy (28). By Carl Djerassi. Opened May 18, 2007. (Closed June 10, 2007)

PLAYS PRODUCED JUNE 1, 2007–MAY 31, 2008

Playwrights Horizons production of **Crazy Mary** (27). By A.R. Gurney. Tim Sanford artistic director, Leslie Marcus managing director, William Russo general manager, in the Mainstage Theater. Opened June 3, 2007. (Closed June 26, 2007)

Pearl	Myra Lucretia Taylor	Jerome	Mitchell Greenberg
Skip	Michael Esper	Mary	Kristine Nielsen
Lydia	Sigourney Weaver		

Direction, Jim Simpson; scenery, John Lee Beatty; costumes, Claudia Brown; lighting, Brian Aldous; sound, Jill BC DuBoff; music, Michael Holland; casting, Alaine Alldaffer; stage management, Janet Takami; press, the Publicity Office, Marc Thibodeau, Michael S. Borowski, Jeremy Shaffer, Matthew Fasano.

Time: Today. Place: Library of a private psychiatric institution in Boston. Presented in two parts.

An allegory on the decline of WASP culture into penury or madness given flesh by a pair of middle age female cousins.

Making amends: Mitchell Greenberg, Sigourney Weaver and Kristine Nielsen in Crazy Mary. *Photo: Joan Marcus*

New York Theatre Workshop production of **Horizon** (31). By Rinde Eckert. James C. Nicola artistic director, Lynn Moffat managing director. Opened June 5, 2007. (Closed July 1, 2007)

Mason Number 1; others .... David Barlow   Mason Number 2; others .... Howard Swain
Reinhart Poole .... Rinde Eckert

  Direction, David Schweizer; choreography, David Barlow; scenery and lighting, Alexander V. Nichols; costumes, David Zinn; sound, Gregory T. Kuhn; music, Mr. Eckert; stage management, Chad Brown and Odessa (Niki) Spruill; press, Richard Kornberg and Associates, Don Summa.

  Presented without intermission.

  Performance piece employing music and memory to evoke a theologian's crises of intellect, conscience and faith.

Brits Off Broadway presentation of the **Stephen Joseph Theatre** production of **Intimate Exchanges** (22). By Alan Ayckbourn. Elysabeth Kleinhans artistic director, Peter Tear executive producer, in association with Stephen Joseph Theatre (Alan Ayckbourn artistic director), in Theater A at 59E59 Theaters. Opened June 14, 2007. (Closed July 1, 2007)

Toby; others .... Bill Champion   Celia; others .... Claudia Elmhirst
  Direction, Mr. Ayckbourn and Tim Luscombe; scenery and costumes, Michael Holt; lighting, Ben Vickers; stage management, Misha Siegel-Rivers; press, Karen Greco.

  Presented in two parts.

  Eight interrelated plays on love and life in which all roles are performed by two actors. The plays are *Events on a Hotel Terrace, Affairs in a Tent, A One Man Protest, Love in the Mist, A Cricket Match, A Game of Golf, A Pageant, A Garden Fete.* First presentation of record was given at Stephen Joseph Theatre in Scarborough, North Yorkshire (6/1982). First US presentation of record was given at the Old Globe in San Diego (12/4/1986–1/11/1987).

Second Stage Theatre production of **eurydice** (80). By Sarah Ruhl. Carole Rothman artistic director, Ellen Richard executive director, in association with Berkeley Repertory Theatre (Tony Taccone artistic director, Susan Medak managing director) and Yale Repertory Theatre (James Bundy artistic director, Victoria Nolan managing director), at Second Stage Theatre. Opened June 18, 2007. (Closed August 26, 2007)

Eurydice .... Maria Dizzia	Orpheus .... Joseph Parks
Loud Stone .... Gian-Murray Gianino	Father .... Charles Shaw Robinson
Little Stone .... Carla Harting	Nasty and Interesting Man;
Big Stone .... Ramiz Monsef	Lord of the Underworld .... Mark Zeisler

Direction, Les Waters; scenery, Scott Bradley; costumes, Meg Neville; lighting, Russell H. Champa; sound, Bray Poor; casting, Tara Rubin Casting, Amy Potozkin, Paul Fouquet; stage management, Michael Suenkel; press, Barlow-Hartman, Michael Hartman, Tom D'Ambrosio, Ryan Ratelle.

Presented without intermission.

In her journey to the Underworld, Eurydice learns poignant lessons about the nature of longing and loss. First presentation of record was given by the Madison Repertory Theatre in Wisconsin (8/29–9/21/2003). The 2007–08 Off Broadway production was first presented at Berkeley Repertory Theatre (10/15–11/21/2004) before a run at Yale Repertory Theatre (9/28–10/14/2006). A 2007–08 *Best Plays* choice (see essay by Celia Wren in this volume).

Roundabout Theatre Company presentation of **Beyond Glory** (69). Solo performance piece by Stephen Lang; based on the book by Larry Smith. Todd Haimes artistic director, Harold Wolpert managing director, Julia C. Levy executive director, in association with the Goodman Theatre (Robert Falls artistic director, Roche Schulfer executive director),

Above-world: Maria Dizzia and Joseph Parks in eurydice. *Photo: Joan Marcus*

Valor incarnate: Stephen Lang in Beyond Glory. *Photo: Joan Marcus*

Tribute Productions and Steven Suskin, in the Laura Pels Theatre at the Harold and Miriam Steinberg Center for Theatre. Opened June 21, 2007. (Closed August 19, 2007)

Performed by Mr. Lang.

Military voices: John Bradford Lloyd, Matt Sincell, Anne Twomey.

Standby: Mr. Lang—Tony Campisi.

Direction, Robert Falls; scenery, Tony Cisek; costumes, David C. Woolard; lighting, Dan Covey; sound, Cecil Averett; music, Robert Kessler and Ethan Neuberg; projections, John Boesche; casting, Carrie Gardner; stage management, James FitzSimmons; press, Boneau/Bryan-Brown, Adrian Bryan-Brown, Matt Polk, Jessica Johnson.

Presented without intermission.

Solo performance piece in which one actor recalls stories of courage in battle that resulted in Medals of Honor bestowed on the characters represented. First presentation of record was given by Tribute Productions at the Women in Military Service for America Memorial Theatre in Arlington National Cemetery (4/2–5/31/2004). A later version was presented at the Goodman Theatre in Chicago (9/20–10/16/2005).

Elvis People (4). By Doug Grissom. Produced by Robert A. Rush at New World Stages 1. Opened June 21, 2007. (Closed June 23, 2007)

John L.; others	Jordan Gelber	Eddie; others	Nick Newell
Susie; others	Jenny Maguire	Mom;others	Nell Page
Stuart; others	David McCann	Dad; others	Ed Sala

Understudies: Kristen Bedard, Ned Noyes.

Direction, Henry Wishcamper; scenery, Cameron Anderson; costumes, Theresa Squire; lighting, Robert P. Robins; sound, Graham Johnson; video, Maya Ciarrocchi; wigs and hair, Erin Kennedy Lunsford; associate producer, Emilee MacDonald; casting, Stephanie Klapper Casting; stage management, Eric Tysinger; press, David Gersten and Associates, David Gersten, Kevin P. McAnarney, Jacob Langfelder.

Presented in two parts.

Homage in a variety of scenes to the hold Elvis Presley—man and myth—retains on American consciousness. First presentation of record was given at the Mill Mountain Playhouse in Roanoke, Virginia (2006).

The Public Theater production of **Romeo and Juliet** (12). Revival of the play by William Shakespeare. Oskar Eustis artistic director, Mara Manus executive director, at the Delacorte Theater. Opened June 24, 2007. (Closed July 8, 2007)

Escalus	Timothy D. Stickney	Capulet	Michael Cristofer
Mercutio	Christopher Evan Welch	Lady Capulet	Opal Alladin
Paris	Dan Colman	Juliet	Lauren Ambrose
Montague	George Bartenieff	Tybalt	Brian Tyree Henry
Lady Montague	Saidah Arrika Ekulona	Nurse	Camryn Manheim
Romeo	Oscar Isaac	Friar Laurence	Austin Pendleton
Benvolio	Owiso Odera	Friar John	Orville Mendoza

Ensemble: Ari Brand, Anthony Carrigan, Tiffany Danielle, Seth Duerr, Quincy Dunn-Baker, Christian Felix, Susan Hyon, Alexander Lane, Orville Mendoza, Jeffrey Omura, Lucas Papaelias, Alex Podulke, Mary Rasmussen, Cornelius Smith Jr., Alexander Sovronsky.

Musicians: Lucas Papaelias guitar; Alexander Sovronsky guitar, flute.

Understudies: Ms. Ambrose—Mary Rasmussen; Mr. Isaac—Cornelius Smith Jr.; Mses. Aladdin, Ekulona—Susan Hyon; Ms. Manheim—Saidah Arrika Ekulona; Mr. Pendleton—Orville Mendoza; Mr. Welch—Quincy Dunn-Baker; Mr. Stickney—Christian Felix; Messrs. Cristofer, Bartenieff, Mendoza—Seth Duerr; Mr. Henry—Alex Podulke; Messrs. Odera and Colman—Anthony Carrigan.

Swing: Tiffany Dannielle.

Direction, Michael Greif; choreography, Sergio Trujillo; scenery, Mark Wendland; costumes, Emilio Sosa; lighting, Donald Holder; sound, Acme Sound Partners; music, Michael Friedman; fight direction, Rick Sordelet; associate producers, Peter DuBois, Heidi Griffiths, Mandy Hackett; casting , Jordan Thaler and Heidi Griffiths; stage management, Michael McGoff; press, Sam Neuman.

Time: Long ago. Place: Verona. Presented in two parts.

Star-crossed lovers die needlessly due to a feud between their families. Believed to have been written in 1594 or early 1595, the first presentation of record was given in a nonextant adaptation by William Davenant (1662). As early as 1597, however, the title page of the first quarto edition claimed that the play had "been often (with great applause) plaid publiquely" by Hunsdon's Men, which were better known as the Chamberlain's Men except for a brief period (7/22/1596–3/17/1597) after Lord Hunsdon's death and before his son succeeded him as chamberlain. First presentation of record in what is now the US was given at the New Theatre in Chapel Street by David Douglass's Company of Comedians (3/4/1762) in an adaptation by David Garrick. Mrs. Douglass played Juliet and her son, Lewis Hallam II, played Romeo. When the 2007–08 production opened at the Delacorte, it was the first presentation of *Romeo and Juliet* in Central Park by the New York Shakespeare Festival in nearly 40 years (8/7–31/1968; 21 performances). In that era, the *Best Plays* editor counted all showings—including previews—as performances. Shows that were cancelled amid a performance due to rain were counted as ½ of a performance. In an attempt to be consistent with our other listings, *Best Plays* now counts performances from the press opening and excludes rain cancellations.

New York City Center Encores! Summer Stars presentation of **Gypsy** (14). Concert version of the musical with book by Arthur Laurents; music by Jule Styne; lyrics by Stephen Sondheim; based on the memoirs of Gypsy Rose Lee. Jack Viertel artistic director, at City Center. Opened July 14, 2007. (Closed July 29, 2007)

Uncle Jocko; Pastey	Jim Bracchitta	Balloon Girl	Katie Micha
Georgie; others	Bill Bateman	Bab Louise	Emma Rowley
Vladimir; others	Kyrian Friedenberg	Baby June	Sami Gayle

Rose	Patti LuPone	East St. Louis	Matty Price
Pop; Cigar	Bill Raymond	Waitress; Renee	Jessica Rush
Tap Dancer	Matthew Lobenhofer	Miss Cratchitt;	
Boy Scout; Charlie	Andy Richardson	Mazeppa	Nancy Opel
Weber; Phil	Brian Reddy	Agnes	Nicole Mangi
Herbie	Boyd Gaines	Majorie May	Alicia Sable
Dainty June	Leigh Ann Larkin	Geraldine	Mindy Dougherty
Louise	Laura Benanti	Edna Mae	Nancy Renee Braun
Yonkers	Pearce Wegener	Carol Ann	Sarah Marie Hicks
L.A.	Steve Konopelski	Betsey Ann	Beckley Andrews
Tulsa	Tony Yazbeck	Tesse Tura	Alison Fraser
Kansas	John Scacchetti	Electra	Marilyn Caskey
Little Rock	Geo Seery		

Direction, Mr. Laurents; choreography, Jerome Robbins, Bonnie Walker; scenery, James Youmans; costumes, Martin Pakledinaz; lighting, Howell Binkley; sound, Dan Moses Schreier; wigs and hair, Paul Huntley; orchestrations, Sid Ramen and Robert Ginzler; music coordinator, Seymour Red Press; music direction, Patrick Vaccariello; dance arrangements, John Kander; stage management, Craig Jacobs; press,

Time: Age of vaudeville. Place: Various theatrical locations. Presented in two parts.

The ultimate stage mother pushes her daughters into the limelight she would like to have for herself. First presentation of record was given in a pre-Broadway run at the Shubert Theatre in Philadelphia (4/13–5/16/1959). The original Broadway production opened at the Broadway Theatre (5/21/1959–7/9/1960) before taking a five-week hiatus and transferring to the Imperial Theatre (8/15/1960–3/25/1961; 702 total performances). The 2007–08 Encores! production later transferred to Broadway, became the fourth revival at that level and received 2008 Tony Awards for best actress (Ms. LuPone), featured actor (Mr. Gaines) and featured actress (Ms. Benanti) in a musical—the biggest sweep of any *Gypsy* production on Broadway. For past productions of *Gypsy*, Tony Awards were given to Angela Lansbury (1975) and Tyne Daly (1990) for their portrayals as Rose. The 1989–90 season also saw the show receive the 1990 Tony Award for best revival (Fran and Barry Weissler, Kathy Levin, Barry Brown). Ethel Merman and Bernadette Peters are the two Broadway Roses not to be honored with Tony Awards.

ACT I

Overture	Orchestra
"May We Entertain You"	Baby June, Baby Louise
"Some People"	Rose
"Some People" (Reprise)	Rose
"Small World"	Rose, Herbie
"Baby June and Her Newsboys"	Baby June, Baby Louise, Newsboys
"Have an Eggroll, Mr. Goldstone"	Rose, Herbie, June, Mr. Goldstone, Boys
"Little Lamb"	Louise
"You'll Never Get Away From Me"	Rose, Herbie
"Dainty June and Her Farmboys"	Dainty June, Farmboys
"If Momma Was Married"	Louise, June
"All I Need Is the Girl"	Tulsa, Louise
"Everything's Coming Up Roses"	Rose

ACT II

Entr'acte	Orchestra
"Madame Rose's Toreadorables"	Louise, Hollywood Blondes
"Together Wherever We Go"	Rose, Herbie, Louise
"You Gotta Get a Gimmick"	Mazeppa, Electra, Tessie Tura
"The Strip"	Louise
"Rose's Turn"	Rose

Irish Repertory Theatre production of **Tom Crean: Antarctic Explorer** (50). Solo performance piece by Aidan Dooley. Charlotte Moore artistic director, Ciarán O'Reilly producing director, in association with Northern Stage, Fairbank Productions and Play on Words Theatre Company, at the Irish Repertory Theatre. Opened July 22, 2007. (Closed September 9, 2007)

Performed by Mr. Dooley.

Direction, scenery and costumes, Mr. Dooley; lighting, Brian Nason; stage management, Janice M. Brandine; press, Shirley Herz Associates, Shirley Herz.

Presented in two parts.

A member of three expeditions that attempted to reach the South Pole tells stories of hardship and courage in the face of danger. Although source material is generally uncredited for this piece, Ciara Dwyer reported in a 2005 interview of Mr. Dooley for the *Sunday Independent* (Ireland) that Michael Smith's book *Tom Crean: Unsung Hero* (2000) "was an enormous help" in creating the work. First presentation of record was an abbreviated version given at the National Maritime Museum in Greenwich, London, as part of an exhibition on the race to the South Pole (9/14/2000). First US presentation of record was given at the Ground Floor Theatre during the 2003 New York International Fringe Festival (8/8–24/2003) where the production received an award in the solo performance category.

New York Theatre Workshop production of **The Black Eyed** (23). By Betty Shamieh. James C. Nicola artistic director, Lynn Moffat managing director. Opened July 31, 2007. (Closed August 19, 2007)

Aiesha	Aysan Celik	Architect	Jeanine Serralles
Tamam	Lameece Issaq	Delilah	Emily Swallow

Direction, Sam Gold; scenery, Paul Steinberg; costumes, Gabriel Berry; lighting, Jane Cox; sound, Darron L. West; stage management, Rachel Zack; press, Richard Kornberg and Associates, Don Summa.

Presented without intermission.

A discussion in a heavenly antechamber among Arab women from across time who debate the morality and social impact of terrorist attacks. First presentation of record was given at the Magic Theatre in San Francisco (5/14/2005) after numerous developmental readings.

The All-American Sport of Bipartisan Bashing (49). Solo performance piece by Will Durst. Produced by Hanging Chad Productions at New World Stages 5. Opened August 15, 2007. (Closed October 14, 2007)

Performed by Mr. Durst.

Direction, Eric Krebs; scenery, Peter Feuchtwanger; press, Keith Sherman and Associates, Keith Sherman, Brett Oberman.

Topical political humor performed by an experienced satirist.

The Public Theater production of **A Midsummer Night's Dream** (16). Revival of the play by William Shakespeare. Oskar Eustis artistic director, Mara Manus executive director, at the Delacorte Theater. Opened August 23, 2007. (Closed September 9, 2007)

Theseus	Daniel Oreskes	Francis Flute	Jesse Tyler Ferguson
Hippolyta	Opal Alladin	Robin Starveling	Ken Cheeseman
Egeus	George Morfogen	Tom Snout	Jason Antoon
Hermia	Mireille Enos	Snug	Keith Randolph Smith
Demetrius	Elliot Villar	Puck	Jon Michael Hill
Lysander	Austin Lysy	First Fairy	Chelsea Bacon
Helena	Martha Plimpton	Oberon	Keith David
Peter Quince	Tim Blake Nelson	Titania	Laila Robins
Nick Bottom	Jay O. Sanders	Philostrate	Herb Foster

Fairies: Simon Garratt, Erica Huang, Cassady Leonard, Lily Maketansky, Lina Silver, Jack Tartaglia.
Ensemble: Christine Corpuz, Ben Huber, Mallory Portnoy.
Understudies: Mses. Corpuz, Portnoy, Mr. Huber.

Direction, Daniel Sullivan; choreography, David Neumann; scenery, Eugene Lee; costumes, Ann Hould-Ward; lighting, Michael Chybowski; sound, Acme Sound Partners; music, Dan Moses Schreier; music direction, Steven Malone; associate producers, Peter DuBois, Mandy Hackett; stage management, James Latus; press, Candi Adams.

Presented in two parts.

Shakespeare's comic take on the transformative—and illusive—power of love. First presentation of record was an adaptation titled *A Play of Robin Goodfellow* at the court of King James I in 1604. The play is believed to have been written for performance at an aristocrat's wedding, probably in 1596, but no record survives. First US presentation of record, likely in the 1816 Frederic Reynolds adaptation as a comic opera, was given at New York's Park Theatre (11/9/1826 and 11/24/1826; 2 performances). The most recent production of *Midsummer* at the Delacorte was a co-production between the Public Theater—then known as the New York Shakespeare Festival—and Teatro do Ornitorrinco for Festival Latino (7/30–11/1991; 12 performances). In that era, the *Best Plays* editor counted all showings—including previews—as performances. In an attempt to be consistent with our other listings, *Best Plays* now counts performances from the press opening and excludes rain cancellations. The 1991 presentation was performed in Portugese without simultaneous translation.

Walmartopia (136). Transfer from Off Off Broadway of the musical with book, music and lyrics by Catherine Capellaro and Andrew Rohn; additional lyrics by Steve Tyska. Produced by WMTopia LLC at the Minetta Lane Theatre. Opened September 3, 2007. (Closed December 30, 2007)

Vicki Latrell	Cheryl Freeman	Dr. Normal; Otis	Stephen DeRosa
Maia Latrell	Nikki M. James	Darin; Alan	Brennen Leath
Miguel; Zeb	Bradley Dean	Sam Walton	Scotty Watson

Ensemble: Sarah Bolt, John Jellison, Andrew Polk, Pearl Sun, Helene Yorke.

Musicians: August Eriksmoen conductor, keyboards; Matt Beck guitar, banjo; David Richards saxophone, clarinet, bass clarinet; Gary Potts bass; Steve Bartosik drums, percussion.

Direction, Daniel Goldstein; choreography, Wendy Seyb; scenery, David Korins; costumes, Miranda Hoffman; lighting, Ben Stanton; sound, Tony Smolenski IV, Walter Trarbach; projections, Leah Gelpe; orchestrations and music direction, Mr. Eriksmoen; wigs and hair, Erin Kennedy Lunsford; stage management, Bess Marie Glorioso; press, O and M Company, Rick Miramontez, Philip Carrubba, Molly Barnett.

Presented in two parts.

A plucky mother in a future time confronts a soul-deadening corporation that threatens to overtake humanity. First presentation of record was given as a one-act by the Mercury Players Theater during its 2004 Playfest in Madison, Wisconsin (9/2004). The piece continued in development with runs in Madison's Bartell Theatre (12/2005–1/2006) and Capitol Theatre (3/2006) before opening at the Harry De Jur Playhouse during the 2006 New York International Fringe Festival (8/16–22/2006; 5 performances). The Fringe cast and creative team were replaced for the transfer to Off Broadway. Brennen Leath died of complications due to diabetes following the September 22 evening performance—the September 23 performances were cancelled. Mr. Leath was replaced October 10 by DeMond B. Nason.

ACT I

"A New Age Has Begun"	Company
"American Dream"	Vicki, Maia, Miguel, Company
"March of the Executives"	Smiley, Company
"Baby Girl"	Vicki, Maia
The Future Is Ours	Dr. Normal, Smiley
"A Woman's Place"	Vicki, Maia, Company
"Flash Them Bootstraps"	Sam, Company
"Heave-Ho"	Dr. Normal, Company

ACT II

"Walmartopia"	Company
"American Dream" (Reprise)	Zeb

"One-Stop Salvation" .... Counselor, Guard, Vicki, Maia, Zeb
"The Future Is Ours" (Reprise) .... Smiley, Lawrence
"Socialist Paradise" .... Vicki, Maia, Zeb
"These Bullets Are Freedom" .... Alan, Daphne, Otis, Company
(music and lyrics by Steve Tyska)
"Consume" and "American Dream" (Reprise) .... Sam, Zeb, Company
"What Kind of Mother?" .... Vicki, Maia
"Outside the Big Box" .... Company

Brooklyn Academy of Music presentation of the **Royal Shakespeare Company** production of **King Lear** (14). Revival of the play by William Shakespeare. Alan H. Fishman chairman, Karen Brooks Hopkins president, Joseph V. Melillo executive producer at the Harvey Theater. Opened September 11, 2007. (Closed September 30, 2007)

King Lear..................................... Ian McKellen	Kent .... Jonathan Hyde
Goneril .... Frances Barber	Gloucester .... William Gaunt
Regan .... Monica Dolan	Edmund .... Philip Winchester
Cordelia ....Romola Garai		

Ensemble: Julian Harries, Guy Williams, Ben Addis, Peter Hinton, Ben Meyjes, Sylvester McCoy.

Direction, Trevor Nunn; scenery and costumes, Christopher Oram; lighting, Neil Austin; sound, Fergus O'Hare; music, Steven Edis; music direction, Jeff Moore; fight direction, Malcolm Ranson; stage management, Simon Ash; press, Sandy Sawotka, Fatima Kafele, John Wyszniewski, Christina Norris.

Presented in two parts.

An aged king disrupts all of civilized society when he injudiciously divides his kingdom and sets in motion grave events. First presentation of record at the court of James I (12/26/1606). First presentation of record in this country at New York's Theatre in Nassau Street (1/14/1754) was influenced by Nahum Tate's 1681 adaptation of *King Lear*. First US presentation of the restored Shakespeare version was given by William Charles Macready at the Park Theatre (9/27/1844). More recent productions have featured Kevin Kline (The Public Theater: 3/7–25/2007; 18 performances) and Christopher Plummer (Lincoln Center Theater: 3/4–4/18/2004; 33 performances) as the old king.

Brooklyn Academy of Music presentation of the **Royal Shakespeare Company** production of **The Seagull** (9). Revival of the play by Anton Chekhov. Alan H. Fishman chairman, Karen Brooks Hopkins president, Joseph V. Melillo executive producer at the Harvey Theater. Opened September 12, 2007. (Closed September 29, 2007)

Arkadina .... Frances Barber	Polina .... Melanie Jessop
Konstantin ....Richard Goulding	Masha .... Monica Dolan
Sorin .... Ian McKellen;	Trigorin .... Gerald Kyd
William Gaunt	Dorn .... Jonathan Hyde
Nina ....Romola Garai	Medvedenko................................. Ben Meyjes
Shamrayev .... Guy Williams		

Direction, Trevor Nunn; scenery and costumes, Christopher Oram; lighting, Neil Austin; sound, Fergus O'Hare; music, Steven Edis; music direction, Jeff Moore; fight direction, Malcolm Ranson; stage management, Simon Ash; press, Sandy Sawotka, Fatima Kafele, John Wyszniewski, Christina Norris.

Presented in two parts.

A self-obsessed actress whose time is nearly past ignores the crisis of her grown son as she tends to her young lover. First US presentation of record was given in Russian at the Russian Lyceum (12/22/1905). First presentation of record in English was given in London by the Adelphi Play Society at the Little Theatre (3/31/1912). The first New York presentation of record in English was given by the Washington Square Players at the Bandbox Theatre (5/22/1916).

Modern pietá: Janel Moloney and Jeremy Shamos in 100 Saints You Should Know. *Photo: Joan Marcus*

Playwrights Horizons production of **100 Saints You Should Know** (16). By Kate Fodor. Tim Sanford artistic director, Leslie Marcus managing director, William Russo general manager, in the Mainstage Theater. Opened September 18, 2007. (Closed September 30, 2007)

Theresa	Janel Moloney	Colleen	Lois Smith
Matthew	Jeremy Shamos	Garrett	Will Rogers
Abby	Zoe Kazan		

Direction, Ethan McSweeny; scenery, Rachel Hauck; costumes, Mimi O'Donnell; lighting, Jane Cox; sound, Matt Hubbs; casting, Alaine Alldaffer; stage management, Michaella K. McCoy; press, the Publicity Office, Marc Thibodeau, Michael S. Borowski, Jeremy Shaffer, Matthew Fasano.

Presented in two parts.

Crises of faith bring people together and divide them. First presentation of record was given by Steppenwolf Theatre Company in Chicago (7/20–8/12/2006). A 2007–08 *Best Plays* choice (see essay by John Istel in this volume).

The Public Theater presentation of **Hair: The American Tribal Love-Rock Musical** (3). Concert version of the musical with book and lyrics by James Rado and Gerome Ragni; music by Galt McDermot. Oskar Eustis artistic director, Mara Manus executive director, at the Delacorte Theater. Opened September 22, 2007. (Closed September 24, 2007)

Crissy .... Allison Case	Sheila .... Karen Olivo
Claude .... Jonathan Groff	Black Boys Trio; Tribe .... Alisan Porter
Father; Margaret Meade .... Andrew Kober	Black Boys Trio; Tribe .... Megan Reinking
Mother .... Megan Lawrence	Woof .... Bryce Ryness
White Boys Trio; Tribe .... Nicole Lewis	White Boys Trio; Tribe .... Saycon Sengbloh
Dionne .... Patina Miller	Jeanie .... Kacie Sheik
Hud .... Darius Nichols	Berger .... Will Swenson

Tribe: Ato Blankson-Wood, Steel Burkhardt, Lauren Elder, Allison Guinn, Anthony Hollock, Kaitlin Kiyan, John Moauro, Brandon Pearson, Paris Remillard, Maya Sharpe, Theo Stockman, Tommar Wilson.

Direction, Diane Paulus; choreography, Karole Armitage; scenery, Scott Pask; costumes, Michael McDonald; lighting, Michael Chybowski; sound, Acme Sound Partners; music direction, Rob Fisher; stage management, Nancy Harrington; press, Candi Adams.

Concert version of the musical dedicated to peace, love and eternal joy. First presentation of record was also the first production in the Public Theater's new building on Lafayette Street in Greenwich Village. *Hair* was performed in the Anspacher Theater and though it began performances October 17, 1967—and that was the date of opening in advertisements—those early performances were previews during which a fair amount of creative turbulence reigned. Critics were asked not to publish before the October 29, 1967, performance. That date is, therefore, the "first presentation of record" (10/29–12/10/1967; 49 performances). The production transferred, under the auspices of Michael Butler, to the nightclub Cheetah (12/22/1967–1/28/1968; 45 performances). After a hunt for a suitable venue and a change of directors—Gerald Freedman was replaced by Tom O'Horgan—the Broadway production opened at the Biltmore Theatre (4/29/1968–7/1/1972; 1,750 performances).

ACT I

"Aquarius" .... Dionne, Tribe
"Donna" .... Berger, Tribe
"Hashish" .... Tribe
"Sodomy" .... Woof, Tribe
"Colored Spade" .... Hud, Tribe
"Manchester, England" .... Claude, Tribe
"I'm Black" .... Hud, Woof, Berger, Claude, Tribe
"Ain't Got No" .... Woof, Hud, Dionne, Tribe
"Sheila Franklin" .... Tribe
"I Believe in Love" .... Sheila, Trio
"Ain't Got No Grass" .... Tribe
"Air" .... Jeanie, Crissy, Dionne
"The Stone Age" .... Berger
"I Got Life" .... Claude, Tribe
"Initials" .... Tribe
"Going Down" .... Berger, Tribe
"Hair" .... Claude, Berger, Tribe
"My Conviction" .... Margaret Mead
"Easy to Be Hard" .... Sheila
"Don't Put It Down" .... Berger, Woof, Tribe Member
"Frank Mills" .... Crissy
"Hare Krishna" .... Tribe
"Where Do I Go" .... Claude and Tribe

ACT II

"Electric Blues" .... Tribe Members
"Oh Great God of Power" .... Tribe
"Black Boys" .... Tribe Members
"White Boys" .... Dionne, Tribe Members
"Walking in Space" .... Tribe
"Minuet" .... Orchestra

"Yes, I's Finished on Y'alls Farmlands" .... Hud, Tribe Members
"Four Score and Seven Years Ago"; "Abie Baby" .... Abraham Lincoln,
Hud, Tribe Members
"Give Up All" .... Buddahdalirama, Woof,
Sheila, Crissy
"Three-Five-Zero-Zero" .... Tribe
"What a Piece of Work Is Man" .... Tribe Members, Claude
"How Dare They Try" .... Tribe
"Good Morning, Starshine" .... Sheila, Tribe
"Ain't Got No" (Reprise) .... Claude, Tribe
"The Flesh Failures" .... Claude, Sheila,
Dionne, Woof
"Eyes Look Your Last" .... Tribe
"Let the Sun Shine In" .... Tribe

New York Theatre Workshop presentation of **The Misanthrope** (55). Revival of the play by Molière; adapted by Tony Harrison. James C. Nicola artistic director, Lynn Moffat managing director. Opened September 24, 2007. (Closed November 11, 2007)

Eliante	Quincy Tyler Bernstine	Acaste	Joan MacIntosh
Clitandre	Jason C. Brown	Oronte	Alfredo Narciso
Alceste	Bill Camp	Philinte	Thomas Jay Ryan
Arsinoé	Amelia Campbell	Célimène	Jeanine Serralles

Direction, Ivo van Hove; scenery and lighting, Jan Versweyveld; costumes, Emilio Sosa; sound, Raul Vincent Enriquez; video, Tal Yarden; dramaturgy, Bart van den Eynde; stage management, Larry K. Ash; press, Richard Kornberg and Associates, Don Summa.

Time: The present. Presented without intermission.

Modern adaptation of Molière's satire on the corruptions of everyday life in which an actor literally lies with garbage. First presentation of the 1666 play in English was given at Broadway's New Amsterdam Theatre with Richard Mansfield as Alceste (4/10–15/1905; 8 performances).

Celia: The Life and Music of Celia Cruz (269). Musical with book by Carmen Rivera and Candido Tirado; music and lyrics by various artists. Produced by Henry Cardenas and David Maldonado at New World Stages 2. Opened September 26, 2007. (Closed May 25, 2008)

Celia Cruz	Xiomara Laugart	Ollita; Assistant	Anissa Gathers
Pedro Knight	Modesto Lacén	Tia Ana; others	Sunilda Caraballo
Nurse	Pedro Capó	Simon; others	Elvis Nolasco
Woman	Selenis Leyva	Announcer; others	Wilson Mendieta

Ensemble: Grizel "Chachi" Del Valle, Sekou McMiller.

Musicians: Isidro Infante conductor, piano; Nelson Jaime trumpet, keyboards; Raul Agráz trumpet; Diomedes Matos bass; Luisito Quinero timbal, percussion; Robert Quintero congas, percussion; Nelson González trés, bongos.

Understudies: Mses. Laugart, Leyva—Anissa Gathers; Ms. Leyva—Sunilda Caraballo; Mr. Lacén—Elvis Nolasco; Mr. Capó—Wilson Mendieta.

Direction, Jaime Azpilicueta; choreography, Maria Torres; scenery, Narelle Sissons; costumes, Haydée Morales; lighting, Sarah Sidman; sound, Bernard Fox; orchestrations, arrangements and music direction, Mr. Infante; projections, Jan Hartley; hair, Ruth Sanchez; executive producer, Daddy Yankee; associate producer, Gerry Fojo; casting, Orpheus Group Casting, Ellyn Long Marshall and Maria E. Nelson; stage management, Elis C. Arroyo; press, Creativelink, Inc., Bianca LaSalle, Soldanela Rivera, Javier Lopez.

Presented in two parts.

Musical based on the life and music of the "Queen of Salsa." Six performances per week were performed in Spanish, two in English.

ACT I

"Toro Mata" .... Celia, Company
"Drume Negrita"; "Canto Lucumí" .... Ollita
"Cumbachero" .... Woman, Celia
"Caramelos" .... Celia
"Burundanga"; "El Yerbero Moderno"; "Que Bueno Baila Usted" .... Celia
"Mexico Lindo" .... Celia
"Cao Cao Maní Picao" .... Celia
"Tu Voz" .... Celia
"Drume Negrita" .... Woman, Ollita
"La Guarachera" .... Celia
"Bemba Colorá" .... Celia, Company

ACT II

"Usted Abusó" .... Woman, Pedro, Nurse
"Isadora Duncan"; "Encantigo"; Guantanamera" .... Celia
"Las Caras Lindas" .... Ollita
"Quimbara" .... Celia
"Cúcala" .... Nurse, Celia
"Canto a la Habana" .... Celia
"Dos Jueyes" .... Celia
"Cuba" .... Ollita
"Soy Antillana"; "La Dicha Mia"; "Cuando Volverás" .... Celia
"Celia's Oye Coma Va" .... Celia
"El Guabá" .... Celia
"Gracias" .... Nurse
"La Negra Tiene Tumbao" .... Celia
"Yo Viviré" .... Celia
"La Vida es un Carnaval" .... Celia, Company

Three Mo' Tenors (142). Musical revue by Marion J. Caffey. Produced by Willette Murphy Klausner at the Little Shubert. Opened September 27, 2007. (Closed January 27, 2008)

Performed by James N. Berger Jr., Duane A. Moody, Victor Robertson; or Kenneth D. Alston Jr., Ramone Diggs, Phumzile Sojola.

Musicians: Keith Burton, Carl Carter, Fabiola Leon, Etienn Litel, Steve Williams.

Direction and choreography, Mr. Caffey; scenery, Michael Carnahan; costumes, Gail Cooper-Hecht; lighting, Richard Winkler; sound, Domonic Sack; music supervision, arrangements and orchestrations, Joseph Joubert; additional arrangements, Danny Holgate, Michael McElroy; music direction, Mr. Burton; press, Keith Sherman and Associates, Scott Klein.

Presented in two parts.

An African-American musical answer to the famed tenors José Carreras, Placido Domingo and Luciano Pavarotti in which the performers sing classical, pop, blues, Broadway and spirituals. First presentation of record was given at the Emerson Majestic Theatre in Boston (5/17–19/2001; 3 performances) in preparation for a tour and public television special. The original tenors in the group were Victor Trent Cook, Roderick Dixon and Thomas Young.

Forbidden Broadway: Rude Awakening (200). Musical revue by Gerard Alessandrini. Produced by John Freedson, Harriet Yellin, Jon B. Platt, in association with Gary Hoffman, Jerry Kravat and Masakazu Shibaoka at the 47th Street Theatre. Opened October 2, 2007. (Closed March 24, 2008)

Performed by Jared Bradshaw, Janet Dickinson, James Donegan, Valerie Fagan, Steve Saari (piano).

Direction, Mr. Alessandrini and Phillip George; scenery, Megan K. Halpern; costumes, Alvin Colt; lighting, Marc Janowitz; sound, Timothy Owen Mazur and Erich Bechtel; music direction, David Caldwell; stage management, Jim Griffith; press, Keith Sherman and Associates, Glenna Freedman, DJ Martin.

Presented in two parts.

A new edition of the long-running spoof of popular theatrical productions and personages. Prior to its opening, there was a title change from *Forbidden Broadway: The Roast of Utopia*. The closing date marks a spring hiatus with a re-opening planned for summer 2008. See Long Runs Off Broadway section of this volume for information on earlier productions.

Greetings From Yorkville (35). Musical with book and lyrics by Anya Turner; music and lyrics by Robert Grusecki. Produced by Who Knows Productions at the Soho Playhouse. Opened October 4, 2007. (Closed November 4, 2007)

Performed by Ms. Turner and Mr. Grusecki.

Direction, Thommie Walsh and Baayork Lee; scenery, Jesse Poleshuck; costumes, Dona Granata; lighting, Natasha Katz; sound, David Stollings; press, Shirley Herz Associates, Shirley Herz, Daniel DeMello.

Presented in two parts.

Autobiographical tale of a songwriting team trying to make it in show business. First presentation of record was given at the Woodstock Fringe Festival in New York (9/2004).

Musical Numbers included: "Greetings From Yorkville," "Secret Song," "Ordinary People," "It's Called a Piano," "The Road," "Greetings From Yorkville" (Reprise), "Life is Good."

The Rise of Dorothy Hale (137). By Myra Bairstow. Produced by Judson Moore, Paolo Montalban, Asset Management Partners, Edmund Gaynes, Aridyne Productions, at St. Luke's Theatre. Opened October 4, 2007. (Closed January 27, 2008)

Frank DeLuca	Michael Badalucco	Dorothy Hale	Laura Koffman
Mitch Davenport	Patrick Boll	Harry Hopkins	Mark LaMura
Frida Kahlo	Sarita Choudhury	Clare Boothe Luce	Sarah Wynter

Direction, Pamela Hall; scenery, Josh Iacovelli; costumes, Rebecca J. Bernstein; lighting, Graham Kindred; casting, Judy Henderson; stage management, C.J. Thom; press, David Gersten and Associates, David Gersten.

Understudy: Messrs. Badalucco, LaMura, Boll—Nicholas Martin-Smith.

Presented in two parts.

Mystery in which a suspect suicide leads to questions about certain relationships among historically prominent persons. Inspired by the 1939 Frida Kahlo painting, *The Suicide of Dorothy Hale*.

*Jump (269). By Yegam Theatre Company. Produced by CAMI Ventures, in association with Yegam Theatre Company, Amuse, New York Networks and Hobijisu, at the Union Square Theatre. Opened October 7, 2007.

Old Man	Woon-Yong Lee	Daughter	Hee-Jeong Hwang
Grandfather	Sang-Cheul Lee	Son-in-Law	Byung-Eun Yoo
Father	Cheol-Ho Lim	Burglar 1	Yun-Gab Hong
Mother	Hyun-Ju Kim	Burglar 2	Seung-Youl Lee
Uncle	Young-Jo Choi		

Alternate cast: Kyung-Ae Hong, Chang-Young Kim, Dong-Kyun Kim, Joo-Sun Kim, Kyung-Hyun Kim, Tae-Sung Kim, Han-Chang Lim.

Direction, Chul-Ki Chol; choreography, Gye-Hwan Park; scenery, Tae-Young Kim; costumes, Dolsilnai; lighting, Sung-Bin Lim and Benjamin Pearcy; sound, Soo-Yong Lee. music, Dong-Joon Lee; press, O and M Company, Rick Miramontez, Molly Barnett.

Presented without intermission.

Slapstick comedy, acrobatics and martial arts spectacle. First presentation of record was given at the Woolim Theater of Seoul (2003).

National Theatre of Greece presentation of **Electra** (6). Revival of the play by Sophocles; translated into modern Greek by Minos Volanakis. Yannis Houvardas artistic director, at City Center. Opened October 10, 2007. (Closed October 14, 2007)

Tutor	Yannis Fertis	Chrysothemis	Kora Karvouni
Orestes	Apostolis Totsikas	Clytemnestra	Karyofyllia Karaabeti
Pylades	Miltos Sotiriadis	Aegisthus	Lazaros Georgakopoulos
Electra	Stefania Goulioti	Musician	Samuel Marieri

Chorus: Margarita Amarantidi, Errika Bigiou, Katerina Daskalaki, Kika Georgiou, Ioanna Zoi Karavasili, Irini Kirmizaki, Christina Maxouri, Lida Maniatakou, Marili Milia, Yota Militsi, Georgina Palaiothodorou, Maria Saltiri, Pinelopi Sergounioti, Mara Vlachaki.

Direction, Peter Stein; choreography, Lia Tsolaki, scenery and costumes, Dionissis Fotopoulos; lighting, Japhy Weideman; music, Alessando Nidi; press, Richard Kornberg and Associates, Laura Kaplow-Goldman.

Presented without intermission.

Modern Greek version of the classic tragedy centering on filial passion and revenge. Believed to have been written toward the end of the fifth century before the common era.

Playwrights Horizons production of **A Feminine Ending** (31). By Sarah Treem. Tim Sanford artistic director, Leslie Marcus managing director, William Russo general manager, in the Peter Jay Sharp Theater. Opened October 17, 2007. (Closed November 11, 2007)

Amanda	Gillian Jacobs	David	Richard Masur
Jack	Alec Beard	Billy	Joe Paulik
Kim	Marsha Mason		

Direction, Blair Brown; scenery, Cameron Anderson; costumes, Michael Krass; lighting, Ben Stanton; sound and music, Obadiah Eaves; casting, Alaine Alldaffer; stage management, Robyn

Define yourself: Richard Masur and Gillian Jacobs in A Feminine Ending. *Photo: Joan Marcus*

Call waiting: Andre Royo in A View From 151st Street. *Photo: Monique Carboni*

Henry; press, the Publicity Office, Marc Thibodeau, Michael S. Borowski, Jeremy Shaffer, Matthew Fasano.

Time: The present. Place: Brooklyn, New York, and New Hampshire. Presented without intermission.

A talented young female composer negotiates the difficulties that exist on her path to artistic development and her detours into personal relationships. First presentation of record was given during Just Add Water/West: A Playwrights' Festival at Portland Center Stage in Oregon (7/22–23/2006).

Labyrinth Theater Company production of **A View From 151st Street** (22). By Bob Glaudini. John Ortiz artistic director, Philip Seymour Hoffman co-artistic director, John Gould Rubin co-artistic director and executive director, in LuEsther Hall at the Public Theater. Opened October 18, 2007. (Closed November 4, 2007)

Dwight	Gbenga Akinnagbe	Monroe	Russell G. Jones
Lena	Liza Colón-Zayas	Mara	Marisa Malone
Delroy	Craig "muMs" Grant	Irene	Elizabeth Rodriguez
Daniel	Juan Carlos Hernandez	Ray	Andre Royo

Musicians: Brian Noll conductor; Andrew Emer, Nir Felder, Q.

Direction, Peter DuBois; scenery, David Korins; costumes, Mimi O'Donnell; lighting, Japhy Weideman; sound, Bart Fasbender; music, Michael Cain; lyrics, Mr. Glaudini; music direction, Paul J. Thompson; stage management, Nicola Rossini; press, O and M Company, Rick Miramontez, Philip Carrubba.

Time: The present: Place: New York City. Presented in two parts.

The mean streets of upper Manhattan are populated by people who combat drugs (or use them), engage in violence (or suffer from it) and yearn for better ways to communicate.

Die Mommie Die! (97). By Charles Busch. Produced by Daryl Roth and Bob Boyett at New World Stages 1. Opened October 21, 2007. (Closed January 13, 2008)

Bootsie Carp	Kristine Nielsen	Angela Arden	Charles Busch
Edith Sussman	Ashley Morris	Sol Sussman	Bob Ari
Tony Parker	Chris Hoch	Lance Sussman	Van Hansis

Standbys: Mses. Nielsen, Morris—Melinda Melfrich.

Direction, Carl Andress; scenery, Michael Anania; costumes, Michael Bottari, Ronald Case, Jessica Jahn; lighting, Ben Stanton; sound, Ken Hypes; music, Lewis Flinn; projections, Chris Kateff; wigs, Katherine Carr; associate producers, Elyse Pasquale, Tim Levy; casting, Mark Simon; stage management, Donald William Myers; press, the Publicity Office, Jeremy Shaffer.

Time: 1967. Place: Beverly Hills, California. Presented without intermission.

Comic thriller in which the cross-dressed leading lady is a modern woman whose homicidal impulses echo Greek tragedy. First presentation of record was given at the Coast Playhouse in West Hollywood under the title *Die! Mommy! Die!* (7/16–8/8/1999). It was later rendered as a 2003 film, with the current spelling of the title.

Roundabout Theatre Company production of **The Overwhelming** (72). By J.T. Rogers. Todd Haimes artistic director, Harold Wolpert managing director, Julia C. Levy executive director, in the Laura Pels Theatre at the Harold and Miriam Steinberg Center for Theatre. Opened October 23, 2007. (Closed December 23, 2007)

Charles Woolsey;		Jack Exley	Sam Robards
Zimbawean Doctor	James Rebhorn	Joseph Gasana	Ron Cephas Jones

Under siege: Sam Robards, Michael Stahl-David, Linda Powell in The Overwhelming. *Photo: Joan Marcus*

Jean-Claude Buisson;
  Jan Verbeçk .... Boris McGiver
Linda White-Keeler .... Linda Powell
Geoffrey Exley .... Michael Stahl-David
Samuel Mizinga .... Charles Parnell

Rwandan Man; others .... Owiso Odera
Gérard .... Chris Chalk
Rwandan Doctor;
  Elise Kayitesi .... Sharon Washington
Emiritha .... Tisola Logan

Understudies: Mses. Powell, Washington, Logan—Chinasa Ogbuagu; Mr. Rebhorn—Peter Bradbury; Mr. Stahl-David—Christopher Abbott; Messrs. Parnell, Jones—Andrew Stewart-Jones; Messrs. Rebhorn, McGiver—Daniel Stewart; Messrs. Chalk, Odera—Maduka Steady.

Direction, Max Stafford-Clark; scenery, Tim Shortall; costumes, Tobin Ost; lighting, David Weiner; sound, Gareth Fry; hair, Justen M. Brosnan; fight direction, Rick Sordelet; casting, Carrie Gardner; stage management, Pat Sosnow; press, Boneau/Bryan-Brown, Adrian Bryan-Brown, Matt Polk, Jessica Johnson.

Time: Early 1994. Place: Kigali, Rwanda. Presented in two parts.

An American family caught in the swirl of political and social turbulence as Rwanda is about to erupt with genocide. First presentation of record was given at the National Theatre in London (5/17–8/30/2006).

*Fuerzabruta (254). Performance piece by Diqui James. Produced by Concert Productions International, Fuerzabruta, Ozono, David Binder at the Daryl Roth Theatre. Opened October 24, 2007.

Performed by Freddy Bosche, Hallie Bulleit, Daniel Case, Michael Hollick, Joshua Kobak, Gwyneth Larsen, Tamara Levinson, Rose Mallare, Brooke Miyasaki, Jon Morris, Jason Novak, Marlyn Ortiz, Kepani Salgado-Ramos.

Direction, Mr. James; costumes, Andrea Matio; lighting, Edi Pampini; sound, Herman Nupieri; music Gaby Kerpel; automation, Alberto Figueiras; stage management, Jeff Benish; press, the Karpel Group, Bridget Klapinski.

Presented without intermission.

Spectacle that demands audience participation in a whirl of sensory stimulation. First presentation of record was given at Buenos Aires (5/2005) before runs in Lisbon and London.

Manhattan Theatre Club production of **The Receptionist** (72). By Adam Bock. Lynne Meadow artistic director, Daniel Sullivan acting artistic director, Barry Grove executive director, at City Center Stage I. Opened October 30, 2007. (Closed December 30, 2007)

Mr. Dart ....Josh Charles
Mr. Raymond .... Robert Foxworth

Beverly Wilkins ....Jayne Houdyshell
Lorraine Taylor .... Kendra Kassebaum

Understudies: Ms. Houdyshell—Susan E. Finch; Messrs. Charles, Foxworth—Tom Hammond; Ms. Kassebaum—Danielle Skraastad.

Direction, Joe Mantello; scenery, David Korins; costumes, Jane Greenwood; lighting, Brian MacDevitt; sound, Darron L. West; casting, David Caparelliotis; stage management, Martha Donaldson; press, Boneau/Bryan-Brown, Chris Boneau, Aaron Meier, Steven Padla, Heath Schwartz, Christine Olver.

Presented without intermission.

It is business as usual for the woman who answers the office phones, but her dawning understanding of what "business" means strikes fear into her heart. First presentation of record was given during a staged reading at the Perry Mansfield New Works Festival (6/16/2006) in Steamboat Springs before a similar staging during the National Playwrights' Conference at the Eugene O'Neill Theater Center (7/13/2006). A 2007–08 *Best Plays* choice (see essay by David Cote in this volume).

Frankenstein (45). Musical with book and lyrics by Jeffrey Jackson; music by Mark Baron; adapted by Gary P. Cohen; based on the book by Mary Shelley. Produced by Gerald Goehring, Douglas C. Evans, Michael F. Mitri, David S. Stone, in association with Barbara and Emery Olcott, at 37 Arts. Opened November 1, 2007. (Closed December 9, 2007)

Victor Frankenstein .... Hunter Foster
Justine Moritz .... Mandy Bruno
Henry Clerval .... Jim Stanek
Elizabeth Lavenza .... Christiane Noll
The Creature .... Steve Blanchard
Caroline .... Becky Barta
Agatha; others .... Erin Clark
William .... Struan Erlenborn
Alphonse .... Eric Michael Gillett
Capt. Walton; Blind Man .... Aaron Serotsky

Ensemble: Nick Cartell, Leslie Henstock, Patrick Mellen.

Musicians: Stephen Purdy conductor, keyboard; John Bowen keyboard; Martyn Axe keyboard; Alan Cohen guitar; Hugh Mason bass; Greg Giannascoli drums, percussion.

Direction, Bill Fennelly; choreography, Kelly Devine; scenery, Kevin Judge; costumes, Emily Pepper; lighting, Thom Weaver; sound, Domonic Sack and Carl Casella; projections, Michael Clark, orchestrations, Richard DeRosa and Mr. Baron; music direction, Stephen Purdy; press, Keith Sherman and Associates.

Presented in two parts.

A new musical version of the familiar tale from the pen of Mary Shelley.

ACT I

Prelude .... Capt. Walton, Victor, Company
"A Golden Age" .... Company
"Amen" .... Condemned Man, Victor, Company
"Birth to My Creation" .... Victor
"Dear Victor" .... Elizabeth, Victor
"The Hands of Time" .... Elizabeth, Henry, Justine, William
"Your Father's Eyes" .... Alphonse
"The Creature's Tale" .... Creature
"The Waking Nightmare" .... Creature

Risqué business: Natalie Venetia Belcon and Marc Kudisch in The Glorious Ones. *Photo: Joan Marcus*

"The Music of Love" .... Blind Man, Agatha, Creature
"Why?" .... William, Justine, Creature,
Victor, Company
"The Proposition" .... Victor, Creature

ACT II

"Happier Day" .... Company
"The Modern Prometheus" .... Victor, Henry, Creature
"The Hands of Time" (Reprise) .... Elizabeth, Victor
"The Workings of the Heart" .... Elizabeth, Victor, Company
"An Angel's Embrace" .... Creature
"The Workings of the Heart" (Reprise) .... Victor
"Your Father's Eyes" (Reprise) .... Alphonse
"These Hands" .... Creature
"The Chase" .... Victor, Company
"The Coming of the Dawn" .... Victor
"Amen" (Reprise) .... Creature, Victor
"The Sorrow Born of Dreams" .... Company

Lincoln Center Theater production of **The Glorious Ones** (72). Musical with book and lyrics by Lynn Ahrens; music by Stephen Flaherty; based on the novel by Francine Prose. André Bishop artistic director, Bernard Gersten executive producer, in the Mitzi E. Newhouse Theater. Opened November 5, 2007. (Closed January 6, 2008)

Flaminio Scala .... Marc Kudisch
Pantalone .... David Patrick Kelly
Columbina .... Natalie Venetia Belcon
Armanda Ragusa .... Julyana Soelistyo
Dottore .... John Kassir
Isabella Andreini; Boy Actor .... Erin Davie
Francesco Andreini;
Comic Servant .... Jeremy Webb

Orchestra: David Holcenberg conductor, piano; Deborah Abramson associate conductor, keyboard 2; Cenovia Cummins violin, mandolin; Katie Schlaikjer cello; Scott Shachter reeds; Will De Vos, French horn; Marc Schmied bass; Norbert Goldberg percussion.

Understudies: Mses. Belcon, Davie—Ana Maria Andricain; Messrs. Kassir, Kelly—Scott Robertson; Mr. Kudisch—Neal Benari; Ms. Soelistyo—Nitya Vidyasagar; Mr. Webb—Chris Peluso.

Direction and choreography, Graciela Daniele; scenery, Daniel Ostling; costumes, Mara Blumenfeld; lighting, Stephen Strawbridge; sound, Scott Stauffer; orchestrations, Michael Starobin; vocal arrangements, Mr. Flaherty; music direction, Mr. Holcenberg; music coordination, John Miller; casting, Stanczyk/Cherpakov Casting; stage management, Michael Brunner; press, Philip Rinaldi, Barbara Carroll.

Time: Late 1500s and beyond. Place: The streets of Italy. Presented without intermission.

A company of strolling players live and love as members of the group create the archetypes for *commedia dell'arte*. First presentation of record was given at Pittsburgh Public Theater (4/28–5/20/2007).

MUSICAL NUMBERS

Prologue: "The Glorious Ones" .... Flaminio, Company
"Making Love" .... Columbina, Flaminio, Company
"Pantalone Alone" .... Pantalone
"The Comedy of Love" .... Pantalone, Armanda Ragusa, Company
Scenario: "The Madness of Columbina" .... Company
"The Glorious Ones" (Reprise) .... Flaminio, Francesco
"Madness to Act" .... Flaminio
"Absalom" .... Francesco
"The Invitation to France" .... Dottore
"Flaminio Scala's Historical Journey to France" .... Company
"Three Lazzi" .... Company
"Armanda's Tarantella" .... Armanda, Men
"Improvisation" .... Flaminio
"The World She Writes" .... Isabella

Family plan: Gilbert Owuor and Brian Tyree Henry in The Brothers Size. Photo: Michal Daniel

"Opposite You" .... Francesco, Isabella
"My Body Wasn't Why" .... Columbina
Scenario: "The Madness of Isabella" .... Company
"Flaminio Scala's Ominous Dream" .... Flaminio, Company
"The World She Writes" (Reprise) .... Francesco
"Rise and Fall" .... Dottore, Company
"The Moon Woman" (A Play) .... Company
"The Glorious Ones" (Reprise) .... Flaminio
"I Was Here" .... Flaminio
"Armanda's Sack" .... Armanda, Company
Finale: "The Comedy of Love" .... Company

The Public Theater production of **The Brothers Size** (56). By Tarell Alvin McCraney. Oskar Eustis artistic director, Mara Manus executive director, in association with the Foundry Theatre (Melanie Joseph artistic director), in the Shiva Theater. Opened November 6, 2007. (Closed December 23, 2007)

Ogun .... Gilbert Owuor   Elegba .... Elliot Villar
Oshoosi .... Brian Tyree Henry   Percussion .... Jonathan M. Pratt

Direction, Tea Alagic; scenery, Peter Ksander and Douglas Stein; costumes, Zane Pihlstrom; lighting, Burke Brown; music, Vincent Olivieri and Mr. Pratt; stage management, Barbara Reo; press, Candi Adams, Sam Neuman.

Presented without intermission.

A pair of African-American brothers face tribulations of temptation and frustration when a third man's presence threatens the family unit. First presentation of record was given during the 2007 Under the Radar Festival at the Public Theater (1/19–28/2007).

Second Stage Theatre production of **Peter and Jerry** (57). By Edward Albee. Carole Rothman artistic director, Ellen Richard executive director, at Second Stage Theatre. Opened November 11, 2007. (Closed December 30, 2007)

Homelife		*The Zoo*	
Ann	Johanna Day	Peter	Bill Pullman
Peter	Bill Pullman	Jerry	Dallas Roberts

Direction, Pam MacKinnon; scenery, Neil Patel; costumes, Theresa Squire; lighting, Kevin Adams; casting, Tara Rubin Casting; stage management, C.A. Clark; press, Barlow-Hartman, Michael Hartman, Tom D'Ambrosio, Ryan Ratelle.

Time: The present. Place: Peter and Ann's Upper East Side living room; Central Park. Presented in two parts.

Mr. Albee's classic 1958 play, *The Zoo Story*, revised and enhanced with a first act titled *Homelife*, which gives a fuller understanding of Peter's existential crisis. The entire work has since been retitled as *At Home at the Zoo*. First presentation of record was given at Hartford Stage (5/28–6/20/2004). A 2007–08 *Best Plays* Special Citation honoree (see essay by Michael Sommers in this volume).

Make Me a Song: The Music of William Finn (55). Musical revue by Rob Ruggiero; music and lyrics by Mr. Finn. Produced by Junkyard Dog Productions, Larry Hirschhorn, Jayson Raitt, Stacey Mindich, Jamie deRoy, Eric Falkenstein, in association with Nick Demos, Francine Bizar, Bob Eckert, Impresario's Choice on Broadway, Eileen T'Kaye,

Death wish: Dallas Roberts in Peter and Jerry.
Photo: Joan Marcus

Barbara Manocherian, Remmel T. Dickinson, at New World Stages 5. Opened November 12, 2007. (Closed December 30, 2007)

Performed by Sandy Binion, D.B. Bonds, Adam Heller, Sally Wilfert, Darren R. Cohen (piano). Understudies: Messrs. Bonds, Heller—Jason Dula; Mses. Binion, Wilfert—Alysha Umphress.

Direction, Mr. Ruggiero; scenery, Luke Hegel-Cantarella; costumes, Alejo Vietti; lighting, John Lasiter; sound, Zachary Williamson; music supervision, Michael Morris; music direction, Mr. Cohen; casting, Stuart Howard, Amy Schecter, Paul Hardt; stage management, Cambra Overend; press, Blue Current Public Relations, Pete Sanders, Andrew Snyder.

Presented without intermission.

Musical revue of Mr. Finn's songs strung together with a narrative. First presentation of record was given at TheaterWorks in Hartford, Connecticut (8/18/2006).

MUSICAL NUMBERS

"Make Me a Song" .... Adam
"Heart and Music" .... Company
(vocal arrangements by Jason Robert Brown)
"Hitchhiking Across America" .... D.B.
(vocal arrangements by Vadim Feichtner)
"Billy's Law of Genetics" .... D.B., Company
(vocal arrangements by Jason Robert Brown)
"Passover" .... Sally
"Republicans Part I" Adam
"Only One" .... Sandy
"I'd Rather Be Sailing"; "Set Those Sails" .... D.B., Sally
(vocal arrangements by Darren R. Cohen, Carmel Dean)
"Republicans Part 2" .... Adam
"Change" .... Sandy, Company
(vocal arrangements by Michael Morris)
"I Have Found" .... Sally
"Republicans Part 3" .... Adam
"You're Even Better Than You Think You Are" .... Company
(vocal arrangements by Michael Starobin, Carmel Dean, Michael Morris)

Classical Theatre of Harlem production of **Black Nativity** (36). Revival of the songplay by Langston Hughes. Alfred Preisser artistic director, Christopher McElroen executive director, at the Duke on 42nd Street. Opened December 1, 2007. (Closed December 30, 2007)

Narrator; Pastor .... Andre De Shields   Mary .... Tracy Jack
Joseph .... Enrique Cruz DeJesus

Ensemble: Melvin Bell III, Ebony Blake, Alexander Elisa, Phyre Hawkins, Laiona Michelle, Nikki Stephenson, Tryphena Wade, Rejinald Woods, Shangilia Youth Choir of Kenya.

Direction, Alfred Preisser; choreography, Ms. Jack; scenery, Troy Hourie; costumes, Kimberly Glennon; lighting, Aaron Black; music direction, Kelvyn Bell; stage management, Elyzabeth Gorman; press, Brett Singer and Associates, Brett Singer.

Presented without intermission.

Religious music and text interweaving Mr. Hughes's original work with contemporary sources. First presentation of record was given in an Off Broadway production at the 41st Street Theatre (12/11/1961–1/6/1962; 32 performances) before a transfer to the York Playhouse (1/9–28/1962; 24 performances). The 41st Street Theatre opened at 125 West 41st Street in April 1957 with a seating capacity of 169. Prior to the 1961 opening, Carmen de Lavallade (Mary) and Alvin Ailey (Joseph) withdrew from the production after the title was changed from *Wasn't It a Mighty Day?* Both performers expressed displeasure with the title change.

Manhattan Theatre Club production of **Pumpgirl** (48). By Abbie Spallen. Lynne Meadow artistic director, Daniel Sullivan acting artistic director, Barry Grove executive director, at City Center Stage II. Opened December 4, 2007. (Closed January 13, 2008)

Troubled threesome: Geraldine Hughes, Hannah Cabell and Paul Sparks in Pumpgirl.
Photo: Joan Marcus

Pumpgirl .... Hannah Cabell   Hammy .... Paul Sparks
Sinead .... Geraldine Hughes

Understudies: Mses. Cabell, Hughes—Jane Pfitsch; Mr. Sparks—Tim Ruddy.

Direction, Carolyn Cantor; scenery, David Korins; costumes, Mimi O'Donnell; lighting, David Weiner; sound, Robert Kaplowitz; casting, Nancy Piccione; stage management, Rachel E. Miller; press, Boneau/Bryan-Brown, Chris Boneau, Aaron Meier, Steven Padla, Heath Schwartz, Christine Olver.

Time: Roundabout now. Place: A border town in Northern Ireland. Presented in two parts.

Three working-class Irish spin yarns of false hope and nameless despair through interwoven monologues. First presentation of record was given by the Bush Theatre at the Traverse Theatre during the 2006 Edinburgh Festival (8/5–27/2006). It was later presented at the Bush's home venue in London (9/12–10/14/2006).

Runt of the Litter (76). Revival of the solo performance piece by Bo Eason. Produced by Forbes Candlish, Dawn Eason, Peter Fitzgerald, Tom Quinn, Larry Safir at 37 Arts. Opened December 9, 2007. (Closed February 24, 2007)

Performed by Mr. Eason.

Direction, Larry Moss; scenery, James Dardenne; costumes, Sports Robe; lighting, David Gipson; sound, Peter Fitzgerald; stage management, Joe Gladstone.

Presented without intermission.

A former professional football player recounts the many challenges of being undersized for his game and feeling underappreciated for it. First presentation of record was given at Stages Repertory Theatre in Houston (2/21–3/18/2001). Later workshopped at the Tamarind Theatre in Los Angeles (4/17–18/2001; 2 performances). First presentation of record in New York was given by MCC Theater (1/31–3/10/2002).

The Public Theater production of **Yellow Face** (39). By David Henry Hwang. Oskar Eustis artistic director, Mara Manus executive director, in association with Center Theatre Group (Michael Ritchie artistic director, Charles Dillingham managing director), in Martinson Hall. Opened December 10, 2007. (Closed January 13, 2008)

Marcus .... Noah Bean	Stuart; others .... Lucas Caleb Rooney
HYH; others .... Francis Jue	Announcer;
Leah; others .... Julienne Hanzelka Kim	Name Withheld
June; others .... Kathryn A. Layng	on Advice of Counsel .... Anthony Torn
DHH .... Hoon Lee	

Direction, Leigh Silverman; scenery, David Korins; costumes, Myung Hee Cho; lighting, Donald Holder; sound; Darron L. West; casting, Jordan Thaler, Heidi Griffiths, Erika Sellin; stage management, Cole P. Bonenberger; press, Candi Adams, Sam Neuman.

Time: 1988 to the present. Place: New York; Los Angeles; Washington, DC; San Francisco; Boston; Guizhou Province; China. Presented in two parts.

An Asian-American playwright finds his identity compromised by relationships within his community and with his wealthy father. First presentation of record was given at Los Angeles's Mark Taper Forum by the Center Theatre Group, in association with East West Players and the Public Theater (5/20–7/1/2007). A 2007–08 *Best Plays* choice (see essay by Dan Bacalzo in this volume).

Playwrights Horizons production of **Doris to Darlene, a Cautionary Valentine** (16). By Jordan Harrison. Tim Sanford artistic director, Leslie Marcus managing director, William Russo general manager, in the Mainstage Theater. Opened December 11, 2007. (Closed December 23, 2007)

Passing strange: Noah Bean and the company in Yellow Face. *Photo: Joan Marcus*

Sampling sounds: Michael Crane, Tobias Segal, Tom Nelis, de'Adre Aziza (kneeling), Laura Heisler and David Chandler in Doris to Darlene, a Cautionary Valentine. *Photo: Joan Marcus*

Doris	de'Adre Aziza	Richard Wagner	David Chandler
Vic Watts	Michael Crane	Young Man	Tobias Segal
King Ludwig II	Laura Heisler	Mr. Campani	Tom Nelis

Direction, Les Waters; scenery, Takeshi Kata; costumes, Christal Weatherly; lighting, Jane Cox; sound, Darron L. West; music, Kirsten Childs; music arrangements, Victor Zupanc; casting, Alaine Alldaffer; stage management, Elizabeth Moreau; press, the Publicity Office, Marc Thibodeau, Michael S. Borowski, Jeremy Shaffer, Matthew Fasano.

Presented in two parts.

Musical inspiration collides across the centuries and its various products are converted into commodities for sale or appropriation.

New York Theatre Workshop production of **Beckett Shorts** (41). Four one-act plays by Samuel Beckett. James C. Nicola artistic director, Lynn Moffat managing director. Opened December 16, 2007. (Closed January 20, 2008)

Act Without Words I

Man	Mikhail Baryshnikov

Act Without Words II

A	Mikhail Baryshnikov
B	David Neumann

Rough for Theatre I

A	Mikhail Baryshnikov
B	Bill Camp

Eh Joe

Joe	Mikhail Baryshnikov
Woman	Karen Kandel

Direction, JoAnne Akalaitis; scenery, Alexander Brodsky; costumes, Kaye Voyce; lighting, Jennifer Tipton; sound, Darron L. West; music, Philip Glass; video, Mirit Tal; stage management, Anthony Cerrato; press, Richard Kornberg and Associates, Don Summa.

Presented without intermission.

Man is fated to struggle ceaselessly for desires just out of reach, while haunted by the internal voices that seem never to still. *Act Without Words I* was first presented as *Acte sans paroles*, part of a double bill with the world premiere of *Fin de partie* (*Endgame*), in French, at the Royal Court Theatre (4/3/1957; 6 performances). Deryk Mendel, for whom the piece was written, performed the role of "Man." Reliable sources conflict on the first presentation of *Act Without Words II*. In Britain, it is reputed to have received its first presentation at the Clarendon Press Institute, Oxford (1959), before a run at the Institute of Contemporary Arts in London (1/25/1960). *The Times* (London) notes, on separate occasions, the "first British production" and the "British premiere" of *Act Without Words II* two years later at In-Stage, Fitzroy Square (7/1/1962) on a triple bill of short pieces directed by Charles Marowitz. Mr. Mendel performed *Act Without Words II* in tandem with the first number at the Ulmer Theater in Ulm-Donau, Germany (6/14/1963). First presentation of *Rough for Theatre I* was given at the Schiller Theater in Hamburg, Germany (1976). *Eh Joe* was created for BBC television and first aired in 1966.

New York Gilbert and Sullivan Players production of **Princess Ida** (3). Revival of the operetta with book by William S. Gilbert; music by Arthur Sullivan. Albert Bergeret artistic director, at City Center. Opened January 4, 2008. (Closed January 12, 2008)

King Hildebrand	Keith Jurosko	Princess Ida	Kimilee Bryant
Hilarion	Colm Fitzmaurice	Lady Blanche	Dianna Dollman
Cyril	Patrick Hogan	Lady Psyche	Shana Farr
Florian	William Whitefield	Melissa	Melissa Attebury
King Gama	Stephen Quint	Sacharissa	Megan Loomis
Arac	David Wannen	Chloe	Rebecca O'Sullivan
Guron	David Auxier	Ada	Victoria Devany
Scynthius	Louis Dall'Ava		

Ensemble: Meredith Borden, Joshua Bouchard, Ted Bouton, Susan Case, Derrick Cobey, Michael Connolly, Michael Galante, Matthew Harrison, Katie Hall, Amy Helfer, Alan Hill, David Macaluso, Robin Mahon, Nick Mannix, Lance Olds, Marcie Passley, Monique Pelletier, Paul Sigrist, Angela Smith, Chris-Ian Sanchez, Amber Smoke.

Daughters of the Plough: Carol Davis, Christi Harrison, Andrea Stryker-Rodda.

Understudies: Ms. Bryant—Shana Farr; Ms. Dollman—Amber Smoke; Mr. Fitzmaurice—Matthew Harrison; Mr. Quint—David Macaluso; Mr. Whitefield—Lance Olds; Ms. Attebury—Amy Helfer; Ms. Farr—Megan Loomis; Messrs. Auxier, Dall'Ava—Joshua Bouchard; Mr. Wannen—David Auxier.

Direction, Mr. Bergeret; choreography, Janis Ansley Ungar; scenery, Albere; costumes; Gail J. Wofford and Stivanello Costume Company; lighting, Sally Small; music direction, Mr. Bergert; stage management, David Sigafoose; press, Peter Cromarty.

Presented in two parts.

A proto-feminist princess forswears the company of men and establishes a school for women, which leads to crossdressed suitors, complications and ultimate compromise. First presentation of record at given at the Savoy Theatre in London (1/5/1884).

ACT I

Overture
"Search Throughout the Panorama" .... Florian, Company
"Now Hearken to My Strict Command" .... Hildebrand, Company
"Today We Meet . . . Ida Was a Twelve Month Old" .... Hilarion
"From the Distant Panorama" .... Company
"We Are Warriors Three" .... Arac, Guron, Scynthius, Company
"If You Give Me Your Attention" .... Gama, Company
"P'raps If You Address the Lady" .... Company

ACT II

"Towards the Empyrean Heights" .... Psyche, Melissa, Sacharissa, Women
"Mighty Maiden With a Mission" .... Women
"Minerva! Oh, Hear Me" .... Princess Ida
"And Thus to Empyrean Heights" .... Women

"Come Mighty Must" .... Lady Blanche
"Gently, Gently" .... Hilarion, Cyril, Florian
"I Am a Maiden" .... Hilarion, Cyril, Florian
"The World Is but a Broken Toy" .... Ida, Hilarion, Cyril, Florian
"A Lady Fair of Lineage High" .... Psyche, Hilarion, Cyril, Florian
"The Woman of the Wisest Wit" .... Melissa, Psyche, Hilarion, Cyril, Florian
"Now Wouldn't You Like" .... Lady Blanche, Melissa
"Merrily Ring the Luncheon Bell" .... Lady Blanche, Cyril, Company
"Would You Know the Kind of Maid" .... Cyril
"Oh Joy! Our Chief Is Saved!" .... Company

ACT III

"Death to the Invader!" .... Melissa, Women
"Whene'er I Spoke" .... Gama
"I Built Upon a Rock!" .... Princess Ida
"When Anger Spreads His Wing" .... Company
"This Helmet, I Suppose" .... Arac, Guron, Scynthius, Company
"This Is Our Duty" .... Company
"With Joy Abiding" .... Ida, Hilarion, Company

New York Gilbert and Sullivan Players production of **The Pirates of Penzance** (5). Revival of the operetta with libretto by William S. Gilbert; music by Arthur Sullivan. Albert Bergeret artistic director, at City Center. Opened January 5, 2008. (Closed January 13, 2008)

Maj. Gen. Stanley	Stephen Quint	Edith	Erika Person
Pirate King	David Wannen	Kate	Melissa Attebury;
Samuel	David Macaluso		Amy Helfer (alt.)
Frederic	Colm Fitzmaurice	Isabel	Robin Mahon;
Police Sgt.	Keith Jurosko;		Meredith Borden (alt.)
	David Auxier (alt.)	Ruth	Angela Smith
Mabel	Laurelyn Watson Chase		

Ensemble: Ashley Adler, David Auxier, Meredith Borden, Cáitlín Burke, Derrick Cobey, Michael Connolly, Louis Dall'Ava, Dianna Dollman, Katie Hall, Matthew Harrison, Amy Helfer, Alan Hill, Lynelle Johnson, Robin Mahon, James Mills, Jenny Millsap, Lance Olds, Rebecca O'Sullivan, Natalie Ross, Paul Sigrist, Sarah Caldwell Smith, Chris-Ian Sanchez, Kathy Tarello, Eric Werner, William Whitefield.

Understudies: Mr. Quint—James Mills; Mr. Wannen—Louis Dall'Ava; Mr. Macaluso—Lance Olds; Mr. Fitzmaurice—Matthew Harrison; Ms. Chase—Sarah Caldwell Smith; Ms. Person—Cáitlín Burke.

Swings: Megan Loomis, Michael Galante.

Direction, Mr. Bergeret; choreography, Bill Fabris; scenery, Lou Anne Gilleland; costumes, Gail J. Wofford; lighting, Sally Small; music direction, Mr. Bergeret, Jeffrey Kresky; stage management, David Sigafoose; press, Peter Cromarty.

Presented in two parts.

An unwilling young pirate renounces his apprenticeship only to discover that duty binds him to the ways of the brigand. First presentation of record was given in New York at the Fifth Avenue Theatre (12/31/1879). It was the fifth collaboration by Messrs. Gilbert and Sullivan and their only work to have its premiere in this country.

ACT I

Overture .... Orchestra
"Pour, O Pour The Pirate Sherry" .... Pirates, Samuel
"When Frederic Was a Little Lad" .... Ruth
"Oh, Better Far to Live and Die" .... Pirate King, Pirates
"Oh, False One, You Have Deceived Me!" .... Frederic and Ruth
"Climbing Over Rocky Mountain" .... Women, Edith, Kate
"Stop, Ladies, Pray!" .... Frederic, Edith, Kate, Women

"Oh, Is There Not One Maiden Breast" .... Frederic, Mabel, Women
"Poor Wand'ring One!" Mabel, Women
"What Ought We to Do" .... Edith, Kate, Women
"How Beautifully Blue the Sky" .... Women, Mabel, Frederic
"Stay, We Must Not Lose Our Senses" .... Frederic, Women, Pirates
"Hold, Monsters!" .... Mabel, Samuel, Major General,
Women, Pirates
"I Am the Very Model of a Modern Major General" .... Major General, Women, Pirates
"Oh, Men of Dark and Dismal Fate" .... Company

ACT II

"Oh, Dry the Glistening Tear" .... Women, Mabel
"Then, Frederic, Let Your Escort Lion-Hearted" .... Major General, Frederic
"When the Foeman Bares His Steel" .... Sergeant, Mabel, Edith, Kate,
Major General, Police, Women
"Now for the Pirates' Lair!" .... Frederic, Pirate King, Ruth
"When You Had Left Our Pirate Fold" .... Ruth, Frederic, Pirate King
"Away, Away! My Heart's on Fire" .... Ruth, Pirate King, Frederic
"All Is Prepared" .... Mabel, Frederic
"Stay, Frederic, Stay!" .... Mabel, Frederic
"No, I Am Brave!" .... Mabel, Sergeant, Police
"When a Felon's Not Engaged in His Employment" .... Sergeant, Police
"A Rollicking Band of Pirates We" .... Pirates, Sergeant, Police
"With Cat-Like Tread, Upon Our Prey We Steal" .... Pirates, Police, Samuel
"Hush, Hush! Not a Word" .... Frederic, Pirates, Police, Major General
"Sighing Softly to the River" .... Major General, Company

Brooklyn Academy of Music presentation of **National Theatre** production of **Happy Days** (27). Revival of the play by Samuel Beckett. Alan H. Fishman chairman, Karen Brooks Hopkins president, Joseph V. Melillo executive producer at the Harvey Theater. Opened January 9, 2008. (Closed February 2, 2008)

Winnie .... Fiona Shaw   Willie .... Tim Potter

Direction, Deborah Warner; scenery, Tom Pye; costumes, Luca Costigliolo; lighting, Jean Kalman; sound, Christopher Shutt; music, Mel Mercier; stage management, Jane Pole; press, Sandy Sawotka, Fatima Kafele, John Wyszniewski, Matthew Yeager.

Presented in two parts.

A woman buried in the earth to her waist carries on, with the dirt rising, because she cannot do otherwise. First presentation of record was given at the Cherry Lane Theatre in a production directed by Alan Schneider (9/17/1961). Walter Kerr famously began his review in the *New York Herald Tribune*, "Well, happy days are gone again" (9/18/1961). Ms. Warner had been earlier barred by Mr. Beckett's estate from staging his work after a controversial 1994 production of *Footfalls* with Ms. Shaw. The 2007–08 Off Broadway production of *Happy Days* was first presented in the National Theatre's Lyttelton (1/24–3/1/2007).

New York Gilbert and Sullivan Players production of **Trial by Jury** (1). Revival of the operetta with libretto by William S. Gilbert; music by Arthur Sullivan. Albert Bergeret artistic director, at City Center. Opened January 10, 2009. (Closed January 10, 2008)

Learned Judge .... Stephen Quint   Jury Foreman .... Ted Bouton
Plaintiff's Counsel .... Richard Holmes   Usher .... David Wannen
Defendant .... Patrick Hogan   Plaintiff .... Laurelyn Watson Chase

Ensemble: David Auxier, Meredith Borden, Susan Case, Michael Connolly, Louis Dall'Ava, Victoria Devany, Dianna Dollman, Michael Galante, Katie Hall, Alan Hill, Lynelle Johnson, Keith Jurosko, Daniel Lockwood, Megan Loomis, David Macaluso, Robin Mahon, Jenny Millsap, Lance Olds, Monique Pelletier, Erika Person, Edward Prostak, Chris-Ian Sanchez, Paul Sigrist, Angela Smith, Michael J. Strone, William Whitefield.

Direction, Mr. Bergeret; choreography, Robin Mahon; costumes, Gail J. Wofford; lighting, Sally Small; music direction, Mr. Bergeret; stage management, David Sigafoose; press, Peter Cromarty.

Time: 1935. Place: A courtroom. Presented without intermission.

First presentation of record was given at the Royalty Theatre in London (3/25/1875). Presented on the same program as *G and S a la Carte* (see below).

MUSICAL NUMBERS

"Hark, the Hour of Ten Is Sounding"	Company
"Is This the Court of the Exchequer?"	Defendant, Company
"When First My Old, Old Love I Knew"	Defendant, Usher, Company
"All Hail Great Judge!"	Company, Judge, Usher
"When I, Good Friends, Was Called to the Bar"	Judge, Company
"Swear Thou the Jury!"	Counsel, Usher, Defendant, Judge, Jury
"Where Is the Plaintiff?"	Counsel, Usher, Bridesmaids, Plaintiff
"Oh, Never, Never, Never"	Judge, Foreman, Plaintiff, Usher, Jury, Bridesmaids
"May It Please You"	Counsel, Plaintiff, Usher, Company
"That She Is Reeling Is Plain to See"	Judge, Foreman, Plaintiff, Counsel, Company
"Oh, Gentlemen, Listen, I Pray"	Defendant, Bridesmaids
"That Seems a Reasonable Proposition"	Judge, Counsel, Company
"A Nice Dilemma" Company	
"I Love Him, I Love Him"	Plaintiff, Defendant, Judge, Company
"Oh, Joy Unbounded"	Company

New York Gilbert and Sullivan Players production of **G and S a la Carte** (1). Musical revue with book by David Auxier; music by Arthur Sullivan; lyrics by William S. Gilbert and others. Albert Bergeret artistic director, at City Center. Opened January 10, 2009. (Closed January 10, 2008)

Richard D'Oyly Carte	Richard Holmes	Arthur Sullivan	Stephen Quint
Helen Lenoir	Erika Person	William S. Gilbert	Keith Jurosko

Direction, Mr. Bergeret; choreography, Robin Mahon; costumes, Gail J. Wofford; lighting, Sally Small; music direction, Mr. Bergeret; stage management, David Sigafoose; press, Peter Cromarty.

Presented without intermission.

A cast party following the opening of Gilbert and Sullivan's *Trial by Jury*. Presented on the same program as *Trial By Jury* (see above).

New York Gilbert and Sullivan Players production of **The Mikado** (1). Revival of the operetta with libretto by William S. Gilbert; music by Arthur Sullivan. Albert Bergeret artistic director, at City Center. Opened January 12, 2008. (Closed January 12, 2008)

The Mikado	Keith Jurosko	Yum-Yum	Laurelyn Watson Chase
Nanki-Poo	Daniel Lockwood	Pitti-Sing	Melissa Attebury
Ko-Ko	David Macaluso	Peep-Bo	Robin Mahon
Pooh-Bah	Louis Dall'Ava	Katisha	Dianna Dollman
Pish-Tush	Edward Prostak		

Ensemble: David Auxier, Susan Case, Derrick Cobey, Michael Connolly, Michael Galante, Robert Garner, Katie Hall, Alan Hill, Lynelle Johnson, Jenny Millsap, Lance Olds, Rebecca O'Sullivan, Monique Pelletier, Paul Sigrist, Chris-Ian Sanchez, Angela Smith, Kathy Glauber Tarello, William Whitefield.

Direction, Mr. Bergeret; scenery, Albere; costumes,Gail J. Wofford and Kayko Nakamura; lighting, Sally Small; music direction, Mr. Bergeret; stage management: David Sigafoose; press, Peter Cromarty.

Presented in two acts.

Star-crossed love and mistaken identity played in a fantasy Japan. First presentation of record at London's Savoy Theatre (3/14/1885).

ACT I

Overture .... Orchestra
"If You Want to Know Who We Are" .... Nanki-Poo, Men
"A Wand'ring Minstrel I" .... Nanki-Poo, Men
"Our Great Mikado, Virtuous Man" .... Pish-Tush, Men
"Young Man, Despair" .... Pooh-Bah, Nanki-Poo, Pish-Tush
"And Have I Journeyed for a Month" .... Nanki-Poo, Pooh-Bah
"Behold the Lord High Executioner" .... Ko-Ko, Men
"As Some Day It May Happen" .... Ko-Ko, Men
"Comes a Train of Little Ladies" .... Women
"Three Little Maids From School Are We" .... Yum-Yum, Peep-Bo,
Pitti-Sing, Women
"So Please You, Sir, We Much Regret" .... Yum-Yum, Peep-Bo, Pitti-Sing,
Pooh-Bah, Women
"Were You Not to Ko-Ko Plighted" .... Yum-Yum, Nanki-Poo
"I Am so Proud" .... Pooh-Bah, Ko-Ko, Pish-Tush
"With Aspect Stern and Gloomy Stride" .... Company

ACT II

"Braid the Raven Hair" .... Pitti-Sing, Women
"The Sun, Whose Rays Are All Ablaze" .... Yum-Yum
"Brightly Dawns Our Wedding Day" .... Yum-Yum, Pitti-Sing,
Nanki-Poo, Pish-Tush
"Here's a How-De-Do!" .... Yum-Yum, Nanki-Poo, Ko-Ko
"Mi-Ya Sa-Ma" .... Mikado, Katisha, Women, Men
"A More Humane Mikado" .... Mikado, Women, Men
"The Criminal Cried as He Dropped Him Down" .... Ko-Ko, Pitti-Sing, Pooh-Bah,
Women, Men
"See How the Fates Their Gifts Allot" .... Mikado, Pitti-Sing, Pooh-Bah,
Ko-Ko, Katisha
"The Flowers That Bloom in the Spring" .... Nanki-Poo, Ko-Ko, Yum-Yum,
Pitti-Sing, Pooh-Bah
"Alone, and Yet Alive!" .... Katisha
"Willow, Tit-Willow" .... Ko-Ko
"There Is Beauty in the Bellow of the Blast" .... Katisha, Ko-Ko
"For He's Gone and Married Yum-Yum" .... Company

Straight Up With a Twist (90). Solo performance piece by Paul Stroili. Produced by David and Hyra George at the Players Theatre. Opened January 24, 2008. (Closed May 4, 2008)

Performed by Mr. Stroili.

Direction, Bill Penton; scenery, Mr. George; costumes, Crystal Thompson; lighting, Christopher Ryan; press, Keith Sherman and Associates, Scott Klein.

Presented without intermission.

A heterosexual explores his Italian-American roots and his penchant for perfectly folded sheets. First presentation of record was given under the title *Renaissance Geek* at Los Angeles's Gascon Center Theatre in 1999 before a run at the Tamarind Theatre (9/14-10/29/2000).

Jerry Springer: The Opera (2). Musical with book and lyrics by Stewart Lee and Richard Thomas; music by Mr. Thomas. Produced by David J. Foster, Jared Geller,

Avalon Promotions, in association with Ruth Hendel and Jonathan Reinis, at Carnegie Hall. Opened January 29, 2008. (Closed January 30, 2008)

Jerry Springer	Harvey Keitel	Chucky; Adam	Sean Jenness
Warm Up Man; Satan	David Bedella	Steve	Sam Kitchin
Zandra; others	Linda Balgord	Peaches	Patricia Phillips
Montel; Jesus	Lawrence Clayton	Baby Jane	Laura Shoop
Shawntel; Eve	Katrina Rose Dideriksen	Andrea; Archangel Michael	Emily Skinner
Dwight; God	Luke Grooms	Tremont; Angel Gabriel	Max von Essen

Ensemble: Katie Banks, Kristy Cates, Patty Goble, Chris Gunn, Celisse Henderson, Robert Hunt, John Eric Parker, Kate Pazakis, Eddie Pendergraft, Richard Poole, Soara-Joye Ross, Tory Ross, Roland Rusinek, John Schiappa, Michael James Scott, Dennis Stowe, Edwin Vega, Sasha Weiss, Jim Weitzer, Betsy Werbel, Lauren Worsham.

Direction, Jason Moore; choreography, Josh Prince; scenery, David Korins; costumes, Ilona Somogyi; lighting, Jeff Croiter; sound, Brian Ronan; video, Aaron Rhyne; hair, Erin Kennedy Lunsford; orchestrations, Martin Koch and Nick Gilpin; music coordination, Michael Keller; music direction, Stephen Oremus; stage management, Evan Ensign.

Presented in two parts.

Musical spoof of a television talk show famed for encouraging—and moralizing on—the basest impulses among members of the American underclass. First presentation of record was given in a workshop at the Battersea Arts Centre in London (8/21–9/2/2001) with Mr. Thomas in the title role. After further development, the production re-opened at Battersea (2/5–23/2002) before a run at the 2002 Edinburgh Festival (8/2–26/2002) and a stand at the National Theatre's Lyttelton (4/9–9/30/2003). The production transferred to the West End's Cambridge Theatre (10/14/2003–2/19/2005; 609 performances) before a 2006 UK tour.

New York City Center Encores! production of **Applause** (5). Concert version of the musical with book by Betty Comden and Adolph Green; music by Charles Strouse; lyrics by Lee Adams. Jack Viertel artistic director, at City Center. Opened February 7, 2008. (Closed February 10, 2008)

Margo Channing	Christine Ebersole	Karen Richards	Kate Burton
Eve Harrington	Erin Davie	Bartender	Gregg Goodbrod
Tony Awards Announcer	Bob Gaynor	Peter	Bob Gaynor
Howard Benedict	Tom Hewitt	Stan Harding	Tony Freeman
Bert	David Studwell	Bonnie	Megan Sikora
Buzz Richards	Chip Zien	Waiters	James Harkness,
Bill Sampson	Michael Park		Steven Sofia
Duane Fox	Mario Cantone	TV Director	J.D. Webster

Ensemble: Cole Burden, John Carroll, Paula Leggett Chase, Susan Derry, Sarah Jane Everman, Tony Freeman, Lisa Gajda, Bob Gaynor, Gregg Goodbrod, Justin Greer, James Harkness, Joe Komara, Raymond J. Lee, Monica L. Patton, Manuel Santos, Jennifer Savelli, Chaunteé Schuler, Steven Sofia, David Studwell, Kevin Vortmann, J.D. Webster, Kristen Beth Williams.

Orchestra: Rob Berman conductor; Suzanne Ornstein concertmistress; Belinda Whitney, Laura Seaton, Maura Giannini, Eric Degioia, Kristina Musser, Fritz Krakowski, Lisa Matricardi, Martin Agee violin; Richard Brice, Crystal Garner, David Blinn viola; Roger Shell, Deborah Sepe cello; John Beal double bass; Andrew Sterman, Edward Salkin, Allen Won, Lino Gomez, John Winder woodwinds; Robert Millikan, Glenn Drewes, Kamau Adilifu trumpet; Bruce Bonvissuto, Wayne Goodman, Dean Plank trombone; Jay Berliner guitar; Steven Freeman piano, organ; Richard Rosenzweig drums; Thad Wheeler percussion; Victoria Drake harp.

Direction and choreography, Kathleen Marshall; scenery, John Lee Beatty; costumes, Martin Pakledinaz; lighting, Kenneth Posner; sound, Peter Hylenski; orchestrations, Philip J. Lang; music direction, Mr. Berman; casting, Jay Binder, Jack Bowdan; stage management, Karen Moore; press, Helene Davis Public Relations.

Presented in two parts.

Women claw their way up and down the ladder of theatrical success in a musical based on the 1950 Bette Davis film, which received six Academy Awards. A 1969-70 *Best Plays* choice, the original Broadway production opened at the Palace Theatre (3/30/1970–7/27/1972; 896 performances). The original production received 1970 Tony Awards in the musical categories of best musical, actress (Lauren Bacall), choreography (Ron Field) and direction (Mr. Field).

ACT I

Overture .... Orchestra
"Backstage Babble" .... Company
"Think How It's Gonna Be" .... Margo, Duane, Eve
"But Alive" .... Margo, Duane, Eve, Company
"But Alive" (Reprise) .... Margo, Duane, Eve, Company
"The Best Night of My Life" .... Eve
"Who's That Girl?" .... Margo, Eve
"Applause" .... Bonnie, Company
(new material arranged by David Chase and orchestrated by Larry Blank)
"Hurry Back" .... Margo
"Fasten Your Seat Belts" .... Buzz, Karen, Howard, Bill,
Duane, Margo, Company
"Welcome to the Theatre" .... Margo

ACT II

Entr'acte .... Orchestra
"Inner Thoughts" .... Karen, Buzz, Margo
"Good Friends" .... Buzz, Margo, Karen
"The Best Night of My Life" (Reprise) .... Eve
"She's No Longer a Gypsy" .... Duane
"One of a Kind" .... Bill, Margo
"One Hallowe'en" .... Eve
"Something Greater" .... Bill, Margo

Brooklyn Academy of Music presentation of the **Chichester Festival Theatre** production of **Macbeth** (40). Revival of the play by William Shakespeare. Alan H. Fishman chairman of the board, Karen Brooks Hopkins president, Joseph V. Melillo executive producer, at the Harvey Theater. Opened February 13, 2008. (Closed March 22, 2008)

Macbeth	Patrick Stewart	Lennox	Mark Rawlings
Lady Macbeth	Kate Fleetwood	Ross	Tim Treloar
Duncan	Paul Shelley	Seyton	Christopher Patrick Nolan
Malcolm	Scott Handy	Witch	Sophie Hunter
Banquo	Martin Turner	Witch; Gentlewoman	Polly Frame
Macduff	Michael Feast	Witch	Niamh McGrady
Lady Macduff	Suzanne Burden		

Direction, Rupert Goold; choreography, Georgina Lamb; scenery and costumes, Anthony Ward; lighting, Howard Harrison; sound and music, Adam Cork; video and projections, Lorna Heavey; fight direction, Terry King; stage management, Jane Pole; press, Sandy Sawotka, Fatima Kafele, John Wyszniewski, Matthew Yeager.

Presented in two parts.

A Scottish thane and his lady wife are seized by a power madness that leads to murder and ruin. First presentation of record was given at the Globe Theatre (4/20/1611) with Richard Burbage in the title role. It is believed, however, to have been given earlier at Hampton Court (8/7/1606). First presentation of record in this country was given at the John Street Theatre (3/3/1768) with Lewis Hallam II in the title role. In May 1849, there were three competing productions in New York, two of which—with the Englishman William Charles Macready and the American Edwin Forrest in the title roles—helped to spark the deadly Astor Place Riots (5/7–10/1849). First presentation of record of the 2007–08 production was given in the Minerva Theatre by the Chichester Festival Theatre (5/25–9/1/2007) before a run in the West End's Gielgud Theatre (9/24–12/1/2007). The Brooklyn Academy of Music presentation transferred to Broadway (4/8–5/24/2008; 52 performances). See Plays Produced on Broadway section of this volume.

Inner glow: Brian d'Arcy James and Alice Ripley in Next to Normal. *Photo: Joan Marcus*

Second Stage Theatre production of **Next to Normal** (38). Musical with book and lyrics by Brian Yorkey; music by Tom Kitt. Carole Rothman artistic director, Ellen Richard executive director, at Second Stage Theatre. Opened February 13, 2008. (Closed March 16, 2008)

Henry	Adam Chanler-Berat	Diana	Alice Ripley
Natalie	Jennifer Damiano	Dr. Madden; Dr. Fine	Asa Somers
Dan	Brian d'Arcy James	Gabe	Aaron Tveit

Musicians: Mary-Mitchell Campbell conductor, piano; Michael Aarons guitar; Christian Hebel violin, keyboard; Ted Mook cello; Randy Landau bass; Damien Bassman drums, percussion.

Understudies: Messrs. Chanler-Berat, Tveit—Corey Boardman; Messrs. James, Somers—Kevin Kern; Ms. Ripley—Jessica Phillips; Ms. Damiano—Morgan Weed.

Direction, Michael Greif; choreography, Sergio Trujillo; scenery, Mark Wendland; costumes, Jeff Mahshie; lighting, Kevin Adams; sound, Brian Ronan; orchestrations, Michael Starobin and Mr. Kitt; music direction, Ms. Campbell; music coordination, Michael Keller; vocal arrangements, AnnMarie Milazzo; stage management, Judith Schoenfeld; press, Barlow-Hartman, Michael Hartman, Tom D'Ambrosio, Michelle Bergmann.

Presented in two parts.

A woman with severe bipolar disorder struggles with delusions and makes life difficult for her family. First presentation of record was a workshop given by Village Theatre in Issaquah, Washington (6/21–23/2005; 3 performances) under the title *Feeling Electric*. Before the title change, the work received further development at TBG Theater under the auspices of the 2005 New York Musical Theatre Festival (9/14–24/2005; 6 performances).

Roundabout Theatre Company production of **Crimes of the Heart** (77). Revival of the play by Beth Henley. Todd Haimes artistic director, Harold Wolpert managing director, Julia C. Levy executive director, in the Laura Pels Theatre at the Harold and Miriam Steinberg Center for Theatre. Opened February 14, 2008. (Closed April 20, 2008)

Lenny Magrath	Jennifer Dundas	Meg Magrath	Sarah Paulson
Chick Boyle	Jessica Stone	Babe Botrelle	Lily Rabe
Doc Porter	Patch Darragh	Barnette Lloyd	Chandler Williams

Understudies: Mses. Rabe, Stone—Jessica Cummings; Messrs. Darragh, Williams—Mycah Hogan; Mses. Paulson, Dundas—Kelly Mares.

Direction, Kathleen Turner; scenery, Anna Louizos; costumes, David Murin; lighting, Natasha Katz; sound and music, John Gromada; wigs, Paul Huntley; fight direction, J. David Brimmer; casting, Tara Rubin Casting, Laura Schutzel; stage management, Charles Means; press, Boneau/Bryan-Brown, Adrian Bryan-Brown, Matt Polk, Jessica Johnson, Amy Kass.

Time: Fall 1974, five years after Hurricane Camille. Place: The Magrath home in Hazelhurst, Mississippi. Presented in two parts.

Three sisters in small Mississippi town battle crises and the petty indignities of life. First presentation of record was given during Actors Theatre of Louisville's third annual Festival of New American Plays (2/1/1979; 12 performances). Manhattan Theatre Club presented the first New York production in a soldout run at its East 73rd Street space (12/9/1980–1/11/1981; 35 performances). A Broadway production was announced three months before Ms. Henley was named the 1981 Pulitzer Prize in Drama honoree. A 1980-81 *Best Plays* choice, the Broadway production played at the John Golden Theatre (11/4/1981–2/13/1983; 535 performances).

Labyrinth Theater Company production of **Unconditional** (24). By Brett C. Leonard. John Ortiz artistic director, Philip Seymour Hoffman co-artistic director, John Gould Rubin co-artistic director and executive director, in LuEsther Hall at the Public Theater. Opened February 18, 2008. (Closed March 9, 2008)

Spike	Chris Chalk	Missy	Anna Chlumsky

Pick-up artist: John Doman and Saidah Arrika Ekulona in Unconditional. *Photo: Monique Carboni*

Zero hero: Joel Hatch in Adding Machine. *Photo: Carol Rosegg*

Lotty	Saidah Arrika Ekulona	Tracie	Yolonda Ross
Gary	Kevin Geer	Keith	John Doman
Daniel	Trevor Long	Newton	Isiah Whitlock Jr.
Jessica	Elizabeth Rodriguez		

Direction, Mark Wing-Davey; scenery, Mark Wendland; costumes, Mimi O'Donnell; lighting, Japhy Weideman; sound, Bart Fasbender; casting, Judith Bowman Casting; stage management, Libby Steiner; press, O and M Company, Rick Miramontez, Philip Carrubba.

Time: The present. Place: New York City. Presented in two parts.

Daily life continuously grinds the human spirit and love is difficult to hold in this drama about a disparate group of New Yorkers who commit acts unspeakable and tender.

*Adding Machine (97). Musical with book by Jason Loewith and Joshua Schmidt; music by Mr. Schmidt; based on *The Adding Machine* by Elmer Rice. Produced by Scott Morfee, Tom Wirtshafter, Margaret Cotter at the Minetta Lane Theatre. Opened February 25, 2008.

Mrs. Zero	Cyrilla Baer	Mr. Two	Roger E. DeWitt
Mr. Zero	Joel Hatch	Mrs. Two	Adinah Alexander
Daisy	Amy Warren	Boss	Jeff Still
Mr. One	Daniel Marcus	Shrdlu	Joe Farrell
Mrs. One	Niffer Clarke		

Musicians: Timothy Splain synthesizer; Andy Boroson piano; Brad "Gorilla" Carbone percussion.

Understudies: Ms. Warren—Adinah Alexander; Messrs. Marcus, DeWitt, Farrell—Randy Blair; Ms. Baer—Niffer Clarke; Mr. Still—Roger E. DeWitt; Mr. Hatch—Daniel Marcus; Mses. Clarke, Alexander—Ariel A. Morgenstern.

Direction, David Cromer; scenery, Takeshi Kata; costumes, Kristine Knanishu; lighting, Keith Parham; sound, Tony Smolenski IV; video, Peter Flaherty; music direction, J. Oconer Navarro;

casting, Pat McCorkle, Joe Lopick; stage management, Richard A. Hodge; press, O and M Company, Rick Miramontez, Jon Dimond.

Time: 1920s. Place: An American city and the afterlife. Presented without intermission.

Trapped in a dead-end existence, a human "machine" cannot break free of society's expectations even when given an opportunity. First presentation of record was given by Next Theatre Company in Evanston, Illinois (2/4–3/4/2007; 23 performances). The musical was inspired by Elmer Rice's *The Adding Machine*, which was first presented under the auspices of the Theatre Guild at the Garrick Theatre for five weeks (3/19–4/19/1923) before a four-week run at the Comedy Theatre (4/23–5/19/1923; 72 total performances). A 2007–08 *Best Plays* choice (see essay by Jeffrey Sweet in this volume).

MUSICAL NUMBERS

Prelude
"In Numbers" .... Mr. One, Mrs. One,
Mr. Two, Mrs. Two

Scene 1: In the Bedroom
"Something to Be Proud Of" .... Mrs. Zero, Mr. One, Mrs. One,
Mr. Two, Mrs. Two

Scene 2: At the Office
"Office Reverie" .... Mr. Zero, Daisy, Mr. One,
Mrs. One, Mr. Two, Mrs. Two
"In Numbers" .... Mr. Zero, Mr. One, Mrs. One,
Mr. Two, Mrs. Two

Scene 3: In the Living Room
"I'd Rather Watch You" .... Daisy
"The Party" .... Mrs. Zero, Mr. One, Mrs. One,
Mr. Two, Mrs. Two

Scene 4: In the Courtroom
"Zero's Confession" .... Mr. Zero, Mr. One, Mrs. One,
Mr. Two, Mrs. Two

Scene 5: In the Jail
"Once More" .... Mr. Zero, Mrs. Zero
"Ham and Eggs!" .... Mr. Zero, Mrs. Zero
"Didn't We?" .... Mr. Zero, Mrs. Zero
"The Gospel According to Shrdlu" .... Shrdlu, Mr. One, Mrs. One,
Mr. Two, Mrs. Two

Scene 6: A Pleasant Place
"Shrdlu's Blues" .... Shrdlu, Mr. Zero, Mr. One,
Mrs. One, Mr. Two, Mrs. Two
"Daisy's Confession" .... Daisy, Mr. Zero
"I'd Rather Watch You" (Reprise) .... Mr. One, Mrs. One,
Mr. Two, Mrs. Two
"Freedom!" .... Mr. One, Mrs. One, Mr. Two,
Mrs. Two, Daisy, Shrdlu, Mrs. Zero

Scene 7: The Machine
"In Numbers" (Reprise) .... Mr. One, Mrs. One,
Mr. Two, Mrs. Two
"Freedom!" (Reprise) .... Mr. Zero
"The Music of the Machine" .... Shrdlu, Mrs. Zero, Mr. One,
Mrs. One, Mr. Two, Mrs. Two

Fabulous Divas of Broadway (61). Solo performance piece by Alan Palmer. Produced by Berlique at St. Luke's Theatre. Opened February 27, 2008. (Closed April 19, 2008)

Performed by Mr. Palmer and Curtis Jerome (piano).

Direction, Mr. Palmer; scenery, Jessa Orr; costumes, C. Buckey; lighting, Peter Ray; music direction, Mr. Jerome; stage management, Kimberly Jade Tompkins; press, the Publicity Office, Michael S. Borowski.

Presented without intermission.

Solo performance piece in which one actor impersonates 32 women in 20 songs that aim to celebrate great female performers of the Broadway stage. First presentation of record was given at Open Stage West in Sherman Oaks, California (9/8–11/25/2007).

Playwrights Horizons production of **Dead Man's Cell Phone** (32). By Sarah Ruhl. Tim Sanford artistic director, Leslie Marcus managing director, William Russo general manager, in the Mainstage Theater. Opened March 4, 2008. (Closed March 30, 2008)

Jean	Mary-Louise Parker	Other Woman	Carla Harting
Gordon	T. Ryder Smith	Hermia	Kelly Maurer
Mrs. Gottlieb	Kathleen Chalfant	Dwight	David Aaron Baker

Direction, Anne Bogart; scenery and costumes, G.W. Mercier; lighting, Brian H. Scott; sound, Darron L. West; casting, Alaine Alldaffer; stage management, Elizabeth Moreau; press, the Publicity Office, Marc Thibodeau, Michael S. Borowski, Jeremy Shaffer, Matthew Fasano.

Presented in two parts.

A woman recovers a man's cellphone moments after his death and becomes the keeper of his legacy. First presentation of record was given at Woolly Mammoth Theatre Company in Washington, DC (6/15–7/14/2007).

New York Theatre Workshop production of **Liberty City** (16). Solo performance piece by Jessica Blank and April Yvette Thompson. James C. Nicola artistic director, Fred Walker interim managing director. Opened March 4, 2008. (Closed March 16, 2008)

Mourning sickness: Kathleen Chalfant, David Aaron Baker and Mary-Louise Parker in Dead Man's Cell Phone. *Photo: Joan Marcus*

Hush-hush: Caralyn Kozlowski, Deborah Sonnenberg and Nancy Ringham in Secrets of a Soccer Mom. *Photo: Carol Rosegg*

Performed by Ms. Thompson.

Direction, Ms. Blank; scenery, Antje Ellermann; costumes, Mattie Ullrich; lighting, David Lander; sound, Jane Shaw; video, Tal Yarden; press, Richard Kornberg and Associates, Don Summa.

Social change and cultural identity engage in a tale of a family's struggle for survival. Developed through a series of readings and workshops that began with Ms. Blank recording interviews of Ms. Thompson about her family and her life experience.

Beebo Brinker Chronicles (63). Transfer from Off Off Broadway of the play by Kate Moira Ryan and Linda S. Chapman; adapted from the writing of Ann Bannon. Produced by Lily Tomlin, Jane Wagner, Harriet Newman Leve, Elyse Singer, Jamie deRoy, Pam Laudenslager, Douglas Denoff, Double Play Connections at 37 Arts. Opened March 5, 2008. (Closed April 27, 2008)

Marcie; others .... Carolyn Baeumler	Beth .... Autumn Dornfeld
Beebo Brinker .... Jenn Colella	Laura .... Xanthe Elbrick
Charlie; Burr .... Bill Dawes	Jack Mann .... David Greenspan

Understudies: Messrs. Dawes, Greenspan—Nick Basta; Mses. Baeumler, Colella, Dornfeld, Ireland—Brownwen Coleman.

Direction, Leigh Silverman; scenery, Rachel Hauck; costumes, Theresa Squire; lighting, Nicole Pearce; sound, Jill BC DuBoff; hair, Rob Greene and J. Jared Janas; casting, Jack Doulin; stage management, Pamela Edington; press, Spin Cycle, Ron Lasko.

Presented without intermission.

Adaptation of popular pulp novels from the 1950s and 1960s that chart the love affairs of Greenwich Village lesbians. First presentation of record was given Off Off Broadway by Hourglass Group at the Fourth Street Theatre (10/1–28/2007).

Secrets of a Soccer Mom (69). By Kathleen Clark. Produced by A-Frame Productions at the Snapple Theater Center. Opened March 5, 2008. (Closed May 4, 2008)

Nancy .... Nancy Ringham   Alison .... Caralyn Kozlowski
Lynn .... Deborah Sonnenberg

Direction, Judith Ivey; scenery, Lex Liang; costumes, Elizabeth Flauto; lighting, Jeff Croiter; sound, Zachary Williamson; stage management, Scott Pegg; press, Barlow-Hartman.

Presented without intermission.

Mothers on a journey of self-discovery confront their need to compete—even against their own children. First presentation of record was given at Fleetwood Stage in New Rochelle (9–10/2003) under the title *Soccer Moms*.

Tim Minchin (34). Solo performance piece by Mr. Minchin. Produced by Phil McIntyre Entertainment at New World Stages 5. Opened March 5, 2008. (Closed April 12, 2008.

Performed by Mr. Minchin.

Direction, Mr. Minchin; lighting, Paul Jones; sound, Zane Birdwell; stage management, Jason Adams.

Presented without intermission.

An Australian writer of comic songs who has the desire to be a rock star, but not the ego, performs his 90-minute act.

The Public Theater production of **Conversations in Tusculum** (24). By Richard Nelson. Oskar Eustis artistic director, Mara Manus executive director, in the Anspacher Theater. Opened March 11, 2008. (Closed March 30, 2008)

Brutus .... Aidan Quinn   Servilia .... Maria Tucci
Porcia .... Gloria Reuben   Cicero .... Brian Dennehy
Cassius .... David Strathairn   Syrus .... Joe Grifasi

Direction, Mr. Nelson; scenery, Thomas Lynch; costumes, Susan Hilferty; lighting, Jennifer Tipton; sound and music, John Gromada; casting, Jordan Thaler, Heidi Griffiths; stage management, Matthew L. Silver; press, Candi Adams, Sam Neuman.

Presented in two parts.

Time: May–September, in the year 45 BCE. Place: Villas and hillsides near Tusculum.

Roman aristocrats debate their course of action in the face of Julius Caesar's imperial designs, drawing political parallels to the modern United States.

The Public Theater production of **Drunk Enough to Say I Love You?** (25). By Caryl Churchill. Oskar Eustis artistic director, Mara Manus executive director, in association with the Royal Court Theatre, in the Newman Theater. Opened March 16, 2008. (Closed April 6, 2008)

Guy .... Samuel West   Sam .... Scott Cohen

Direction, James Macdonald; scenery, Eugene Lee; costumes, Susan Hilferty; lighting, Peter Mumford; sound, Danny Erdberg; music, Matthew Herbert; stage management, Michael McGoff; press, Candi Adams, Sam Neuman.

Presented without intermission.

Allegory on the "special relationship" between the US and the UK as a pair of male lovers, with Britain portrayed as a needy puppy who never protests enough. First presentation of record was given at the Royal Court Theatre (11/22–12/22/2006).

*Jackie Mason: The Ultimate Jew (78). Solo performance piece by Mr. Mason. Produced by Jyll Rosenfeld, in association with Allen Spivak, Adam Spivak and Larry Magid, at New World Stages 1. Opened March 18, 2008.

Performed by Mr. Mason.

Fast friends? Gideon Banner and Michael Esper in The Four of Us. *Photo: Joan Marcus*

Bridezilla night: Maria Dizzia, Cassie Beck, Sue Jean Kim and Barrett Foa in The Drunken City. *Photo: Joan Marcus*

Direction, Mr. Mason; scenery, Brian Webb; lighting, Paul Miller; sound, Ryan Powers; stage management, Steve Sabaugh; press, David Gersten and Associates.

Presented in two parts.

The latest of Mr. Mason's comedy shows. Before this run, he had 10 Broadway stands. The first was a play titled *A Teaspoon Every Four Hours*, presented at the ANTA Playhouse—now the August Wilson Theatre—for one performance (6/14/1969) following 97 previews. His most recent Broadway run was *Jackie Mason: Freshly Squeezed* (3/23–9/4/2005; 172 performances).

Manhattan Theatre Club production of **The Four of Us** (64). By Itamar Moses. Lynne Meadow artistic director, Daniel Sullivan acting artistic director, Barry Grove executive producer, at City Center Stage II. Opened March 25, 2008. (Closed May 18, 2008)

Benjamin .... Gideon Banner   David .... Michael Esper

Understudy: Messrs. Banner, Esper—Eli James.

Direction, Pam MacKinnon; scenery and costumes, David Zinn; lighting, Russell H. Champa; sound, Daniel Baker; casting, Nancy Piccione; production stage management, Robyn Henry; press, Boneau/Bryan-Brown, Chris Boneau, Aaron Meier, Heath Schwartz, Christine Olver.

Presented without intermission.

Two writers who are friends find their relationship strained as one becomes a wealthy literary star and the other struggles. First presentation of record was given by American Conservatory Theater's First Look series at the Zeum Theater in San Francisco (1/2005) before a production at the Old Globe in San Diego (2/8–3/11/07). Prior to the Off Broadway production, there was a Philadelphia presentation by 1812 Productions (5/18–6/17/2007).

Playwrights Horizons production of **The Drunken City** (31). By Adam Bock. Tim Sanford artistic director, Leslie Marcus managing director, William Russo general manager, in the Peter Jay Sharp Theater. Opened March 26, 2008. (Closed April 20, 2008)

Melissa .... Maria Dizzia   Eddie .... Barrett Foa
Marnie .... Cassie Beck   Frank .... Mike Colter
Linda .... Sue Jean Kim   Bob .... Alfredo Narciso

Direction, Trip Cullman; choreography, John Carrafa; scenery, David Korins; costumes, Jenny Mannis; lighting, Matthew Richards; sound, Bart Fasbender; music, Michael Friedman; casting, Alaine Alldaffer; stage management, Bess Marie Glorioso; press, the Publicity Office, Marc Thibodeau, Michael S. Borowski, Jeremy Shaffer, Matthew Fasano.

Presented without intermission.

Brides-to-be on the town in the big city begin to reconsider choices they have made. First presentation of record was given by the Kitchen Theatre Company in Ithaca, New York (7/9–30/2005).

New York City Center Encores! production **Juno** (5). Concert version of the musical with book by Joseph Stein; music and lyrics by Marc Blitzstein; based on the play *Juno and the Paycock* by Sean O'Casey; concert adaptation, David Ives. Jack Viertel artistic director, at City Center. Opened March 27, 2008. (Closed March 30, 2008)

Sullivan .... Timothy Shew   Jerry Devine .... Michael Arden
Mrs. Maisie Madigan .... Rosaleen Linehan   Charlie Bentham .... Clarke Thorell
Mrs. Coyne .... Kay Walbye   Foley .... Greg Stone
Mrs. Brady .... Louisa Flaningam   "Captain" Jack Boyle ...... Conrad John Schuck
Miss Quinn .... Jennifer Smith   "Joxer" Daly .... Dermot Crowley
Robbie Tancred .... Kurt Froman   First IRA Man .... Kevin Vortmann
Mrs. Tancred .... Annie McGreevey   Second IRA Man .... Patrick Wetzel
Mary Boyle .... Celia Keenan-Bolger   Irish Tenor .... J. Maxwell Miller
Johnny Boyle .... Tyler Hanes   Policeman .... Jay Lusteck
Juno Boyle .... Victoria Clark

Ensemble: Timothy W. Bish, Troy Edward Bowles, Pamela Brumley, Callie Carter, Leah Edwards, Ryan Jackson, Jay Lusteck, Mary MacLeod, Melissa Rae Mahon, J. Maxwell Miller, Pamela Otterson, John Selya, Timothy Shew, Greg Stone, Megan Thomas, Kevin Vortmann, Alan M-L Wager, Patrick Wetzel.

Orchestra: Eric Stern conductor; Martin Agee concertmaster; Maura Giannini, Christoph Franzgrote, Kristina Musser, Laura Seaton, Robert Zubrycki, Ann Labin, Michael Roth, Marti Sweet violin; Richard Brice, Shelley Holland-Moritz, Chris Jenkins viola; Deborah Assael-Migliore, Anja Wood cello; John Beal double bass; Susan Rotholtz, Diane Lesser, Steven Kenyon, Richard Heckman, Robert DeBellis, John Campo woodwinds; Russ Rizner, French horn; John Dent, Phil Granger trumpet; Bruce Bonvissuto, Jack Schatz trombone; Jay Berliner guitar, banjo, mandolin; Mark Mitchell piano; William Schimmel accordion; Billy Miller drums, percussion.

Direction, Garry Hynes; choreography, Warren Carlyle; scenery, John Lee Beatty; costumes, Toni-Leslie James; lighting, Ken Billington; sound, Scott Lehrer; orchestrations, Robert Russell Bennett, Mr. Blitzstein and Hershy Kay; music direction, Mr. Stern; music coordination, Seymour Red Press; casting, Jay Binder, Mark Brandon; stage management, Karen Moore; press, Helene Davis Public Relations.

Time: 1921. Place: Dublin. Presented in two parts.

Musical adaptation of Mr. O'Casey's play about the Irish underclass during some of the worst times of the "troubles." Developed as *Daarlin' Man*, the title was changed a few weeks before the first performances on the road at the National Theatre in Washington, DC (1/17–1/31/1959). *Juno* later played the Shubert Theatre in Boston (2/4–28/1959) before the Broadway opening at the Winter Garden Theatre (3/9–21/1959; 16 performances). Shirley Booth (Juno Boyle) and Melvyn Douglas ("Captain" Jack Boyle) starred in the production.

ACT I

Overture	Orchestra
"We're Alive"	Company
"I Wish It So"	Mary
"Song of the Ma"	Juno
"We Can Be Proud"	Policeman, Sullivan, First IRA Man
"Daarlin' Man"	Captain, Joxer, Company
"One Kind Word"	Jerry
"Old Sayin's"	Captain, Juno
"What Is the Stars?"	Captain, Joxer
"Old Sayin's" (Reprise)	Juno, Captain
"Poor Thing"	Mrs. Madigan, Mrs. Coyne, Mrs. Brady, Miss Quinn
"My True Heart"	Mary, Charlie
"On a Day Like This"	Juno, Mary, Joxer, Captain, Company

ACT II

Entr'acte	Orchestra
"Bird Upon the Tree"	Juno, Mary
"Music in the House"	Captain, Company
"It's Not Irish"	Irish Tenor, Company
"The Liffey Waltz"	Juno, Company
"Hymn"	First IRA Man, Company
Ballet: "The Ballad of Johnny Boyle"	Johnny, Robbie, Company
"Poor Thing" (Reprise)	Mrs. Madigan, Mrs. Coyne, Mrs. Brady, Miss Quinn
"Farewell, Me Butty"	Captain, Joxer
"For Love"	Mary
"One Kind Word" (Reprise)	Jerry
"I Wish It So"	Mary
"Lament"	Juno
"Bird Upon the Tree" (Reprise)	Mary, Juno
Finale	Company

Acts of contrition: Michael Shannon and Ellen Burstyn in The Little Flower of East Orange. *Photo: Monique Carboni*

The Public Theater and **Labyrinth Theater Company** production of **The Little Flower of East Orange** (33). By Stephen Adly Guirgis. Oskar Eustis artistic director, Mara Manus executive director for the Public Theater; John Ortiz artistic director, Philip Seymour Hoffman co-artistic director, John Gould Rubin co-artistic director and executive director for Labyrinth Theater Company; in Martinson Hall. Opened April 6, 2008. (Closed May 4, 2008)

Therese Marie .... Ellen Burstyn	Dr. Shankar .... Ajay Naidu
Aunt Margaret; others .... Elizabeth Canavan	Francis James .... Howie Seago
Magnolia; others .... Liza Colón-Zayas	Danny .... Michael Shannon
Det. Baker; others .... Arthur French	David Halzig; others .... Sidney Williams
Nadine; Cathleen .... Gillian Jacobs	Espinosa; Surgeon 2 .... David Zayas

Direction, Philip Seymour Hoffman; choreography, Barry McNabb; scenery, Narelle Sissons; costumes, Mimi O'Donnell; lighting, Japhy Weideman; sound and music, David Van Tieghem; casting, Jordan Thaler, Heidi Griffiths; stage management, Monica Moore; press, Candi Adams, Sam Neuman, O and M Company, Rick Miramontez, Philip Carrubba.

Time: The present and the past. Place: New York City. Presented in two parts.

A family whose matriarch is dying comes to terms with the passionate, contradictory emotions that drive their anger and grief.

Brooklyn Academy of Music presents the **Baxter Theatre Centre** production of **Sizwe Banzi Is Dead** (10). Revival of the play by Athol Fugard, John Kani and Winston Ntshona. Alan H. Fishman chairman of the board, Karen Brooks Hopkins president, Joseph V. Melillo executive producer, at the Harvey Theater. Opened April 8, 2008. (Closed April 19, 2008)

Styles;   Robert Zwelinzima;
  Buntu .... John Kani   Sizwe Banzi .... Winston Ntshona

Direction, Aubrey Sekhabi; scenery and costumes, Messrs. Kani and Ntshona; lighting, Mannie Manim; stage management, Mary Susan Gregson; press, Sandy Sawotka, Fatima Kafele, John Wyszniewski, Matthew Yeager.

Presented without intermission.

In apartheid-era South Africa, a man must be complicit in self-erasure in order to "survive." First presentation of record was given at the Space Theatre in Cape Town, South Africa (10/8/1972). The production later opened at the Royal Court's Theatre Upstairs (9/20/1973) before a transfer to the Royal Court mainstage (1/8/1974) and a subsequent move to the West End's Ambassadors Theatre (4/10–6/29/1974). First New York presentation of record was given on Broadway at the Edison Theatre (11/13/1974–5/18/1975; 159 performances). Messrs. Kani and Ntshona, who created the roles in the original production in Cape Town, London and New York, both received 1975 Tony Awards in acting for their performances in *Sizwe Banzi Is Dead* (rendered *Sizwe Bansi Is Dead* in early citations) and in *The Island*, which played in repertory that season. Upon their return to South Africa, the actors were arrested following a performance of the play that was deemed "highly inflammatory, vulgar and abusive" by the authorities. A global outcry led to their release—and expulsion from the Transkei "tribal homeland"—after 15 days in solitary confinement. The 2007–08 production was a revival that began at Baxter Theatre Centre, Cape Town (7/11–8/5/2006) before its run at the National Theatre's Lyttelton (3/19–4/4/2007).

*Lincoln Center Theater production of **The New Century** (55). By Paul Rudnick. André Bishop artistic director, Bernard Gersten executive producer, in the Mitzi E. Newhouse Theater. Opened April 14, 2008.

Helene Nadler .... Linda Lavin   Joann Milderry .... Christy Pusz
David Nadler; Shane .... Mike Doyle   Barbara Ellen Diggs .... Jayne Houdyshell
Mr. Charles .... Peter Bartlett   Announcer .... Jordan Dean

Understudies: Mses. Lavin, Houdyshell—Maggie Burke; Mr. Doyle—Jordan Dean; Mr. Bartlett—Jay Rogers; Ms. Pusz—Robyn Kramer.

Direction, Nicholas Martin; scenery, Allen Moyer; costumes, William Ivey Long; lighting, Kenneth Posner; sound and music, Mark Bennett; casting, Daniel Swee; stage management, Stephen M. Kaus; press, Philip Rinaldi, Barbara Carroll.

Time: The present. Place: Long Island; Florida; Illinois, Manhattan. Presented in two parts.

Four short plays (*Pride and Joy*, *Mr. Charles, Currently of Palm Beach*, *Crafty* and *The New Century*) that celebrate the growing mainstream experience of homosexuals in contemporary culture. First presentation of record of *Mr. Charles* was given at Ensemble Studio Theatre during Series A of its Marathon '98 (5/6–6/14/1998). First presentation of record of *Pride and Joy* was given at Pace University as one of the Downtown Plays under the auspices of the Drama Dept.—the theater company, not a department of the university—during the Tribeca Theatre Festival (10/21–31/2004).

*Manhattan Theatre Club production of **From Up Here** (54). By Liz Flahive. Lynne Meadow artistic director, Daniel Sullivan acting artistic director, Barry Grove executive producer, in association with Ars Nova, at City Center Stage I. Opened April 16, 2008.

Kate .... Jenni Barber   Charlie .... Will Rogers
Caroline .... Arija Bareikis   Kenny .... Tobias Segal
Lauren .... Aya Cash   Mr. Goldberger; Stevens .... Joel Van Liew
Daniel .... Brian Hutchison   Grace .... Julie White

Understudies: Messrs. Rogers, Segal—Ben Hollandsworth; Mses. Barber, Cash—Amelia Jean; Mses. Bareikis, White—Colleen Quinlan; Messrs. Hutchison, Van Liew—Baylen Thomas.

Direction, Leigh Silverman; scenery, Allen Moyer; costumes, Mattie Ullrich; lighting, Pat Collins; sound, Jill BC DuBoff; music, Tom Kitt; casting, David Caparelliotis, Nancy Piccione; stage management, David H. Lurie; press, Boneau/Bryan-Brown, Chris Boneau, Aaron Meier, Heath Schwartz, Christine Olver.

Collateral damage: Julie White and Tobias Segal in From Up Here. *Photo: Joan Marcus*

Time: Now. Place: The suburban Midwest. Presented without intermission.

A teenage boy and his family suffer continuing repercussions of an act of violence perpetrated by him. First presentation of record was given as a workshop at Ars Nova's Next Step program (11/2006) after development in the organization's Out Loud reading series.

Brooklyn Academy of Music presentation of **Endgame** (20). Revival of the play by Samuel Beckett. Alan H. Fishman chairman; Karen Brooks Hopkins president; Joseph V. Melillo executive producer, in the Harvey Theater. Opened April 30, 2008. (Closed May 18, 2008)

Clov .... Max Casella   Nell .... Elaine Stritch
Nagg .... Alvin Epstein   Hamm .... John Turturro

Direction, Andrei Belgrader; scenery, Anita Stewart; costumes, Candice Donnelly; lighting, Michael Chybowski; stage management, James Latus; press, Sandy Sawotka, Fatima Kafele, John Wyszniewski, Matthew Yeager.

Presented without intermission.

Human existence in a void without hope. First presentation of record was given in French under the title *Fin de partie*, in French, at the Royal Court Theatre (4/3/1957; 6 performances). First New York presentation of record was given Off Broadway at the Cherry Lane Theatre in a production directed by Alan Schneider with Mr. Epstein in the role of Clov (1/28–4/20/1958; 96 performances).

New York Philharmonic presentation of **Camelot** (5). Concert version of the musical with book and lyrics by Alan Jay Lerner; music by Frederick Loewe; based on the novel *The Once and Future King* by T.H. White; adapted by Lonnie Price. Zarin Mehta president and executive director, at Avery Fisher Hall. Opened May 7, 2008. (Closed May 10, 2008)

Merlyn	Stacy Keach	Lancelot	Nathan Gunn
King Arthur	Gabriel Byrne	Squire Dap	Weston Wells Olson
Guenevere	Marin Mazzie	Pellinore	Christopher Lloyd
Sir Dinadan	Christopher Sieber	Lady Anne	Jane Brockman
Sir Lionel	Marc Kudisch	Mordred	Bobby Steggert
Sir Sagramore	Will Swenson	Morgan le Fey	Fran Drescher
Nimue	Erin Morley	Tom of Warwick	Rishi Mutalik
Page	Justin Stein		

Direction, Mr. Price; choreography, Josh Prince; scenery, James Noone; costumes, Tracy Christensen; lighting, Paul Miller; sound, Peter Fitzgerald; orchestrations, Robert Russell Bennett and Philip J. Lang; music direction, Paul Gemignani; stage management, Peter Hanson; press, Kate Merlino.

Time: Long ago. Place: Camelot; France. Presented in two parts.

King Arthur, Guinevere and Lancelot in an ancient tale of love and betrayal. First announced under the title *Jenny Kiss'd Me* in April 1959, it became *Camelot* by the end of October that year. A play similarly titled—*Jenny Kissed Me* by Jean Kerr—had appeared on Broadway in 1948 for 20 performances (it is also the title of a well-known 19th century poem by Leigh Hunt). First presentation of record was given at the O'Keefe Centre for the Performing Arts in Toronto (10/1–22/1960) before a run at Boston's Shubert Theatre (10/28–11/26/1960). Dates shifted for the embattled show, which had a huge Broadway advance of at least $3 million, as the show needed to be trimmed from three-and-a-half hours to a more manageable length, Mr. Lerner suffered a bleeding ulcer in Toronto that required hospitalization and director Moss Hart suffered a heart attack. The original Broadway production opened at the Majestic Theatre (12/3/1960–1/5/1963; 873 performances) with Julie Andrews, Richard Burton, Robert Goulet, Roddy McDowell and John Cullum. It received 1961 Tony Awards for best actor in a musical (Mr. Burton), scenic design (Oliver Smith), costume design (Adrian, Tony Duquette) and music direction (Franz Allers).

Musical numbers included: "Camelot," "I Wonder What the King Is Doing Tonight," "If Ever I Would Leave You," "What Do the Simple Folk Do?," "The Lusty Month of May," "How to Handle a Woman."

New York City Center Encores! production of **No, No, Nanette** (5). Concert version of the musical with book by Otto Harbach and Frank Mandel; music by Vincent Youmans; lyrics by Irving Caesar and Mr. Harbach; adapted by Burt Shevelove; concert adaptation, David Ives. Jack Viertel artistic director, at City Center. Opened May 8, 2008. (Closed May 12, 2008)

Pauline	Rosie O'Donnell	Tom Trainor	Shonn Wiley
Lucille Early	Beth Leavel	Nanette	Mara Davi
Sue Smith	Sandy Duncan	Flora Latham	Angel Reda
Jimmy Smith	Charles Kimbrough	Betty Brown	Jennifer Cody
Billy Early	Michael Berresse	Winnie Winslow	Nancy Anderson

Ensemble: David Baum, Jacob ben Widmar, Brandon Davidson, Leah Edwards, Sara Edwards, Zak Edwards, Mary Giattino, Luke Hawkins, Matthew J. Kilgore, Cara Kjellman, Todd Lattimore, Deborah Lew, Ryan Malyar, Brent McBeth, Alessa Neeck, Carolann M. Sanita, Kiira Schmidt, Chad Seib, Kelly Sheehan, Anna Aimee White.

Orchestra: Rob Fisher conductor; Suzanne Ornstein concertmistress, violin; Martin Agee, Mineko Yajima, Maura Giannini, Christoph Franzgrote, Kristina Musser, Lisa Matricardi, Robert Zubrycki violin; Richard Brice, Richard Sortomme, Shelley Holland-Moritz, Richard Dolan viola, violin; Roger Shell, Deborah Assael-Migliore cello; John Seal double bass; Jay Berliner guitar, banjo, ukulele; Lawrence Feldman, Steven Kenyon, Dennis Anderson, Lino Gomez, Ronald Jannelli woodwinds; Russ Rizner, French horn; Robert Millikan, Glenn Drewes, John Chudoba trumpet; Bruce Bonvissuto, Dean Plank trombone; Joseph Thalken piano; John Redsecker percussion.

Direction, Walter Bobbie; choreography, Randy Skinner; scenery, John Lee Beatty; costumes, Gregg Barnes; lighting, Ken Billington; sound, Scott Lehrer; orchestrations, Ralph Burns, Luther Henderson; music direction, Mr. Fisher; music coordination, Seymour Red Press; casting, Jay Binder, Jack Bowdan; stage management, Karen Moore; press, Helene Davis Public Relations.

Time: 1925. Place: A weekend in early summer. Presented in three parts.

A nostalgic reprisal of the 1971 revival of a 1925 musical about the many paths to love (and money). First presentation of record was given at the Harris Theatre in Chicago (5/4/1924–4/11/1925) before a tour to Milwaukee, Detroit and other stops. A second company started in Detroit during the Chicago run and moved to Philadelphia for an extended run. A West Coast company began in Los Angeles at the Mason Theatre (3/9–7/4/1925) before a run in San Francisco with a London company opening days later at the Palace Theatre (3/11/1925). Producer H.H. Frazee reportedly was earning $25,000 per week in profit from the show several months before it opened on Broadway. *No, No, Nanette* is based on underlying sources including a Frazee production of *My Lady Friends*, which was a Broadway success in the 1919–20 season despite shedding numerous authors in development. The production of *Nanette* has been long (and probably falsely) associated with the sale of Babe Ruth to the New York Yankees in the spring of 1920 because of a purported need Frazee—who owned the Boston Red Sox in those days—had to raise money for *Nanette*. The sale certainly was effected to be rid of the troublesome Ruth as a Frazee employee, but it is also possible that the money was needed to pay for the purchase of Broadway's Harris Theatre, which became the Frazee in September 1920. Another possibility is that the gradual evolution of *Lady Friends* into *Nanette* led to a conflation of the two by angry Red Sox fans. The original Broadway production of *No, No, Nanette* opened at the Globe Theatre (9/16/1925–6/19/1926; 321 performances). As adapted by Mr. Shevelove, the 1971 Broadway revival was to have been directed and choreographed by Busby Berkeley. Although Mr. Berkeley received "supervision" credit, the famed film choreographer became ill early in the process and was not much of a factor. The revival played at the 45th Street Theatre (1/19/1971–2/3/1973; 861 performances) and received 1971 Tony Awards for best actress in a musical (Helen Gallagher), featured actress in a musical (Patsy Kelly), choreography (Donald Saddler) and costumes (Raoul Pène Du Bois).

ACT I

Overture .... Orchestra
"Too Many Rings Around Rosie" .... Lucille, Men
"I've Confessed to the Breeze" .... Tom, Nanette
"The Call of the Sea" .... Billy, Women
"I Want to Be Happy" .... Jimmy, Nanette,
Sue, Company
"No, No, Nanette" .... Nanette, Tom, Men
Finaletto .... Tom, Nanette, Company

ACT II

"Peach on the Beach" .... Nanette, Company
"The Three Happies" .... Jimmy, Flora,
Betty, Winnie
"Tea for Two" .... Tom, Nanette, Company
"You Can Dance With Any Girl" .... Lucille, Billy
Finaletto .... Company

ACT III

Entr'acte .... Orchestra
"Telephone Girlie" .... Billy, Betty,
Flora, Winnie
The "Where-Has-My-Hubby-Gone?" Blues .... Lucille, Men
"Waiting for You" .... Tom, Nanette
"Take a Little One-Step" .... Sue, Company
(lyrics by Zelda Sears)
Finale .... Company

*Brits Off Broadway presentation of a **Traverse Theatre Company** production of **Damascus** (23). By David Greig. Elysabeth Kleinhans artistic director, Peter Tear executive producer, in Theater A at 59E59 Theaters. Opened May 11, 2008.

Muna .... Nathalie Armin   Paul .... Ewen Bremner

Wasim .... Alex Elliott   Zakaria .... Khalid Laith
Elena .... Dolya Gavanski

Direction, Philip Howard; scenery and costumes, Anthony MacIlwaine; lighting, Chahine Yavroyan; sound, Graham Sutherland; music and arrangements, Jon Beales; stage management, Amy Kaskeski; press, Karen Greco, Kelly Davis.

Presented in two parts.

A hapless Scotsman in Syria writes English language "learning systems" that do not take Arab cultural difference into account—and love may yet bloom. First presentation of record was given at Traverse Theatre during the 2007 Edinburgh Festival (8/5–26/2007). It was revived for an international tour to the Harborfront Centre in Toronto (4/22–26/2008) before its run during Brits Off Broadway.

*Lincoln Center Theater production of **John Lithgow: Stories by Heart** (5). Solo performance piece by Mr. Lithgow. André Bishop artistic director, Bernard Gersten executive producer, in the Mitzi E. Newhouse Theater. Opened May 12, 2008.

Performed by Mr. Lithgow.

Direction, Jack O'Brien; stage management, Brandon Kahn; press, Philip Rinaldi, Barbara Carroll.

Presented without intermission.

A meditation on the art and essence of storytelling in which Mr. Lithgow recites tales favored by his family past and present.

*Second Stage Theatre production of **Good Boys and True** (15). By Roberto Aguirre-Sacasa. Carole Rothman artistic director, Ellen Richard executive director, at Second Stage Theatre. Opened May 19, 2008.

Justin .... Christopher Abbott   Brandon .... Brian J. Smith
Cheryl .... Betty Gilpin   Elizabeth .... J. Smith-Cameron
Maddy .... Kellie Overbey   Coach Shea .... Lee Tergesen

Direction, Scott Ellis; scenery, Derek McLane; costumes, Tom Broecker; lighting, Kenneth Posner; music, Lewis Flinn; casting, Mele Nagler; stage management, Diane DiVita; press, Barlow-Hartman, Michael Hartman, Tom D'Ambrosio, Michelle Bergmann.

Presented without intermission.

Secrets, lies and brutality in an overprivileged prep school force a mother to confront difficult truths about her son. First presentation of record was given as a staged reading at the Eugene O'Neill Theater Center during the National Playwrights' Conference (7/18/2007 and 7/20/2007; 2 performances). First production of record was presented at Steppenwolf Theatre Company, Chicago (12/21/2007–2/16/2008). See the listings in the Season Around the United States section for more information on these presentations.

CAST REPLACEMENTS
AND TOURING COMPANIES

○ ○ ○ ○ ○

Compiled by Jennifer Ashley Tepper

T HE FOLLOWING IS a list of the major cast replacements of record in productions that opened during the current and in previous seasons, and other New York shows that were on a first-class tour in 2007–2008.

The name of each major role is listed in *italics* beneath the title of the play in the first column. In the second column directly opposite appears the name of the actor who created the role in the original New York production (whose opening date appears in *italics* at the top of the column). Indented immediately beneath the original actor's name are the names of subsequent New York replacements—with the date of replacement when available.

The third column gives information about first-class touring companies. When there is more than one roadshow company, #1, #2, etc., appear before the name of the performer who created the role in each company (and the city and date of each company's first performance appears in *italics* at the top of the column). Subsequent replacements are also listed beneath names in the same manner as the New York companies, with dates when available.

ALTAR BOYZ

	New York 3/1/05	*Chicago 6/10/06*
Matthew	Scott Porter	Matthew Buckner
	James Royce Edwards 2/9/06	
	John Selya 4/3/06	
	Kyle Dean Massey	
	Matthew Buckner	
	Chad Doreck 9/3/07	
	Michael Kadin Craig 3/31/08	
Mark	Tyler Maynard	Ryan J. Ratliff
	Danny Calvert 7/12/05	
	Tyler Maynard 1/9/06	
	Zach Hannah	
	Ryan J. Ratliff	
Luke	Andy Karl	Jesse JP Johnson
	James Royce Edwards	
	Andrew C. Call 2/9/06	
	Landon Beard	
	Andrew C. Call 9/21/07	

	Jesse JP Johnson	
	Neil Haskell 4/22/08	
Abraham	David Josefsberg	Nick Blaemire
	Dennis Moench	Ryan Strand
	Eric Schneider	
	Ryan Strand	
Juan	Ryan Duncan	Jay Garcia
	Nick Sanchez	
	Clyde Alves	
	Ryan Duncan 5/1/06	
	Shaun Taylor Corbett 7/3/06	
	Jay Garcia	
	Mauricio Perez	

AUGUST: OSAGE COUNTY

New York 12/4/07

Little Charles	Ian Barford
Violet Weston	Deanna Dunagan
Johnna Monevata	Kimberly Guerrero
Charlie Aiken	Francis Guinan
Steve Heidebrecht	Brian Kerwin
Beverly Weston	Dennis Letts
	Munson Hicks 1/28/08
	Michael McGuire 3/1/08
Jean Fordham	Madeleine Martin
	Molly Ranson
Karen Weston	Mariann Mayberry
Barbara Fordham	Amy Morton
Ivy Weston	Sally Murphy
Bill Fordham	Jeff Perry
Mattie Fae Aiken	Rondi Reed
Sheriff Deon Gilbeau	Troy West
	Scott Jaeck

AVENUE Q

	New York 7/31/03	*San Diego 6/30/07*
Princeton; Rod	John Tartaglia	Robert McClure
	Barrett Foa 2/1/05	
	Howie Michael Smith 7/3/06	
Brian	Jordan Gelber	Cole Porter
	Evan Harrington	
Kate Monster; Lucy	Stephanie D'Abruzzo	Kelli Sawyer
	Mary Faber 12/26/05	
	Kelli Sawyer 10/30/06	
	Mary Faber	
	Sarah Stiles 12/29/07	
Nicky; Trekkie	Rick Lyon	Christian Anderson
	Christian Anderson 7/5/05	

	Rick Lyon 5/2/06 Robert McClure 10/30/06 David Benoit	
Christmas Eve	Ann Harada Ann Sanders 10/26/04 Ann Harada 1/25/05 Ann Sanders	Angela Ai
Gary Coleman	Natalie Venetia Belcon Haneefah Wood Rashidra Scott 12/17/07	Carla Renata

BEAUTY AND THE BEAST

New York 4/18/94
Closed 7/29/07

Beast	Terrence Mann Jeff McCarthy Chuck Wagner James Barbour Steve Blanchard Jeff McCarthy 2/17/04 Steve Blanchard 4/13/04
Belle	Susan Egan Sarah Uriarte Berry Christianne Tisdale Kerry Butler Deborah Gibson Kim Huber Toni Braxton Andrea McArdle Sarah Litzsinger Jamie-Lynn Sigler Sarah Litzsinger 2/11/03 Megan McGinnis 4/15/03 Christy Carlson Romano 2/17/04 Brooke Tansley 9/14/04 Ashley Brown 9/20/05 Sarah Litzsinger 5/30/06 Sarah Uriarte Berry 9/19/06 Deborah Lew 12/26/06 Anneliese van der Pol 4/3/07
Lefou	Kenny Raskin Harrison Beal Jamie Torcellini Jeffrey Schecter Jay Brian Winnick 11/12/99 Gerard McIsaac Brad Aspel Steve Lavner Aldrin Gonzalez
Gaston	Burke Moses Marc Kudisch Steve Blanchard Patrick Ryan Sullivan Christopher Sieber Chris Hoch 12/10/02

Grant Norman
Donny Osmond 9/19/06
Stephen R. Buntrock 12/26/06
Chris Hoch
Donny Osmond

Maurice

Tom Bosley
  MacIntyre Dixon
  Tom Bosley
  Kurt Knudson
  Timothy Jerome
  JB Adams 11/12/99
  Jamie Ross

Cogsworth

Heath Lamberts
  Peter Bartlett
  Robert Gibby Brand
  John Christopher Jones
  Jeff Brooks 11/12/99
  Christopher Duva
  Jonathan Freeman 11/26/06

Lumiere

Gary Beach
  Lee Roy Reams
  Patrick Quinn
  Gary Beach
  Meshach Taylor
  Patrick Page
  Paul Schoeffler
  Patrick Page
  Bryan Batt
  Rob Lorey 5/7/02
  David DeVries
  Peter Flynn
  Jacob Young 5/9/05
  John Tartaglia 11/21/06
  David DeVries 5/22/07

Babette

Stacey Logan
  Pamela Winslow
  Leslie Castay
  Pam Klinger
  Louisa Kendrick
  Pam Klinger
  Meredith Inglesby

Mrs. Potts

Beth Fowler
  Cass Morgan
  Beth Fowler
  Barbara Marineau 11/12/99
  Beth Fowler
  Cass Morgan
  Alma Cuervo 2/17/04
  Jeanne Lehman 11/10/05

CHICAGO

New York 11/14/96

Roxie Hart

Ann Reinking
  Marilu Henner
  Karen Ziemba

Belle Calaway
Charlotte d'Amboise
Sandy Duncan 8/12/99
Belle Calaway 1/18/00
Charlotte d'Amboise 3/24/00
Belle Calaway
Nana Visitor
Petra Nielsen 10/8/01
Nana Visitor 11/19/01
Belle Calaway 1/13/02
Denise Van Outen 3/18/02
Belle Calaway 4/22/02
Amy Spanger 8/6/02
Belle Calaway
Tracy Shayne 4/15/03
Melanie Griffith 7/11/03
Charlotte d'Amboise 10/7/03
Bianca Marroquin 12/15/03
Gretchen Mol 1/5/04
Charlotte d'Amboise 3/1/04
Tracy Shayne
Charlotte d'Amboise
Brooke Shields 9/5/05
Robin Givens
Tracy Shayne
Charlotte d'Amboise
Rita Wilson 6/12/06
Bianca Marroquin
Bebe Neuwirth 12/31/06
Bianca Marroquin 4/23/07
Lisa Rinna 6/19/07
Michelle DeJean 8/7/07
Tracy Shayne 9/4/07
Michelle DeJean 9/11/07

Velma Kelly   Bebe Neuwirth
Nancy Hess
Ute Lemper
Bebe Neuwirth
Ruthie Henshall 5/25/99
Mamie Duncan-Gibbs 10/26/99
Bebe Neuwirth 1/18/00
Donna Marie Asbury 3/23/00
Sharon Lawrence 4/11/00
Vicki Lewis
Jasmine Guy
Bebe Neuwirth
Donna Marie Asbury
Deidre Goodwin
Vicki Lewis
Deidre Goodwin 6/29/01
Anna Montanaro 7/9/01
Deidre Goodwin 9/14/01
Donna Marie Asbury
Roxane Carrasco 1/13/02
Deidre Goodwin 3/18/02
Stephanie Pope
Roxane Carrasco
Caroline O'Connor 11/8/02

Brenda Braxton 3/3/03
Deidre Goodwin 6/24/03
Reva Rice 10/7/03
Brenda Braxton 1/1/04
Pia Dowes 4/8/04
Brenda Braxton 5/16/04
Terra C. MacLeod 7/27/04
Donna Marie Asbury 2/14/05
Brenda Braxton 2/21/05
Luba Mason 6/28/05
Brenda Braxton
Robin Givens
Brenda Braxton
Amra-Faye Wright
Brenda Braxton 4/17/06
Terra C. MacLeod 2/21/08
Brenda Braxton 3/7/08
Mya Harrison 5/12/08
Nancy Lemenager 5/19/08

Billy Flynn　　　　James Naughton
Gregory Jbara
Hinton Battle
Alan Thicke
Michael Berresse
Brent Barrett
Robert Urich 1/11/00
Clarke Peters 2/1/00
Brent Barrett 2/15/00
Chuck Cooper
Brent Barrett 7/2/01
Chuck Cooper 8/27/01
George Hamilton 11/12/01
Eric Jordan Young 1/18/02
Ron Raines 3/26/02
George Hamilton 5/21/02
Michael C. Hall 8/8/02
Destan Owens
Taye Diggs
Billy Zane 11/8/02
Kevin Richardson 1/20/03
Clarke Peters
Gregory Harrison
Brent Barrett 6/2/03
Patrick Swayze 12/15/03
James Naughton 1/5/04
Norm Lewis 2/2/04
Christopher Sieber 3/23/04
Tom Wopat 5/16/04
Christopher Sieber 6/17/04
Marti Pellow 8/3/04
Wayne Brady 9/7/04
Tom Wopat 12/7/04
Brent Barrett 1/4/05
Christopher McDonald 7/1/05
Huey Lewis 11/18/05
John O'Hurley 1/16/06
Obba Babatunde 4/17/06
Usher 8/22/06

Christopher McDonald 10/15/06
Huey Lewis 11/20/06
Philip Casnoff 1/12/06
Joey Lawrence 5/4/07
Harry Hamlin 6/19/07
Tom Wopat 8/7/07
George Hamilton 9/14/07
Brian McKnight 10/8/07
Maxwell Caulfield 11/19/07
Jeff McCarthy 12/7/07
John Schneider 1/14/08

Amos Hart   Joel Grey
Ernie Sabella
Tom McGowan
P.J. Benjamin
Ernie Sabella 11/23/99
P.J. Benjamin
Tom McGowan
P.J. Benjamin
Raymond Bokhour 7/30/01
P.J. Benjamin 8/13/01
Rob Bartlett
P.J. Benjamin 3/3/03
Raymond Bokhour
P.J. Benjamin
Raymond Bokhour
Kevin Chamberlin 6/12/06
Rob Bartlett
Vincent Pastore 11/19/07
Ron Orbach 1/28/08

Matron   Marcia Lewis
Roz Ryan
Marcia Lewis
Roz Ryan
Marcia Lewis
Roz Ryan
Marcia Lewis
Jennifer Holliday 6/18/01
Marcia Lewis 8/27/01
Roz Ryan 11/16/01
Michele Pawk 1/14/02
Alix Korey 3/4/02
B.J. Crosby 3/3/03
Angie Stone 4/15/03
Camille Saviola 6/10/03
Debbie Gravitte 12/15/03
Roz Ryan 3/15/04
Carol Woods
Roz Ryan
Anne L. Nathan 9/13/04
Carol Woods 1/31/05
Anne L. Nathan 2/21/05
Mary Testa
Carol Woods
Debra Monk 9/5/06
Lillias White 1/31/07
Roz Ryan

Adriane Lenox 8/7/07
Roz Ryan 10/1/07
Aida Turturro 11/19/07

Mary Sunshine   D. Sabella
J. Loeffelholz
R. Bean
A. Saunders
J. Maldonado
R. Bean
A. Saunders 1/2/02
R. Bean 1/14/02
M. Agnes
D. Sabella 3/24/03
R. Bean 5/17/04
R. Lowe
D. Sabella-Mills 8/28/07

A CHORUS LINE
New York 8/5/06

Bobby   Ken Alan
Will Taylor 7/24/07

Don   Brad Anderson
Jason Patrick Sands 7/24/07

Zach   Michael Berresse
Mario Lopez 4/15/08
Grant Turner 5/13/08

Diana   Natalie Cortez

Cassie   Charlotte d'Amboise

Maggie   Mara Davi
Melissa Lone 7/24/07

Val   Jessica Lee Goldyn
Jenifer Foote

Sheila   Deidre Goodwin

Larry   Tyler Hanes
Nick Adams 7/24/07

Richie   James T. Lane

Mark   Paul McGill

Judy   Heather Parcells

Greg   Michael Paternostro
Michael Gruber 7/24/07

Bebe   Alisan Porter
Krysta Rodriguez 7/24/07

Mike   Jeffrey Howard Schecter

Connie   Yuka Takara
J. Elaine Marcos 12/4/06
Lisa Ho
J. Elaine Marcos 7/24/07

Paul   Jason Tam
Bryan Knowlton 7/24/07

Kristine   Chryssie Whitehead
Katherine Tokarz 7/24/07

| *Al* | Tony Yazbeck | |
| | Kevin B. Worley 7/3/07 | |

THE COLOR PURPLE

	New York 12/1/05	*Chicago 4/17/07*
	Closed 2/24/08	
Celie	LaChanze	Jeannette I. Bayardelle
	Jeannette I. Bayardelle 11/7/06	Kenita R. Miller
	Kenita R. Miller 2/20/07	
	Fantasia Barrino 4/10/07	
	Zonya Love 1/9/08	
Shug Avery	Elisabeth Withers-Mendes	Michelle Williams
	Angela Robinson 2/1/08	Angela Robinson
Mister	Kingsley Leggs	Rufus Bonds Jr.
Sophia	Felicia P. Fields	Felicia P. Fields
	NaTasha Yvette Williams 1/30/07	
	Chaka Khan 1/9/08	
Nettie	Renee Elise Goldsberry	LaToya London
	Darlesia Cearcy 1/17/07	
Harpo	Brandon Victor Dixon	Stu James
	Chaz Lamar Shepherd	
	Bebe Winans 1/9/08	
Old Mister	Lou Meyers	Adam Wade
	Larry Marshall	

COMPANY

	New York 11/29/06
	Closed 7/1/07
Robert	Raúl Esparza
Harry	Keith Buterbaugh
Peter	Matt Castle
Paul	Robert Cunningham
Marta	Angel Desai
Kathy	Kelly Jeanne Grant
Sarah	Kristin Huffman
Susan	Amy Justman
Amy	Heather Laws
	Jane Pfitsch
Jenny	Leenya Rideout
David	Fred Rose
Larry	Bruce Sabath
April	Elizabeth Stanley
Joanne	Barbara Walsh

CURTAINS

	New York 3/22/07
Lt. Frank Cioffi	David Hyde Pierce

Carmen Bernstein	Debra Monk
Georgia Hendricks	Karen Ziemba
Aaron Fox	Jason Danieley
Niki Harris	Jill Paice
	Erin Davie 2/15/08
Christopher Belling	Edward Hibbert
Daryl Grady	John Bolton
Johnny Harmon	Michael X. Martin
Oscar Shapiro	Michael McCormick
Bobby Pepper	Noah Racey
	David Elder
Sidney Bernstein	Ernie Sabella
	Gerry Vichi 1/8/08
Bambi Bernet	Megan Sikora

THE DROWSY CHAPERONE

	New York 5/1/06	Toronto 9/19/07
	Closed 12/30/07	
Janet Van De Graff	Sutton Foster	Andrea Chamberlain
	Janine LaManna 4/17/07	
	Mara Davi 7/31/07	
Man in Chair	Bob Martin	Bob Martin
	Jonathan Crombie 3/20/07	Jonathan Crombie
	John Glover 4/17/07	
	Jonathan Crombie 8/21/07	
	Bob Saget 10/19/07	
Mrs. Tottendale	Georgia Engel	Georgia Engel
	Jo Anne Worley 4/17/07	
	Cindy Williams 12/11/07	
Underling	Edward Hibbert	Robert Dorfman
	Peter Bartlett 1/16/07	
George	Eddie Korbich	Richard Vida
	Patrick Wetzel 5/22/07	
Feldzieg	Lenny Wolpe	Cliff Bemis
	Gerry Vichi 6/5/07	
The Drowsy Chaperone	Beth Leavel	Nancy Opel
Aldopho	Danny Burstein	James Moye
		Dale Hensley
Robert Martin	Troy Britton Johnson	Mark Ledbetter

THE FANTASTICKS

	New York 8/23/06
Matt	Santino Fontana
	Douglas Ullman Jr.
	Anthony Fedorov 5/1/07
	Nick Spangler 7/30/07
	Douglas Ullman Jr. 10/29/07
	Nick Spangler
Luisa	Sara Jean Ford

                            Julie Craig
                            Betsy Morgan
                            Whitney Bashor
                            Julie Craig 7/30/07
                            Whitney Bashor 11/5/07
                            Julie Craig 1/15/08
El Gallo   Burke Moses
                            Ivan Hernandez 9/17/07
                            Burke Moses 10/29/07
Hucklebee   Leo Burmester
                            John Deyle
Bellomy   Martin Vidnovic
Henry   Thomas Bruce (Tom Jones)
                            William Tost
Mortimer   Robert R. Oliver
Mute   Douglas Ullman Jr.
                            Nick Spangler
                            Jordan Nichols 7/30/07

GREASE
                            New York 8/19/07
Danny Zuko   Max Crumm
Sandy Dumbrowski   Laura Osnes
Doody   Ryan Patrick Binder
Miss Lynch   Susan Blommaert
Vince Fontaine   Jeb Brown
Teen Angel   Stephen R. Buntrock
Roger   Daniel Everidge
                            Will Blum 5/26/08
Patty Simcox   Allison Fischer
Cha-Cha   Natalie Hill
Marty   Robyn Hurder
Jan   Lindsay Mendez
Betty Rizzo   Jenny Powers
Sonny Latierri   Jose Restrepo
Kenickie   Matthew Saldivar
Eugene   Jamison Scott
Frenchy   Kirsten Wyatt

HAIRSPRAY
                            New York 8/15/02
Tracy Turnblad   Marissa Jaret Winokur
                            Kathy Brier 8/12/03
                            Carly Jibson 5/4/04
                            Marissa Jaret Winokur 6/8/05
                            Shannon Durig
                            Marissa Perry 4/15/08

Edna Turnblad	Harvey Fierstein
	Michael McKean 5/4/04
	Bruce Vilanch
	John Pinette 9/6/05
	Blake Hammond
	Paul C. Vogt 1/30/07
	George Wendt 10/23/07
Wilbur Turnblad	Dick Latessa
	Peter Scolari
	Todd Susman
	Stephen DeRosa 9/6/05
	Jere Burns
	Jerry Mathers 6/5/07
	Jim J. Bullock 9/18/07
Amber Von Tussle	Laura Bell Bundy
	Tracy Jai Edwards 7/14/03
	Jordan Ballard
	Becky Gulsvig
	Brynn O'Malley
	Ashley Spencer 7/24/07
Velma Von Tussle	Linda Hart
	Barbara Walsh 7/14/03
	Leah Hocking
	Liz Larsen
	Leah Hocking 3/13/06
	Isabel Keating 6/6/06
	Michele Pawk 8/21/07
	Mary Birdsong
	Karen Mason 4/8/08
Link Larkin	Matthew Morrison
	Richard H. Blake 1/13/04
	Andrew Rannells
	Ashley Parker Angel
Motormouth Maybelle	Mary Bond Davis
	Darlene Love
	Jenifer Lewis 4/22/08
Seaweed	Corey Reynolds
	Chester Gregory II 7/14/03
	Tevin Campbell 12/13/05
Penny Pingleton	Kerry Butler
	Jennifer Gambatese 6/15/04
	Brooke Tansley 4/11/04
	Jennifer Gambatese 6/15/04
	Tracy Miller
	Diana DeGarmo 2/7/06
	Haylie Duff 7/18/06
	Diana DeGarmo
	Alexa Vega 2/13/07
	Niki Scalera
Corny Collins	Clarke Thorell
	Jonathan Dokuchitz 1/13/04
	Lance Bass 8/14/07
Little Inez	Danelle Eugenia Wilson
	Aja Maria Johnson 7/19/03
	Nia Imani Soyemi

I LOVE YOU, YOU'RE PERFECT, NOW CHANGE

New York 8/1/96

Man #1   Jordan Leeds
                Danny Burstein 10/1/96
                Adam Grupper 8/22/97
                Gary Imhoff 2/9/98
                Adam Grupper 4/1/98
                Jordan Leeds 3/17/99
                Bob Walton 10/27/00
                Jordan Leeds 1/30/01
                Darrin Baker 1/29/02
                Danny Burstein 4/12/02
                Jordan Leeds 6/3/02
                Will Erat 12/20/05
                Ron Bohmer 3/20/06
                Will Erat
                Jim Stanek
                Frank Vlastnik 10/1/07

Man #2   Robert Roznowski
                Kevin Pariseau 5/25/98
                Adam Hunter 4/20/01
                Sean Arbuckle 9/23/02
                Frank Baiocchi 2/17/03
                Colin Stokes 10/10/03
                Jamie LaVerdiere
                Adam Arian
                Brian McElroy 1/29/07
                Jonathan Rayson 10/26/07

Woman #1   Jennifer Simard
                Erin Leigh Peck 5/25/98
                Kelly Anne Clark 1/10/00
                Andrea Chamberlain 3/13/00
                Lori Hammel 11/4/00
                Andrea Chamberlain 1/29/01
                Amanda Watkins 8/24/01
                Karyn Quackenbush 1/2/02
                Marissa Burgoyne 8/9/02
                Andrea Chamberlain 12/17/02
                Karyn Quackenbush 2/17/03
                Sandy Rustin 6/13/03
                Andrea Chamberlain 11/19/04
                Jordan Ballard
                Jodie Langel
                Courtney Balan 12/8/06
                Amy White
                Christy Faber 1/14/08

Woman #2   Melissa Weil
                Cheryl Stern 2/16/98
                Mylinda Hull 9/17/00
                Melissa Weil 2/9/01
                Evy O'Rourke 3/13/01
                Marylee Graffeo 6/11/01
                Cheryl Stern 1/18/02
                Marylee Graffeo 3/11/02
                Janet Metz 4/26/02

Anne Bobby 12/17/02
Janet Metz 3/3/03
Anne Bobby 5/23/05

JERSEY BOYS

	New York 11/6/05	*San Francisco 12/1/06*
Frankie Valli	John Lloyd Young	Jarrod Spector
	Michael Longoria 11/29/07	Christopher Kale Jones
		Joseph Leo Bwarie
Tommy DeVito	Christian Hoff	Deven May
	Dominic Nolfi	Jeremy Kushnier
Bob Gaudio	Daniel Reichard	Erich Bergen
	Sebastian Arcelus 1/10/08	Andrew Rannells
Nick Massi	J. Robert Spencer	Michael Ingersoll
		Steve Gouveia

LEGALLY BLONDE

	New York 4/29/07
Elle Woods	Laura Bell Bundy
Warner Huntington III	Richard H. Blake
Emmett Forrest	Christian Borle
Paulette	Orfeh
Professor Callahan	Michael Rupert
Vivienne Kensington	Kate Shindle
Brooke Wyndam	Nikki Snelson
	Michelle Kittrell 4/9/08
	Beth Curry 4/23/08
	Nicolette Hart 5/7/08
Margot	Annaleigh Ashford
	Haven Burton 9/26/07
	Kate Rockwell 5/13/08
Serena	Leslie Kritzer
	Tracy Jai Edwards 8/15/07
Pilar	DeQuina Moore
	Asmeret Ghebremichael 7/2/07
Enid	Natalie Joy Johnson
Kyle	Andy Karl

LES MISÉRABLES

	New York 11/9/06
	Closed 1/6/08
Jean Valjean	Alexander Gemignani
	Drew Sarich 7/23/07
	John Owen-Jones 10/23/07
Inspector Javert	Norm Lewis
	Ben Davis 4/24/07
	Drew Sarich (alt.)
	Robert Hunt 7/6/07
Fantine	Daphne Rubin-Vega

	Lea Salonga 3/6/07
	Judy Kuhn 10/23/07
Marius	Adam Jacobs
Cosette	Ali Ewoldt
	Leah Horowitz
Eponine	Celia Keenan-Bolger
	Mandy Bruno 4/24/07
	Megan McGinnis 6/18/07
Madame Thernardier	Jenny Galloway
	Ann Harada 4/24/07
Thernardier	Gary Beach
	Chip Zien 6/29/07
Enjolras	Aaron Lazar
	Max von Essen 4/24/07

THE LION KING

	New York 11/13/97	*#1 Gazelle Company* *#2 Cheetah Company*

Rafiki	Tsidii Le Loka
	Thuli Dumakude 11/11/98
	Sheila Gibbs
	Nomvula Dlamini
	Tshidi Manye
		#1 Futhi Mhlongo
		    Phindile Mkhize
		#2 Thandazile A. Soni
		    Gugwana Dlamini

Mufasa	Samuel E. Wright
	Alton Fitzgerald White
	Nathaniel Stampley
		#1 Alton Fitzgerald White
		    Thomas Corey Robinson
		    L. Steven Taylor
		    Dionne Randolph
		#2 Rufus Bonds Jr.
		    Nathaniel Stampley
		    Geno Segers

Sarabi	Gina Breedlove Meena T. Jahi 8/4/98 Denise Marie Williams Meena T. Jahi Robyn Payne Jean Michelle Grier	#1 Jean Michelle Grier Lashanda Reese-Fletcher #2 Marvette Williams

Zazu	Geoff Hoyle
	Bill Bowers 10/21/98
	Robert Dorfman
	Tony Freeman
	Adam Stein
	Jeffrey Binder
		#1 Jeffrey Binder
		    Mark Cameron Pow
		#2 Derek Hasenstab
		    Timothy McGeever
		    Michael Dean Morgan

Scar	John Vickery
	Tom Hewitt 10/21/98
	
	Derek Smith
	Patrick Page
	Derek Smith
	Patrick Page
	Dan Donohue 10/9/07
	Derek Smith 3/30/08
		#1 Patrick Page
		    Dan Donohue
		    Timothy Carter
		#2 Larry Yando
		    Kevin Gray

Banzai	Stanley Wayne Mathis Keith Bennett 9/30/98	#1 James Brown-Orleans Randy Donaldson

	Leonard Joseph	#2 Melvin Abston
	Curtiss I'Cook	Rudy Roberson
	Rodrick Covington	
	Benjamin Sterling Cannon	
	James Brown-Orleans	
Shenzi	Tracy Nicole Chapman	#1 Jacquelyn Renae Hodges
	Vanessa S. Jones	Kimberly Hebert Gregory
	Lana Gordon	Jayne Trinette
	Marlayna Sims	#2 Shaullanda Lacombe
	Bonita J. Hamilton	Danielle Lee Greaves
		Jacquelyn Renae Hodges
Ed	Kevin Cahoon	#1 Wayne Pyle
	Jeff Skowron 10/21/98	Michael Nathanson
	Jeff Gurner	#2 Brian Sills
	Timothy Gulan	Robbie Swift
	Thom Christopher Warren	
	Enrique Segura	
Timon	Max Casella	#1 John Plumpis
	Danny Rutigliano 6/16/98	Mark Shunock
	John E. Brady	#2 Benjamin Clost
	Danny Rutigliano	Adam Hunter
		Damian Baldet
		John Gardiner
Pumbaa	Tom Alan Robbins	#1 Ben Lipitz
		#2 Bob Amaral
		Phil Fiorini
		Bob Amaral
Simba	Jason Raize	#1 Alan Mingo Jr.
	Christopher Jackson	S.J. Hannah
	Josh Tower	Dashaun Young
	Wallace Smith	#2 Brandon Victor Dixon
	Dashaun Young 11/2/07	Brandon Louis
	Wallace Smith 12/30/07	Wallace Smith
		Clifton Oliver
Nala	Heather Headley	#1 Kissy Simmons
	Mary Randle 7/7/98	Lisa Nicole Wilkerson
	Heather Headley 12/8/98	Adrienne Muller
	Bashirrah Creswell	Chauntee Schuler
	Sharon L. Young	Erica Ash
	Renée Elise Goldsberry	#2 Adia Ginneh Dobbins
	Kissy Simmons	Ta'rea Campbell

MAMMA MIA!

	New York 10/18/01	*#1 US Tour*
		#2 Las Vegas
Donna Sheridan	Louise Pitre	#1 Dee Hoty
	Dee Hoty 10/22/03	Laurie Wells
	Carolee Carmello 10/20/04	Mary Jayne Raleigh
	Michele Pawk 10/19/05	#2 Tina Walsh
	Corinne Melancon	Jacqueline Holland
	Leah Hocking	Carol Linnea Johnson
	Carolee Carmello	
Sophie Sheridan	Tina Maddigan	#1 Chilina Kennedy
	Jenny Fellner 10/22/03	Carrie Manolakos

	Sara Kramer 10/20/04	Vicki Noon
	Carey Anderson 10/19/05	#2 Jill Paice
		Suzie Jacobsen Balser
		Kelly Anise Daniells
		Libby Winters
Tanya	Karen Mason	#1 Cynthia Sophiea
	Jeanine Morick	Lisa Mandel
	Tamara Bernier	Christine Sherrill
	Judy McLane 10/20/04	#2 Karole Foreman
	Joan Hess	Reyna Von Vett
	Summer Rognlie	Vicki Van Tassel
	Judy McLane 9/26/07	
Rosie	Judy Kaye	#1 Rosalyn Rahn Kerins
	Harriett D. Foy	Laura Ware
	Liz McCartney 10/20/04	Allison Briner
	Olga Merediz 10/19/2005	#2 Jennifer Perry
	Gina Ferrall	Kristine Zbornik
		Robin Baxter
Sky	Joe Machota	#1 P.J. Griffith
	Aaron Staton	Corey Greenan
	Andy Kelso 10/19/05	Timothy Ware
		#2 Victor Wallace
		Patrick Sarb
Sam Carmichael	David W. Keeley	#1 Gary Lynch
	John Hillner	Sean Allan Krill
	David W. Keeley	#2 Nick Cokas
	John Hillner	Lewis Cleale
	Daniel McDonald 10/20/04	Rick Negron
	John Dossett 10/19/05	Rob Sutton
	David McDonald	
	Christopher Shyer 9/26/07	
Harry Bright	Dean Nolen	#1 Michael DeVries
	Richard Binsley	Ian Simpson
	Michael Winther	#2 Michael Piontek
	David Beach 10/20/04	Andy Taylor
	Michael Mastro	T. Scott Cunningham
	Ben Livingston 9/26/07	
Bill Austin	Ken Marks	#1 Craig Bennett
	Adam LeFevre	Milo Shandel
	Mark L. Montgomery	#2 Mark Leydorf
	Pearce Bunting	Patrick Gallo
		Jefferson Slinkard
		Ron McClary

MARY POPPINS

New York 11/16/06

Mary Poppins	Ashley Brown
George Banks	Daniel Jenkins
Bert	Gavin Lee
Winifred Banks	Rebecca Luker
Jane Banks	Katherine Doherty
	Kathryn Faughnan
	Delaney Moro

Alexandra Berro
Nicole Bocchi
Lila Coogan
Devynn Pedell

Michael Banks   Matthew Gumley
Henry Hodges
Alexander Scheitinger
Jacob Levine
Daniel Marconi

THE PHANTOM OF THE OPERA

New York 1/26/88   *#1 National Tour*
                            #2 Las Vegas (95 minutes)

The Phantom	Michael Crawford	#1 Franc D'Ambrosio
	Thomas James O'Leary	Brad Little
	Hugh Panaro 2/1/99	Ted Keegan
	Howard McGillin 8/23/99	Brad Little
	Brad Little	Ted Keegan
	Howard McGillin	Brad Little
	Hugh Panaro 4/14/03	Gary Mauer
	Howard McGillin 12/22/03	John Cudia
	Hugh Panaro 1/5/04	#2 Brent Barrett (alt.)
	Howard McGillin	#2 Anthony Crivello (alt.)
	Gary Mauer	
	Howard McGillin	
	John Cudia 5/22/08	
Christine Daaé	Sarah Brightman	#1 Tracy Shane
	Sandra Joseph 1/29/98	Kimilee Bryant
	Adrienne McEwan 8/2/99	Amy Jo Arrington
	Sarah Pfisterer 1/17/00	Rebecca Pitcher
	Sandra Joseph 10/30/00	Kathy Voytko
	Sarah Pfisterer 8/6/01	Julie Hanson
	Elizabeth Southard 3/25/02	Rebecca Pitcher
	Lisa Vroman 4/22/02	Lisa Vroman
	Sandra Joseph 6/10/03	Rebecca Pitcher
	Jennifer Hope Wills 12/12/06	Marie Danvers
		Jennifer Hope Wills
		Marni Raab
		#2 Sierra Boggess (alt.)
		#2 Elizabeth Loyacano (alt.)
		Kristi Holden
Christine Daaé (alt.)	Patti Cohenour	#1 Tamra Hayden
	Adrienne McEwan	Marie Danvers
	Sarah Pfisterer	Megan Starr-Levitt
	Adrienne McEwan	Marni Raab
	Lisa Vroman 10/30/00	Elizabeth Southard
	Adrienne McEwan 7/9/01	Sarah Lawrence
	Julie Hanson 9/20/03	
	Elizabeth Loyacano 12/8/07	
Raoul	Steve Barton	#1 Ciaran Sheehan
	Gary Mauer 4/19/99	Jason Pebworth 1/29/97
	Jim Weitzer 4/23/01	Jim Weitzer
	Michael Shawn Lewis 11/2/01	Jason Pebworth 7/22/98
	John Cudia 4/7/03	Richard Todd Adams 3/31/99
	Jim Weitzer 10/3/03	Jim Weitzer 1/12/00

John Cudia 12/21/03
Tim Martin Gleason 5/27/05
Michael Shawn Lewis
Tim Martin Gleason

John Cudia
Tim Martin Gleason
Jim Weitzer
Adam Monley
Michael Gillis
Greg Mills
#2 Tim Martin Gleason

RENT

New York 4/29/96

Roger Davis

Adam Pascal
  Norbert Leo Butz
  Richard H. Blake (alt.)
  Manley Pope 6/1/02
  Sebastian Arcelus 12/30/02
  Ryan Link 9/8/03
  Jeremy Kushnier 11/14/03
  Carey Shields 1/18/05
  Will Chase 12/26/05
  Tim Howar 1/30/06
  Adam Pascal 7/30/07
  Declan Bennett 10/8/07
  Will Chase 5/5/08

Mark Cohen

Anthony Rapp
  Jim Poulos
  Trey Ellett 5/15/00
  Matt Caplan 6/1/02
  Joey Fatone 8/5/02
  Matt Caplan 12/23/02
  Drew Lachey 9/10/04
  Matt Caplan 3/14/04
  Christopher J. Hanke 8/5/06
  Anthony Rapp 7/30/07
  Harley Jay 10/8/07
  Adam Kantor 3/24/08

Tom Collins

Jesse L. Martin
  Michael McElroy
  Rufus Bonds Jr. 9/7/99
  Alan Mingo Jr. 4/10/00
  Mark Leroy Jackson 1/15/01
  Mark Richard Ford 2/3/02
  Destan Owens 8/16/04
  Mark Richard Ford 12/20/04
  Destan Owens
  Troy Horne 11/27/06
  Michael McElroy

Benjamin Coffin III

Taye Diggs
  Jacques C. Smith
  Stu James 3/13/00
  D'Monroe
  Stu James 11/29/04
  D'Monroe
  Rodney Hicks 9/13/07

Joanne Jefferson

Fredi Walker
  Gwen Stewart

Alia León
Kenna J. Ramsey
Danielle Lee Greaves 10/4/99
Natalie Venetia Belcon 10/2/00
Myiia Watson-Davis 6/1/02
Merle Dandridge 10/28/02
Kenna J. Ramsey 3/3/03
Merle Dandridge
Nicole Lewis
Kenna J. Ramsey 11/29/05
Tonya Dixon 11/13/06
Merle Dandridge

Angel Schunard Wilson Jermaine Heredia
  Wilson Cruz
  Shaun Earl
  Jose Llana
  Jai Rodriguez
  Andy Señor 1/31/00
  Jai Rodriguez 3/10/02
  Andy Señor 2/17/03
  Jai Rodriguez 7/05/04
  Andy Señor 7/19/04
  Jai Rodriguez 8/2/04
  Justin Johnston 8/16/04
  Andy Señor 3/15/04
  Justin Johnston

Mimi Marquez Daphne Rubin-Vega
  Marcy Harriell 4/5/97
  Krysten Cummings
  Maya Days
  Loraine Velez 2/28/00
  Karmine Alers 6/1/02
  Krystal L. Washington 5/15/03
  Melanie Brown 4/19/04
  Krystal L. Washington 8/23/04
  Jamie Lee Kirchner
  Antonique Smith 3/6/07
  Tamyra Gray 5/29/07

Maureen Johnson Idina Menzel
  Sherie René Scott
  Kristen Lee Kelly
  Tamara Podemski
  Cristina Fadale 10/4/99
  Maggie Benjamin 6/1/02
  Cristina Fadale 10/28/02
  Maggie Benjamin
  Melanie Brown
  Maggie Benjamin 4/19/04
  Kelly Karbacz 7/19/04
  Maggie Benjamin
  Ava Gaudet
  Maggie Benjamin 10/5/06
  Nicolette Hart 1/8/07
  Eden Espinosa 5/30/08

SPAMALOT

	New York 3/17/05	#1 Boston 3/7/06 #2 Las Vegas 3/31/07 (90 minutes)

King Arthur	Tim Curry
	John Bolton 7/22/05
	Tim Curry 8/9/05
	Simon Russell Beale 12/20/05
	Harry Groener 4/25/06
	Jonathan Hadary 10/31/06
		#1 Michael Siberry
		   Gary Beach 3/4/08
		   Jonathan Hadary 9/2/08
		   Richard Chamberlain 1/20/09
		#2 John O'Hurley

Lady of the Lake	Sara Ramirez Lauren Kennedy 12/20/05 Marin Mazzie 10/31/06 Hannah Waddingham 1/13/08	#1 Pia C. Glenn Esther Stilwell #2 Nikki Crawford

Sir Dennis Galahad	Christopher Sieber
	Lewis Cleale 7/5/06
	Christopher Sieber 5/1/07
	Bradley Dean 3/25/08
		#1 Bradley Dean
		   Ben Davis
		   Anthony Holds
		#2 Edward Staudenmayer

Sir Robin	David Hyde Pierce
	Martin Moran 4/4/06
	Clay Aiken 1/18/08
	Robert Petkoff 5/6/08
		#1 David Turner
		   James Beaman
		   Robert Petkoff
		#2 Harry Bouvy

Sir Lancelot	Hank Azaria Alan Tudyk 8/6/05 Hank Azaria 12/2/05 Steve Kazee 4/4/06 Chris Hoch 10/3/06 Richard Holmes	#1 Richard Holmes Patrick Heusinger #2 J. Anthony Crane
Patsy	Michael McGrath David Hibbard Michael McGrath	#1 Jeff Dumas Brad Bradley #2 Justin Brill
Sir Bedevere	Steve Rosen Jeffrey Kuhn Brad Oscar 12/18/07 Steve Rosen 4/29/08	#1 Christopher Gurr #2 Randal Keith
Prince Herbert	Christian Borle Tom Deckman	#1 Tom Deckman Christopher Sutton #2 Steven Strafford

SPRING AWAKENING

	New York 12/10/06
Georg	Skylar Astin
Martha	Lilli Cooper
Adult Women	Christine Estabrook Kate Burton 12/21/07 Christine Estabrook
Moritz	John Gallagher Jr. Blake Bashoff 12/18/07
Ernst	Gideon Glick Blake Daniel

Melchior	Jonathan Groff
	Kyle Riabko 5/23/08
Otto	Brian Charles Johnson
Wendla	Lea Michele
	Alexandra Socha 5/20/08
Ilse	Lauren Pritchard
	Emma Hunton 2/19/08
Adult Men	Stephen Spinella
	Glenn Fleshler
Anna	Phoebe Strole
Hanschen	Jonathan B. Wright
	Matt Doyle
Thea	Remy Zaken

TARZAN

New York 5/10/06
Closed 7/8/07

Tarzan	Josh Strickland
Jane	Jenn Gambatese
Kerchak	Shuler Hensley
	Robert Evan 3/28/07
Kala	Merle Dandridge
Terk	Chester Gregory II

THE 25TH ANNUAL PUTNAM COUNTY SPELLING BEE

	New York 5/2/05 *Closed 1/20/08*	Baltimore 9/19/06
William Barfee	Dan Fogler	Eric Peterson
	Josh Gad 1/31/06	Dan Fogler 5/24/07
	Jared Gertner 1/30/07	Eric Roediger
Marcy Park	Deborah S. Craig	Katie Boren
	Greta Lee 4/17/07	Deborah S. Craig 5/24/07
		Katie Boren
Leaf Coneybear	Jesse Tyler Ferguson	Michael Zahler
	Barrett Foa 6/25/06	Jesse Tyler Ferguson 5/24/07
	Stanley Bahorek 4/17/07	Andrew Keenan-Bolger
Rona Lisa Peretti	Lisa Howard	Jennifer Simard
	Lucia Spina 10/19/06	Sally Wilfert 4/11/07
	Jennifer Simard 4/17/07	Lisa Howard 5/24/07
		Sally Wilfert
Olive Ostrovsky	Celia Keenan-Bolger	Lauren Worsham
	Jessica-Snow Wilson 9/19/06	Celia Keenan-Bolger 5/24/07
	Jenni Barber 4/17/07	Vanessa Ray
Mitch Mahoney	Derrick Baskin	Alan H. Green
	James Monroe Inglehart 4/17/07	Derrick Baskin 5/24/07
		Alan H. Green
		Kevin Smith Kirkwood
Chip Tolentino	Jose Llana	Miguel Cervantes

	Aaron J. Albano 4/17/07	Jose Llana 5/24/07
		Justin Keyes
Douglas Panch	Jay Reiss	James Kall
	Greg Stuhr 10/25/06	Jay Reiss 5/24/07
	Mo Rocca 4/17/07	James Kall
	Darrell Hammond 6/12/07	
	Daniel Pearce	
Logainne S.	Sarah Saltzberg	Sarah Stiles
	Sara Inbar 4/17/07	Sarah Saltzberg 5/24/07
		Dana Steingold

WICKED

	New York 10/30/03	*#1 Toronto 3/9/05*
		#2 Chicago 7/13/05
		#3 Los Angeles 2/21/07
Glinda	Kristin Chenoweth	#1 Kendra Kassebaum
	Jennifer Laura Thompson 7/20/04	Megan Hilty
	Megan Hilty 5/31/04	Christina DeCicco
	Kate Reinders 5/30/05	#2 Kate Reinders
	Kendra Kassebaum	Stacie Morgain Lewis
	Annaleigh Ashford 10/9/07	Erin Mackey
	Kendra Kassebaum 5/14/08	#3 Megan Hilty
Elphaba	Idina Menzel	#1 Stephanie J. Block
	Eden Espinosa 6/15/04	Julia Murney 3/8/06
	Idina Menzel 7/6/04	Victoria Matlock
	Shoshana Bean 1/11/05	Shoshana Bean 9/6/06
	Eden Espinosa 1/10/06	Victoria Matlock
	Ana Gasteyer 10/10/06	#2 Ana Gasteyer
	Julia Murney 1/9/07	Kristy Cates 1/24/05
	Stephanie J. Block 10/9/07	Dee Roscioli
		#3 Eden Espinosa
Wizard of Oz	Joel Grey	#1 David Garrison
	George Hearn 7/20/04	P.J. Benjamin 3/8/06
	Ben Vereen 5/31/05	#2 Gene Weygandt
	David Garrison 4/4/06	Peter Kevoian
	Lenny Wolpe 7/10/07	#3 John Rubinstein
Madame Morrible	Carole Shelley	#1 Carol Kane
	Rue McClanahan 5/31/05	Carole Shelley
	Carol Kane	Alma Cuervo
	Jayne Houdyshell	Barbara Tirrell
	Carole Shelley 8/28/07	#2 Rondi Reed
	Miriam Margolyes 1/22/08	Carole Shelley
		Barbara Robertson
		#3 Carol Kane
Fiyero	Norbert Leo Butz 12/21/04	#1 Derrick Williams
	Taye Diggs 1/18/05	Sebastian Arcelus 3/8/06
	Norbert Leo Butz 1/20/05	Clifton Hall
	Joey McIntyre 7/20/04	#2 Derrick Williams
	David Ayers 1/11/05	#3 Kristoffer Cusick
	Derrick Williams 1/10/06	
	Sebastian Arcelus 1/9/07	
	Derrick Williams 12/18/07	
	David Burnham 1/8/08	
Boq	Christopher Fitzgerald	#1 Logan Lipton

	Randy Harrison 6/22/04	Kirk McDonald
	Christopher Fitzgerald 7/27/04	#2 Telly Leung
	Robb Sapp 1/4/05	Adam Flemming
	Jeffrey Kuhn 1/11/05	#3 Adam Wylie
	Robb Sapp	
	Logan Lipton 8/8/06	
	Ben Liebert	
Dr. Dillamond	William Youmans	#1 Timothy Britten Parker
	Sean McCourt	K. Todd Freeman
	Steven Skybell	Tom Flynn
		#2 Steven Skybell
		Timothy Britten Parker
		K. Todd Freeman
		#3 Timothy Britten Parker
Nessarose	Michelle Federer	#1 Jenna Leigh Green
	Cristy Candler 1/10/06	Jennifer Waldman 3/8/06
	Jenna Leigh Green 3/14/06	Deedee Magno Hall
	Cristy Candler	#2 Heidi Kettenring
		Summer Naomi Smart
		#3 Jenna Leigh Green

FIRST-CLASS NATIONAL TOURS

ANNIE

Seattle 8/21/05

Annie	Marissa O'Donnell
	Madison Kerth
Miss Hannigan	Alene Robertson
	Victoria Oscar
	Alene Robertson
	Kathie Lee Gifford
	Alene Robertson
	Lynn Andrews
Daddy Warbucks	Conrad John Schuck
	David Barton
Rooster Hannigan	Scott Willis
	Zander Meisner
Lily St. Regis	Mackenzie Phillips
	Julie Cardia
	Ashley Puckett Gonzales
	Cheryl Hoffman
FDR	Allan Baker
	Jeffrey B. Duncan
Sandy	Lola

CAMELOT

San Jose 1/30/07

King Arthur	Michael York
	Lou Diamond Phillips 9/11/07
Guenevere	Rachel York
	Rachel de Benedet 9/11/07

Lancelot	James Barbour
	Matt Bogart 9/11/07
Mordred	Shannon Stoeke

THE LIGHT IN THE PIAZZA

San Francisco 8/1/06

Clara	Elena Shaddow
Fabrizio	David Burnham
Margaret	Christine Andreas
Franca	Laura Griffith
Giuseppe	Jonathan Hammond
Signor Naccarelli	David Ledingham
Roy Johnson	Brian Sutherland
Signora Naccarelli	Diane Sutherland

SWEENEY TODD

Boston 10/23/07

Sweeney Todd	David Hess
	Alexander Gemignani
Lovett	Judy Kaye
Johanna	Lauren Molina
Anthony	Benjamin Magnuson
Beggar Woman	Diana DiMarzio
Jonas	John Arbo
Judge Turpin	Keith Buterbaugh
Beadle	Benjamin Eakeley
Tobias	Edmund Bagnell
Pirelli	Katrina Yaukey

WHO'S AFRAID OF VIRGINIA WOOLF?

Washington, DC 1/4/07

Martha	Kathleen Turner
George	Bill Irwin
Honey	Kathleen Early
Nick	David Furr

THE SEASON OFF
OFF BROADWAY

THE SEASON OFF OFF BROADWAY

○ ○ ○ ○ ○ *By Sylviane Gold* ○ ○ ○ ○ ○

IF ANYONE NEEDED a reminder of how much (and how little) has changed since an assortment of theater outsiders—audacious writers, gonzo directors, adventurous audiences—created what we now think of as Off Off Broadway, it arrived November 1, 2007, when the *New York Times* reported that Tom O'Horgan, in failing health and dire financial straits, was selling his possessions after abandoning New York for a condo in Sarasota.

If a movement as disorderly and tatterdemalion as OOB can be said to have founding fathers and mothers, O'Horgan must surely be counted among them. He had been there for the early days at Caffe Cino and Judson Poets and La MaMa. He had been there when the surge of experimentation overflowed from downtown and reached Broadway: in 1971, four shows he had directed—*Hair, Lenny, Jesus Christ Superstar* and *Inner City*—were running there, each marked with his almost feral brand of theatricality. As economic stakes uptown began to balloon and artistic possibilities dwindled, he had returned to his roots, lending his extravagant, body-centric style to plays and musicals in out-of-the-way theaters and, yes, in his loft.

Now, at 83, he was suffering from Alzheimer's, his loft had been sold, and his collection of theater posters, props and musical instruments—he had begun his career as a composer—were to be auctioned off. It was a sad tale from a human perspective, of course. But it also underscored the extent to which radical innovation and boldness of approach had been re-marginalized in the decades since the theater first welcomed its rebellious orphans. When John Gruen interviewed O'Horgan for the *New York Times Magazine*, in 1972, the wilderness years for OOB already seemed on the verge of becoming history. "We did all that at a time when you couldn't do crazy things anywhere else," O'Horgan told him, referring to *Futz* and *Tom Paine* and the rest of his pre-*Hair* output. "I'm probably more outrageous on Broadway than I ever was downtown."

Thirty-five years later, in the 2007–2008 season, it was clear that the 1970s had become distant history. Downtown theater was still filtering uptown, however sporadically. And, as Charles Isherwood pointed out in a

May essay in the Arts and Leisure section of the *New York Times*, established companies operating under Equity's Off Broadway contracts were increasingly foraging among the OOB upstarts to fill out their schedules. But most of the work that managed to find a berth at a mainstream institution—Liz Flahive's *From Up Here*, for example, which landed at Manhattan Theatre Club via Ars Nova—fit there comfortably, without stretching anyone's boundaries. The idea that a director might be more outrageous in an uptown theater than he or she could be downtown seemed downright laughable. (By the same token, remember what it takes these days just to *be* outrageous: Jim Simpson's revival of Peter Handke's *Offending the Audience*, at the Flea in January, revealed just how much harder it is to offend us these days than it was in the past.)

Much of the original impetus—and shock value—of OOB derived from the desire to overturn traditional structures of storytelling, to replace them with something more urgent and less predictable, more visceral and less cerebral. But storytelling of one kind or another is still at the heart of the theater enterprise, and several productions this season took on its very essence. Most notable, perhaps, was the story-theater treatment Elevator Repair Service gave the dense, famously enigmatic first section of *The Sound and the Fury* at New York Theatre Workshop in April. (Its sponsorship of the ERS production came as NYTW was curtailing its own activities: with the income stream from the 10-year Broadway run of *Rent* coming to an end, it was forced to trim staff and cut budgets.)

In *The Sound and the Fury*, actors took turns reading out the text of the novel—every word—as their colleagues, regularly switching roles, enacted the elusive memories taking shape in Benjy Compson's addled brain. "Director John Collins proves that William Faulkner's book suits the theater like a dream," wrote Jeremy McCarter in *New York*, and Ben Brantley agreed in the *Times*, calling *The Sound and the Fury* an opportunity "to rediscover some of the thrill that came with encountering and gradually embracing one of the great achievements of Western literature for the first time."

Last season's New Georges hit, *God's Ear*, by Jenny Schwartz, brought yet another kind of unorthodox narrative to the stage when it moved to the Vineyard Theatre in April. With its jangling poetry of cliché and everyday verbiage pouring from a family reeling after the death of a child, it wowed the critics again. Schwartz is "a playwright to reckon with," wrote Alexis Soloski in the *Village Voice* when the play had its premiere at the East 13th Street Theatre at the tail end of last season. This season, Isherwood commended Schwartz and her director, Anne Kauffman, for sustaining "the tension between wild originality and the agony of the mundane."

The storytelling was also wild in Enda Walsh's *The Walworth Farce*, directed by Mikel Murfi at St. Ann's Warehouse. The convoluted comedy focuses on the bizarre playacting ritual of an Irish family in London. McCarter's *New York* review noted the work's debts to Joe Orton and Martin McDonagh, but called it "largely, admirably, original."

Comfort with the unknown is Off Off Broadway's signature aesthetic.

Family Ties

> JESSE: Henry David Thoreau brought his laundry home to his mother the entire time he lived on Walden Pond.
>
> —From *Hunting and Gathering* by Brooke Berman

FOR ALL OF THE NARRATIVE liberties taken by *Sound and Fury*, *God's Ear*, and *Walworth*, these productions and their dissection of family strife arise from a long, venerable theater tradition. *August: Osage County* may have garnered most of the hype this season, but it was hardly the only locale for twisted parents and maimed children. In the New Group production of *Things We Want*, by Jonathan Marc Sherman, three variously codependent brothers grappled with the fallout from their parents' suicides. Ethan Hawke directed Paul Dano, Peter Dinklage and Josh Hamilton as the brothers and helped Zoe Kazan—the gifted young granddaughter of Elia—advance closer to the stage stardom that seems her inevitable fate.

The grasping, cantankerous members of Horton Foote's Gordon clan clashed over their inheritance in the Best Play *Dividing the Estate*, which Primary Stages presented to great acclaim at 59E59. (See Garrett Eisler's essay in this volume.) The large cast, headed by Elizabeth Ashley and directed by Michael Wilson, etched yet another chapter—this one oddly comic—in Foote's multiplay account of life in a small Texas town. New England had its share of rancid relationships, too. Lucy Thurber traveled to a rural, poverty-stricken town in western Massachusetts for the unhappy tribe she chronicled in *Scarcity*, which opened at the Atlantic Theater Company in September with television's Kristen Johnston and Michael T.

Weiss, and film's Jesse Eisenberg as members of the troubled family. At Theatre Row's Lion, *The Main(e) Play*, by Chad Beckim, had the hero coming home for Thanksgiving only to find the locks had been changed.

In the multigenerational, multimedia family saga *Imminence*, by the Talking Band's Paul Zimet, the rupturing of the family was echoed at La MaMa in Nic Ularu's breakaway set. And no retrospective of pain would be complete without a word or two from Neil LaBute. He briefly dissected a marriage in *The Great War*, with Laila Robins and Grant Shaud as the sadly mismatched pair, as part of an Ensemble Studio Theatre marathon evening. And in June at MCC Theater, his home base, LaBute probed another wretched family: *In a Dark Dark House* told the horror-laced story of two brothers sharing a woeful past.

Two women were at the heart of *The Shape of Metal*, by Irish playwright Thomas Kilroy, which was part of the Brits Off Broadway festival at 59E59. Roberta Maxwell, playing a sculptor under Brian Murray's direction, evoked what Caryn James described in the *Times* as "a selfish wreck of a mother." The original dysfunctional family—now living in the suburbs and spouting rock songs by Gordon Is a Mime—put in an appearance at PS 122 in the bizarrely entertaining *Oedipus Loves You* by Gavin Quinn and Simon Doyle. "From Ireland by way of Mars," *Variety*'s Sam Thielman wrote of the production, which cast Tiresias as a family therapist and turned Greek tragedy into Jerry Springer—or was it the other way around?

Of course, not all stage families this season were toxic. The New Group's *Rafta, Rafta* took a lighter look at the inevitable conflicts between parent and child. Written by Ayub Khan-Din and directed by Scott Elliott, the play transposes Bill Naughton's 1963 newlyweds-without-privacy comedy *All in Good Time* to a working-class Anglo-Indian family in northern England. In another Primary Stages offering, *Hunting and Gathering*, Brooke Berman took a wry look at a segment of New York's homeless population—not the penniless in the streets but the underfinanced young adults who bounce from share to sublet to housesit and for whom family is both an irritant and a safety net. Leigh Silverman directed Michael Chernus, Jeremy Shamos, and two young women well-equipped in the family department: Meryl Streep's daughter Mamie Gummer and James Naughton's daughter Keira.

Life in Wartime

OFF OFF BROADWAY theatergoers looking for misery had plenty of misbegotten marriages, abused children and failed relationships from which to choose. But these private woes began to look almost comforting beside the daunting public dilemmas that found their way to the stage. The country's disastrous adventure in Iraq received less and less attention in the news media, but it spawned multiple theater productions, some of them new and directly inspired by the war, some of them old and retrofitted in order to comment on it. The Signature Theatre Company launched its season-long exploration of Charles Mee's *oeuvre* with *Iphigenia 2.0*, in which Agamemnon begins by saying, "There are acts / that will set an empire on a course / that will one day / bring it to an end." Even *Queens Boulevard*, Mee's seemingly nonpolitical musical set in New York's most diverse borough, prodded audiences gently to ruminate about America's relationship with Asia. (Mee's exuberant theatrical imagination was also on view at the Brooklyn Academy of Music, where his Joseph Cornell bouquet, *Hotel Cassiopeia*, kicked off the theater segment of the Next Wave festival in October, and at 3LD Art and Technology Center, which presented his multimedia extravaganza *Fire Island* in April.)

Like *Iphigenia*, David Greenspan's dazzling *Old Comedy After Aristophanes' Frogs* exploded classic forms to address current concerns. Directed at Classic Stage Company by Target Margin's artistic director David Herskovits, it was the final installment in the company's two-year reconsideration of Greek theater. At the Henry Street Settlement, Waterwell revived its own reconsideration of Aeschylus, *The Persians: A Comedy About War With Five Songs*. To Caryn James, who reviewed many of the season's OOB offerings for the *Times*, the preoccupation with the Greeks was directly related to the Iraq conflict and the issues raised by war in a democracy.

But the war was addressed in other genres as well. It was surely no accident of timing that brought Joe Tantalo's Godlight Theatre production of Eric Simonson's adaptation of the classic 1969 antiwar novel by Kurt Vonnegut, *Slaughterhouse Five or: The Childen's Crusade*, to 59E59 in January. Andy Webster, writing in the *Times,* found it "skillfully adapted" and "meticulously choreographed." Vonnegut was writing about World War II, but the audience likely was thinking about Iraq. In Michael Murphy's new play, which ran at the Clurman in March, the Vietnam conflict stands in for Iraq: *The Conscientious Objector* was a smooth inquiry into Martin Luther King's opposition to that unpopular war. Iraq also came disguised as World War I in Stephen Massicotte's biting look at two of its embittered, disillusioned veterans, Robert Graves and T.E. Lawrence, in *The Oxford Roof Climber's Rebellion,* presented in October by Urban Stages. Massicotte aptly summarized the general tenor in a couple of sentences from Robert Graves: "An enemy killed is an enemy created. Every pace you march into another man's home is one pace farther from your own."

Sometimes, the war onstage did not have a name. The mythical, battle-ravaged country in Howard Barker's 1992 allegory, *A Hard Heart,* at the Clurman in November, furnished Kathleen Chalfant, as its queen, an occasion for one of her brilliant performances. And an unnamed country suffering the aftermath of combat and ethnic cleansing was the setting for *War*, the 2003 play by the Swedish writer Lars Norén, given its American premiere in February at Rattlestick Playwrights Theater.

At other times, Iraq came up only in passing, a dour, jolting surprise in material not specifically tied to it: Annie Dorsen's nose-thumbing satire of commercialization, *Democracy in America,* at PS 122, interpolated a pair of Abu Ghraib photos into the set. The bizarrely accoutered young heroine of *Alice Unwrapped*, Laura Harrington and Jenny Giering's seemingly whimsical slice of the Zipper's Inner Voices: Solo Musicals event, was not that bizarre, given that her father was missing in Iraq. Bickering relatives in Mike Leigh's comic play about a Jewish family in London, *2000 Years*, chimed in on the war and the future of Israel in a New Group production at the Acorn Theater. And Cindy Sheehan's opposition to George W. Bush was included among the protests of union organizers, abolitionists and suffragists in the Culture Project's production of Rob Urbinati's *Rebel Voices* in November.

Most often, however, playwrights waded directly into the quagmire with no apologies. With its Iraq veterans starkly recounting their experiences while a fantasia of their storied regiment's military history unfolds around them, Gregory Burke's *Black Watch*, directed by John Tiffany, reminded Brantley of the *Times* of "the transporting power that is unique to theater." Acclaimed at the 2006 Edinburgh Festival Fringe, the show was presented in October at St. Ann's Warehouse. In the Lucille Lortel Award honoree for outstanding play, *Betrayed,* the *New Yorker* writer George Packer traced America's abandonment of its most vulnerable allies in the true stories of three Iraqi translators who worked for the government; Adam Feldman, writing in *Time Out New York,* praised the Culture Project production for its "sobering impact" and "solemn dignity," while Charles Isherwood called it "heart-rending" in the *Times*. At the Fire Dept., a series of dramatic bits and pieces by writers such as Jessica Blank and José Rivera were grouped under the rubric *At War: American Playwrights Respond to Iraq* and presented in rotating rep by actors including Bobby Cannavale, Bebe Neuwirth and David Strathairn. In a 59E59 offering, *Flags,* the pseudonymous Jane Martin called attention to the families who have sacrificed their men and women while "most of the rest of us sigh and . . . change the channel or head to the mall."

Less explicit but no less pointed, *The Leopard and the Fox* by Rajiv Joseph dissected the military coup in Pakistan that overthrew the regime of Zulfiqar Ali Bhutto for October audiences at the Barrow Group. The Abingdon Theatre Company weighed in the same month with Tom Coash's *Cry Havoc,* about a naïve English translator visiting Egypt.

Naomi Wallace took a broadly critical view with *The Fever Chart: Three Visions of the Middle East*, directed by Jo Bonney and presented in May at the Public. In *Variety*, Sam Thielman noted the trilogy's reliance on "the good old binary opposition" of "cruel Israelis and saintly Palestinians," but welcomed Wallace's "engagement with the wider world."

Perhaps the most poignant effort to depict the torment of Iraq on stage had to be John Belluso's *The Poor Itch*, about a veteran disabled both physically and emotionally by his service. Because Belluso died before completing it, the play was presented at the Public Lab in March as an unorthodox collage of various drafts, notes and elisions, each shift indicated by the ringing of a bell. Andy Propst's review in the *Village Voice* admired Lisa Peterson's direction and the "exceptional performances" of Christopher Thornton and Deirdre O'Connell as the soldier and his mother.

In Europe, of course, there is a long and deep tradition of political theater, so it is no surprise that Middle Eastern politics and culture figured heavily this spring in the fifth annual Brits Off Broadway festival at 59E59. With actors in whiteface and using cardboard cutout props under the direction of Muriel Romanes, Torben Betts "shakes the daylights out of the smarmy idea of freedom," said Andrea Stevens in the *Times* of his allegorical *The Unconquered*. In Mike Bartlett's *Artefacts,* the gap separating a British teen from her Iraqi father stood in for the West's failure to understand the land it chose to invade. And the Dutch writer Adelheid Roosen brought another take to the subject in October, when her *Vagina Monologues*-inspired play *The Veiled Monologues*, in which Muslim women talk about their sexuality, came to St. Ann's Warehouse in repertory with *Is. Man*, about honor killings, both under her direction.

Even musical theater became an arena for antiwar politics. Untitled Theater Company #61 tried turning Kurt Vonnegut's 1963 doomsday novel, *Cat's Cradle*, into a calypso musical with a score by Henry Akona and direction by the adapter, Edward Einhorn. "The novel's themes of war, extremism and impotent leadership are disturbingly contemporary," wrote Raven Snook in *Time Out New York*, but the general verdict was that Untitled had overreached. Book writer Clay McLeod Chapman and composer Kyle Jarrow got a better reception for their dark musical about a captured journalist and contractor held in a war-torn land in the offbeat, rock-inflected *Hostage*

Song, directed by Oliver Butler at the Kraine. At La MaMa ETC, in December, Oren Safdie's book and Ronnie Cohen's songs took a somewhat lighter approach to the Middle East in *West Bank, UK*, a look at 100 years of Jewish-Muslim interaction through an ongoing battle for a London apartment.

La MaMa, of course, has been an OOB force for decades. This season, as usual, it provided showcases for veterans such as the extraordinary puppeteer Theodora Skipitares, who presented her take on *Medea*. There was also exotica such as *The Sejny Chronicles*, a musical postcard from a multi-ethnic town on the border of Poland, Lithuania and Belarus—as well as work by a horde of theatrical newbies. One of them was the journalist, novelist and screenwriter Jimmy Breslin, whose *Love Lasts on Myrtle Avenue* opened in December under the direction of George Ferencz.

Breslin's foray into a new form was business as usual for OOB. Familiar names often turn up in new contexts, and in 2007–08, actors tried directing, other scribes jumped into playwriting and dramaturgs unearthed forgotten works by writers best remembered for novels or films. The gifted actress Judith Ivey started the season in June directing twisty suspense in Marisa Wegrzyn's *The Butcher of Baraboo* at Second Stage Uptown and then in March showed her comedy chops with Kathleen Clark's *Secrets of a Soccer Mom* at the Snapple Theater Center. Ethan Coen, of the Academy Award-winning Coen Brothers, made his debut as a playwright in January with *Almost an Evening*, an anthology of three metaphysical playlets directed by Neil Pepe at the Atlantic Theater Company's Stage 2. Reviewing for the *Times*, Brantley was reminded of the "urbane, mindteasing divertissements that once flourished Off Broadway." The tart little comedies, featuring a choleric turn by F. Murray Abraham as Jehovah, moved to 45 Bleecker for an extended stay. Shortly before he died, another filmmaker, Anthony Minghella, was given a local stage production at Atlantic Stage 2. A selection of his one-acts were collected under the title *Politics of Passion*; their unifying theme of miscommunication was particularly well exemplified in *Cigarettes and Chocolate*, which centers on a woman who stops speaking for Lent.

For Ernest Hemingway completists, the Mint Theater Company unearthed the novelist's play *The Fifth Column*, about a pair of reporters during the Spanish Civil War—any resemblance to the author and Martha Gellhorn was presumably not coincidental. And they produced the rarely seen play *The Power of Darkness*, Leo Tolstoy's 1886 study of a nefarious peasant. But yes, some of the season's new plays came from new writers. The Roundabout Theatre Company, for decades a conservative purveyor of the tried-and-true—often with a big-name star attached—joined the development process. The company transformed its 62-seat black box theater in the Harold and Miriam Steinberg Center for Theatre, previously used for educational programs, into Roundabout Underground, dedicated to the untried and unknown. The project began in October with a splash: Jason Moore directed Stephen Karam's *Speech and Debate*, a spiffy debut play about a group of high school misfits that Caryn James called "funny and cliché-free" and "brilliantly performed" in her *Times* review.

Older Kids on the Block

THE SEASON ALSO afforded retrospective looks at some of the theater's living treasures. In April Edward Albee directed a brilliant cast in a double bill of his one-acts, *The American Dream* and *The Sandbox*, at the Cherry Lane Theatre. Ben Brantley, writing in the *Times*, was particularly taken with Judith Ivey's imperious Mommy, "pricelessly portrayed . . . with the purring contentment of a cat who has eaten an entire aviary of canaries." Early work—maybe too early, according to James—from the mid-1960s, when Tom Stoppard was trying his hand at television plays, arrived at the Boomerang Theatre Company in September under the umbrella title *Stoppard Goes Electric*. In November, Theatre for a New Audience presented Adrienne Kennedy's searing memory play about segregation and hate, *The Ohio State Murders*, at the Duke, with the extraordinary LisaGay Hamilton playing the author's alter ego. Hamilton's performance, directed by Evan Yionoulis, received an Obie Award for acting, while Kennedy collected another for lifetime achievement.

Speaking of lifetime achievement, the Living Theatre was back in October with *Maudie and Jane*, a two-hander by Luciano Nattino based on a Doris Lessing novel about a pair of very different women who become friends. James, reviewing in the *Times*, was awed by the energy and bravery of 81-year-old Judith Malina, "still dancing around the stage, taking off her clothes, doing her best to shake up the world."

The Kitchen played host to David Greenspan's gloss on the *Poetics* of Aristotle and Gerald Else's commentaries, *The Argument*, and his adaptation of Plato's *Symposium*, titled *Dinner Party*, both directed by Herskovits. "Greenspan always seems to be in motion of some kind, seducing us through abstruse passages with a clap, a snap, a histrionic flourish of the hand," wrote Isherwood of *The Argument*. Obie judges were impressed too, and gave him a special citation. Another OOB favorite, David Gordon, turned up at the Kitchen with his *Uncivil Wars: Collaborating With Brecht and Eisler*, based on Michael Feingold's translation of Brecht's *The Roundheads and the Pointheads*.

Will Eno, whose blazingly original way with words was encouraged by Albee, returned to the boards with *Oh the Humanity and other exclamations*, an anthology of five short plays at the Flea Theater. Brian Hutchinson and Marisa Tomei, under the direction of Jim Simpson, provided an hour of what Isherwood described in the *Times* as "playfully profound theater." As the Flea's artistic director, Simpson also presented new work from another writer with a unique style, Adam Rapp. In *Bingo With the Indians*, Rapp—who had just opened the wackier-than-usual *American Sligo* at Rattlestick—gave a dark and antic spin to that tired old imperative, "Let's put on a show," adding larceny to the mix as a theater troupe plots to steal the proceeds of a bingo game.

Hey, Kids!

"LET'S PUT ON A SHOW" has long been the animating spirit behind OOB's most dedicated troupes. And they, too, contributed memorably to the season. Richard Foreman and the Ontological-Hysteric Theater celebrated their 40th anniversary with a typically exuberant mix of serious fun, *Deep Trance Behavior in Potatoland*, in January at St. Mark's Church. The Wooster Group delved into the DNA of theater itself with its October production of what Brantley likened to a karaoke *Hamlet*: grainy film of John Gielgud's 1964 Broadway production starring Richard Burton juxtaposed with live actors, including Scott Shepherd in the title role, attempting a facsimile onstage. The peripatetic company presented *Hamlet* at the Public, but announced what Elizabeth LeCompte called "a trial marriage" with the Baryshnikov Arts Center. The company would still borrow other spaces, she said, but would become a regular tenant at Baryshnikov's home base, 37 Arts, in a 299-seat space to be named for Jerome Robbins.

Less venerable than the Wooster Group but OOB-worthies nonetheless, Richard Maxwell and his New York City Players arrived at the Performing Garage in November with his new musical, *Ode to the Man Who Kneels*. Filtering the conventions and archetypes of the American West through his poor-theater sensibility, Maxwell "uncovers unexpected textures by magnifying the banal," wrote Brantley in his *Times* rave.

The next month, another offbeat musical, *The Slug Bearers of Kayrol Island*, brought the deadpan world of Ben Katchor's droll cartoons to the Vineyard Theatre. Composer Mark Mulcahy, director Bob McGrath, and designers Jim Findlay and Jeff Sugg all entered the spirit of Katchor's two-dimensional world, and the result, said Brantley, was "an answered prayer for anyone who has dreamed of living inside a graphic novel." The clever, eye-popping designs by Findlay and Sugg won an Obie, a Lortel and a Henry Hewes Design Award. Another entry in the Vineyard's extraordinary season, Julia Cho's quietly riveting drama *The Piano Teacher*, also drew notice from the awards panels: Elizabeth Franz's cozy (and then chilling) portrayal of Mrs. K., the title character, was honored by the Lortel Awards and the Drama League.

Primary Stages, which ended its season with a Lortel Award for outstanding body of work, had begun its stellar year in August with Michael Hollinger's absorbing *Opus*, a drama about internecine conflicts that consume a string quartet. Directed by Terrence J. Nolan, who steered the world premiere at Philadelphia's Arden Theatre Company, the play offered an insider's look at the delicate structure of an artistic entity—a mysterious web of ego, neurosis, and talent. Mahira Kakkar was especially impressive as the young interloper who joins the group in an emergency.

Another OOB stalwart, MCC Theater, followed its production of LaBute's *Dark Dark House* (mentioned above) with Jim Knable's whimsical comedy, *Spain*. In Knable's play, Annabella Sciorra played host to a Spanish inquisition—of sorts—as a conquistador in full armor (Michael Aronov) and a Mayan priest (Lisa Kron) invaded her messy life. Sciorra was followed in February by Lynn Redgrave, in another star turn. Mick Gordon and AC Grayling's *Grace* is ostensibly about a confirmed atheist whose grown son announces that he wants to enter the priesthood. But, wrote Isherwood, it devolved into an inquiry into "whether religious belief is an irrational superstition . . . or an ineradicable human need."

The Atlantic Theater Company's highly successful season included *Parlour Song* by Jez Butterworth, a surreal deconstruction of a middle-age, middlebrow marriage that inspired Brantley to write, "Now *this* is adult entertainment." Neil Pepe directed the fine cast, which included filmdom's Emily Mortimer making her New York stage debut. The season finale, Conor McPherson's spellbinding *Port Authority*, was another acting tour de force, with Brian d'Arcy James, John Gallagher Jr., and Jim Norton as three Dubliners talking about their thwarted lives.

For all the heterogeneity of these OOB entities, there were still niches that needed filling. The Negro Ensemble Company, a history-changing catalyst in the American black theater, reconstituted itself in Harlem with *Webeime*, a musical collage by Layon Gray. Performed by the Black Gents of Hollywood, it drew an encouraging pat on the back from Neil Genzlinger in the *Times*. The National Black Theatre gave 1977 Tony Award-winner Trazana Beverley the opportunity to star in Euripides's *Medea*. And the Women's Project continued its advocacy on behalf of women playwrights.

This year's crop included Catherine Trieschmann's *Crooked*, about a mismatched friendship between two teenaged girls in Mississippi. Caryn James in the *Times* called the play, which mines themes of religious fundamentalism and homosexuality, "a gem of a discovery."

Song of Myself

IN FEBRUARY, the Kraine Theater presented a hardbitten musical about the legal problems of the insane, *Attorney for the Damned*, with book and lyrics by Denis Woychuk and music by Rob McCulloch. Woychuk, owner of the Kraine, is a former lawyer who had earlier turned his experiences with mental patients into a memoir of the same title. He was not the only one delving into autobiography OOB. At Theater for the New City, Carla Cantrelle showed off her aerialist skills along with her playwriting with *Looking Up*, a two-character work about a trapeze artist finding her way in the city—and in life—after leaving the circus. James Braly turned his somewhat hair-raising personal story into *Life in a Marital Institution*, a one-man show at 59E59 that he described as "20 years of monogamy in one terrifying hour." In January, the vehement monologist Mike Daisey unleashed his threnody for his chosen art form, *How Theater Failed America*, at the Public as part of the Under the Radar festival. And David Rothenberg, who decades ago had produced *Fortune and Men's Eyes*, returned with *The Castle* at New World Stages, in which four ex-convicts recounted their difficulties after prison.

For those reticent about committing overt autobiography, there was always biography. The season had its share of plays looking back at the lives of crucial men and women of history and literature. Michael O. Smith performed his one-man show about Teddy Roosevelt, *The Bully Pulpit*, in a respectable run at the Beckett. In a less commercial vein, Medicine Show Theatre presented *On the Border*, Howard Pflanzer's fantasmagoric account of the last night of Walter Benjamin's life. At the Atlantic, the invaluable Peter Parnell returned to the stage in December with *Trumpery*, his fascinating inquiry into the influence of personality and politics on Charles Darwin's epochal work on evolution. David Esbjornson directed Michael Cristofer and a supporting cast of impressive depth, with Santo Loquasto's richly imagined set giving physical dimension to the play's twin realms, nature and civilization. The contrasts were just as stark in *New Jerusalem*. David Ives's bracing play at Classic Stage Company about Baruch de Spinoza, faith and apostasy, prompted Michael Feingold to praise "the sheer brainy delight of Ives's script" in his *Village Voice* review. Jeremy Strong, under the direction of Walter Bobbie, received a Lortel nomination for his portrayal of the 17th-century Jewish philosopher as young upstart.

Joining this heavy-duty male roster was the celebrated Russian poet Anna Akhmatova, brought to life at Theater for the New City by television actress Rebecca Schull, author and star of *On Naked Soil: Imagining Anna Akhmatova*. Thanks to the New Georges, there was also Rose Mary Woods, whose role in history might be forgotten if not for the fact that, as Richard M. Nixon's White House secretary, she tried to take the blame for the eighteen-and-a-half-minute gap in the Watergate tapes. She was played at several stages of her life by Kristin Griffith—in a "commanding performance," wrote Neil Genzlinger in the *Times*—in *Stretch (a fantasia)*, by Susan Bernfield.

From Paris, Tokyo, Warsaw—With Greasepaint

IN JULY, the 2007 Lincoln Center Festival imported Robert Wilson's cruelly glamorous evocation of the fables of La Fontaine, a low-comedy kabuki classic and a raft of Spanish-language theater from Argentina, Chile, Mexico and Spain. *Les Fables de La Fontaine*, created for the Comédie-Française and performed by members of the company, impressed Ben Brantley as "an act of prestidigitation" in its balance "of Baroque elegance and primal ferocity." *Hokaibo*, written in 1784 but updated for maximum comic effect by Nakamura Kanzaburo XVIII, the artistic director and star of Tokyo's Heisei Nakamura-za, brought the elegance of kabuki to bear on a comic tale of lechery and honor. (Later in the season, kabuki fans were treated to Theatre of a Two-Headed Calf's Obie-honored, punk-flavored adaptation of Chikamatsu's *Drum of the Waves of Horikawa* at Here Arts Center.)

Elegance was quite beside the point in *Divinas Palabras*, a gruesome catalogue of human cruelty written in 1920 by Ramón del Valle-Inclán and performed with élan by the Centro Dramático Nacional of Madrid. The Mexican company Teatro de Ciertos Habitantes also did a play about a gruesome subject, but it took a more-or-less comic view of the 18th-century fad for castrating boys to preserve their glorious singing voices. *De Monstruos y Prodigios: La Historia de los Castrati* (*Monsters and Prodigies: The History of the Castrati*) by Jorge Kuri was given a "madcap" staging, wrote Wilborn Hampton in the *Times*. The Argentine company Proyecto Chejov performed *Un Hombre que se Ahoga* (*A Man Who Drowns*), the company's capsule version of *The Three Sisters*, with roaring energy and sex-change casting—an approach, wrote Ginia Bellafante in the *Times*, that "never rises above the level of a stunt."

The fall brought the Next Wave to the Brooklyn Academy of Music, with theatrical goodies from Poland, Germany and France. Reviewing for the *Times,* Jason Zinoman found Hanoch Levin's *Krum* an "assured tragicomedy" balancing "a rueful humor with an emotionally wrenching sadness" in the production by TR Warszawa and Stary Teatr of Krakow. Hamburg's Thalia Theater presented a starkly modernist *Lulu* that framed Wedekind's archetypal vamp, Caryn James wrote, as "more careless than seductive." And that master of theatrical legerdemain, James Thiérrée, brought enough rope to hang himself and then some in *Au Revoir Parapluie.* But as usual, his interests were life and laughter as he coaxed the mass of cord into surprising transformations.

In January, the Public launched its fourth annual Under the Radar festival, an array of new work curated by Mark Russell, formerly of PS 122. The offerings included *In Spite of Everything*, by the Bay Area hiphop theater troupe Suicide Kings; *Stoop Stories*, by 1995 Obie Award-winner Dael Orlandersmith; and *Generation Jeans*, from the Belarus Free Theatre. But the most buzz was probably generated by *Poetics: A Ballet Brut*, a cult item that was revived after receiving four performances in 2006–07. Created and performed by Nature Theater of Oklahoma, it was a wordless compendium of gestures derived purely by chance—thank you, John Cage and Merce Cunningham—from the spinning of a six-sided top. It was also, not coincidentally, the complete opposite of *No Dice*, which the company had just finished performing in what had been a children's gymnasium in Tribeca.

Commissioned by the Soho Rep and created by Kelly Copper and Pavol Liska, the Nature Theater of Oklahoma founders, *No Dice* was a three-and-a-half hour torrent of conversation recited verbatim from the taped phone calls of the company's family and friends—"an epic of the everyday," Liska called it in an interview with the *Voice*'s Brian Parks. Claudia La Rocco, writing in the *Times*, had another description: "wondrous." She left "blissful and sated, yet wanting more." The Obie Award judges would soon be honoring *No Dice* with a special citation. Clearly, the company was on its way to a secure place in the OOB firmament. But when Parks asked Liska about their next project, he had no answer. "If we knew what the next show was," Liska told him, "we'd probably do something else."

That lust for experimentation and comfort with the unknown are what OOB has always been about. It links Liska and Copper back to Tom O'Horgan and the other restless souls who started the whole business way back when; to Foreman, LeCompte and Mee, who have been carrying forward this tradition of the untraditional; and to the next generation that will ultimately replace them. When O'Horgan talked to Gruen in 1972, he thought that chain was coming to an end. "Let's face it," he had said. "There is no more avant-garde, there is no more underground. Everything has surfaced. There just isn't any point going into some loft now, and putting on some crazy play." Tell it to the Nature Theater of Oklahoma.

PLAYS PRODUCED OFF OFF BROADWAY
AND ADDITIONAL NYC PRESENTATIONS
○ ○ ○ ○ ○
Compiled by Vivian Cary Jenkins and Sheryl Arluck

BELOW IS A broad sampling of 2007–2008 Off Off Broadway productions in New York. There is no definitive "Off Off Broadway" area or qualification. To try to define or regiment it would be untrue to its fluid, often exploratory purpose. This listing of hundreds of works produced by scores of OOB groups is as inclusive as reliable sources and space allow. This section pertains to professional theater in New York that is covered by neither Broadway nor full Off Broadway contracts.

The more active and established producing groups are identified in **bold face type**, in alphabetical order, with artistic policies and the names of company leaders given whenever possible. Each group's 2007–08 schedule, with emphasis on new plays, is listed with play titles in CAPITAL LETTERS. Often these are works-in-progress with changing scripts, casts and directors, sometimes without an engagement of record (but an opening or early performance date is included when available).

Many of these Off Off Broadway groups have long since outgrown a merely experimental status and offer programs that are the equal—and in many cases the superior—of anything in the New York theater. These listings include special contractual arrangements such as the showcase code, letters of agreement (allowing for longer runs and higher admission prices than usual) and, closer to the edge of commercial theater, so-called "mini-contracts." Certain productions of companies below may be found in the Plays Produced Off Broadway section when performances per week or size of venue indicate such a shift. Available data has been compiled from press representatives, company managers and publications of record.

A large selection of developing groups and other shows that made appearances Off Off Broadway during the season under review appears under the "Miscellaneous" heading at the end of this listing. Festival listings include samples of the schedules offered and are sometimes limited to the title and author of the work listed to allow for the inclusion of more works.

Amas Musical Theatre. Dedicated to bringing people of all races, creeds, colors and national origins together through the performing arts. Donna Trinkoff producing artistic director, Jan Hacha managing director.

WANDA'S WORLD. Musical with book by Eric H. Weinberger; music and lyrics by Beth Falcone. January 23, 2008. Direction and choreography, Lynne Taylor-Corbett; scenery, Beowulf Boritt; costumes, Jennifer Caprio; lighting, Aaron Spivey; sound, Brett Jarvis; projections, Matthew Myhrum; music direction, Doug Oberhamer; stage management, Brian Westmoreland. With Lakisha Anne Bowen, Jennifer Bowles, Michael Dexter, James Royce Edwards, Leo Ash Evens, Devin Ilaw, Heather Jane Rolff, Sandie Rosa, Christine Scharf, Christopher Vettel, Valerie Wright. Presented in association with Terry Schnuck.

Atlantic Theater Company. Produces new plays and reinterpretations of classics that speak in a contemporary voice on issues reflecting today's society. Neil Pepe artistic director, Andrew D. Hamingson managing director.

10 MILLION MILES. Musical with book by Keith Bunin; music and lyrics by Patty Griffin. June 14, 2007. Direction, Michael Mayer; scenery, Derek McLane; costumes, Michael Krass; lighting, Jules Fisher and Peggy Eisenhauer; sound, Brian Ronan; music direction, Tim Weil; stage management, James Harker. With Irene Molloy, Matthew Morrison, Skipp Sudduth, Mare Winningham. Presented in association with Ira Pittelman and Tom Hulce.

SCARCITY. By Lucy Thurber. September 20, 2007. Direction, Jackson Gay; scenery, Walt Spangler; costumes, Ilona Somogyi; lighting, Jason Lyons; sound, Daniel Baker; music, Jason Mills; stage management, Marion Friedman. With Meredith Brandt, Jesse Eisenberg, Kristen Johnston, Maggie Kiley, Miriam Shor, Todd Weeks, Michael T. Weiss.

TRUMPERY. By Peter Parnell. December 5, 2007. Direction, David Esbjornson; scenery, Santo Loquasto; costumes, Jane Greenwood; lighting, James F. Ingalls; sound, Obadiah Eaves; stage management, Matthew Silver. With Bianca Amato, Michael Countryman, Michael Cristofer, Timothy Deenihan, Manoel Felciano, Neal Huff, Peter Maloney, Jack Tartaglia, Paris Rose Yates.

Family feud: Meredith Brandt, Kristen Johnston, Jesse Eisenberg and Michael T. Weiss in Scarcity. *Photo: Doug Hamilton*

Not touching: Chris Bauer and Emily Mortimer in Parlour Song. *Photo: Doug Hamilton*

PARLOUR SONG. By Jez Butterworth. March 5, 2008. Direction, Neil Pepe; scenery, Robert Brill; costumes, Sarah Edwards; lighting, Kenneth Posner; sound, Obadiah Eaves; stage management, Freda Farrell. With Chris Bauer, Jonathan Cake, Emily Mortimer.

PORT AUTHORITY. By Conor McPherson. May 21, 2008. Direction, Henry Wishcamper; scenery, Takeshi Kata, costumes, Jenny Mannis; lighting, Matthew Richards; sound, Bart Fasbender; stage management, Mary Kathryn Flynt. With Brian d'Arcy James, John Gallagher Jr., Jim Norton.

STAGE 2.
HUMAN ERROR. By Keith Reddin. August 8, 2007. Direction, Tracy Brigden; scenery, Luke Hegel-Cantarella; costumes, Markas Henry; lighting, Jeff Croiter; sound and music, Eric Shim; stage management, Jillian M. Oliver. With Meg Gibson, Tim Guinee, Ray Anthony Thomas.

ALMOST AN EVENING. Three one-act plays by Ethan Coen. WAITING. FOUR BENCHES. DEBATE. January 22, 2008. Direction, Neil Pepe; scenery, Riccardo Hernandez; costumes, Ilona Somogyi; lighting, Donald Holder; sound, Eric Shim; fight direction, J. David Brimmer; stage management, Marion Friedman. With F. Murray Abraham, Jonathan Cake, J.R. Horne, Jordan Lage, Mark Linn-Baker, Elizabeth Marvel, Mary McCann, Del Pentecost, Joey Slotnick. Presented in association with Art Meets Commerce.

Brooklyn Academy of Music Next Wave Festival. Since 1983, this annual festival has presented hundreds of cutting-edge events, including dozens of world premieres. With its focus on leading international artists, it is one of the world's largest and most prestigious festivals of contemporary performing arts. Alan H. Fishman chairman of the board; Karen Brooks Hopkins president; Joseph V. Melillo executive producer.

HOTEL CASSIOPEIA. By Charles L. Mee. October 9, 2007. Direction, Anne Bogart; scenery, Neil Patel; costumes, James Schuette; lighting, Brian H. Scott; sound, Darron L. West; projections, Greg King; dramaturgy, Adrien-Alice Hansel; stage management, Elizabeth

Moreau. With Akiko Aizawa, J. Ed. Araiza, Michi Barall, Leon Ingulsrud, Ellen Lauren, Barney O'Hanlon, Stephen Webber. Presented in association with SITI Company.

KRUM. By Hanoch Levin. October 17, 2007. Direction, Krzysztof Warlikowski; scenery and costumes, Malgorzata Szczesniak; lighting, Felice Ross. With Jacek Poniedzialek, Malgorzata Rolniatowska, Magdalena Cielecka, Malgorzata Hajewska-Krzysztofik, Anna Radwan-Gancarczyk, Danuta Stenka, Redbad Klijnstra, Marek Kalita, Zygmunt Malanowicz, Adam Nawojczyk, Pawel Kruszelnicki, Miron Hakenbeck. Presented in association with TR Warszawa and Stary Teatr, Krakow.

LULU. By Frank Wedekind. November 27, 2007. Direction, Michael Thalheimer; scenery, Olaf Aktmann; costumes, Barbara Drosihn; lighting, Stefan Bolliger; music, Bert Wrede; video, Alexander du Prel; stage management, Thoralf Kunze. With Christoph Bantzer, Michael Benthin, Andreas Döhler, Maren Eggert, Markus Graf, Fritzi Haberlandt, Norman Hacker, Felix Knopp, Hans Low, Peter Moltzen, Helmut Mooshammer, Harald Weiler. Presented in association with Thalia Theater, Hamburg.

AU REVOIR PARAPLUIE. By James Thiérrée. December 4, 2007. Direction and scenery, Mr. Thiérrée; costumes, Victoria Thiérrée and Manon Gignoux; lighting, Jérôme Sabre; sound, Thomas Delot; stage management, Marc Moura and Guillaume Pissembon. With Kaori Ito, Magnus Jakobsson, Satchie Noro, Maria Sendow, Mr. Thiérrée.

Classic Stage Company. Reinventing and revitalizing the classics for contemporary audiences. Brian Kulick artistic director, Jessica R. Jenen executive director.

RICHARD III. Revival of the play by William Shakespeare. November 13, 2007. Direction, Brian Kulick and Michael Cumpsty; scenery, Mark Wendland; costumes, Oana Botez-Ban; lighting, Brian H. Scott; sound Jorge Muelle; music, Mark Bennett. With Craig Baldwin, Steven Boyer, Mr. Cumpsty, Philip Goodwin, Chad Hoeppner, Paul Lazar, Roberta Maxwell, KK Moggie, Andy Phelan, Michael Potts, Judith Roberts, Maria Tucci, Graham Winton.

NEW JERUSALEM. By David Ives. January 13, 2008. Direction, Walter Bobbie; scenery, John Lee Beatty; costumes, Anita Yavich; lighting, Ken Billington; sound, Acme Sound Partners; stage management, Robyn Henry. With Richard Easton, Fyvush Finkel, David Garrison, Jenn Harris, Michael Izquierdo, Natalia Payne, Jeremy Strong.

THE SEAGULL. By Anton Chekhov; translated by Paul Schmidt. March 13, 2008. Direction, Viacheslav Dolgachev; scenery, Santo Loquasto; costumes, Suzy Benzinger, lighting; Brian MacDevitt; sound, Jorge Muelle; stage management, Michaella K. McCoy. With Bill Christ, Alan Cumming, Kelli Garner, Ryan Homchick, John Christopher Jones, Greg Keller, Marjan Neshat, Ryan O'Nan, Annette O'Toole, David Rasche, Dianne Wiest.

OLD COMEDY AFTER ARISTOPHANES'S FROGS. By David Greenspan. May 11, 2008. Direction, David Herskovits; scenery, David Evans Morris; costumes, Meredith Palin; lighting, Lenore Doxsee; sound, Alex Hawthorn, Mr. Herskovits and Kate Marvin; music, Thomas Cabaniss; music direction, David Rosenmeyer; stage management, Ryan C. Durham. With Purva Bedi, Davina Cohen, Charlie Hudson III, Michael Levinton, Derek Lucci, Pedro Pascal, Tina Shepard, Anthony Mark Stockard. Presented in association with Target Margin Theater.

Ensemble Studio Theatre. Membership organization of playwrights, actors, directors and designers dedicated to supporting individual theater artists and developing new works. Stages more than 300 projects each season, ranging from readings to fully mounted productions. William Carden artistic director, Paul A. Slee executive director.

MARATHON 2007 (SERIES B). June 15–30, 2007.
PRICELESS. By Elizabeth Diggs. Direction, Mary B. Robinson. With Craig Anthony Grant, Morgan Hallett, Michael Izquierdo. BEIRUT ROCKS. By Israel Horovitz. Direction, Jo Bonney. With Enver Gjokaj, Marin Ireland, Stephanie Janssen, Frank Solorzano. SELF-PORTRAIT IN A BLUE ROOM. By Daniel Reitz. Direction, Pamela Berlin. With Larry Pine, Chris Stack. CASTING. By Amy Fox. Direction, Nela Wagman. With Polly Adams, Sutton Crawford, Noah Fleiss, Alfredo Narciso. MILTON BRADLEY. By Peter Sagal. Direction, Susan Einhorn. With Jason Schuchman, Stephen Singer.

LUCY. By Damien Atkins. October 29, 2007. Direction, William Carden; scenery, Ryan Kravetz; costumes, Suzanne Chesney; lighting, Chris Dallos; sound, David Lawson; stage management, Jeff Davolt. With Lucy DeVito, Christopher Duva, Lisa Emery, Keira Naughton, Scott Sowers.

ON THE WAY TO TIMBUKTU. Solo performance piece by Petronia Paley. December 8, 2007. Direction, Talvin Wilks; scenery and lighting, Maruti Evans, costumes, Suzanne Chesney, music, Min Xiao-Fen; stage management, Jennifer Conley Darling. With Ms. Paley.

THICKER THAN WATER 2008. February 4–March 1, 2008.
508. By Amy Herzog. Direction, Marlo Hunter. With Julie Fitzpatrick, Miguel Govea. LA FÊTE. By Daria Polatin. Direction, R.J. Tolan. With Geneva Carr, Lucy DeVito, Grant Shaud. FOR CANDY. By Michael Sendrow. Direction, Marlo Hunter. With David Gelles-Hurwitz, Grant Shaud. IT'LL SOON BE HERE. Musical with book by Delaney Britt Brewer; music by Eric Kuehnemann. Direction, Abigail Zealey Bess. With Jenny Greer, Debbie Lee Jones, Lance Rubin. RED BLUE AND PURPLE. By Justin Deabler. Direction, Michael Goldfried. With Miguel Govea, Kelli Lynn Harrison. CO-OP. Musical with book by Courtney Lauria and Matt Schatz; music and lyrics by Mr. Schatz. Direction, Jordan Young. With Steve Boyer, Julie Fitzpatrick. BOTH. By Emily Chadick Weiss. Direction, Alexa Polmer. With Steve Boyer, David Gelles-Hurwitz, Jenny Greer, Lance Rubin, Maureen Sebastian.

FIRST LIGHT FESTIVAL WORKSHOPS 2008. April 7–May 3, 2008.
PURE. By Rey Pamatmat. April 11, 2008. Direction, Carlos Armesto. CASE STUDY. By Amy Fox. April 18, 2008. Direction, William Carden. ADA. Opera with book and lyrics by Margaret Vandenburg, music by Kim Sherman. April 25, 2008. Direction, Lisa Rothe. THE FLOWER HUNTER. May 1, 2008. By Romulus Linney. Direction, Jamie Richards. THE PHYSICISTS. By Friedrich Dürrenmatt. May 3, 2008. Direction, Mary B. Robinson. With Laurence Luckinbill, Peter Maloney, James Rebhorn.

MARATHON 2008 (SERIES A). May 8–May 31, 2008.
AN UPSET. By David Auburn. Direction, Harris Yulin. With Darren Goldstein, Matt Lauria. CHRISTMAS PRESENT. By Amy Herzog. Direction, R.J. Tolan. With Julie Fitzpatrick, Jake Hoffman. A LITTLE SOUL-SEARCHING. By Willie Reale. Direction, Evan Cabnet; music, Patrick Barnes. With Michael Potts, Karen Trott. TOSTITOS. By Michael John Garcés. Direction, May Adrales. With Berrett Doss, Jenny Gomez, Andres Munar, Howard Overshown. WEDDING PICTURES. By Quincy Long. Direction, Kathleen Dimmick. With Autumn Dornfeld, Eric Gilde, Jacob Hawkins, Petronia Paley.

MARATHON 2008 (SERIES B). May 23–June 20, 2008.
THE GREAT WAR. By Neil LaBute. Direction, Andrew McCarthy. With Laila Robins, Grant Shaud. OCTOBER/NOVEMBER. By Anne Washburn. Direction, Ken Rus Schmoll. With Amelia McClain, Gio Perez. OKAY. By Taylor Mac. HAPPY BIRTHDAY WILLIAM ABERNATHY. By Lloyd Suh. With Joe Ponazecki. IDEOGRAM. By David Zellnik. Direction, Abigail Zealey Bess.

The Flea Theater. Formed to present distinctive, cutting-edge work that raises the standards of Off Off Broadway. Jim Simpson artistic director, Carol Ostrow producing director.

AMERICA LOVESEXDEATH. Solo performance piece by Billy the Mime. September 6, 2007. Direction, Billy the Mime; scenery, Kyle Chepulis; costumes, Eleni J. Christou; lighting, Brian Aldous; sound, Josh Higgason; music, Gary Stockdale; stage management, Yvonne Perez. With Billy the Mime.

BINGO WITH THE INDIANS. By Adam Rapp. November 9, 2007. Direction, Mr. Rapp, scenery, John McDermott; costumes, Daphne Javitch; lighting, Miranda Hardy; sound, Brandon Wolcott; stage management, Rachel Sterner. With Cooper Daniels, Corinne Donly, Evan Enderle, Ben Horner, Missel Leddington. Jessica Pohly, Rob Yang.

SEATING ARRANGEMENTS. By Erik Pold, Stine Worm Sorensen, Allan Richard Jensen and the Bats; adapted from the work of Karen Blixen. October 10, 2007. Direction, Mr. Pold; scenery Mr. Sorensen; music, Sylvia Mincewicz, Max Jenkins and Bobby Moreno.With

Donal Brophy, Jane Elliot, Ben Horner, Mr. Jenkins, Jocelyn Kuritsky, Nana Mensah, Ms. Mincewicz, Mr. Moreno. Presented in association with Pold Worm Jensen.

OH THE HUMANITY AND OTHER EXCLAMATIONS. Five one-act plays by Will Eno. November 29, 2007. Direction, Jim Simpson; scenery, Kyle Chepulis; costumes, Claudia Brown; lighting, Brian Aldous; sound, Jill BC DuBoff, stage management, Lindsay Stares. BEHOLD THE COACH IN A BLAZER, UNINSURED. With Brian Hutchinson. LADIES AND GENTLEMEN, THE RAIN. With Brian Hutchinson, Marisa Tomei. ENTER THE SPOKESWOMAN, GENTLY. With Marisa Tomei. THE BULLY COMPOSITION. With Brian Hutchinson, Marisa Tomei. OH, THE HUMANITY. With Brian Hutchinson, Marisa Tomei, Drew Hildebrand.

OFFENDING THE AUDIENCE. By Peter Handke. January 21, 2008. Direction, Jim Simpson; stage management, Joanna Leigh Congalton. With Raniah Al-Sayed, Ivory Aquino, Felipe Bonilla, Jon Cage, Jaime Carrillo, Dan Cozzens, Yung-I Chang, Erwin Falcon, Drew Hildebrand, Emily Hyberger, Alexis Macnab, Bobby Moreno, Chance Mullen, Lisa Pettersson, Rachael Richman, Erin Roth, John Russo, Sarah Sakaan, Annie Scott, Sarah Silk, Ronald Washington, Jeff Worden.

LOWER NINTH. By Beau Willimon. February 28, 2008. Direction, Daniel Goldstein; scenery, Donyale Werle; costumes, Heather Dunbar; lighting, Ben Stanton; sound, Jill BC DuBoff; music, Aaron Mecht; stage management, Jess Johnston. With Gbenga Akinnagbe, Gaius Charles, James McDaniel.

THE BREAK UP. By Tommy Smith. THE HAPPY SAD. By Ken Urban. March 22, 2008. Direction, Sherri Kronfeld; scenery, John McDermott; costumes, Erin Elizabeth Murphy; lighting, Ben Kato; sound, Brandon Wolcott; stage management, Teddy Nicholas. With Felipe Bonilla, Havilah Brewster, Jane Elliot, Pete Forester, Tom Lipinski, Stephen O'Reilly, John Russo, Annie Scott, Ronald Washington.

Intar. One of the country's longest-running Latino theaters producing in English, the company nurtures the professional development of Latino theater artists and works to produce innovative plays that reflect diverse perspectives. Eduardo Machado artistic director.

NIGHT OVER TAOS. By Maxwell Anderson. October 1, 2007. Direction, Estelle Parsons; scenery, Peter Larkin; costumes, Michael Krass; lighting, Howard S. Thies; sound, Erich Bechtel; music, Yukio Tsuji; stage management, Alan Fox. With Juan Luis Acevedo, David Anzuelo, Cheryl Lynn Bowers, Miriam Colón Valle, Hortencia Colorado, Emilio Delgado, Shawn Elliott, Yaremis Felix, Marshall Factora, Michael Frederic, James Gale, Sarah Nina Hayon, Maria Helan, Mercedes Herrero, Irma-Estel LaGuerre, Jack Landron, Bryant Mason, Ron Moreno, Veronica Reyes, Mike Roche, Sibyl Santiago, Mickey Solis, Liam Torres, Ricardo Valdez, Erin Wagner, Teresa Yenque.

ALL EYES AND EARS. By Rogelio Martinez. May 5, 2008. Direction, Eduardo Machado; scenery and lighting, Maruti Evans; costumes, Michael Bevins; sound, Elizabeth Rhodes; stage management, Michael Alifanz. With Martín Solá, Terumi Matthews, Christina Pumariega, Liam Torres, Maria Helan, Ed Vassallo.

Irish Repertory Theatre. Brings works by Irish and Irish-American playwrights to a wider audience and develops new works focusing on a wide range of cultural experience. Charlotte Moore artistic director, Ciarán O'Reilly producing director.

NEW WORKS READING SERIES. June 29, 2007–May 23, 2008. GIRLS AND DOLLS. By Lisa McGee. June 29, 2007. With Laura Heisler, Samantha Soule. O GO MY MAN. By Stella Feehily. Friday, July 27, 2007. With Mia Barron, Denis Butkus, Bianca Amato, Mattie Hawkinson, Roxanna Hope, David Pittu, Amanda Quaid, Reg Rogers. THE AVENUE. By Christian O'Reilly. August 24, 2007. With Seán Gormley, Derek Lucci, Paula McGonagle, Gordana Rashovich, Tommy Schrider. SIX CONVERSATIONS ABOUT LOVE. By Ionna Anderson. September 28, 2007. With Becky Ann Baker, Rosalyn Coleman, Patricia Conolly, Peter Rogan. HANG LENNY POPE. By Chris O'Connell. October 26, 2007.

With Jennifer Dundas, Luke Farrell Kirby, Ciarán O'Reilly, Annie Purcell. CHERRY SMOKE. By Jim McManus. November 16, 2007. With Zachary Booth, Mahira Kakkar, Louisa Krause, Benjamin Walker. CRUMBLE (LAY ME DOWN JUSTIN TIMBERLAKE). By Sheila Callaghan. December 14, 2007. With Bianca Amato, Denis Butkus, Catherine Curtin, David Greenspan, Laura Heisler. DUCK. By Stella Feehily. January 25, 2008. With Aya Cash, Orlagh Cassidy, Jarlath Conroy, Mattie Hawkinson, Sean Fredricks, David C. Wells. MONGED. By Gary Duggan. February 22, 2008. With Gideon Glick, Austin Lysy, James McMenamin. FOR NINA. By Robert Emmet Lunney. March 28, 2007. With Lisa Emery, Peter Friedman, Steven Goldstein, Louisa Krause, Larry Pine, Jennifer Van Dyck. THE ELECTRIC CENTURY. By Andrew Case. April 25, 2008. With Fred Applegate, Meg Gibson, Salvatore Inzerillo, Stephen Kunken, Sarah Lord, KK Moggie, Jay Patterson. HORSE LATITUDES. By Hilary Fannin. May 23, 2008. With Zachary Booth, Charlotte Colavin, Patricia Conolly, Michael Countryman, Patch Darragh, Maria Dizzia, Greg Keller, Susan Louise O'Connor.

SIVE. By John B. Keane. September 27, 2007. Direction, Ciarán O'Reilly; scenery, Charles Corcoran; costumes, Martha Hally; lighting, Jason Lyons; sound, Zachary Williamson; stage management, April Ann Kline. With James Barry, Donie Carroll, Terry Donnelly, Patrick Fitzgerald, Christopher Joseph Jones, Aidan Redmond, Wrenn Schmidt, Mark Thornton, Fiana Toibin.

A CHILD'S CHRISTMAS IN WALES. By Dylan Thomas; adapted by Charlotte Moore. 'Twas the Night Before Christmas. By Clement Clarke Moore; adapted by Ms. Moore. December 5, 2007. Direction and scenery, Ms. Moore; costumes, David Toser; lighting, Mac Smith, music, Ken Darby, music direction, John Bell; stage management, Rhonda Picou. With Kerry Conte, Bonnie Fraser, Justin Packard, Joshua Park, Ashley Robinson.

THE DEVIL'S DISCIPLE. By George Bernard Shaw. December 13, 2007. Direction and scenery, Tony Walton; costumes, Mr. Walton and Rebecca Lustig; lighting, Brian Nason; sound, Zachary Williamson; fight direction, Rick Sordelet; stage management, Christine Lemme. With Curzon Dobell, Jonathan Donahue, Jenny Fellner, Sean Gormley, Cristin Milioti, Craig Pattison, Lorenzo Pisoni, Darcy Pulliam, Robert Sedgwick, John Windsor-Cunningham, Richard B. Watson.

TAKE ME ALONG. Musical with book by Joseph Stein and Robert Russell; music and lyrics by Bob Merrill; based on *Ah, Wilderness!* by Eugene O'Neill. February 28, 2008. Direction, Charlotte Moore; choreography, Barry McNabb, scenery, James Morgan; costumes, Linda Fisher; lighting, Mary Jo Dondlinger; sound, Zachary Williamson; music direction, Mark Hartman; stage management, Rhonda Picou. With Anastasia Barzee, Donna Bullock, Dewey Caddell, Teddy Eck, Beth Glover, Justin Packard, William Parry, Noah Ruff, Emily Skeggs, Gordon Stanley, Don Stephenson.

PRISONER OF THE CROWN. By Richard F. Stockton; additional material, Richard T. Herd. May 22, 2008. Direction, Ciarán O'Reilly; scenery, Charles Corcoran; costumes, David Toser; lighting, Brian Nason; sound, Zachary Williamson; stage management, Elis C. Arroyo. With Peter Cormican, Patrick Fitzgerald, Philip Goodwin, Emma O'Donnell, Tim Ruddy, Ian Stuart, John Vennema, John Windsor-Cunningham.

La MaMa Experimental Theatre Club (ETC). A workshop for experimental theater of all kinds. Ellen Stewart founder and director.

Schedule included:
ALL HER FACES–A PORTRAIT OF DUSTY SPRINGFIELD. By Anthony Inneo. June 1, 2007. Direction, Mr. Inneo; choreography, Gregory Daniels; sound, Adam Farquharson; music direction, Jo Lynn Burks. With Steve Bartosik, Sandra Caldwell, Lauren Echo, Amy Lou Fox, Sean Jenness, Isabel Santiago, Louis Tucci.

GOLONDRINA (SWALLOW). By Aminta de Lara. June 7, 2007. Direction, Diana Chery and Ms. de Lara; music, Maria Eugenia Atilano. With Ms. de Lara, Ana Munoz.

DELTA. By Petar Todorov and Gregor Kamnikar. September 20, 2007. Direction and choreography, Messrs. Todorov and Kamnikar; costumes, Marina Yaneva and Hannah Schwartz. With Desislava Mincheva, Lyudmila Miteva, Toni Pashova.

A GLOBAL DIONYSUS IN NAPOLI. By Paolo Favero. September 21, 2007. Direction, Giuliana Ciancio and Nicola Ciancio; costumes, Daniela Ciancio; lighting, Michelangelo Campanale. With Marcello Colasurdo, Vernon Douglas, Marco Messina.

CARAVAGGIO CHIAROSCURO. Musical with book by Gian Marco Lo Forte; music and lyrics by Duane Boutte. September 27, 2007. Direction, George Drance; scenery, Mr. Lo Forte; costumes, Denise Greber; lighting, Federico Restrepo; music direction, Jason Sagebiel; stage management, Karina Martins. With Mr. Boutte, Dana Cote, Sara Galassini, Silvia Giampaola, Jeffrey Glaser, Erika Iverson, Ralph Martin, Elizabeth Mutton, Matt Nasser, Graham Skipper, Kat Yew.

IPHIGENIA AT AULIS. By Euripides; adapted by Wlodzimierz Staniewski. October 7, 2007. Direction, Mr. Staniewski; choreography, Julia Bui-Ngoc; costumes, Monika Onoszko; lighting, Grzegorz Podbieglowski; sound, Maciej Znamierowski; music, Zygmunt Konieczny. With Maniucha Bikont, Charlie Cattrall, Karolina Cicha, Anna Dabrowska, Mariusz Golaj, Joanna Holcgreber, Benedict Hotchins, Justyna Jary, Tanushka Marah, Agnieszka Mendel, Marcin Mrowca, Jacek Timingeriu, Barbara Wesolowska.

THE USUAL FREAK SHOW. By Jeffrey Essmann. November 2, 2007. With Mr. Essman, Michael John LaChiusa.

EXPERIMENTS NEW PLAY READING SERIES. October 18–December 10, 2007.
PLAINS. By Stacia Saint Owens. With Nick Denning, Juliet O'Brien, Julie Rosier. WAITING FOR MERT. By Michael Zettler. October 18, 2007. With Alexander Alioto, Peter McCabe. THE WARZONE IS MY BED. By Yasmine Beverly Rana. October 20, 2007. With Alexander Alioto, Sheila Dabney, Jason Howard, John-Andrew Morrison, Candace Reid, Jenne Vath. TENTAGATNET. By Peter Dizozza. October 21, 2007. With Leslie Ann Hendricks, John Andrew Morrison, Sonja Perryman, Chris Zorker. SCHRODINGER'S CAT. By Stan Kaplan. October 21, 2007. With Timothy Doyle. AUDITIONING ANGELS. By Pieter-Dirk Uys. October 25, 2007. With Sheila Dabney, Peter McCabe, Sonja Perryman, Will Rhys, Jenne Vath. THE LOST CITIES OF ASHER. By Adam Kraar. November 12, 2007. Direction, Lorca Peress. With John FitzGibbon, Melissa Kraus, Mikel Sarah Lambert, Valorie Niccore, Tanya Perez, Patricia Randell.

LOVE LASTS ON MYRTLE AVENUE. By Jimmy Breslin. December 10, 2007. Direction, George Ferencz. With Joe Gioco, Nell Gwynn, Leslie Ann Hendricks, Cam Korman, Peter McCabe, Chuck Montgomery, Susan Patrick, Jim Seaman, Jenne Vath, T.D. White, Chris Zorker.

BABA AND THE TREE OF LIFE. By Edgar Nkosi White. February 11, 2008. Direction, Danna Manno. With Gerald Asbell Jr., Camille Gaston, Chénana Manno, John Andrew Morrison, Solomon Tosin, Jenne Vath.

LUCKY PATRON FOR THE ARTS. By C.S. Hanson. May 12, 2008. Direction, George Ferencz. Rajesh Bose, Jason Howard, LeeAnne Hutchinson, Peter McCabe, Carolina McNeely, John-Andrew Morrison, Allen Lewis Rickman, Jenne Vath.

WEST BANK, UK. Musical with book by Oren Safdie; music and lyrics by Ronnie Cohen. December 2, 2007. Direction, Mr. Safdie; choreography, Wendy Seyb; scenery, Michael V. Moore; costumes, Greco; lighting, Matt Berman; music direction, Scott Baldyga. With Jeremy Cohen, Mike Mosallam, Anthony Patellis, Michelle Solomon.

THE HONOR AND GLORY OF WHALING. By Michael Gorman. December 28, 2007. Direction, George Ferencz; scenery, Marguerite White; costumes, Sarah Boyden; lighting, Carla Bosnjak; sound, Tim Schellenbaum; music, Tonya Ridgely. With David Bennett, David Branch, Ruth Coughlin, J.P. Guimont, Al Joyce, Michael Kimball, Anita Menotti.

THE JACK OF TARTS. Musical with book and lyrics by Chris Tanner and Eric Wallach; music and lyrics by Paul Johnson. January 31, 2008. Direction and choreography, Mr. Wallach. With Lance Cruce, Michael Lynch, Julie Atlas Muz, Mr. Tanner.

IMMINENCE. By Paul Zimet. February 15, 2008. Direction, Mr. Zimet; choreography, Hilary Easton; scenery, Nic Ularu; costumes, Kiki Smith; lighting, Carol Mullins; music, Peter Gordon and Ellen Maddow; projections, Kit Fitzgerald. With William Badgett, David Brooks,

Amelia Campbell, Kim Gambino, Lula Graves, Kristine Lee, Ms. Maddow, Greg Manley, Steven Rattazzi, Tina Shepard, the Talking Band.

THE CHERRY ORCHARD SEQUEL. By Nic Ularu. February 24, 2008. Direction, Mr. Ularu; scenery, Carl Hamilton and Craig Vetter; costumes, Kimi Maeda; lighting, James Hunter; sound, Walter Clissen; stage management, K. Dale White. With John-Patrick Driscoll, Zachary T. Hanks, Robert Hungerford, Robyn Hunt, Richard Jennings, Paul Kaufman, Patrick Michael Kelly, Steve Pearson.

SEVEN DAYS. By Shlomi Moskovitz; translated by Anthony Berris. March 13, 2008. Direction, Geula Jeffet Attar and Victor Attar; choreography, Neta Pulvermacher; music, Yuval Mesner; scenery, Robert Eggers; lighting, Watoku Ueno. With Mr. Attar, Deborah Carlson, Ofrit Shiran Peres, Udi Razzin.

MEDEA. By Euripides; translated and adapted by Theodora Skipitares. March 13, 2008. Direction, Ms. Skipitares; lighting, Pat Dignan, music, Tim Shellenbaum; projections, Kay Hines; puppets, Cecilia Schiller. With Ms. Skipitares.

RAILROAD BACKWARD. By Kestutis Nakas. March 21, 2008. Direction, Mr. Nakas. With Chris Amos, Kent Brown, Samantha Grisafe, John David Hall, Frederick Harris, Mr. Nakas, Edgar Oliver, Nicky Paraiso.

THE SEJNY CHRONICLES. By Bozena Szroeder; translated by Danuta Borchardt. April 10, 2008. Direction, Ms. Szroeder. With Aleksandra Tomal, Edyta Rogucka, Dominika Turowicz, Aleksandra Kotarska, Katarzyna Ostrowska, Dagmara Nieszczerzewska, Ula Kapp, Aleksandra Szruba, Jakub Ostrowski, Artur Mazewski, Robert Ogurkis, Patryk Zubowicz, Piotr Szroeder, Michal Pawlowski.

BROTHERS. By Andrea Paciotto; based on a poem by Ellen Stewart and the Old Testament. April 24, 2008. Direction, Ms. Paciotto; music, Jan H. Klug. With Dejan Andric, Thikomir Dakic, Nikolina Djordjievic, Marko Dukic, Dragana Maric, Ana Radovanovic, Boris Savija, Dejan Zoric.

Lincoln Center Festival 2007. July 10–29, 2007. An annual international summer arts festival offering classic and contemporary work. Nigel Redden artistic director.

GEMELOS. By Laura Pizarro and Juan Carlos Zagal; based on a novel by Agota Kristof. July 10, 2007. Direction, Ms. Pizarro and Mr. Zagal; scenery and costumes, Rodrigo Bazaes, Eduardo Jiménez, Ms. Pizarro, Messrs. Zagal and Lorca; music, Mr. Zagal. With Diego Fonticella, Ms. Pizarro, Mr. Zagal. Presented in association with Compañia Teatro Cinema of Chile.

FABLES DE LA FONTAINE. By Jean de La Fontaine; translated for supertitles by Mike Sens. July 10, 2007. Direction, scenery and lighting, Robert Wilson; costumes, Moidele Bickel; music, Michael Galasso; masks, Kuno Schlegelmilch; dramaturgy, Ellen Hammer. With Christian Blanc, Cécile Brune, Charles Chemin, Christine Fersen, Grégory Gadebois, Françoise Gillard, Gérard Giroudon, Nicolas Lormeau, Madeleine Marion, Laurent Natrella, Céline Samie, Bakary Sangaré, Léonie Simaga, Laurent Stocker, Coraly Zahonero. Presented in association with the Comédie-Française.

BOOK OF LONGING. By Philip Glass and Leonard Cohen. July 14, 2007. Direction, Susan Marshall; scenery, Christine Jones; costumes, Kasia Walicka Maimone; lighting, Scott Zielinski, music direction, Michael Riesman. With Will Erat, Timothy Fain, Mr. Glass, Tara Hugo, Daniel Keeling, Eleonore Oppenheim, Dominique Plaisant, Mr. Riesman, Mick Rossi, Kate St. John, Andrew Sterman, Wendy Sutter.

RENJISHI (THE THREE LIONS). July 16, 2007. Direction, Nakamura Kanzaburo XVIII. With Nakamura Kantaro II, Mr. Kanzaburo, Nakamura Shichinosuke II. Presented in association with Heisei Nakamura-za.

HOKAIBO. By Nakawa Shimesuke; translated by Linda Hoaglund. July 17, 2007. Direction, Kushida Kazuyoshi; choreography, Fujima Kanjuro; costumes, Arai Kumiko, Hiruta Noritaka, Kurosaki Atsuhiro; lighting, Saito Shigeo; stage management, Takeshiba Tokutaro. With Nakamura Hashinosuke, Kataoka Kamezo, Nakamura Kantaro, Nakamura Kanzaburo,

Nakamura Senjaku, Nakamura Shichinosuke, Sasano Takashi, Bando Yajuro, Paul Lazar. Presented in association with Heisei Nakamura-za.

DE MONSTRUOS Y PRODIGIOS: LA HISTORIA DE LOS CASTRATI. By Jorge Kuri and Claudio Valdés Kuri. July 20, 2007. Direction, Mr. Valdés Kuri. With Edwin Calderón, Miguel Angel Lopez, Javier Medina, Kaveh Parmas, Raúl Román, Luis Fernando Villegas, Gastón Yanes. Presented in association with Teatro de Ciertos Habitantes of Mexico.

UN HOMBRE QUE SE AHOGA; based on *The Three Sisters* by Anton Chekhov. July 17, 2007. Direction and scenery, Daniel Veronese; lighting, Gonzalo Córdova. With Osvaldo Bonet, Silvina Bosco, Claudio Da Passano, Adriana Ferrer, Gabriella Ferraro, Malena Figó, Maria Figueras, Fernando Llosa, Maria Lubos, Pablo Messiez, Elvira Onetto, Silvina Sabater, Luciano Suardi, Claudio Tolcachir. Presented in association with Proyecto Chejov of Argentina.

DIVINAS PALABRAS. By Ramón Maria del Valle-Inclán; adapted by Juan Mayorga. July 26, 2007. Direction, Gerardo Vera; scenery, Richardo Sánchez Cuerda and Mr. Vera; costumes, Alejandro Andújar; lighting, Juan Gómez-Conejo; music, Luis Delgado; video, Alvaro Luna. With Fidel Almansa, Ester Bellver, Sonsoles Benedicto, Miriam Cano, Paco Dénize, Charo Gallego, Gabriel Garbisu, Carlota Gaviño, Emilio Gavira, Elisabet Gelabert, Elena Gonzalez, Alicia Hermida, Daniel Holguín, Javier Lara, Jesús Noguero, Pietro Olivera, Idola Ruiz de Lara, Sergio Sánchez, Fernando Sansegundo, Julieta Serrano, Julia Trujillo, Pablo Vásquez, Abel Vitón. Presented in association with Centro Drámatico Nacional of Spain.

MCC Theater. Brings together exceptional theater artists to produce works that encourage a re-examination of the world in which we live through the unique perspectives of extraordinary writers. Robert LuPone and Bernard Telsey artistic directors, William Cantler associate artistic director, Blake West executive director.

IN A DARK DARK HOUSE. By Neil LaBute. June 7, 2007. Direction, Carolyn Cantor; scenery, Beowulf Boritt; costumes, Jenny Mannis; lighting, Ben Stanton; sound and music, Rob

Family secret: Ron Livingston and Frederick Weller in In a Dark Dark House. *Photo: Joan Marcus*

The conquered: Veanne Cox and Annabella Sciorra in Spain. *Photo: Joan Marcus*

Kaplowitz; stage management, Joel Rosen. With Louisa Krause, Ron Livingston, Frederick Weller. Presented in association with the Lucille Lortel Foundation.

SPAIN. By Jim Knable. October 30, 2007. Direction, Jeremy Dobrish; scenery, Beowulf Boritt; costumes, Jenny Mannis; lighting, Michael Gottlieb; sound, Jill BC DuBoff; fight direction, Rick Sordelet; stage management, Alexis R. Prussack. With Michael Aronov, Veanne Cox, Erik Jensen, Lisa Kron, Annabella Sciorra.

GRACE. By Mick Gordon and AC Grayling. February 11, 2008. Direction, Joseph Hardy; scenery, Tobin Ost; costumes, Alejo Vietti; lighting, Matthew Richards; sound, Fabian Obispo; stage management, Robert Bennett. With Philip Goodwin, Oscar Isaac, Robert Emmet Lunney, KK Moggie, Lynn Redgrave.

Mint Theater Company. Committed to bringing new vitality to worthy but neglected plays. Jonathan Bank artistic director.

THE RETURN OF THE PRODIGAL. By St. John Hankin. June 6, 2007. Direction, Jonathan Bank; scenery and costumes, Clint Ramos; lighting, Tyler Micoleau; sound, Jane Shaw; stage management, Kimothy Cruse. With Bradford Cover, Tandy Cronyn, Leah Curney, Roderick Hill, Richard Kline, Kate Levy, Lee Moore, Margot White.

THE POWER OF DARKNESS. By Leo Tolstoy; translation by Martin Platt. September 6, 2007. Direction, Mr. Platt; scenery, Bill Clarke, costumes, Holly Poe Durbin; lighting, Jeff Nellis; music, Ellen Mandel; stage management, Allison Deutsch. With Mark Alhadeff, Lisa Altomare, Jennifer Bissell, Steve Brady, Peter Bretz, Randy Danson, Matthew A.J. Gregory, Letitia Lange, Anne Letscher, Peter Levine, Angela Reed, Jeff Steitzer, Alok Tewari, Goldie Zwiebel.

THE FIFTH COLUMN. By Ernest Hemingway. March 27, 2008. Direction, Jonathan Bank; scenery, Vicki R. Davis; costumes, Clint Ramos; lighting, Jeff Nellis; sound, Jane Shaw; dramaturgy, Juan Salas; stage management, Allison Deutsch. With James Andreassi, Heidi

Armbruster, Kelly AuCoin, Ryan Duncan, Ronald Guttman, John Patrick Hayden, Joe Hickey, Carlos Lopez, Ned Noyes, Maria Parra, Joe Rayome, Nicole Shalhoub, Teresa Yenque.

New Dramatists. An organization devoted to playwrights. Members may use the facilities for projects ranging from private readings of their material to public scripts-in-hand readings. Listed below are readings open to the public during the season under review. Todd London artistic director, Joel K. Ruark executive director.

STEP ASIDE. By Barry Kaplan and William McDaniel. June 12, 2007. With Elliot Villar, Eddie Brown, Nondumiso Tembe, Ken Robinson, Stacey Linnartz, Amirah Vann, Carter Gill.

BERNICE BOBS HER HAIR. By Julia Jordan and Adam Gwon. June 20–28, 2007. Direction, Joe Calarco. With Jill Abramovitz, Kenneth Boys, Charlie Brady, Will Erat, Leah Horowitz, Maria Thayer, Debra Wiseman Tobias, Kate Wetherhead, Wayne Wilcox.

A NIGHT IN THE OLD MARKETPLACE. By Glen Berger and Frank London. June 29, 2007. Direction, Alex Aron. With Manu Narayan, David Margulies, Steven Rattazzi, Valerie Geffner, Lori Prince, Susan Louise O'Connor, Erik Liberman.

WHOLEHEARTED. By Quincy Long. August 6, 2007. Direction, Kathleen Dimmick. With Paul Sparks, Zabryna Guevara, Guy Boyd, William Youmans, Peter Gerety, Clea Lewis, Phyllis Somerville.

NEW PLAYWRIGHT WELCOME. September 10, 2007. GREEN GIRL. By Sarah Hammond. Direction, Kristin Horton. With Maggie Fine, Robert Beitzel.THE DINOSAUR WITHIN. By John Walch. Direction, Shana Gold. With Brenda Wehle, Leon Addison Brown. KITCHEN TABLE. By Eugenie Chan. Direction, Shelley Butler. With Christopher Larkin, Ali Ahn, Natalie Kim, Hoon Lee, Michi Barall. MADAGASCAR. By J.T. Rogers. Direction, Gus Reyes. With Marin Ireland, Mary Beth Peil, Larry Pine. DIAGRAM OF A PAPER AIRPLANE. By Carlos Murillo. Direction, Mr. Murillo. With David Greenspan, Rafael Baez. GOD SAVE GERTRUDE. By Deborah Stein. Direction, Lear deBessonet. With Maria Cellaria, Lucas Near-Verbrugghe. THIS SUMMER. By Julie Marie Myatt. Direction, Melissa Kievman. With Lynn Cohen, Ronald Cohen.

WATERSHED. By Matthew Maguire. October 4, 2007. Direction, Mr. Maguire. With Annie Parisse, Paul Sparks, Rocco Sisto.

GRADUATION FESTIVAL. October 15–26, 2007. OVERDRIVE. By Dominic Taylor. Direction, Mr. Taylor. With Charles Parnell, Julia Knight, Gerardo Rodriquez, Kibibi Dillon. AUTODELETE. By Honor Molloy. Direction, Adam Greenfield. With John Keating, Gretchen Krich, Jerry Manning, Alejandro Morales, Mallery Avidon. STRIPPING THE CORPSE. By Julie Hebert. MARY PEABODY IN CUBA. By Anne Garcia Romero. Direction, Leah Gardiner. With Mandy Gonzalez, Kelly Eubanks, Diane Ciesla, Alfredo Narciso, Alvaro Mendoza, Sara Sirota, Ron Riley, Lauren Munger. CURRENT NOBODY. By Melissa James Gibson. With Christina Kirk. THE OCTOBER CRISIS (TO LAURA). By Alejandro Morales. Direction, Scott Ebersold. With Mercedes Herrero, Melanie Kann, Mark H. Dold, Matthew Dellapina, Polly Lee. FUBAR. By Karl Gajdusek. Direction, Drew Barr. With Juliana Francis, Joel de la Fuente, Michael Laurence, Katie Sigismund, Lou Sumrall. INSTRUCTIONS FOR BREATHING. By Caridad Svich. Direction, Daniella Topol. With Michael Tisdale, Carla Harting, Alfredo Narciso, Polly Lee, Gerardo Rodriguez, Julia Weldon.

PURE CONFIDENCE. By Carlyle Brown. November 5–7, 2007. With Gavin Lawrence, William Parry, John Horton, Maureen Silliman, Heather Alicia Simms, Ron Riley, Barbara McCulloh.

THE QUESTION OF GOD. By Mark St. Germain. November 8, 2007. Direction, Mr. St. Germain. With Robert Zuckerman and Jack Gilpin.

ANGELA'S MIXTAPE. By Eisa Davis. November 10–12, 2007. Direction, Liesl Tommy. With Brenda Thomas, Michelle Hurd, Adrienne Hurd, and Rebecca Naomi Jones.

SONS. By Oni Faida Lampley. November 12, 2007. Direction, Leah Gardiner. With Nedra McClyde, Seth Gilliam, Chad Goodridge, Will Jackson Harper, Elaina Erika Davis, Kibibi Dillon.

BRIGHT CAPTIVES. By Gordon Dahlquist. November 13, 2007. Direction, Mr. Dahlquist. With Maria Dizzia, Jeff Biehl, Molly Powell, John McAdams, Frank Deal, Maria Striar, Joe Goodrich.

THE PEARL MERCHANT. By Brie Walker. November 16, 2007. Direction, Pat Golden. With Maria Dizzia, Greg Steinbruner, Kristin Griffith, Tamilla Woodard.

SEVEN. By Anna Deavere Smith, Ruth Margraff, Gail Kriegel, Carol K. Mack, Susan Yankowitz, Catherine Filloux, Paula Cizmar. November 19, 2007. Direction, Evan Yionoulis. With Phyllis Johnson, Lanna Joffrey, Socorro Santiago, Barbara Sims, Jolly Abraham, Ching Valdes-Aran, Meg Gibson.

LEAVING EDEN. By Chiori Miyagawa. November 27, 2007. Direction, Alice Reagan. With Sue Jean Kim, Luis Vega, Noel Velez, Jon Krupp, Ching Valdes-Aran, Rebecca Lingafelter, Riddick Marie, Birgit Huppuch.

THE DAY OF THE PICNIC. By Russell Davis. November 29, 2007. Direction, Rebecca Lynn Brown. With Kevin Bergen, Owiso Odera, Nancy Boykin, Ronald Cohen, Lynn Cohen, Mahira Kakkar, Novella Nelson.

PLAYTIME. December 3–15, 2007. DEAR SARA JANE. By Victor Lodato. December 13, 2007. Direction, Jackson Gay. With Marin Ireland. HORSEDREAMS. By Dael Orlandersmith. December 14, 2007. Direction, Gordon Edelstein. With Dael Orlandersmith, Victor Slezak, Jeremy Allen White. THE JESUS YEAR. By Brooke Berman. December 14, 2007. Direction, Trip Cullman. With Mia Barron, Maria Dizzia, Lucas Papaelias, Angela Pietropinto, Eddie Kaye Thomas. THE MIRACLE AT NAPLES. By David Grimm. December 15, 2007. Direction, Peter DuBois. With Colby Chambers, Manoel Felciano, Marin Ireland, Dick Latessa, Pedro Pascal, Angela Pietropinto, Christina Pumariega. SONS OF LIBERTY. By Mark St. Germain and John Markus. December, 20, 2007. Direction, Bob Balaban. With Tom Aldredge, Larry Block, Amelia Campbell, Dan Lauria, Peter Maloney, Wallace Shawn, William Wise, Christopher Evan Welch. DAPHNE DOES DIM SUM. By Eugenie Chan. January 4–7, 2008. Direction, Kate Lyn Reiter. With Raul Aranas, Wai Ching Ho, Virginia Wing, Henry Yuk. THE EXTINCTION OF FELIX GARDEN. By Sarah Hammond. January 16, 2008. Direction, Wendy McClellan. With Aysan Celik, Michael Ray Escamilla, Lynn Cohen, Cyrus Hernstadt, Keith Randolph Smith

I'LL BE SEEING YOU. By Leah Hendrick. January 18, 2008. Direction, Matthew Maquire. With Arthur French, Bob Braswell, Eliza Baldi, Rashaad Ernesto Green, Judith Roberts, Edward O'Blenis.

THE FIRST BORN. By Harding Lemay. January 29, 2008. Direction, Tom Ferriter. With Douglas Taurel, Annie Kozuch, Paul Newport, Jillie Simon, Marian Seldes, James Patrick Early.

THE LISTENER OF JUNK CITY. By Liz Duffy Adams and John Hodian. February 8, 2008. Direction, Wendy McClellan. With Gabrielle Stravelli, David Ruffin, Bill Gross, Jose Llana, Keira Keeley.

1:23. By Carson Kreitzer. February 11, 2008. Direction, Mark Wing-Davey. With Eva Kaminsky, Deborah Knox, Rege Lewis, Michael Pemberton, Shirley Roeca.

BLUE GROTTO. By Taylor Mac. February 22, 2008. Direction, Josh Hecht. With Judith Roberts, Leslie Lyles, Ashlie Atkinson.

MIND THE GAP. By Kara Manning. March 24, 2008. Direction, Hal Brooks. With Reed Birney, Kristin Griffith, Creighton James, Matthew Rauch, Nalini Sharma.

KILL TO EAT. By Caridad Svich. March 31, 2008. Direction, Jean Randich. With Raul Castillo, Jocelyn Kuritsky, Bryant Mason, Alfredo Narciso, Juliana Francis Kelly.

RUNWAY 69. By Carson Kreitzer and Erin Kamler. April 1–3, 2008. Direction, Wendy McClellan With Marie-France Arcilla, Tracee Beazer, Erik Liberman, April Matthis, Javier Munoz, Jim Price, David Ruffin, Elise Santora, Emily Simoness, Gabrielle Stravelli, Mark Stringham, Kendall Rileigh.

DOUBLE TIME. By John Walch and Nile Rodgers. April 4, 2008. Direction, Lynne Taylor-Corbett. With Rodney Hicks, Idara Victor, Bobby Steggert, Lakisha Anne Bowen,

Joel Blum, Charlie Pollock, David Boyd, Chase Steele Greye, Albert Christmas, Anthony Santos, Arthur French.

PURE AND SIMPLE. By Jim Nicholson. April 10, 2008. Direction, James Dacre. With Annika Boras, Bill Buell, Kyle Knauf, Elena McGhee.

TELA BELLA. By Clare Drobot April 18, 2008. Direction, Jade King Carroll. With Richard Bekins, Cherise Booth, Timothy Fannon, Creighton James, Yuri Skujins, Sandra Struthers.

WALLFLOWER. By Deborah Stein. April 28, 2008. Direction, Wendy McClellan. With Annie Purcell, Brandon Espinoza, Aya Cash.

THE BOOK OF LAMBERT. By Leslie Lee. April 28, 2008. Direction, Cyndy A. Marion. With Jay Ward, Rebecca Thomas, Heather Massie, Arthur French, Marjorie Johnson, Scott Sortman, Pamela Monroe, Carolyn Michelle Smith, Christopher Johnson.

THE MIKE AND MORGAN SHOW. By Raphael Bob-Waksberg. May 30, 2008. Direction, Kip Fagan. With Adam Goldman, Eloise Mumford.

New Federal Theatre. Dedicated to integrating minorities into the mainstream of American theater through the training of artists and the presentation of plays by minorities and women. Woodie King Jr. producing director.

THREE TRAVELERS. By Richard Abrons. January 24, 2008. Direction, Jay Broad; scenery, Don Llewellyn; costumes, Karen Perry; lighting, David F. Segal; sound, Sean O'Halloran; stage management, Jacqui Casto. With Judith Lightfoot Clark, Kenneth Maharaj, Kathleen McNenny, Stephen Schnetzer.

SWEET MAMA STRINGBEAN. By Beth Turner. April 9, 2008. Direction, Elizabeth Van Dyke; choreography, Mickey Davidson; scenery, Ademola Olugebefola; costumes, Carolyn Adams; lighting, Shirley Prendergast; sound, Sean O'Halloran; stage management, Bayo. With Cjay Hardy Philip, Marishka Shanice Phillip, Sandra Reaves-Phillips, Gary E. Vincent, Darryl Jovan Williams.

New York Theatre Workshop. Dedicated to nurturing artists at all stages of their careers and to developing provocative new works. James C. Nicola artistic director.

THE SOUND AND THE FURY (APRIL SEVENTH, 1928). By Elevator Repair Service; based on the book by William Faulkner. April 29, 2008. Direction, John Collins; scenery, David Zinn; costumes, Colleen Werthmann; lighting, Mark Barton; sound, Matt Tierney; stage management, Sarah C. Hughes. With Mike Iveson, Vin Knight, Aaron Landsman, April Matthis, Annie McNamara, Randolph Curtis Rand, Greig Sargeant, Kate Scelsa, Kaneza Schaal, Susie Sokol, Tory Vazquez, Ben Williams. Presented in association with Elevator Repair Service.

The New Group. Provides an artistic home for fresh acting, writing and design talent. Committed to cultivating a young and diverse theatergoing audience. Scott Elliott artistic director, Geoffrey Rich executive director.

THINGS WE WANT. By Jonathan Marc Sherman. November 7, 2007. Direction, Ethan Hawke; scenery Derek McLane; costumes, Mattie Ullrich; lighting, Jeff Croiter; sound, Daniel Baker; stage management, Valerie A. Peterson. With Paul Dano, Peter Dinklage, Josh Hamilton, Zoe Kazan. Presented in association with Janice Montana.

2000 YEARS. By Mike Leigh. February 7, 2008. Direction, Scott Elliott; scenery, Derek McLane; costumes, Mimi O'Donnell, lighting, Jason Lyons, sound, Ken Travis; music, Klezmatics; stage management, Valerie A. Peterson. With Yuval Boim, David Cale, Laura Esterman, Jordan Gelber, Merwin Goldsmith, Cindy Katz, Natasha Lyonne, Richard Masur.

RAFTA, RAFTA. By Ayub Khan-Din; based on the play *All in Good Time* by Bill Naughton. May 8, 2008. Direction, Scott Elliott; scenery, Derek McLane; costumes, Theresa Squire; lighting, Jason Lyons, sound; Shane Rettig; music, DJ Rekha; stage management, Valerie A. Peterson. With Utkarsh Ambudkar, Satya Bhabha, Sarita Choudhury, Ranjit Chowdhry, Manish Dayal, Sakina Jaffrey, Sean T. Krishnan, Reshma Shetty, Alok Tewari, Alison Wright.

Drinkin' 'n' thinkin': Paul Dano and Peter Dinklage in Things We Want. *Photo: Carol Rosegg*

No kvetching: Natasha Lyonne, Cindy Katz, Laura Esterman and Jordan Gelber in 2000 Years. *Photo: Carol Rosegg*

Pan Asian Repertory Theatre. Creates opportunities for Asian-American artists to perform under the highest professional standards while promoting plays by and about Asians and Asian Americans. Tisa Chang founding artistic director.

THE JOY LUCK CLUB. By Susan Kim; adapted from the novel by Amy Tang. November 7, 2007. Direction, Tisa Chang; scenery, Kaori Akazawa; costumes, Carol Pelletier; lighting, Victor En Yu Tan; sound, Peter Griggs and Tyrone Sanders; stage management, James W. Carringer. With Tina Chilip, Lydia Gaston, Wai Ching Ho, Carol A. Honda, Sacha Iskra, Scott Klavan, Han Nah Kim, Dian Kobayashi, Kathleen Kwan, Ming Lee, Rosanne Ma, Tom Matsusaka, Les J.N. Mau, Tran T. Thuc Hanh, Virginia Wing.

THE MISSING WOMAN. By Nguyen Thi Minh Ngoc April 7, 2008. Direction, Ms. Ngoc; scenery and costumes, Kim B; lighting, Joyce Liao; stage management, Elis C. Arroyo. With Ngoc Dang, My Hang, Tran Thuc Hanh, Le Leon, Thanh Loc, Ms. Ngoc, Hai Phuong. Presented in association with the Institute for Vietnamese Culture and Education.

Performance Space 122. Provides artists of a wide range of experience an opportunity to develop work and find an audience. Vallejo Gantner artistic director.

Schedule included:

THE DEVIL ON ALL SIDES. By Fabrice Melquiot; translated by Ben Yalom. June 12, 2007. Direction, Mr. Yalom; sound and music, Dan Cantrell and Patrick Kaliski. With Debórah Eliezer, Stephen Jacob, Brian Livingston, Ryan O'Donnell, Nora El Samahy, Joseph William.

ST. JOAN OF THE STOCKYARDS. By Bertolt Brecht; adapted by Lear deBessonet. June 18. 2007. Direction, Mr. deBessonet; choreography, Tracy Bersley; scenery, Justin Townsend; lighting, Peter Ksander, sound, Mark Huang; music, Kelley McRae. With Kate Benson, Mike Crane, Jessica Green, Jonathan Green, Pete McCain, Nate Schenkkan, Kristen Sieh, Richard Toth.

500 CLOWN FRANKENSTEIN. By Molly Brennan, Adrian Danzig, Leslie Buxbaum Danzig and Paul Kalina. December 12, 2007. Direction, Ms. Danzig; scenery, Dan Reilly; costumes, Tatjana Radisic; lighting, Ben Wilhelm; stage management, Angela Renaldo. With Ms. Brennan, Messrs. Danzig, Kalina.

HELLO FAILURE. By Kristen Kosmas. March 6, 2008. Direction, Ken Rus Schmoll. With Michael Chick, Benjamin Forster, Janna Gjesdal, Megan Hart, Joan Jubett, Kristen Kosmas, Matthew Maher, Aimee Phelan-Deconinck, Tricia Rodley, Maria Striar.

BRIDE. By Kevin Augustine. March 19, 2008. Direction, Mr. Augustine and Ken Berman; choreography, James Graber, scenery, Tom Lee; costumes, Shima Ushiba and Caroline Walter; lighting, Miranda Hardy; sound, David Malloy, music, Andrea La Rose, video; Mr. Lee; puppets, Mr. Augustine; stage management, Paloma H. Wake. With Mr. Augustine, Lindsey Briggs, Frankie Cordero, James Graber, Alissa Hunnicutt, Nina Kyle, Rob Lok, Jamie Moore, Jessica Scott, Gloria Sun.

DEMOCRACY IN AMERICA. By Annie Dorsen. April 3, 2008. Direction, Ms. Dorsen. With Philippa Kaye, Okwui Okpokwasili, Anthony Torn.

VENGEANCE CAN WAIT. By Yukiko Motoya; translated by Kyoko Yoshida and Andy Bragen. April 25, 2008. Direction, Jose Zayas. With Pun Bandhu, Paul H. Juhn, Jennifer Lim, Becky Yamamoto.

REMEMBER THIS MOMENT. By Gabri Christa and Niles Ford. May 1, 2008. Direction and choreography, Ms. Christa and Mr. Ford; video, Marilys Ernst. With Ms. Christa and Mr. Ford.

OEDIPUS LOVES YOU. By Gavin Quinn and Simon Doyle. May 21, 2008. Direction, Mr. Quinn; scenery, Andrew Clancy; costumes, Helen McCusker; lighting, Aedin Cosgrove; sound, Jimmy Eadie; music, Gordon Is a Mime; stage management, Rob Usher. With Ned Dennehy, Aoife Duffin, Bush Moukarzel, Gina Moxley, Dylan Tighe.

THE EUTHANASIST. Solo performance piece by Liza Lentini. May 31, 2008. Direction. Alan Miller; scenery, Adam Dugas; lighting, Diana Kesselschmidt; projections, Pam Kray; music, Paul Cantelon. With Monika Schneider.

Ping Chong and Company. Creates inter-disciplinary theatre works exploring the intersections of history, race and culture in the modern world. Ping Chong founder and artistic director, Bruce Allardice managing director.

> DELTA RISING. By Ping Chong and Talvin Wilks. May 28, 2008. Direction, Messrs. Chong and Wilks; lighting, Brant Thomas Murray; projection, Maya Ciarocchi; stage management, Jennifer Conley Darling. With Shermel Carthan, Gene Dattel, Edena Hines, Toni Seawright, Virginia Wing.

Primary Stages. Dedicated to new American plays, the company works with emerging playwrights through commissions and the Dorothy Strelsin New American Writers Group. Casey Childs executive producer, Andrew Leynse artistic director.

> OPUS. By Michael Hollinger. August 7, 2007. Direction, Terrence J. Nolan; scenery, Jim Kronzer; costumes, Anne Kennedy; lighting, Justin Townsend; sound, Jorge Cousineau; stage management, Fred Hemminger. With David Beach, Mahira Kakkar, Michael Laurence, Douglas Rees, Richard Topol. Presented in association with Jamie deRoy.

> DIVIDING THE ESTATE. By Horton Foote. September 27, 2007. Direction, Michael Wilson; scenery, Jeff Cowie; costumes, David C. Woolard; lighting, Rui Rita; sound and music, John Gromada; fight direction, B.H. Barry; stage management, Cole P. Bonenberger. With Devon Abner, Elizabeth Ashley, James DeMarse, Hallie Foote, Arthur French, Penny Fuller, Lynda Gravátt, Virginia Kull, Maggie Lacey, Nicole Lowrance, Gerald McRaney, Jenny Dare Paulin, Keiana Richàrd. First presentation of record was given at McCarter Theatre Center (3/31–4/16/1989; 16 performances). A 2007–08 *Best Plays* choice (see essay by Garrett Eisler in this volume).

> HUNTING AND GATHERING. By Brooke Berman. February 3, 2008. Direction, Leigh Silverman; scenery, David Korins, costumes, Miranda Hoffman; lighting, Ben Stanton; sound, Robert Kaplowitz; stage management, Kate Hefel. With Michael Chernus, Mamie Gummer, Keira Naughton, Jeremy Shamos.

Changing tune: David Beach, Richard Topol, Douglas Rees and Michael Laurence in Opus. *Photo: James Leynse*

Property panic: Michael Chernus and Jeremy Shamos in Hunting and Gathering. *Photo: James Leynse*

SOMETHING YOU DID. By Willy Holtzman. April 1, 2008. Direction, Carolyn Cantor; scenery, Eugene Lee; costumes, Jenny Mannis; lighting, Jeff Croiter; sound and music, Lindsay Jones; stage management, Samone B. Weissman. With Jordan Charney, Joanna Gleason, Adriane Lenox, Portia, Victor Slezak. Presented in association with Nancy Cooperstein and Betty Ann Besch Solinger.

The Public Theater. Special projects, in addition to its regular Off Broadway productions. Oskar Eustis artistic director, Mara Manus executive director.

UNDER THE RADAR. January 9–20, 2008.
Schedule included:
CHURCH. By Young Jean Lee. January 9, 2008. Direction, Ms. Lee. With Brian Bickerstaff, Weena Pauly, Katy Pyle, Katie Workum.

TERMINUS. By Mark O'Rowe. January 9, 2008. Direction, Mr. O'Rowe. With Andrea Irvine, Aidan Kelly, Eileen Walsh.

THIS PLACE IS A DESERT. By Jay Scheib and Leah Gelpe. January 9, 2008. Direction, Mr. Scheib. With Sarita Choudhury, April Sweeney.

BETWEEN THE DEVIL AND THE DEEP BLUE SEA. By Suzanne Andrade. January 9, 2008. Direction, Ms. Andrade and Paul Barritt. With Mses. Andrade, Appleton, Henley.

DISINFORMATION. By Tommy Smith. January 10, 2008. Direction, Mr. Smith. With Orianna Herman, Amy O'Neal, Reggie Watts.

BIG, 3RD EPISODE (HAPPY/END). By Superamas. January 10, 2008.

IN SPITE OF EVERYTHING. By The Suicide Kings. January 10, 2008. Direction, Marc Bamuthi Joseph. With Jamie DeWolf, Rupert Estanislao, Geoff Trenchard.

LOW: MEDITATIONS TRILOGY PART I. Solo performance piece by Rha Goddess. January 10, 2008. Direction, Chay Yew. With Ms. Goddess.

POETICS: A BALLET BRUT. By Kelly Copper and Pavol Liska. January 10, 2008. Direction, Ms. Copper and Mr. Pavol. With Nature Theater of Oklahoma.

REGURGITOPHAGY. Solo performance piece by Michel Melamed. January 10, 2008. Direction, Alessandra Colasanti, Marco Abujamra and Mr. Melamed. With Mr. Melamed.

STOOP STORIES. Solo performance piece by Dael Orlandersmith. January 10, 2008. With Ms. Orlandersmith.

TROJAN WOMEN. By Euripides; adapted by Alfred Preisser. January 10, 2008. Direction, Mr. Preisser; choreography, Tracy Jack. With Zenzele Cooper, Michael Early, Christel Halliburton, Zainab Jah, Ty Jones, Linda Kurlioff, Amanda Marie, Lizan Mitchell, Sipiwe Moyo, Alexander Mulzac, Angela D. Polite, Brandi Rhonme, Sui-Lin Robinson, Kiat Sing Teo, Nabil Vilas, Tryphena Wade. Presented in association with the Classical Theatre of Harlem.

GENERATION JEANS. By Belarus Free Theatre. January 11, 2008. With Nikolai Khalezin.

SMALL METAL OBJECTS. By Back to Back Theatre. January 11, 2008. With Simon Laherty, Sonia Tubin.

HOW THEATER FAILED AMERICA. Solo performance piece by Mike Daisey. January 13, 2008. Direction, Jean-Michele Gregory. With Mr. Daisey.

PUBLIC LAB. Presented in association with Labyrinth Theater Company. February 4–June 29, 2008.

MOM, HOW DID YOU MEET THE BEATLES? By Adam P. Kennedy and Adrienne Kennedy. February 10, 2008. Direction, Peter DuBois; scenery and costumes, Alexander Dodge; lighting, Michael Chybowski; sound, Walter Trarbach; stage management, Elizabeth Miller. With William Demeritt, Brenda Pressley.

THE POOR ITCH. By John Belluso. March 19, 2008. Direction, Lisa Peterson scenery, Rachel Hauck; costumes, Gabriel Berry; lighting, Ben Stanton; sound and music, Robert Kaplowitz; fight direction, Thomas Schall; stage management, Katrina Lynn Olson. With Michael Chernus, Alicia Goranson, Marc Damon Johnson, Piter Marek, Deirdre O'Connell, John Ottavino, Susan Pourfar, Renaldy Smith, Christopher Thornton.

THE CIVILIANS' PARIS COMMUNE. By Steven Cosson and Michael Friedman. April 4, 2008. Direction, Mr.Cosson; scenery, Alexander Dodge; costumes, Sarah Beers; lighting, Thomas Dunn; sound, Ken Travis. With Kate Buddeke, Aysan Celik, Nina Hellman, Dan Lipton, Jeanine Serralles, Brian Sgambati, Jeremy Shamos, Emily Tepe, Sam Breslin Wright.

THE FEVER CHART: THREE VISIONS OF THE MIDDLE EAST. By Naomi Wallace. May 6, 2008. Direction, Jo Bonney; scenery, Rachel Hauck; costumes, Ilona Somogyi; lighting, Lap Chi Chu; sound, Christian Fredrickson; stage management, Christina Lowe. With Natalie Gold, Lameece Issaq, Omar Metwally, Arian Moayed, Waleed F. Zuaiter.

THE GOOD NEGRO. By Tracey Scott Wilson. May 20, 2008. Direction, Liesl Tommy; scenery and costumes, Clint Ramos, lighting, Lap Chi Chu; sound, Daniel Baker. With Joniece Abbott-Pratt, Francois Battiste, J. Bernard Calloway, Lizzy Cooper Davis, Anthony Mackie, LeRoy McClain, Brian Wallace, Myk Watford.

Puerto Rican Traveling Theatre. Professional company presenting English and Spanish productions of Puerto Rican and Hispanic playwrights, emphasizing subjects of relevance today. Miriam Colón Valle founder and producer.

THREE CALLA LILLIES. By Abniel Marat; translated by Charles Philip Thomas. April 17, 2008. Direction, Josean Ortiz; scenery, Ann Bartek; lighting, Wilburn Bonnell. With Dalia Davi, Crystal Espinal, Elvira Franco, Gabriela Lugo, Sophia Angelica Nitkin, Susan Rybin.

DINNER FOR TWO (CENA PARA DOS). By Santiago Moncada; translated by Charles Philip Thomas. May 15, 2008. Direction, Tony Mata; scenery, Christina Gould; costumes, Summer Lee Jack, lighting, Scott Cally. With Angelica Ayala, Jezabel Montero, Fred Valle.

Roundabout Theatre Company. Committed to teaming great theatrical works with the industry's finest artists to re-energize classic plays and musicals. Roundabout Underground is designed to foster new works by emerging playwrights. Todd Haimes artistic director, Harold Wolpert managing director, Julia C. Levy executive director.

ROUNDABOUT UNDERGROUND.
SPEECH AND DEBATE. By Stephen Karam. October 29, 2007. Direction, Jason Moore; choreography, Boo Killebrew; scenery, Anna Louizos; costumes, Heather Dunbar; lighting, Justin Townsend; sound and projections, Brett Jarvis; stage management, James FitzSimmons. With Susan Blackwell, Jason Fuchs, Gideon Glick, Sarah Steele.

Signature Theatre Company. Makes an extended commitment to a playwright's body of work, engaging the writer in every aspect of the creative process. James Houghton artistic director.

IPHIGENIA 2.0. By Charles L. Mee. August, 26, 2007. Direction and choreography, Tina Landau; scenery, Blythe R.D. Quinlan; costumes, Anita Yavich; lighting, Scott Zielinski; sound, Jill BC DuBoff; stage management, Winnie Y. Lok. With Jimonn Cole, Will Fowler, J.D. Goldblatt; Chasten Harmon, Jesse Hooker, Emily Kinney, Louisa Krause, Kate Mulgrew, Tom Nelis, Angelo Niakas, Seth Numrich, Rocco Sisto.

QUEENS BOULEVARD (THE MUSICAL). By Charles L. Mee. December 3, 2007. Direction, Davis McCallum; choreography, Peter Pucci; scenery, Mimi Lien; costumes, Christal Weatherly, lighting, Marcus Doshi; sound, Ken Travis; video, Joseph Spirito; music direction, Matt Castle; arrangements, Michael Friedman; stage management, Winnie Y. Lok. With Amir Arison, Michi Barall, Satya Bhabha, Marsha Stephanie Blake, Bill Buell, Demosthenes Chrysan, Geeta Citygirl, Emily Donahoe, William Jackson Harper, Jodi Lin, Arian Moayed, Debargo Sanyal, Jon Norman Schneider, Ruth Zhang.

PARADISE PARK. By Charles L. Mee. February 12, 2008. Direction, Daniel Fish; choreography, Peter Pucci; scenery, David Zinn; costumes, Kaye Voyce; lighting, Mark Barton; sound, Elizabeth Rhodes; music, Bill Schimmel; video, Joshua Thorson; stage management, Winnie Y. Lok. With Vanessa Aspillaga, Satya Bhabha, Veanne Cox, Gian Murray Gianino. William Jackson Harper, Christopher McCann, Paul Mullins, Alan Semok, Laurie Williams.

Soho Rep. Dedicated to the development and production of exuberant, unconventional new plays. Sarah Benson artistic director, Alexandra Conley executive director.

PHILOKTETES. By John Jesurun. October 13, 2007. Direction and scenery by Mr. Jesurun; costumes, Ruth Pongstaphone; lighting, Jeff Nash; production stage manager, Andrea Jess Berkey. With William Badgett, Louis Cancelmi, Jason Lew.

NO DICE. By Nature Theater of Oklahoma. December 8, 2007. Direction, Pavol Liska and Kelly Copper; scenery and costumes, Peter Nigrini; music, Lumberob, Kristin Worrall; stage management, Kell Condon. With Anne Gridley, Thomas Hummel, Robert M. Johanson, Zachary Oberzan, Kristin Worrall.

Theater for the New City. Developmental theater and new experimental works. Crystal Field executive director.

Schedule included:
THE POISON MAN. By Eugenia Macer-Story. June 7, 2007. Direction, Ms. Macer-Story; scenery and lighting, Jason Sturm; stage management, Adrian Gallard. With Steve Greenstein, Von Duvois Jacobs, Ilana Landecker, Primy Rivera, Nate Steinwachs, Renee Valenti, Katie Yamulla.

EMERGENCY CONTRACEPTION. September 13, 2008. Musical with book and lyrics by Sara Cooper; music by Chris Shimojima. Direction, Ms. Cooper; music direction, Marc

Taking command: Rocco Sisto and Tom Nelis in Iphigenia 2.0. *Photo: Carol Rosegg*

New family: Amir Arison and Michi Barall in Queens Boulevard (the musical). *Photo: Carol Rosegg*

Giosi; stage management, Michelle Gaidos. With Sara Cooper, Noah DeBiase, Brian Griffin, Teresa Jusino, Hannah Kim, Michael Rehse, Elysia Segal.

THE SORDID PERILS OF ACTUAL EXISTENCE. By Andy Reynolds and Tom Gladwell. November 15, 2007. Direction, Mr. Gladwell; scenery, Donald L. Brooks; costumes, Carol Sherry; stage management, Meagan Walker. With Crystal Field, Dick Morrill, Mr. Reynolds, Laura Wickens.

QUEENS OF HEART. By Sabura Rashid-Huggins. December 20, 2007. Direction, Ms. Rashid-Huggins. With Kyle Brown, John Goodlow, Angela Rostick, Ria Wilkerson, Lisa-Roxanne Walter.

LOOKING UP. By Carla Cantrelle. February 18, 2008. Direction, Giovanna Sardelli; scenery and lighting, Nathan Elsener; sound, Christopher A. Granger; stage management, Emily Glinick. With Ms. Cantrelle, Bryant Mason.

THE FURTHER ADVENTURES OF UNCLE WIGGILY: WINDBLOWN VISITORS. Musical with book and lyrics by Laurel Hessing; music by Arthur Abrams. March 2, 2008. Direction, Crystal Field. With Clara Ruf Maldonado, Craig Meade, John Prayer, Primy Rivera, Elizabeth Ruf, Michael Vazquez.

SEX! DRUGS! AND UKULELES! Musical with book and lyrics by Uke Jackson; music by Terry Waldo. March 13, 2008. Direction, Victor Maog; choreography, Celia Rowlson-Hall; scenery, Mark Marcante; costumes, Susan Gittins; sound, Richard Reta. With Christian Baskous, Meg Cavanaugh, John Forkner, Allison Lind.

ON NAKED SOIL: IMAGINING ANNA AKHMATOVA. By Rebecca Schull. April 12, 2008. Direction, Susan Einhorn; scenery, Ursula Belden; costumes, Mimi Maxmen; lighting, Victor En Yu Tan; sound, Megan Henninger; video, Aaron Rhyne; dramaturgy, Robert Blacker; stage management, Katherine Wallace. With Sue Cremin, Lenore Loveman, Ms. Schull.

Theatre for a New Audience. Founded in 1979, the company's mission is to energize the performance and study of Shakespeare and classic drama. Jeffrey Horowitz founding artistic director, Dorothy Ryan managing director.

THE OHIO STATE MURDERS. By Adrienne Kennedy. November 4, 2007. Direction, Evan Yionoulis; scenery, Neil Patel; costumes, Emilio Sosa, lighting, Chris Akerlind; sound and music, Mike Yionoulis and Sarah Pickett. With Cherise Boothe, LisaGay Hamilton, Kobi Libii, Aleta Mitchell, Julia Pace Mitchell, Saxon Palmer.

OROONOKO. By Biyi Bandele; adapted from the work of Aphra Behn. February 10, 2008. Direction, Kate Whoriskey; choreography, Warren Adams; scenery, John Arnone; costumes, Emilio Sosa; lighting, Donald Holder; sound, Fabian Obispo; fight direction Rick Sordelet; stage management, Renee Lutz. With Che Ayende, David Barlow, Gregory Derelian, Ira Hawkins, Jordan C. Haynes, Albert Jones, Ezra Knight, Graeme Malcolm, LeRoy McClain, Toi Perkins, Christen Simon, John Douglas Thompson.

ANTONY AND CLEOPATRA. Revival of the play by William Shakespeare. April 3, 2008. Direction, Darko Tresnjak; choreography, Peggy Hickey; scenery, Alexander Dodge; costumes, Linda Cho; lighting, York Kennedy; sound, Jane Shaw; fight direction, Rick Sordelet; stage management, Renee Lutz. With Nathan Blew, Jeffrey Carlson, Christine Corpuz, Marton Csokas, Gregory Derelian, Grant Goodman, Randy Harrison, James Knight, George Morfogen, Ryan Quinn, Laila Robins, Michael Rogers, Christian Rummel, Matthew Schneck, Christen Simon, Erik Singer, John Douglas Thompson, Lisa Velten Smith.

Vineyard Theatre. Dedicated to new work, bold programming and the support of artists. A center for the creation of new plays and musicals, the company has premiered provocative, groundbreaking works by both new and established writers. Douglas Aibel artistic director, Jennifer Garvey-Blackwell executive director.

THE PIANO TEACHER. By Julia Cho. November 18, 2007. Direction, Kate Whoriskey; scenery, Derek McLane; costumes, Ilona Somogyi; lighting, David Weiner; sound and music, Obadiah Eaves; stage management, Bryce McDonald. With John Boyd, Elizabeth Franz, Carmen M. Herlihy.

THE SLUG BEARERS OF KAYROL ISLAND. Musical with book and lyrics by Ben Katchor; music by Mark Mulcahy. February 12, 2008. Direction, Bob McGrath; choreography, John Carrafa; scenery, Jim Findlay and Jeff Sugg; costumes, Mattie Ullrich; lighting, Russell H. Champa; sound, David Arnold and Brett Jarvis; music direction, Erik James, stage management, Megan Smith. With Stephen Lee Anderson, Tom Riis Farrell, Jody Flader, Peter Friedman, Matt Pearson, Bobby Steggert, Will Swenson.

GOD'S EAR. By Jenny Schwartz. April 17, 2008. Direction, Anne Kauffman; scenery, Kris Stone; costumes, Olivera Gajic; lighting, Tyler Micoleau; sound, Leah Gelpe; songs, Michael Friedman; additional lyrics, Ms. Schwartz; stage management, Megan Schwartz. With Gibson Frazier, Judith Greentree, Christina Kirk, Raymond McAnally, Matthew Montelongo, Monique Vukovic, Rebecca Wisocky. Presented in association with New Georges.

The Women's Project. Nurtures, develops and produces plays written and directed by women. Julie Crosby producing artistic director, Julia Miles founding artistic director.

WAPATO. By Peggy Stafford. December 7, 2008. Direction, Rebecca Patterson; scenery, Marion Williams; costumes, Jenny C. Fulton; lighting, Dawn Chiang; sound, Jane Shaw; stage management, Jack Gianino. With Kathleen Butler, Nancy Franklin, Lucy Martin, Dale Soules, Kaipo Schwab. Presented as part of Hothouse, the new-play development series.

SAND. By Trista Baldwin. February 10, 2008. Direction, Daniella Topol; scenery, Anita Fuchs; costumes, Clint Ramos; lighting, Traci Klainer; sound, Daniel Baker; music, Broken Chord Collective; fight direction, J. David Brimmer; dramaturgy, Megan E. Carter; stage management, Jack Gianino. With Alec Beard, Angela Lewis, Pedro Pascal.

CROOKED. By Catherine Trieschmann. April 20. 2008. Direction, Liz Diamond; scenery, Jennifer Moeller; costumes, Ilona Somogyi; lighting, S. Ryan Schmidt; sound and music, Jane Shaw; stage management, Jack Gianino. With Betsy Aidem, Carmen M. Herlihy, Cristin Milioti.

CORPORATE CARNIVAL. By Megan E. Carter, Julie Crosby, Jyana S. Gregory and Andy Paris. May 14, 2008. Direction, Ms. Gregory; scenery and costumes, Junghyun Georgia Lee; sound and music, Fitz Patton. With David Anzuelo, Karen Grenke, Andrew Grusetskie, Mr. Paris, Richard Saudek, Meghan Williams, Lisa Rafaela Clair, Prudence Heyert, Megan Raye Manzi, Austin Sanders, Jeff Wills.

The Wooster Group. Ensemble of artists collaborating on the development and production of theatre pieces that respond to the evolving culture. Elizabeth LeCompte director.

HAMLET. Revival of the play by William Shakespeare. October 31, 2007. Direction, Elizabeth LeCompte; scenery, Ruud van den Akker; costumes, Claudia Hill; lighting, Jennifer Tipton and Gabe Maxson; sound, Geoff Abbas, Joby Emmons and Matt Schloss; music, Fischerspooner, Warren Fischer; fight direction, Felix Ivanov; stage management, Buzz Cohen. With Dominique Bousquet, Ari Fliakos, Alessandro Magania, Daniel Pettrow, Bill Raymond, Scott Shepherd, Casey Spooner, Kate Valk, Judson Williams. Presented in association with the Public Theater and St. Ann's Warehouse.

York Theatre Company. Dedicated to the development of small-scale musicals, to the rediscovery of underappreciated musicals from the past and to serving the community through educational initiatives. James Morgan producing artistic director.

MUSICALS IN MUFTI. June 15–July 29, 2007. *Schedule included:*

IT'S A BIRD . . . IT'S A PLANE . . . IT'S SUPERMAN! Musical with book by David Newman and Robert Benton; music by Charles Strouse; lyrics by Lee Adams. June 15, 2007. Direction, Stuart Ross. With Shoshana Bean, Stan Chandler, Lea DeLaria, Scot Fedderly, Cheyenne Jackson, Rachel Jones, Jean Louisa Kelly, Rodney Peck, Amy Ryder, David Rasche, Katherine Von Till, Michael Winther.

I AND ALBERT. Musical with book by Jay Presson Allen; music by Charles Strouse; lyrics by Lee Adams. June 29, 2007. Direction, Michael Montel. With Nancy Anderson, Edwin

Cahill, Roger E. DeWitt, Nick Galbraith, Ken Krugman, Lorinda Lisitza, Gabriella Malek, Stephen Mo Hanan, Brooke Sunny Moriber, Adam Riegler, Mackenzie Thomas, Gerrett VanderMeer, Sasha Weiss, Nick Wyman.

BAJOUR. Musical with book by Ernest Kinoy; music and lyrics by Walter Marks. July 13, 2007. Direction, Stuart Ross; music direction, Mark Hartman. With Talia Barzilay, Thom Christopher, Angel Desai, Erick Devine, Michael Iannucci, Don Mayo, Nancy McCall, Nicholas Rodriguez, Teri Ralston, Deone Zanotto.

THE DAY BEFORE SPRING. Musical with book and lyrics by Alan Jay Lerner; music by Frederick Loewe. July 27, 2007. Direction, David Glenn Armstrong; music direction, Aaron Gandy. With David Abeles, Richard Todd Adams, Hunter Bell, Summer Broyhill, Janine DiVita, Ashlee Fife, Robyn Kramer, Daniel C. Levine, Orville Mendoza, Lindsay Packard, Tia Speros, Amanda Watkins, Ed Watts, Mark York.

MUSICALS IN MUFTI FALL SERIES. September 14–October 28, 2007.

ZORBA. Musical with book by Joseph Stein; music by John Kander; lyrics by Fred Ebb; based on the novel by Nikos Kazantzakis. September 14, 2007. Direction, Steven Yuhasz; music direction, Patrick Vaccariello. With Raymond Bokhour, Jane Brockman, Joseph Cullinane, Vince D'Elia, Robin De Jesús, Beth Fowler, Denis Lambert, Jeff McCarthy, Ken McMullen, Crista Moore, Emily Skinner, Aaron Ramey, Tina Stafford, Deone Zanotto.

ENTER LAUGHING. Musical with book by Joseph Stein; music and lyrics by Stan Daniels. September 28, 2007. Direction, Stuart Ross; music direction, Matt Castle. With Bruce Adler, Jill Eikenberry, Josh Grisetti, Kaitlin Hopkins, George S. Irving, Robb Sapp, Emily Shoolin, Kelly Sullivan, Michael Tucker.

THE BODY BEAUTIFUL. Musical with book by Joseph Stein, with Will Glickman; music by Jerry Bock; lyrics by Sheldon Harnick. October 12, 2007. Direction, David Glenn Armstrong; music direction, John Bell. With Stephen Bienskie, Laura Marie Duncan, Ryan Duncan, Amy Goldberger, Cady Huffman, Capathia Jenkins, Jonathan Kay, Megan Lawrence, Mike McGowan, Brad Oscar, John Eric Parker, Patrick Richwood, Angie Schworer, Jim Sorensen.

THE BAKERS WIFE. Musical with book by Joseph Stein; music and lyrics by Stephen Schwartz. October 26, 2007. Direction, Gordon Greenberg; music direction, Mark Hartman. With Wendi Bergamini, Kevin Cahoon, Jacque Carnahan, Rick Crom, Betsy DiLellio, Joy Franz, Laurent Giroux, Renée Elise Goldsberry, Mitchell Greenberg, Gay Marshall, Michael Medeiros, John O'Creagh, Richard Pruitt, Maureen Silliman, Max von Essen, Lenny Wolpe, Clinton Zugel.

MISCELLANEOUS

ABINGDON THEATRE COMPANY. Schedule included: *The Greenhouse Effect*. Solo performance piece by Michael Deep. June 12, 2007. Direction, Kate Buhmann; with Mr. Deep. *The People vs. Mona*. Musical with book by Jim Wann and Patricia Miller; music and lyrics by Mr. Wann. July 12, 2007. Direction, Laura Standley; with Dan Bailey, Richard Binder, Jason Chimonides, Karen Culp, Natalie Douglas, Marcie Henderson, Ritt Henn, Omri Schein, Mariand Torres, David Jon Wilson. *Sin* by Wendy MacLeod. July 24, 2007. Direction, Jordana Kritzer; with Christopher Armond, Amy Broder, Henry Caplan, Megan Hill, Kelly Miller, Carter Roy, Collin Mackenzie Smith, Douglas Scott Sorenson. *The Cascade Falls* by Adam Michael Cohen. August 24, 2007. Direction, Ryan Hemphill; with Lucas Beck, Kirsten Scoles, Sam Whitten. *The Goldman Project* by Staci Swedeen. October 3, 2007. Direction, Joe Brancato; with Tony Guncler, Anita Keal, Bernadette Quigley. *Cry Havoc* by Tom Coash. October 28, 2007. Direction, Kim T. Sharp; with Keith Merrill, Pamela Paul, Sameer Sheikh. *Another Vermeer* by Bruce J. Robinson. April 6, 2008. Direction, Kelly Morgan; with Dan Cordie, Thom Christopher, Justin Grace, Christian Pedersen, Austin Pendleton.

ACCESS THEATER. Schedule included: *Shirley at the Tropicana*. Solo performance piece by Amanda Ronconi. October 27, 2007. Direction, Joan Evans; with Ms. Ronconi. *The Danish Mediations/Slots* by Sergei Burbank. August 16, 2007. Directed by Adam Karsten; with Anna Kull, Fayna Sanchez, Jason Updike. *Departures* by Kristen Palmer. October 7, 2007. Direction, Kyle Ancowitz; with Keira Keeley, Travis York. *Local Story* by Kristen Palmer. November 30, 2007. Direction, Susanna

L. Harris; with Havilah Brewster, Marielle Heller, Keira Keeley, Ben Scaccia, Mark Watson, Travis York. *Euphoric Tendencies* by Tanya Marten. March 6, 2008. Direction, Jonathan Marten; with Katherine Barron, Lizzie Czerner, Nicole Godino, Dona Elena Hatcher, Johnny Blaze Leavitt, Tanya Marten, Jonathan Marten, Gary Mink, Carol Padiernos, Dayle Pivetta, Bella Vendramini, Ceren Zorlu. *How to Be a Doll* by Alissa Riccardelli. March 13, 2008. Direction, Genevieve Gearheart; with Carissa Cordes, Annie Harrison, Cindy Kawasaki, Ouida Maedel, Lucy McRae, Sharla Meese, Erinina Marie Ness, Aubrey Snowden. *When Is a Clock* by Matthew Freeman. April 19, 2008. Direction, Kyle Ancowitz; with Beau Allulli, David DelGrosso, Laura Desmond, Tracey Gilbert, Ian Gould, Tom Staggs, Matthew Trumbull.

THE ACTORS COMPANY THEATRE (TACT). Schedule included: *The Runner Stumbles* by Milan Stitt. November 4, 2007. Direction, Scott Alan Evans; with Mary Bacon, Jamie Bennett, Cynthia Darlow, Christopher Halladay, Chris Hietikko, Julie Jesneck, Christina Bennett Lind, Greg McFadden, Mark L. Montgomery, James Murtaugh, Ashley West. *The Eccentricities of a Nightingale* by Tennessee Williams. May 5, 2008. Direction, Jenn Thompson; with Mary Bacon, Nora Chester, Cynthia Darlow, Francesca Di Mauro, Todd Gearhart, Larry Keith, Darrie Lawrence, Greg McFadden, John Plumpis, James Prendergast, Scott Schafer.

ALTERED STAGES. Schedule included: *If Wishes Were Horses* by Kari Floren. June 7, 2007. Direction, Julia Gibson; with Robertson Carricart, Suzanne Grodner, Michael McKenzie. *True Genius* by David Holstein. September 25, 2007. Direction, Jill Sierchio; with Nancy Evans, Tyler S. Gulizio, Regina Myers, Ken Scudder, Perry Tiberio. *Mark Twain's Blues*. Musical with book by Walt Stepp; music and lyrics by Messrs. Stepp and Twain. February 21, 2008. Direction, Tom Herman; with Bonne Kramer, Lance Olds, Barry Phillips, Bill Tatum.

AMERICAN THEATRE OF ACTORS. Schedule included: *The Possibilities* by Howard Barker. September 27, 2007. Direction, Albert Aeed; with Michael Benjamin, Jeremy Brenna, Marilyn Duryea, Lori Feller, Ramesh Ganeshram, Rodney Hakim, Charles Hendricks, Angus Hepburn, Malina Linkas, Maureen Mooney, Alison Ostergaard, Carly Robbins, Fred Rueck, John Stagnari, Molly Rydzel, Reema Zaman. *Save the World* by Chris Kipiniak. January 19, 2008. Direction, Michael Barakiva; with Craig Bridger, Charrisa Chamorro, Christine Corpuz, Noshir Dalal, Kelly Hutchinson, Danielle Skraastad, Jonathan Woodward.

ARCLIGHT. Schedule included: *If Truth Be Known* by Judi Komaki. June 4, 2007. Direction, Christine Simpson; with Constance Boardman, James Patrick Earley, Lydia Gaston, Bea Soong. *Edge*. Solo performance piece by Paul Alexander. September 9, 2007. Direction, Mr. Alexander; with Angelica Torn. *The Boycott*. Solo performance piece by Kathryn Blume. October 24, 2007. Direction, Jason Jacobs; with Ms. Blume. *The Puppetmaster of Lodz* by Gilles Segal; translated by Tonen Sara O'Connor. December 3, 2007. Direction, Bruce Levitt; with Daniel Damiano, Herbert Rubens, Suzanne Toren, Robert Zukerman. *The Set Up* by James Lindenberg. April 30, 2008. Direction, Mr. Lindenberg; with Scott Cunningham, Jennifer Danielle, Major Dodge, Mr. Lindenberg, Tracy Weiler, Tara Westwood.

ARS NOVA. Schedule included: *Tongues Will Wag*. Solo performance piece by Mike Daisey. January 14, 2008. *Boom* by Peter Sinn Nachtreib. March 20, 2008. Direction, Alex Timbers; with Megan Ferguson, Lucas Near-Verbrugghe, Susan Wands.

ATLANTIC STAGE 2 THEATER. Schedule included: *Politics of Passion:* Truly, Madly, Deeply; Hang Up; Cigarettes and Chocolate *by Anthony Minghella. June 26, 2007*. Direction, Cheryl Faraone; with MacLeod Andrews, David Barlow, Colby DiSarro, Michael Wrynn Doyle, Cassidy Freeman, Tara Giordano, Laura Harris, Jesse Hooker, Lauren Turner Kiel, Willie Orbison, Julia Proctor, James Matthew Ryan. *No End of Blame* by Howard Barker. June 27, 2007. Direction, Richard Romagnoli; with MacLeod Andrews, Bill Army, Megan Byrne, Alex Cranmer, Caitlin Dennis, Alex Draper, Christopher Duva, Lucas Kavner, Jeanne LaSala, Julia Proctor, Peter Schmitz, Alec Strum, Sally Swallow. *Girl Gang*. Musical with book by Mark W. Knowles; music and lyrics by David G. Smith. September 27, 2007. Direction, Mr. Knowles; with Megan Byrne, Alex Draper, Christopher Duva, Jeanne LaSala, Peter B. Schmitz.

AXIS THEATRE COMPANY. Schedule included:*A Glance at New York* by Benjamin A. Baker. October 13, 2007. Direction, Randy Sharp; with Brian Barnhart, Marlene Berner, Regina Betancourt, David Crabb, George Demas, Britt Genelin, Laurie Kilmartin, Edgar Oliver, Marc Palmieri, Jim Sterling, Ian Tooley. *Seven in One Blow, or the Brave Little Kid* by Axis Theatre Company; adapted from the fairy tale by The Brothers Grimm. December 7, 2007. Direction, Randy Sharp; with Brian Barnhart, David Crabb, George Demas, Deborah Harry, Lynn Mancinelli, Sue Ann Molinell, Edgar Oliver, Marc Palmieri, Abigail Savage, Jim Sterling. *Carpenters Gold* by Robert Cucuzza. March 13, 2008. Direction, Mr. Cucuzza; with Ella Bole, Gina Guarnieri, Patrick Long, Rebecca Lukens, Hagar Moor, Cori-Ann Roublick, Josh Wolinsky.

BANK STREET THEATRE. Schedule included: *Morning Star* by Sylvia Regan. July 2, 2007. Direction, Dan Wackerman; with Lena Kaminsky, David Lavine, Geany Masai, Allan Mirchin, Steve Sterner, Caroline Tamas, Darcy Yellin, Josh Philip Weinstein. *A Good Farmer* by Sharyn Rothstein. September 25, 2007. Direction, Matthew Arbour; with Jacqueline Duprey, Sharon Eisman, Andrew Giarolo, Borden Hallowes. *The Turn of the Screw* by Henry James; adapted by Jeffrey Hatcher. November 2, 2007. Direction, Don K. Williams; with Steve Cook, Melissa Pinsly.

THE BARROW GROUP (TBG). Schedule included: *The Leopard and the Fox* by Rajiv Joseph. October 17, 2007. Direction, Giovanna Sardelli; with Michael Crane, Andrew Guilarte, Sanjiv Jhaveri, Rock Kohli, Ramiz Monsef, Gita Reddy, David Sajadi. *Gray Area* by John Ahlin. February 18, 2008. Direction, Seth Barrish; with Mr. Ahlin, Aaron Goodwin, Keith Jochim, Taylor Ruckel. *Shapeshifter* by Jonathan Wallace. March 9, 2008. Direction, Glory Sims Bowen; with Jennifer Boehm, V. Orion Delwaterman, Shane Jerome, Yvonne Roen, Shelley Virginia.

BARROW STREET THEATRE. Schedule included: *Gone Missing*. Musical with book by The Civilians; music and lyrics by Michael Friedman. June 24, 2007. Direction, Steven Cosson; with Emily Ackerman, Damian Baldet, Jennifer Morris, Stephen Plunkett, Robbie Sublett, Colleen Werthmann. *The/King/Operetta* by Waterwell. July 7, 2007. Direction, Tom Ridgely; with Hanna Cheek, Rodney Gardiner, Arian Moayed, Mr. Ridgely, Kevin Townley. *TraumNovela* by Juan Borona, Cris Buchner and Bettina Sheppard; music and lyrics by Ms. Sheppard. September 26, 2007. Direction, Ms. Buchner; with Mayumi Asada, Danilo Barbieri, Meg Benfield, Becca Blackwell, Anthony Castellanos, Evan Edwards, Jason Garcia Ignacio, Anna Kepe, Shelly Ley, Brittany Mayer, Damian Norfleet, Steven W. Nielsen, Lauren Rodriguez, Ms. Sheppard, Heather White. *The Nuclear Family* by Jimmy Ray Bennett, John Gregorio and Stephen Guarino. September 20, 2007. Direction, Matthew Loren Cohen; with Messrs. Cohen, Bennett, Gregorio, Guarino. *The Jesus Factor*. Solo performance piece by Brian Dykstra. February 7, 2008. Direction, Margaret Perry; with Mr. Dykstra.

BARUCH PERFORMING ARTS CENTER. Schedule included: *Blind Mouth Singing* by Jorge Ignacio Cortinas. September 19, 2007. Direction, Ruben Polendo; with Alexis Camins, Mia Katigbak, Sue Jean Kim, Orville Mendoza, Jon Norman Schneider. *The Actor's Rap* by J. Kyle Manzay. January 31, 2008. Direction, Mr. Manzay; with Shaun Cruz, Carmen Gill, Glenn Gordon, Mr. Manzay.

BRICK THEATRE. Schedule included: THE PRETENTIOUS FESTIVAL. June 1–July 1, 2007. *Between the Legs of God by* Art Wallace. Direction, Mr. Wallace; with Ursula Cataan, Heath Kelts, Devon Hawks Ludlow, Mike Rutkoski, Adam Swiderski, Trav S.D. *Commedia dell'Artemisia by* Kiran Rikhye. Direction, Jon Stancato; with David Bengali, Layna Fisher, Cameron J. Oro, Liza Wade White. *Dinner at Precisely Eight-Thirteen*. Musical *with book and lyrics by* Lisa Ferber, *music by* Paul Nelson. *Direction,* Elizabeth London; with Ivanna Cullinan, Jennifer Houston, Greg LoProto, Erin Blair O'Malley, Baz Snider, Ryan Stadler, Moira Stone. *The Hobo Got Too High* by Marc Spitz. August 10, 2007. Direction, Ian W. Hill; with Rasheed Hinds, Mr. Hill, Roger Nasser, Jessica Savage. *Love, Death and Vengeance* by Daniel Kelley. December 6, 2007. Direction, Anthony C.E. Nelson; with Ben Correale, Katie Hartman, Katie Holland, John Moreno, Rachel Risen, Leah Rudick, Henry Zebrowski.

CHASHAMA. Schedule included: *Dark of the Moon* by Howard Richardson and William Berney. June 15, 2007. Direction, Ian R. Crawford; with Adalgiza Chemountd, Renee Delio, Sarah Hayes Donnell, Noah Dunham, Adam Fujita, Matthew Hadley, Russel Harder, Jessica Howell, Chris Masullo, Brendan Norton, Katey Parker, Amanda Peck, Minna Richardson, Jake Thomas, Dennis X. Tseng. *Becca and Heidi*. Solo performance piece by Sharon Eberhardt. August 12, 2007. Direction, Blake Lawrence; with Linday Anderson. *Long Distance* by Bridgette Dunlap. August 9, 2007. Direction, Ms. Dunlap and Alexis Grausz; with Diana Lynne Drew, Kathryn Ekblad, Charley Layton, Madeleine Maby, Sara Montgomery, Elizabeth Neptune, Hugh Scully, Jake Thomas, Jesse Wilson.

CHERRY LANE THEATRE. Schedule included: TONGUES: READING SERIES. June 4–12, 2007. *Smoke in the Mountains* by Beau Willimon. Direction, Sam Gold; with Michael Chernus, Patch

Darragh, Austin Lysy, James Seol, Paul Sparks. *No Stallions in Manhattan* by Jane Ann Crum. Direction, Loretta Greco. *Loons* by Rob Ackerman. Direction, Jamie Richards; with Kevin Geer, Cynthia Harris, Robert Hogan, Jared McGuire, Caroline Rhea, Grant Shaud. VENGEANCE. October 9–December 1, 2007. *Rats* by Ron Fitzgerald. Direction, Alex Kilgore and Ari Edelson; with Michael Mosley, David Ross. *Squalor* by Gina Gionfriddo. Direction, Alex Kilgore and Ari Edelson; with Carrie Shaltz, David Wilson Barnes. *Skin and Bones* by Julian Sheppard. Direction, Alex Kilgore and Ari Edelson; with Michael Mosley, Lisa Joyce. *Specter* by Neena Beber. Direction, Alex Kilgore and Ari Edelson; with David Wilson Barnes, Carrie Shaltz. *Giftbox* by Francine Volpe. Direction, Alex Kilgore and Ari Edelson; with David Wilson Barnes, Lisa Joyce, Michael Mosley, David Ross, Carrie Shaltz. *Hoodoo Love* by Katori Hall (Lynn Nottage, mentor). November 1, 2007. Direction, Lucie Tiberghien; with Keith Davis, Marjorie Johnson, Angela Lewis, Kevin Mambo. *Killing the Boss* by Catherine Filloux. February 12, 2008. Direction, Jean Randich; with Alexis Camins, Sue Cremin, John Daggett, Edward Hajj, Mercedes Herrero, Orville Mendoza, Dale Soules. MENTOR PROJECT 2008. March 26–May 17, 2008. *The Woodpecker* by Samuel Brett Williams (Charles Fuller, mentor). March 26, 2008. Direction, Drew DeCorleto; with Stephanie Cannon, Dan Moran, Cosmo Pfeil, Debargo Sanyal, Matt Unger. *The Young Left* by Greg Keller (Gretchen Cryer, mentor). April 15, 2008. Direction, Kip Fagan; with Mark Alhadeff, Michael Crane, Diane Davis, Keira Keeley, Joe Tippett, Elisabeth Waterston. *Jailbait* by Deirdre O'Connor (Michael Weller, mentor). May 6, 2008. Direction, Suzanne Agins; with David Wilson Barnes, Flora Diaz, Peter O'Connor, Natalia Payne. *The American Dream* and *The Sandbox* by Edward Albee. April 9, 2008. Direction, Mr. Albee; with George Bartenieff, Kathleen Butler, Judith Ivey, Lois Markle, Daniel Shevlin, Harmon Walsh, Jesse Williams.

CLASSICAL THEATRE OF HARLEM. Schedule included: *Emancipation* by Ty Jones. April 17, 2008. Direction, Christopher McElroen; with Happy Anderson, Jenny Bennett, Gisela Chipe, Michael E. Cummings, Mr. Jones, James Jorsling, Stephen Conrad Moore, Jason Podplesky, Angela D. Polite, Wayne Pyle, Sean Patrick Reilly, James Singletary, Lelund Durond Thompson.

CLEMENTE SOTO VELEZ CULTURAL CENTER (CSV). Schedule included: ID AMERICA FESTIVAL. November 9–21, 2007. AMERICAN CULTURE. Direction, Kerry Whigham. *Asparagus* by Schatzie Schaefers. *Bobby Hebert* by Samuel Brett Williams. *Close Encounter* by Amy Tofte. *Human Resources* by Mike Folie. *Interpreting a Dream* by Judy Klass. *The New Sign* by K. Biadaszkiewicz. *Please Pass the Salt* by Debbie Wiess. *Shift: A Political Allegory* by Jordan Smedberg. With Janice Amano, Daryl Denner, Brittany Felton, Alexandra Henrikson, Roger Lirtsman, Stacy Osei-Kuffour, Wil Petre, Paola Poucel, Julian Schwartz, Yesenia Tromp, Kyle Walters, Kristina Wilson. AMERICAN DREAMS. Direction, Josh Gelb. *Alarm* by Paul Moulton. *Appetite* by Caren Skibell. *Night Before Last* by Doug Reed. *Normal Is a Country* by Steven Schutzman. *Onus On Us* by Cheryl Games. *Peace Talk* by James McLindon. *Prospect Park* by Brendan O'Brien. *Upgrade* by Albert Pergande. With Veronica Bruce, Dominique Fishback, Dina Kirschenbaum, Adam Laupus, Mark Lindberg, Molly Pope, Karina Richardson, Anna Savant. AMERICAN PSYCHE. Direction, Deena Selenow. *Followed* by Edith Weisso. *Here to Serve You* by Barbara Lindsay. *Moment* by Matt Haldeman. *Run of the River* by William Kovacsik. *Simultaneity* by Melanie Wallner. *Soapbox* by Carl Brandt Long. *Superhero* by Mark Harvey Levine. *To Darfur* by Erik Christian Hanson. With Colin Fisher, Julie Katz, Pearce Larson, Michael Mergo, Chelsea Palano, Elizabeth Romanski, Nandini Sonnad, Phillip W. Weiss, Hallie York. ID AMERICA FESTIVAL READINGS. November 9–21, 2007. ASSIMILATION IN AMERICA. Direction, Michael Melamedoff. *An American Christmas* by Jenni Berman Eng. *Apologies to Vietnam* by C.S. Hanson. With Francis Benhamou, Seiko Carter, Alan Cross, David Hollander, DeVon Jackson, Carol Jacobanis, John Lavelle, Natalie Silverlieb. ATTITUDES TOWARDS RACE. Direction, Patty Montesi. *Cultural Diversity Ate My Lunch* by Alonzo Lamont Jr. *One Night at Fern's* by Darren Canady. With Enid Deja Aramburu, Amanda Marklin, Azania Dungee, Elliott Chisholm, Maggie Low, John Wellington-Simon. PHARMAPSYCHOLOGY IN AMERICA. Direction, Jesse Edward Rosbrow. *Orientation Day* by Chris Shaw Swanson. *The Seven Second Itch* by Stephen J. Miller. With Nicolette Callaway, Michael Climek, Mim Granahan, Rich Lovejoy, Samantha Mason, Gregg David Shore, Alexander Yakovleff, Morgan Anne Zipf.

CLUBBED THUMB. Schedule included: *Amazons and Their Men* by Jordan Harrison. January 5, 2008. Direction, Ken Rus Schmoll; with Gio Perez, Heidi Schreck, Brian Sgambati, Rebecca Wisocky.

COLLECTIVE UNCONSCIOUS. Schedule included: THE UNDERGROUNDZERO FESTIVAL. July 19–August 5, 2007. *Let Us Go Then You and I* based on the works of Samuel Beckett. Direction,

James Dacre; with Eliza Bell, Becky Flaum, Erin Layton. *Why He Drinks Coffee* by Josh Koenigsberg. Direction, Matt Torney; with Adam Radford, Josh Sauerman, Allison Weisgall. *Journey to the End of Night* by Jason Lindner. Direction, Joshua Carlebach. *Sick: Sick of it All* by Caleb Hammond. Direction, Mr. Hammond; with Kim Carpenter, Jeff Clarke, Dan Cozzens, Jordan Harrison, Aimee Phelan-Deconinck, Jorge Rubio, Eric Dean Scott. *Things Are Going to Change, I Can Feel It* by Michael Smart. November 6, 2007. Direction, JJ Lind; with Max Dana, Brady Jenkins, Ainna Manapat, Liz Vacco. *Sherri Zahad and Her Arabian Knights*, based on Richard F. Burton's translation of *The Arabian Knights*. April 13, 2008. Direction, Yvan Greenberg; with Corey Dargel, Sheila Donovan, Oleg Dubson, Andrew Gilchrist.

THE CULTURE PROJECT. Schedule included: WOMEN CENTER STAGE FESTIVAL. June 18–July 11, 2007. *Political Subversities* by Elizabeth Swados. *Scarlet Letter* by Nathaniel Hawthorne; adapted by Carol Gilligan. Direction, Leigh Silverman; with Marisa Tomei, David Strathairn. *Till the Break of Dawn* by Danny Hoch. September 13, 2007. Direction, Mr. Hoch; with Bambadjan Bamba, Dominic Colon, Matthew-Lee Erlbach, Gwendolen Hardwick, Jimmie James, Jaymes Jorsling, Maribel Lizardo, Flaco Navaja, pattydukes, Johnny Sanchez, Luis Vega. *Rebel Voices* by Rob Urbinati; adapted from the book *Voices of a People's History* by Howard Zinn and Anthony Arnove. November 18, 2007. Direction, Will Pomerantz and Mr. Urbinati; with Opal Alladin, Tim Cain, Staceyann Chin, Morgan Hallett, Lenelle Moise, Allison Moorer, Thom Rivera. *Betrayed* by George Packer; based on his article *Betrayed: The Iraqis Who Trusted America the Most*. February 5, 2008. Direction, Pippin Parker; with Jeremy Beck, Aadya Bedi, Mike Doyle, Ramsey Faragallah, Sevan Greene, Waleed F. Zuaiter. WOMEN CENTER STAGE FESTIVAL. April 8–April 28, 2008. *Expatriate* by Lenelle Moïse. Direction, Tamilla Woodard; with Ms. Moïse, Karla Mosely. *I Have Been to Hiroshima Mon Amour* by Chiori Miyagawa. Direction, Jean Wagner. *A State of Innocence* by Naomi Wallace. Direction, Suzana Berger. *Mwena* by Nick Mwaluko. Direction, Alicia Dhyana House. *Warriors Don't Cry*. Solo performance piece by Eisa Davis. April 25, 2008. With Ms. Davis.

DIXON PLACE. Schedule included: *O Yes I Will* by Deb Margolin. September 27, 2007. Direction, Merri Milwe; with Ms. Margolin, Troy Mercier.

DR2. Schedule included: *The Fabulous Life of a Size Zero* by Marissa Kamin. June 14, 2007. Direction, Ben Rimalower; with Brenda Black, Anna Chlumsky, Gillian Jacobs, Kate Reinders, Christopher Sloan, Brian J. Smith. *Masked* by Ilan Hatsor; translated by Michael Taub. August 2, 2007. Direction, Ami Dayan; with Sanjit DeSilva, Daoud Heidami, Arian Moayed. *Artfuckers* by Michael Domitrovich. February 19, 2008. Direction, Eduardo Machado; with Asher Grodman, Tuomas Hiltunen, Will Janowitz, Jessica Kaye, Nicole LaLiberte.

EAST 13TH STREET THEATRE. Schedule included: *Uncle Vanya* by Anton Chekhov. June 20, 2007. Direction, Rachel Chavkin; with Gillian Chadsey, Libby King, Marjo-Riikka Makela.

EMERGING ARTISTS THEATRE COMPANY. Schedule included: 2007 FALL EATFEST. October 16–November 4, 2007. *The List* by Kristyn Leigh Robinson. Direction, Molly Marinik; with Scott Katzman, Maya Rosewood. *Water and Discarded Hair* by Jessamyn Fiore. Direction, Kel Haney; with Tracee Chimo, William Connell. *National Treasure* by Jon Spano. Direction, Derek Jamison; with Valerie David, Marc Garber. *Emily Breathes* by Matt Casarino. Direction, Ryan Hilliard; with Hunter Gilmore, Greg Homison. *Stray* by Corey Rieger. Direction, Roberto Cambeiro; with Jane Altman, Ron Bopst, William Reinking. *Clothes Encounter* by David Almeida and Stephen J. Miller. Direction, Nick Micozzi; with Amy Bizjak, Bryan Kaplan. *Den of Iniquity* by Patrick Gabridge. Direction, Ian Streicher Gerald; with Andrea Alton, Jess Phillips, William Reinking. *For the Good of the Nation* by Jeff Hollman. Direction, Eric Chase; with Enid Cortes, Paul Herbig, Justin Maruri, Jason O'Connell. *The Gipper* by Peter Levine. Direction, Deb Guston; with Vivian Meisner, Peter Treitler. *Lucky Day* by Mark Lambeck. Direction, Jonathan Warman; with Wayne Henry, Karen Stanion. *Safe* by D.W. Gregory. Direction, Ian Streicher; with Tom Greenman, Janelle Lannan. 2008 TRIPLE THREAT FESTIVAL. February 9–March 2, 2008. *Claymont* by Kevin Brofsky. Direction, Derek Jamison; with Wynne Anders, Ron Bopst, Glory Gallo, Jason Hare, Rebecca Hoodwin, Aimee Howard, Stephen Sherman. *Sisters' Dance* by Sarah Hollister. Direction, Paul Adams; with Blanche Cholet, Laura Fois, Janice Mann, Nick Ruggeri, Chuck Saculla. SPRING EATFEST. April 15–May 5, 2008. *Islands of Repair* by Leslie Bramm. Direction, Melissa Attebery. *The Letter* by Chuck Rose. Directed by Rasa Allan Kazlas. *Onions* by FJ Hartland. Direction, Dan Dinero. *Antiques* by Stan Lachow. Direction, James Jaworski. *Break* by J. Stephen Brantley. Direction, Jonathan Warman. *Undercurrents* by Marc Castle. Direction, Roberto Cambeiro. *Fast Light and*

Brilliant by Richard Martin. Direction, Ian Streicher. *George and Bill are Friends* by Susan West Chamberlin. Direction, Molly Marinik.

59E59 THEATERS. Schedule included: BRITS OFF BROADWAY. *Rabbit* by Nina Raine. Direction, Ms. Raine; with Ruth Everett, Adam James, Hilton McRae, Charlotte Randle, Alan Westaway, Susannah Wise. EAST TO EDINBURGH FESTIVAL. July 10–July 29, 2007. *Inside Private Lives* by Kristin Stone. Direction, Lee Michael Cohn; with Leonora Gershman, Maddisen Krown, Adam LeBow, Yee Yee Lee, Mary MacDonald, Eileen O'Connell, Paul Ryan, Bryan Safi, David Shofner, Kristin Stone, Sheila Wolf. *The Boys Next Door* by Tom Griffin. Direction, Christian Galpin and Benjy Schirm; with Christopher Mack, Renee Miller, Elizabeth Olson, Holly Payne-Strange, Mike Pfaff, Ed Sorrell, Tom Wilson. *Mod.* Musical with book by Paul Andrew Perez; music and lyrics by George Griggs. Direction, Chantel Pascente; with Christine Barnwell, Alexa Bonaros, Lucy Braid, Lizzie Campolongo, Andre Catrini, Susannah Genty-Waksberg, Mike Greco, Jasmine Schwab, Amy Secunda, Sarah Shankman, Craig Sogel, Rachel Warren. *Tender* by Shapour Benard. Direction, Julie Baber; with Andrea Dionne, Kelly Dwyer, Amber Gray, Kellie McCants. *The Nina Variations* by Steven Dietz. Direction, Douglas Rome; with Josh Berrent, Hannah Blechman, Kathleen Burnard, Lindsay Ferris, Sammi Grozbean, Nazzi Haririnia, Andy Hirsch, Mimi Lynch, Seph Normandy, Ella Robertson, Sarah Russell, Katy Summerlin, Liz Venz, Sam Wharton. SUMMER SHORTS FESTIVAL. August 2–30, 2007. *Amici, Ascoltat* by Warren Leight. Direction, Evan Yionoulis; with Tony Campisi, Derek Lucci. *Afternoon Tea.* Musical with book and lyrics by Eduardo Machado; music by Skip Kennon. Direction, Billy Hopkins; with John Hickok, Ann Talman. *Rain, Heavy at Times* by Leslie Lyles. Direction, Billy Hopkins; with Stephanie Cannon, Judith Roberts, Mark Elliot Wilson. *Real World Experience* by Michael Domitrovich. Direction, Eduardo Machado; with J.J. Kandel, Nicole LaLiberte, David Marcus. *Skin Deep* by Tina Howe. Direction, Laura Barnett; with James Katharine Flynn, Joe Kolbow, Grant Shaud. *Merwins Lane* by Keith Reddin. Direction, Billy Hopkins; with Clara Hopkins Daniels, J.J. Kandel. *Father's Day* by John Augustine. Directed by Daniel Winerman; with Colby Chambers, Catherine Curtin, Chris Wright. *The Hanging of Razor Brown* by Le Wilhelm. August 5, 2007. Direction, Merry Beamer; with Nick Giello, John Mervini, Anastasia Morsucci, Tracy Newirth, Jon Oak, Lynn Osborn, Erin Singleton, Jaclyn Sokol. *The Shattering of the Golden Pane* by Le Wilhelm. August 19, 2007. Direction, Gregg David; with Kristin Carter, Mark A. Kinch, Kevin Perri, Kirstin Walsh. *The Shape of Metal* by Thomas Kilroy. September 12, 2007. Direction, Brian Murray; with Julia Gibson, Roberta Maxwell, Molly Ward. *Flags* by Jane Martin. September 15, 2007. Direction, Henry Wishcamper; with Ryan Johnston, Steven Klein, Karen Landrey, Stephen Mendillo, Chris Mulkey. *Widows* by Ariel Dorfman. January 10, 2008. Direction, Hal Brooks; with Josh Alexander, Mark Alhadeff, Ching Valdes-Aran, Veronica Cruz, Sam Dingman, Sarah Nina Hayon, Mercedes Herrero, Guiesseppe Jones, Ana Cruz Kayne, Ephraim Lopez, Melissa Miller, James Saba, Joaquin Torres, Audrey Lynn Weston. *Slaughterhouse Five or: The Children's Crusade* by Kurt Vonnegut; adapted by Eric Simonson. January 22, 2008. Direction, Joe Tantalo; with David Bartlett, Ashton Crosby, Darren Curley, Gregory Konow, Deanna McGovern, Dustin Olson, Nick Paglino, Aaron Paternoster, Michael Shimkin, Michael Tranzilli. *The Jazz Age* by Allan Knee. February 14, 2008. Direction, Christopher McElroen; with Amy Rutberg, PJ Sosko, Dana Watkins. *Life in a Marital Institution.* Solo performance piece by James Braly. February 24, 2008. Direction, Hal Brooks; with Mr. Braly. *Rainbow Kiss* by Simon Farquhar. March 12, 2008. Direction, Will Frears; with Michael Cates, Robert Hogan, Charlotte Parry, Peter Scanavino. *Missives* by Garret Jon Groenveld. March 23, 2008. Direction, Elysabeth Kleinhans; with Shamika Cotton, Richard Gallagher, Peter Kleinhans, Jay Randall, Ryan Tresser, Ashley West. BRITS OFF BROADWAY. April 23–June 29, 2008. *Yellow Moon* by David Greig. Direction, Guy Hollands; with Nalini Chetty, Keith MacPherson, Beth Marshall, Andrew Scott Ramsay. *The Unconquered* by Torben Betts. Direction, Muriel Romanes; with Neal Barry, Nicola Harrison, Alexandra Mathie, Neil McKinven. *Artefacts* by Mike Bartlett. Direction, James Grieve; with Mouna Albakry, Karen Ascoe, Amy Hamdoon, Peter Polycarpou, Lizzy Watts. *Blink* by Ian Rowlands. Direction, Steve Fisher; with Rhian Blythe, Lisa Palfrey, Sion Pritchard.

FLORENCE GOULD HALL. Schedule included: *The Vultures* by Henri Becque. October 1, 2007. Direction, Jim Simpson; with Gerry Bammon, Jacqueline Chambord, Maria Dizzia, Ron Fabor, Bebe Neuwirth, Annie Parisse, Kathleen Turner, James Waterston, Mark Zeisler, the Bats.

45 BLEECKER. Schedule included: *Wake Up.* Solo performance piece by Karen Finley. October 21, 2007. Direction, Ms. Finley; with Ms. Finley. *Silence! The Musical.* Musical with book by Hunter

Bell; music and lyrics by Jon Kaplan and Al Kaplan; adapted from Thomas Harris's novel, *Silence of the Lambs*. September 19, 2007. Direction, Christopher Gattelli; with Harry Bouvy, Stephen Bienskie, Deidre Goodwin, Jenn Harris, Jeff Hiller, Lisa Howard, Paul Kandel, Howard Kaye. *The Turn of the Screw* by Jeffrey Hatcher. October 19, 2007. Direction, Marc Silberschatz; with Erin Cunningham, Tim Scott. *At War: American Playwrights Respond to Iraq* by Jessica Blank and Erik Jensen, Bathsheba Doran, Cory Hinkle, Rajiv Joseph, Ryan Kelly, Peter Maloney, Jose Rivera, Lynn Rosen, Jonathan Schaefer. January 21, 2008. Direction, Erica Gould; with Jennifer Albano, Jessica Blank, Bobby Cannavale, Janeane Garofalo, Erica Gould, Josh Hamilton, Judith Hawking, Korey Jackson, Erik Jensen, Amanda Marikar, Bebe Neuwirth, Denis O'Hare, Derek Phillips, Steven Rattazzi, Gloria Reuben, Jake Robards, Audrey Rosenberg, Daniel Sunjata, David Strathairn, Jonathan Schaefer, Jeremy Schwartz, Michael Warner, Jeremy Webb.

45TH STREET THEATRE. Schedule included: *The Second Tosca* by Tom Rowan. June 13, 2007. Direction, Kevin Newbury; with Jeremy Beck, Tug Coker, Rachel de Benedet, Mark Light-Orr, Melissa Picarello, Vivian Reed, Carrington Vilmont. *You May Go Now* by Bekah Brunstetter. September 9, 2007. Directed Georgie Broadwater; with Justin Blanchard, Ginger Eckert, Melinda Helfrich, Ben Vershbow. *Arpeggio* by David Stallings. November 3, 2007. Direction, Cristina Alicea; with Jonathan Albert, Allison Ikin, Kristina Kohl, Marino Antonio Miniño, Andy Travis. *Fugitive Songs*. Musical with music by Chris Miller; lyrics by Nathan Tysen. March 9, 2008. Direction, Joe Calarco; with D.B. Bonds, Halle Petro, Todd E. Pettiford, Ben Roseberry, Lucia Spina. *American Girls* by Hilary Bettis. April 6, 2008. Direction, Jeff Cohen; with Ms. Bettis, Kira Sternbach.

47TH STREET THEATRE. Schedule included: *Dai (enough)*. Solo performance piece by Iris Bahr. November 19, 2007. With Ms. Bahr.

14TH STREET THEATER. Schedule included: *Have You Seen Steve Steven?* by Ann Marie Healy. September 17, 2007. Direction, Anne Kauffman; with Brandon Bales, Frank Deal, Tom Riis Farrell, Alissa Ford, Kate Hampton, Jocelyn Kuritsky, Matthew Maher, Carol Rosenfeld, Stephanie Wright Thompson. *Celebration*. Musical with book and lyrics by Tom Jones; music by Harvey Schmidt. December 27, 2007. Direction, Erin Smiley; with Kristen Alberda, Tom Berger, Nathan Bovos, George Croom, Ben Griessmeyer, Liz Kimball, Kristian Lazzaro, Stefanie O'Connell, Kasey Williams, Joshua Robinson. *Bordertown* by Steve Ives. April 24, 2008. Direction, Tom Berger; with Michael Bertolini, Claro de los Reyes, Nick Fondulis, Cary Hite, Michael Kinsbaker, Marta Kuersten, TD White, Kasey Williams.

FOURTH STREET THEATRE. Schedule included: *The Beebo Brinker Chronicles* by Kate Moira Ryan. October 1, 2007. Direction, Leigh Silverman; with Carolyn Baeumler, Autumn Dornfeld, David Greenspan, Marin Ireland, Anna Foss Wilson.

GENE FRANKEL THEATRE. Schedule included: *Purple Hearts* by Burgess Clark. September 5, 2007. Direction, David Epstein; with Dan Patrick Brady, Kevin T. Collins, Anneka Fagundes, Cecilla Frontero, Ryan Serhant, Rebecca White. *I Used to Write on Walls* by Bekah Brunstetter. October 11, 2007. Direction, Isaac Byrne and Diana Basmajian; with Darcie Champagne, Ellen David, Maggie Hamilton. *Journey to the End of the Night*. Solo performance piece adapted from the life and novel of Louis-Ferdinand Céline; text adapted by Jason Lindner. January 10, 2008. Direction, Joshua Carlebach; with Richard Crawford. *Does Anyone Know Sarah Paisner?* by Jennifer Lane. February 16, 2008. Direction, Elyzabeth Gorman; with Maggie Benedict, David Beukema, Keenan Caldwell, Nathaniel P. Claridad, Alana Jackler, Sadrina Johnson, Yvette King, Kathryn Merry, David Stallings, Sandy Travis, Jason Odell Williams. *Chamber Music* by Arthur Kopit. April 11, 2008. Direction, Robert F. Cole; with Omar Abdali, Victoria Boomsma, Margie Catov, Petra Kipke, Judy Merrick, Julianne Nelson, Dan Snow, Laura Spaeth, Luanne Surace, Kim Vasquez. *The Day the Whores Came Out to Play Tennis* by Arthur Kopit. April 11, 2008. Direction, John Scheffler; with Robert F. Cole, Bill Krakauer, Thomas S. Nielsen, Paul Pricer, Jonathan Pereira, Zachary Zito. *Two Rooms* by Lee Blessing. May 8, 2008. Direction, James Phillip Gates; with Tori Davis, Garrett Lee Hendricks, Tracy Hostmyer, Joe Osheroff.

HARLEM REPERTORY THEATRE. Schedule included: *Finian's Rainbow*. Musical with book by E.Y. Harburg and Fred Saidy; music by Burton Lane; lyrics by Mr. Harburg. July 21, 2007. Direction, Keith Lee Grant; with Daniel Fergus, Greer Samuels, John Wiethorn. *Tambourines to Glory* by Langston Hughes. August 10, 2007. Direction, Keith Lee Grant, with Romeo Ballantine, Alexandra Bernard, Lynette Braxton.

HENRY STREET SETTLEMENT. Schedule included: *Hostages* by Clay McLeod Chapman. October 27, 2007. Direction, Oliver Butler; with *Hannah Bos, Hanna Cheek, Abe Goldfarb, Paul Thureen. At the Seashore* by Libby Emmons. October 27, 2007. Direction, Peter Sanfilippo; with Alex Goode, Emily Season, Eric Yellin. *The Persians: A Comedy About War With Five Songs* by Waterwell; adapted from Aeschylus. October 31, 2007. Direction, Kevin Townley; with Hanna Cheek, Rodney Gardiner, Arian Moayed. *Ixomia* by Eric Sanders. November 1, 2007. Direction, Stephen Brackett; *with Adam Belvo, Estelle Collins, Jared Culverhouse, Danny Defarri, Julie Lake, Orion Taraban, Philip Taratula, Sarah Turner, Cole Wimpee.*

HERE ARTS CENTER. Schedule included: *White Hot* by Tommy Smith. June 20, 2007. Direction, May Adrales; with Ben Beckley, Mary Jane Gibson, Joel Israel, Patricia Nelson. *Goodbye April, Hello May* by Ethan Lipton. June 28, 2007. Direction, Patrick McNulty; with Albert Aeed, Bill Coelius, Gibson Frazier, Kelly Mares, Maria Striar. *What Happened When* by Daniel Talbott. July 5, 2007. Direction, Brian Roff; with Jimmy Davis, Jacob Fishel. *Drum of the Waves of Horikawa* by Theatre of a Two-Headed Calf; adapted from the play by Monzaemon Chikamatsu. October 24, 2007. Direction, Brooke O'Harra; with Jess Barbagallo, Heidi Schreck.

HUDSON GUILD THEATRE. Schedule included: *Love, Life and Redemption* by Setor Attipoe. July 30, 2007. Direction, Mr. Attipoe; with Amy Chang, Tommy Connati, Dayna Dayson, Laura Lamberti, Marlana Marie, Mavis Martin, Altagracia Nova, John Rankin, Melissa Scott, Steven Sirkis, Tunde Somade. *The Colored Museum* by George C. Wolfe. January 10, 2008. Direction, Jason Summers; with James Edward Becton, Suzanne Harvin, Be Rivers, Marlana Marie, Erica Young.

IRISH ARTS. Schedule included: *Rock Doves* by Marie Jones. September 6, 2007. Direction, Ian McElhinney; with Natalie Brown, Johnny Hopkins, Marty Maguire, Tim Ruddy.

THE KITCHEN. Schedule included: *The Argument* by David Greenspan; based on Aristotle's *Poetics* and the commentary of Gerald Else. June 16, 2007. Direction, David Herskovits; with Mr. Greenspan, Han Nah Kim, Diana Konopka, Mary Neufeld, Steven Rattazzi, Greig Sargeant, Stephanie Weeks, Ian Wen. *Dinner Party* by David Greenspan; adapted from Plato's *Symposium*. June 16, 2007. Direction, David Herskovits; with David Greenspan, Han Nah Kim, Diana Konopka, Mary Neufeld, Steven Rattazzi, Greig Sargeant, Stephanie Weeks, Ian Wen. *Uncivil Wars: Collaborating With Brecht and Eisler* by David Gordon; based on *The Roundheads and the Pointheads* by Bertolt Brecht as translated by Michael Feingold. December 13, 2007. Direction, Mr. Gordon; with Autumn Dornfeld, Norma Fire, John Kelly, Derek Lucci, Estelle Parsons, Robert LaVelle, Valda Setterfield.

KRAINE THEATER. Schedule included: *Mercy Thieves* by Mark Kilmurry. October 11, 2007. Direction, Craig Baldwin, with Nico Evers-Swindell, Emma Jackson, Victoria Roberts, Nick Stevenson, Jeremy Waters. *Boys' Life* by Howard Korder. January 22, 2008. Direction, Dena Kology; with Ed Davis, Abigail Flynn, Kendra Holton, Ms. Kology, Sarah Matthay, Ryan Nicholoff, Chris Worley. *Attorney for the Damned*. Musical with book by Denis Woychuk; music by Rob McCulloch. March 15, 2008. Direction, Stephen Vincent Brennan; with Denny Blake, Maria Dalbotten, Brian Ferrari, Ray Fisher, Lee Goffin-Bonnenfant, Norma Gomez, Rob Hunter, Boskim Jeon, Allison Johnson, Patrick Mattingly, Amanda Ochoa, Juliana Smith, Teddy Williams. *Hostage Song*. Musical with book by Clay McLeod Chapman; music and lyrics by Kyle Jarrow. April 3, 2008. Direction, Oliver Butler; with Paul Bates, Hannah Bos, Hanna Cheek, Abe Goldfarb, Kyle Jarrow, Drew St. Aubin, Jonathan Sherrill, Paul Thureen.

LARK PLAY DEVELOPMENT CENTER. Schedule included: PLAYWRIGHTS WEEK FESTIVAL. September 26–October 1, 2007. Schedule included: *Sand* by Trista Baldwin. Direction, Daniella Topol. *Velocity* by Daniel Macdonald. Direction, Sturgis Warner. *Nobody* by Richard Allen. Direction, Timothy Douglas. *Children at Play* by Jordan Seavey. Direction, Jackson Gay. *Gary* by Melinda Lopez. Direction, Victor Maog. *Pistachio Stories* by Laura Shamas. Direction, Kip Fagan.

THE LIVING THEATRE. Schedule included: *Mysteries and Smaller Pieces* by The Living Theatre. October 14, 2007. Direction, Judith Malina and Gary Brackett. *Maudie and Jane* by Luciano Nattino. November 30, 2007. Direction, Hanon Reznikov; with Judith Malina, Pat Russell.

MANHATTAN THEATRE SOURCE. Schedule included: *Universal Robots* by Mac Rogers. July 9, 2007. Direction, Mr. Rogers; with Esther Barlow, Jason Howard, David Ian Lee, Michelle O'Connor, Ridley Parson, Nancy Sirianni, Tarantino Smith, Ben Sulzbach, Jennifer Gordon Thomas, James

Wetzel. *Wicked Tavern Tales* by Greg Oliver Bodine. October 17, 2007. Direction, Amber Estes; with Libby Collins, Brianna Hansan, Ridley Parson, Kevin G. Shinnick, Nancy Sirianni. *Prayer* by Jonathan Kravetz. December 9, 2007. Direction, Damon Krometis; with James Edward Becton, Daniel Owen Dungan, Marisa Merrigan, Kevin G. Shinnick, Tobias Squier-Roper, Joe Tippett. *Kitty and Lina* by Manuel Igrejas. April 3, 2008. Direction, Lory Henning; with Jennifer Boutell, Marilyn Bernard.

MA-YI THEATRE COMPANY. Schedule included: *The Children of Vonderly* by Lloyd Suh. October 4, 2007. Direction, Ralph B. Pena; with Lynn Cohen, Jackie Chung, Graeme Gillis, William Jackson Harper, Stephen Jutras, Hoon Lee, Shawn Randall, Maureen Sebastian. *Note to Self* by Vincent Marano. February 27, 2008. Direction, Mr. Marano; with Jerry Ferris, Christina Romanello.

MCGINN/CAZALE. Schedule included: MUSICALS TONIGHT. September 25, 2007–April 27, 2008. *Half a Sixpence.* Musical with book by Beverley Cross; music and lyrics by David Heneker. Direction, Thomas Sabella-Mills; with Danny Beiruti, Sean Bell, Amy Griffin, Kathryn Holtkamp, Jenna Coker-Jones, Robert Lydiard, Michael Jennings Mahoney, Patti Perkins, Jon Peterson, Roger Rifkin, Sara Sawyer, Doug Shapiro, Deborah Jean Templin, Christine Walker, Erika Zabelle, Anthony Zillmer. *The Chaos Theories* by Alexander Dinelaris. October 25, 2007. Direction, Mr. Dinelaris and Steward M. Schulman; with Richard Bekins, Max Darwin, Alison Fraser, Todd Gearhart, Ted Koch, Amanda Mantovani, Darcie Siciliano, Maryann Towne. *Deathbed* by Mark Schultz. January 31, 2008. Direction, Wendy C. Goldberg; with Ross Bickell, Charlotte Booker, Emily Donahoe, Clifton Guterman, Ryan King, Brandon Miller, Patricia Randell, Christa Scott-Reed, Jonathan Walker.

MEDICINE SHOW THEATRE. Schedule included: *The Theory of Color* by Lella Heins. July 20, 2007. Direction, Alexander Harrington; with Alexandra Devin, Celeste Moratti, James Nugent, Niall O'Hegerty, Charlotte Patton, Kathryn Savannah, Geoff Wigdor. *One Nation Under* by Andrea Lepcio. August 9, 2007. Direction, Tye Blue; with Christopher Abbott, J'nelle Bobb-Semple, Adrienne Hurd, Toks Olagundoye, Peter Reznikoff, Chrystal Stone. *The Sheik* by Deloss Brown. September 12, 2007. Direction, Mr. Brown; with Jules Hartley, Jacqueline Herbach, Marc Palmieri, Jack Perry, Amber Voiles. *On the Border* by Howard Pflanzer. November 24, 2007. Direction, Barbara Vann; with Elaine Evans, Felix Gard, Mike Lesser, Lauren LoGiudice, Monica Lynch, Vince Phillip, Charles J. Roby, Lutin Tanner, Alok Tewari.

METROPOLITAN PLAYHOUSE. Schedule included: *Margaret Fleming* by James A. Herne. September 28, 2007. Direction, Alex Roe; with Sidney Fortner, Peter Judd, Teresa Kelsey, Margaret Loesser Robinson, Marshall Sharer, Scott Sortman, Todd Woodard. THE PIONEER. Five plays by Eugene O'Neill. November 9, 2007. *Before Breakfast*; *Ile*; *The Movie Man*; *The Web*; *The Last Will and Testament of Silverdene Emblem O'Neill*. Direction, Mark Harborth; with Ron Dreyer, Andrew Firda, David Patrick Ford, Sidney Fortner, Michael Hardart, Keri Setaro. *Year One of the Empire* by Elinor Fuchs and Joyce Antler. February 29, 2008. Direction, Alex Roe; with Michael Durkin, David Patrick Ford, Michael Hardart, Gregory Jones, J.M. McDonough, John Tobias. *The Devil and Tom Walker* by Washington Irving; adapted by Anthony P. Pennino. April 25, 2008. Direction, Yvonne Conybeare; with Michael Durkin, Justin Flagg, Erik Gratton, Rebecca Hart, Sarah Hund, Michael-Jerome Johnson.

MIDTOWN INTERNATIONAL THEATRE FESTIVAL. July 16–August 5, 2007. Schedule included: *All the King's Women* by Luigi Jannuzzi. Direction, Branan Whitehead; with Jessica Asch, Rebecca Bateman, Alisha Campbell, Craig Clary, Salomé M. Krell. *The Conjugality Test* by Michael Lazan. Direction, David Gautschy; with Warren Katz, Ed Kershen, Amanda Sayle, Jacqueline Sydney, Shaun Bennet Wilson. *The Executioner* by Jon Kern. Direction, Pedro Salazar. With Sebastián Cruz, Kelly Eubanks, Melinda Helfrich, Walker Lewis, Tania Molina, Ed Perez, Sam Sadigurski, Scott Sweatt, Isaac Hirotsu Woofter. *Five by Three* by Nicole Greevy, Uma Incrocci, Erica Jensen. Direction, Mses. Greevy and Jensen; with Mike Caban, William Franke, Deborah Green, Ms. Greevy, Armistead Johnson, Sarah Malkin, Kirk McGee, Christian Pedersen, Ninon Rogers, Alison Saltz, Andi Teran, Dan Truman, Melanie Wehrmacher. *I'm in Love With Your Wife* by Alex Goldberg. Direction, Tom Wojtunik; with Shane Jacobsen, Katie Kreisler, Ron Palillo, Ean Sheehy, Marion Wood, Monica Yudovich. *The Last One Left* by Jason Pizzarello. Direction, Dev Bondarin; with Phil Bartolf, Marco Formosa, Deborah Johnstone, Maria McConville, John Stillwaggon, Emily Zempel. *Patriot Acts* by Marshall Jones III. Direction, Rice Rosetti; with Julie Cotton, Deidre Da Silva, Nick Farco, Andrew Kaempfer, Asad Khan, Sarah Koestner, Stacie Lents, Paul O'Connor, Shanti Wesley. *The Secrets of Women* by Meri Wallace. Direction, Leah Bonvissuto; with Anne Ackerman, Sabrina

Bogen, Allison Colby, Maureen Griffin, Angus Hepburn, Erin Leigh, Annalisa Loeffler, Torey Marks. *Stray Dog Hearts* by Padraic O'Reilly. Direction, Jennifer Gelfer; with Marc Santa Maria, Kimberly Bailey, Rainbow Dickerson, Mike DiGiacinto, Stephen Jutras. *Take Me America*. Musical with book and lyrics by Bill Nabel; music by Bob Christianson. Direction, Gregg Wiggans; with Ana Andricain, Eric Chan, Michelle Liu Coughlin, Jan Leslie Harding, Mike Mitchell Jr., Ellen Mittenthal, Natasha Tabandera, Ernest Williams. *Webeime* by Layon Gray. Direction, Mr. Gray; with Justin Biko, Mr. Gray, Jay Jones, Eddie Lewis, Jason McGhee, Lamman Rucker, Thom Scott, Donn Swaby.

NATIONAL ASIAN AMERICAN THEATER COMPANY (NAATCO). Schedule included: *The House of Bernarda Alba* by Federico Garcia Lorca; adapted by Chay Yew. June 4, 2007. Direction, Mr. Yew; with Ching Valdes-Aran, Kati Kuroda, Natsuko Ohama, Ali Ahn, Carmen M. Herlihy, Maile Holck, Mia Katigbak, Sue Jean Kim, Jeanne Sakata, Sophia Skiles. *Falsettoland*. Musical with book by James Lapine and William Finn; music and lyrics by Mr. Finn. June 14, 2007. Direction, Alan Muraoka; with MaryAnn Hu, Christine Toy Johnson, Francis Jue, Jason Ma, Manu Narayan, Ann Sanders, Ben Wu.

NATIONAL BLACK THEATRE. Schedule included: *Black Man Rising* by James Chapymy. October 17, 2007. Direction, Patricia R. Floyd; with Neil Dawson, Larry Floyd, Lawrence Saint-Victor, Melvin Shambry, Juson Williams. *Medea* by Euripides; translated by Nicholas Rudall. February 19, 2008. Direction, Petronia Paley; with Trazana Beverley, David Heron, Mary E. Hodges, Sharita Hunt, Marishka Phillips, Beverley Prentice, Ian Stuart, Bryan Webster, Renauld White, Dathan B. Williams, David D. Wright, Natasha Yannacanedo, Ma'at Zachary.

NEW GEORGES. Schedule included: *Good Heif* by Maggie Smith. October 8, 2007. Direction, Sarah Cameron Sunde; with Paul Klementowicz, April Matthis, John McAdams, Barbara Pitts, Yves Rene, Christopher Ryan Richards. *Stretch (a fantasia)* by Susan Bernfield. May 5, 2008. Direction, Emma Griffin; with Eric Clem, Kristin Griffith, Brian Gerard Murray, Evan Thompson.

NEW YORK CITY PLAYERS. Schedule included: *Ode to the Man Who Kneels*. Musical with book, music and lyrics by Richard Maxwell. Direction, Mr. Maxwell; with Jim Fletcher, Anna Kohler, Emily Cass McDonnell, Greg Mehrten, Brian Mendes.

NEW WORLD STAGES. Schedule included: *My First Time* by Ken Davenport. July 28, 2007. Direction, Mr. Davenport; with Bill Dawes, Josh Heine, Kathy Searle, Cydnee Welburn. *The Castle* by David Rothenberg with Vilma Ortiz Donovan, Kenneth Harrigan, Angel Ramos and Casimiro Torres. April 27, 2008. Direction, Mr. Rothenberg; with Ms. Donovan, Messrs. Harrigan, Ramos and Torres.

NEW YORK INTERNATIONAL FRINGE FESTIVAL. August 10–26, 2007. Schedule included: *And Somewhere Men Are Laughing* by Jeff Mandels. Direction, Bill Russell; with John Fugelsang, Hunter Gallagher, Paul Iacono, Carol Lempert, Katie Neil, Jana Robbins, Brian Shepard. *As Far As We Know* by the Torture Project Ensemble and Christina Gorman. Direction, Laurie Sales; with Sara Kathryn Bakker, Michael Battelli, Faith Catlin, Alex Cherington, Lea McKenna Garcia, Abby Royle, Kelly Van Zile, Joseph Varca, Jeff Wills. *Bash'd!: A Gay Rap Opera* by Chris Craddock and Nathan Cuckow. Direction, R.M. Jenkins; with Messrs. Craddock and Cuckow. *A Beautiful Child* by Truman Capote. Direction, Linda Powell; with Maura Lisabeth Malloy, Joel Van Liew. *Bombs in Your Mouth* by Corey Patrick. Direction, Joseph Ward; with Cass Buggé, Mr. Patrick. *Dirt*. Solo performance piece by Robert Schneider; translated by Paul F. Dvorak. Direction, David Robinson; with Christopher Domig. *Double Vision* by Barbara Blumenthal-Ehrlich. Direction, Ari Laura Kreith; with Rebecca Henderson, Shane Jacobsen, Linda Jones, Quinn Mattfeld, Christopher McCann, Sarah Silk. *Elephant in the Room!* by Dan Fogler; based on *Rhinoceros* by Eugene Ionesco. Direction, Mr. Fogler; with Randy Baruh, Jordan Gelber, Kate Gersten, Johnny Giacolone, Lennon Parham, Sarah Saltzberg, Ariel Shafir, Dennis Staroselsky, Law Tarello, Bjorn Thorstad, Ivy Vahanian. *End's Eve: The Feast of 2012* by Hilary Park and Jennifer Gnisci. Direction, Erik Slavin; with Devon Berkshire, Nic Few, Patrick Knighton, Ethan Matthews, Chance Mullen, Lauren Orkus, Tony Naumovsky, Tim Smallwood, Marnye Young. *Hillary Agonistes* by Nick Salamone. Direction, Jon Lawrence Rivera; with Priscilla Barnes, Rebecca Metz, Nick Salamone. *Jamaica, Farewell*. Solo performance piece by Debra Ehrhardt. Direction, Monique Lai; with Ms. Ehrhardt. *Jaspora*. Solo performance piece by Nancy Moricette. Direction, Ilknur River Ozgur; with Ms. Moricette. *Jazz Hand: Tales of a One Armed Woman* by Mary Theresa Archbold and Pat Shay. Direction, Kevin Allison; with Ms. Archbold, Mr. Shay. *Lights Rise on Grace* by Chad Beckim. Direction, Robert

O'Hara; with Ali Ahn, Alexander Alioto, Jaime Lincoln Smith. *Mary Brigit Poppleton Is Writing a Memoir* by Madeline Walter. Direction, Heidi Handelsman; with Allison Altman, Daleelah Sada Johnson, Russell Johnson, Julie Marcus, Allyson Morgan, Doug Roland, Evan Silverman, Patrick Stewart, Isaiah Tanenbaum. *Naked in a Fishbowl* by Katharine Heller, Brenna Palughi, Lynne Rosenberg, Lauren Seikaly. Direction, Hugh Sinclair; with Mses. Heller, Palughi, Rosenberg, Seikaly. *Night* by Philip Gerson. Direction, Michael Lilly; with Grant Aleksander, Josh Clayton, Jenn Miller Cribbs, Veronica Cruz, Laurence Lau, Maureen Mueller. *Paper Son.* Solo performance piece by Byron Yee. *Piaf: Love Conquers All* by Roger Peace. Direction, Naomi Emmerson; with Ms. Emmerson. *Riding the Bull* by August Schulenburg. Direction, Kelly O'Donnell; with Will Ditterline, Liz Dailey. *Roxy Font* by Liza Lentini. Direction, Ian Belton; with Pepper Binkley, Shalita Grant, Roger Lirtzman, Tim McGeever, Liz Thompson. *Stock Home* by Alex Goldberg. Direction, Seth Soloway; with Lauren Cook, Megan Tusing, Mather Zickel.

NEW YORK MUSICAL THEATRE FESTIVAL (NYMF). September 17–October 7, 2007. Schedule included: *Sherlock Holmes (The Early Years).* Musical with book by Kate Ferguson and Robert Hudson; music by Jared M. Dembowski; lyrics by Susanna Pearse. Direction, Nona Lloyd; with William Connell, Sarah Glendening, Scott Gofta, Nicholas Kohn, Gavin Lodge, Mike Masters, Susan Louise O'Connor, Robyne Parrish, William Ryall, Elizabeth Shepherd, Laura Shoop, Michael St. John, Doug Trapp. *Back Home: The War Brides Musical.* Musical with book by Ronald Sproat, music by Christopher Berg, lyrics by Frank Evans. Direction, Bick Goss; with Raissa Katona Bennett, Jeff Scot Carey, Joe Danbusky, Jenn Zarine Habeck, Adam J. MacDonald, Kristin Maloney, Vanessa June Marshall, Christina Morrell, Danielle Erin Rhodes, Steve Sterner. *Gemini the Musical.* Musical with book by Albert Innaurato; music and lyrics by Charles Gilbert. Direction, Mark Robinson; with Bethe Austin, Joel Blum, Kirsten Bracken, Linda Hart, Jonathan Kaye, Dan Micciche, Ryan Reid. *Mud Donahue and Son.* Musical with book by Jeff Hochhauser, music by Bob Johnston; lyrics by Messrs. Johnston and Hochhauser; based on *Letters of a Hoofer to His Ma* by Jack Donahue. Direction, Lynne Taylor-Corbett; with Karen Murphy, Shonn Wiley. *Sympathy Jones.* Musical with book by Brooke Pierce; music and lyrics by Masi Asare. Direction, Sarah Gurfield; with Jimmy Ray Bennett, Christopher Carl, Tony Chiroldes, Thursday Farrar, Amanda Ryan Paige, Glenn Peters, Charlie Pollock, Kate Shindle. *Going Down Swingin'.* Musical with book and lyrics by Matt Boresi, music by Peter Hilliard. Direction, Jenny Lord; with Stacie Bono, Tom Deckman, George McDaniel, Meredith Patterson, Hardy Rawls, Marla Schaffel, Christopher Shyer, James Stovall. *Love Sucks.* Musical with book and lyrics by Stephen O'Rourke; music by Brandon Patton. Direction, Andrew Goldberg; with Kim Gatewood, Rebecca Hart, Caryn Havlik, Robert Andrew Marnell, Athena Reich, Heather Robb, Andrew M. Ross, Debargo Sanyal, Nicholas Webber, Jason Wooten. *Such Good Friends.* Musical with book, music and lyrics by Noel Katz. Direction, Marc Bruni; with Joshua Campbell, Michael Thomas Holmes, Laura Jordan, Liz Larsen, Dirk Lumbard, Shannon O'Bryan, Brad Oscar, Jeff Talbot, Blake Whyte, Lynn Wintersteller. *The Boy in the Bathroom.* Musical with book by Michael Lluberes; music by Joe Maloney; lyrics by Messrs. Lluberes and Maloney. Direction, Mr. Lluberes; with Ana Nogueira, Mary Stout, Michael Zahler. *Platforms.* Musical with book by Delaney Britt Brewer, music by Brent Lord. Direction, Holly-Anne Ruggiero; with Ted Levy, Deborah Yates. *With Glee.* Musical with book, music and lyrics by John Glee. Direction, Ryan Mekenian; with Justin Bellero, Greg Kenna, Liz Kerins, Dan Lawler, Michael Miller, Kevin Murphy, Ryan Speakman. *The Beastly Bombing.* Musical with book and lyrics by Julien Nitzberg; music by Roger Neill. Direction, Mr. Nitzberg, with Andrew Ableson, Joel Bennett, Curt Bonnem, Kate Gabrielle Feld, Heather Marie Marsden, Aaron Matijasic, Jesse Merlin, John Quale, Natalie Salins, Jacob Sidney, Russell Steinberg. *Unlock'd.* Musical with book and lyrics by Sam Carner; music by Derek Gregor. Direction, Igor Goldin; with Sarah Jane Everman, Jackie Burns, Alison Cimmet, Maria Couch, William Thomas Evans, Chris Gunn, Mary Catherine McDonald, Christopher Totten, Jim Weitzer, Darryl Winslow. *Bernice Bobs Her Mullet.* Musical by Joe Major; based on *Bernice Bobs Her Hair* by F. Scott Fitzgerald. Direction, Andy Sandberg; with Nick Cearley, Katrina Rose Dideriksen, Jeff Hiller, Hollie Howard, Garrett Long, Ann Morrison, Brandon Wardell, Lauren Worsham. *The Good Fight.* Musical with book and lyrics by Nick Enright; music by David King. Direction, Crispin Taylor; with Bernard Angel, Eliza Anderson, Brad Carroll, Zack Curran, Chrystal de Grussa, Brent Dolahenty, Stuart Fisher, Keane Fletcher, Lachlan Gillespie, Gemma-Ashley Kaplan, Gareth Keegan, Suzie Mathers, Matthew McFarlane, Stephanie Morrison, Vanessa Raspa, Caleb Rixon, Kathryn Sgroi, Liz Stiles. *The Piper.* Musical with book, music and lyrics by Marcus Hummon. Direction, Michael Bush; with Nancy Anderson, Sean Attebury, Cole

Burden, Daren de Paul, Tom Galantich, Trisha Jeffrey, Jillian Louis, T. J. Mannix, Christiane Noll, Catherine LaVelle, Patrick Ryan. *Tully (In No Particular Order)*. Musical with book by Joshua William Gelb; music by Stephanie Johnstone; lyrics by Mr. Gelb and Ms. Johnstone. Direction, Mr. Gelb; with Adam Hose, Autumn Hurlbert, David McGee, Austin Miller, Evan Jay Newman, Owen O'Malley, Kate Rockwell. *The Yellow Wood*. Musical with book by Michelle Elliott; music by Danny Larsen; lyrics by Ms. Elliott and Mr. Larsen. Direction, B.D. Wong; with Jill Abramovitz, Randy Blair, Patrick Boll, Sean Bradford, Scot Fedderly, Mary Ann Hu, Caissie Levy, Elizabeth Lundberg, Dennis Moench, Marnie Schulenburg, Yuka Takara, Jason Tam. *Petite Rouge*. Musical with book, music and lyrics by Joan Cushing; adapted from Little Red Riding Hood by Mike Artell. Direction, Michael J. Bobbitt; with Billy Bustamante, Cyana Cook, Felicia Curry, L.C. Harden, Tracy McMullan, Bobby Smith.

NICU'S SPOON THEATRE COMPANY. Schedule included: *Kosher Harry* by Nick Grosso. October 12, 2007. Direction, Stephanie Barton-Farcas and Aaron Kubey; with Wynne Anders, Michael DiMartino, Darren Fudenske, Jennifer Giroux, Shira Grabelsky, Andrew Hutcheson, Sherrie Morgan, Alvaro Sena. *Elizabeth Rex* by Timothy Findley. April 4, 2008. Direction, Joanne Zipay; with Stephanie Barton-Farcas, Rebecca Challis, Oliver Conant, Michael Digoia, Bill Galarno, Melanie Horton, Andrew Hutcheson, Merle Louise, Sammy Mena, Scott Nogi, Tim Romero, Alvaro Sena, David Tully.

NUYORICAN POET'S CAFÉ. Schedule included: *Body Parts* by Ishmael Reed. October 25, 2007. Direction, Rome Neal; with Henry Afro-Bradley, Samia Axudo, Rod Bladel, Reggie Buckingham, Wendy Callard-Booz, Dan Campanelli, Steve Cromity, Megan C. Jackson, Patrick Lam, D.J. Lapite, Karen Denise Page, Robert Turner.

OHIO THEATER. Schedule included: *Bad Jazz* by Robert Farquhar. November 11, 2007. Direction, Trip Cullman; with Rob Campbell, Colby Chambers, Darren Goldstein, Marin Ireland, Ryan O'Nan, Susie Pourfar.

ONTOLOGICAL-HYSTERIC THEATER. Schedule included: *Famous Actors* by Kara Feely. June 14, 2007. Direction, Ms. Feely; with Ross Beschler, Avi Glickstein, Annie Kunjappy, Daniel Allen Nelson, Jessica Grace Pagan, Zuzanna Szadkowski. *The Art of Memory* by Tanya Calamoneri. July 12, 2007. Direction, Kenn Watt; with Ms. Calamoneri, Heather Harpham, Lisa Ramirez, Cassie Terman. *Dysphoria* by Alec Duffy. August 2, 2007. Direction, Mr. Duffy; with David Frank, Masayasu Nakanishi, Nisi Sturgis, Amy Laird Webb, Marshall York. *Deep Trance Behavior in Potatoland* by Richard Foreman. January 22, 2008. Direction, Mr. Foreman; with Sarah Dahlen, Joel Israel, Caitlin McDonough Thayer, Fulya Peker, Caitlin Rucker. *Vicious Dogs on Premises* by Saviana Stanescu. May 30, 2008. Direction, Dan Safer; with Heather Christian, Sean Donovan, Mike Mikis, Mr. Safer, Laura Berlin Stinger.

PEARL THEATRE COMPANY. Schedule included: *Hamlet*. Revival of the play by William Shakespeare. September 11, 2007. Direction, Shepard Sobel; with Jolly Abraham, Robin Leslie Brown, Bradford Cover, Dominic Cuskern, Jimmy Davis, TJ Edwards, R.J. Foster, Robert Hock, Regi Huc, Kenneth Lee, Sean McNall, Eduardo Placer, David Sedgwick, Christopher Thornton, David L. Townsend. *The Constant Couple* by George Farquhar. November 25, 2007. Direction, Jean Randich; with Jolly Abraham, Rachel Botchan, Robin Leslie Brown, Joanne Camp, Bradford Cover, Dominic Cuskern, Meg McCrossen, Sean McNall, Orville Mendoza, Jack Moran, John Pasha, Eduardo Placer, Caleb Rupp, David L. Townsend. *The Mandrake* by Niccolo Machiavelli; translated by Peter Constantine. January 20, 2008. Direction, Jim Calder; with Rachel Botchan, Bradford Cover, Dominic Cuskern, TJ Edwards, Rocelyn Halili, Edward Seamon, Carol Schultz, Erik Steele. *Ghosts* by Henrik Ibsen. March 9, 2008. Direction, Regge Life: with Joanne Camp, TJ Edwards, John Behlmann, Tom Galantich, Keiana Richàrd. *The Importance of Being Earnest* by Oscar Wilde. April 27, 2008. Direction, J.R. Sullivan; with Ali Ahn, Rachel Botchan, Joanne Camp, Bradford Cover, Dominic Cuskern, TJ Edwards, Sean McNall, Carol Schultz.

PHOENIX THEATRE ENSEMBLE. Schedule included: *CEO and Cinderella*. Solo performance piece by Angela Madden. January 24, 2008. Direction, Barbara Bosch; with Ms. Madden. *The Lifeblood* by Glyn Maxwell. February 1, 2008. Direction, Robert Hupp; with Brian Costello, Jolie Garrett, Douglas McKeown, Joseph J. Menino, Jason O'Connell, Craig Smith, Elise Stone, Mark Waterman. *I Have Before Me a Remarkable Document Given to Me by a Young Lady From Rwanda* by Sonja Linden. April 12, 2008. Direction, Elise Stone; with Joseph J. Menino, Susan Heyward.

PRODUCERS CLUB. Schedule included: *Uncommon Women and Others* by Wendy Wasserstein. July 13, 2007. Direction, Tony White; with Jovanka Ciares, Mary Jane Gocher, Deidre Johnson, Jerrah Kohn, Rachel Lande, Jenny Levine, Gabrielle Rosen, Megan Sambataro, Colleen Summa, Kasey Williams. *The Housedress* by Gerard Denza. November 1, 2007. Direction, Mr. Denza; with R. Ross Pivec, Phil Strumolo, J.C. Whittaker. *Monkey Trick* by Brad Saville. February 28, 2008. Direction, Mr. Saville; with Penny Bittone, Anne Fidler, David Marcus.

PROSPECT THEATER COMPANY. Schedule included: *The Rockae*. Musical with music and lyrics by Peter Mills; adapted by Mr. Mills and Cara Reichel from *The Bacchae* by Euripides. September 15, 2007. Direction, Ms. Reichel; with Meghan McGeary, Gordon Stanley. *The Blue Flower*. Musical with book, music and lyrics by Jim Bauer; additional material, Ruth Bauer. February 2, 2008. Direction and choreography, Will Pomerantz; with Nancy Anderson, Jason Collins, Jamie LaVerdiere, Meghan McGeary, Marcus Neville, Robert Petkoff, Eric Starker. *Honor*. Musical with book, music and lyrics by Peter Mills and Cara Reichel. April 19, 2008. Direction, Ms. Reichel; with Alan Ariano, Eymard Cabling, Ariel Estrada, Ali Ewoldt, Steven Eng, Christine Toy Johnson, Brian Jose, Ming Lee, Jaygee Macapugay, Doan MacKenzie, Mel Maghuyop, Diane V. Phelan, Romney Piamonte, Vincent Rodriguez, David Shih, Whitney Lee, Allan Mangaser, Toshiji Takeshima, Robert Torigoe.

RATTLESTICK THEATER. Schedule included: *Badge* by Matthew Schneck. June 18, 2007. Direction, Jenn Thompson; with Glynis Bell, Tara Falk, Darrell James, Greg McFadden. *American Sligo* by Adam Rapp. September 24, 2007. Direction, Mr. Rapp; with Guy Boyd, Marylouise Burke, Michael Chernus, Emily Cass McDonnell, Megan Mostyn-Brown, Paul Sparks, Matthew Stadelmann. *Rag and Bone* by Noah Haidle. November 20, 2007. Direction, Sam Gold; with Michael Chernus, Kevin Jackson, Deirdre O'Connell, Matthew Stadelmann, Henry Stram, Audrey Lynn Weston, David Wohl. *War* by Lars Norén; translated by Marita Lindholm Gochman. February 11, 2008. Direction, Anders Cato; with Ngozi Anyanwu, Rosalyn Coleman, Flora Diaz, Laith Nakli, Alok Tewari. *Steve and Idi* by David Grimm. May 5, 2008. Direction, Eleanor Holdridge; with Michael Busillo, Mr. Grimm, Greg Keller, Zachary Knower, Evan Parke.

RED BULL THEATER. Schedule included: REVELATION READINGS. October 1, 2007–January 21, 2008. *Desdemona* by Paula Vogel. October 1, 2007. Direction, Jesse Berger; with Mamie Gummer, Jessica Hecht, Jennifer Ikeda. *The Changeling* by Thomas Middleton and William Rowley. October 8, 2007. Direction Karin Coonrod; with Juliana Francis, David Patrick Kelly, Kevin Massey, Griffin Matthews, Matthew Rauch, John Douglas Thompson. Tony Torn, Molly Ward. *Tallgrass Gothic* by Melanie Marnich. October 22, 2007. Direction, Leigh Silverman; with Michael Cerveris, Michael Chernus. *The Just* by Albert Camus; adapted by Anthony Clarvoe. October 29, 2007. Direction, Ethan McSweeny; with Neal Huff, Meg Fee, Ellen McLaughlin, Michael Stuhlbarg. *The Rover* by Aphra Behn. November 12, 2007. Direction, Eleanor Holdridge; with Daniel Breaker, Carla Harting. *The Lady's Not for Burning* by Christopher Fry. November 26, 2007. Direction, Joseph Hardy; with Richard Easton, Lynn Redgrave. *Edward II* by Christopher Marlowe; adapted by Bertolt Brecht. January 7, 2008. Direction, Michael Sexton; with Hannah Cabell, Michael Cerveris, Davis Hall, Jason Butler Harner, Randy Harrison, Derek Lucci, Denis O'Hare, Matthew Rauch, Daniel Stewart. *Don't Fuck With Love* by Kay Matschullat; adapted from Alfred de Musset. January 14, 2008. Direction, Lear deBessonet; with Mary Bacon, Michael Crane, Geraint Wyn Davies, Adam Green, Keiko Green, Michael Izquierdo, Merritt Janson, Jeanine Serralles. *The Cardinal* by James Shirley. January 21, 2008. Direction, Carl Forsman; with Eric Alba, Heidi Armbruster, William Connell, Frank Deal, Ben Hollandsworth, Brian Hutchison, Stephanie Janssen, Brad Makarowski, Michael Mastro, Scott Parkinson, Joey Parsons, Ross Raines, Matthew Rauch, Roger Rees, Thomas Jay Ryan, Sarah Stockton. *Edward II* by Christopher Marlowe; adapted by Garland Wright. December 15, 2007. Direction, Jesse Berger; with Arthur Bartow, Rob Breckenridge, Wesley Broulik, Joseph Costa, William DeMerritt, Michael Gotch, Davis Hall, Lucas Hall, Randy Harrison, James Knight, Claire Lautier, Terence MacSweeny, Raum-Aron, Derrick LeMont Sanders, Raphael Nash Thompson, Patrick Vaill, Marc Vietor.

RED ROOM. Schedule included: *Night of Nigro* by Don Nigro. August 2, 2007. Direction, Greg T. Parente and Erica Terpening-Romeo; with Toni-Ann Gardiner, Tamara Geisler, Alice Kremelberg, Thomas James Lombardo, Mr. Parente, Ashley Ramos, Ms. Terpening-Romeo. *Say Your Prayers, Mug!* by Todd Michael. October 4, 2007. Direction, Mr. Michael; with Jimmy Blackman, Jill Yablon. *The Hand That Feeds You* by Greg Turner. February 7, 2008. Direction, Sara Sahin; with Nathan Dame, Ellen Lanese, Michael Judson Pace, Patrick Stafford.

ROY ARIAS STUDIOS AND THEATRES. Schedule included: *The Red Lamp* by Hilliard Booth. July 25, 2007. Direction, Patrick Mills; with Himyo Green, Shashone Lambert, William Sudan Mason, Maisha Meloncon, Tiffany Raelynn, Dwight Ali Williams. *Providence: There Is No Such Thing as Coincidence* by Cody Daigle. February 9, 2008. Direction, Ian R. Crawford; with Anthony Crep, Kathryn Ekblad, Douglas Scott Sorenson, Aly Wirth. *White Widow*. Musical with book, music and lyrics by Paul Dick. May 9, 2008. Direction, Elizabeth Falk; with Dave Adamick, Elizabeth Daniels, Christopher deProphetis, Claybourne Elder, Phil Franzese, Nick Gaswirth, Chris Gleim, Emilio Magnotta, Katherine Malak, Erin Mosher, Phil Olejack, Michael Padgett, Jeremy Pasha, Thomas Rainey, Tim Realbuto, Jacob Reilly, Kristin Katherine Shields, Amy Elaine Warner, Cassie Wooley, Michael Yeshoin.

ST. ANN'S WAREHOUSE. Schedule included: *The Veiled Monologues* by Adelheid Roosen. October 5, 2007. Direction, Ms. Roosen; with Oya Capelle, Nazmiye Oral, Meral Polat. In repertory with *Is. Man* by Adelheid Roosen. October 6, 2007. Direction, Ms. Roosen; with Oya Capelle, Nazmiye Oral, Meral Polat. *Black Watch* by Gregory Burke. October 20, 2007. Direction, John Tiffany; with David Colvin, Ali Craig, Emun Elliott, Ryan Fletcher, Jack Fortune, Paul Higgins, Henry Pettigrew, Paul Rattray, Nabil Stuart, Jordan Young. *The Walworth Farce* by Enda Walsh. April 18, 2008. Direction, Mikel Murfi; with Denis Conway, Garrett Lombard, Tadhg Murphy, Mercy Ojelade.

SECOND STAGE UPTOWN. Schedule included: *The Butcher of Baraboo* by Marisa Wegrzyn. June 11, 2007. Direction, Judith Ivey; with Ashlie Atkinson, Michael Countryman, Ali Marsh, Debra Jo Rupp, Welker White. *Election Day* by Josh Tobiessen. August 1, 2007. Direction, Jeremy Dobrish; with Michael Ray Escamilla, Halley Feiffer, Adam Green, Lorenzo Pisoni, Katharine Powell.

78TH STREET THEATRE LAB. Schedule included: *Botanical Gardens* by Todd Logan. September 9, 2007. Direction, Rob Urbinati; with Anne Carney, Malachy Cleary. *Atomic Farmgirl* by C. Denby Swanson; adapted from the memoir by Teri Hein. November 16, 2007. Direction, Brooke Brod; with Hamilton Clancy, Melissa Condren, Brad Coolidge, Dawn Evans, Dennis Gagomiros, Jane Guyer, Karen Kitz, David Marantz, Maria McConville, Kathleen O'Grady. *An Eclectic Evening of Shorts* by Kia Corthron, Carol Hall, Jeffrey Sweet, Gary Garrison, Roland Tec, Hilary Chaplain, David Engel, Kristine Niven, Margo Hammond. March 27, 2008. Direction, Bob Berky, Janice Goldberg, Maggie Lally, Kathryn Long, John Monteith, Michael Rock, Mark Robinson, Tlaloc Rivas; with Michelle Best, DK Bowser, Ms. Chaplain, Mr. Engel, Leo Ash Evens, Jim Ewing, Justin Greer, Ms. Hammond, Frank Hankey, Kaitlin Hopkins, Jackie Jenkins, Carol Lempert, Ms. Niven, Sara Pauley, Jim Price, Chris Stack, Scotty Watson, Cotton Wright.

SNAPPLE THEATER CENTER. Schedule included: *Secrets of a Soccer Mom* by Kathleen Clark. March 5, 2008. Direction, Judith Ivey; with Caralyn Kozlowski, Nancy Ringham, Deborah Sonnenberg.

SOHO PLAYHOUSE. Schedule included: *The Toad Poems* by Gerald Locklin and George Carroll. June 15, 2007. Direction, Ian Morgan; with John Wojda, Barbara Pitts, Marina Squerciati. *Flanagan's Wake* by Bonnie Shadrake and Amy Binns-Calvey. October 6, 2007. Direction, Ms. Binns-Calvey; with Michael Connell, Aaron Costa Ganis, Abigail Dierdre Gullo, Walker Hare, Kieran Kenny, Casey McClellan, Maeve Price. *Every Girl Gets Her Man* by Emma Sheanshang. March 9, 2008. Direction, Michael Melamedoff; with Danny Bernardy, Cass Buggé, Amy Flanagan, Anna Margaret Hollyman, Chloe Whiteford, Sarah Wilson. *Substitution* by Anton Dudley. May 4, 2008. Direction, Katherine Kovner; with Kieran Campion, Shana Dowdeswell, Brandon Espinoza, Jan Maxwell.

SOHO THINK TANK. Schedule included: ICE FACTORY 2007. July 4, 2007–August 18, 2007. Schedule included: *No More Pretending* by Kirk Wood Bromley. Direction, Howard Thoresen; with Meg MacCary. *Vampire University* by John Kaplan. Direction, Desmond Mosley; with Tom Bonner, Renee-Michele Brunet, Kristin Ciccone, Emily Kron, Skyler McLean, Stephanie Marie Williams. *Me* by Kirk Wood Bromley. May 4, 2008. Direction, Alec Duffy; with Arthur Aulisi, Lora Chio, Drew Cortese, Sarah Engelke, Josh Hartung, Bob Laine, Meagan Prahl, Dan Renkin, Annie Scott, Erwin Thomas, Paula Wilson, Brenda Withers, Marshall York.

STUDIO DANTE. Schedule included: *From Riverdale to Riverhead* by Anastasia Traina. June 2, 2007. Direction, Nick Sandow; with Catherine Curtin, Ken Forman, Bess Rous, Annabella Sciorra, Angelica Torn. *The Joke* by Sam Marks. October 20, 2007. Direction, Sam Gold; with Jordan Gelber, Thomas Sadoski. *Sisters, Such Devoted Sisters*. Solo performance piece by Russell Barr. January 26, 2008. Direction, Michael Imperioli; with Mr. Barr.

SYMPHONY SPACE. Schedule included: *Surface to Air* by David Epstein. July 11, 2007. Direction, James Naughton; with Bruce Altman, Larry Bryggman, James Colby, Marisa Echeverria, Cady Huffman, Lois Smith, Mark J. Sullivan.

THEATER BREAKING THROUGH BARRIERS (TBTB). Schedule included: *The Rules of Charity* by John Belluso. June 3, 2007. Direction, Ike Schambelan; with George Ashiotis, Brian Bielawski, Hollis Hamilton, Gregg Mozgala, Pamela Sabaugh, Nicholas Viselli. Romeo and Juliet. Revival of the play by William Shakespeare. March 5, 2008. Direction, Ike Schambelan; with George Ashiotis, Gregg Mozgala, Nicholas Viselli, Emily Young.

THEATRE AT ST. CLEMENT'S. Schedule included: *The Screwtape Letters* by C.S. Lewis. November 8, 2007. Direction, Jeffrey Fiske; Max McLean, Karen Eleanor Wright.

THEATRE ROW THEATRES. Schedule included: THE SUMMER PLAY FESTIVAL. July 10–August 5, 2007. Schedule included: *Alice in War* by Steven Bogart. Direction, Alice Reagan. *Blueprint* by Bixby Elliot. Direction, Jonathan Silverstein. *Cipher* by Cory Hinkle. Direction, Kip Fagan. *Devil Land* by Desi Moreno-Penson. Direction, Jose Zayas. *Flesh and the Desert* by Carson Kreitzer. Direction, Beth Milles. *The Gabriels* by Van Badham. Direction, Rebecca Patterson. *Half of Plenty* by Lisa Dillman. Direction, Meredith McDonough. *Lower Ninth* by Beau Willimon. Direction, Daniel Goldstein. *minor gods* by Charles Forbes. Direction, Gaye Taylor Upchurch. *Missing Celia Rose* by Ian August. Direction, Adam Immerwahr. *My Wandering Boy* by Julie Marie Myatt. Direction, John Gould Rubin. *The Nightshade Family* by Ruth McKee. Direction, Shelley Butler. *Not Waving* by Ellen Melaver. Direction, Douglas Mercer. *Novel* by Anna Ziegler. Direction, Michael Goldfried. *Unfold Me* by Joy Tomasko. Direction, Linsay Firman. *Vrooommm! A NASComedy* by Janet Allard. Direction, David Lee. THE ACORN. *Guilty* by Nancy Manocherian. July 5, 2007. Direction, Kira Simring; with Jason A. Bishop, Tracee Chimo, Mary Ann Conk, Glory Gallo, Ken Hypes, Heather Kenzie, Ms. Manocherian, Ned Massey, Tim McMath, Ms. Simring, Darnell Williams. THE BECKETT. *Apartment 3A* by Jeff Daniels. February 1, 2008. Direction, Owen M. Smith; with Philip J. Cutrone, Marianna McClellan, Doug Nyman, Jay Rohloff, Vincent Vigilante. *U.S. Drag* by Gina Gionfriddo. March 1, 2008. Direction, Trip Cullman; with Tanya Fischer, Logan Marshall Green, Rebecca Henderson, Lisa Joyce, James Martinez, Michael Mosley, Matthew Stadelmann, Audrey Lynn Weston. *The Bully Pulpit*. Solo performance piece by Michael O. Smith. May 14, 2008. Direction, Byam Stevens; with Mr. Smith. THE CLURMAN. *The Maddening Truth* by David Hay. January 15, 2008. Direction, Carl Forsman; with Peter Benson, Richard Bekins, William Connell, Lisa Emery, Terry Layman. *The Conscientious Objector* by Michael Murphy. March 18, 2008. Direction, Carl Forsman; with Chad Carstarphen, Jimonn Cole, John Cullum, Brian Hicks, Jonathan Hogan, Rachel Leslie, James Miles, Steve Routman, Geddeth Smith, Harold Suratt, DB Woodside. *The Coffee Trees* by Arthur Giron. October 3, 2007. Direction, Marion Castleberry; with Teddy Canez, Chris Ceraso, Angela Clemente, Elizabeth A. Davis, Dan Domingues, Annie Henk, Veronica Matta, Steven Pounders, Victor Truro. *A Hard Heart* by Howard Barker. November 11, 2007. Direction, Will Pomerantz; with Kathleen Chalfant, Melissa Friedman, Dion Graham, Alex Organ, Thom Sesma, James Wallert, Sarah Winkler. *The Maddening Truth*. Solo performance piece by David Hay. January 30, 2008. Direction, Carl Forsman; with Lisa Emery. THE KIRK. *Reconstructing Mama*. Musical with book by Stephen Svoboda; music by N. David Williams; lyrics by Messrs. Svoboda and Williams. August 12, 2007. Direction, Mr. Svoboda; with Lauren Connolly, Danny Marr, Ariana Shore, Chris Teutsch, Jonathan White. *Pied-a-Terre* by John Anastasi. December 6, 2007. Direction, Tom Ferriter; with Jessica McKee, Robin Riker, John Howard Swain. *Anchors* by Tony Zertuche. February 9, 2008. Direction, Eliza Beckwith; with Bryan Close, Helen Coxe, Andrew Eisenman, Laura Hall, Kyle Masteller, Banaue Miclat, Raushanah Simmons, Renaldy Smith, Kristin Villanueva. *Umbrella* by L. Pontius. April 15, 2008. Direction, Padraic Lillis; with Christa Kimlicko Jones, Judson Jones. THE LION. *Fair Game* by Karl Gajdusek. August 20, 2007. Direction, Andrew Volkoff; with Joy Franz, Caralyn Kozlowski, Ray McDavitt, Sarah-Doe Osborne, Brian Sgambati. *None of the Above* by Jenny Lyn Bader. October 10, 2007. Direction, Julie Kramer; with Adam Green, Halley Feiffer. *Acts of Love* by Kathryn Chetkovich. November 6, 2007. Direction, Marc Geller; with Andrew Dawson, Andrew Rein, Abby Royle, Diane Tyler. *The Main(e) Play* by Chad Beckim. January 23, 2008. Direction, Robert O'Hara; with Alexander Alioto, Curran Connor, Susan Dahl, Michael Gladis, Allyson Morgan. *Affluenza!* by James Sherman. March 13, 2008. Direction, Maura Farver; with Nancy Evans, Paul Herbig, Philipe D. Preston, Michael Saenz, Stephen Squibb, Mary Willis White.

13TH STREET REPERTORY COMPANY. Schedule included: *Nunchuck Ninja Nuns* by Lauren M. Cavanaugh. March 14, 2008. Direction, Michael Flanagan; with Kalina Dalton, Errol W. Greaves, Ari Jacobson, Lindsay Johnston, Frank Juste, Katie Nelson-Croner, Danielle Newell, Grace M. Trulli. *A Muse in Manhattan* by Terence Patrick Hughes. April 30, 2008. Direction, Mr. Hughes; with Jeremy Ellison Gladstone, Jack Wann, Susan Stout, Ziad Ghanem. *No More Waiting.* Musical with book and lyrics by Chris Widney; music by David Christian Azarow. May 30, 2008. Direction, Samantha Saltzman; with Brian C. Curl, Dustin J. Harder, Jeni Incontro, Benj Mirman, Jenny Paul.

3LD ART AND TECHNOLOGY CENTER. Schedule included: *Doppelganger* by Simon Heath. June 30, 2007. Direction, Manny Bocchieri; with Metha Brown, Heather Carmichael, Jermaine Chambers, Matt Hanley. *(Rus)h* by James Scruggs. March 1, 2008. Direction, Kristin Marting; with Marc Bovino, Chandra Thomas, Dax Valdes, Luis Vega, Lathrop Walker. *Fire Island* by Charles L. Mee. April 10, 2008. Direction, by Kevin Cunningham; with Tina Alexis Allen, Kiku Collins, Livia de Paolis, Allison Keating, Joshua Koehn, Albert Kuvezin, Jenny Lee Mitchell, Kate Moran, Jon Okabayashi, Stephen Payne, Aldo Perez, Gautham Prasad, Matthew Talmage, David Tirosh, Victor Weinstock, Catherine Yeager. *Architecting* by Davey Anderson, Dave Polato, Lucy Kendrick Smith and Nathan Wright. May 14, 2008. Direction, Rachel Chavkin; with Jessica Almasy, Frank Boyd, Jill Frutkin, Libby King, Jake Margolin, Kristen Sieh.

TRANSPORT GROUP. Schedule included: *Crossing Brooklyn.* Musical with book and lyrics by Laura Harrington; music by Jenny Giering. October 28, 2007. Direction, Jack Cummings III; with J. Bradley Bowers, Jenny Fellner, Blythe Gruda, Susan Lehman, Bryce Ryness, Clayton Dean Smith, Ken Triwush, Kate Weiman, Jason F. Williams. *Marcy in the Galaxy.* Musical with book, music and lyrics by Nancy Shayne. April 6, 2008. Direction, Jack Cummings III; with Janet Carroll, Donna Lynne Champlin, Jenny Fellner, Mary-Pat Green, Jonathan Hammond, Teri Ralston.

T. SCHREIBER STUDIO. Schedule included: *Sister Cities* by Colette Freedman. October 26, 2007. Direction, Cat Parker; with Emberli Edwards, Jamie Neumann, Ellen Reilly, Judith Scarpone, Maeve Yore. *The Night of the Iguana* by Tennessee Williams. March 1, 2008. Direction, Terry Schreiber; with Peter Aguero, Bruce Colbert, Ian Campbell Dunn, Loren Dunn, Denise Fiore, Peter Judd, Alecia Medley, Armando Merlo, Pat Patterson, Derek Roché, Janet Saia, Jenny Strassburg, Gail Willwerth Upp, Guito Wingfield.

UNDER ST. MARKS. Schedule included: *Unaccessorized.* Solo performance piece by Rich Kiamco. June 5, 2007. Direction, Dan Bacalzo; with Mr. Kiamco. *I Google Myself* by Jason Schafer. June 14, 2007. Direction, Jason Jacobs; with Tim Cusack, John Gardner, Reed Prescott. *And We All Wore Leather Pants* by Robert Attenweiler. September 6, 2007. Direction, John Patrick Hayden; with Becky Benhayon, Danny Bruckert, Ariana Shore, Joe Stipek. *Kinderspiel* by Kiran Rikhye. October 4, 2007. Direction, Jon Stancato; with Sam Dingman, Layna Fisher, Cameron J. Oro, Alexia Vernon.

URBAN STAGES. Schedule included: *The Oxford Roof Climber's Rebellion* by Stephen Massicotte. October 12, 2007. Direction, Roger Danforth; with Dylan Chalfy, Stafford Clark-Price, Tom Cleary, Erin Moon, George Morfogen. *The Blue Bird.* Musical by Stanton Wood and Lori Laster; with music by Colm Clark; adapted from the play by Maurice Maeterlinck. December 14, 2007. Direction; Heath Cullens; with Ronit Aranoft, Drew Battles, Diana Buirski, Jenny Gammello, Francis Mateo, Maureen Silliman. *27 Rue de Fleurus.* Musical with book by Ted Sod; music by Lisa Koch; lyrics by Mr. Sod and Ms. Koch. March 6, 2008. Direction, Frances Hill; with Sarah Chalfy, Susan Haefner, Barbara Rosenblat, Cheryl Stern, Emily Zacharias.

THE VACLAV HAVEL FESTIVAL. Schedule included: October 26–November 26, 2007. *Audience*, translated by Jan Novák. Direction, Edward Einhorn; with Dan Leventritt, Scott Simpson. *The Garden Party*, translated by Jan Novák. Direction, Andrea Boccanfuso; with James Bentley, Sergei Burbank, John Kohan, Michael Marion, David Nelson, Steve Russo, Alley Scott, Laura Stockton, Kristine Waters. *The Increased Difficulty of Concentration*, translated by Stepan Simek. Direction, Yolanda Hawkins; with John Hagan, Brad Holbrook, Shira Kobren, Meret Oppenheim, David Ott, Matthew Park, Amy Quint, Kate Reilly. *Largo Desolato*, translated by Tom Stoppard. Direction, Eva Burgess; with Jennifer Boutell, Joshua Briggs, Nancy Nagrant, Jon Okabayashi, Brian Quirk, Erik Kever Ryle, Greg Skura, Skyler Sullivan, Janet Ward. *The Memo*, translated by Paul Wilson. Direction, Edward Einhorn; with Peter Bean, V. Orion Delwaterman, Ryan Dutcher, Talaura Harms, Uma Incrocci, Alice Starr McFarland, Skid Maher, Tom McCarten, Josh Mertz, Shelley Ray, Leah Reddy, Andrew Rothkin, Josh Silverman, Ken Simon, Maxwell Zener. *Protest*, translated by Jan

Novák. Direction, Robert Lyons; with Andy Paris, Richard Toth. *Temptation*, translated by Marie Winn. Direction, Ian W. Hill; with Fred Backus, Eric C. Bailey, Aaron Baker, Danny Bowes, Walter Brandes, Maggie Cino, Tim Cusack, Jessi Gotta, Christiaan Koop, Roger Nasser, Timothy McCown Reynolds, Alyssa Simon.

WALKERSPACE. Schedule included: *Cat's Cradle*. Musical by Henry Akona; adapted by Edward Einhorn from the novel by Kurt Vonnegut. February 23, 2008. Direction Mr. Einhorn; with Sean Allison, Michael Bertolini, John Blaylock, Katherine Boynton, Jerome Brooks, Daryl Brown, Rosalynd Darling, Sarah Engelke, Andrew Haserlat, Sheila Johnson, Jenny McClintock, Martin J. Mitchell, Paul Pricer, Michelle Rabbani, Timothy McCown Reynolds, Horace V. Rogers, Phoebe Silva, Josh Silverman, Darius Stone, Barry Weil, Sandy York.

MICHAEL WELLER THEATRE. Schedule included: *Two Thirds Home* by Padraic Lillis. July 26, 2007. Direction, Giovanna Sardelli; with Peggy J. Scott, Aaron Roman Weiner, Ryan Woodle. *A Yorkshire Fairie Tale* by Thomas H. Diggs. October 1, 2007. Direction, Nancy Robillard; with Jessica Arinella, Matthew G. Rashid. *War Uncensored* by Andrew Carroll. November 8, 2007. Direction, Diana Basmajian; with Marinda Thea Anderson, Joseph Ditmyer, Mark Emerson, Megan Hart, Derrence Washington. *Tender* by Abi Morgan. January 23, 2008. Direction, Kevin O'Rourke; with Betsy Aidem, Noel Joseph Allain, Torsten Hillhouse, Aylsia Reiner, John Rothman, Sarah Megan Thomas, Jeffrey Woodard. *Sunday on the Rocks* by Theresa Rebeck. February 14, 2008. Direction, Bryn Boice; with Lauren Bauer, Leslie Dock, Kelly Howe, Melissa Menzie.

WEST END THEATRE. Schedule included: *Time is the Mercy of Eternity* by Deb Margolin. April 21, 2008. Direction, Marc Stuart Weitz; with Curzon Dobell, Lisa Kron, Khris Lewin, Claire Siebers. *The Witlings* by Frances Burney. May 16, 2008. Direction, Deborah Philips; with George Drance, Casey Groves, Erika Iverson, Wendy Mapes, Frank Mihelich, Rachel Benbow Murdy, Elizabeth Mutton, Gabriel Portuondo, Margi Sharp, Graham Skipper.

WHERE EAGLES DARE THEATRE. Schedule included: *Mothergun* by Christine Evans. June 4, 2007. Direction, Joya Scott; with Claro de los Reyes, Danielle Eliav, David Roberts, Michael R. Rosete. *Barcinda Forest* by Janeen Stevens. April 20, 2008. Direction, Barry Gomolka; with James A. Clark, Sean Demers, Johnny Ferro, Erin Fogel, Ashley Noel Jones, Manny Liyes, Elda Luisi, Jorge Tapia, Mary Trotter.

WINGS THEATRE COMPANY. Schedule included: *The Engagement: A Snatch of Life in 3 Acts* by Carolyn M. Brown and Denise E. Womack. June 15, 2007. Direction, Ms. Womack; with Lashambi Britton, Stephanie Gilchrist, Candice Hassell, Celine Justice, Jamil Mangan, Lorraine Mattox, Kianné Muschett, Tim Romero, Shanell Sapp, Tyron Saulsbury. *Auntie Mayhem* by David Pumo. September 6, 2007. Direction, Donna Jean Fogel; with Moe Bertran, Ivan Davila, Mark Finley, Jason Flores, Carl K. Li, Andre Myers. *DiMaggio: The Man Behind the Myth*. Musical with book, music and lyrics by Robert Mitchell. November 29, 2007. Direction, Don Johanson; with Alissa Alter, Michael Basile, Pamela Brumley, Peter Carrier; Andrew Claus, Joe Cummings, Anna Hanson, Robert Kalman, Stephanie Martinez, John Moss, Matthew Naclerio, Stephen Nichols, Christopher Vettel. *Questa* by Victor Bumbalo. March 1, 2008. Direction, Jeffrey Corrick; with Krista Amigone, Dana Benningfield, Jason Alan Griffin, John Haggerty, Jeremiah Maestas, G. Alverez Reid, Danny Wildman.

WORKSHOP THEATER. Schedule included: *The Guest at Central Park West* by Levy Lee Simon. February 25, 2008. Direction, Thomas Cote; with Harvy Blanks, Curt Bouril, Jed Dickson, Erinn Holmes, John Marshall Jones, Trish McCall, Tracy Newirth. *Domino Courts* by William Hauptman. March 20, 2008. Direction, Michael Mislove; with Michele Ammon, Elizabeth Irene, Curtis Nielsen, Shade Vaughn. *Still Lives* by Paul Hancock. April 4, 2008. Direction, Jocelyn Sawyer; with Jeff Berg, Bridget Barkan, Ashley Davis, Jerzy Gwiazdowski, Tim Intravia, Alixandra Liiv, Candace Thaxton.

ZIPPER THEATER. Schedule included: *The Sensuous Woman* by Margaret Cho. October 6, 2007. Direction, Randall Rapstine; with Ms. Cho, Princess Farhana, Kurt Hall, Ian Harvie, Selene Luna, Dirty Martini, Liam Sullivan, Diana Yanez. *Vita and Virginia* by Eileen Atkins. February 25, 2008. Direction, Pamela Berlin; with Kathleen Chalfant, Patricia Elliot. INNER VOICES: SOLO MUSICALS. May 12, 2008. *Tres Ninas* by Ellen Fitzhugh and Michael John LaChiusa. Direction, Jonathan Butterrell; with Victoria Clark. *Alice Unwrapped* by Laura Harrington and Jenny Giering. Direction, Jeremy Dobrish; with Jennifer Damiano. *A Thousand Words Come to Mind* by Michele Lowe and Scott Davenport Richards. Direction, Jack Cummings III; with Barbara Walsh.

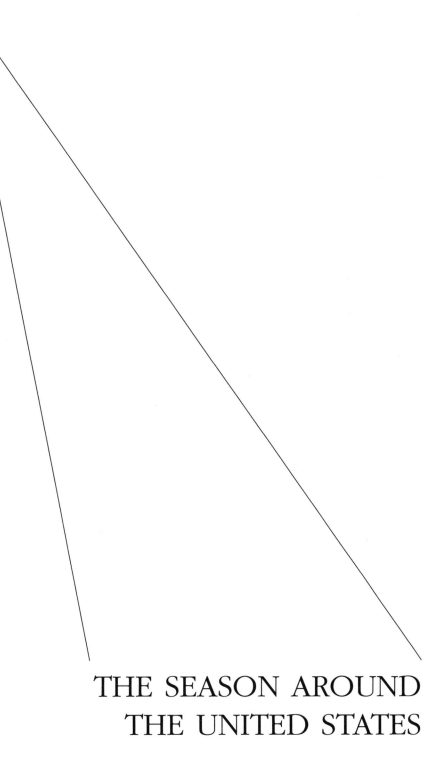

THE SEASON AROUND
THE UNITED STATES

STEINBERG/AMERICAN THEATRE CRITICS
NEW PLAY AWARD AND CITATIONS
○ ○ ○ ○ ○
A DIRECTORY OF NEW
UNITED STATES PRODUCTIONS

THE AMERICAN THEATRE CRITICS ASSOCIATION (ATCA) is the organization of drama critics in all media throughout the United States. One of the group's stated purposes is "To increase public awareness of the theater as a national resource." To this end, ATCA has annually cited outstanding new plays produced around the US, which were excerpted in our series beginning with the 1976–1977 volume. As we continue our policy of celebrating playwrights and playwriting in *Best Plays*, we offer essays on the recipients of the 2008 Harold and Mimi Steinberg/ATCA New Play Award and Citations. The Steinberg/ATCA New Play Award of $25,000 was given to Moisés Kaufman for his play *33 Variations*. The Steinberg/ATCA New Play Citations were given to Deborah Zoe Laufer for *End Days* and Sarah Ruhl for *Dead Man's Cell Phone*. Citation honorees receive prizes of $7,500 each.

The ATCA awards are funded by the Harold and Mimi Steinberg Charitable Trust, which supports theater throughout the United States with its charitable giving. The awards were renamed this year, putting the Steinberg family name first, to honor the trust's renewed (and enhanced) commitment to the honors. The Steinberg/ATCA New Play Award and Citations are given in a ceremony at Actors Theatre of Louisville. Essays in the next section—by Nelson Pressley (*The Washington Post*), Christine Dolen (*The Miami Herald*) and Peter Marks (*The Washington Post*)—celebrate the Steinberg/ATCA Citation honorees.

ATCA's 15th annual M. Elizabeth Osborn Award for a new playwright was voted to Elyzabeth Gregory Wilder for *Gee's Bend*, which was produced in 2007 by the Alabama Shakespeare Festival.

The process of selecting these outstanding plays is as follows: any American Theatre Critics Association member may nominate the first full professional production of a finished play (not a reading or an airing as a play-in-progress) that premieres outside New York City during the calendar year under consideration.

Nominated 2007 scripts were studied and discussed by the New Plays Committee chaired by William F. Hirschman (*South Florida Sun-Sentinel*). The committee included ATCA members Misha Berson (*The Seattle Times*), Michael Elkin (*Jewish Exponent,* Philadelphia), Jay Handelman (*Sarasota Herald Tribune*), Pam Harbaugh (*Florida Today*), George Hatza (*Reading Eagle*), Chad Jones (*The Oakland Tribune*), Elizabeth Keill, (*Independent Press*, New Jersey) Wendy Parker (*Village Mill*, Virginia), Michael Sander (*Back Stage*) and Herbert Simpson (*City Newspaper*, Rochester).

Committee members made their choices on the basis of script rather than production. If the timing of nominations and openings prevents some works from being considered in any given year, they may be eligible for consideration the following year if they have not since moved to New York City.

2008 Steinberg/ATCA New Play Award

33 VARIATIONS
By Moisés Kaufman

○ ○ ○ ○ ○

Essay by Nelson Pressley

> KATHERINE: Variation form allows the composer to slow down time, to pierce the waltz and enter the minutae that life, in its haste, robs us of. One could say that variation form allows us to experience every moment in the waltz.

THE FERVENT EXPLORATION of possibilities is writer-director Moisés Kaufman's theme in *33 Variations*, his drama about a modern musicologist studying Beethoven's famous *Diabelli Variations* for piano, and that ever-questing spirit marked the play's development process, as well. The drama was a departure for Kaufman: For the first time, he was writing a play—inventing characters and situations—and creating a new work outside the bounds of his Tectonic Theater Project. To a significant extent, *33 Variations* represents Kaufman stretching beyond the documentary-fueled process that characterized *The Laramie Project* and *Gross Indecency: The Three Trials of Oscar Wilde*.

Yet Kaufman, 43 when this drama premiered at Arena Stage in August 2007 (in a co-production with Tectonic), did not entirely abandon old habits. He did his homework and then some, digging deep into a genuine musical mystery: why did Ludwig van Beethoven, at the height of his powers, compose 33 variations on a minor waltz by music publisher and impresario Anton Diabelli?

That project began as a publishing gimmick by Diabelli, who supplied his own simple three-minute waltz and recruited dozens of Viennese composers to offer a single variation each. (The result, Diabelli reckoned, would yield a publishing bonanza.) That Beethoven labored for years and produced a landmark of the form without leaving a definitive record of why—in fact, leaving a provocative gap that Kaufman cannily exploits—led Kaufman to his fugue-like consideration of creativity, the struggle for control, mortality and the mystery of human motivation.

Research led to seldom-seen Beethoven manuscripts, and Kaufman the director showed Kaufman the writer how to render this material with

Scholarly seeker: Mary Beth Peil and Graeme
Malcolm in 33 Variations. *Photo: Scott Suchman*

flair. Kaufman's staging at Arena made artful use of sheet music projections, as well as of a concert pianist (Diane Walsh) who played the variations as needed. Reviewing the show for the *Washington Post*, Peter Marks wrote that Kaufman turned the stage into "an exquisite teaching tool." Kaufman includes a note in the script: "There are two more characters in the play: one, the music of Beethoven's *Diabelli Variations*, and two, the images of the original Beethoven sketches projected throughout the piece." The music, printed and played, is indeed influential, supplying an energy that ranges from inspired frenzy to poignant grace as characters face deep loss.

The play's four-year development began at the Sundance Institute and, after the Arena premiere, continued at San Diego's La Jolla Playhouse. This string of workshops and meetings generated a working archive that Kaufman often expanded during rehearsal. According to dramaturg Mark Bly, Kaufman began the Arena production with a 100-page "play document" and another 130 pages of what were termed "unused moments" created by Kaufman with actors in various workshops along the way. "I think that the moment you take one fact and pin it up against another, you're creating a narrative," Kaufman told me in an interview for the *Washington Post*. That the actors were doing a lot of this pinning and re-pinning very late in the process was unnerving to some in the cast, a peril that Kaufman monitored closely. Still, he acknowledged an affinity for the quest, laughing as he said, "We get into a room, we throw text around, we play; we're a mess until a couple of days before tech!"

THE TWO-ACT PLAY is indeed comprised of 33 scenes as it follows the waning months of Dr. Katherine Brandt, a musicologist who appears to be in two places at once as the drama starts.

> KATHERINE: (*in her own world*) Let us begin with the primary cause of things.
> Let us begin with how something came about.
> Why it came about.
> And became what it is.

Kaufman: "We get into a room, we throw text around, we play."

CLARA: Mom.

KATHERINE: (*still in her own world*) It begins with a music publisher, in Vienna. In 1819.

CLARA: Mom.

KATHERINE: (*still in her own world*) The music publisher has written a small waltz that he hopes will . . .

CLARA: MOM!

KATHERINE: (*is brought back to the present by Clara*) What is it?

CLARA: Have you heard a word I said?

KATHERINE: Yes.

CLARA: What did I say?

KATHERINE: You said that they'd call us in soon.

CLARA: No. I said that everyone else who was here before us has gone in. So we're next.

Clara is Katherine's grown daughter, and they are in a hospital waiting room; Katherine has Lou Gehrig's disease (amyotrophic lateral sclerosis). Clara doesn't think her mother should travel to Bonn for research, but Katherine—professionally dedicated and intellectually rigorous to the point of seeming more attached to her work than to her job-hopping daughter—will not be deterred. The nurse they see, a competent but bashful man named Mike, sides with Katherine. As Clara impatiently takes him aside, Katherine continues to address the audience, describing Vienna and introducing Diabelli in terse expository dialogue that straddles the centuries:

> DIABELLI: An invitation!
> To the fifty GREATEST composers in Vienna.
> "My Dear musicians,
> I am enclosing in this letter a new waltz of my own making."
>
> KATHERINE: He was a great music publisher but not so great a composer.

Thus does Katherine open a portal to 19th century Vienna while bluntly establishing her fascination with Beethoven's obsession. Clara, like Katherine, initially addresses the audience directly, explaining that her overachieving mother earned her PhD in record time even as Clara was an infant. That the play is ultimately a mother-daughter story would be hard to divine at this point, but it will become apparent that Katherine views Clara much as she thinks Beethoven regarded Diabelli's charming but decidedly minor waltz. Katherine's attention gravitates toward greatness and Clara disappoints.

The scene shifts to a grumpy Beethoven (Graeme Malcolm, severe in a greatcoat and gray wig) working on Variation 1, then returns to the present as Katherine packs for Germany. Clara offers to quit her costume-design job and accompany her mother, but Katherine complains that Clara will

Love music: Greg Keller and Laura Odeh in 33 Variations. *Photo: Scott Suchman*

never excel if she keeps switching careers. Clara counters that she enjoys mastering something, then moving on. She prefers variations, in other words, though she doesn't put it that way. "Why," Clara asks, "is that any less rigorous than what you do?"

As Katherine declines with ALS, so Beethoven slips into deafness and bouts of madness; Kaufman closely links the minds and bodies of these two temporally separate characters throughout the play. These demanding figures set a heady tone, and the performances enthrall each time they sweep the audience along in the throes of creative or critical discovery. After Kaufman cuts to a second "meet cute" between Clara and Mike (coincidentally stuck in a laptop repair line—their romance is sincere and wry, if not always fresh), we follow Katherine to Bonn and into the Beethoven archives supervised by a stern German librarian named Gertie. There Katherine gets her sought-after glimpse of the recesses of Beethoven's genius.

> GERTIE: This document records his compositional decisions.
>
> (*GERTIE turns the page. A projection of a full page of a sketch appears.*)
>
> Some of these phrases have never been played before.
> Here, this one has never been recorded.
> Look here.
>
> (*Projection. We see the phrase of music in Beethoven's handwriting. It is a zoomed in portion of a sketch for Variation 12.*)
>
> GERTIE: You are hearing an original composition of Beethoven never before heard, except by the people who have read this book!
> (*The pianist plays the phrase that's never been heard before.*)

Who but Kaufman would seek—and find—such thrills in a library? Yet the vividly staged discovery, with Jeff Sugg's sheet music projections dancing across the surface of Derek McLane's elegant set of mobile shelves, yields the same frisson generated by the famous scene of Mozart feverishly dictating to Salieri in *Amadeus*. Kaufman goes the Peter Shaffer play one better, however, by adding the visual element of the projected notes. "It's like looking over his shoulder as he composed," Katherine says a few moments later, as she and Gertie (and the surprised, rapt audience) examine the sketchbook revisions.

KAUFMAN WORKS IN PARALLELS—more variations—shifting from Katherine's study of Beethoven's notations to Clara's discovery of meaning in her mother's most recent e-mail, which is uncharacteristically filled with typos. Likewise, as Katherine fears losing university support, so Beethoven disrespects a patron. As he defensively demonstrates the riches he has mined from just three notes of Diabelli's waltz, he offers a choice that echoes the concerns of artists across the eras: "You can have that, or you can have me talking to the count."

As Mike and Clara edge crablike toward a deeper relationship, Katherine and Gertie strike up a friendship, although both bonds are extremely tentative. Clara is hesitant with Mike because she fears complications as her mother declines, and no one is closer to Katherine than Beethoven, which is illustrated in a stark scene as she undergoes X-rays. In a bit of magic realism, Katherine finds solace resting on the composer himself, who, passing through her medical procedure, is absorbed in his own world. "It's the first time we see the depth of her sadness," Kaufman writes in a program note, and Mary Beth Peil's light, yet commanding performance as Katherine indeed begins to give way to the vulnerability that will characterize Act II.

The Act I curtain is a flurry of urgent dialogue that repeats and merges melodramatically, closing with Beethoven's and Katherine's joint plea as their illnesses close in: "I must have the chance to finish this work." In terms of high drama, the play, like its two towering central figures, has nearly peaked already. Yet if Act I is about the excitement of creation and discovery, Act II explores decay and the difficulty of accepting the end. It demonstrates a seize-the-day sentiment that would make Thornton Wilder smile.

Beethoven's deafness compels him to take questions via notebook, while Katherine's disease threatens her with a speech device that can delivers words typed onto a keyboard. (That Mike uses this gizmo to declare his love for Clara is characteristic of their offbeat relationship, which consistently offers sweet-natured comic counterpoint.) A bizarre laughing fit shows Katherine suffering from "emotional incontinence," answered by Beethoven scrawling on the shutters of yet another rented house from which he will be evicted. If the parallelism begins to seem schematic, as more than one critic suggested—the generally admiring Bob Mondello noted the pattern was "so insistent that the underlying structure begins to seem overly pat," a point echoed by Marks—it may be an inevitable hazard of the variation form. Looking twice, and seeing differently, is the point of Beethoven's exercise—and Kaufman's.

Katherine begins to see things afresh personally as an unlucky new discovery sets her back professionally, and her revelation once again is brought to light by music. Beethoven, again scaling the creative heights as he works on Variation 32, talks out his progressions while the audience luxuriates in the playing by Walsh, and the composer's commentary prefigures what remains of the play: "The world is condensing, refining itself. Then a C flat diminished chord, forcing us toward a resolution. Then an augmented chord. Then again softer and almost disappearing . . ."

KATHERINE IS DYING, and has asked Gertie to give her a lethal dose of morphine after it becomes clear she can no longer communicate. Clara is bitter that her mother cut her out of this plan—even Mike is in on it—but Katherine explains herself to Gertie, saying that her daughter "doesn't see me. You see a musicologist. She sees a patient." Gertie sensibly replies, "She sees her mother," but Katherine's tart and unyielding nature shoves even this ally aside.

Alone, Katherine contemplates Variation 24 as her pointedly prosaic counterparts, Mike and Clara, make love. "How," Katherine asks, recognizing that this was the beginning of the end for Beethoven and the Variations, "does one begin to let go?" Health fails again and she meets Beethoven as she undergoes an MRI. "Oh, I was so hoping I wouldn't hallucinate," she deadpans. "It doesn't look good in a scholar." Finally given her opportunity to speak with the composer, though, the subject isn't music; it's surrender.

Still, it isn't Beethoven who springs the mystery open for Katherine: it is Clara, who absent-mindedly sings Diabelli's waltz because it is melodic—an enjoyable dance. Katherine discovers her thesis at last. As peace and reconciliation descend on all of the characters, they reinforce Katherine's observation on the unique capability of the variation form, which she calls "an exercise in reclaiming all that is fleeting."

Near the play's final moments, Clara delivers Katherine's last public lecture. Katherine is dead, and the words that opened the play are revealed as Beethoven's, now recycled as a kind of benediction. All that remains is a final closing dance, with Beethoven and Katherine ultimately striding side by side as the scene fades to black. The message may appear sentimental, but as Beethoven discovered a complex musical universe from Diabelli, so Kaufman, appropriating the methods of scholarship and the language of music, dances a sophisticated waltz around a timeless theme.

2008 Steinberg/ATCA New Play Citation

DEAD MAN'S CELL PHONE
By Sarah Ruhl

○ ○ ○ ○ ○

Essay by Peter Marks

> MRS. GOTTLIEB: I did not raise my children with any religion. Perhaps I should have. Certain brands of guilt can be inculcated in a secular way but other brands of guilt can only be obtained with reference to the metaphysical.

AS A VIRTUOSO of snap judgments, Mrs. Gottlieb, the stern dowager of Sarah Ruhl's *Dead Man's Cell Phone*, renders a funny, off-the-cuff impression of Jean, the enigmatic younger woman who has wangled a dinner invitation to her grand house:

> MRS. GOTTLIEB: You're very comforting. I don't know why. You're like a very small casserole—has anyone ever told you that?

Jean's reaction is a deadpan "No," but an audience's is more demonstrative: we chuckle, caught off-guard yet again by the peculiar enchantments of the words Ruhl places on characters' lips. Something about equating Jean with a classic dish of slow-cooked ingredients—albeit in "a very small" portion—suggests a flavorful hidden truth about Jean, just as it evokes something surprisingly poetic about Mrs. Gottlieb. And, of course, about Ruhl, too. The dramatist's evident epigrammatic gift, her ability to evoke the quirky curlicues of everyday conversation and to make the most casual observations somehow redolent of personality, is a quality encountered again and again in Ruhl's absurdist, tragicomic works.

It is a signature trait as well of *Dead Man's Cell Phone*, one of the wryest comedies to date by the author of *Passion Play: a Cycle, eurydice* (honored elsewhere in this volume) and *The Clean House*—the last a finalist for the 2005 Pulitzer Prize, a Citation honoree for the 2005 Steinberg/ATCA New Play Award and a 2006–07 Best Play. *Dead Man's Cell Phone* cheekily uses that ubiquitous electronic device as a spiritual conveyance, showing us how portable intimacy has become in modern times, how we can insinuate ourselves into one another's lives as quickly as one can enter a number on speed-dial.

Other women: Jennifer Mendenhall and Polly Noonan in Dead Man's Cell Phone. *Photo: Stan Barouh*

In typical Ruhlian fashion, however, *Dead Man's Cell Phone* does not lend itself to easy categorization. Ruhl's ethereal style is all her own. The play is at once a social satire, a flight of philosophical fancy and a love story. Its dramatic structure, as in her other works, is a porous fabric through which her characters pass as they reveal arcane details about themselves and more incisive truths about the world around them. The locales of *Dead Man's Cell Phone*, for instance, encompass the mundane and the supernatural, places both out of our daily travels and our imaginations, ranging from a dreary cafe to a chamber off the beaten path of the afterlife.

What binds Ruhl's sometimes unruly narratives is her skill at making connections, at taking us to odd corners of the cosmos in works that are playful and often symbol-laden, but always authentic-feeling. At the center of *Dead Man's Cell Phone* is the exploration of a basic human tendency, a weakness to which any of us might succumb: escaping, for however brief an interlude, into the life of someone else.

THE MECHANISM FOR this examination is the intrusive, handheld apparatus that in Ruhl's construct has all but eradicated privacy—has reduced what is public, in a sense, to a cellular level. As the indignant Mrs. Gottlieb declares, after a cell phone rings during her son's memorial service:

MRS. GOTTLIEB: There are only one or two sacred places left in the world today. Where there is no ringing. The theater, the church and the toilet. But some people actually answer their phones in the shitter these days. Some people really do so. How many of you do? Raise your hand if you've answered your cell phone while you were quietly urinating. Yes, I thought so. My God.

It is, in fact, the ringing of a cell phone that sets the events of the play in motion. Jean, the central character, described in the stage directions as having "an insular quality, as though she doesn't want to take up space," is sitting in a virtually empty cafe, drinking coffee, when a phone begins to

The story Ruhl devises comes from a dark place, a precinct of loneliness.

ring repeatedly at another table. It so happens that the phone's owner, Gordon, seated with his back to the audience, is dead. Jean doesn't know this when she utters the play's opening line, "Excuse me—are you going to get that?" Soon enough, she realizes that Gordon has gone to his reward, and unwittingly bequeathed his beckoning cell phone to Jean, who is given a choice: let it ring, or let it lead it to something new.

Are you the type who would answer a stranger's phone? And if you are, what on earth would you say to the caller? These are merely the first of many questions *Dead Man's Cell Phone* provokes. For Jean, as you have surely guessed, does not resist that urge to see who is on the other end of the line. As a result of this simple act of nosiness, she begins to reveal the ways in which she is a woman of considerably more complicated impulses, inclinations and insecurities than the audience possibly could have foreseen.

Dead Man's Cell Phone made its official debut June 16, 2007, at the Woolly Mammoth Theatre Company in Washington, D.C., under the direction of Rebecca Bayla Taichman, a frequent Ruhl collaborator. The company, which specializes in contemporary American plays, many of them world premieres, had a history with Ruhl, too, having staged a production of *The Clean House* two years earlier with Taichman as director.

The six-member cast featured several fine Washington actors, including Rick Foucheux as Gordon and Sarah Marshall as Mrs. Gottlieb, Gordon's mother. Naomi Jacobson played Gordon's wife, Hermia; Bruce Nelson was Gordon's brother, Dwight; and Jennifer Mendenhall portrayed a character identified only as the Other Woman. Anchoring the production was the

Jean of Polly Noonan, a comic actress of impish, off-center appeal, who appears regularly in Ruhl's productions and whom the playwright has described as one of her muses.

For Woolly's sleek downtown Washington space, designed in the courtyard style of the Cottesloe Theatre at London's National Theatre, designer Neil Patel conceived a set that could function as a neutral backdrop for the diverse geography of *Cell Phone*: an imposing, semicircular wall of white brick. It was especially effective for a scene in which Jean and Gordon finally met, not in heaven, but in a sterile custom-made room in hell resembling the cafe where Gordon ordered his last meal. Jean has arrived here, Gordon explains, because "When you die you go straight to the person you most loved, right back to the very moment, the very place, you decided you loved them."

A play of whimsical dimension gives designers special creative license, and here, costume designer Kate Turner-Walker outfits the rich women of the story in evocatively chic suits and dresses. Best are the ensembles for Mrs. Gottlieb, the severity of whose look is reflected in her elaborate furs and decorous eyewear.

Ice queen: Sarah Marshall, Bruce Nelson and Polly Noonan in Dead Man's Cell Phone. *Photo: Stan Barouh*

THE STORY RUHL devises comes from a dark place, a precinct of loneliness. For in answering Gordon's cell phone, Jean not only embarks on an elaborate ruse, pretending to have been a part of Gordon's life, but also creates a purpose to her own existence that otherwise has eluded her. She comes to revel in her role as a sort of angel of consolation for Gordon's survivors—the comforting casserole on a messy banquet table of grief.

The fact is, however, Jean is a better liar than judge of character. Gordon, we learn over the course of *Dead Man's Cell Phone*, was cold, unfaithful and in a deeply questionable line of work: he had a worldwide business in the trafficking of human organs. Not a fellow to whom you'd especially want to devote a pool of tears.

The first part of the play is the amusing chronicle of Jean's baroque pretense, which she finds very easy to perpetrate. On top of everything else, Gordon practiced all kinds of deception himself—and so his relatives offer no resistance to the idea that the woman in possession of his cell phone must be who she says she is. (One of the satisfactions of the work is the rendering of this biting family portrait—particularly of the hilarious Mrs. Gottlieb, a chew-'em-up-and-spit-'em-out matriarch whose diet aptly enough consists entirely of charred meats.)

Jean, for her part, proves to be quick on her feet, able to intuit what Gordon's relations need to hear. Ruhl allows you to see how someone's cell phone could serve as an entry pass to all the intimate nooks and crannies of a life. In this case, those details include a mistress—the aforementioned Other Woman—who seeks out the keeper of the cell phone. Jean takes on as a sacred trust the job of Gordon's mouthpiece—which means she concocts her own fairy tale version of Gordon's thoughts and motives.

> OTHER WOMAN: Gordon and I—we were—well—you know. And so I wanted to know . . . this is going to sound sentimental . . . I wanted to know his last words.
>
> JEAN: That's not sentimental.
>
> OTHER WOMAN: I hate sentiment.
>
> JEAN: I don't think that's sentimental. Really, I don't.
>
> OTHER WOMAN: So. His last words.
>
> JEAN: Gordon mentioned you before he died. Well, he more than mentioned you. He said: Tell her that I love her. And then he turned his face away and died.
>
> OTHER WOMAN: He said that he loved me.
>
> JEAN: Yes.

> OTHER WOMAN: I waited for such a long time. And the
> words—delivered through another woman. What a shit.

How gullible we are, the play seems to be saying, and how easily we will believe a reasonable facsimile of what we suspect to be true. We learn only one biographical fact about Jean, that she works in the office of a Holocaust Museum. It is, of course, a telling detail, as the play revolves to some degree around the notion of how we will be recalled after we die—if we will be recalled at all. Ruhl ties this idea in technological ribbons, suggesting that the digital age clouds rather than clarifies our sense of what we mean, have meant, to each other.

> JEAN: I want to remember everything. Even other people's memories.
>
> DWIGHT: These digital cameras—you know—and all the digital-stuff—the informational bits—flying through the air—no one wants to remember. People say I love you—on cell phones—and where does it go? No paper. Remembering requires paper.

IT IS A MEASURE of Gordon's furtive character that Jean's charade is never uncovered. So tenuous were his bonds to his loved ones that when Jean invents a deathbed keepsake for each of them, they are mollified by the silliest of gifts: To Hermia, his widow, Jean bequeaths the salt shaker that had been on the table at which he died. And she's made happy by it.

Ruhl likes to linger in the chasms of her characters' desperation. It is as if each one in *Dead Man's Cell Phone* is serving a term in solitary confinement, hopeful for emotional parole, unsure it will ever come. The loneliest character of all is Gordon, whom we meet in a monologue at the top of Act II, as he attempts to persuade us that morally questionable decisions are thoroughly appropriate in a morally relativistic universe.

> GORDON: Truth for its own sake—I've never understood the concept. Morality can be measured by results: how good do you make people feel? You make them feel good? Then you're a good man.

By Gordon's lights, Jean is a very good woman. She fabricates aspects of a Gordon who never was, and for her efforts she confers a sense of well-being on the household, cracking the lonely shells of its denizens and establishing a loving relationship for herself, in the arms of Dwight. So perhaps, re-assembling all those airborne informational bits according to her own artful fiction, Jean has developed something better than actual memory. That's the irony that manages to ring through Ruhl's intriguing act of imagination.

2008 Steinberg/ATCA New Play Citation

END DAYS

By Deborah Zoe Laufer

○ ○ ○ ○ ○

Essay by Christine Dolen

RACHEL: Nelson says it's a wonderful time to be alive. Isn't that amazing? That he really feels that way? I always thought that optimism and joy were a sign of low intellect. But he seems fairly bright. When I'm with him, I almost feel hopeful. But then I go home and my mother is waiting for the apocalypse like it's a Greyhound Bus.

THROUGHOUT THE EARLY scenes of Deborah Zoe Laufer's *End Days*, an intelligent and "open-hearted" (her description) comedy that had its world premiere at Florida Stage in October 2007, the optimism to which its angriest character refers is in extremely short supply. Set mostly in the Stein family's condo, two years after the terrorist attacks of September 11, 2001, *End Days* is a contemplation of the resulting shift in our collective psyche. Laufer does not explore just the fear, dread and depression that are predictable reactions to unimaginable catastrophe—although those feelings are laced through her script. More significantly and humorously, the playwright imagines how the traumatized try to get their world to make sense again.

That Laufer could find redemptive laughter in such a subject is not surprising. The Juilliard-educated former actress and standup comic turned to playwriting after her two sons were born. Her full-length plays—*The Last Schwartz* (2002), *The Gulf of Westchester* (2004), *Fortune* (2005), *End Days* (2007) and the upcoming *Out of Sterno* (scheduled for Maine's Portland Stage in March 2009)—are topical, insightful, observant and, though full of the conflict that makes for good drama, pleasurably amusing.

Laufer found a kindred theatrical spirit in Louis Tyrrell, the founder and artistic director of Florida Stage. Located in the wealthy oceanside community of Manalapan, south of Palm Beach, the 250-seat theater is among Florida's best. Tyrrell's longtime mission has been to present new work by playwrights with distinctive voices. Laufer, whose *Last Schwartz*, *Gulf of Westchester* and *End Days* all had their first productions at Florida Stage, is one of Tyrrell's most notable finds. Due to Florida Stage's partnership

The clash: Michaela Cronan and Scott Borish in End Days. *Photo: Sigvision Photography*

with the National New Play Network—whose members stage "rolling world premieres" at multiple theaters and allow playwrights to refine their work through succeeding productions—Laufer's work has had life at theaters throughout the country.

IN *END DAYS*, Sylvia Stein (Elizabeth Dimon) is a woman in her 40s and the formerly atheist daughter of Orthodox Jewish parents. Trying to find meaning and salvation for her family in the post-September 11 world, she has become the most fervent kind of evangelical Christian, a born-again soul who literally walks with (and sips coffee with and talks to) Jesus. The savior is played by an actor (Terry Hardcastle) who also plays another iconic character, physicist Stephen Hawking. These two characters—one religious, the other a scientist—function as imaginary but vividly interacting "friends" to the mother and daughter in the play's grieving family.

Sylvia's husband Arthur (Jim Shankman) is not so much unresponsive as immobilized. He was once the workaholic senior vice-president of a company in the World Trade Center. Sixty-six people were in his office on the day the Twin Towers collapsed; he was the lone survivor. He has been in his bathrobe since, barely eating or bathing, trapped in a cocoon of despair and desolation. The Steins' 16-year-old daughter Rachel (Michaela Cronan) copes with the loss of her parents, who are present physically (except when Sylvia and Jesus go evangelizing) but not emotionally, transformed into unavailable strangers. Going "Goth," Rachel keeps her hostile attitude at a boil. Even so, she attracts the attention of the new kid in school, her neighbor Nelson Steinberg.

A fractured family searches for safe haven from terror and sorrow.

Nelson (Scott Borish) is an orphan, a boy whose mother died when he was young. That trauma triggered a lifelong habit: He wears versions of the Elvis Halloween costume his mom gave him when he was five. Nelson's father remarried, then *he* died. Now Nelson lives with his stepmother and her new Jewish husband. Ever agreeable, Nelson prepares for a three-years-late bar mitzvah, whenever his fellow students are not beating the tar out of him for coming to school in a Vegas-era Elvis suit.

THAT IS HOW Laufer begins the play, with Nelson crooning his own lame ode to the Goth girl at the center of his fantasies. First one milk carton comes flying at him, followed by taunts, followed by a dairy barrage and Nelson's hasty exit.

In the Stein family's kitchen and den, Laufer introduces Sylvia, Arthur and Jesus. Rousing Arthur from his stupor (he has slept slumped on the kitchen table), Sylvia cheerfully outlines her plans for the day:

> SYLVIA: We're going door to door on West Lake this morning. You should join me. And then this afternoon, we're back in front of the triple X video store on Townsend. The first day we prayed there, twenty-two sinners went in. Last night it was less than ten. It's the miracle of prayer.

As Jesus, Sylvia's spiritual king, helps her tote bibles, that other "king" comes calling. Nelson puts his best I'm-crushing-on-your-daughter foot forward, and his enthusiastic reaction to Sylvia's explanation of the coming Rapture makes her think she's got a live one. The boy awkwardly tries to make conversation with Arthur, quickly figuring out that Rachel's father is clinically depressed. Arthur, he suggests, should look into getting some help. When Arthur dismisses his concern, Nelson replies:

> NELSON: That's exactly what my father said, and then one morning we found him hanging from the basement ceiling pipes. None of us saw it coming. So you really can't take these things too lightly. (*There is a long stunned silence.*) That was inappropriate, wasn't it? Too much information. Didn't read the signs. Sorry about that.

Rachel enters and recoils at seeing the Elvis freak in her kitchen. She confronts her father about his ennui, his failure to bring food into the house, his obvious odor. Sylvia invites Nelson to share the good news at her church's healing service on Sunday and—again, ever agreeable—he accepts, though he explains that he is also committed to Hebrew school on the weekends. Rachel and Sylvia revisit what is obviously an ongoing argument: mother trying to "save" her daughter, embarrassed daughter wondering what happened to the woman who used to argue "religion is all bullshit."

In the school cafeteria, Nelson chats with Rachel. He downplays his role as a human target of his fellow students and keeps talking as she tries to ignore him. Then he introduces Rachel to the work of the man who will become as much her hero as Jesus is Sylvia's. Calling Stephen Hawking's *A*

Help us, anyone: Elizabeth Dimon, Scott Borish and Michaela Cronan in End Days. *Photo: Susan Lerner Photography*

Brief History of Time the "greatest book ever written," he gives an indifferent Rachel the briefest summary of its ideas and a short Hawking bio. Reluctantly, she agrees to borrow the book. Then, after an explanation of just why he wears an Elvis outfit, Nelson points out something he finds truly amazing: He, Elvis and Hawking all share the same January 8 birthday. Rachel, ever droll, suggests that perhaps Nelson should consider dressing up like Hawking.

LAUFER NOW BEGINS accelerating the action with shorter scenes. Outside the adult-video store, Sylvia is parked on a folding chair. Enter Jesus, toting coffee for them both. Letting us know that Jesus is, for Sylvia, as real as Arthur or Rachel, Laufer has the two talk, a giddy Sylvia declaring his transformative power:

> SYLVIA: [. . .] Before you came into my life, there's no way in heck I would be out here sipping coffee in broad daylight where any drive-by shooter could take me out. And now—let 'em try. Death is just a gateway to a lifetime with you.

After school, Nelson pays the still-not-dressed Arthur a visit. And in an empty hallway at school, Rachel gets her own surprise visitor: Hawking, in his trademark wheelchair, speaking in a monotone via his computer. She panics, not just because she has been smoking weed but because she fears she's turning into a "nut" like her mother. From the start, Laufer establishes that Hawking has an edge Jesus does not. When Rachel mentions that she is reading *A Brief History of Time*, Hawking asks whether she bought the book. After she says it belongs to Nelson, Hawking replies:

> STEPHEN: You should buy it. I like it w hen people buy it.

Jumping to Nelson and Arthur shopping for cereal at the supermarket, Laufer has Arthur acknowledge the effects of his former workaholism and his present depression on Rachel. He shares a small part of his September 11 story with Nelson, touching on his grief and guilt. And Nelson, upbeat Nelson, suggests that the first step toward recovery might be cereal, lots of it, so he and the Steins can eat breakfast together every morning.

Next, the Steins and Nelson are back at the condo after the Sunday-morning service, Nelson "healed" from his Elvis suit-induced injuries. When they're alone, Rachel calls him on his little miracle, labeling him a "God whore" and arguing that he can't be Jewish on Saturday and evangelical on Sunday. Back and forth they go, Nelson confessing his crush on her, Rachel admitting that she read Hawking's book. Transported, in full science-geek mode, he tells her about the Large Hadron Collider in Switzerland. This works like an aphrodisiac on Rachel, who kisses him repeatedly.

Later, Arthur gets Nelson to sing some of his Torah portion—which he does a la Elvis—then offers to coach him. Nelson sees the stirrings of a man coming back to life, and the two celebrate over cereal. Behind Starbucks, Rachel is partaking of more marijuana and chatting up her new guru. Hawking explains his version of end days to her, one not nearly as rapturous as the saved flying up to heaven.

In the final scene of Act I, Sylvia pesters Jesus, manipulating him into telling her exactly when the Rapture will happen—which is Wednesday. She begs him not to leave her family behind. But he takes his leave, observing that he has to go in order to come back.

AS ACT II BEGINS, it is two days and counting until Armageddon. Sylvia, far from being able to keep Jesus's confidence, has told "a few people" that the Rapture is just around the corner—her minister, the congregation, anyone who reads the Penny Saver, all the folks who grabbed one of her flyers outside the grocery store. Rachel is, no surprise, mortified. Sylvia begs her daughter to stay home from school Wednesday so that they can all go to heaven together. Arthur, on the road to emotional recovery as evidenced by his stocking of the refrigerator and cupboards, wonders if the milk will keep while they are away.

Nelson arrives, and after Sylvia explains what is about to happen, he offers to bring his special dip with onion soup and water chestnuts to the family's pre-Rapture vigil. Rachel strikes a bargain with her mother: If she stays home and Jesus doesn't show by midnight Wednesday, Sylvia will give it all up: Jesus. Evangelizing. The works.

When Nelson returns for the vigil he is—surprise!—not wearing the Elvis outfit. As with Arthur's shopping, it is a sign of healing. Sylvia asks for prayer and repentance; the others keep going on tangents, until finally she thunders:

> SYLVIA: *Just ask for forgiveness all right!?* Could you all just ask Jesus for forgiveness? This really doesn't have to be so complicated! If you could all just FOCUS and get your minds off dip and waffles and chips and your Uncle Morty, if you could all just FOCUS, maybe you could be forgiven and saved and raptured and not left to burn in the fiery furnace of hell on Earth!!! Okay?

The family and the boy who adores them pass the night noshing, watching *Left Behind*, sleeping, talking about faith and science, and revisiting the past. A thunderstorm, complete with hail, seems to Sylvia to be the beginning of the end. But the long day and night bring something else: emotional revelations, real vulnerability and a new beginning.

In *End Days*, Laufer creates a fractured family searching for a safe haven, people trying to escape overwhelming terror and sorrow through religion, science or other means. The answer she suggests, similar to Dorothy's "there's no place like home" in *The Wizard of Oz*, is that salvation can happen anywhere—even in a condo—if we will only connect, support and love one another.

A DIRECTORY OF NEW
UNITED STATES PRODUCTIONS
○ ○ ○ ○ ○
Compiled by Jennifer Ashley Tepper

THIS LISTING INCLUDES professional productions that opened during the June 1, 2007–May 31, 2008 season. Its focus is on new plays—and other productions of note—by a variety of resident companies around the United States. Production information listed here in alphabetical order, by state, was obtained from the producing organizations included and from editorial research in various databases. Resident theaters producing new plays and operating under contracts with Actors' Equity Association are queried for this comprehensive directory. Active US theater companies not included in this list may not have presented new (or newly revised) scripts during the year under review or had not submitted production information by July 1, 2008. Productions listed below are world premieres, US premieres, regional premieres, substantial revisions or otherwise worthy of note. Relatively new plays that have received widespread production are not listed here due to space and other considerations. Theaters in the US are encouraged to submit proposed listings of new works, new adaptations and other productions of significant concept or cast to the editor of *The Best Plays Theater Yearbook* series.

ALABAMA

Alabama Shakespeare Festival, Montgomery
Geoffrey Sherman producing artistic director

ROCKET CITY. By Mark Saltzman. April 20, 2008 (world premiere). Direction, David Ellenstein; scenery, Michael Schweikardt; costumes, Susan Branch; lighting, Mike Post; sound, Richelle Thompson; dramaturgy, Susan Willis; stage management, Sarah Lee Howell.

Amy Lubin	Lori Prince	Harry S. Truman; others	Paul Hopper
Major Hamilton Pike Jr.	Fletcher McTaggart	General Barklee; others	Ralph Elias
Jed Kessler	Daniel Cameron Talbott	Susanna Pruitt; Sarah	Greta Lambert
Wernher Von Braun	Matt Bradford Sullivan	Bertina Dupray; others	Suzanna Hay
Israel Watkins	James Bowen		

ALABAMA

ARIZONA

Arizona Theatre Company, Tucson

David Ira Goldstein artistic director, Jessica L. Andrews managing director

THE CLEAN HOUSE. By Sarah Ruhl. April 5, 2008. Direction, Jon Jory; scenery, Neil Patel; costumes, Lorraine Venberg; lighting, Brian J. Lilienthal; sound, Matt Callahan; stage management, Glenn Bruner. Presented in association with Actors Theatre of Louisville.

Lane .... Felicity La Fortune	Ana .... Rae C Wright
Virginia .... Kate Goehring	Ensemble .... Charlotte Bernhardt,
Charles .... Bernard Burak Sheredy	Julie Marie Garrison
Matilde............................... Alexandra Tavares	

ARKANSAS

Arkansas Repertory Theatre, Little Rock

Robert Hupp producing artistic director

IT HAPPENED IN LITTLE ROCK. By Rajendra Ramoon Maharaj. September 14, 2007 (world premiere). Direction, Mr. Maharaj; choreography, Michael Susko; music direction, Charles Creath; scenery, Mike Nichols; costumes, Leslie Bernstein; lighting, Matthew Webb; sound, M. Jason Pruzin; stage management, Brian Westmoreland.

Performed by Julian Rebolledo, Taïfa Harris, Nick Petrie, Mary-Pat Green, Arthur W. Marks, Gia McGlone, J. Bernard Calloway, Shannon Lamb, Vanessa Lemonides, Steve Hudelson, Destan Owens.

Presented without intermission.

CALIFORNIA

American Conservatory Theater, San Francisco

Carey Perloff artistic director, Heather Kitchen executive director

THE IMAGINARY INVALID. By Molière; adapted by Constance Congdon. June 13, 2007. Direction, Ron Lagomarsino; scenery, Erik Flatmo; costumes, Beaver Bauer; lighting, Nancy Schertler; sound and music, Fabian Obispo; music direction, Frank Johnson; dramaturgy, Michael Paller; stage management, Kimberly Mark Webb.

Argan .... John Apicella	Dr. Purgeon .... Steven Anthony Jones
Beline .... René Augesen	M. De Bonnefoi;
Angelique .... Allison Jean White	M. Fleurant .... Anthony Fusco
Cleante .... Jud Williford	Toinette .... Nancy Dussault
Claude de Aria .... Gregory Wallace	

Ensemble: Margarett Head, Maureen McVerry, Brian Stevens.

Presented in two parts.

ARIZONA – ARKANSAS – CALIFORNIA

BRAINPEOPLE. By José Rivera. February 2, 2008. Direction, Chay Yew; scenery, Daniel Ostling; costumes, Lydia Tanji; lighting, Paul Whitaker; sound, Cliff Caruthers; dramaturgy, Michael Paller; stage management, June Palladino.

Mayannah	Lucia Brawley	Rosemary	René Augesen
Ani	Sona Tatoyan		

Presented without intermission.

CURSE OF THE STARVING CLASS. May 30, 2008. By Sam Shepard. Direction, Peter DuBois; scenery, Loy Arcenas; costumes, Lydia Tanji; lighting, Japhy Weideman; sound, Fabian Obispo; stage management, Elisa Guthertz.

Wesley	Jud Williford	Ellis	Rod Gnapp
Ella	Pamela Reed	Malcolm	Craig Marker
Emma	Nicole Lowrance	Emerson	T. Edward Webster
Taylor	Dan Hiatt	Slater	Howard Swain
Weston	Jack Willis		

Presented in two parts.

Berkeley Repertory Theatre
Tony Taccone artistic director, Susan Medak managing director

TAKING OVER. By Danny Hoch. January 16, 2008 (world premiere). Direction, Tony Taccone; scenery and costumes, Annie Smart; lighting, Alexander V. Nichols; stage management, Michael Suenkel.

Performed by Mr. Hoch.
Presented without intermission.

TRAGEDY: A TRAGEDY. By Will Eno. March 19, 2008. Direction, Les Waters; scenery, Antje Ellermann; costumes, Meg Neville; lighting, Matt Frey; sound, Cliff Caruthers; stage management, Michael Suenkel.

Frank in the Studio	David Cromwell	Constance	
Michael;		at the Home	Marguerite Stimpson
Legal Advisor	Max Gordon Moore	Witness	Danny Wolohan
John in the Field	Thomas Jay Ryan		

Presented without intermission.

Center Theatre Group, Los Angeles
Michael Ritchie artistic director

CLAY. By Matt Sax. September 19, 2007. Directon, Eric Rosen; scenery, Walt Spangler; lighting, Howell Binkley; sound and orchestrations, Joshua Horvath; stage management, Elizabeth Atkinson; in the Kirk Douglas Theatre. Presented in association with Chicago's About Face Theatre and Lookingglass Theatre Company.

Performed by Mr. Sax.
Presented without intermission.

EN UN SOL AMARILLO. By César Brie. October 28, 2007. Direction, Mr. Brie; scenery, Gonzalo Callejas; costumes, Soledad Ardaya and Danuta Zarzyka; lighting and sound,

CALIFORNIA

Giampaolo Nalli and Ms. Zarzyka; in the Kirk Douglas Theatre. Presented in association with Teatro de los Andes of Bolivia.

Performed by Lucas Achirico, Daniel Aguirre, Gonzalo Callejas, Alice Guimaraes.

Presented without intermission.

THE HISTORY BOYS. By Alan Bennett. November 14, 2007. Direction, Paul Miller; scenery, Bob Crowley; lighting, Mark Henderson; sound, Colin Pink and Jon Gottlieb; music, Richard Sisson; video, Ben Taylor and Austin Switser; stage management, James T. McDermott; in the Ahmanson Theater.

Hector	Dakin Matthews	Dakin	Seth Numrich
Irwin	Peter Paige	Lockwood	Adam Armstrong
Mrs. Lintott	Charlotte Cornwell	Posner	Alex Brightman
Headmaster	H. Richard Greene	Rudge	Cord Jackman
Akthar	Ammar Ramzi	Scripps	Brett Ryback
Crowther	Demond Robertson	Timms	Sean Marquette

Ensemble: John Apicella, Ryder Bach, Andrew McClain, Edward Tournier, Elizabeth West.

Presented in two parts.

BLOODY BLOODY ANDREW JACKSON. Musical with book by Alex Timbers; music and lyrics by Michael Friedman. January 2, 2008 (world premiere). Direction, Mr. Timbers; choreography, Kelly Devine; scenery, Robert Brill; costumes, Emily Rebholz; lighting, Jeff Croiter; sound, Bart Fasbender; projections, Jake Pinholster; music direction and orchestrations, Gabriel Kahane; stage management, David S. Franklin; in the Kirk Douglas Theatre. Presented in association with the Public Theater, New York.

Andrew Jackson	Benjamin Walker	Red Eagle	Greg Hildreth
Rachel	Anjali Bhimani	Van Buren	Brian Hostenske
Lyncoya	Sebastian Gonzalez	Calhoun	Adam O'Byrne
Clay	Will Greenberg		

Ensemble: Will Collyer, Diane Davis, Zack DeZon, Erin Felgar, Kristin Findley, Jimmy Fowlie, Patrick Gomez, Matthew Rocheleau, Ben Steinfeld, Ian Unterman, Taylor Wilcox.

Presented without intermission.

TWO UNRELATED PLAYS BY DAVID MAMET. By Mr. Mamet. May 18, 2008. Direction, Neil Pepe; scenery, Takeshi Kata; costumes, Ilona Somogyi; lighting, Christopher Akerlind; sound, Cricket S. Myers; production stage manager, David S. Franklin; in the Kirk Douglas Theatre.

The Duck Variations

Emil Varec	Harold Gould	George S. Aronovitz	Michael Lerner

Keep Your Pantheon

Strabo	Ed O'Neill	Titus	J.J. Johnston
Pelargon	David Paymer	Lupus Albus Secundus	Dominic Hoffman
Philius	Michael Cassidy	Quintus Magnus	Steven Goldstein
Ramus	Jack Wallace	Herald	Vincent Guastaferro

Presented in two parts.

CALIFORNIA

East West Players, Los Angeles
Tim Dang producing artistic director

DURANGO. By Julia Cho. September 19, 2007. Direction, Chay Yew; scenery, Donna Marquet; costumes, Dori Quan; lighting, Jose Lopez; projections, Jason Thompson; sound, John Zalewski; stage management, Seth Kolarsky.

Boo-Seng Lee	Nelson Mashita	Jerry; Ned	John Apicella
Isaac Lee	Jin Suh	Red Angel; Bob	Alex Klein
Jimmy Lee	Ryan Cusino		

Presented without intermission.

DAWN'S LIGHT. By Jeanne Sakata. November 7, 2007 (world premiere). Direction, Jessica Kubzansky; scenery and projections, Naiko Nezu; costumes, Soojin Lee; lighting, Jeremy Pivnick; sound, John Zalewski; stage management, Nate Genung.

Gordon Hirabayashi .... Ryun Yu

Presented without intermission.

VOICES FROM OKINAWA. By Jon Shirota. February 13, 2008 (world premiere). Direction, Tim Dang; scenery, Mina Kinukawa; costumes, Soojin Lee; lighting, Guido Girardi; sound, Dave Iwataki; stage management, Ondina V. Dominguez.

Kama	Joseph Kim	Hitoshi	Atsushi Hirata
Obaa-san	Amy Hill	Harue	Teruko Kataoka
Takeshi	Taishi Mizuno	Namiye	Mari Ueda
Keiko	Sachiko Hayashi	Yasunobu	Kotaro Watanabe

PIPPIN. Musical with book by Roger O. Hirson; music and lyrics by Stephen Schwartz. May 14, 2008. Direction, Tim Dang; music direction, Marc Macalintal; choreography, Blythe Matsui and Jason Tyler Chong; scenery and projections, Alan E. Muraoka; costumes, Naomi Yoshida; lighting, Dan Weingarten; stage management, Ronn Gosswick.

Leading Player	Marcus Choi	Catherine	Maegan McConnell
Pippin	Ethan Le Phong	Berthe	Gedde Watanabe
Charles	Mike Hagiwara	Lewis	Cesar Cipriano
Fastrada	Jenn Aedo	Theo	William Jay

Ensemble: Kari Lee Cartwright, Ryyn Chua, Blythe Matsui, Mike Moh, Chloe Stewart.
Presented in two parts.

Geffen Playhouse, Los Angeles
Gilbert Cates producing director

THIRD. By Wendy Wasserstein. September 19, 2007. Direction, Maria Mileaf; scenery, Vince Mountain; costumes, Alex Jaeger; lighting, David Lander; music, Michael Roth; stage management, Dana Victoria Anderson.

Nancy	Jayne Brook	Laurie	Christine Lahti
Third	Matt Czuchry	Jack	M. Emmet Walsh
Emily	Sarah Drew		

Presented in two parts.

CALIFORNIA

THE QUALITY OF LIFE. By Jane Anderson. October 10, 2007 (world premiere). Direction, Ms. Anderson; scenery, Francois-Pierre Couture; costumes, Christina Haatainen Jones; lighting, Jason H. Thompson; sound, Karl Lundeberg; stage management, Anna Belle Gilbert.

Bill	Scott Bakula	Jeannette	Laurie Metcalf
Neil	Dennis Boutsikaris	Dinah	JoBeth Williams

Presented in two parts.

SOME GIRLS. By Neil LaBute. February 6, 2008. Direction, Mr. LaBute; scenery, Sibyl Wickersheimer; costumes, Lynette Meyer; lighting, Kristie Roldan; sound, Cricket Myers; production stage manager, Mary Michele Miner.

Lindsay	Rosalind Chao	Tyler	Justina Machado
Guy	Mark Feuerstein	Bobbi	Jaime Ray Newman
Sam	Paula Cale Lisbe		

Presented without intermission.

JOAN RIVERS: A WORK IN PROGRESS BY A LIFE IN PROGRESS. By Ms. Rivers, Douglas Bernstein and Denis Markell. February 13, 2008 (world premiere). Direction, Bart DeLorenzo; scenery, Tom Buderwitz; costumes, Christina Haatainen Jones; lighting, Rand Ryan; sound, John Ballinger; projections, Austin Switser; stage management, Elizabeth A. Brohm.

Herself	Joan Rivers	Svetlana	Emily Kosloski
Evan	Tara Joyce	Kenny	Adam Kulbersh

Ensemble: Dorie Barton, Leo Marks, Melissa Rivers.

Presented without intermission.

Laguna Playhouse, Laguna Beach
Andrew Barnicle artistic director

THE VERDI GIRLS. By Bernard Farrell. June 3, 2007 (world premiere). Direction, Andrew Barnicle; scenery, Dwight Richard Odle; costumes, Julie Keen; lighting, Paulie Jenkins; sound, David Edwards; stage management, Rebecca Michelle Green.

Linda	Elyse Mirto	Oliver	Gregory North
Breda	Katharine McEwan	Mario	Vasili Bogazianos
Pete	Bo Foxworth	Mrs. Green	Patricia Cullen
Patricia	Traci L. Crouch		

Presented in two parts.

TRANCED. By Bob Clyman. January 5, 2008 (world premiere). Direction, Jessica Kubzansky; scenery, Narelle Sissons; costumes, Julie Keen; lighting, Jeremy Pivnick; sound, David Edwards; stage management, Rebecca Michelle Green.

Dr. Philip Malaad	Thomas Fiscella	Beth	Ashley West Leonard
Azmera	Erica N. Tazel	Logan	Andrew Borba

Presented in two parts.

CALIFORNIA

RED HERRING. By Michael Hollinger. February 16, 2008. Direction, Andrew Barnicle; scenery, Bruce Goodrich; costumes, Julie Keen; lighting, Paulie Jenkins; sound, David Edwards; stage management, Vernon Willet.

Maggie Pelletier	Kirsten Potter	James Appel; others	Brett Ryback
Frank Keller; others	Brendan Ford	Mrs. Kravitz; others	DeeDee Rescher
Lynn McCarthy; Clerk	Traci L. Crouch	Andrei Borchevsky; others	Tom Shelton

Presented in two parts.

BROWNSTONE. By Catherine Butterfield. March 29, 2008 (world premiere). Direction, Ms. Butterfield; scenery, Lauren Helpern; costumes, Julie Keen; lighting, Paulie Jenkins; sound, David Edwards; stage management, Rebecca Michelle Green.

Davia	Deborah Puette	Deena	Dorothea Harahan
Stephen	Brian Rohan	Jessica	Laurie Naughton
Maureen	Kim Shively	Jason	Gino Anthony Pesi

Presented in two parts.

La Jolla Playhouse
Christopher Ashley artistic director, Steven B. Libman managing director

CARMEN. Musical with book by Sarah Miles; music by John Ewbank; lyrics by AnnMarie Milazzo; based on Prosper Mérimée's *Carmen*. June 17, 2007. Direction, Franco Dragone; choreography, Ms. Miles; scenery, Klara Zieglerova; costumes, Suzy Benzinger; lighting, Christopher Akerlind; music direction, Jeffrey Klitz; fight direction, Steve Rankin; stage management, Phyllis Schray.

Carmen	Janien Valentine	Zuniga	Neal Benari
Jose	Ryan Silverman	Lillias Pastia	Genson Blimline
Escamillo	Victor Wallace	Garcia	Caesar Samayoa
Micaela	Shelley Thomas		

Ensemble: Iresol Cardona, Gabriel Croom, Noemi Del Rio, Maria Eberline, Tony Falcon, Jacqui Graziano, Shannon Lewis, Jorge E. Maldonado, Michelle Marmolejo, Rocio Ponce, Marcos Santana, Carlos Sierra-Lopez, Natalia Zisa.

Musical numbers included: "Espana Viva (The Living Spain)," "In the Place of Good Men," "This Is Not Our Last Goodbye," "God Will Make Us Men," "Your Heart at All Cost," "Carmen's Theme," "Freedom Is Now," "Gordo," "Ah Men," "The Factory Fight," "What Is Worth a Life?," "Injusticia," "Ah Men" (Reprise), "The Letter," "A Free Man Today," "The Desert," "To Say Goodbye," "Tavern Dance," "Ole," "This Dance Is Not Over," "The Prayer," "I Will Love You Always—Lullaby," "Touch the Sun," "The Ritual," "Jose's Freedom," "What I See," "What Is My Heart?," "The Last Kick," "This Dance Is Beginning," "I Will Love You Always," "Finale—What I See."

Presented in two parts.

THE DECEPTION. By Marivaux; adapted by Steven Epp and Dominique Serrand. July 22, 2007. Direction, Mr. Serrand; scenery, David Coggins; costumes, Sonya Berlovitz; lighting, Marcus Dilliard; sound, Zachary Humes; stage management, Benjamin McGovern. Presented in association with Theatre de la Jeune Lune, Minneapolis.

Chevalier	Merritt Janson	Trivelin	J.C. Cutler
Lelio	Casey Greig	Arlequino	Nathan Keepers
The Countess	Emily Gunyou Halaas		

CALIFORNIA

Ensemble: Dorian Christian Baucum, Michelle Diaz, Liz Elkins, Larry Herron, Brandon D. Taylor.

Presented in two parts.

THE ADDING MACHINE. By Elmer Rice. September 16, 2007. Direction, Daniel Aukin; scenery, Andrew Lieberman; costumes, Maiko Matsushima; lighting, Japhy Weideman; sound, Colbert S. Davis IV; music, Cassia Streb; stage management, Anjee Nero.

Mr. Zero	Richard Crawford	Shrdlu	Joshua Everett Johnson
Daisy; Mrs. Two	Diana Ruppe	Mrs. Zero	Jan Leslie Harding

Ensemble: Walter Belenky, Molly Fite, Liz Jenkins, Rufio Lerma, Paul Morgan Stetler, Peter Wylie.

Presented in two parts.

MOST WANTED. Musical with book by Jessica Hagedorn; music by Mark Bennett; lyrics by Mr. Bennett and Ms. Hagedorn. October 2, 2007. Direction, Michael Greif; choreography, Javier Velasco; scenery, Steven C. Kemp; costumes, Clint Ramos; lighting, Tom Ontiveros; sound, Philip G. Allen; music direction and arrangements, Charlie Alterman; orchestrations, Dan Lipton; dramaturgy, Shirley Fishman; stage management, J. Philip Bassett. A Page to Stage Workshop production.

Lee Reyes; Apolo Serra	Arthur Acuña	Teresa Reyes; Apolonia Serra	Leah Hocking
Elizabeth Mitchell	Merle Dandridge	Daddyo; others	Peter Kapetan
Angie Reyes; others	Zandi De Jesus	Stormy Leather	Ken Page
Chris Bradley; Javier Luna	Danny Gurwin	Daddyo; others	David Nathan Perlow
Daddyo; others	Michael Grant Hall	Danny Reyes	Daniel Torres
Soprano; others	Kathleen Halm		

Presented in two parts.

CRY-BABY. Musical with book by Mark O'Donnell and Thomas Meehan; music and lyrics by Adam Schlesinger and David Javerbaum; based on the film by John Waters. November 18, 2007. Direction, Mark Brokaw; choreography, Rob Ashford; scenery, Scott Pask; costumes, Catherine Zuber; lighting, Howell Binkley; sound, Peter Hylenski; music direction and incidental music, Lynne Shankel; orchestrations, Christopher Jahnke; stage management, Mahlon Kruse.

Wade "Cry-Baby" Walker	James Snyder	Dupree	Chester Gregory II
Allison	Elizabeth Stanley	Pepper	Carly Jibson
Mrs. Vernon-Williams	Harriet Harris	Wanda	Lacey Kohl
Baldwin	Christopher J. Hanke	Mona	Cristen Paige
Lenora	Alli Mauzey	Judge Stone	Richard Poe

Ensemble: Cameron Adams, Ashley Amber, Nick Blaemire, Michael Buchanan, Eric L. Christian, Colin Cunliffe, Joanna Glushak, Stacey Todd Holt, Michael D. Jablonski, Marty Lawson, Spencer Liff, Courtney Laine Mazza, Mayumi Miguel, Tory Ross, Eric Sciotto, Peter Matthew Smith, Allison Spratt, Charlie Sutton.

Musical numbers included: "The Anti-Polio Picnic," "Watch Your Ass," "One Tear," "I'm Infected," "Squeaky Clean," "Let's Disappear," "Jukebox Jamboree," "Screw Loose," "Class Dismissed," "Baby Baby Baby Baby Baby (Baby Baby)," "Can I Kiss You . . .?," "I'm Infected" (Reprise), "You Can't Beat the System," "Misery, Agony, Helplessness, Hopelessness, Heartache and Woe," "All in My Head," "Jailyard Jubilee," "A Little Upset," "I Did Something Wrong . . . Once," "Thanks for the Nifty Country!," "This Amazing Offer," "Do That Again," "Nothing Bad's Ever Gonna Happen Again."

CALIFORNIA

THE SEVEN. Musical with book and lyrics by Will Power; music by Mr. Power, Will Hammond and Justin Ellington; adapted from Aeschylus's *Seven Against Thebes*. February 17, 2008. Direction, Jo Bonney; choreography, Bill T. Jones; scenery, Richard Hoover; costumes, Emilio Sosa; lighting, David Weiner; sound, Darron L. West; projections, Robin Silvestri; music direction, Daryl Waters; stage management, Wendy Ouellette. Presented in association with New York Theatre Workshop.

Oedipus	Edwin Lee Gibson	Tydeus	Flaco Navaja
Eteocles	Benton Greene	Right Hand	Bernard White
Polynices	Jamyl Dobson	DJ	Chinasa Ogbuagu

Ensemble: Uzo Aduba, Dashiell Eaves, Shaneeka Harrell, Postell Pringle, Pearl Sun, Charles Turner.

Presented in two parts.

Magic Theatre, San Francisco
Chris Smith artistic director, David Jobin managing director

EXPEDITION 6. By Bill Pullman. September 15, 2007 (world premiere). Direction, Mr. Pullman; choreography, Robert Davidson; scenery and lighting, Kate Boyd; costumes, Callie Floor; sound, Sara Huddleston; music, Gary Grundei; stage management, Angela Nostrand. Presented in association with Chabot Space and Science Center.

Performed by Arwen Anderson, John Behlmann, Sally Clawson, Nora El Samahy, Karl Hanover, Robert Karma Robinson, Brent Rose, Justin Walvoord.

Presented in two parts.

THE CROWD YOU'RE IN WITH. By Rebecca Gilman. November 17, 2007. Direction, Amy Glazer; scenery, Erik Flatmo; costumes, Meg Neville; lighting, Kurt Landisman; sound, Sara Huddleston; stage management, Angela Nostrand.

Jasper	T. Edward Webster	Karen	Lorri Holt
Melinda	Makela Spielman	Tom	Charles Shaw Robinson
Dan	Kevin Rolston	Dwight	Chris Yule
Windsong	Allison Jean White		

Presented without intermission.

TERRITORIES. By Betty Shamieh. January 19, 2008. Direction, Jessica Heidt; choreography, Monique Jenkinson; scenery, Melpomene Katakalos; costumes, Fumiko Bielefeldt; lighting, Ray Oppenheimer; sound, Will McCandless; stage management, Karen Runk.

Saladin	Alfredo Narciso	Reginald	Rod Gnapp
Alia	Nora el Samahy		

Presented without intermission.

TIR NA NOG. By Edna O'Brien; based on her novel *The Country Girls*. March 1, 2008. Direction, Chris Smith; choreography, Jean Butler; scenery, Annie Smart; costumes, Cassandra Carpenter; lighting, Kurt Landisman; sound, Sara Huddleston; music direction, Mary Pitchford; stage management, Angela Nostrand.

Performed by Deborah Black, Anne Darragh, Matt Foyer, Robert Parsons, Ms. Pitchford, Summer Serafin, Cat Thompson, Michael Louis Wells, Allison Jean White.

Presented in two parts.

CALIFORNIA

OCTOPUS. By Steve Yockey. May 17, 2008. Direction, Kate Warner; scenery, Erik Flatmo; costumes, Alexae Visel; lighting, Jarrod Fischer; sound, Sara Huddleston; stage management, Angela Nostrand. Presented in association with Encore Theatre Company.

Blake	Patrick Alparone	Andy	Brad Erickson
Kevin	Eric Kerr	Telegram Delivery Boy	Rowan Brooks
Max	Liam Vincent		

Presented without intermission.

Marin Theatre Company, Mill Valley
Jasson Minadakis artistic director, Ryan Rilette managing director

LOVE SONG. By John Kolvenbach. September 11, 2007. Direction, Jasson Minadakis; scenery, Eric Sinkkonen; costumes, Laura Hazlett; lighting, Kurt Landisman; sound, Steve Schoenbeck; dramaturgy, Maryanne Olson; stage management, Risa Aratyr.

Beane	Darren Bridgett	Harry	Steve Irish
Joan	Julia Brothers	Waiter	Will Springhorn Jr.
Molly	Jody Flader		

Presented without intermission.

FOUND OBJECTS. By Kenn Rabin. October 10, 2007 (world premiere). Direction, Robin Stanton; lighting, Selena Young; projections, Kurt Wobken; dramaturgy, Maryanne Olson; stage management, Courtney Ames.

Patricia	Julia Brothers	David	Tim Kniffin
Martin	Michael Keys Hall	Chloe	Summer Serafin

LOVERS AND EXECUTIONERS. By John Strand. November 20, 2007. Direction, Josh Costello; scenery, Steve Coleman; costumes, Fumiko Bielefeldt; lighting, Lucas Krech; sound, Chris Houston; stage management, Risa Aratyr.

Constance	Alexandra Creighton	Beatrice	Gwen Loeb
Bernard	Jackson Davis	Julie; Frederick	Lisa Anne Porter
Don Lope	Lance Gardner	Octavius	Liam Vincent
Guzman	Gary Grossman		

SAID SAÏD. By Kenneth Lin. February 5, 2008. Direction, Jasson Minadakis; scenery, John Wilson; costumes, Michele Wynne; lighting, Kurt Landisman; sound, Chris Houston; stage management, Peter Royston.

Garcet	Marvin Greene	Sarah	Delia McDougall
Emily	Danielle Levin	Saïd	Jarion Monroe

LOVE PERSON. By Aditi Brennan Kapil. April 27, 2008. Direction, Gia Forakis; scenery, Eric Sinkkonen; costumes, Michele Wynne; lighting, Stephanie Buchner; sound and music, Chris Houston; choreography, Sally Christian; video, Erin Gilley; dramaturgy, Maryanne Olson; stage management, Risa Aratyr.

Vic	Emily Morrison	Maggie	Cathleen Riddley
Ram	Janak Ramachandran	Free	Mary Colleen Vreeland

CALIFORNIA

New Conservatory Theatre Center, San Francisco
Ed Decker artistic and executive director

HOLDING THE MAN. By Tommy Murphy; adapted from a novel by Timothy Conigrave. September 29, 2007. Direction, Matthew Graham Smith; scenery, Jon Wai-keung Lowe; costumes, Prem Lathi.

Tim Conigrave .... Ben Randle   John Caleo .... Bradly Mena
    Ensemble: Danielle Perata, Dennis Parks, Nicole Lungerhausen, Wesley Cayabyab.
    Presented in two parts.

Pasadena Playhouse
Sheldon Epps artistic director, Brian Colburn managing director

MATTER OF HONOR. By Michael J. Chepiga. August 31, 2007. Direction, Scott Schwartz; scenery, Robert Brill; costumes, Maggie Morgan; lighting, Donald Holder; sound and music, Mark Bennett; stage management, Charles M. Turner III.

Johnson C. Whittaker .... Cedric Sanders   Schofield .... Richard Doyle
Chase .... Eric Lutes   Stanton .... Steve Coombs
    Ensemble: Ryan J. Hill, Steve Holm, John O'Brien, Adam J. Smith, Bryan Watkins.
    Presented without intermission.

RAY CHARLES LIVE! Musical by Suzan Lori-Parks. November 9, 2007 (world premiere). Direction, Sheldon Epps; choreography, Kenneth L. Roberson; scenery, Riccardo Hernandez; costumes, Paul Tazewell; lighting, Donald Holder; sound, Carl Casella and Domonic Sack; video, Austin Switser; music direction, Rahn Coleman; stage management, Lurie Horns Pfeffer. Presented in association with Benjamin Productions, Baldwin Entertainment Group, Joe Adams and Ray Charles Enterprises.

Ray Charles .... Brandon Victor Dixon   Margie Hendricks .... Sabrina Sloan
Della B .... Nikki Renee Daniels   Ahmet Ertegun .... Daniel Tatar
Retha Robinson .... Yvette Cason   Jeff Brown................................ Harrison White
Mary Ann Fisher .... Angela Teek   Tom Dowd .... Matthew Benjamin
    Ensemble: NRaca, Phillip Atmore, Aaron Brown, Christopher Brown, Meloney Collins, Tara Cook, Wilkie Ferguson, Dionne Figgins, Matthew Koehler, Sylvia MacCalla, Yusuf Nasir, Maceo Oliver, Jeremiah Whitfield-Pearson, Leslie Stevens, Rocklin Thompson, Ricke Vermont.
    Musical numbers included: "What'd I Say," "What Kind of Man Is This," "Barrelhouse Blues," "Drifting Blues," "Drown in My Own Tears," "One Mint Julep," "Them That Got," "Blue Moon of Kentucky," "Leave My Woman Alone," "Mess Around," "Angels Are Watching Over Me," "Hallelujah, I Love Her So," "Mary Ann," "I Got a Woman," "Let the Good Times Roll," "Don't Set Me Free," "Tell the Truth," "I Can't Stop Loving You," "Moving On," "Hard Times" (Instrumental), "What'd I Say" (Reprise), "Unchain My Heart," "Georgia on My Mind," "Bye, Bye Love," "Born to Lose," "Drown in My Own Tears" (Reprise), "Hit the Road, Jack," "You Don't Know Me," "What'd I Say" (Reprise).
    Presented in two parts.

MASK. Musical with book by Anna Hamilton Phelan; music by Barry Mann; lyrics by Cynthia Weil; based on the film of the same title. March 21, 2008. Direction, Richard Maltby Jr.; choreography, Patti Colombo; scenery, Robert Brill; costumes, Maggie Morgan;

CALIFORNIA

lighting, David Weiner; sound, Peter Fitzgerald; projections, Austin Switser; music direction, Joseph Church; orchestrations, Steve Margoshes; arrangements, Mr. Mann; stage management, Joe Witt.

Rusty Dennis	Michelle Duffy	Rocky Dennis	Allen E. Read
Gar	Greg Evigan	Diana Archer	Sarah Glendening
Dozer	Michael Lanning		

Ensemble: Alec Barnes, Brad Blaisdell, Katy Blake, Ryan Castellino, Diane Delano, Chris Fore, Krysten Leigh Jones, Mark Luna, Heather Marie Marsden, Shanon Mari Mills, Suzanne Petrela, Ethan Le Phong, Jolene Purdy, James Leo Ryan, Matthew Stocke.

Musical numbers included: "Come Along for the Ride," "The Way I See It," "Every Birth," "Three to Six Months," "Do It for Love," "Close to Heaven," "You Know I Would," "Azusa High," "A Woman So Beautiful," "Azusa High" (Revised), "Look at You," "Beautiful World," "I Can't," "After Goodbye," "Days of Miracles," "Wherever This Road Goes," "Planet Vulkturn," "Long Last Ride/Finale."

Presented in two parts.

San Jose Repertory Theatre
Timothy Near artistic director, Nick Nichols managing director

THE TRIUMPH OF LOVE. By Lillian Groag; adapted from Marivaux; translated by Frederick Kluck. September 28, 2007. Direction, Ms. Groag; scenery, Kate Edmunds; costumes, Raquel Barreto; lighting, Russell H. Champa; sound, Jeff Mockus; dramaturgy, Kirsten Brandt and Dan Venning; stage management, Laxmi Kumaran. Presented in association with California Shakespeare Theater.

Dimas	Ron Campbell	Leonide	Stacy Ross
Corine	Catherine Castellanos	Arlecchino	Danny Scheie
Hermocrates	Dan Hiatt	Agis	Jud Williford
Leontine	Domenique Lozano		

Presented in two parts.

THIS WONDERFUL LIFE. By Steve Murray. November 30, 2007. Direction, Kirsten Brandt; scenery, Robin Roberts; costumes, Brandin Baron; lighting and projections, David Lee Cuthbert; sound, Jeff Mockus; stage management, Laxmi Kumaran.

Performed by Mark Setlock.

Presented without intermission.

TRANCED. By Robert Clyman. February 1, 2008. Direction, Barbara Damashek; scenery, Kris Stone; costumes, B. Modern; lighting, Daniel Ordower; sound, Jeff Mockus; stage management, Laxmi Kumaran.

Azmera	Kenya Brome	Philip	Thom Rivera
Logan	James Carpenter	Beth	Stacy Ross

SOUVENIR. By Stephen Temperley. March 28, 2008. Direction, R. Hamilton Wright; scenery, Edie Whitset; costumes, Marcia Dixcy Jory; lighting, Rick Paulson; sound, Steve Schoenbeck; stage management, Laxmi Kumaran.

Florence Foster Jenkins	Patti Cohenour	Cosme McMoon	Mark Anders

CALIFORNIA

THE STRANGE CASE OF DR. JEKYLL AND MR. HYDE. By Jeffrey Hatcher; adapted from the novella by Robert Louis Stevenson. May 16, 2008 (world premiere). Direction, David Ira Goldstein; scenery, Kent Dorsey; costumes, Anna Oliver; lighting, Dawn Chiang; sound, Brian Jerome Peterson; music, Roberta Carlson; fight direction, Ken Merckx; stage management, Laxmi Kumaran. Presented in association with the Arizona Theatre Company.

Performed by Anna Bullard, Stephen D'Ambrose, Alan Kaiser, Carrie Paff, Danielle Perata, Mark Anderson Phillips, Ken Ruta, Mr. Wright.

Presented in two parts.

The Old Globe, San Diego
Louis G. Spisto executive producer, Darko Tresnjak resident artistic director

A CATERED AFFAIR. Musical with book by Harvey Fierstein; music and lyrics by John Bucchino; based on the film by Gore Vidal and the teleplay by Paddy Chayefsky. September 30, 2007. Direction, John Doyle; scenery, David Gallo; costumes, Ann Hould-Ward; lighting, Brian MacDevitt; sound, Dan Moses Schreier; projections, Zachary Borovay; music direction, Constantine Kitsopoulos; orchestrations, Don Sebesky; stage management, Claudia Lynch. Presented in association with Jujamcyn Theaters, Jordan Roth, Harvey Entertainment, Ron Fierstein, Richie Jackson, Daryl Roth, Tulchin/Bartner/ATG and O'Boyle/Stevens.

Aggie Hurley	Faith Prince	Sam; Mr. Halloran	Philip Hoffman
Tom Hurley	Tom Wopat	Alice; Army Sergeant	Katie Klaus
Winston	Harvey Fierstein	Delores; Caterer	Heather MacRae
Janey Hurley	Leslie Kritzer	Myra; Saleswoman	Kristine Zbornik
Ralph Halloran	Matt Cavenaugh	Pasha; Mrs. Halloran	Lori Wilner

Presented without intermission.

IN THIS CORNER. By Steven Drukman. January 10, 2008. Direction, Ethan McSweeny; scenery, Lee Savage; costumes, Tracy Christensen; lighting, Tyler Micoleau; sound, Lindsay Jones; fight direction, Steve Rankin; stage management, Diana Moser.

Joe Louis	Dion Graham	Reporter; Jacobs	David Deblinger
Max Schmeling	Rufus Collins	Nurse; others	Katie Barrett
Announcer; others	T. Ryder Smith	Boxer	John Keabler
Blackburn; Pastor	Al White		

Presented in two parts.

THE AMERICAN PLAN. By Richard Greenberg. February 28, 2008. Direction, Kim Rubinstein; scenery, Wilson Chin; costumes, Emily Pepper; lighting, Chris Rynne; sound, Paul Peterson; stage management, Leila Knox.

Lili Adler	Kate Arrington	Eva Adler	Sandra Shipley
Nick Lockridge	Patrick Zeller	Gil Harbison	Michael Kirby
Olivia Shaw	Sharon Hope		

Presented in two parts.

DANCING IN THE DARK. Musical with book by Douglas Carter Beane; music by Arthur Schwartz; lyrics by Howard Dietz; based on Betty Comden and Adolph Green's 1953

CALIFORNIA

film, *The Band Wagon*. March 13, 2007 (world premiere). Direction, Gary Griffin; choreography, Warren Carlyle; scenery, John Lee Beatty; costumes, David C. Woolard; lighting, Ken Billington; sound, Brian Ronan; music direction, Don York; orchestrations, Larry Hochman; stage management, Daniel S. Rosokoff.

Tony Hunter	Scott Bakula	Paul Byrd	Sebastian La Cause
Gabrielle Gerard	Mara Davi	Lily Marton	Beth Leavel
Lester Marton	Adam Heller	Jeffrey Cordova	Patrick Page
Hal Meadows	Benjamin Howes		

Ensemble: Jacob ben Widmar, Brandon Bieber, Robin Campbell, Angie Canuel, Rachel Coloff, Dylis Croman, Nicolas Dromard, Adam Perry, Eric Santagta, Kiira Schmidt, Branch Woodman, Ashley Yeater.

Musical numbers included: "That's Entertainment!," "Triplets," "The Pitch," "Got a Bran' New Suit," "By Myself," "Something You Never Had Before," "You and the Night and the Music," "You and the Night and the Music" (Reprise), "I Love Louisa," "New Sun in the Sky," "Louisiana Hayride," "Something to Remember You By," "Rhode Island Is Famous for You," "I Guess I'll Have to Change My Plan," "Sweet Music," "Something You Never Had Before" (Reprise), "A Shine on Your Shoes," "Dancing in the Dark," "That's Entertainment!" (Reprise).

Presented in two parts.

BEETHOVEN, AS I KNEW HIM. By Hershey Felder; based on the work of Gerhard von Breuning. May 8, 2008 (world premiere). Direction, Joel Zwick; scenery, Francois-Pierre Couture; costumes, Carole Boue; lighting, Richard Norwood; sound, Erik Carstensen; music, Beethoven; projections, Andrew Wilder and Christopher Ash; stage management, GiGi Garcia

Performed by Mr. Felder.

Presented without intermission.

South Coast Repertory, Costa Mesa
David Emmes producing artistic director, Martin Benson artistic director

SHIPWRECKED! AN ENTERTAINMENT—THE AMAZING ADVENTURES OF LOUIS DE ROUGEMONT (AS TOLD BY HIMSELF). By Donald Margulies. September 29, 2007 (world premiere). Direction, Bart DeLorenzo; scenery, Keith E. Mitchell; costumes, Candice Cain; lighting, Rand Ryan; sound and music, Steven Cahill; puppets, Christine Marie; stage management, Erin Nelson.

Louis de Rougemont	Gregory Itzin	Player 2	Michael Daniel Cassady
Player 1	Melody Butiu		

Presented without intermission.

A FEMININE ENDING. By Sarah Treem. January 12, 2008 (West Coast premiere). Direction, Timothy Douglas; scenery, Tony Cisek; costumes, Candice Cain; lighting, Peter Maradudin; music, Vincent Olivieri; sound, Colbert S. Davis IV; stage management, Julie Haber. Presented in association with Portland Center Stage.

Amanda	Brooke Bloom	Billy	Jedadiah Schultz
Kim	Amy Aquino	Jack	Peter Katona
David	Alan Blumenfeld		

Presented without intermission.

CALIFORNIA

CULTURE CLASH IN AMERICCA. By Culture Clash (Richard Montoya, Ric Salinas and Herbert Siguenza). March 21, 2008. Direction, David Emmes; scenery and costumes, Angela Balogh Calin; lighting, Lonnie Raphael Alcaraz; sound, B.C. Keller; stage management, Conwell Worthington III.

> Performed by Richard Montoya, Ric Salinas, Herbert Siguenza.
> Presented in two parts.

TheatreWorks, Palo Alto
Robert Kelley artistic director, Phil Santora managing director

EMMA. Musical with book, music and lyrics by Paul Gordon; adapted from the novel by Jane Austen. August 25, 2007 (world premiere). Direction, Robert Kelley; choreography, MaryBeth Cavanaugh; scenery, Joe Ragey; costumes, Fumiko Bielefeldt; lighting, Steven B. Mannshardt; sound, Cliff Caruthers; music direction, William Liberatore; orchestrations, Mr. Gordon; additional arrangements, Mr. Liberatore and David Kreppel; dramaturgy, Vickie Rozell; stage management, Jaimie L. Johnson.

Emma	Lianne Marie Dobbs	Harriet Smith	Dani Marcus
Mr. Woodhouse	George Ward	Frank Churchill	Travis Poelle
Mr. Knightley	Timothy Gulan	Jane Fairfax	Mindy Lym
Miss Bates	Suzanne Grodner	Robert Martin;	
Mrs. Bates;		Servant	Nick Nakashima
Housekeeper	Laurie Strawn	Mrs. Elton;	
Mr. Elton	Brian Herndon	Mrs. Churchill	Danielle Levin
Mr. Weston	Richard Frederick	Butler; Minister	Sean Patrick Murtagh
Mrs. Weston	Alison Ewing		

> Presented in two parts.

COLORADO

Denver Center Theatre Company
Kent Thompson artistic director

OUR HOUSE. By Theresa Rebeck; conceived by Ms. Rebeck and Daniel Fish. January 18, 2008 (world premiere). Direction, Mr. Fish; scenery, Andrew Lieberman; costumes, Kaye Voyce; lighting, Scott Zielinski; sound, Richard M. Scholwin; fight direction, Geoffrey Kent; stage management, Christi B. Spann.

Wes	Danny Mastrogiorgio	Grigsby	Suzy Jane Hunt
Jennifer	Molly Ward	Vincent	Haynes Thigpen
Merv	Rob Campbell	Stu	Jonathan Fried
Alice	Kate Nowlin	Assistant	Jennifer Le Blanc

> Presented without intermission.

LYDIA. By Octavio Solis. January 24, 2008 (world premiere). Direction, Juliette Carillo; scenery, Antje Ellermann; costumes, Christal Weatherly; lighting, Charles R. MacLeod; sound, Kimberly Fuhr; music, Chris Webb; fight direction, Geoffrey Kent; stage management, Lyle Raper.

CALIFORNIA – COLORADO

Ceci	Onahoua Rodriguez	Claudio	Ricardo Gutierrez
Misha	Carlo Alban	Alvaro	Christian Barillas
Rene	Rene Millan	Lydia	Stephanie Beatriz
Rosa	Catalina Maynard		

Presented in two parts.

PLAINSONG. By Eric Schmiedl; based on the novel by Kent Haruf. January 31, 2008 (world premiere). Direction, Kent Thompson; scenery, Vicki Smith; costumes, Susan E. Mickey; lighting, Don Darnutzer; sound, Craig Breitenbach; music, Gary Grundei; fight direction, Geoffrey Kent; stage management, Christopher C. Ewing.

Tom Guthrie	John Hutton	Victoria Roubideaux	Tiffany Ellen Solano
Ike	Gabe Antonelli;	Maggie Jones	Kathleen McCall
	Ian Frazier	Raymond McPherson	Mike Hartman
Bobby	Keean Johnson;	Harold McPherson	Philip Pleasants
	Jeremy Singer		

Ensemble: Josh Clayton, Stephanie Cozart, Michael J. Fulvio,Sam Gregory, David Ivers, Lauren Klein, Kendra Kohrt, Jeremiah Miller, Randy Moore, Leslie O'Carroll, Erik Sandvold, Danielle Slavick.

Presented in three parts.

CONNECTICUT

Eugene O'Neill Theater Center, Waterford
Preston Whiteway executive director

National Playwrights' Conference, Wendy C. Goldberg artistic director

END DAYS. By Deborah Zoe Laufer. July 5, 2007. Direction, Rebecca Bayla Taichman. Performed by Peter Friedman, Zoe Lister Jones, Ryan King, Caitlin O'Connell, David Ross.

THE VELVET RUT. By James Still. July 6, 2007. Direction, Lisa Peterson. Performed by Clifton Guterman, Lenny Von Dohlen.

THE WOODPECKER. By Samuel Brett Williams. July 11, 2007. Direction, Jesse Berger. Performed by Christian Conn, Deirdre O'Connell.

THE CROWD YOU'RE IN WITH. By Rebecca Gilman. July 12, 2007. Direction, Wendy C. Goldberg. Performed by Mike Doyle, Ryan King, Amy Redford, John Rothman, Makela Spielman, Tom Story.

GOOD BOYS AND TRUE. By Roberto Aguirre-Sacasa. July 18, 2007. Direction, Peter DuBois. Performed by Rebecca Brooksher, Ravenna Fahey, Kevin Geer, Billy Magnussen, Peter Stadlen, Julie White.

THE BOOK CLUB PLAY. By Karen Zacarías. July 19 2007. Direction, Bruce Sevy. Performed by Cherise Booth, Mike Doyle, Amy Redford, Makela Spielman, Tom Story, Jennifer Van Dyck.

COLORADO – CONNECTICUT

GUARDIANS. By Lucy Caldwell. July 25, 2007. Direction, Carey Perloff. Performed by Jeremy Bobb, Rebecca Brooksher. Presented in association with the Druid Theatre Company, Galway.

THE BALLAD OF EMMETT TILL. By Ifa Bayeza. July 26, 2007. Direction, Kate Whoriskey. Performed by Nicoye Banks, Cherise Booth, Daniel Breaker, Alexis Brown, Matt D'Amico, Colman Domingo, Nic Few, John Jellison, Warner Miller, Thomas Sadoski, Myra Lucretia Taylor, Jonathan Walker, Jess Weixler, John Wesley. Presented in association with the Goodman Theatre, Chicago.

National Music Theatre Conference, Paulette Haupt artistic director

NOTES TO MARIANNE. Musical with book, music and lyrics by David Rossmer and Dan Lipton. July 14, 2007. Direction, Benjamin Endsley Klein; music direction, Fred Lassen. Performed by Jenny Fellner, Suzan Postel, Monique French, Jason Wooten, Dennis Parlato, Andrew Samonsky, Ken Triwush, Eric Bondoc, Alicia Irving.

RED EYE OF LOVE. Musical with book and lyrics by Arnold Weinstein and John Wulp; music by Jan Warner; adapted from a play by Mr. Weinstein. July 21, 2007. Direction, Ted Sperling; music direction, Rob Berman. Performed by Cheyenne Jackson, Elizabeth Stanley, Joe Grifasi, Cole Burden, Kimberly Chesser, Harris Doran, Anne Kittredge, Jason Ma, Monique Midgette, Paul Stovall.

Goodspeed Musicals, East Haddam
Michael P. Price executive director

HAPPY DAYS. Musical with book by Garry Marshall; music and lyrics by Paul Williams. August 9, 2007. Direction, Gordon Greenberg; choreography, Michele Lynch; scenery, Walt Spangler; costumes, David C. Woolard; lighting, Jeff Croiter; sound, Randy Hansen; music direction, Shawn Gough; music supervision, John McDaniel; stage management, Bradley G. Spachman; in the Norma Terris Theatre, Chester.

Fonzie	Joey Sorge
Richie Cunningham	Rory O'Malley
Pinky Tuscadero	Felicia Finley
Howard Cunningham	Patrick Garner
Marion	Cynthia Ferrer
Joanie	Natalie Bradshaw
Ralph Malph	Todd Buonopane
Potsie	Christopher Ruth
Chachi	Eric Schneider
Arnold	Michael J. Farina
Lori Beth	Julia Burrows
Pinkette Lola	Andrea Dora
Pinkette Sally	Lauren Parsons
Jumpy Malachi	Tom Plotkin
Count Malachi	Andrew Varela

Presented in two parts.

13. Musical with book by Dan Elish and Robert Horn; music and lyrics by Jason Robert Brown. May 9, 2008. Direction, Jeremy Sams; choreography, Christopher Gattelli; scenery and costumes, David Farley; lighting, Brian MacDevitt; sound, Jon Weston; music direction, Tom Kitt; orchestrations and arrangements, Mr. Brown; stage management, Rick Steiger; in the Norma Terris Theatre, Chester.

Evan Goldman	Graham Phillips; Hudson Thames
Archie	Aaron Simon Gross
Patrice	Allie Trimm
Brett	Eric Nelsen
Lucy	Elizabeth Egan Gillies
Kendra	Ashton Smalling
Charlotte	Ariana Grande

CONNECTICUT

Molly .... Caitlin Gann	Bill .... Joey LaVarco
Cassie .... Taylor Bright	Malcolm .... Kyle Crews
Steve .... Eamon Foley	Eddie .... Alberto Calderon

Musical numbers included: "Thirteen," "Becoming a Man," "I've Got a Feeling," "Get Me What I Need," "What It Means to Be a Friend," "All Hail the Brain," "Getting Ready," "Any Minute," "Here I Come," "Anything You Want," "Bad Bad News," "Tell Her," "Big Day," "Perfect Pieces," "It Can't Be True," "If That's What It Is," "A Little More Homework."

Presented in two parts.

Hartford Stage, Hartford

Michael Wilson artistic director, Michael Stotts managing director

OUR TOWN. By Thornton Wilder. September 7, 2007. Direction, Gregory Boyd; scenery, Jeff Cowie; costumes, Alejo Vietti; lighting, Rui Rita; sound and music, John Gromada; stage management, Tree O'Halloran.

Stage Manager .... Hal Holbrook	George Gibbs .... Donovan Patton
Dr. Gibbs .... Ross Bickell	Rebecca Gibbs .... Erin S. Courtney
Joe Crowell .... Jacob Lombardi	Emily Webb .... Ginna Carter
Howie Newsome .... Bill Kux	Editor Webb .... Frank Converse
Mrs. Gibbs .... Josie de Guzman	Simon Stimson .... Noble Shropshire
Mrs. Webb .... Annalee Jefferies	

Ensemble: Jordan Cyr, Andrew Shipman, Nafe Katter, Bill Kux, Charlotte Booker, Robert Hannon Davis, Jacob Lombardi, Justin Fuller, Michael Angelo Morlani, Tom Libonate.

Presented in three parts.

CHICK, THE GREAT OSRAM. By David Grimm. October 19, 2007. Direction, Michael Wilson; scenery, Tony Straiges; costumes, David C. Woolard; lighting, Rui Rita; sound and music, John Gromada; stage management, Gregory R. Covert.

Chick .... Robert Sella	Helen .... Enid Graham

Presented without intermission.

ZERLINE'S TALE. By Jeremy Sams; adapted from a story by Hermann Broch. January 19, 2008. Direction, Michael Wilson; scenery, Alexander Dodge; costumes, Jane Greenwood; lighting, Howell Binkley; sound and music, John Gromada; stage management, Linda Marvel.

Zerline .... Elizabeth Ashley	Man .... Jon David Casey

Presented without intermission.

THE BLUEST EYE. By Lydia R. Diamond; adapted from the novel by Toni Morrison. February 27, 2008. Direction, Eric Ting; scenery, Scott Bradley; costumes, Toni-Leslie James; lighting, Russell H. Champa; sound and music, Michael Bodeen and Rob Milburn. Presented in association with the Long Wharf Theatre.

Mama; Woman .... Miche Braden	Soaphead Church; Daddy .... Ellis Foster
Mrs. Breedlove; Woman .... Oni Faida Lampley	Pecola .... Adepero Oduye
Claudia .... Bobbi Baker	Freida; Darlene .... Ronica V. Reddick
Cholly .... Leon Addison Brown	Maureen Pearl; others .... Shelley Thomas

Presented without intermission.

CONNECTICUT

Long Wharf Theatre, New Haven

Gordon Edelstein artistic director, Joan Channick managing director

THE PRICE. By Arthur Miller. October 31, 2007. Direction, Gordon Edelstein; scenery, Eugene Lee; costumes, Jessica Ford; lighting, Michael Chybowski; sound, Corrine K. Livingston; stage management, Charles M. Turner.

Victor Franz	Marco Barricelli	Gregory Solomon	David Margulies
Esther Franz	Kate Forbes	Walter Franz	Jeff McCarthy

Presented in two parts.

LET ME DOWN EASY. By Anna Deavere Smith. January 16, 2008. Direction, Stephen Wadsworth; scenery, David Rockwell; costumes, Ann Hould-Ward; lighting, David Lander; sound, David Budries; projections, Jan Hartley; dramaturgy, Dorrine Kondo and Alisa Solomon; stage management, Diane DiVita. Presented in association with Daryl Roth.

Performed by Ms. Deavere Smith.

Presented in two parts.

Westport Country Playhouse

Joanne Woodward and Anne Keefe artistic directors,
Jodi Schoenbrun Carter managing director

MARY'S WEDDING. By Stephen Massicotte. June 23, 2007. Direction, Tazewell Thompson; scenery, Donald Eastman; costumes, Linda Cho; lighting, Robert W. Henderson; sound, Fabian Obispo; stage management, Cole P. Bonenberger.

Mary; Flowers	Hannah Cabell	Charlie	Lee Aaron Rosen

Presented without intermission.

SEDITION. By David Wiltse. August 4, 2007 (world premiere). Direction, Tazewell Thompson; scenery, Donald Eastman; costumes, Ilona Somogyi; lighting, Robert Wierzel; sound and music, Fabian Obispo; stage management, Katherine Lee Boyer.

Megrim	Jeffrey DeMunn	Harriet Schrag	Hannah Cabell
Andrew Schrag	Chris Sarandon	Tellig	Bryant Martin
Cassidy	Mark Shanahan	Chancellor	Colin McPhillamy

Presented in two parts.

BEING ALIVE. Musical revue by Billy Porter; based on works by Stephen Sondheim; additional text by William Shakespeare. August 26, 2007 (world premiere). Direction, Mr. Porter; choreography, AC Ciulla; scenery, Allen Moyer; costumes, Anita Yavich; lighting, Kevin Adams; sound, Brett Jarvis; music direction, Mark Berman; music supervision, James Sampliner; orchestrations, Mr. Sampliner and Michael McElroy; stage management, Peter Wolf.

Performed by Natalie Venetia Belcon, Chuck Cooper, Joshua Henry, N'Kenge, Leslie Odom Jr., Ken Robinson, Rema Webb.

Musical numbers included: "Take Me to the World," "Children Will Listen," "Giants in the Sky," "Not While I'm Around," "Anyone Can Whistle," "I Know Things Now," "Pretty Women, "Everybody Ought to Have a Maid," "What Can You Lose, Not a Day Goes By," "There Won't Be Trumpets," "Getting Married Today," "I Wish I Could Forget You," "Is This What You Call Love," "Stay With

CONNECTICUT

Me," "No More," "There's Something About a War," "More," "I Remember," "Losing My Mind," "Something Just Broke," "Live, Laugh, Love," "No One Is Alone," "Send in the Clowns," "Move On," "Fear No More," "Being Alive," "Sunday."

Presented without intermission.

VIGIL. By Morris Panych. March 1, 2008. Direction, Stephen DiMenna; scenery, Andromache Chalfant; costumes, Ilona Somogyi; lighting, Ben Stanton; sound, Daniel Baker; music, Broken Chord Collective; stage management, Cole P. Bonenberger.

Kemp .... Timothy Busfield   Grace .... Helen Stenborg

Presented in two parts.

Yale Repertory Theatre, New Haven

James Bundy artistic director, Victoria Nolan managing director

RICHARD II. By William Shakespeare. September 27, 2007. Direction, Evan Yionoulis; scenery, Brenda Davis; costumes, Melissa E. Trn; lighting, Ji Youn Chang; sound, Sarah Pickett; music, Mike Yionoulis; production stage manager, James Mountcastle.

Richard II .... Jeffrey Carlson	Duchess of Gloucester;	
Henry Bolingbroke .... Billy Eugene Jones	Duchess of York .... Caroline Stefanie Clay	
John of Gaunt;	Earl of Northumberland .... Jonathan Fried	
Gardener .... Alvin Epstein	Lord Willoughby .... Edward O'Blenis	
Duke of York .... George Bartenieff	Bishop of Carlisle .... Christopher McHale	
Thomas Mowbray .... Christopher Grant	Duke of Aumerle .... Allen E. Read	
Queen Isabelle .... Caitlin Clouthier	Exton .... Alex Knox	

Ensemble: Brian Robert Burns, Kristjiana Gong, Christopher McFarland, Dan Moran, Josh Odsess-Rubin, Joseph Parks, Joe Tapper.

Presented in two parts.

THE EVILDOERS. By David Adjmi. January 24, 2008 (world premiere). Direction, Rebecca Bayla Taichman; scenery, Riccardo Hernandez; costumes, Susan Hilferty; lighting, Stephen Strawbridge; sound, Bray Poor; stage management, Joanne E. McInerney.

Carol .... Johanna Day	Judy .... Samantha Soule
Martin .... Matt McGrath	Jerry .... Stephen Barker Turner

Presented in two parts.

A WOMAN OF NO IMPORTANCE. By Oscar Wilde. March 27, 2008. Direction, James Bundy; scenery, Lauren Rockman, costumes, Anya Klepikov; lighting, Ola Braten; sound, Jana Hoglund; dramaturgy, Amy Boratko and Jennifer Shaw; stage management, Sarah Hodges.

Performed by René Augesen, Judith-Marie Bergan, Will Connolly, John Patrick Doherty, Kate Forbes, Geordie Johnson, Felicity Jones, Patricia Kilgarriff, John Little, Anthony Newfield, Bryce Pinkham, Terence Rigby, Michael Rudko, Erica Sullivan, Liz Wisan.

Presented in two parts.

BOLEROS FOR THE DISENCHANTED. By José Rivera. May 1, 2008 (world premiere). Direction, Henry Godinez; music, Gustavo Leone; scenery, Linda Buchanan; costumes, Yuri Cataldo; lighting, Joseph Appelt; sound, Veronika Vorel; music, Gustavo Leone; stage management, Danielle Federico.

CONNECTICUT

Flora; Eve .... Sona Tatoyan
Donna Milla; Flora .... Adriana Sevan
Don Fermin; Eusebio .... Gary Perez
    Presented in two parts.

Manuelo; Priest .... Felix Solis
Petra; Monica .... Lucia Brawley
Eusebio; Oskar .... Joe Minoso

DELAWARE

Delaware Theatre Company, Wilmington
Anne Marie Cammarato producing director

THE DIARY OF ANNE FRANK. By Frances Goodrich and Albert Hackett; adapted by
Wendy Kesselman. October 20, 2007. Direction, Meredith McDonough; scenery, Kevin
Judge; costumes, Emily Pepper; lighting, Thom Weaver; sound and music, Fabian Obispo;
stage management, Brian V. Klinger.

Anne Frank .... Sara Kapner
Otto Frank .... Joel Leffert
Edith Frank .... Dori Legg
Margot Frank .... Nikki Coble
Miep Gies .... Maggie Kettering
Peter Van Daan ...... Henry Raphael Glovinsky
    Presented in two parts.

Mr. Kraler .... Michael Boudewyns
Mrs. Van Daan .... Geraldine Librandi
Mr. Van Daan .... Paul L. Nolan
Mr. Dussel .... John Morrison
First Man .... Dan Rich
Second Man .... David Sweeny

DISTRICT OF COLUMBIA

Arena Stage, Washington
Molly Smith artistic director, Stephen Richard executive director

33 VARIATIONS. By Moisés Kaufman. August 30, 2007. Direction, Mr. Kaufman; scenery,
Derek McLane; costumes, Janice Pytel; lighting, David Lander; sound, Andre Pluess;
projections, Jeff Sugg; stage management, Meghan Gauger. Presented in association
with Tectonic Theater Project.

Anton Diabelli .... Don Amendolia
Mike Clark .... Greg Keller
Gertie Ladenborger .... Susan Kellermann
Beethoven .... Graeme Malcolm
    Presented in two parts.

Clara Brandt .... Laura Odeh
Katherine Brandt .... Mary Beth Peil
Anton Schindler .... Erik Steele
Pianist .... Diane Walsh

THE WOMEN OF BREWSTER PLACE. Musical with book, music and lyrics by Tim
Acito; based on the novel by Gloria Naylor. October 26, 2007. Direction, Molly Smith;
choreography, Kenneth L. Roberson; scenery, Anne Patterson; costumes, Paul Tazewell;
lighting, Michael Gilliam; sound, Garth Hemphill; music direction, William Foster
McDaniel; orchestrations, Mr. Acito and Mr. McDaniel; dramaturgy, Otis Ramsey-Zoe;
stage management, Amber Dickerson. Presented in association with Alliance Theatre
Company, Atlanta; see Alliance listing for cast and musical numbers.

DELAWARE – DISTRICT OF COLUMBIA

CHRISTMAS CAROL 1941. Musical with book by James Magruder; music by Henry Krieger; lyrics by Susan Birkenhead; adapted from the story by Charles Dickens. November 23, 2007 (world premiere). Direction, Molly Smith; choreography, Parker Esse; scenery, William Schmuck; costumes, Vicki R. Davis; lighting, John (Jock) Munro; sound and orchestrations, Garth Hemphill; projections, Adam Larsen; music direction, George Fulginiti-Shakar; dramaturgy, Mark Bly; stage management, Susan R. White.

Albert Schroen;
  Mr. Bates .... Christopher Bloch
Butch Schroen;
  Prime Strube .... Clinton Brandhagen
Carolyn Schroen .... Mollie Clement
Recruiting Officer 1;
  others .... Daniel Eichner
Elijah Strube .... James Gale
Donald; Bartender .... Tim Getman
Hazel B; Fan .... Tara Giordano
  Presented in two parts.

Young Boy; others .... C.J. Harrison-Davies
Winged Victory;
  Kay .... Gia Mora
Freedom; Mrs. Bates .... Connan Morrissey
Marley; others .... Hugh Nees
Henry Schroen .... Lawrence Redmond
Margarette Schroen .... Nancy Robinette
Grant Yagel; others .... Clay Steakley
Sally Dunlavey;
  Ghost of Grief .... Bayla Whitten

Shakespeare Theatre Company, Washington
Michael Kahn artistic director

TAMBURLAINE. By Christopher Marlowe; adapted by Michael Kahn. November 7, 2007. Direction, Mr. Kahn; choreography, Daniel Pelzig; scenery, Lee Savage; costumes, Jennifer Moeller; lighting, Mark McCullough; music, Karl Lundeberg; fight direction, Rick Sordelet; stage management, M. William Shiner.

Tamburlaine .... Avery Brooks
Zenocrate .... Mia Tagano
Bajazeth .... David McCann

Zabina .... Franchelle Steward Dorn
Mycetes .... Floyd King

Ensemble: Craig Wallace, Terence Archie, Danyon Davis, Kurt Uy, Scott Jaeck, David Emerson Toney, James Denvil, Jonathan Earl Peck, John Lescault, Christopher Marino, Jefferson A. Russell, Robert Jason Jackson, James Konicek, Amy Kim Waschke, David Sabin, Jay Whittaker, Abe Cruz, Kaytie Morris, Kaitlin Manning, Jeremy Pryzby, JJ Area, Chris Crawford, Blake DeLong, Adriano Gatto, Kenric Green, Austin Herzing, Anthony Jackson, Jair Kamperveen, Kevin Pierson, Majed Sayess, Michael Bunting.
  Presented in two parts.

EDWARD II. By Christopher Marlowe; adapted by Michael Kahn. November 9, 2007. Direction, Gale Edwards; choreography, Daniel Pelzig; scenery, Lee Savage; costumes, Murell Horton; lighting, Mark McCullough; fight direction, Rick Sordelet; stage management, M. William Shiner.

Edward II .... Wallace Acton
Queen Isabella .... Deanne Lorette

Gaveston .... Vayu O'Donnell
Mortimer .... Andrew Long

Ensemble: Craig Wallace, Terence Archie, Danyon Davis, Kurt Uy, Scott Jaeck, David Emerson Toney, James Denvil, Jonathan Earl Peck, John Lescault, Christopher Marino, Jefferson A. Russell, Robert Jason Jackson, James Konicek, Amy Kim Waschke, David Sabin, Jay Whittaker, Abe Cruz, Kaytie Morris, Kaitlin Manning, Jeremy Pryzby, JJ Area, Chris Crawford, Blake DeLong, Adriano Gatto, Kenric Green, Austin Herzing, Anthony Jackson, Jair Kamperveen, Kevin Pierson, Majed Sayess, Michael Bunting.
  Presented in two parts.

DISTRICT OF COLUMBIA

Studio Theatre, Washington

Joy Zinoman founding artistic director, Keith Alan Baker managing director

BREATH, BOOM. By Kia Corthron. December 16, 2007. Direction, Rahaleh Nassri; scenery, Eric Van Wyk; costumes, Brandee Mathies; lighting, Harold Burgess; sound, Erik Trester; fight direction, Joel David Santer.

Prix	Roxi Trapp-Dukes	Mother	Monique Page
Shondra; Pepper	Shannon Dorsey	Jupiter	Lanett Proctor
Angel	Juliana Edeke	Comet	Natasha Rothwell
Denise	Nicki Gonzales	Jerome	Theodore Snead
Malika; Socks	Tiffany Jillian Green	Cat	Ashley Ware
Jo	Tonya Upshur Hartwell	Fuego	Abby Wood
Girl	Stefanee Martin		

Presented in two parts.

THE BROTHERS SIZE. By Tarell Alvin McCraney. January 6, 2008. Direction, Tea Alagic; scenery, Peter J. Ksander; costumes, Zane Philstrom; lighting, Burke Brown.

Oshoosi Size	Brian Tyree Henry	Elegba	Elliot Villar
Ogun Size	Gilbert Owuor		

Presented without intermission.

Theater J, Washington

Ari Roth artistic director, managing director Patricia Jenson

ACCIDENT. By Amy Ziff. September 10, 2007 (world premiere). Direction, Rebecca Asher; lighting, Garth Dolan; stage management, Lindsay Miller.

Performed by Ms. Ziff.

DAVID IN SHADOW AND LIGHT. Musical with book and lyrics by Yehuda Hyman; music by Daniel Hoffman. May 18, 2008 (world premiere). Direction, Nick Olcott; music direction, George Fulginiti-Shakar; choreography, Peter DiMuro and Shula Strassfeld; scenery, Misha Kachman; costumes, Reggie Ray; lighting, Colin K. Bills; sound, Matt Otto; masks, Michelle Elwyn; puppets, Ksenya Litvak; fight direction, Paul Gallagher; stage management, Maribeth Chaprnka.

King David	Matt Pearson	Goliath	Russell Sunday
Jonathan	Will Gartshore	Batsheva	Peggy Yates
Angel Metatron	Donna Migliaccio	Adam	Norman Aronovic
Uriah	Lawrence Redmond	Nathan	Matthew Anderson
King Saul	Bobby Smith	Michal	Carolyn Agan

Presented in two parts.

Woolly Mammoth Theatre Company, Washington

Howard Shalwitz artistic director, Jeffrey Herrmann managing director

CURRENT NOBODY. By Melissa James Gibson. November 4, 2007 (world premiere). Direction, Daniel Aukin; scenery, Tony Cisek; costumes, Helen Q. Huang; lighting,

DISTRICT OF COLUMBIA

Colin K. Bills; sound, Ryan Rumery; projections, Jake Pinholster; fight direction, John Gurski; dramaturgy, Elissa Goetschius.

Od .... Jesse Lenat	Jo .... Kathryn Falcone
Bill .... Michael Willis	Suzie .... Jessica Dunton
Tel .... Casie Platt	Pen .... Christina Kirk
Joe .... Deb Gottesman	

Presented without intermission.

THE K OF D. By Laura Schellhardt. January 19, 2008 (world premiere). Direction, John Vreeke; scenery and costumes, Marie-Noelle Daigneault; lighting, Andrew Griffin; sound, Matt Otto.

Performed by Kimberly Gilbert.
Presented in two parts.

STUNNING. By David Adjmi. March 16, 2008 (world premiere). Direction, Anne Kauffman; scenery, Daniel Conway; costumes, Helen Q. Huang; lighting, Colin K. Bills; sound, Ryan Rumery; stage management, Rebecca Berlin.

Lily .... Laura Heisler	Blanche .... Quincy Tyler Bernstine
Shelly .... Gabriela Fernandez-Coffey	Ike .... Michael Gabriel Goodfriend
Claudine .... Abby Wood	JoJo .... Clinton Brandhagen

Presented in two parts.

FLORIDA

Florida Stage, Manalapan
Louis Tyrrell producing director, Nancy Barnett managing director

END DAYS. By Deborah Zoe Laufer. October 19, 2007 (world premiere). Direction, Louis Tyrrell; scenery and lighting, Richard Crowell; costumes, Erin Amico; sound, Matt Kelly; stage management, James Danford.

Nelson Steinberg .... Scott Borish	Jesus;
Rachel Stein .... Michaela Cronan	Stephen Hawking .... Terry Hardcastle
Sylvia Stein .... Elizabeth Dimon	Arthur Stein .... Jim Shankman

Presented in two parts.

THE COUNT. By Roger Hedden. January 25, 2008 (world premiere). Direction, Louis Tyrrell; scenery, Richard Crowell; costumes, Nelson Fields; lighting, Suzanne M. Jones; sound, Matt Kelly; stage management, James Danford.

The Count .... Dan Leonard	Michael .... Warren Kelley
Jane Gray .... Deborah Hazlett	Connie .... Lois Markle
Lester .... Richard Henzel	Monty .... Michael Marotta

Presented in two parts.

WARD 57. By Jessica Goldberg. March 21, 2008. Direction, Michael Bigelow Dixon; scenery, Victor Becker; costumes, Marcia Dixcy Jory; lighting, Jim Fulton; sound, Matt Kelly; stage management, Susan Clement Jones.

DISTRICT OF COLUMBIA – FLORIDA

Pvt. Anthony Small .... Buddy Haardt
Capt. Gray Whitrock .... Brandon Morris
Wendy Hoffman .... Aditi Brennan Kapil
    Presented without intermission.

Eric .... Sid Solomon
Lydia Whitrock .... Bonni Allen

ORDINARY NATION. By Carter W. Lewis. May 9, 2008. Direction, Louis Tyrrell; scenery, Richard Crowell; costumes, Erin Amico; lighting, Michael Jon Burris; sound, Matt Kelly; stage management, James Danford.

G.J. Jones .... Dan Leonard
Frankie Jones .... Emily Zimmer
Nation Jones .... Joe Kimble
    Presented in two parts.

Allison Jones .... Annie Fitzpatrick
Gibb Aston .... Peter Thomasson

Florida Studio Theatre, Sarasota
Richard Hopkins artistic director, Rebecca Langford managing director

PURE CONFIDENCE. By Carlyle Brown. December 5, 2007. Direction, Kate Alexander; scenery, Jack Magaw; costumes, Marcella Beckwith; lighting, Martin E. Vreeland; stage management, Stacy A. Blackburn.

Auctioneer; Clerk .... Dean Bowden
Mattie .... Barbara Bradshaw
Caroline .... Melanna Gray
    Presented in two parts.

Simon Cato .... Gavin Lawrence
Dewitt; Reporter .... Richard McWilliams
Col. Johnson .... Ed Schiff

THE MIAMIANS. By Michael McKeever. April 2, 2008. Direction, Kate Alexander; scenery, Nayna Ramey; costumes, Marcella Beckwith; lighting, Martin E. Vreeland; stage management, Karin J. Ivester.

Adelle .... Laquayva Anthony
Jackson .... Kenajuan Bentley
Leo .... Matthew DeCapua
    Presented in two parts.

Isaac ....Jon Kohler
Marta .... Marina Re
Luis .... David Perez-Ribada

GEORGIA

Alliance Theatre Company, Atlanta
Susan V. Booth artistic director, managing director Thomas Pechar

THE WOMEN OF BREWSTER PLACE. Musical with book, music, and lyrics by Tim Acito; based on the novel by Gloria Naylor. September 12, 2007 (world premiere). Direction, Molly Smith; choreography, Kenneth L. Roberson; scenery, Anne Patterson; costumes, Paul Tazewell; lighting, Darren W. McCroom; sound, Garth Hemphill; music direction, William Foster McDaniel; orchestrations, Mr. Acito and Mr. McDaniel; dramaturgy, Celise Kalke; stage management, Susan R. White. Presented in association with Arena Stage, Washington, DC.

Sophie .... Cheryl Alexander
Mrs. Browne .... Terry Burrell

Tee ....Suzzanne Douglas
Mattie .... Tina Fabrique

Lorraine .... Harriett D. Foy	Kiswana .... Monique L. Midgette
Wanda .... Eleasha Gamble	Cora Lee .... Tijuana T. Ricks
Etta Mae .... Marva Hicks	Lucielia .... Shelley Thomas

Musical numbers included: "The End of the Line," "How Do We Get Through to You?," "Makin' the Rounds," "Kiswana Browne," "Adding It Up," "Oh, Etta Mae," "Then Know This," "Dumbass," "Man of God," "Sing, Billie," "Leave the Light On," "A Midsummer Night's Dream," "This Ain't a Prayer," "The Street Protest," "Smile," "Welcome to the DMV," "That Girl Is Gonna Be Trouble," "How I Hate It When the World Gets Into You," "Getting Freaky With Me," "The Tenants' Association Meeting," "Ghosts With Paper Bones," "Was There a Moment When?," "If You Want Me to Be Strong," "Because My Soul Is Dry," "Tear Down the Wall," "Save Your Rain."

Presented in two parts.

IN THE RED AND BROWN WATER. By Tarell Alvin McCraney. February 6, 2008 (world premiere). Direction, Tina Landau; scenery, Mimi Lien; costumes, Jessica Jahn; lighting, Scott Zielinski; sound, Mimi Epstein; dramaturgy, Celise Kalke; stage management, Pat A. Flora.

Egungun .... William Cobbs	O Li Roon; Man .... Daniel Thomas May
Shango .... Rodrick Covington	Oya .... Kianné Muschett
Mama Moja; Woman .... Chinai J. Hardy	Shun .... Carra Patterson
Elegba .... Jon Michael Hill	Aunt Elegua .... Heather Alicia Simms
Ogun .... Andre Holland	Nia .... Sharisa Whatley

Presented in two parts.

EURYDICE. By Sarah Ruhl. March 19, 2008. Direction, Richard Garner; scenery, Kat Conley; costumes, Miranda Hoffman; lighting, Justin Townsend; sound, Clay Benning; music, Kendall Simpson; dramaturgy, Celise Kalke; stage management, lark hackshaw.

Orpheus ....Justin Adams	Eurydice .... Melinda Helfrich
Nasty and Interesting Man;	Little Stone .... Paul Hester
Lord of Underworld .... Andrew Benator	Father ....Chris Kayser
Big Stone .... Neal A. Ghant	Loud Stone .... Courtney Patterson

ILLINOIS

About Face Theatre, Chicago

Eric Rosen artistic director, Heather Schmucker interim executive director

WEDDING PLAY. By Eric Rosen. November 4, 2007 (world premiere). Direction, Mr. Rosen; scenery, Meghan Raham; costumes, Janice Pytel; lighting, Christopher Ash; sound, Josh Hovarth and Rick Sims; stage management, Jonathan Templeton. Presented in association with Steppenwolf Theatre Company; in the Steppenwolf Garage.

Abbas.................................... Kareem Bandealy	Jon Kay .... Joe Dempsey
Thalia...Lesley Bevan	Kenny Mace .... Craig Spidle
Adam Mace .... Sean Cooper	Tom Braddle .... Benjamin Sprunger

Presented in two parts.

Court Theatre, Chicago

Charles Newell artistic director, Dawn J. Helsing executive director

THYESTES. By Seneca; translated by Caryl Churchill. September 29, 2007. Direction, JoAnne Akalaitis; scenery, Kaye Voyce; lighting, Jennifer Tipton; sound and music, Andre Pluess; stage management, Ellen Hay.

Thyestes .... James Krag	Ghost of Tantalus .... Lance Stuart Baker
Atreus .... Mick Weber	Fury; Minister .... Wandachristine
Young Tantalus .... Charlie Bazzell;	Messenger .... Wilson Cain III
Connor Hernandez	

Ensemble: Scott Baity Jr., Elizabeth Laidlaw.

Presented without intermission.

CAROUSEL. Musical with book and lyrics by Oscar Hammerstein II; music by Richard Rodgers; based on *Liliom* by Ferenc Molnar, as adapted by Benjamin F. Glazer. March 15, 2008. Direction, Charles Newell; choreography, Randy Duncan; scenery, John Culbert; costumes, Jacqueline Firkins; lighting, Mark McCullough; sound, Joshua Horvath and Ray Nardelli; music direction and orchestrations, Doug Peck; stage management, Ellen Hay. Presented in association with Long Wharf Theatre, New Haven.

Billy Bigelow .... Nicholas Belton	Nettie; others .... Ernestine Jackson
Julie Jordan .... Johanna McKenzie Miller	Jigger Craigin .... Matthew Brumlow
Carrie Pipperidge .... Jessie Miller	Enoch Snow .... Rob Lindley
Mrs. Mullin;	Louise .... Laura Scheinbaum
Heavenly Friend .... Hollis Resnik	

Ensemble: Sean Blake, Ben Dicke, Carol Angeli Feiger, Neil Friedman, Jess Godwin, Tommy Rapley, Travis Turner.

Presented in two parts.

FIRST BREEZE OF SUMMER. By Leslie Lee. May 24, 2008. Direction, Ron OJ Parson; scenery, Jack Magaw; costumes, Christine Pascual; lighting, Marc Stubblefield; sound and music, Joshua Horvath and Ray Nardelli; dramaturgy, Jocelyn Prince.

Gremmar .... Pat Bowie	Lucretia .... Cynthia Kaye McWilliams
Harper Edwards .... Ronald Conner	Milton Edwards .... A.C. Smith
Lou Edwards .... Calvin Dutton	Nate Edwards .... Brian Weddington
Briton; Joe .... Jonathan Eliot	Hattie Edwards .... Jacqueline Williams
Aunt Edna Marsha .... Marsha Estell	Reverend Mosely .... Alfred H. Wilson
Sam Greene .... Taj McCord	Hope; Gloria .... Ebony Wimbs

Presented in two parts.

The Goodman Theatre, Chicago

Robert Falls artistic director, Roche Schulfer executive director

MIRROR OF THE INVISIBLE WORLD. By Mary Zimmerman; adapted from the epic poem *Haft Paykar* by Nizami Ganjavi. July 2, 2007. Direction, Ms. Zimmerman; scenery, Daniel Ostling; costumes, Mara Blumenfeld; lighting, John Culbert; sound and music, Michael Bodeen; arrangements, Mr. Bodeen, Gary Kalar, Ronnie Malley, Eve Monzingo; stage management, Alden Vasquez.

ILLINOIS

King Bahram .... Faran Tahir
Indian Princess;
    others .... Anjali Bhimani
Greek Princess;
    others .... Atley S. Loughridge
Moorish Princess;
    others .... Charlette Speigner
Russian Princess;
    others .... Sofia Jean Gomez
    Presented in two parts.

Turkish Princess;
    others .... Stacey Yen
Chinese Princess;
    others .... Lisa Tejero
Persian Princess;
    others .... Nicole Shalhoub

PASSION PLAY: A CYCLE IN THREE PARTS. By Sarah Ruhl. September 24, 2007. Direction, Mark Wing-Davey; scenery, Allen Moyer; costumes, Gabriel Berry; lighting, James F. Ingalls; sound, Cecil Averett; projections, Ruppert Bohle; stage management, Joseph Drummond.

Carpenter 1;
    Townsman .... Brendan Averett
John; others .... Joaquin Torres
Carpenter 2;
    Townsman .... Keith Kupferer
Pontius; others .... Brian Sgambati
Visiting Friar; others .... Alan Cox
    Presented in three parts.

Village Idiot; Violet .... Polly Noonan
Director .... Craig Spidle
Mary 2 .... Nicole Wiesner
Mary 1 .... Kristen Bush
Machinist; others .... John Hoogenakker
Queen Elizabeth; others .... T. Ryder Smith

THE COOK. By Eduardo Machado. October 29, 2007. Direction, Henry Godinez; scenery, Todd Rosenthal; costumes, Ana Kuzmanic; lighting, Robert Christen; sound, Ray Nardelli and Andre Pluess; music, Gustavo Leone.

Gladys .... Karen Aldridge
Carlos .... Edward F. Torres
Adria; Lourdes .... Maricela Ochoa
    Presented in two parts.

Julio .... Philip James Brannon
Elena; Rosa .... Monica Lopez

TALKING PICTURES. By Horton Foote. February 4, 2008. Direction, Henry Wishcamper; scenery, Tom Burch; costumes, Birgit Rattenborg Wise; lighting, Robert Christen; sound, Richard Woodbury; stage management, Kimberly Osgood.

Katie Bell Jackson .... Lee Stark
Vesta .... Kathleen Romond
Myra .... Jenny McKnight
Mr. Jackson .... Jason Wells
Mrs. Jackson .... Judy Blue
Willis .... Philip Earl Johnson
    Presented in two parts.

Estaquio .... Gabriel Notarangelo
Pete .... Bubba Weiler
Gladys .... Audrey Francis
Ashenback .... E. Vincent Teninty
Gerard .... Dan Waller

Lookingglass Theatre Company, Chicago

David Catlin artistic director, Rachel E. Kraft executive director

HEPHAESTUS: A GREEK MYTHOLOGY CIRCUS TALE. By Tony Hernandez; narration by Mr. Hernandez, Heidi Stillman and Kerry Catlin; lyrics by Rick Sims. January 16, 2008. Direction, Mr. Hernandez and Ms. Stillman; choreography, Lijana

ILLINOIS

Wallenda-Hernandez; scenery and lighting, Brian Sidney Bembridge; costumes, Ms. Wallenda-Hernandez; sound, Joshua Horvath and Ray Nardelli; music, Messrs. Horvath, Nardelli, Kevin O'Donnell, Andre Pluess; stage management, Patia Bartlett. Presented in association with Silverguy Entertainment.

Hephaestus	Tony Hernandez	Aphrodite; Thetis	Anya Stankus
Hera	Lijana Wallenda-Hernandez	Iris	Anna Vigeland
Ares	Almas Meirmanov	Little Girl	Abigail Droeger

Ensemble: Jarret Daiper, Nich Galzin, Rick Kubes, Richie McGuire, Viktoria Grimmy, Rani Waterman, Akemi Berry, Natalie Cook, Carolina Gwinn, Kate Hartgering, Hannah Jarvis, Simone Lazar, Meredith Taylor, Meredith Tomlins.

Presented in two parts.

Northlight Theatre, Skokie
BJ Jones artistic director, Timothy J. Evans executive director

THE MISER. By Molière; translated and adapted by James Magruder. October 10, 2007. Direction, Mark E. Lococo; scenery, Tim Morrison; costumes, Rachel Anne Healy; lighting, Diane Fairchild; sound, Lindsay Jones; stage management, Rita Vreeland.

S. Anselme; others	Patrick Clear	Cleante	Lea Coco
Elise	Kate Fry	Maitre Jacques	Bob Fairbrook
Valere	Timothy Edward Kane	La Fleche; others	Dieterich Gray
Harpagon	Gene Weygandt	Brindavoine	Mark Mysliwiec
Frosine	Jacqueline Williams	Mariane	Erica Peregrine

Presented in two parts.

BETTER LATE. By Larry Gelbart and Craig Wright. April 9, 2008 (world premiere). Direction, BJ Jones; scenery, Jack Magaw; costumes, Rachel Laritz; lighting, JR Lederle; sound and music, Rob Milburn and Michael Bodeen; projections, Stephan Mazurek; stage management, Laura D. Glenn.

Julian	Mike Nussbaum	Lee	John Mahoney
Nora	Linda Kimbrough	Billy	Steve Key

Presented without intermission.

Steppenwolf Theatre Company, Chicago
Martha Lavey artistic director, David Hawkanson executive director

THE CRUCIBLE. By Arthur Miller. September 23, 2007. Direction, Anna D. Shapiro; scenery, Todd Rosenthal; costumes, Virgil Johnson; lighting, Donald Holder; sound, Michael Bodeen and Rob Milburn; fight direction, Chuck Coyl; stage management, Michelle Medvin.

Rev. Parris	Ian Barford	Thomas Putnam	John Lister
Betty Parris	Lee Stark	Mercy Lewis	Lucy Carapetyan
Tituba	Ora Jones	Mary Warren	Alana Arenas
Abigail Williams	Kelly O'Sullivan	John Proctor	James Vincent Meredith
Susanna Walcott	Mildred Marie Langford	Rebecca Nurse	Mary Seibel
Ann Putnam;		Giles Corey	Maury Cooper
Sarah Good	Ginger Lee McDermott	Rev. John Hale	Tim Hopper

ILLINOIS

Elizabeth Proctor .... Sally Murphy	Judge Hathorne .... Tim Edward Rhoze
Francis Nurse .... Leonard J. Kraft	Deputy Gov. Danforth .... Francis Guinan
Ezekial Cheever .... Alan Wilder	Hopkins .... Justin James Farley
John Willard .... Chike Johnson	

Presented in two parts.

GOOD BOYS AND TRUE. By Roberto Aguirre-Sacasa. December 21, 2007 (world premiere). Direction, Pam McKinnon; scenery, Todd Rosenthal; costumes, Nan Cibula-Jenkins; lighting, Ann G. Wrightson; sound and music, Rob Milburn and Michael Bodeen; stage management, Christine D. Freeburg.

Brandon Hardy .... Stephen Louis Grush	Maddy Emerson .... Kelli Simpkins
Elizabeth Hardy .... Martha Lavey	Justin Simmons .... Tim Rock
Coach Russell Shea .... John Procaccino	Cheryl Moody .... Kelly O'Sullivan

Ensemble: Nick Horst, Mark Minton.

Presented in two parts.

CARTER'S WAY. By Eric Simonson. March 8, 2008. Direction, Mr. Simonson; scenery, Neil Patel; costumes, Karin Kopischke; lighting, Keith Parham; sound, Barry G. Funderburg; music, Darrell Leonard; dramaturgy, Edward Sobel; fight direction, Robin H. McFarquhar; stage management, Malcolm Ewen.

Pewee Abernathy .... K. Todd Freeman	Eunice Fey .... Anne Adams
Oriole Carter .... James Vincent Meredith	Boss Jack Thorpe .... Robert Breuler
Marilyn Stokes .... Ora Jones	Corky; others .... Scott Cummins
Johnny Russo .... Keith Kupferer	

Ensemble: Calvin Dutton, Curtis M. Jackson, Michael Pogue.

Presented in two parts.

DEAD MAN'S CELL PHONE. By Sarah Ruhl. April 5, 2008. Direction, Jessica Thebus; scenery, Scott Bradley; costumes, Linda Roethke; lighting, James F. Ingalls; music, Andre Pluess and Ben Sussman; stage management, Christine D. Freeburg.

Mrs. Gottlieb .... Molly Regan	Dwight .... Coburn Goss
Jean .... Polly Noonan	Hermia .... Mary Beth Fisher
Gordon .... Marc Grapey	Other Woman .... Sarah Charipar

Ensemble: Geraldine Dulex, Ben Whiting.

Presented in two parts.

Victory Gardens Theater, Chicago

Dennis Zacek artistic director, Marcelle McVay managing director

I SAILED WITH MAGELLAN. By Claudia Allen; adapted from the novel by Stuart Dybek. June 18, 2007 (world premiere). Direction, Sandy Shinner; scenery, Jeff Bauer; costumes, Carol J. Blanchard; lighting, Rita Pietraszek; sound, Andre Pluess; projections, Mike Tutaj; stage management, Tina M. Jach.

Perry .... Bubba Weiler	Moms .... Morgan McCabe
Teen Perry .... Justin Cholewa	Zip .... Rob Riley
Sir; Teo .... Marc Grapey	Joe; others .... Desmin Borges
Mick; Ralphie .... Josh Akerlow	Palooka; others .... Michael Liu
Lefty .... Lance Stuart Baker	Camille; others .... Laura Scheinbaum

ILLINOIS

THE DEFIANT MUSE. By Nicholas A. Patricca. October 1, 2007 (world premiere). Direction, Andrea J. Dymond; choreography, Wilfredo Rivera; scenery, Keith Pitts; costumes, Judith Lundberg; lighting, Charles Cooper; sound and music, Joe Cerqua; fight direction, Nick Sandys; stage management, Tina M. Jach.

Sor Juana	Lisa Tejero	Fernandez	Desmin Borges
Don Juan	Dan Kenney	Gongora	Ricardo Gutierrez
Lisi; Elvira	Dawn Alden	Nunez	Kenn E. Head

Presented in two parts.

A PARK IN OUR HOUSE. By Nilo Cruz. November 5, 2007. Direction, Dennis Zacek; scenery, Samuel Ball; costumes, Judith Lundberg; lighting, Patrick Chan; sound, Mikhail Fiksel. Presented in association with Teatro Vista.

Ofelina	Charin Alvarez	Pilar	Marcela Muñoz
Hilario	Gustavo Mellado	Cousin Fifo	Joe Minoso
Camilo	Bubba Weiler	Dimitri	Lance Stuart Baker

Presented in two parts.

A BIG BLUE NAIL. By Carlyle Brown. February 4, 2008 (world premiere). Direction and scenery, Loy Arcenas; costumes, Meghan Raham; lighting, Jesse Klug; sound, Rob Milburn and Michael Bodeen; stage management, Ellyn Costello.

Henson	Anthony Fleming III	Tupi	Scott Baity Jr.
Peary	Larry Neumann Jr.	Josephine Peary	Laura T. Fisher
Future	Bethanny Alexander		

Inuits: Esteban Andres Cruz, Joseph Anthony Foronda, Narciso Lobo, Remigio Ortiz.
Presented in two parts.

FOUR PLACES. By Joel Drake Johnson. April 7, 2008 (world premiere). Direction, Sandy Shinner; scenery, Jack Magaw; costumes, Carol J. Blanchard; lighting, Avraham Mor; sound, Andre Pluess; stage management, Tina M. Jach.

Peggy	Mary Ann Thebus	Ellen	Meg Thalken
Warren	Peter Burns	Barb	Jennifer Avery

Presented without intermission.

KENTUCKY

Actors Theatre of Louisville
Marc Masterson artistic director, Jennifer Bielstein executive director

32nd Annual Humana Festival of New American Plays. February 24–March 30, 2008.

GREAT FALLS. By Lee Blessing. February 27, 2008 (world premiere). Direction, Lucie Tiberghien; scenery, Paul Owen; costumes, Lorraine Venberg; lighting, Brian J. Lilienthal; sound, Matt Callahan; music, Brian Callahan; dramaturgy, Amy Wegener; stage management, Kathy Preher.

Monkey Man	Tom Nelis	Bitch	Halley Wegryn Gross

Time: The present. Place: The great northwest. Presented without intermission.

ILLINOIS – KENTUCKY

BECKY SHAW. By Gina Gionfriddo. March 2, 2008 (world premiere). Direction, Peter DuBois; scenery, Paul Owen; costumes, Jessica Ford; lighting, Brian J. Lilienthal; sound, Benjamin Marcum; fight direction, Lee Look; dramaturgy, Adrien-Alice Hansel; stage management, Michael D. Domue.

Suzanna Slater	Mia Barron	Andrew Porter	Davis Duffield
Max Garrett	David Wilson Barnes	Becky Shaw	Annie Parisse
Susan Slater	Janis Dardaris		

Time: The present. Place: New York, Rhode Island, Florida. Presented in two parts.

THIS BEAUTIFUL CITY. Musical with book by Steve Cosson and Jim Lewis; music and lyrics by Michael Friedman. March 5, 2008. Direction, Mr. Cosson; choreography, Chase Brock; scenery and video, Debra Booth; costumes, Lorraine Venberg; lighting, Deb Sullivan, sound, Matt Callahan; music direction, Scott Anthony; dramaturgy, Jocelyn Clarke and Adrien-Alice Hansel; stage management, Debra Anne Gasper. Presented in association with the Civilians and the Studio Theatre, Washington, DC.

Performed by Emily Ackerman, Marsha Stephanie Blake, Ian Brennan, Brad Heberlee, Dori Legg, Stephen Plunkett, Elizabeth Gilbert, Katie Gould, Andy Lutz, Bing Putney, Ashley Robinson, Matthew Sa, Scott Anthony, Anthony Gantt, Ben Short.

Time: Before and after the 2006 election. Place: Colorado Springs. Presented in two parts.

THE BREAK/S. By Marc Bamuthi-Joseph. March 8, 2008 (world premiere). Direction, Michael John Garcés; choreography, Stacey Printz; scenery, Michael B. Raiford; costumes, Jessica Ford; lighting, Brian J. Lilienthal; sound, Paul Doyle; video, David Szlasa; film, Eli Jacobs-Fantauzzi; music, Ajayi Jackson; arrangements, DJ Excess and Tommy Shepherd; dramaturgy Brian Freeman and Julie Felise Dubiner; stage management, Lori M. Doyle. Presented in association with the Living Word Project and MAPP International Productions.

Performed by Messrs. Bamuthi-Joseph, Excess, Shepherd.

Presented without intermission.

ALL HAIL HURRICANE GORDO. By Carly Mensch. March 13, 2008. Direction, Sean Daniels; scenery, Paul Owen; costumes, Lorraine Venberg; lighting, Deb Sullivan; sound, Matt Callahan; fight direction, Lee Look; dramaturgy, Julie Felise Dubiner; stage management, Paul Mills Holmes. Presented in association with the Cleveland Play House.

Chaz	Matthew Dellapina	India	Tracee Chimo
Gordo	Patrick James Lynch	Oscar	William McNulty

Time: The present. Place: New York City suburbs. Presented in two parts.

NEIGHBORHOOD 3: REQUISITION OF DOOM. By Jennifer Haley. March 18, 2008. Direction, Kip Fagan; scenery, Michael B. Raiford; costumes, Jessica Ford; lighting, Brian J. Lilienthal; sound, Benjamin Marcum; fight direction, Lee Look; dramaturgy, Amy Wegener; stage management, Bethany Ford.

Steve; others	John Leonard Thompson	Makaela; others	Reyna de Courcy
Leslie; others	Kate Hampton	Walkthroughs	William McNulty
Trevor; others	Robin Lord Taylor		

Presented without intermission.

KENTUCKY

Ten-Minute Plays. March 29, 2008.

IN PARIS YOU WILL FIND MANY BAGUETTES BUT ONLY ONE TRUE LOVE. By Michael Lew. March 29, 2008. Direction, Sean Daniels; scenery, Brenda Ellis; costumes, Emily Ganfield; lighting, Paul Werner; sound, Benjamin Marcum; dramaturgy, Adrien-Alice Hansel; stage management, Debra Anne Gasper.

Lindy .... Brandie Moore   Ryan .... Christopher Scheer
Liz .... Jessica Lauren Howell
    Time: The present. Place: Paris. Presented without intermission.

ONE SHORT SLEEPE. By Naomi Wallace. March 29, 2008. Direction, Marc Masterson; scenery, Paul Owen; costumes, Susan Neason; lighting, Paul Werner; sound, Benjamin Marcum; dramaturgy, Adrien-Alice Hansel; stage management, Debra Anne Gasper.

Basheer .... Ramiz Monsef
    Time: Then and now. Presented without intermission.

DEAD RIGHT. By Elaine Jarvik. March 29, 2008. Direction, Marc Masterson; scenery, Paul Owen; costumes, Susan Neason; lighting, Paul Werner; sound, Benjamin Marcum; dramaturgy, Adrien-Alice Hansel; stage management, Debra Anne Gasper.

Penny .... Dori Legg   Bill .... William McNulty
    Time: The present. Place: Penny and Bill's kitchen. Presented without intermission.

TONGUE, TIED. By M. Thomas Cooper. March 29, 2008. Direction, Marc Masterson; scenery, Paul Owen; costumes, Susan Neason; lighting, Paul Werner; sound, Benjamin Marcum; dramaturgy, Adrien-Alice Hansel; stage management, Debra Anne Gasper.

Tina .... Emily Ackerman   Tom .... Stephen Plunkett
    Time: The present. Place: A psychiatrist's waiting room. Presented without intermission.

MARYLAND

Center Stage, Baltimore
Irene Lewis artistic director, Michael Ross managing director

THESE SHINING LIVES. By Melanie Marnich. April 30, 2008 (world premiere). Direction, David Schweizer; scenery, Alexander Dodge; costumes, Anita Yavich; lighting, Justin Townsend; sound, Rob Milburn and Michael Bodeen; dramaturgy, Gavin Witt; stage management, Mike Schleifer.

Catherine Donohue .... Emma Joan Roberts   Pearl .... Cheryl Lynn Bowers
Tom Donohue .... Jonathan C. Kaplan   Frances .... Kate Gleason
Mr. Reed .... Erik Lochtefeld   Charlotte .... Kelly McAndrew
    Presented without intermission.

KENTUCKY – MARYLAND

Round House Theatre, Bethesda
Blake Robison producing artistic director

REDSHIRTS. By Dana Yeaton. October 17, 2007. Direction, Lou Bellamy; scenery, C. Lance Brockman; costumes, Matthew J. LeFebvre; lighting, Michelle Habeck; sound, Martin Gwinup; stage mangement, Maribeth Chaprnka; in the Silver Spring theater. Presented in association with Penumbra Theatre, St. Paul. See Penumbra listing for cast list.

THE BOOK CLUB PLAY. By Karen Zacarías. February 6, 2008 (world premiere). Direction, Nick Olcott; scenery, James Kronzer; costumes, Rosemary Pardee; lighting, Colin K. Bills; sound, Matthew M. Nielson; projections, JJ Kaczynski; stage management, Jennifer Schwartz; in the Bethesda theater.

Ana	Lise Bruneau	Jen	Connan Morrissey
Lily	Erika Rose	Alex	Matthew Detmer
Will	Sasha Olinick	Interviewees	Sarah Marshall
Rob	Jason Paul Field		

Presented in two parts.

LORD OF THE FLIES. By Nigel Williams; adapted from the novel by William Golding. April 2, 2008. Direction, Blake Robison; choreography, Kelly Mayfield; scenery and lighting, Kevin Rigdon; costumes, Trish Rigdon; sound, Matthew Nielson; stage management, Jennifer Schwartz; in the Bethesda theater.

Ralph	Alexander Strain	Simon	Matt Farabee
Jack	Evan Casey	Henry	Abe Cruz
Piggy	Craig Pattison	Maurice	Clay Steakley
Roger	Patrick Elliott	Bill	Ryan Nealy
Sam	Michael Grew	Perceval	Sean McCoy
Eric	Kyle Schliefer		

Presented in two parts.

MASSACHUSETTS

Actors' Shakespeare Project, Boston
Benjamin Evett artistic director, Sara Stackhouse executive producer

MACBETH. By William Shakespeare. October 20, 2007. Direction, Adrianne Krstansky; choreography, Sarah Hickler; scenery, Susan Zeeman Rogers; costumes, Anna-Alisa Belous; lighting, Jeff Adelberg; sound, David Wilson; stage management, Tom Helmer.

Macbeth	Marya Lowry	Macduff	Sarah Newhouse
Lady Macbeth	Paula Plum	Ross; doctor	Candice Brown
King Duncan; others	Bobbie Steinbach	Angus; others	Victoria Bucknell
Witch One; others	Denise Cormier	Lennox; Gentlewoman	Ruby Rose Fox
Witch Three; others	Jessica Kochu	Malcolm	Robin JaVonne Smith
Banquo	Jacqui Parker		

Presented in two parts.

MARYLAND – MASSACHUSETTS

THE TEMPEST. By William Shakespeare. March 16, 2008. Direction, Patrick Swanson; choreography, Sarah Hickler; scenery, David R. Gammons; costumes, Seth Bodie; lighting, Jeff Adelberg; music direction, Eric McDonald; stage management, Adele Nadine Traub.

Prospero .... Alvin Epstein
Ariel .... Marianna Bassham
Caliban .... Benjamin Evett
Miranda .... Mara Sidmore
Ferdinand .... Jason Bowen
Alonso .... David Gullette
Trinculo .... John Kuntz
Gonzalo .... Walter Locke
Antonio .... Richard Snee
Stephano .... Robert Walsh
Sebastian .... Antonio Ocampo-Guzman
Adrian .... Daniel Berger-Jones

Presented in two parts.

American Repertory Theatre, Cambridge

Gideon Lester acting artistic director, Robert J. Orchard executive director

DONNIE DARKO. By Marcus Stern; adapted from the screenplay by Richard Kelly. October 31, 2007. Direction, Mr. Stern; scenery, Matt McAdon; costumes, Clint Ramos; lighting, Scott Zielinski; sound, David Remedios and Mr. Stern; stage management, Katherine Shea. Presented in association with Matthew Garrity.

Donnie Darko .... Dan McCabe
Gretchen Ross .... Flora Diaz
Rose Darko .... Paula Langton
Eddie Darko .... Will LeBow
Samantha Darko .... Carolyn McCandlish
Elizabeth Darko .... Angela Nahigian
Dr. Lilian Thurman .... Mara Sidmore
Jim Cunningham .... Thomas Derrah
Kitty Farmer .... Karen MacDonald
Principal Cole .... Remo Airaldi
Rabbit; Frank .... Perry Jackson

Karen Pomeroy;
  Linda Connie .... Sarah Jorge Leon
Dr. Monitoff;
  Larry Ricky .... DeLance Minifee
Seth Devlin .... Thomas Kelley
Joanie; Lanky .... Kathy Lebrón
Cherita Chin .... Talisa Friedman
Roberta Sparrow .... Greta Merchant
Sparkle Motion Dancers .... Gillian Gordon,
                                                           Lisa Woods

Presented without intermission.

COPENHAGEN. By Michael Frayn. January 9, 2008. Direction, Scott Zigler; scenery and costumes, David Reynoso; lighting, Kenneth Helvig; sound, David Remedios; dramaturgy, Katie Rasor; stage management, Amy James.

Niels Bohr .... Will LeBow
Margarethe Bohr .... Karen MacDonald

Werner Heisenberg .... John Kuntz

Presented in two parts.

JULIUS CAESAR. By William Shakespeare. February 13, 2008. Direction, Arthur Nauzyciel; scenery, Riccardo Hernandez; costumes, James Schuette; lighting, Scott Zielinski; sound, David Remedios; stage management, Chris De Camillis. Presented in association with the Centre Dramatique National of Orléans, France.

MASSACHUSETTS

Mark Anthony	James Waterston	Cicero	Jeremy Geidt
Marcus Brutus	Jim True-Frost	Decius Brutus	Neil Patrick Stewart
Julius Caesar	Thomas Derrah	Casca	Remo Airaldi
Cassius	Mark L. Montgomery	Trebonius	Daniel Le
Octavius	Thomas Kelley	Soothsayer	Kunal Prasad
Portia; Calpurnia	Sara Kathryn Bakker	Metellus Cimber	Gardiner Comfort
Cinna	Perry Jackson	Lucius	Jared Craig
Lepidus	Will LeBow		

Musicians: Eric Hofbauer, Blake Newman, Mariane Solivan.

Presented in two parts.

CARDENIO. By Stephen Greenblatt and Charles L. Mee. May 14, 2008 (world premiere). Direction, Les Waters; choreography, Doug Elkins; scenery, Annie Smart; costumes, Christal Weatherly; lighting, James F. Ingalls; sound, David Remedios; stage management, Chris De Camillis.

Will	Thomas Kelley	Susanna	Leenya Rideout
Anselmo	Mickey Solis	Luisa	Karen MacDonald
Camila	Sarah Baskin	Alfred	Will LeBow
Sally	Liz Wilson	Melchiore	Thomas Derrah
Edmund	Nathan Keepers	Simonetta	Rebecca Luttio
Doris	Maria Elena Ramirez	Rudi	Remo Airaldi

Presented in two parts.

Barrington Stage Company, Sheffield
Julianne Boyd artistic director

CALVIN BERGER. Musical with book, music and lyrics by Barry Wyner. July 3, 2007. Direction, Stephen Terrell; scenery, Brian Prather; costumes, Amela Baksic; lighting, Scott Pinkney; music direction, Justin Paul; stage management, Jamie Rose Thoma.

Calvin	David Perlman	Matt	Aaron Tveit
Rosanna	Elizabeth Lundberg	Bret	Gillian Goldberg

Presented in two parts.

FUNKED UP FAIRY TALES. Musical with book, music and lyrics by Kirsten Childs. August 8, 2007. Direction, Kevin Del Aguila; scenery, Brian Prather; costumes, Matthew Hemesath; lighting, Jeff Davis; sound, Daniel A. Little; music direction, Darren R. Cohen; stage management, Jamie Rose Thoma.

Performed by Christy McIntosh, Rashidra Scott, Alysha Umphress, Edwina Findley, Heath Calvert, Desmond Green.

Musical numbers included: "Prelude," "Three Magical Fairies," "Ersilia's Dream," "Family Honor," "I Wanna Get Married Momma (Even Though I'm a Pig)," "Don't Look for Nothin' That Can't Be Found," "Tammi-Lynn," "The Moon and the Stars," "The Carter Hall Ball," "Hey Beyonce," "Intervention," "Thrill of Love," "Reality Show Wife," "Brag on Your Daughters," "Straw Into Gold," "On Bended Knee," "Rumpelstiltskin," "Hand Over the Baby," "Epilogue."

Presented without intermission.

MASSACHUSETTS

Berkshire Theatre Festival, Stockbridge
Kate Maguire executive director

ONE FLEW OVER THE CUCKOO'S NEST. By Dale Wasserman; adapted from the novel by Ken Kesey. July 13, 2007. Direction, Eric Hill; scenery, Karl Eigsti; costumes, Jessica Risser-Milne; lighting, Matthew E. Adelson; sound, J Hagenbuckle; stage management, Alan Filderman.

Randle P. McMurphy	Jonathan Epstein	Martini	Robert Serrell
Nurse Ratched	Linda Hamilton	Cheswick	E. Gray Simons III
Billy Bibbit	Randy Harrison	Aide Williams; Turkle	Anthony Stockard
Dr. Spivey	Ron Bagden	Candy Starr	Crystal Bock
Chief Bromden	Austin Durant	Aide Warren	Sheldon Best
Scanlon	Jerry Krasser	Ruckley	Stew Nantell
Dale Harding	Tommy Schrider		

Ensemble: Rebecca Leigh Webber
Presented in two parts.

EDUCATING RITA. By Willy Russell. August 22, 2007. Direction, Richard Corley; scenery, Joseph Varga; costumes, Sarah Reever; lighting, Holly Blomquist; sound and music, Joe Cerqua; stage management, Stephen Horton.

Frank	Jonathan Epstein	Rita	Tara Franklin

Presented in two parts.

MY PAL GEORGE. By Rick Cleveland. July 5, 2007 (world premiere). Direction, Eric Simonson; scenery, Dave Brooks; lighting, Erik M. Seidel; sound, Craig Kaufman.

Performed by Mr. Cleveland.

Huntington Theatre Company, Boston
Nicholas Martin artistic director, Michael Maso managing director

THE 39 STEPS. By Patrick Barlow; based on the book by John Buchan. September 19, 2007. Direction, Maria Aitken; scenery and costumes, Peter McKintosh; lighting, Kevin Adams; sound, Mic Pool; stage management, Nevin Hedley.

Richard Hannay	Charles Edwards	Clowns	Cliff Saunders,
Annabella; others	Jennifer Ferrin		Arnie Burton

Presented in two parts.

BRENDAN. By Ronan Noone. October 24, 2007 (world premiere). Direction, Justin Waldman; scenery, Alexander Dodge; costumes, Mariann Verheyen; lighting, Jeff Croiter; sound, Fitz Patton; stage management, Eileen Ryan Kelly.

Brendan	Dashiell Eaves	Daisy; others	Kathleen McElfresh
Woman	Nancy E. Carroll	Steveo; others	Ciaran Crawford
Fred; others	Cliff Odle	Rose	Natalie Gold
Josh; others	Tommy Schrider	Maria	Kelly McAndrew
Bum; others	Bradley Thoennes		

Presented without intermission.

MASSACHUSETTS

STREAMERS. By David Rabe. November 14, 2007. Direction, Scott Ellis; scenery, Neil Patel; costumes, Tom Broecker; lighting, Jeff Croiter; sound, John Gromada; stage management, Stephen M. Kaus.

Richie	Hale Appleman	Martin	Charlie Hewson
Cokes	Larry Clarke	Rooney	John Sharian
Carlyle	Ato Essandoh	Roger	J.D. Williams
Billy	Brad Fleischer		

Ensemble: Cobey Mandarino, Augustus Kelley, John Diket, M. Zach Bubolo.

Presented in two parts.

THIRD. By Wendy Wasserstein. January 9, 2008. Direction, Richard Seer; scenery, Ralph Funicello; costumes, Robert Morgan; lighting, Matthew Richards; sound, Bruce Ellman; stage management, Stephen M. Kaus.

Laurie Jameson	Maureen Anderman	Nancy Gordon	Robin Pearson Rose
Emily	Halley Feiffer	Voices	Alex Mickiewicz,
Woodson Bull III	Graham Hamilton		Libby Woodbridge
Jack Jameson	Jonathan McMurtry		

Presented in two parts.

SHINING CITY. By Conor McPherson. March 12, 2008. Direction, Robert Falls; scenery, Santo Loquasto; costumes, Kaye Voyce; lighting, Christopher Akerlind; sound, Obadiah Eaves; stage management, Eileen Ryan Kelly.

Laurence	Keith Gallagher	Ian	Jay Whittaker
John	John Judd	Naesa	Nicole Wiesner

Presented without intermission.

THE CRY OF THE REED. By Sinan Ünel. April 9, 2008. Direction, Daniel Goldstein; scenery, Eugene Lee; costumes, Laurie Churba; lighting, Michael Chybowski; sound and music, Eric Shim; fight direction, Thomas Schall; stage management, Gail P. Luna.

Hakan; Kadir	Amir Arison	Ayla	Cigdem Onat
Sevgi	Lisa Birnbaum	Philip	Darren Pettie
Josh	Sean Dugan	Nabil	Rafi Silver
Tariq; others	Laith Nakli		

Presented in two parts.

SHE LOVES ME. Musical with book by Joe Masteroff; music by Jerry Bock; lyrics by Sheldon Harnick; based on a play by Miklos Laszlo. May 21, 2008. Direction, Nicholas Martin; choreography, Denis Jones; scenery, James Noone; costumes, Robert Morgan; lighting, Kenneth Posner and Philip Rosenberg; sound, Drew Levy and Tony Smolenski IV; music direction, Charlie Alterman; stage management, Matthew L. Silver.

Georg Nowack	Brooks Ashmanskas	1st Customer	Nancy E. Carroll
Busboy	Jason Babinsky	2nd Customer	Rosie Hunter
Amalia Balash	Kate Baldwin	3rd Customer	Sarah Turner
Arpad Laszlo	Jeremy Beck	4th Customer	Monique Alhaddad
Steven Kodaly	Troy Britton Johnson	5th Customer	Ashley Arcement
Mr. Maraczek	Dick Latessa	Headwaiter	Marc Vietor
Keller	Josh Mertz	Ensemble	Aldrin Gonzalez,
Ladislav Sipos	Mark Nelson		Warner Kiernan
Ilona Ritter	Jessica Stone		

MASSACHUSETTS

North Shore Music Theatre, Beverly

Jon Kimbell artistic director

THE THREE MUSKETEERS. Musical with book by Peter Raby; music by George Stiles; lyrics by Paul Leigh; based on the novel by Alexandre Dumas. August 23, 2007. Direction, Francis Matthews; choreography, Dennis Callahan; scenery and costumes, Lez Brotherston; lighting, Hugh Vanstone; sound, John A. Stone; music direction, Dale Rieling; orchestrations, David Shrubsole; fight direction, Bryce Bermingham; stage management, Bethany Ford. Presented in association with Greg Schaffert and Frank A. Martin.

Aramis	Kevyn Morrow	Planchet	Steven Booth
Athos	John Schiappa	Bonacieux	Jeff Edgerton
Porthos	Jimmy Smagula	Constance	Jenny Fellner
D'Artagnan	Aaron Tveit	Father; Treville	Kingsley Leggs
Milady	Kate Baldwin		

Ensemble: Chad Ackerman, Mark Aldrich, Adam Alexander, Becky Barta, Mr. Bermingham, Allison Blackwell, Mick Bleyer, Heather Koren, Nick Dalton, Holly Davis, Constantine Germanacos, Emily Harvey, David Mann, Jonathan Sanford, Matt Stokes, Anne Tolpegin.

Musical numbers: "Riding to Paris," "The Like of a Musketeer," "The Challenges," "Count Me In," "Any Day," "Paris by Night," "To the Rescue," "Doing Very Well Without You," "Ride On," "Gentlemen," "Time," "A Good Old-Fashioned War," "Who Could Have Dreamed of You," "Take a Little Wine," "No Gentlemen," "Pour La France," "Lilacs," "Beyond the Walls."

Presented in two parts.

Williamstown Theatre Festival

Nicholas Martin artistic director, Deborah Fehr general manager

HERRINGBONE. Musical with book by Tom Cone; music by Skip Kennon; lyrics by Ellen Fitzhugh; based on a play by Mr. Cone. June 15, 2007. Direction, Roger Rees; choreography, Darren Lee; scenery, Neil Patel; costumes, William Ivey Long; lighting, Frances Aronson; sound, Nick Borisjuk; music direction, Dan Lipton; stage management, David H. Lurie.

Herringbone .... B.D. Wong

Presented in two parts.

DISSONANCE. By Damian Lanigan. June 29, 2007 (world premiere). Direction, Amanda Charlton; scenery, Andrew Layton; costumes, Jennifer Caprio; lighting, Marcus Doshi; sound, Bart Fasbender; stage management, Robyn Henry.

James	Daniel Gerroll	Beth	Alicia Witt
Hal	Thomas Sadoski	Jonny	Patch Darragh
Paul	Rufus Collins		

Presented in two parts.

THE FRONT PAGE. By Ben Hecht and Charles MacArthur. July 5, 2007. Direction, Ron Daniels; scenery, Riccardo Hernandez; costumes, Linda Cho; lighting, Charles Foster; sound, Nick Borisjuk; stage management, Adam Grosswirth.

Wilson	Brian Hutchison	Endicott	Joe Plummer

MASSACHUSETTS

Murphy	Ted Koch	Sheriff Hartman	Wayne Knight
McCue	Matthew Rauch	Peggy Grant	Amanda Leigh Cobb
Schwartz	Rod McLachlan	Mrs. Grant	Kay Walbye
Kruger	Michael Braun	Mayor	Tom Bloom
Bensinger	Robert Stanton	Mr. Pincus	John Cariani
Woodenshoes Eichorn	Greg Hildreth	Earl Williams	Bill Cwikowski
Diamond Louis	Sean Patrick Reilly	Walter Burns	Richard Kind
Hildy Johnson	Jason Butler Harner	Carl	Cary Donaldson
Jennie	Anne O'Sullivan	Frank	Patrick James Lynch
Mollie Malloy	Kathy McCafferty		

Presented in three parts.

VILLA AMERICA. By Crispin Whittell. July 12, 2007 (world premiere). Direction, Mr. Whittell; scenery, Mimi Lien; costumes, Emily Pepper; lighting, Thom Weaver; sound, Nick Borisjuk; stage management, Gregory T. Livoti.

Gerald Murphy	Karl Kenzler	Pablo Picasso	David Deblinger
Honoria; Sara Murphy	Jennifer Mudge	Ernest Hemingway	Matthew Bomer
F. Scott Fitzgerald	Nate Corddry	Mrs. Murphy; others	Charlotte Booker

Presented in two parts.

BLITHE SPIRIT. By Noel Coward. July 19, 2007. Direction, Maria Mileaf; scenery, Neil Patel; costumes, Katherine Roth; lighting, Nicole Pearce; sound, Fitz Patton; stage management, David H. Lurie.

Edith	Jenn Harris	Mrs. Bradman	Adriane Lenox
Ruth	Jessica Hecht	Madame Arcati	Wendie Malick
Charles	Bernard White	Elvira	Kate Jennings Grant
Dr. Bradman	Michael Boatman		

Presented in two parts.

PARTY COME HERE. Musical with book by Daniel Goldfarb; music and lyrics by David Kirshenbaum. July 26, 2007 (world premiere). Direction, Christopher Ashley; choreography, Dan Knechtges; scenery, G.W. Mercier; costumes, David C. Woolard; lighting, Howell Binkley; sound, Jim van Bergen; music direction, Vadim Feichtner; orchestrations, Lynne Shankel; arrangements, Carmel Dean; stage management, Gail Eve Malatesta.

Jack	Hunter Foster	Kate	Kate Reinders
Liberty	Kaitlin Hopkins	Volere	Chauntee Schuler
Wood	Adam Heller	Orlando	Malcolm Gets

Ensemble: Jordan Barbour, Clifton Alphonzo Duncan, Kate Roberts, Sarah Turner.

Musical numbers included: "Miracles Happen," "Making the Leap," "That's What I Want," "The Party Come Here," "Life Is a Coconut," "The Boy Who Could Also Disappear," "You're a Jew," "Fall in Deep," "Volere's Prayer," "A Hymn for Ethel," "In Rio," "Everybody Hates," "Woman on a Rampage," "Come Out of Your Cave," "Vision of Beauty," "Give Me a Sign."

Presented in two parts.

THE CORN IS GREEN. By Emlyn Williams. August 2, 2007. Direction, Nicholas Martin; scenery, James Noone; costumes, Jeff Mahshie; lighting, Frances Aronson; sound, Drew Levy; stage management, Stephen M. Kaus.

John Goronwy Jones	Rod McLachlan	Miss Ronberry	Kathy McCafferty

MASSACHUSETTS

Idwal Morris .... Blake Segal
Sarah Pugh .... Amanda Leigh Cobb
Groom .... Patrick James Lynch
Squire .... Dylan Baker
Bessie Watty .... Ginnifer Goodwin
Mrs. Watty .... Becky Ann Baker
Miss Moffat .... Kate Burton
    Presented in three parts.

Morgan Evans .... Morgan Ritchie
Robbart Robbatch .... Greg Hildreth
Glyn Thomas .... Barnett Cohen
Will Hughes .... Jordan Dean
John Owen .... Joe Tippett
Old Tom .... Tom Bloom

THE PHYSICISTS. By Friedrich Dürrenmatt; translation by James Kirkup. August 8, 2007. Direction, Kevin O'Rourke; scenery, Alexander Dodge; costumes, Deborah Brothers; lighting, Colin K. Bills; sound, David Sanderson; stage management, Jenny Dewar.

Police Doctor;
  Mrs. Rose .... Meggie Nidever
Blocker; Murillo .... Kaveh Landsverk
Inspector Fox .... John Feltch
Sister Boll .... Morgan Phillips-Spotts
Herbert George Butler
  (Newton) .... Roger Rees
    Presented in two parts.

Doctor von Zahnd .... Brenda Wehle
Ernest Henry Ernesti
  (Einstein) .... Mark Blum
Deacon Rose;
  Louis Sievers .... Cary Donaldson
Jonathan Wm. Mobius .... Rob Campbell
Monica Stettler .... Lydia Barnett-Mulligan

CRIMES OF THE HEART. By Beth Henley. August 9, 2007. Direction, Kathleen Turner; scenery, Kris Stone; costumes, Christal Weatherly; lighting, Charles Foster; sound, Drew Levy; stage management, Adam Grosswirth.

Lenny Magrath .... Jennifer Dundas
Chick Boyle .... Kali Rocha
Doc Porter .... Patch Darragh
    Presented in two parts.

Meg Magrath .... Sarah Paulson
Babe Botrelle .... Lily Rabe
Barnette Lloyd .... Chandler Williams

THE AUTUMN GARDEN. By Lillian Hellman. August 16, 2007. Direction, David Jones; scenery, Thomas Lynch; costumes, Ilona Somogyi; lighting, David Weiner; sound, John Gromada; stage management, Matthew L. Silver.

Rose Griggs .... Maryann Plunkett
Mary Ellis .... Elizabeth Franz
Gen. Benjamin Griggs .... Brian Kerwin
Edward Crossman .... Rufus Collins
Frederick Ellis .... Eric Murdoch
Carrie Ellis .... Cynthia Mace
    Presented in three parts.

Sophie Tuckerman .... Mamie Gummer
Leon .... Rama C. Marshall
Constance Tuckerman .... Allison Janney
Nicholas Denery .... John Benjamin Hickey
Nina Denery .... Jessica Hecht
Hilda .... Brooke Parks

MICHIGAN

Purple Rose Theatre Company, Chelsea
Guy Sanville artistic director, Jeff Daniels executive director

SEA OF FOOLS. By Matt Letscher. June 30, 2007 (world premiere). Direction, Mr. Letscher; scenery, Vincent Mountain; costumes, Christianne Myers; lighting, Reid G. Johnson; sound, Quintessa Gallinat; stage management, Michelle DiDomenico.

MASSACHUSETTS – MICHIGAN

Performed by Sandra Birch, Grant R. Krause, John Lepard, Janet Maylie, Suzi Regan, John Seibert, Guy Sanville, Clyde Brown.

THE POETRY OF PIZZA. By Deborah Breevort. October 12, 2007 (world premiere). Direction, Guy Sanville; scenery, Bartley H. Bauer; costumes, Meghann O'Malley-Powell; lighting, Dana White; sound, Tom Whalen; stage management, Heather A. Hummel.

Performed by Sarah Benoit, Sandra Birch, Ruth Crawford, David Daoust, Grant R. Krause, Hugh Maguire, Qarie Marshall, Michelle Mountain.

VINO VERITAS. By David MacGregor. January 25, 2008 (world premiere). Direction, Guy Sanville; scenery, Daniel C. Walker; costumes, Christianne Myers; lighting, Dana White; sound, Quintessa Gallinat; stage management, Michelle DiDomenico.

Performed by Quetta Carpenter, Tommy A. Gomez, Suzi Regan, Phil Powers.

GROWING PRETTY. By Carey Crim. April 5, 2008 (world premiere). Direction, Michelle Mountain; scenery, Vincent Mountain; costumes, Meghann O'Malley-Powell; lighting, Dana White; sound, Quintessa Gallinat; stage management, Stephanie Buck.

Performed by Matt Gwynn, Stacie Hadgikosti, Grant R. Krause, Hugh Maguire, Michael Brian Ogden, Rhiannon R. Ragland.

MINNESOTA

The Guthrie Theater, Minneapolis
Joe Dowling artistic director

THE HOME PLACE. By Brian Friel. September 28, 2007. Direction, Joe Dowling; scenery, Frank Hallinan Flood; costumes, Monica Frawley; lighting, Matthew Reinert; sound, Reid Rejsa; stage management, Russell W. Johnson.

Christopher Gore	Simon Jones	Sally Cavanagh	Maggie Chestovich
Margaret O'Donnell	Sarah Agnew	Clement O'Donnell	Charles Keating
Dr. Richard Gore	Richard S. Iglewski	David Gore	Michael Bakkensen
Con Doherty	Matthew Amendt	Tommy Boyle	Samuel Finnegan Pearson
Johnny MacLoone	James Ramlet	Maisie McLaughlin	Juliet Paulson;
Perkins	Steve Lewis		Scarlett Thompson
Mary Sweeney	Virginia S. Burke		

Presented in three parts.

PEN. By David Marshall Grant. November 7, 2007. Direction and scenery, Rob Melrose; costumes, Christine Richardson; lighting, Frank Butler; sound, C. Andrew Mayer; dramaturgy, Michael Lupu; stage management, Michele Harms.

Matt	Marc Halsey	Jerry	Philip Callen
Helen	Michelle Barber		

Presented in two parts.

PEER GYNT. By Henrik Ibsen; translated and adapted by Robert Bly. January 18, 2008. Direction, Tim Carroll; scenery and costumes, Laura Hopkins; lighting, Stan Pressner; music, Claire van Kampen; sound, Scott W. Edwards; stage management, Chris A. Code.

Peer Gynt .... Mark Rylance
Asa .... Isabell Monk O'Connor
Troll Princess .... Tracey Maloney
Solveig .... Miriam Silverman

Ensemble: Phyllis Wright, Tyson Forbes, Matthew Amendt, Mark Rosenwinkel, Jonas Goslow, Richard Ooms, Bill McCallum, Michelle O'Neill, Catherine Johnson Justice, Maha Chehlaoui, Jim Lichtscheidl, Alexis Gaither, Marisa Jacobus, Mac Rasmus, Jake Speikers.

Presented in two parts.

Penumbra Theatre, St. Paul
Lou Bellamy artistic director

REDSHIRTS. By Dana Yeaton. September 6, 2007 (world premiere). Direction, Lou Bellamy; scenery, C. Lance Brockman; costumes, Matthew J. LeFebvre; lighting, Michelle Habeck; sound, Martin Gwinup; stage management, Ronald Alois Schultz. Presented in association with Round House Theatre, Bethesda.

Dante Greene .... James T. Alfred
Tyrell Moore .... James Craven
Tori .... Kimberly Gilbert
Jahzeel Wilson .... Cedric Mays
Dale Mayo .... Will Sallee
Audrey Yantz .... Kimberly Schraf
Charlene Bigelow .... Regina Marie Williams
Curtis Combs .... Ahanti Young

Presented in two parts.

GEM OF THE OCEAN. By August Wilson. April 25, 2008. Direction, Lou Bellamy; scenery and costumes, Matthew J. LeFebvre; lighting, Michelle Habeck; sound, Malo Adams; stage management, Mary K. Winchell. Presented in association with the Guthrie Theater.

Solly Two Kings .... James Craven
Eli .... Abdul Salaam El Razzac
Rutherford Selig .... Terry Hempleman
Aunt Ester .... Marvette Knight
Citizen Barlow .... Cedric Mays
Caesar .... T. Mychael Rambo
Black Mary .... Austene Van

Presented in two parts.

Theatre de la Jeune Lune, Minneapolis
Barbra Berlovitz, Steven Epp, Vincent Gracieux, Robert Rosen, Dominique Serrand
artistic directors

THE DECEPTION. By Steven Epp and Dominique Serrand; adapted from *La Fausse Suivante* by Marivaux. October 13, 2007. Direction, Mr. Serrand; scenery, David Coggins; costumes, Sonya Berlovitz; lighting, Marcus Dilliard. Presented in association with La Jolla Playhouse.

Trivelin .... Steven Epp
Lelio .... Casey Greig
Contessa .... Emily Gunyou Halaas
Chevalier .... Merritt Janson
Arlequino .... Nathan Keepers

Ensemble: Eleanor Caudill, Kaila Frymire, J.J. Johnson, Michael Kelley, Sheila Regan.

Presented in two parts.

FISHTANK. By Dominique Serrand, Steven Epp and Nathan Keepers. February 16, 2008.

Harry .... Nathan Keepers
Coco .... Jennifer Baldwin Peden

MINNESOTA

Jules .... Dominique Serrand   Jim .... Steven Epp

MISSOURI

The Repertory Theatre of St. Louis
Steven Woolf artistic director, Mark D. Bernstein managing director

THE VERTICAL HOUR. By David Hare. January 18, 2008. Direction, Jim O'Connor; scenery and costumes, Marie Anne Chiment; lighting, Mark Wilson; stage management, Champe Leary.

Oliver Lucas .... Anderson Matthews   Philip Lucas .... Jeremiah Wiggins
Nadia Blye .... Gloria Biegler   Terri Scholes .... Jamie Lynn Concepcion
Dennis Dutton .... Brian White
   Presented in two parts.

NEW JERSEY

Centenary Stage Company, Hackettstown
Carl Wallnau producing director, Catherine Rust associate artistic director

DAPHNE DOES DIM SUM. By Eugenie Chan. February 22, 2008 (world premiere). Direction, Kate Lyn Reiter; costumes, Julie Sharp.

Alan .... Alan Ariano   Bessie .... Kitty Mei-Mei Chen
Daphne .... Shigeko Sara Suga   Waiter .... Michael R. Rosete
   Presented without intermission.

Women Playwrights Series. April 9–April 23, 2008.
A DEATH DEFYING ACT. By Barbara Lindsay. April 9, 2009.
STRANGE WEATHER. By Renee Flemings. April 16, 2008.
YOU MAY GO NOW. By Bekah Brunstetter. April 23, 2008.

George Street Playhouse, New Brunswick
David Saint artistic director, Todd Schmidt managing director

OSCAR AND THE PINK LADY. By Eric-Emmanuel Schmitt. January 18, 2008. Direction, Frank Dunlop; scenery, Michael Vaughn Sims; costumes, Jane Greenwood; lighting, Christopher J. Bailey; sound, Lindsay Jones.

   Performed by Rosemary Harris.
   Presented in two parts.

THE SCENE. By Theresa Rebeck. February 29, 2008. Direction, Jeremy B. Cohen; scenery, Kris Stone; costumes, Miranda Hoffman; lighting, Robert Wierzel; sound, Lindsay Jones. Presented in association with Hartford Stage.

MINNESOTA – MISSOURI – NEW JERSEY

Clea .... Christy McIntosh	Stella .... Henny Russell
Charlie .... Matthew Arkin	Lewis .... Liam Craig

Presented in two parts.

ROGER IS DEAD. By Elaine May. April 11, 2008 (world premiere). Direction, Ms. May; scenery, R. Michael Miller; costumes, Michael Sharpe and Devon Painter; lighting, Phil Monat; sound, Carl Casella.

Doreen .... Marlo Thomas	Michael .... Mark Blum
Carla .... Julia Brothers	Roger .... Tom Bloom
Freddie .... Carman Lacivita	Old Woman .... Patricia O'Connell

Presented without intermission.

McCarter Theatre Center, Princeton
Emily Mann artistic director, Jeffrey Woodward managing director

STICK FLY. By Lydia R. Diamond. September 15, 2007. Direction, Shirley Jo Finney; scenery, Felix E. Cochren; costumes, Karen Perry; lighting, Victor En Yu Tan; sound, Darron L. West; stage management, Cheryl Mintz.

Cheryl Washington ....Julia Pace Mitchell	Flip LeVay .... Javon Johnson
Taylor Scott .... Michole Briana White	Joseph LeVay .... John Wesley
Kent LeVay (Spoon) .... Kevin T. Carroll	Kimber Davies .... Monette Magrath

Presented in two parts.

TARTUFFE, OR THE IMPOSTOR. By Molière; translated into English by Richard Wilbur. October 12, 2007. Direction, Daniel Fish; scenery, John Conklin; costumes, Kaye Voyce; lighting, Jane Cox; sound, Karin Graybash; video, Alexandra Eaton; dramaturgy, Janice Paran; stage management, Alison Cote.

Mariane .... Michelle Beck	Damis .... Nick Westrate
Cleante .... Christopher Donahue	Valere .... Daniel Cameron Talbott
Tartuffe .... Zach Grenier	Dorine .... Sally Wingert
M. Loyal .... Andy Paterson	Police Officer .... Tom Story
Orgon .... Michael Rudko	Mme. Pernelle .... Beth Dixon
Elmire .... Christina Rouner	

Presented in two parts.

ME, MYSELF AND I. By Edward Albee. January 25, 2008 (world premiere). Direction, Emily Mann; scenery, Thomas Lynch; costumes, Jennifer von Mayrhauser; lighting, Kenneth Posner; sound, Darron L. West; stage management, Cheryl Mintz.

OTTO .... Michael Esper	otto .... Colin Donnell
Mother .... Tyne Daly	Maureen .... Charlotte Parry
Doctor .... Brian Murray	Man .... Stephen Payne

Presented in two parts.

THE MAD 7. By Yehuda Hyman; adapted from a tale by Rabbi Nachman of Breslov. February 22, 2008 (world premiere). Direction, Mara Isaacs; choreography, Mr. Hyman; scenery, Narelle Sissons; costumes, Kristin Fiebig; lighting, Mary Louise Geiger; sound, Karin Graybash; video, Seth Mellman; stage management, Lauren Kurinskas.

Performed by Mr. Hyman.

NEW JERSEY

2008 Steinberg/ATCA Honorees

Steinberg Prize: Greg Keller, Mary Beth Peil and Don Amendolia in 33 Variations *at Arena Stage. Photo: Scott Suchman*

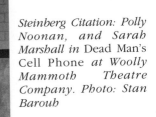

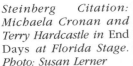

Steinberg Citation: Polly Noonan, and Sarah Marshall in Dead Man's Cell Phone *at Woolly Mammoth Theatre Company. Photo: Stan Barouh*

Steinberg Citation: Michaela Cronan and Terry Hardcastle in End Days *at Florida Stage. Photo: Susan Lerner*

ARGONAUTIKA. By Mary Zimmerman; translated by David R. Slavitt and Peter Green from texts by Gaius Valerius Flaccus and Apollonius of Rhodes. March 21, 2008. Direction, Ms. Zimmerman; scenery, Daniel Ostling; costumes, Ana Kuzmanic; lighting, John Culbert; sound and music, Andre Pluess and Ben Sussman; puppetry, Michael Montenegro. Presented in association with Berkeley Repertory Theatre, Shakespeare Theatre Company of Washington, DC, and Lookingglass Theatre Company of Chicago.

Hylas; Dymas	Justin Blanchard	Medea; ensemble	Atley S. Loughridge
Pelias; ensemble	Allen Gilmore	Meleager; ensemble	Andy Murray
Athena	Sofia Jean Gomez	Hercules; Aietes	Søren Oliver
Pollux; ensemble	K.C. Jackson	Idmon; ensemble	Jesse J. Perez
Castor; ensemble	Chris Kipiniak	Jason	Jake Suffian
Aphrodite; ensemble	Tessa Klein	Hera	Lisa Tejero
Andromeda; ensemble	Ronete Levenson	Amycus; ensemble	Jason Vande Brake

Presented in two parts.

A SEAGULL IN THE HAMPTONS. By Emily Mann; adapted from *The Seagull* by Anton Chekhov. May 9, 2008 (world premiere). Direction, Ms. Mann; scenery, Eugene Lee; costumes, Jennifer von Mayrhauser; lighting, Jane Cox; sound, Karin Graybash; music, Baikida Carroll; stage management, Cheryl Mintz.

Maria	Maria Tucci	Ben	Larry Pine
Nicholas	Brian Murray	Lorenzo	Daniel Oreskes
Alex	Stark Sands	Paula	Jacqueline Antaramian
Nina	Morena Baccarin	Milly	Laura Heisler
Philip	David Andrew Macdonald	Harold	Matthew Maher

Presented in two parts.

New Jersey Repertory Company, Long Branch
Suzanne Barabas artistic director, Gabor Barabas executive producer

AND HER HAIR WENT WITH HER. By Zina Camblin. January 19, 2008 (world premiere). Direction, Kamilah Forbes; scenery, Charles Corcoran; costumes, Patricia E. Doherty; lighting, Jill Nagle; sound, Jessica Paz; stage management, Rose Riccardi.

Performed by Ms. Camblin and MaConnia Chesser.
Presented without intermission.

Shakespeare Theatre of New Jersey, Madison
Bonnie J. Monte artistic director

THE TIME OF YOUR LIFE. By William Saroyan. September 8. 2007. Direction, Paul Mullins; scenery, James Wolk; costumes, Lora LaVon; lighting, Michael Giannitti; sound, Karin Graybash; stage management, Josiane M. Lemieux.

Joe	Andrew Weems	Harry	Blake Hackler
Nick	Gregory Derelian	Wesley	Anthony Stokes
Arab	Paul Meshejian	Lorene	Megan Irene Davis
Newsboy	Michael Mungiello	Blick	Christopher Burns
Tom	Ned Noyes	Mary L.	Allison Daugherty
Kitty Duval	Sofia Jean Gomez	McCarthy	John Nahigian
Dudley	Salvatore Cacciato	Krupp	Sean Mahan

NEW JERSEY

Kit Carson .... Edmond Genest
Sailor .... John Niahigian
Elsie .... Jennifer Gawlik
Killer .... Megan Irene Davis
  Presented in two parts.

Killer's Sidekick .... Allison Daugherty
Society Lady .... Carole Caton
Society Gentleman .... Barry Smith

HENRY VI: BLOOD AND ROSES. By William Shakespeare; adapted by Brian B. Crowe. October 13, 2007. Direction, Mr. Crowe; scenery, Michael Schweikardt; costumes, Dane Laffrey; lighting, S. Ryan Schmidt; sound, Guy Sherman; fight direction, Doug West; stage management, Kathy Snyder.

Talbot; others .... Clark Carmichael
York; Whitmore .... Rufus Collins
Warder; others .... Tristan Colton
Henry V (voice) .... David Conrad
Exeter; Horner .... Frank Copeland
Warder; others .... Jordan Coughtry
Servingman; others .... Will Davis
Somerset .... Joe Discher
Lady in Waiting;
  Lady Grey .... Maurine Evans
Henry VI .... Ryan Farley
Gloucester; others .... John Hickok
Servingman; others .... Roderick Lapid
Mayor of London;
  others .... Terence MacSweeny
  Presented in two parts.

Young Henry;
  Edward .... Daniel Marconi
Sir William;
  Lord Saye .... Garth McCardle
Suffolk; others .... Fletcher McTaggart
Winchester; others .... William Metzo
Captain; others .... Jed Peterson
Margaret .... Angela Pierce
Servingman; others .... Tom Robenolt
Dame Eleanor; others .... Patricia Skarbinski
Rutland .... Theodore Thurlow
Warwick; Jack Cade .... Scott Whitehurst
Nun; others .... Jo Williamson
Hume; others .... Derek Wilson

NEW YORK

Studio Arena Theatre, Buffalo

Kathleen Gaffney artistic director, Iain Campbell managing director

DON'T TALK TO THE ACTORS. By Tom Dudzick. September 15, 2007 (world premiere). Direction, Thomas Caruso; scenery, Troy Hourie; costumes, Donna McCarthy; lighting, John Saunders; sound, Rick Menke; stage management, Marianne Montgomery.

Performed by Denny Dillon, Richard Kline, Lewis J. Stadlen, Dana Powers Acheson, Polly Lee, Peter Stadlen.

Syracuse Stage

Timothy Bond producing artistic director, Jeffrey Woodward managing director

THE BOMB-ITTY OF ERRORS. Musical by Jordan Allen-Dutton, Jason Catalano, Gregory J. Qaiyum and Erik Weiner; music by Jeffrey Qaiyum. March 14, 2008. Direction, Andy Goldberg; scenery, Shoko Kambara; costumes, Amelia Dombrowski; lighting, Aaron Spivey; sound, Jonathan Hertner; stage management, Adam Ganderson.

Antipholus of Syracuse .... Jason Babinsky
Antipholus of Ephesus .... James Barry
Dromio of Syracuse .... Darian Dauchan

Dromio of Ephesus .... Griffin Matthews
DJ .... Kheedim Oh

NEW JERSEY – NEW YORK

OHIO

Cincinnati Playhouse in the Park

Edward Stern producing artistic director, Buzz Ward executive director

THE BLONDE, THE BRUNETTE AND THE VENGEFUL REDHEAD. By Robert Hewett. January 17, 2008. Direction, Mark Lamos; scenery, Andrew Jackness; costumes, Candice Donnelly; lighting, Thomas C. Hace; sound, David Stephen Baker; music, John Gromada; video, Peter Nigrini; stage management, Andrea L. Shell.

> Performed by Annalee Jefferies.
> Presented in two parts.

A SLEEPING COUNTRY. By Melanie Marnich. March 27, 2008 (world premiere). Direction, Mark Rucker; scenery, Rachel Hauck; costumes, Katherine Roth; lighting, Phil Monat; sound and music, Ryan Rumery; stage management, Wendy J. Dorn.

Isabella Orsini	Kate Levy	Greg; others	Andy Paris
Midge; others	Susan Louise O'Connor	Julia Fracassi	Dana Slamp

AROUND THE WORLD IN 80 DAYS. By Mark Brown; adapted from the novel by Jules Verne. May 15, 2008. Direction, Michael Evan Haney; scenery, Joseph P. Tilford; costumes, David Kay Mickelsen; lighting, Betsy Adams; sound, David Andrew Levy; music, Mark Parenti; stage management, Andrea L. Shell.

James Forster;		Passepartout;	
others	Lauren Elise McCord	John Sullivan	Evan Zes
Gauthier Ralph; others	Jay Russell	Andrew Stuart; others	John Keating
Phileas Fogg	Daniel Freedom Stewart		

> Ensemble: Margaret-Ellen Jeffreys, Mark Parenti
> Presented in two parts.

The Cleveland Play House

Michael Bloom artistic director, Kevin Moore managing director

SHERLOCK HOLMES: THE FINAL ADVENTURE. By Steven Dietz; adapted from the play by Arthur Conan Doyle and William Gillette. October 17, 2007. Direction, Tim Ocel; scenery, Rob Koharchik; costumes, Pamela Scofield; lighting, Peter West; sound, Scotty Iseri; music, Andrew Hopson; fight direction, John Stead; .

Dr. Watson	Nick Berg Barnes	King of Bohemia	Remi Sandri
Prof. Moriarty	Timothy Crowe	James Larrabee;	
Madge Larrabee	Catherine Lynn Davis	Policeman	Matthew Schneck
Irene Adler	Krista Hoeppner	Sid Prince; others	Jim Wisniewski
Sherlock Holmes	Christian Kohn		

> Presented in two parts.

THE CHOSEN. By Aaron Posner and Chaim Potok; adapted from the novel by Mr. Potok. November 7, 2007. Direction, Seth Gordon; scenery, Michael B. Raiford; costumes, David Kay Mickelsen; lighting, Michael Lincoln; sound, James C. Swonger; stage management, John Godbout.

Reb Saunders .... Kenneth Albers
Danny Saunders .... Andrew Pastides
Reuven Malter .... Adam Richman
Young Reuven Malter .... Jeremy Rishe
David Malter .... George Roth
    Presented in two parts.

GEE'S BEND. By Elyzabeth Gregory Wilder. February 6, 2008. Direction, Shirley Jo Finney; scenery, Michael Vaughn Sims; costumes, Myrna Colley-Lee; lighting, Victor En Yu Tan; sound, James C. Swonger; stage management, John Godbout.

Nella .... Shanesia Davis
Macon .... Wendell B. Franklin
Sadie .... Erika LaVonn
Alice; Asia .... Wanda Christine
    Presented without intermission.

FusionFest 2008. April 23–May 11, 2008. Schedule included:

RUNT OF THE LITTER. By Bo Eason. May 1, 2008. Direction, Larry Moss.
    Performed by Mr. Eason.

A HANDSOME WOMAN RETREATS. By Kim Wayans. April 30, 2008. Direction, Iona Morris.
    Performed by Ms. Wayans.

IN THE CONTINUUM. By Danai Gurira and Nikkole Salter. April 29, 2008.
    Performed by Ms. Gurira and Ms. Salter.

THE OBSERVATORY. By Greg Germann. May 5, 2006. Direction, Michael Bloom.
    Performed by Sean Haberle, John Hines, Blake Lindsley, Kelly Mares.

THE LUNACY. By Sandra Perlman. May 10, 2006. Direction, Mark Alan Gordon.
    Performed by Amanda Duffy, Dan Hammond, Michael Regnier.

SAM AND LUCY. By Brooke Berman. May 11, 2006. Direction, Seth Gordon.
    Performed by Thomas Degnan; Bruce MacVittie, Andrew May, Elizabeth Ann Townsend, Melynee Weber.

A WORLD BENEATH. By Neena Beber. May 17, 2006. Direction, Seth Gordon.
    Performed by Michael Chernus, Marin Ireland, Dorothy Silver, T. Ryder Smith.

AMERICANS. By Eric Schlosser. May 18, 2006. Direction, Seth Gordon.
    Performed by Mark Alan Gordon, Jeff Grover, Charles Kartali, Annie Paul, George Roth, Reuben Silver, Dudley Swetland, Elizabeth Ann Townsend, Tom Woodward.

OREGON

Oregon Shakespeare Festival, Ashland
Bill Rauch artistic director, Paul Nicholson executive director

WELCOME HOME, JENNY SUTTER. By Julie Marie Myatt. February 24, 2008 (world premiere). Direction, Jessica Thebus; scenery, Richard L. Hay; costumes, Lynn Jeffries; lighting, Allen Lee Hughes; sound and music, Paul James Prendergast; fight direction, John Sipes; dramaturgy, Lue Morgan Douthit.

Jenny Sutter .... Gwendolyn Mulamba
Lou .... Kate Mulligan
Buddy .... David Kelly
Donald .... Gregory Linington

OHIO – OREGON

Hugo .... Cameron Knight   Cheryl .... K.T. Vogt
    Presented without intermission.

Portland Center Stage
Chris Coleman artistic director, Greg Phillips executive director

A FEMININE ENDING. By Sarah Treem. February 8, 2008. Direction, Timothy Douglas; scenery, Tony Cisek; costumes, Candice Cain; lighting, Peter Maradudin; sound, Colbert S. Davis IV; music, Vincent Olivieri; stage management, Jamie Hill. Presented in association with South Coast Repertory, Costa Mesa.

Amanda .... Brooke Bloom   Kim .... Sharonlee McLean
Jack .... Michael Borrelli   David .... Ken Land
Billy .... Jedadiah Schultz
    Presented without intermission.

SOMETIMES A GREAT NOTION. By Ken Kesey; adapted by Aaron Posner. April 4, 2008. Direction, Mr. Posner; scenery, Tony Cisek; costumes, Jeff Cone; lighting, Dan Covey; sound, Casi Pacillo; music, Jim Ragland.

Henry Stamper .... Tobias Andersen   Henderson: others .... Chris Murray
Joe Ben .... Andy Paterson   Newton; others .... Scott Coopwood
Vivian .... Sarah Grace Wilson   Sorenson; others .... Tim True
Leland .... Karl Miller   Walker; others .... Todd Van Voris
Hank .... P.J. Sosko   Floyd; others .... Jim Wisniewski
Gibbons; others .... Kevin-Michael Moore
    Presented in two parts.

PENNSYLVANIA

Arden Theatre Company, Philadelphia
Terrence J. Nolen producing artistic director, Amy L. Murphy managing director

WITTENBERG. By David Davalos. January 23, 2008 (world premiere). Direction, J.R. Sullivan; scenery and lighting, Michael Philippi; costumes, Elizabeth Covey; sound, Jorge Cousineau; stage management, Patricia G. Sabato.

Hamlet .... Shawn Fagan   Eternal Feminine .... Kate Udall
John Faustus .... Scott Greer   Martin Luther .... Greg Wood
    Presented in two parts.

City Theatre Company, Pittsburgh
Tracy Brigden artistic director, Greg Quinlan managing director

MOTHER TERESA IS DEAD. By Helen Edmunson. October 10, 2007. Direction, Tracy Brigden; scenery, Tony Ferrieri; costumes, Angela M. Vesco; lighting, Andrew David Ostrowski; sound, Elizabeth Atkinson; stage management, Patti Kelly.

Jane .... Rebecca Harris   Mark .... Sam Redford

PENNSYLVANIA

Frances .... Kristen Griffiths   Srinivas .... Nehal Joshi
    Presented in two parts.

THE 13TH OF PARIS. By Mat Smart. January 30, 2008 (world premiere). Direction, Melia Bensussen; scenery, Judy Gailen; costumes, Pei-Chi Su; lighting, Andrew David Ostrowski; sound, Joe Pino; stage management, Patti Kelly.

Vincent .... Matthew Dellapina   Chloe .... Bridget Connors
Annie .... Theo Allyn   Jessica .... Jenny Wales
Jacques .... Edmond Genest   William .... Gregory Johnstone
    Presented without intermission.

InterAct Theatre Company, Philadelphia
Seth Rozin producing artistic director, Dave Brown managing director

LAST OF THE BOYS. By Steven Dietz. October 24, 2007. Direction, Paul Meshejian; scenery, Matt Saunders; costumes, Millie Hiibel; lighting, Josh Schulman; sound, Christopher Colucci; stage management, Michele Traub.

Ben .... Dan Kern   Lorraine .... Susan Moses
Jeeter ....Jack Hoffman   Young Soldier .... David Strattan White
Salyer .... Karen Peakes
    Presented in two parts.

BLACK GOLD. By Seth Rozin. January 30, 2008 (world premiere). Direction, Mr. Rozin; scenery, Marka Suber; costumes, Karen Ledger; lighting, Peter Whinnery; sound, Nick Rye; dramaturgy, Peter Bonilla; stage management, Michele Traub.

Performed by Craig Allen Edwards, Delanté G. Keys, Kaci M. Fannin, Sean Christopher Lewis, Maureen Torsney-Weir, Tim Moyer.

Presented without intermission.

HOUSE, DIVIDED. By Larry Loebell. May 28, 2008 (world premiere). Direction, Seth Rozin; scenery, Dirk Durossett; costumes, Susan Smythe; lighting, Peter Whinnery; sound, Shannon Zura; stage management, Michele Traub.

Lou Goldstein .... David Howey   Oren Goldstein .... Davy Raphaely
Doug Goldstein .... Paul Meshejian   Young Doug Goldstein .... Noah Herman
Paul Goldstein .... Dan Hodge   Young Lou Goldstein .... Robert T. DaPonte
    Presented in two parts.

The People's Light and Theatre Company, Malvern
Abigail Adams artistic director, Grace E. Grillet managing director

SIX CHARACTERS IN SEARCH OF AN AUTHOR. By Luigi Pirandello; adapted by Louis Lippa. October 12, 2007. Direction; Ken Marini; scenery, Arthur R. Rotch; costumes, Marla J. Jurglanis; lighting, Dennis Parichy; sound, Charles Brastow; stage management, Kate McSorley.

Lead Actor.................................... Kevin Bergen   Director .... Peter DeLaurier
Young Actress............................. Elena Bossler   Young Actor............................ Mark Del Guzzo
Stepdaughter .... Kim Carson   Lead Actress .... Melanye Finister

PENNSYLVANIA

Little Girl .... Julia Giampietro
Son .... Evan Jonigkeit
Stage Manager .... Cathy Simpson
Assistant Stage Manager ...... Matt Mezzacappa
Young Boy .... Connor Murtaugh
    Presented in two parts.

Harry Andrews .... Gregory Scott Miller
Father .... Stephen Novelli
Mother .... Ceal Phelan
Madame Pace .... Marcia Saunders

TREASURE ISLAND. Musical with book by Kathryn Petersen; music and lyrics by Michael Ogborn; adapted from the novel by Robert Louis Stevenson. November 17, 2007 (world premiere). Direction, David Bradley; choreography, Samantha Bellomo; scenery, James F. Pyne Jr.; costumes, Rosemarie E. McKelvey; lighting, Paul Hackenmueller; sound, Charles T. Brastow; music direction, David Ames; dramaturgy, Elizabeth Pool; stage management, Mr. Brastow.

Mother Hawkins .... Mark Lazar
Jamie Hawkins .... Erin Weaver
Captain Smilenot .... Pete Pryor
Evelyn Treelawnee .... Susan McKey
Squire Treelawnee .... Tom Teti
Long John Silver .... Ian Bedford
Dr. Livesee .... Ben Dibble
    Presented in two parts.

Mama Kura .... Joilet Harris
Polly the Parrot .... Maggie Fitzgerald
Ezekial Machete Scabbs .... Chris Faith
Tinnitus Tom .... Matt Hultgren
Israel Chopped Hand .... Justin Jain
Hackin Devil Dan .... Jefferson Haynes

CRISPIN: THE CROSS OF LEAD. By Avi; adapted by Russell Davis. January 18, 2008. Direction, Andy Belser; scenery, Randy Ward; costumes, Marla J. Jurglanis; lighting, John Ambrosone; sound and music, John Nuhn; dramaturgy, Megan Monahan; stage management, Kate McSorley.

Cerdic; others .... Josh Beckel
Crispin .... Erin Brueggemann
Widow Daventry;
    others .... Kathleen Lisa Clarke
Priest; others .... Nathan Dryden
Father Quinel;
    others .... Michael Lopez
    Presented in two parts.

Bear .... Christopher Patrick Mullen
John Aycliffe .... Stephen Novelli
Goodwife Peregrine;
    others .... Julianna Zinkel

GETTING NEAR TO BABY. By Audrey Couloumbis; adapted by Y York. March 28, 2008 (world premiere). Direction, Abigail Adams; scenery, Jim Kronzer; costumes, Marla J. Jurglanis; lighting, Dennis Parichy; sound and music, Christopher Colucci; dramaturgy, Elizabeth Pool; stage management, Kate McSorley.

Little Sister .... Maggie Fitzgerald
Willa Jo .... Claire Inie-Richards
Lucy Wainwright .... Susan McKey

Uncle Hob .... Christopher Patrick Mullen
Aunt Patty .... Mary Elizabeth Scallen

Philadelphia Theatre Company
Sara Garonzik producing artistic director, Diane Claussen managing director

BEING ALIVE. Musical revue by Billy Porter; based on works by Stephen Sondheim; additional text by William Shakespeare. October 31, 2007. Direction, Mr. Porter; choreography, AC Ciulla; scenery, Allen Moyer; costumes, Anita Yavich; lighting, Kevin

PENNSYLVANIA

Adams; sound, Robert J. Killenberger; music supervision, James Sampliner; music direction, Ethan Popp; orchestrations, Michael McElroy and Joseph Joubert; dramaturgy, Warren Hoffman; stage management, Victoria L. Hein.

Performed by Bryan Terrell Clark, Chuck Cooper, Vanita Harbour, Patina Renea Miller, Jesse Nager, Leslie Odom Jr., Nandi Walker, Rema Webb.

Presented without intermission.

M. BUTTERFLY. By David Henry Hwang. January 23, 2008. Direction, Joe Calarco; choreography, Chu Shan Zhu; scenery, Michael Fagin; costumes, Helen Huang; lighting, Chris Lee; sound, Matthew Nielson; music, Robert Maggio; dramaturgy, Warren Hoffman; stage management, Victoria L. Hein.

Marc; others	Jared Michael Delaney	Comrade Chin; others	Doan Ly
Rene Gallimard	Christopher Innvar	Renee; others	Anne Marie Nest
Song Liling	Telly Leung	Ambassador Toulon;	
Dancer	Wen Tao Li	others	Larry Petersen
Dancer	Ying Chun Li	Helga Gallimard	Susan Wilder

Presented in two parts.

THIRD. By Wendy Wasserstein. March 26, 2008. Direction, Mary B. Robinson; scenery, James Noone; costumes, Karen Ann Ledger; lighting, Russell H. Champa; sound, Fitz Patton; music, Robert Maggio; dramaturgy, Warren Hoffman; stage management, Victoria L. Hein.

Emily	Jennifer Blood	Jack	Ben Hammer
Nancy	Melanye Finister	Laurie	Lizbeth Mackay
Third	Will Fowler		

Presented in two parts.

THE HAPPINESS LECTURE. By Bill Irwin. May 21, 2008 (world premiere). Scenery, Kelly Hanson; costumes, Rebecca Lustig; lighting, Nancy Schertler; sound and video, Jorge Cousineau; music, John Forster; dramaturgy, Warren Hoffman; stage management, Nancy Harrington.

Performed by Mr. Irwin, Ephrat Asherie, Nichole Canuso, Jennifer Childs, Melanie Cotton, Aaron Cromie, Lee Ann Etzold, Makoto Hirano, Cori Olinghouse, Dawn Falato.

Presented without intermission.

Prince Music Theater, Philadelphia
Marjorie Samoff producing director

A NIGHT IN THE OLD MARKETPLACE. Musical with book and lyrics by Glen Berger; music by Frank London; adapted from the play by I.L. Peretz. October 6, 2007 (world premiere). Direction, Alexandra Aron; choreography, Karen Getz; scenery, Lauren Halpern; costumes, Levi Okunov; lighting, Tyler Micoleau; sound, Nick Kourtides; music direction, Eric Barnes; stage management, Michael Andrew Rodgers.

Badkhn	Ray Wills	Sheyndele; others	Deborah Grausman
Nosn	Steven Rattazzi	Gargoyle	Charlotte Cohn
Recluse (Itzhak)	Guil Fisher		

Ensemble: Melinda Blake, Matthew Burrow, Elisa Matthews, Nicholas F. Saverine.
Musicians: Eric Barnes, Skip Heller, Lidia Kaminska, Gregg Mervine, Jim Parker.

PENNSYLVANIA

The Wilma Theater, Philadelphia

Blanka Zizka and Jiri Zizka artistic directors, James Haskins managing director

AGE OF AROUSAL. By Linda Griffiths. December 12, 2007. Direction, Blanka Zizka; scenery, Matthew Saunders; costumes, Janus Stefanowicz; lighting, Russell H. Champa; sound and music, Troy Herion; stage management, Patreshettarlini Adams.

Everard Barfoot	Eric Martin Brown	Mary Barfoot	Mary Martello
Alice Madden	Monique Fowler	Monica Madden	Larisa Polonsky
Rhoda Nunn	Krista Hoeppner	Virginia Madden	Roxanne Wellington

Presented in two parts.

YING TONG: A WALK WITH THE GOONS. By Roy Smiles. February 20, 2008. Direction, Jiri Zizka; scenery, David P. Gordon; costumes, Janus Stefanowicz; lighting, Jerold R. Forsyth; sound, Jorge Cousineau; stage management, Patreshettarlini Adams.

Peter Sellers	Steven Beckingham	Harry Secombe	Ed Jewett
Spike Milligan	David Beach	Wallace Greenslade	Colin McPhillamy

Presented in two parts.

RHODE ISLAND

Trinity Repertory Company, Providence

Curt Columbus artistic director, Michael Gennaro executive director

SOME THINGS ARE PRIVATE. By Deborah Salem Smith. February 20, 2008 (world premiere). Directon, Laura Kepley; scenery, Wilson Chin; costumes, William Lane; lighting, Brian J. Lilienthal; sound, Peter Sasha Hurowitz; projections, Jamie Jewett.

Sally Mann	Anne Scurria	Thomas Kramer	Stephen Thorne

Narrators: Janice Duclos, Rachael Warren, Richard Donnelly.

Presented without intermission.

PARIS BY NIGHT. Musical with book and lyrics by Curt Columbus; music by Andre Pluess and Amy Warren. April 30, 2008 (world premiere). Direction and choreography, Birgitta Victorson; scenery, Eugene Lee; costumes, William Lane; lighting, Deb Sullivan; sound, Peter Sasha Hurowitz; music direction, Michael Rice; stage management, Lori Lundquist.

Buck	James Royce Edwards	Marie	Rachael Warren
Sam	Joe Wilson Jr.	Henriette	Janice Duclos
Harry	Stephen Berenson	Patrick	Stephen Thorne
Frank	Mauro Hantman	Le Mec	Timothy John Smith

Ensemble: Lynette R. Freeman-Maiga, Michael Propster, Adam Suritz, Charise Greene, Jude Sandy, Erin Tchoukaleff.

Presented in two parts.

PENNSYLVANIA – RHODE ISLAND

TEXAS

Alley Theatre, Houston
Gregory Boyd artistic director, Dean R. Gladden managing director

THE SCENE. By Theresa Rebeck. October 31, 2007. Direction, Jeremy B. Cohen; scenery and lighting, Kevin Rigdon; costumes, Alejo Vietti; sound and music, Paul James Prendergast; stage management, Rebecca C. Monroe.

Charlie	Jeffrey Bean	Lewis	Liam Craig
Clea	Elizabeth Bunch	Stella	Elizabeth Rich

Time: The present. Place: New York City. Presented in two parts.

THE LIEUTENANT OF INISHMORE. By Martin McDonagh. January 30, 2008. Direction, Gregory Boyd; scenery and lighting, Kevin Rigdon; costumes, Judith Dolan; sound, Garth Hemphill; fight direction, Steve Rankin and Waldo Warshaw; stage management, Elizabeth M. Berther.

Donny	John Tyson	Mairead	Elizabeth Bunch
Davey	Brandon Hearnsberger	Christy	Todd Waite
Padraic	Chris Hutchison	Brendan	Jeffrey Bean
James	Justin Doran	Joey	John Paul Green

Time: 1993. Place: Inishmore, County Galway, Ireland. Presented in two parts.

UNDERNEATH THE LINTEL. By Glen Berger. March 26, 2008. Direction, Alex Harvey; scenery and lighting, Kevin Rigdon; costumes, Blair Gulledge; sound, Daniel Baker; music, Andy Statman; projections, Clint Allen; stage management, Elizabeth M. Berther.

The Librarian .... John Tyson
Time: Now. Place: Here. Presented without intermission.

THE GERSHWINS' AN AMERICAN IN PARIS. Musical with book by Ken Ludwig; music and lyrics by George Gershwin and Ira Gershwin. May 18, 2008 (world premiere). Direction, Gregory Boyd; choreography, Randy Skinner; scenery, Douglas W. Schmidt; costumes, Carrie Robbins; lighting, Paul Gallo; sound, Tom Morse; music supervision and arrangements, Rob Berman; music direction, Andrew Bryan; orchestrations, Doug Besterman and Larry Blank; fight direction, B.H. Barry; stage management, Peter Wolf.

Achille	Jeremy Benton	Janelle	Alison Levenberg
Dominique	Sae La Chin	Bastien	Joseph Medeiros
Desiree	Erin Crouch	Mimi	Shannon M. O'Bryan
Preston	Jeffry Denman	Miss Klemm	Kerry O'Malley
Hamish	Stephen DeRosa	Louis Goldman	Ron Orbach
Julienne	Lianne Marie Dobbs	Jean Paul	James Patterson
Hermia	Felicia Finley	Yvette	Meredith Patterson
Michel Gerard	Harry Groener	Yves	Wes Pope
Victor Spinelli	Michael Thomas Holmes	Pierre	Benjie Randall
Emil	Drew Humphrey	Chloe	Kristen J. Smith
Francoise	Wendy James	Raymond	J.D. Webster
Hilda	Alix Korey	Monique; Hedda	Kristen Beth Williams
Rene; Georges	Tony Lawson		

Swings: Sara Brians, Matthew Kirk.

TEXAS

Musical numbers included: "Funny Face," "Fidgety Feet," "Wake Up Brother and Dance," "Meadow Serenade," "(I'll Build A) Stairway to Paradise," "(I've Got) Beginner's Luck," "Love Walked In," "Clap Yo' Hands," "'S Wonderful," "Delishious," "An American In Paris," "Fascinating Rhythm," "They All Laughed," "Nice Work If You Can Get It," "Just Another Rhumba," "Treat Me Rough," "Isn't It A Pity?," "The Bad, Bad Men," "Boy! What Love Has Done To Me!," "Home Blues."

Rude Mechanicals, Austin

Madge Darlington, Lana Lesley, Kirk Lynn, Sarah Richardson, Shawn Sides
producing artistic directors

THE METHOD GUN. By Kirk Lynn. April 2, 2008 (world premiere). Direction, Shawn Sides; scenery, Leilah Stewart; costumes, Laura Cannon, lighting, Brian Scott; sound and music, Graham Reynolds; video, Michael Mergen and Lowell Bartholomee; dramaturgy, Ellie McBride; stage management, Jazz Miller.

Performed by Ms. Cannon, Thomas Graves, Lana Lesley, Jason Liebrecht, Ms. Sides.

VIRGINIA

Signature Theatre, Arlington

Eric Schaeffer artistic director, Maggie Boland managing director

THE WITCHES OF EASTWICK. Musical with book and lyrics by John Dempsey; music by Dana P. Rowe; based on the novel by John Updike and the Warner Bros. film. June 15, 2007. Direction, Eric Schaeffer; choreography, Karma Camp; scenery, Walt Spangler; costumes, Alejo Vietti; lighting, Chris Lee; sound, Matt Rowe; music direction, Jon Kalbfleisch; orchestrations, Bruce Coughlin; stage management, Kerry Epstein. Presented in association with Cameron Mackintosh.

Darryl Van Horne	Marc Kudisch	Fidel	Scott J. Strasbaugh
Alexandra Spofford	Emily Skinner	Little Girl	Brittany O'Grady
Jane Smart	Christiane Noll	Gina Marino	Tammy Roberts
Sukie	Jacquelyn Piro Donovan	Joe Marino	David Covington
Felicia Gabriel	Karlah Hamilton	Greta Neff	Amy McWilliams
Clyde Gabriel	Harry A. Winter	Raymond Neff	Jeremy Benton
Michael Spofford	James Gardiner	Frank Ogden	Diego Prieto
Jennifer Gabriel	Erin Driscoll	Brenda Parsley	Sherri L. Edelen
Rebecca Barnes	Brianne Cobuzzi	Ed Parsley	Thomas Adrian Simpson
Toby Bergman	Matt Conner	Marge Perley	Ilona Dulaski

Presented in two parts.

THE WORD BEGINS. By Steve Connell and Sekou (tha misfit). October 8, 2007 (world premiere). Direction, Robert Egan; scenery and costumes, Myung Hee Cho; lighting, Chris Lee; sound, Adam Phalen; projections, Michael Clark; stage management, Taryn J. Colberg. Presented in association with Prana Theatre Group.

Performed by Mr. Connell and Sekou (tha misfit).

Presented without intermission.

THE STUDIO. By Christopher d'Amboise. November 6, 2007. Direction and choreography, Mr. d'Amboise; scenery, Chris Barreca; costumes, Kelly Crandall; lighting, Mark Lanks; sound and music, Jeremy Lee; stage management, Kerry Epstein.

Emil	Stephen Lee Anderson	Jackie	Tyler Hanes
Lisa	Chryssie Whitehead		

Presented without intermission.

GLORY DAYS. Musical with book by James Gardiner; music and lyrics by Nick Blaemire. January 20, 2008. Direction, Eric Schaeffer; choreography, Matthew Gardner; scenery, James Kronzer; costumes, Sasha Ludwig-Siegel; lighting, Mark Lanks; sound, Matt Rowe; music direction, Derek Bowley, arrangements and orchestrations, Jesse Vargas; stage management, Jess W. Speaker III.

Will	Steven Booth	Skip	Adam Halpin
Andy	Andrew C. Call	Jack	Jesse JP Johnson

Presented without intermission.

KISS OF THE SPIDER WOMAN. Musical with book by Terrence McNally; music by John Kander; lyrics by Fred Ebb; based on the novel by Manuel Puig. March 16, 2008. Direction, Eric Schaeffer; choreography, Karma Camp; scenery, Adam Koch; costumes, Anne Kennedy; lighting, Chris Lee; sound, Matt Rowe; music direction, Jon Kalbfleisch; stage management, Kerry Epstein.

Molina	Hunter Foster	Esteban	Christopher Bloch
Valentin	Will Chase	Marcos	Andy Brownstein
Aurora; Spider Woman	Natascia Diaz	Marta	Erin Driscoll
Warden	Steven Cupo	Molina's Mother	Channez McQuay

Ensemble: James Gardiner, Danny Binstock, Kurt Boehm, Matt Conner, L.C. Harden Jr., Stephen Gregory Smith.

Presented in two parts.

THE VISIT. Musical with book by Terrence McNally; music by John Kander; lyrics by Fred Ebb; based on the play by Friedrich Dürrenmatt, as adapted by Maurice Valency. May 28, 2008. Direction, Frank Galati; choreography, Ann Reinking; scenery, Derek McLane; costumes, Susan Hilferty; lighting, Howell Binkley; sound, Matt Rowe; music supervision and arrangements, David Loud; orchestrations, Michael Gibson and Larry Hochman; stage management, Kerry Epstein.

Claire	Chita Rivera	Young Claire	Mary Ann Lamb
Anton	George Hearn	Doctor	Jerry Lanning
Mayor	Mark Jacoby	Jacob Chicken	Ryan Lowe
Annie	Bethe B. Austin	Matilda	Karen Murphy
Townsperson	Leslie Becker	Townsperson	Brianne Moore
Young Anton	D.B. Bonds	Townsperson	Christy Morton
Louis Perch	Matthew Deming	Kurt	Brian O'Brien
Benny	Alan H. Green	Ottilie	Cristen Paige
Rudi	James Harms	Karl	Kevin Reed
Priest	Michael Hayward-Jones	Policeman	Hal Robinson
Lenny	Howard Kaye	Schoolmaster	Jeremy Webb
Evgeny	Doug Kreeger		

Presented in two parts.

VIRGINIA

WASHINGTON

ACT Theatre, Seattle
Kurt Beattie artistic director, Kevin M. Hughes managing director

FIRST CLASS. By David Wagoner. August 2, 2007 (world premiere). Direction, Kurt Beattie; scenery, Carey Wong; costumes, Deb Trout; lighting, Rick Paulsen; sound, Eric Chappelle; stage management, Michael Paul.

Theodore Roethke .... John Aylward

FATHERS AND SONS. By Michael Bradford. May 1, 2008 (world premiere). Direction, Valerie Curtis-Newton; scenery, Matt Smucker; costumes, Melanie Taylor-Burgess; lighting, LB Morse; sound, Eric Chappelle; stage management, Jeffrey K. Hansen.

Leon	William Hall Jr.	Yvette	Tracey A. Leigh
Marcus	Reginald André Jackson	Bernard	Wilbur Penn

5th Avenue Theatre, Seattle
David Armstrong producing artistic director, Marilynn Sheldon managing director

LONE STAR LOVE. Musical with book by Robert Horn and John L. Haber; music and lyrics by Jack Herrick; based on William Shakespeare's *The Merry Wives of Windsor*. September 19, 2007. Direction and choreography, Randy Skinner; scenery, Derek McLane; costumes, Jane Greenwood; lighting, Ken Billington and Paul Miller; sound, Tom Morse; music direction, Mr. Herrick; stage management, Rolt Smith. Presented in association with Mary Ann Anderson, Frank Golden, Frederic B. Vogel, Linda Wright.

Col. John Falstaff	Randy Quaid	Margaret Anne Page	Dee Hoty
Frank Ford	Robert Cuccioli	MissAnne Page	Kara Lindsay
Agnes Ford	Lauren Kennedy	Miss Quickly	Ramona Keller
George Page	Dan Sharkey		

Ensemble: Nick Sullivan, Brandon Williams, Drew McVety, Chad Seib, Ryan Murray, Miguel A. Romero, Stacey Harris, Monica Patton, Amanda Lea Lavergne, Chris Frank, Mr. Herrick, Emily Mikesell, Clarke Thorell, Sam Bardfeld, Gary Bristol, Shannon Ford.

Presented in two parts.

Intiman Theatre, Seattle
Bartlett Sher artistic director, Kevin Maifeld interim managing director

UNCLE VANYA. By Anton Chekhov; adapted by Craig Lucas. June 16, 2007. Direction, Bartlett Sher; scenery, John McDermott; costumes, Deb Trout; lighting, Brian MacDevitt; music, Adam Guettel; sound, Joseph Swartz; stage management, Claire E. Zawa.

Serebriakov	Allen Fitzpatrick	Telegin	Todd Jefferson Moore
Sonya	Kristin Flanders	Vanya	Mark Nelson
Astrov	Tim Hopper	Nanny	Paula Nelson
Maria	Lori Larsen	Worker	Carter J. Davis
Elena	Samantha Mathis	Ensemble	Mark Carr, Chad W. Evans

WASHINGTON

PRAYER FOR MY ENEMY. By Craig Lucas. August 3, 2007 (world premiere). Direction, Bartlett Sher; scenery, John McDermott; costumes, Catherine Zuber; lighting, Stephen Strawbridge; sound, Stephen LeGrand; stage management, Lisa Ann Chernoff.

Billy Noone	Daniel Zaitchik	Austin	John Procaccino
Tad Voelkl	James McMenamin	Karen	Cynthia Lauren Tewes
Dolores Endler	Kimberly King	Marianne	Chelsey Rives

Presented without intermission.

NAMASTE MAN. By Andrew Weems. June 4, 2008 (world premiere). Direction, Bartlett Sher; scenery and costumes, Elizabeth Caitlin Ward; lighting, Greg Sullivan; sound, Peter John Still; dramaturgy, Mame Hunt; stage management, Lisa Ann Chernoff.

Performed by Andrew Weems.
Presented without intermission.

Seattle Repertory Theatre
David Esbjornson artistic director, Benjamin Moore managing director

THE BREACH. By Catherine Filloux, Tarell Alvin McCraney and Joe Sutton. January 16, 2008. Direction, David Esbjornson; choreography, Sonia Dawkins; scenery, Dana Perreault; costumes, Elizabeth Hope Clancy; lighting, James F. Ingalls; sound and music, Mark Bennett; fight direction, Geoff Alm; stage management, Elisabeth Farwell; in the Bagley Wright Theatre.

Mac	Eric Ray Anderson	Linda; Quan, older	Crystal Fox
Editor	John Aylward	Pere Leon	William Hall Jr.
Quan	Michelove René Bain	Water	Nike Imoru
Lynch	Michael Braun	Severance	Hubert Point-Du Jour
Francis	Kelly Conway	Aunt Sis	Michele Shay

Presented in two parts.

BY THE WATERS OF BABYLON. By Robert Schenkkan. February 6, 2008. Direction, Richard Seyd; choreography, Olivier Wevers; scenery, Michael Ganio; costumes, Frances Kenny; lighting, York Kennedy; sound, Christopher Walker; projections, Peter Bjordahl; stage management, JR Welden; in the Leo K. Theatre.

Catherine	Suzanne Bouchard	Arturo .... Armando Durán

Presented in two parts.

THE IMAGINARY INVALID. By Molière; adapted by Constance Congdon. February 27, 2008. Direction, David Schweizer; choreography, Wade Madsen; scenery, Riccardo Hernandez; costumes, David C. Woolard; lighting, Alexander V. Nichols; sound, Matt Starritt and Eyvind Kang; music, Mr. Kang; stage management, Michael John Egan; in the Bagley Wright Theatre.

Claude de Aria; others	Ian Bell	Argan	Rocco Sisto
Béline; others	Julie Briskman	Cleante; others	Andrew William Smith
M. de Bonnefoi; others	Bradford Farwell	Angélique; others	Zoë Winters
Dr. Purgeon; others	David Pichette	M. Fleurant; others	Brandon Whitehead
Toinette; others	Alice Playten		

Presented in two parts.

WASHINGTON

HOW? HOW? WHY? WHY? WHY? By Kevin Kling. March 19, 2008 (world premiere). Direction, David Esbjornson; lighting, Jessica Trundy; sound, Eric Chapelle; puppetry, Dmitri Carter; stage management, Amy Poisson; in the Leo Kreielsheimer Theatre.

Performed by Kevin Kling, Simone Perrin.
Presented without intermission.

THE CURE AT TROY. By Seamus Heaney. April 9, 2008. Direction, Tina Landau; scenery, Blythe Quinlan; costumes, Anita Yavich; lighting, Scott Zielinski; sound and music, Josh Schmidt; stage management, Elisabeth Farwell; in the Bagley Wright Theatre.

Chorus	Guy Adkins	Chorus	Jon Michael Hill
Odysseus	Hans Altwies	Philoctetes	Boris McGiver
Chorus	Ben Gonio	Neoptolemus	Seth Numrich

Presented without intermission.

WISCONSIN

Milwaukee Repertory Theater
Joseph Hanreddy artistic director

THE NIGHT IS A CHILD. By Charles Randolph-Wright. March 14, 2008 (world premiere). Direction, Timothy Douglas; choreography, Simone Ferro; scenery, Tony Cisek; costumes, Tracy Dorman; lighting, Michael Gilliam; sound, Ray Nardelli; stage management, Richelle Harrington Calin.

Todd	Jonathan Gillard Daly	Michael; Brian	Tyler Pierce
Bia	Lanise Antoine Shelley	Joel	Antonio Edwards Suarez
Henrique	Bruno Irizarry	Bartender	Jonathan Dickson
Jane	Monette Magrath	Drunk; Taxi Driver	Shelley Wilson
Harriet	Elizabeth Norment		

Presented in two parts.

ARMADALE. By Wilkie Collins; adapted by Jeffrey Hatcher. April 25, 2008 (world premiere). Direction, Joseph Hanreddy; choreography, Ed Burgess; scenery, Michael Ganio; costumes, Martha Hally; lighting, Noele Stollmack; sound and music, Barry G. Funderburg; stage management, Briana J. Fahey.

Rogers; Young Pedgift	Gerard Neugent	Allan Armadale	Brian Vaughn
Milroy; Downward	James Pickering	Miss Thorpe-Ambrose;	
Mrs. Milroy;		others	Marybeth Gorman
Mrs. Oldershaw	Rose Pickering	Ozias Midwinter	Michael Gotch
Rev. Decimus Brock;		Joseph; Old Pedgift	Steve Pickering
Bashwood	Peter Silbert	Nellie Milroy; Ursula	Emily Trask
Lydia Gwilt	Deborah Staples		

Presented in two parts.

FACTS AND
FIGURES

LONG RUNS ON BROADWAY

○ ○ ○ ○ ○

THE FOLLOWING SHOWS have run 500 or more continuous performances in a single production, usually the first, not including previews or extra nonprofit performances, allowing for vacation layoffs and special one-booking engagements, but not including return engagements after a show has gone on tour. In all cases, the numbers were obtained directly from the show's production offices. Where there are title similarities, the production is identified as follows: (p) straight play version, (m) musical version, (r) revival, (tr) transfer.

THROUGH MAY 31, 2008

PLAYS MARKED WITH ASTERISK WERE STILL PLAYING JUNE 1, 2008

Plays	Performances
*The Phantom of the Opera	8,643
Cats	7,485
Les Misérables	6,680
A Chorus Line	6,137
Oh! Calcutta! (r)	5,959
Beauty and the Beast	5,461
*Rent	5,009
*Chicago (m)(r)	4,786
*The Lion King	4,371
Miss Saigon	4,097
42nd Street	3,486
Grease	3,388
Fiddler on the Roof	3,242
Life With Father	3,224
Tobacco Road	3,182
Hello, Dolly!	2,844
*Mamma Mia!	2,734
My Fair Lady	2,717
The Producers	2,502
*Hairspray	2,393
Annie	2,377
Cabaret (r)	2,377
Man of La Mancha	2,328
Abie's Irish Rose	2,327
Oklahoma!	2,212
Smokey Joe's Cafe	2,036
*Avenue Q	1,996
Pippin	1,944
South Pacific	1,925
The Magic Show	1,920
*Wicked	1,893
Aida	1,852
Deathtrap	1,793

Plays	Performances
Gemini	1,788
Harvey	1,775
Dancin'	1,774
La Cage aux Folles	1,761
Hair	1,750
The Wiz	1,672
Born Yesterday	1,642
The Best Little Whorehouse in Texas	1,639
Crazy for You	1,622
Ain't Misbehavin'	1,604
Mary, Mary	1,572
Evita	1,567
The Voice of the Turtle	1,557
Jekyll & Hyde	1,543
Barefoot in the Park	1,530
Brighton Beach Memoirs	1,530
42nd Street (r)	1,524
Dreamgirls	1,522
Mame (m)	1,508
Grease (r)	1,505
Same Time, Next Year	1,453
Arsenic and Old Lace	1,444
The Sound of Music	1,443
Me and My Girl	1,420
How to Succeed in Business Without Really Trying	1,417
Hellzapoppin'	1,404
The Music Man	1,375
Funny Girl	1,348
Mummenschanz	1,326
*Spamalot	1,317
Movin' Out	1,303
Angel Street	1,295

427

Plays	Performances	Plays	Performances
Lightnin'	1,291	Chicago (m)	898
Promises, Promises	1,281	Applause	896
The King and I	1,246	Can-Can	892
Cactus Flower	1,234	Carousel	890
Sleuth	1,222	I'm Not Rappaport	890
Torch Song Trilogy	1,222	Hats Off to Ice	889
1776	1,217	Fanny	888
Equus	1,209	Children of a Lesser God	887
Sugar Babies	1,208	Follow the Girls	882
Guys and Dolls	1,200	Kiss Me, Kate (m)(r)	881
Amadeus	1,181	City of Angels	878
Cabaret	1,165	Camelot	873
Mister Roberts	1,157	I Love My Wife	872
Annie Get Your Gun	1,147	The Bat	867
Guys and Dolls (r)	1,144	My Sister Eileen	864
The Seven Year Itch	1,141	No, No, Nanette (r)	861
The 25th Annual		Ragtime	861
Putnam County Spelling Bee	1,136	Song of Norway	860
Bring in 'da Noise,		Chapter Two	857
Bring in 'da Funk	1,130	A Streetcar Named Desire	855
Butterflies Are Free	1,128	Barnum	854
Pins and Needles	1,108	Comedy in Music	849
Plaza Suite	1,097	Raisin	847
Fosse	1,092	Blood Brothers	839
They're Playing Our Song	1,082	You Can't Take It With You	837
Grand Hotel (m)	1,077	La Plume de Ma Tante	835
Kiss Me, Kate	1,070	Three Men on a Horse	835
Don't Bother Me, I Can't Cope	1,065	The Subject Was Roses	832
The Pajama Game	1,063	Black and Blue	824
*Jersey Boys	1,050	The King and I (r)	807
Shenandoah	1,050	Inherit the Wind	806
Annie Get Your Gun (r, 2)	1,045	Anything Goes (r)	804
The Teahouse of the August Moon	1,027	Titanic	804
Damn Yankees	1,019	No Time for Sergeants	796
Contact	1,010	Fiorello!	795
Never Too Late	1,007	Where's Charley?	792
Big River	1,005	The Ladder	789
The Will Rogers Follies	983	Fiddler on the Roof (r, 4)	781
Any Wednesday	982	Forty Carats	780
Sunset Boulevard	977	Lost in Yonkers	780
The Odd Couple	966	The Prisoner of Second Avenue	780
Urinetown	965	M. Butterfly	777
A Funny Thing Happened		The Tale of the Allergist's Wife	777
on the Way to the Forum	964	Oliver!	774
Anna Lucasta	957	The Pirates of Penzance (1980 r)	772
Kiss and Tell	956	The Full Monty	770
Show Boat (r)	949	Woman of the Year	770
Dracula (r)	925	My One and Only	767
Bells Are Ringing	924	Sophisticated Ladies	767
The Moon Is Blue	924	Bubbling Brown Sugar	766
Beatlemania	920	Into the Woods	765
Proof	917	State of the Union	765
The Elephant Man	916	Starlight Express	761
Kiss of the Spider Woman	906	The First Year	760
Thoroughly Modern Millie	903	Broadway Bound	756
Luv	901	You Know I Can't Hear You	
The Who's Tommy	900	When the Water's Running	755

Plays	Performances
Two for the Seesaw	750
Joseph and the Amazing Technicolor Dreamcoat (r)	747
Death of a Salesman	742
For Colored Girls . . .	742
Sons o' Fun	742
Candide (m, r)	740
Gentlemen Prefer Blondes	740
The Man Who Came to Dinner	739
Nine	739
Call Me Mister	734
Victor/Victoria	734
West Side Story	732
High Button Shoes	727
Finian's Rainbow	725
Claudia	722
The Gold Diggers	720
Jesus Christ Superstar	720
Carnival	719
The Diary of Anne Frank	717
A Funny Thing Happened on the Way to the Forum (r)	715
I Remember Mama	714
Tea and Sympathy	712
Junior Miss	710
Footloose	708
Last of the Red Hot Lovers	706
The Secret Garden	706
Company	705
Seventh Heaven	704
Gypsy (m)	702
The Miracle Worker	700
That Championship Season	700
The Music Man (m)(r)	698
Da	697
Cat on a Hot Tin Roof	694
Li'l Abner	693
The Children's Hour	691
Purlie	688
Dead End	687
The Lion and the Mouse	686
White Cargo	686
Dear Ruth	683
East Is West	680
Come Blow Your Horn	677
The Most Happy Fella	676
The Drowsy Chaperone	674
Defending the Caveman	671
The Doughgirls	671
*A Chorus Line (r)	670
The Impossible Years	670
Irene	670
Boy Meets Girl	669
The Tap Dance Kid	669
Beyond the Fringe	667
Who's Afraid of Virginia Woolf?	664
Blithe Spirit	657

Plays	Performances
A Trip to Chinatown	657
The Women	657
Bloomer Girl	654
The Fifth Season	654
Rain	648
Witness for the Prosecution	645
Call Me Madam	644
*Mary Poppins	643
Janie	642
The Green Pastures	640
Auntie Mame (p)	639
A Man for All Seasons	637
Jerome Robbins' Broadway	634
The Fourposter	632
Dirty Rotten Scoundrels	627
The Music Master	627
The Color Purple	910
The Tenth Man	623
The Heidi Chronicles	621
Is Zat So?	618
Anniversary Waltz	615
The Happy Time (p)	614
Two Gentlemen of Verona (m)	614
Separate Rooms	613
Affairs of State	610
Oh! Calcutta! (tr)	610
Star and Garter	609
The Mystery of Edwin Drood	608
The Student Prince	608
Sweet Charity	608
Bye Bye Birdie	607
Riverdance on Broadway	605
Irene (r)	604
Sunday in the Park With George	604
Adonis	603
Broadway	603
Peg o' My Heart	603
Master Class	601
Street Scene (p)	601
Flower Drum Song	600
Kiki	600
A Little Night Music	600
Art	600
Agnes of God	599
Don't Drink the Water	598
Wish You Were Here	598
Sarafina!	597
A Society Circus	596
*Spring Awakening (m)	595
Absurd Person Singular	591
A Day in Hollywood/ A Night in the Ukraine	588
The Me Nobody Knows	586
The Two Mrs. Carrolls	585
Kismet (m)	583
Gypsy (m, r)	582
Brigadoon	581

Plays	*Performances*	*Plays*	*Performances*
Detective Story	581	What a Life	538
No Strings	580	Crimes of the Heart	535
Brother Rat	577	Damn Yankees (r)	533
Blossom Time	576	The Unsinkable Molly Brown	532
Pump Boys and Dinettes	573	The Red Mill (r)	531
Show Boat	572	Rumors	531
The Show-Off	571	A Raisin in the Sun	530
Sally	570	Godspell (tr)	527
Jelly's Last Jam	569	Fences	526
Golden Boy (m)	568	The Solid Gold Cadillac	526
One Touch of Venus	567	Doubt, a Parable	525
The Real Thing	566	Biloxi Blues	524
Happy Birthday	564	Irma La Douce	524
Look Homeward, Angel	564	The Boomerang	522
Morning's at Seven (r)	564	Follies	522
The Glass Menagerie	563	Rosalinda	521
I Do! I Do!	560	The Best Man	520
Wonderful Town	559	Chauve-Souris	520
The Last Night of Ballyhoo	557	Blackbirds of 1928	518
Rose Marie	557	The Gin Game	517
Strictly Dishonorable	557	Side Man	517
Sweeney Todd	557	Sunny	517
The Great White Hope	556	Victoria Regina	517
A Majority of One	556	Fifth of July	511
The Sisters Rosensweig	556	Half a Sixpence	511
Sunrise at Campobello	556	The Vagabond King	511
Toys in the Attic	556	The New Moon	509
Jamaica	555	The World of Suzie Wong	508
Stop the World—I Want to Get Off	555	The Rothschilds	507
Florodora	553	On Your Toes (r)	505
Noises Off	553	Sugar	505
Ziegfeld Follies (1943)	553	The Light in the Piazza	504
Dial "M" for Murder	552	Shuffle Along	504
Good News	551	Up in Central Park	504
Peter Pan (r)	551	Carmen Jones	503
How to Succeed in Business		Saturday Night Fever	502
Without Really Trying (r)	548	The Member of the Wedding	501
Let's Face It	547	Panama Hattie	501
Milk and Honey	543	Personal Appearance	501
Within the Law	541	Bird in Hand	500
Pal Joey (r)	540	Room Service	500
The Sound of Music (r)	540	Sailor, Beware!	500
What Makes Sammy Run?	540	Tomorrow the World	500
The Sunshine Boys	538		

LONG RUNS OFF BROADWAY

Plays	Performances
The Fantasticks	17,162
*Tubes	8,849
*Perfect Crime	8,617
*Stomp	6,008
*I Love You, You're Perfect, Now Change	4,937
Tony 'n' Tina's Wedding	4,914
Nunsense	3,672
*Naked Boys Singing!	2,690
The Threepenny Opera	2,611
De La Guarda	2,473
Forbidden Broadway 1982–87	2,332
Little Shop of Horrors	2,209
Godspell	2,124
Vampire Lesbians of Sodom	2,024
Jacques Brel	1,847
Forever Plaid	1,811
Vanities	1,785
Menopause: The Musical	1,724
You're a Good Man, Charlie Brown	1,597
The Donkey Show	1,488
The Blacks	1,408
The Vagina Monologues	1,381
One Mo' Time	1,372
Grandma Sylvia's Funeral	1,360
*Altar Boyz	1,358
Let My People Come	1,327
Late Nite Catechism	1,268
Driving Miss Daisy	1,195
The Hot l Baltimore	1,166
I'm Getting My Act Together and Taking It on the Road	1,165
Little Mary Sunshine	1,143
Steel Magnolias	1,126
El Grande de Coca-Cola	1,114
The Proposition	1,109
Our Sinatra	1,096
Beau Jest	1,069
Jewtopia	1,052
Tamara	1,036
One Flew Over the Cuckoo's Nest (r)	1,025
Slava's Snowshow	1,004
The Boys in the Band	1,000
Fool for Love	1,000
Other People's Money	990
Forbidden Broadway: 20th Anniversary Celebration	983
Cloud 9	971
Secrets Every Smart Traveler Should Know	953
Sister Mary Ignatius Explains It All for You & The Actor's Nightmare	947
Your Own Thing	933
Curley McDimple	931

Plays	Performances
Leave It to Jane (r)	928
Hedwig and the Angry Inch	857
Forbidden Broadway Strikes Back	850
When Pigs Fly	840
The Mad Show	871
Scrambled Feet	831
The Effect of Gamma Rays on Man-in-the-Moon Marigolds	819
Forbidden Broadway: Special Victims Unit	816
Over the River and Through the Woods	800
A View From the Bridge (r)	780
The Boy Friend (r)	763
True West	762
Forbidden Broadway Cleans Up Its Act!	754
Isn't It Romantic	733
Dime a Dozen	728
The Pocket Watch	725
The Connection	722
The Passion of Dracula	714
Love, Janis	713
Adaptation & Next	707
Oh! Calcutta!	704
Scuba Duba	692
The Foreigner	686
The Knack	685
Fully Committed	675
The Club	674
The Balcony	672
Penn & Teller	666
Dinner With Friends	654
*My Mother's Italian, My Father's Jewish, and I'm in Therapy	649
America Hurrah	634
Cookin'	632
The Fantasticks (r)	628
Oil City Symphony	626
The Countess	618
The Exonerated	608
Drumstruck	607
Hogan's Goat	607
Beehive	600
Criss Angel Mindfreak	600
The Trojan Women	600
The Syringa Tree	586
The Dining Room	583
Krapp's Last Tape & The Zoo Story	582
Three Tall Women	582
The Dumbwaiter & The Collection	578
Forbidden Broadway 1990	576
Dames at Sea	575

NEW YORK DRAMA CRITICS' CIRCLE
1935–1936 TO 2007–2008
○ ○ ○ ○ ○

LISTED BELOW ARE the New York Drama Critics' Circle Awards from 1935–1936 through 2007–2008 classified as follows: (1) Best American Play, (2) Best Foreign Play, (3) Best Musical, (4) Best, Regardless of Category (this category was established by new voting rules in 1962–63 and did not exist prior to that year).

1935–36 (1) *Winterset*

1936–37 (1) *High Tor*

1937–38 (1) *Of Mice and Men*, (2) *Shadow and Substance*

1938–39 (1) No award, (2) *The White Steed*

1939–40 (1) *The Time of Your Life*

1940–41 (1) *Watch on the Rhine*, (2) *The Corn Is Green*

1941–42 (1) No award, (2) *Blithe Spirit*

1942–43 (1) *The Patriots*

1943–44 (2) *Jacobowsky and the Colonel*

1944–45 (1) *The Glass Menagerie*

1945–46 (3) *Carousel*

1946–47 (1) *All My Sons*, (2) *No Exit*, (3) *Brigadoon*

1947–48 (1) *A Streetcar Named Desire*, (2) *The Winslow Boy*

1948–49 (1) *Death of a Salesman*, (2) *The Madwoman of Chaillot*, (3) *South Pacific*

1949–50 (1) *The Member of the Wedding*, (2) *The Cocktail Party*, (3) *The Consul*

1950–51 (1) *Darkness at Noon*, (2) *The Lady's Not for Burning*, (3) *Guys and Dolls*

1951–52 (1) *I Am a Camera*, (2) *Venus Observed*, (3) *Pal Joey* (Special citation to *Don Juan in Hell*)

1952–53 (1) *Picnic*, (2) *The Love of Four Colonels*, (3) *Wonderful Town*

1953–54 (1) *The Teahouse of the August Moon*, (2) *Ondine*, (3) *The Golden Apple*

1954–55 (1) *Cat on a Hot Tin Roof*, (2) *Witness for the Prosecution*, (3) *The Saint of Bleecker Street*

1955–56 (1) *The Diary of Anne Frank*, (2) *Tiger at the Gates*, (3) *My Fair Lady*

1956–57 (1) *Long Day's Journey Into Night*, (2) *The Waltz of the Toreadors*, (3) *The Most Happy Fella*

1957–58 (1) *Look Homeward, Angel*, (2) *Look Back in Anger*, (3) *The Music Man*

1958–59 (1) *A Raisin in the Sun*, (2) *The Visit*, (3) *La Plume de Ma Tante*

1959–60 (1) *Toys in the Attic*, (2) *Five Finger Exercise*, (3) *Fiorello!*

1960–61 (1) *All the Way Home*, (2) *A Taste of Honey*, (3) *Carnival*

1961–62 (1) *The Night of the Iguana*, (2) *A Man for All Seasons*, (3) *How to Succeed in Business Without Really Trying*

1962–63 (4) *Who's Afraid of Virginia Woolf?* (Special citation to *Beyond the Fringe*)

1963–64 (4) *Luther*, (3) *Hello, Dolly!* (Special citation to *The Trojan Women*)

1964–65 (4) *The Subject Was Roses*, (3) *Fiddler on the Roof*

1965–66 (4) *The Persecution and Assassination of Marat as Performed by the Inmates of the Asylum of Charenton Under the Direction of the Marquis de Sade*, (3) *Man of La Mancha*

1966–67 (4) *The Homecoming*, (3) *Cabaret*

1967–68 (4) *Rosencrantz and Guildenstern Are Dead*, (3) *Your Own Thing*

1968–69 (4) *The Great White Hope*, (3) *1776*

1969–70 (4) *Borstal Boy*, (1) *The Effect of Gamma Rays on Man-in-the-Moon Marigolds*, (3) *Company*

1970–71 (4) *Home*, (1) *The House of Blue Leaves*, (3) *Follies*

1971–72 (4) *That Championship Season*, (2) *The Screens* (3) *Two Gentlemen of Verona* (Special citations to *Sticks and Bones* and *Old Times*)

1972–73 (4) *The Changing Room*, (1) *The Hot l Baltimore*, (3) *A Little Night Music*

1973–74 (4) *The Contractor*, (1) *Short Eyes*, (3) *Candide*

1974–75 (4) *Equus* (1) *The Taking of Miss Janie*, (3) *A Chorus Line*

433

1975–76 (4) *Travesties*, (1) *Streamers*, (3) *Pacific Overtures*

1976–77 (4) *Otherwise Engaged*, (1) *American Buffalo*, (3) *Annie*

1977–78 (4) *Da*, (3) *Ain't Misbehavin'*

1978–79 (4) *The Elephant Man*, (3) *Sweeney Todd, the Demon Barber of Fleet Street*

1979–80 (4) *Talley's Folly*, (2) *Betrayal*, (3) *Evita* (Special citation to Peter Brook's Le Centre International de Créations Théâtrales for its repertory)

1980–81 (4) *A Lesson From Aloes*, (1) *Crimes of the Heart* (Special citations to *Lena Horne: The Lady and Her Music* and the New York Shakespeare Festival production of *The Pirates of Penzance*)

1981–82 (4) *The Life & Adventures of Nicholas Nickleby*, (1) *A Soldier's Play*

1982–83 (4) *Brighton Beach Memoirs*, (2) *Plenty*, (3) *Little Shop of Horrors* (Special citation to Young Playwrights Festival)

1983–84 (4) *The Real Thing*, (1) *Glengarry Glen Ross*, (3) *Sunday in the Park With George* (Special citation to Samuel Beckett for the body of his work)

1984–85 (4) *Ma Rainey's Black Bottom*

1985–86 (4) *A Lie of the Mind*, (2) *Benefactors* (Special citation to *The Search for Signs of Intelligent Life in the Universe*)

1986–87 (4) *Fences*, (2) *Les Liaisons Dangereuses*, (3) *Les Misérables*

1987–88 (4) *Joe Turner's Come and Gone*, (2) *The Road to Mecca*, (3) *Into the Woods*

1988–89 (4) *The Heidi Chronicles*, (2) *Aristocrats* (Special citation to Bill Irwin for *Largely New York*)

1989–90 (4) *The Piano Lesson*, (2) *Privates on Parade*, (3) *City of Angels*

1990–91 (4) *Six Degrees of Separation*, (2) *Our Country's Good*, (3) *The Will Rogers Follies* (Special citation to Eileen Atkins for her portrayal of Virginia Woolf in *A Room of One's Own*)

1991–92 (4) *Dancing at Lughnasa*, (1) *Two Trains Running*

1992–93 (4) *Angels in America: Millennium Approaches*, (2) *Someone Who'll Watch Over Me*, (3) *Kiss of the Spider Woman*

1993–94 (4) *Three Tall Women* (Special citation to Anna Deavere Smith for her unique contribution to theatrical form)

1994–95 (4) *Arcadia*, (1) *Love! Valour! Compassion!* (Special citation to Signature Theatre Company for outstanding artistic achievement)

1995–96 (4) *Seven Guitars*, (2) *Molly Sweeney*, (3) *Rent*

1996–97 (4) *How I Learned to Drive*, (2) *Skylight*, (3) *Violet* (Special citation to *Chicago*)

1997–98 (4) *Art*, (1) *Pride's Crossing*, (3) *The Lion King* (Special citation to the revival production of *Cabaret*)

1998–99 (4) *Wit*, (3) *Parade*, (2) *Closer* (Special citation to David Hare for his contributions to the 1998–99 theater season: *Amy's View*, *Via Dolorosa* and *The Blue Room*)

1999–00 (4) *Jitney*, (3) *James Joyce's The Dead*, (2) *Copenhagen*

2000–01 (4) *The Invention of Love*, (1) *Proof*, (3) *The Producers*

2001–02 (4) *Edward Albee's The Goat, or Who is Sylvia?* (Special citation to Elaine Stritch for *Elaine Stritch at Liberty*)

2002–03 (4) *Take Me Out*, (2) *Talking Heads*, (3) *Hairspray*

2003–04 (4) *Intimate Apparel* (Special citation to Barbara Cook for her contribution to the musical theater)

2004–05 (4) *Doubt, a Parable*, (2) *The Pillowman*

2005–06 (4) *The History Boys*, (3) *The Drowsy Chaperone*

2006–07 (4) *The Coast of Utopia*, (1) *Radio Golf* (3) *Spring Awakening* (Special citation to the Broadway revival of *Journey's End*)

2007–08 (4) *August: Osage County*, (3) *Passing Strange*

NEW YORK DRAMA CRITICS' CIRCLE
2007–2008

○ ○ ○ ○ ○

AT ITS MAY 12, 2008, meeting the New York Drama Critics' Circle chose honorees for best play and best musical. The first ballot saw seven works receive votes for best play: Tracy Letts's *August: Osage County*, George Packer's *Betrayed*, Gregory Burke's *Black Watch*, Adrienne Kennedy's *The Ohio State Murders*, Tom Stoppard's *Rock 'n' Roll*, Conor McPherson's *The Seafarer* and Elevator Repair Service's adaptation of the William Faulkner novel, *The Sound and the Fury*. Letts's play missed a majority on the first ballot by two votes when *August: Osage County* received only 10 of the 22 votes cast. The first play-ballot resulted in the tallies that follow: *August: Osage County* 10 (Melissa Rose Bernardo, *Entertainment Weekly*; David Cote, *Time Out New York*; Joe Dziemianowicz, *Daily News*; Robert Feldberg, *The Record*; Adam Feldman, *Time Out New York*; Michael Kuchwara, The Associated Press; David Rooney, *Variety*; Frank Scheck, *New York Post*; Linda Winer, *Newsday*; Richard Zoglin, *Time*), *Black Watch* 4 (Eric Grode, *The New York Sun*; John Heilpern, *The New York Observer*; Jeremy McCarter, *New York*; Michael Sommers, *The Star-Ledger*), *The Seafarer* 3 (Elysa Gardner, *USA Today*; Jacques le Sourd, Gannett newspapers; Terry Teachout, *The Wall Street Journal*), *Rock 'n' Roll* 2 (Clive Barnes, *New York Post*; David Sheward, *Back Stage*), *Betrayed* 1 (John Simon, Bloomberg.com), *Ohio State Murders* 1 (Michael Feingold, *The Village Voice*) and *The Sound and the Fury* 1 (Hilton Als, *The New Yorker*). A procedural second ballot determined that an award should be given, so a third, weighted ballot was undertaken.

The third ballot added more plays to the mix as second and third choices were included by the voting critics. The 10 who voted for *August: Osage County* on the first ballot were joined by eight critics who placed the Letts play in either the second (Barnes, Gardner, Grode, Sheward, Sommers and Teachout) or third (Feingold and McCarter) position on their ballots. Als, Heilpern, le Sourd and Simon all declined to include the Pulitzer Prize-winning play among their top three choices. On the third best-play ballot *The Seafarer* placed second; *Rock 'n' Roll* finished third. As a result of the ranked ballot, 12 additional plays were nominated: Michael Murphy's *The Conscientious Objector*, Horton Foote's *Dividing the Estate*, Sarah Ruhl's *eurydice*, Liz Flahive's *From Up Here*, Jenny Schwartz's *God's Ear*, Charles L. Mee's *Iphigenia 2.0*, J.T. Rogers's *The Overwhelming*, Adam Bock's *The Receptionist*, Patrick Barlow's adaptation of the Alfred Hitchcock film of the John Buchan novel, *The 39 Steps*, Peter Parnell's *Trumpery*, Enda Walsh's *The Walworth Farce*, David Henry Hwang's *Yellow Face*.

During a discussion of foreign plays, the group decided to hold *Black Watch* in abeyance until a return engagement planned for the 2008–2009 season because too few members had seen the work to give it proper consideration. As foreign-play balloting unfolded, four members (Heilpern, Rooney, Winer and Zoglin) offered no candidate for the honor and Feingold was the lone supporter of Robert Farquhar's *Bad Jazz*. The frontrunners in the foreign-play category were *Rock 'n' Roll* 9 (Als, Barnes, Feldberg, Feldman, Grode, Kuchwara, McCarter, Sheward, Simon) and *The Seafarer* 8 (Bernardo, Cote, Dziemianowicz, Gardner, le Sourd, Scheck, Sommers, Teachout). When neither play attained a majority, a second vote tabled the foreign-play discussion for the season under review.

In the best-musical category, three ballots were necessary to name an honoree. The first ballot included six nominated works: *Passing Strange* 11 (Als, Cote, Dziemianowicz, Feingold, Feldberg, Gardner, le Sourd, McCarter, Sheward, Sommers, Winer), *Adding Machine* 7 (Feldman, Heilpern, Kuchwara, Rooney, Scheck, Simon, Teachout), *A Catered Affair* 1 (Barnes), *Next to Normal* 1 (Bernardo), *Gone Missing* 1 (Grode), *The Little Mermaid* 1 (Zoglin). *In the Heights* had been eligible (and nominated) during the 2006–2007 season. Failing to attain a majority by a single vote on the first ballot, *Passing Strange* outpaced *Adding Machine* on the third ballot, which included an additional eight musicals in the ranked polling: Christopher Durang and Peter Melnick's *Adrift in Macao*; Mark O'Donnell, Thomas Meehan, David Javerbaum and Adam Schlesinger's adaptation of John Waters's *Cry-Baby*; Waterwell's *The/King/Operetta*; William Finn's *Make Me a Song*; Nature Theater of Oklahoma's *Poetics: A Ballet Brut*; Ben Katchor and Mark Mulcahy's *The Slug Bearers of Kayrol Island*; Douglas Carter Beane, Jeff Lynne and John Farrar's adaptation of *Xanadu* and Mel Brooks and Thomas Meehan's *Young Frankenstein*. Five of the voters (Barnes, Bernardo, Heilpern, Kuchwara and Simon) declined to list *Passing Strange* among their ranked choices on the third ballot while four (Dziemianowicz, Feldberg, Gardner and le Sourd) omitted *Adding Machine* from their final tally.

Honorees received their accolades at an Algonquin cocktail party May 19, 2008.

PULITZER PRIZE WINNERS
1916–1917 TO 2007–2008

1916–17   No award
1917–18   *Why Marry?* by Jesse Lynch Williams
1918–19   No award
1919–20   *Beyond the Horizon* by Eugene O'Neill
1920–21   *Miss Lulu Bett* by Zona Gale
1921–22   *Anna Christie* by Eugene O'Neill
1922–23   *Icebound* by Owen Davis
1923–24   *Hell-Bent fer Heaven* by Hatcher Hughes
1924–25   *They Knew What They Wanted* by Sidney Howard
1925–26   *Craig's Wife* by George Kelly
1926–27   *In Abraham's Bosom* by Paul Green
1927–28   *Strange Interlude* by Eugene O'Neill
1928–29   *Street Scene* by Elmer Rice
1929–30   *The Green Pastures* by Marc Connelly
1930–31   *Alison's House* by Susan Glaspell
1931–32   *Of Thee I Sing* by George S. Kaufman, Morrie Ryskind, Ira and George Gershwin
1932–33   *Both Your Houses* by Maxwell Anderson
1933–34   *Men in White* by Sidney Kingsley
1934–35   *The Old Maid* by Zoe Akins
1935–36   *Idiot's Delight* by Robert E. Sherwood
1936–37   *You Can't Take It With You* by Moss Hart and George S. Kaufman
1937–38   *Our Town* by Thornton Wilder
1938–39   *Abe Lincoln in Illinois* by Robert E. Sherwood
1939–40   *The Time of Your Life* by William Saroyan
1940–41   *There Shall Be No Night* by Robert E. Sherwood
1941–42   No award
1942–43   *The Skin of Our Teeth* by Thornton Wilder
1943–44   No award
1944–45   *Harvey* by Mary Chase
1945–46   *State of the Union* by Howard Lindsay and Russel Crouse
1946–47   No award
1947–48   *A Streetcar Named Desire* by Tennessee Williams
1948–49   *Death of a Salesman* by Arthur Miller
1949–50   *South Pacific* by Richard Rodgers, Oscar Hammerstein II and Joshua Logan
1950–51   No award
1951–52   *The Shrike* by Joseph Kramm
1952–53   *Picnic* by William Inge

1953–54   *The Teahouse of the August Moon* by John Patrick
1954–55   *Cat on a Hot Tin Roof* by Tennessee Williams
1955–56   *The Diary of Anne Frank* by Frances Goodrich and Albert Hackett
1956–57   *Long Day's Journey Into Night* by Eugene O'Neill
1957–58   *Look Homeward, Angel* by Ketti Frings
1958–59   *J.B.* by Archibald MacLeish
1959–60   *Fiorello!* by Jerome Weidman, George Abbott, Sheldon Harnick and Jerry Bock
1960–61   *All the Way Home* by Tad Mosel
1961–62   *How to Succeed in Business Without Really Trying* by Abe Burrows, Willie Gilbert, Jack Weinstock and Frank Loesser
1962–63   No award
1963–64   No award
1964–65   *The Subject Was Roses* by Frank D. Gilroy
1965–66   No award
1966–67   *A Delicate Balance* by Edward Albee
1967–68   No award
1968–69   *The Great White Hope* by Howard Sackler
1969–70   *No Place To Be Somebody* by Charles Gordone
1970–71   *The Effect of Gamma Rays on Man-in-the-Moon Marigolds* by Paul Zindel
1971–72   No award
1972–73   *That Championship Season* by Jason Miller
1973–74   No award
1974–75   *Seascape* by Edward Albee
1975–76   *A Chorus Line* by Michael Bennett, James Kirkwood, Nicholas Dante, Marvin Hamlisch and Edward Kleban
1976–77   *The Shadow Box* by Michael Cristofer
1977–78   *The Gin Game* by D.L. Coburn
1978–79   *Buried Child* by Sam Shepard
1979–80   *Talley's Folly* by Lanford Wilson
1980–81   *Crimes of the Heart* by Beth Henley
1981–82   *A Soldier's Play* by Charles Fuller
1982–83   *'night, Mother* by Marsha Norman
1983–84   *Glengarry Glen Ross* by David Mamet
1984–85   *Sunday in the Park With George* by James Lapine and Stephen Sondheim
1985–86   No award

1986–87 *Fences* by August Wilson

1987–88 *Driving Miss Daisy* by Alfred Uhry

1988–89 *The Heidi Chronicles* by Wendy Wasserstein

1989–90 *The Piano Lesson* by August Wilson

1990–91 *Lost in Yonkers* by Neil Simon

1991–92 *The Kentucky Cycle* by Robert Schenkkan

1992–93 *Angels in America: Millennium Approaches* by Tony Kushner

1993–94 *Three Tall Women* by Edward Albee

1994–95 *The Young Man From Atlanta* by Horton Foote

1995–96 *Rent* by Jonathan Larson

1996–97 No award

1997–98 *How I Learned to Drive* by Paula Vogel

1998–99 *Wit* by Margaret Edson

1999–00 *Dinner With Friends* by Donald Margulies

2000–01 *Proof* by David Auburn

2001–02 *Topdog/Underdog* by Suzan-Lori Parks

2002–03 *Anna in the Tropics* by Nilo Cruz

2003–04 *I Am My Own Wife* by Doug Wright

2004–05 *Doubt, a Parable* by John Patrick Shanley

2005–06 No Award

2006–07 *Rabbit Hole* by David Lindsay-Abaire

2007–08 *August: Osage County* by Tracy Letts

2008 TONY AWARDS

○ ○ ○ ○ ○

THE AMERICAN THEATRE WING'S 62nd annual Tony Awards, named for Antoinette Perry, are presented in recognition of distinguished achievement in the Broadway theater. The Broadway League (Nina Lannan, chairman)—which changed its name from the League of American Theatres and Producers on December 18, 2007—and the American Theatre Wing (Sondra Gilman, chairman; Doug Leeds, president) present these awards, founded by the Wing in 1947. Legitimate theater productions opening in 34 eligible Broadway theaters during the present Tony season—May 10, 2007 to May 7, 2008—were considered by the Tony Awards Nominating Committee (appointed by the Tony Awards Administration Committee) for the awards in 26 competitive categories. The 2007–2008 Nominating Committee consisted of Joe Benincasa, Robert Callely, Betty Corwin, Jacqueline Z. Davis, Michael D. Dinwiddie, Teresa Eyring, Sue Frost, Andrew Jackness, Betty Jacobs, Geoffrey Johnson, Robert Kamlot, Michael Kantor, Howard Marren, Laurence Maslon, Phyllis Newman, Lynn Nottage, Gilbert Parker, Roger Rees, Jonathan Reynolds, Donald Saddler, Steven Suskin, Tom Viola and Kimberlee Wertz.

The Tony Awards are voted from the list of nominees by members of the theater and journalism professions: the governing boards of the five theater artists' organizations (Actors' Equity Association, the Dramatists' Guild, the Society of Stage Directors and Choreographers, United Scenic Artists and the Casting Society of America), members of the designated first night theater press, the board of directors of the American Theatre Wing and the membership of the Broadway League. Because of fluctuation in these groups, the size of the Tony electorate varies from year to year. For the 2007–2008 season there were 795 qualified Tony voters.

The 2007–2008 nominees follow, with winners in each category listed in **bold face type**.

PLAY (award goes to both author and producer). **August: Osage County by Tracy Letts, produced by Jeffrey Richards, Jean Doumanian, Steve Traxler, Jerry Frankel, Ostar Productions, Jennifer Manocherian, the Weinstein Company, Debra Black, Daryl Roth, Ronald and Marc Frankel, Barbara Freitag, Rick Steiner, Staton Bell Group, the Steppenwolf Theatre Company**. *Rock 'n' Roll* by Tom Stoppard, produced by Bob Boyett and Sonia Friedman Productions, Ostar Productions, Roger Berlind, Tulchin/Bartner, Douglas G. Smith, Dancap Productions, Jam Theatricals, the Weinstein Company, Lincoln Center Theater, the Royal Court Theatre London. *The Seafarer* by Conor McPherson, produced by Ostar Productions, Bob Boyett, Roy Furman, Lawrence Horowitz, Jam Theatricals, Bill Rollnick, Nancy Ellison Rollnick, James D'Orta, Thomas S. Murphy, Ralph Guild, Jon Avnet, Philip Geier, Keough Partners, Eric Falkenstein, Max OnStage, the National Theatre of Great Britain. *The 39 Steps* by Patrick Barlow, produced by Roundabout Theatre Company, Todd Haimes, Harold Wolpert, Julia C. Levy, Bob

Boyett, Harriet Newman Leve, Ron Nicynski, Stewart F. Lane, Bonnie Comley, Manocherian Golden Prods., Olympus Theatricals, Douglas Denoff, Marek J. Cantor, Pat Addiss, Huntington Theatre Company, Nicholas Martin, Michael Maso, Edward Snape for Fiery Angel Ltd.

MUSICAL (award goes to the producer). *Cry-Baby* produced by Adam Epstein, Allan S. Gordon, Élan V. McAllister, Brian Grazer, James P. MacGilvray, Universal Pictures Stage Productions, Anne Caruso, Adam S. Gordon, Latitude Link, the Pelican Group, Philip Morgaman, Andrew Farber, Richard Mishaan. **In the Heights produced by Kevin McCollum, Jeffrey Seller, Jill Furman, Sander Jacobs, Goodman/Grossman, Peter Fine, Everett/Skipper.** *Passing Strange* produced by the Shubert Organization, Elizabeth Ireland McCann LLC, Bill Kenwright, Chase Mishkin, Barbara and Buddy Freitag, Broadway Across America, Emily Fisher Landau, Peter May, Boyett Ostar, Larry Hirschhorn, Janet Pailet, Steve Klein, Elie Hirschfeld, Jed Bernstein, Spring Sirkin, Ruth Hendel, Vasi Laurence, Pat Flicker Addiss, Wendy Federman, Jacki Barlia Florin, Joey Parnes, the Public Theater, the Berkeley Repertory Theatre. *Xanadu* produced by Robert Ahrens, Dan Vickery, Tara Smith, B. Swibel, Sarah Murchison, Dale Smith.

BOOK OF A MUSICAL. Mark O'Donnell and Thomas Meehan for *Cry-Baby*. Quiara Alegría Hudes for *In the Heights*. **Stew** for *Passing Strange*. Douglas Carter Beane for *Xanadu*.

ORIGINAL SCORE (music and/or lyrics). David Javerbaum and Adam Schlesinger (music and lyrics) for *Cry-Baby*. **Lin-Manuel Miranda (music and lyrics)** for *In the Heights*. Alan Menken (music), Howard Ashman and Glenn Slater (lyrics) for *The Little Mermaid*. Stew and Heidi Rodewald (music), Stew (lyrics) for *Passing Strange*.

REVIVAL OF A PLAY (award goes to the producer). ***Boeing-Boeing* produced by Sonia Friedman Productions, Bob**

Boyett, Act Productions, Matthew Byam Shaw, Robert G. Bartner, the Weinstein Company, Susan Gallin, Mary Lu Roffe, Broadway Across America, Tulchin/Jenkins/DSM, the Araca Group. *The Homecoming* produced by Jeffrey Richards, Jerry Frankel, Jam Theatricals, Ergo Entertainment, Barbara and Buddy Freitag, Michael Gardner, Herbert Goldsmith Productions, Terry E. Schnuck, Harold Thau, Michael Filerman, Lynne Peyser, Ronald Frankel, David Jaroslawicz, Love Bunny Entertainment. *Les Liaisons Dangereuses* produced by Roundabout Theatre Company, Todd Haimes, Harold Wolpert, Julia C. Levy. *Macbeth* produced by Duncan C. Weldon and Paul Elliott, Jeffrey Archer, Bill Ballard, Terri and Timothy Childs, Rodger Hess, David Mirvish, Adriana Mnuchin, Emanuel Azenberg, BAM, the Chichester Festival Theatre.

REVIVAL OF A MUSICAL. *Grease* produced by Paul Nicholas and David Ian, Nederlander Presentations Inc., Terry Allen Kramer, Robert Stigwood. *Gypsy* produced by Roger Berlind, the Routh-Frankel-Baruch-Viertel Group, Roy Furman, Debra Black, Ted Hartley, Roger Horchow, David Ian, Scott Rudin, Jack Viertel. ***South Pacific* produced by Lincoln Center Theater, André Bishop, Bernard Gersten, Bob Boyett**. *Sunday in the Park With George* produced by Roundabout Theatre Company, Todd Haimes, Harold Wolpert, Julia C. Levy, Bob Boyett, Debra Black, Jam Theatricals, Stephanie P. McClelland, Stewart F. Lane, Bonnie Comley, Barbara Manocherian, Jennifer Manocherian, Ostar Productions, the Menier Chocolate Factory, David Babani.

LEADING ACTOR IN A PLAY. Ben Daniels in *Les Liaisons Dangereuses*, Laurence Fishburne in *Thurgood*, **Mark Rylance** in ***Boeing-Boeing***, Rufus Sewell in *Rock 'n' Roll*, Patrick Stewart in *Macbeth*.

LEADING ACTRESS IN A PLAY. Eve Best in *The Homecoming*, **Deanna Dunagan** in ***August: Osage County***, Kate Fleetwood in *Macbeth*, S. Epatha Merkerson in *Come Back, Little Sheba*, Amy Morton in *August: Osage County*.

LEADING ACTOR IN A MUSICAL. Daniel Evans in *Sunday in the Park With George*, Lin-Manuel Miranda in *In the Heights*, Stew in *Passing Strange*, **Paulo Szot** in ***South Pacific***, Tom Wopat in *A Catered Affair*.

LEADING ACTRESS IN A MUSICAL. Kerry Butler in *Xanadu*, **Patti LuPone** in ***Gypsy***, Kelli O'Hara in *South Pacific*, Faith Prince in *A Catered Affair*, Jenna Russell in *Sunday in the Park With George*.

FEATURED ACTOR IN A PLAY. Bobby Cannavale in *Mauritius*, Raúl Esparza in *The Homecoming*, Conleth Hill in *The Seafarer*, **Jim Norton** in ***The Seafarer***, David Pittu in *Is He Dead?*

FEATURED ACTRESS IN A PLAY. Sinead Cusack in *Rock 'n' Roll*, Mary McCormack in *Boeing-Boeing*, Laurie Metcalf in *November*, Martha Plimpton in *Top Girls*, **Rondi Reed** in ***August: Osage County***.

FEATURED ACTOR IN A MUSICAL. Daniel Breaker in *Passing Strange*, Danny Burstein in *South Pacific*, Robin De Jesús in *In the Heights*, Christopher Fitzgerald in *Young Frankenstein*, **Boyd Gaines** in ***Gypsy***.

FEATURED ACTRESS IN A MUSICAL. de'Adre Aziza in *Passing Strange*, **Laura Benanti** in ***Gypsy***, Andrea Martin in *Young Frankenstein*, Olga Merediz in *In the Heights*, Loretta Ables Sayre in *South Pacific*.

SCENIC DESIGN OF A PLAY. Peter McKintosh for *The 39 Steps*, Scott Pask for *Les Liaisons Dangereuses*, **Todd Rosenthal** for ***August: Osage County***, Anthony Ward for *Macbeth*.

SCENIC DESIGN OF A MUSICAL. David Farley, Timothy Bird and the Knifedge Creative Network for *Sunday in the Park With George*, Anna Louizos for *In the Heights*, Robin Wagner for *Young Frankenstein*, **Michael Yeargan** for ***South Pacific***.

COSTUME DESIGN OF A PLAY. Gregory Gale for *Cyrano de Bergerac*, Rob Howell for *Boeing-Boeing*, **Katrina Lindsay** for

Les Liaisons Dangereuses, Peter McKintosh for *The 39 Steps*.

COSTUME DESIGN OF A MUSICAL. David Farley for *Sunday in the Park With George*, Martin Pakledinaz for *Gypsy*, Paul Tazewell for *In the Heights*, **Catherine Zuber** for ***South Pacific***.

LIGHTING DESIGN OF A PLAY. **Kevin Adams** for ***The 39 Steps***, Howard Harrison for *Macbeth*, Donald Holder for *Les Liaisons Dangereuses*, Ann G. Wrightson for *August: Osage County*.

LIGHTING DESIGN OF A MUSICAL. Ken Billington for *Sunday in the Park With George*, Howell Binkley for *In the Heights*, **Donald Holder** for ***South Pacific***, Natasha Katz for *The Little Mermaid*.

SOUND DESIGN OF A PLAY. Simon Baker for *Boeing-Boeing*, Adam Cork for *Macbeth*, Ian Dickinson for *Rock 'n' Roll*, **Mic Pool** for ***The 39 Steps***.

SOUND DESIGN OF A MUSICAL. Acme Sound Partners for *In the Heights*, Sebastian Frost for *Sunday in the Park With George*, **Scott Lehrer** for ***South Pacific***, Dan Moses Schreier for *Gypsy*.

DIRECTION OF A PLAY. Maria Aitken for *The 39 Steps*, Conor McPherson for *The Seafarer*, **Anna D. Shapiro** for ***August: Osage County***, Matthew Warchus for *Boeing-Boeing*.

DIRECTION OF A MUSICAL. Sam Buntrock for *Sunday in the Park With George*, Thomas Kail for *In the Heights*, Arthur Laurents for *Gypsy*, **Bartlett Sher** for ***South Pacific***.

CHOREOGRAPHY. Rob Ashford for *Cry-Baby*, **Andy Blankenbuehler** for ***In the Heights***, Christopher Gattelli for *South Pacific*, Dan Knechtges for *Xanadu*.

ORCHESTRATIONS. Jason Carr for *Sunday in the Park With George*, **Alex Lacamoire** and **Bill Sherman** for ***In the Heights***, Stew and Heidi Rodewald for *Passing Strange*, Jonathan Tunick for *A Catered Affair*.

SPECIAL AWARD. **Robert Russell Bennett** (1894–1981) for his historic contribution to the musical theater in the field of orchestrations.

LIFETIME ACHIEVEMENT. **Stephen Sondheim**.

REGIONAL THEATRE. **Chicago Shakespeare Theater**, Chicago, Illinois.

TONY AWARD WINNERS, 1947–2008

L ISTED BELOW ARE the Antoinette Perry (Tony) Award winners in the catgories of Best Play and Best Musical from the time these awards were established in 1947 until the present.

1947—No play or musical award
1948—*Mister Roberts*; no musical award
1949—*Death of a Salesman*; *Kiss Me, Kate*
1950—*The Cocktail Party*; *South Pacific*
1951—*The Rose Tattoo*; *Guys and Dolls*
1952—*The Fourposter*; *The King and I*
1953—*The Crucible*; *Wonderful Town*
1954—*The Teahouse of the August Moon*; *Kismet*
1955—*The Desperate Hours*; *The Pajama Game*
1956—*The Diary of Anne Frank*; *Damn Yankees*
1957—*Long Day's Journey Into Night*; *My Fair Lady*
1958—*Sunrise at Campobello*; *The Music Man*
1959—*J.B.*; *Redhead*
1960—*The Miracle Worker*; *Fiorello!* and *The Sound of Music* (tie)
1961—*Becket*; *Bye Bye Birdie*
1962—*A Man for All Seasons*; *How to Succeed in Business Without Really Trying*
1963—*Who's Afraid of Virginia Woolf?*; *A Funny Thing Happened on the Way to the Forum*
1964—*Luther*; *Hello, Dolly!*
1965—*The Subject Was Roses*; *Fiddler on the Roof*
1966—*The Persecution and Assassination of Marat as Performed by the Inmates of the Asylum of Charenton Under the Direction of the Marquis de Sade*; *Man of La Mancha*
1967—*The Homecoming*; *Cabaret*
1968—*Rosencrantz and Guildenstern Are Dead*; *Hallelujah, Baby!*
1969—*The Great White Hope*; *1776*
1970—*Borstal Boy*; *Applause*
1971—*Sleuth*; *Company*
1972—*Sticks and Bones*; *Two Gentlemen of Verona*

1973—*That Championship Season*; *A Little Night Music*
1974—*The River Niger*; *Raisin*
1975—*Equus*; *The Wiz*
1976—*Travesties*; *A Chorus Line*
1977—*The Shadow Box*; *Annie*
1978—*Da*; *Ain't Misbehavin'*
1979—*The Elephant Man*; *Sweeney Todd, the Demon Barber of Fleet Street*
1980—*Children of a Lesser God*; *Evita*
1981—*Amadeus*; *42nd Street*
1982—*The Life & Adventures of Nicholas Nickleby*; *Nine*
1983—*Torch Song Trilogy*; *Cats*
1984—*The Real Thing*; *La Cage aux Folles*
1985—*Biloxi Blues*; *Big River*
1986—*I'm Not Rappaport*; *The Mystery of Edwin Drood*
1987—*Fences*; *Les Misérables*
1988—*M. Butterfly*; *The Phantom of the Opera*
1989—*The Heidi Chronicles*; *Jerome Robbins' Broadway*
1990—*The Grapes of Wrath*; *City of Angels*
1991—*Lost in Yonkers*; *The Will Rogers Follies*
1992—*Dancing at Lughnasa*; *Crazy for You*
1993—*Angels in America, Part I: Millennium Approaches*; *Kiss of the Spider Woman*
1994—*Angels in America, Part II: Perestroika*; *Passion*
1995—*Love! Valour! Compassion!*; *Sunset Boulevard*
1996—*Master Class*; *Rent*
1997—*The Last Night of Ballyhoo*; *Titanic*
1998—*Art*; *The Lion King*
1999—*Side Man*; *Fosse*
2000—*Copenhagen*; *Contact*
2001—*Proof*; *The Producers*

2002—*The Goat, or Who is Sylvia*; *Thoroughly Modern Millie*

2003—*Take Me Out*; *Hairspray*

2004—*I Am My Own Wife*; *Avenue Q*

2005—*Doubt, a Parable*; *Monty Python's Spamalot*

2006—*The History Boys*; *Jersey Boys*

2007—*The Coast of Utopia*; *Spring Awakening*

2008—*August: Osage County*; *In the Heights*

2008 LUCILLE LORTEL AWARDS

○ ○ ○ ○ ○

T HE LUCILLE LORTEL AWARDS for outstanding Off Broadway achievement were established in 1985 by a resolution of the League of Off Broadway Theatres and Producers, which administers them and has presented them annually since 1986. Eligible for the 23rd annual awards in 2008 were Off Broadway productions that opened between April 1, 2007 and March 31, 2008.

PLAY. **Betrayed** by George Packer.

MUSICAL. **Adding Machine**. Book by Jason Loewith and Joshua Schmidt, music by Joshua Schmidt.

SOLO. **Dai (enough)** by Iris Bahr.

REVIVAL. **The Ohio State Murders** by Adrienne Kennedy, produced by Theatre for a New Audience.

ACTOR. **Joel Hatch** in *Adding Machine*.

ACTRESS. **Elizabeth Franz** in *The Piano Teacher*.

FEATURED ACTOR. **Francis Jue** in *Yellow Face*.

FEATURED ACTRESS. **Mare Winningham** in *10 Million Miles*.

DIRECTION. **David Cromer** for *Adding Machine*.

CHOREOGRAPHY. **Peter Pucci** for *Queens Boulevard (the musical)*.

SCENERY. **Jim Findlay** and **Jeff Sugg** for *The Slug Bearers of Kayrol Island*.

COSTUMES. **Michael Bottari**, **Ronald Case** and **Jessica Jahn** for *Die Mommie Die!*

LIGHTING. **Keith Parham** for *Adding Machine*.

SOUND. **Jorge Cousineau** for *Opus*.

BODY OF WORK. **Primary Stages**.

EDITH OLIVER AWARD. **Theodore Mann**.

UNIQUE THEATRICAL EXPERIENCE. **Horizon** by Rinde Eckert, produced by New York Theatre Workshop.

LORTEL AWARD WINNERS 1986–2008

L ISTED BELOW ARE the Lucille Lortel Award winners in the categories of Outstanding Play and Outstanding Musical from the time these awards were established until the present.

1986—*Woza Africa!*; no musical award
1987—*The Common Pursuit*; no musical award
1988—No play or musical award
1989—*The Cocktail Hour*; no musical award
1990—No play or musical award
1991—*Aristocrats*; *Falsettoland*
1992—*Lips Together, Teeth Apart*; *And the World Goes 'Round*
1993—*The Destiny of Me*; *Forbidden Broadway*
1994—*Three Tall Women*; *Wings*
1995—*Camping With Henry & Tom*; *Jelly Roll!*
1996—*Molly Sweeney*; *Floyd Collins*
1997—*How I Learned to Drive*; *Violet*
1998—*Gross Indecency*, and *The Beauty Queen of Leenane* (tie); no musical award

1999—*Wit*; no musical award
2000—*Dinner With Friends*; *James Joyce's The Dead*
2001—*Proof*; *Bat Boy: The Musical*
2002—*Metamorphoses*; *Urinetown*
2003—*Take Me Out*; *Avenue Q*
2004—*Bug*; *Caroline, or Change*
2005—*Doubt, a Parable*; *The 25th Annual Putnam County Spelling Bee*
2006—*The Lieutenant of Inishmore*; *The Seven*
2007—*Stuff Happens*; *In the Heights, Spring Awakening*
2008—*Betrayed*; *Adding Machine*

HAROLD AND MIMI STEINBERG
NEW PLAY AWARD AND CITATIONS
PRINCIPAL CITATIONS AND AMERICAN THEATRE CRITICS
ASSOCIATION NEW PLAY AWARD WINNERS, 1977–2008
○ ○ ○ ○ ○

THE AMERICAN THEATRE CRITICS ASSOCIATION (ATCA) has cited one or more outstanding new plays in United States theater since the 1976–1977 season. The principal honorees have been honored in *The Best Plays Theater Yearbook* since the first year. In 1986 the ATCA New Play Award was given for the first time, along with a $1,000 prize. The award and citations were renamed the American Theatre Critics/Steinberg New Play Award and Citations in 2000 when the Harold and Mimi Steinberg Charitable Trust committed $25,000 per year to the honors. Beginning with the 2006 honors, the awards were renamed the **Harold and Mimi Steinberg/American Theatre Critics Association New Play Award and Citations** to reflect an increased financial commitment of $40,000 per year from the Trust. (See essays on the 2008 Steinberg/ATCA honorees in the Season Around the United States section of this volume.) The award dates were renumbered beginning with the 2000–2001 *Best Plays* volume to correctly reflect the year in which ATCA conferred the honor.

NEW PLAY CITATIONS (1977–1985)
1977—*And the Soul Shall Dance* by Wakako Yamauchi
1978—*Getting Out* by Marsha Norman
1979—*Loose Ends* by Michael Weller
1980—*Custer* by Robert E. Ingham
1981—*Chekhov in Yalta* by John Driver and Jeffrey Haddow
1982—*Talking With* by Jane Martin
1983—*Closely Related* by Bruce MacDonald
1984—*Wasted* by Fred Gamel
1985—*Scheherazade* by Marisha Chamberlain

NEW PLAY AWARD (1986–1999)
1986—*Fences* by August Wilson
1987—*A Walk in the Woods* by Lee Blessing
1988—*Heathen Valley* by Romulus Linney
1989—*The Piano Lesson* by August Wilson
1990—*2* by Romulus Linney
1991—*Two Trains Running* by August Wilson
1992—*Could I Have This Dance?* by Doug Haverty
1993—*Children of Paradise: Shooting a Dream* by Steven Epp, Felicity Jones, Dominique Serrand and Paul Walsh
1994—*Keely and Du* by Jane Martin
1995—*The Nanjing Race* by Reggie Cheong-Leen

1996—*Amazing Grace* by Michael Cristofer
1997—*Jack and Jill* by Jane Martin
1998—*The Cider House Rules, Part II* by Peter Parnell
1999—*Book of Days* by Lanford Wilson.

ATCA/STEINBERG NEW PLAY AWARD AND CITATIONS

2000—*Oo-Bla-Dee* by Regina Taylor
    Citation: *Compleat Female Stage Beauty* by Jeffrey Hatcher
    Citation: *Syncopation* by Allan Knee
2001—*Anton in Show Business* by Jane Martin
    Citation: *Big Love* by Charles L. Mee
    Citation: *King Hedley II* by August Wilson
2002—*The Carpetbagger's Children* by Horton Foote
    Citation: *The Action Against Sol Schumann* by Jeffrey Sweet
    Citation: *Joe and Betty* by Murray Mednick
2003—*Anna in the Tropics* by Nilo Cruz
    Citation: *Recent Tragic Events* by Craig Wright
    Citation: *Resurrection Blues* by Arthur Miller
2004—*Intimate Apparel* by Lynn Nottage
    Citation: *Gem of the Ocean* by August Wilson
    Citation: *The Love Song of J. Robert Oppenheimer* by Carson Kreitzer
2005—*Singing Forest* by Craig Lucas
    Citation: *After Ashley* by Gina Gionfriddo
    Citation: *The Clean House* by Sarah Ruhl

HAROLD AND MIMI STEINBERG/ATCA NEW PLAY AWARD AND CITATIONS

2006—*A Body of Water* by Lee Blessing
    Citation: *Radio Golf* by August Wilson
    Citation: *Red Light Winter* by Adam Rapp
2007—*Hunter Gatherers* by Peter Sinn Nachtrieb
    Citation: *Guest Artist* by Jeff Daniels
    Citation: *Opus* by Michael Hollinger
2008—*33 Variations* by Moisés Kaufman
    Citation: *Dead Man's Cell Phone* by Sarah Ruhl
    Citation: *End Days* by Deborah Zoe Laufer

ADDITIONAL PRIZES AND AWARDS 2007–2008

THE FOLLOWING IS a list of major awards for achievement in the theater this season. The names of honorees appear in **bold type**.

2006–2007 GEORGE JEAN NATHAN AWARD. For dramatic criticism. **H. Scott McMillin** (posthumous).

27TH ANNUAL WILLIAM INGE THEATRE FESTIVAL AWARD. For distinguished achievement in American theater. **Christopher Durang**. Otis Guernsey New Voices Award: **Adam Bock**.

2008 M. ELIZABETH OSBORN AWARD. Presented by the American Theatre Critics Association to an emerging playwright. **Elyzabeth Gregory Wilder** for *Gee's Bend*.

30TH ANNUAL KENNEDY CENTER HONORS. For distinguished achievement by individuals who have made significant contributions to American culture through the arts. **Leon Fleisher**, **Steve Martin**, **Diana Ross**, **Martin Scorsese**, **Brian Wilson**.

2007 NATIONAL MEDALS OF THE ARTS. For individuals and organizations who have made outstanding contributions to the excellence, growth, support and availability of the arts in the United States, selected by the President from nominees presented by the National Endowment. **Morten Lauridsen**, **N. Scott Momaday**, **Roy R. Neuberger**, **R. Craig Noel**, **Les Paul**, **Henry Steinway**, **George Tooker**, **University of Idaho Lionel Hampton International Jazz Festival**, **Andrew Wyeth**.

2008 DRAMATISTS' GUILD AWARDS. Wendy Wasserstein Award: **Laura Jacqmin**. Elizabeth Hull–Kate Warriner Award, Frederick Loewe Award for Dramatic Composition, Flora Roberts Award and Lifetime Achievement Award postponed until fall 2008.

2008 HENRY HEWES DESIGN AWARDS. For design originating in the US, selected by a committee comprising Jeffrey Eric Jenkins (chairman), Dan Bacalzo, David Barbour, David Cote, Tish Dace, Glenda Frank, Mario Fratti, and Joan Ungaro. Scenery: **Mark Wendland** for *Next to Normal*, *Richard III* and *Unconditional*. Costumes: **Katrina Lindsay** for *Les Liaisons Dangereuses*. Lighting: **Donald Holder** for *Cyrano de Bergerac*, *Les Liaisons Dangereuses* and *South Pacific*. Notable effects: **Jim Findlay** and **Jeff Sugg** for the projection designs in *The Slug Bearers of Kayrol Island*.

30TH ANNUAL SUSAN SMITH BLACKBURN PRIZE. For women who have written works of outstanding quality for the English-speaking theater. Honoree: **Judith Thompson** for *Palace of the End*. Special commendations: **Lisa McGee** for *Girls and Dolls*, **Jenny Schwartz** for *God's Ear*, **Polly Stenham** for *That Face*.

64TH ANNUAL CLARENCE DERWENT AWARDS. Given to a female and a male performer by Actors' Equity Association based on New York work that demonstrates promise. **Zoe Kazan** and **Michael Esper**.

2008 RICHARD RODGERS AWARDS. For productions and staged readings of musicals in nonprofit theaters, administered by the American Academy of Arts and Letters and selected by a jury including Stephen Sondheim (chairman), Lynn Ahrens, John Guare, Sheldon Harnick, Richard Maltby Jr. and John Weidman. Staged reading awards: *Alive at Ten* by **Kirsten A. Guenther** and **Ryan Scott Oliver**; *Kingdom* by **Aaron Jafferis** and **Ian Williams**; *See Rock City and Other Destinations* by **Brad Alexander** and **Adam Mathias**.

74TH ANNUAL DRAMA LEAGUE AWARDS. For distinguished achievement in the American theater. Play: *August: Osage County*. Musical: *A Catered Affair*. Revival of a play: *Macbeth*. Revival of a musical: *South Pacific*. Performance: **Patti LuPone** in *Gypsy*. Achievement in musical theater: **Paul Gemignani**. Julia Hansen Award: **Bartlett Sher**. Unique contribution to the theater: **Ellen Stewart**.

2008 NEW DRAMATISTS LIFETIME ACHIEVEMENT AWARD. To an individual who has made an outstanding artistic contribution to the American theater. **Harvey Fierstein**.

18TH ANNUAL ED KLEBAN AWARDS. To individuals deemed the most promising lyricists and librettists in the musical theater. Administered by New Dramatists. Lyricist: **David Lindsay-Abaire**. Librettist (tie): **Laura Harrington**; **Bill Solly** and **Donald Ward**.

2008 *THEATRE WORLD* AWARDS. For outstanding debut performers in Broadway or Off Broadway theater during the 2007–2008 season, selected by a committee including Peter Filichia, Harry Haun, Matthew Murray, Frank Scheck, Michael Sommers, Douglas Watt and Linda Winer. **de'Adre Aziza** for *Passing Strange*, **Cassie Beck** for *Drunken City*, **Daniel Breaker** for *Passing Strange*, **Ben Daniels** for *Les Liaisons Dangereuses*, **Deanna Dunagan** for *August: Osage County*, **Hoon Lee** for *Yellow Face*, **Alli Mauzey** for *Cry-Baby*, **Jenna Russell** for *Sunday in the Park With George*, **Mark Rylance** for *Boeing-Boeing*, **Loretta Ables Sayre** for *South Pacific*, **Jimmi Simpson** for *The Farnsworth Invention*, **Paulo Szot** for *South Pacific*.

53RD ANNUAL DRAMA DESK AWARDS. For outstanding achievement in the 2007–2008 season, voted by an association of New York drama reporters, editors and critics from nominations made by a committee. New play: *August: Osage County*. New musical: *Passing Strange*. Revival of a play: *Boeing-Boeing*. Revival

of a musical: *South Pacific*. Revue: *Forbidden Broadway: Rude Awakening*. Book of a musical: **Douglas Carter Beane** for *Xanadu*. Music: **Stew** and **Heidi Rodewald** for *Passing Strange*. Lyrics: **Stew** for *Passing Strange*. Actor in a play: **Mark Rylance** in *Boeing-Boeing*. Actress in a play: **Deanna Dunagan** in *August: Osage County*. Featured actor in a play: **Conleth Hill** in *The Seafarer*. Featured actress in a play: **Linda Lavin** in *The New Century*. Actor in a musical: **Paulo Szot** in *South Pacific*. Actress in a musical: **Patti LuPone** in *Gypsy*. Featured actor in a musical: **Boyd Gaines** in *Gypsy*. Featured actress in a musical: **Laura Benanti** in *Gypsy*. Solo performance: **Laurence Fishburne** in *Thurgood*. Director of a play: **Anna D. Shapiro** for *August: Osage County*. Director of a musical: **Bartlett Sher** for *South Pacific*. Choreography: **Rob Ashford** for *Cry-Baby*. Orchestrations: **Jason Carr** for *Sunday in the Park With George*. Scenery (play): **Scott Pask** for *Les Liaisons Dangereuses*. Scenery (musical): **Michael Yeargan** for *South Pacific*. Costumes: **Katrina Lindsay** for *Les Liaisons Dangereuses*. Lighting: **Kevin Adams** for *The 39 Steps*. Sound: **Scott Lehrer** for *South Pacific*. Projection and video: Timothy Bird and the **Knifedge Creative Network** for *Sunday in the Park With George*. Unique Theatrical Experience: *The 39 Steps*. Ensemble performance: The casts of *The Homecoming* and *The Dining Room*. Special awards: **Edward Albee, James Earl Jones, 59E59 Theaters** and **Playwrights Horizons**.

58TH ANNUAL OUTER CRITICS' CIRCLE AWARDS. For outstanding achievement in the 2007–2008 season, voted by critics on out-of-town periodicals and media. Broadway play: *August: Osage County*. Off Broadway play: *Dividing the Estate*. Revival of a play: *The Homecoming*. Actor in a play: **Kevin Kline** in *Cyrano de Bergerac*. Actress in a play: **Deanna Dunagan** in *August: Osage County*. Featured actor in a play: **James Earl Jones** in *Cat on a Hot Tin Roof*. Featured actress in a play: **Laurie Metcalf** in *November*. Director of a play: **Anna D. Shapiro** for *August: Osage County*. Broadway musical (tie): *Xanadu* and *Young Frankenstein*. Score (tie): *Adding Machine* and *Next to Normal*. Off-Broadway musical: *Adding Machine*. Revival of a musical: *South Pacific*. Actor in a musical: **Paulo Szot** in *South Pacific*. Actress in a musical: **Patti LuPone** in *Gypsy*. Featured actor in a musical: **Danny Burstein** in *South Pacific*. Featured actress in a musical: **Laura Benanti** in *Gypsy*. Director of a musical: **Bartlett Sher** for *South Pacific*. Choreography: **Rob Ashford** for *Cry-Baby*. Scenery: **David Farley** and **Timothy Bird** for *Sunday in the Park With George*. Costumes: **Katrina Lindsay** for *Les Liaisons Dangereuses*. Lighting: **Ken Billington** for *Sunday in the Park With George*. Solo performance: **Laurence Fishburne** in *Thurgood*. John Gassner Playwriting Award: **Liz Flahive** for *From Up Here*.

53RD ANNUAL *VILLAGE VOICE* OBIE AWARDS. For outstanding achievement in Off and Off Off Broadway theater. Performance: **LisaGay Hamilton** for *The Ohio State Murders*, **Kate Mulgrew** for *Iphigenia 2.0*, **Francis Jue** for *Yellow Face*, **Rebecca Wisocky** for *Amazons and Their Men*, **Joel Hatch** for *Adding Machine*, **Heidi Schreck** for *Drum of the Waves of Horikawa*. Performance (sustained excellence): **Veanne Cox**, **Sean McNall**. Performance (ensemble): *Passing Strange* (**de'Adre Aziza, Daniel Breaker, Eisa Davis, Colman Domingo, Chad Goodridge, Rebecca Naomi Jones, Stew**). Direction: **Krzysztof Warlikowski** for *Krum*, **David Cromer** for *Adding Machine*. Playwriting: **Horton Foote** for *Dividing the Estate*, **David Henry Hwang** for *Yellow Face*. Design (sustained excellence): **Jane Greenwood** (costumes) and **David Zinn** (scenery and costumes). Design (scenery): **Takeshi Kata** (scenery) and **Keith Parham** (lighting) for *Adding Machine*, Peter Ksander (scenery) for *Untitled Mars (This Title May Change)*, **Ben**

Katchor (drawings) and **Jim Findlay** and **Jeff Sugg** (scenery and projections) for *The Slug Bearers of Kayrol Island*. New Theater Piece: **Stew, Heidi Rodewald** and **Annie Dorsen** for *Passing Strange*.

Special Citations: **Nature Theater of Oklahoma** for *No Dice*, **David Greenspan** for *The Argument*. Ross Wetzsteon Award: **Cherry Lane Theatre Mentor Project**. Lifetime Achievement: **Adrienne Kennedy**. Grants: **Keen Company, Theatre of a Two-Headed Calf**.

18TH ANNUAL CONNECTICUT CRITICS' CIRCLE AWARDS. For outstanding achievement in Connecticut theater during the 2007–2008 season. Production of a play: **TheaterWorks** for *Blackbird*. Production of a musical (tie): **Goodspeed Musicals** for *1776*, **Ivoryton Playhouse** for *Joseph and the Amazing Technicolor Dreamcoat*. Actress in a play: **Patricia Kilgarriff** in *A Woman of No Importance*. Actor in a play: **Michael Countryman** in *Shipwrecked*. Actress in a musical: **Jessie Mueller** in *Carousel*. Actor in a musical: **Peter A. Carey** in *1776*. Direction of a play: **Michael Wilson** for *The Milk Train Doesn't Stop Here Anymore*. Direction of a musical: **Rob Ruggiero** for *1776*. Choreography: **Michele Lynch** for *Happy Days*. Scenery: **Riccardo Hernandez** for *The Evildoers*. Costumes: **Anya Klepikov** for *A Woman of No Importance*. Lighting: **Tyler Micoleau** for *Shipwrecked*. Sound: **David Remedios** for *No Exit*, Hartford Stage. Ensemble performance: **Lucia Brawley, Joe Minoso, Gary Perez, Adriana Sevan, Felix Solis, Sona Tatoyan** in *Boleros for the Disenchanted*.

Roadshow: **The Bushnell** for *The Drowsy Chaperone*. Debut award: **Beth Wittig** in *Blackbird*. Tom Killen Memorial Award: **Gordon Edelstein**, Long Wharf Theatre.

26TH ANNUAL ELLIOT NORTON AWARDS. For outstanding contribution to the theater in Boston, voted by a Boston Theater Critics Association Selection Committee comprising Terry Byrne, Carolyn Clay, Iris

Fanger, Louise Kennedy, Joyce Kulhawik, Sandy MacDonald, Robert Nesti, Ed Siegel and Caldwell Titcomb. Sustained Excellence: **Nicholas J. Martin**. New Script: **Paul Grellong** for *Radio Free Emerson*, Sandra Feinstein-Gamm Theatre. Musical production: *A Marvelous Party: The Noel Coward Celebration*, American Repertory Theatre. Visiting production: *My Fair Lady*, Broadway Across America. Large resident production: *Present Laughter*, Huntington Theatre Company. Midsize resident production: *The Clean House*, New Repertory Theatre. Small resident production: *Angels in America*, Boston Theatre Works. Local fringe production: *The Kentucky Cycle*, Zeitgeist Stage Company/Way Theatre Artists. Solo performance: **Nilaja Sun** in *No Child . . .*, American Repertory Theatre. Actor (large company): **Max Wright** in *No Man's Land*, American Repertory Theatre. Actor (small or midsize company): **Maurice E. Parent** in *Angels in America*, Boston Theatre Works; *The Wild Party*, New Repertory Theatre; *Some Men*, SpeakEasy Stage Company. Actress (large company): **Nancy E. Carroll** in *Brendan* and *Present Laughter*, Huntington Theatre Company. Actress (small or midsize company): **Rachel Harker** in *A Streetcar Named Desire*, New Repertory Theatre; *A Pinter Duet*, Downstage @ New Rep; *The Cutting*, Stoneham Theatre. Musical performance: **Lisa O'Hare** in *My Fair Lady*, Broadway Across America. Director (large company): **David Wheeler** for *No Man's Land*, American Repertory Theatre. Director (midsize company): **Paul Daigneault** for *Parade, Some Men, Zanna, Don't!*, SpeakEasy Stage Company. Director (small or fringe company): **Jason Southerland** and **Nancy Curran Willis** for *Angels in America*, Boston Theatre Works. Choreography: **Patti Colombo** for *Seven Brides for Seven Brothers*, North Shore Music Theatre. Design (large company): **Alexander Dodge** for scenery in *Brendan* and *Present Laughter*, Huntington Theatre Company. Design (small or midsize company): **Cristina Todesco** for scenery, **Deb Sullivan** for

lighting and **Jamie Whoolery** for projections in *The Clean House*, New Repertory Theatre.

24TH ANNUAL HELEN HAYES AWARDS. In recognition of excellence in Washington, DC, theater, presented by the Washington Theatre Awards Society.

Resident productions—Play: *Macbeth*, Synetic Theater. Musical: *Reefer Madness*, Studio Theatre 2nd Stage. Lead actress, musical: **Heidi Blickenstaff** in *Meet John Doe*, Ford's Theatre. Lead actor, musical: **Marc Kudisch** in *The Witches of Eastwick*, Signature Theatre (Virginia). Lead actress, play: **Nancy Robinette** in *Souvenir: A Fantasia on the Life of Florence Foster Jenkins*, Studio Theatre. Lead actor, play: **J. Fred Shiffman** in *Souvenir: A Fantasia on the Life of Florence Foster Jenkins*, Studio Theatre. Supporting actress, musical (tie): E. Faye Butler in *Saving Aimee*, Signature Theatre (Virginia); **Karlah Hamilton** in *The Witches of Eastwick*, Signature Theatre (Virginia). Supporting actor, musical: **Erik Liberman** in *Merrily We Roll Along*, Signature Theatre (Virginia). Supporting actress, play: **Kate Eastwood Norris** in *She Stoops to Comedy*, Woolly Mammoth Theatre Company. Supporting actor, play (tie): **Daniel Escobar** in *She Stoops to Comedy*, Woolly Mammoth Theatre Company; **Philip Fletcher** in *Macbeth*, Synetic Theater. Director, play: **Paata Tsikurishvili** for *Macbeth*, Synetic Theater. Director, musical (tie): **Keith Alan Baker, Ryan Christie** and **Matthew Gardiner** for *Reefer Madness*, Studio Theatre 2nd Stage; **Eric Schaeffer** for *Meet John Doe*, Ford's Theatre. Scenery: **Neil Patel** for *Dead Man's Cell Phone*, Woolly Mammoth Theatre Company. Costumes: **Reggie Ray** for *Souvenir: A Fantasia on the Life of Florence Foster Jenkins*, Studio Theatre. Lighting: **Colin K. Bills** for *Dead Man's Cell Phone*, Woolly Mammoth Theatre Company. Sound: **Irakli Kavsadze** and **Paata Tsikurishvili** for *Macbeth*, Synetic Theater. Choreography: **Irina Tsikurishvili** for *Macbeth*, Synetic Theater. Musical direction (tie): **Jon Kalbfleisch** for *Merrily We Roll Along*, Signature Theatre (Virginia); **Christopher Youstra** for *Titanic*, Toby's Dinner Theatre.

Non-resident productions—Production: *Avenue Q* produced by the National Theatre. Lead actress: **Cherry Jones** in *Doubt, a Parable*, the National Theatre. Lead actor: **Bill Irwin** in *Who's Afraid of Virginia Woolf?*, the Kennedy Center. Supporting performer: **Caroline Stefanie Clay** in *Doubt, a Parable*, the National Theatre.

Charles MacArthur Award for outstanding new play: **Sarah Ruhl** for *Dead Man's Cell Phone*, Woolly Mammoth Theatre Company.

Canadian Embassy Award for outstanding ensemble: *Hamlet . . . the rest is silence*, Synetic Theater.

39TH ANNUAL JOSEPH JEFFERSON AWARDS. For achievement in Chicago theater during the 2006–2007 season, given by the Jefferson Awards Committee in 30 competitive categories. Of the 49 producing organizations considered during the season under review, 14 companies were honored. Honors were well distributed among organizations with Steppenwolf Theatre Company receiving six awards for *August: Osage County* and Porchlight Music Theatre Chicago following closely with five. The Goodman Theatre and Marriott Theatre each received four awards as Northlight Theatre and Writers' Theatre celebrated a pair of honors each. Lookingglass Theatre Company also received two awards, one in collaboration with About Face Theatre. Six other theaters were honored in the competitive categories. Jackie Taylor received a special award honoring her work celebrating the contributions of African Americans through theater. The awards ceremony was held October 29, 2007, at Skokie's North Shore Center for the Performing Arts.

Resident productions—New work (play): *August: Osage County* by **Tracy Letts**, Steppenwolf Theatre Company. New work (musical): *The Adding Machine* by **Joshua Schmidt** and **Jason Loewith**, Next Theatre Company. New Adaptation: *Argonautika: The Voyage of Jason and the Argonauts* by **Mary Zimmerman**, Lookingglass Theatre Company. Play: *August: Osage County*, Steppenwolf Theatre Company. Musical:

Ragtime, Porchlight Music Theatre Chicago. Revue: *The All Night Strut!*, Marriott Theatre. Director, play: **Anna D. Shapiro**, *August: Osage County*, Steppenwolf Theatre Company. Director, musical: **L. Walter Stearns**, *Ragtime*, Porchlight Music Theatre Chicago. Ensemble: *August: Osage County*, Steppenwolf Theatre Company. Director, revue: **Marc Robin**, *The All Night Strut!*, Marriott Theatre. Actor in a principal role, play: **Ben Carlson**, *Hamlet*, Chicago Shakespeare Theater. Actress in a principal role, play: **Deanna Dunagan**, *August: Osage County*, Steppenwolf Theatre Company. Actor in a supporting role, play: **Maury Cooper**, *The Price*, Shattered Globe Theatre. Actress in a supporting role, play: **Penny Slusher**, *Another Part of the Forest*, Writers' Theatre. Actor in a principal role, musical: **David Hess**, *Shenandoah*, Marriott Theatre. Actress in a principal role, musical: **Ernestine Jackson**, *Raisin*, Court Theatre. Actor in a supporting role, musical: **Aaron Graham**, *Ragtime*, Porchlight Music Theatre Chicago. Actress in a supporting role, musical: **Sara R. Sevigny**, *Assassins*, Porchlight Music Theatre Chicago. Actor in a revue: **"Mississippi" Charles Bevel**, *Fire on the Mountain*, Northlight Theatre. Actress in a revue: **Molly Andrews**, *Fire on the Mountain*, Northlight Theatre. Solo (tie): **Lance Stuart Baker**, *Thom Pain (based on nothing)*, Theater Wit; **Matt Sax**, *Clay*, About Face Theatre and Lookingglass Theatre Company. Scenery: **Todd Rosenthal**, *August: Osage County*, Steppenwolf Theatre Company. Costumes: **Mara Blumenfeld**, *Mirror of the Invisible World*, the Goodman Theatre. Lighting: **John Culbert**, *Mirror of the Invisible World*, the Goodman Theatre. Sound: **Richard Woodbury**, *King Lear*, the Goodman Theatre. Choreography: **Marc Robin, Beverly Durand, Mark Stuart Eckstein, Sylvia Hernandez-DiStasi** and **Sasha Vargas**, *The All Night Strut!*, Marriott Theatre. Musical direction: **Eugene Dizon**, *Ragtime*, Porchlight Music Theatre Chicago. Original incidental music: **Michael Bodeen**, *Mirror of the Invisible*

World, the Goodman Theatre.   Cameo: **Douglas Vickers**, *The Best Man*, Remy Bumppo Theatre Company. Puppet Design: **Michael Montenegro**, *The Puppetmaster of Lodz*, Writers' Theatre. Special award: **Jackie Taylor**, founding executive director of Black Ensemble Theater, for dedicated leadership in celebrating the contributions of African Americans through theater.

35TH ANNUAL JOSEPH JEFFERSON CITATIONS. For outstanding achievement in professional productions during the 2007–2008 season of Chicago-area theaters not operating under union contracts. The committee saw 143 productions created by 61 producing entities. Honors were bestowed June 9, 2008, at Park West in Chicago. Production, play: ***The Island of Dr. Moreau***, Lifeline Theatre. Production, musical (tie): ***Jerry Springer: The Opera***, Bailiwick Repertory Theatre; ***1776***, Signal Ensemble Theatre. Ensemble: ***Machos***, Teatro Luna. Director, play: **Greg Kolack**, *columbinus*, Raven Theatre. Director, musical: **Fred Anzevino**, *Cabaret*, Theo Ubique Theatre Company, Beverle Bloch and Michael James. New work: **Teatro Luna** and **Coya Paz**, *Machos*, Teatro Luna. New adaptation: **Robert Kauzlaric**, *The Island of Dr. Moreau*, Lifeline Theatre. Actress in a principal role, play: **Vanessa Greenway**, *The Constant Wife*, Griffin Theatre Company. Actress in a principal role, musical: **Elizabeth Lanza**, *Can-Can*, Circle Theatre. Actor in a principal role, play: **Sam Wootten**, *Gross Indecency: The*

Three Trials of Oscar Wilde, Bohemian Theatre Ensemble. Actor in a principal role, musical: **Jeremy Trager**, *Cabaret*, Theo Ubique Theatre Company, Beverle Bloch and Michael James. Actress in a supporting role, play: **Kathleen Ruhl**, *Dolly West's Kitchen*, TimeLine Theatre Company. Actress in a supporting role, musical: **Danielle Brothers**, *Cabaret*, Theo Ubique Theatre Company, Beverle Bloch and Michael James. Actor in a supporting role, play (tie): **Hans Fleischmann**, *In a Dark Dark House*, Profiles Theatre; **Ron Wells**, *A Prayer for My Daughter*, Mary-Arrchie Theatre Co. Actor in a supporting role, musical: **Jeremy Rill**, *Jerry Springer: The Opera*, Bailiwick Repertory Theatre. Scenery: **Michael Menendian** and **Leif Olsen**, *The Night of the Iguana*, Raven Theatre. Costumes: **Elizabeth Shaffer**, *An Ideal Husband*, Circle Theatre. Lighting: **Kevin D. Gawley**, *The Island of Dr. Moreau*, Lifeline Theatre. Sound: **Stephen Ptacek**, *Faster*, the side project. Choreography: **Brenda Didier**, *The Life*, Bohemian Theatre Ensemble. Original incidental music: **Victoria DeIorio**, *The Island of Dr. Moreau*, Lifeline Theatre; **Gregor Mortis** and **Mikhail Fiksel**, *A Lie of the Mind*, Strawdog Theatre Company; **Kevin O'Donnell**, *The Nutcracker*, The House Theatre of Chicago. Music direction: **Joshua Stephen Kartes**, *Cabaret*, Theo Ubique Theatre Company, Beverle Bloch and Michael James. Mask design: **Kimberly G. Morris**, *The Island of Dr. Moreau*, Lifeline Theatre.

THE THEATER HALL OF FAME

○○○○○

THE THEATER HALL OF FAME was created in 1971 to honor those who have made outstanding contributions to the American theater in a career spanning at least 25 years. Honorees are elected annually by members of the American Theatre Critics Association, members of the Theater Hall of Fame and theater historians. Names of those elected in 2007 and inducted January 28, 2008 appear in *bold italics*.

GEORGE ABBOTT	ETHEL BARRYMORE	PETER BROOK
MAUDE ADAMS	JOHN BARRYMORE	JOHN MASON BROWN
VIOLA ADAMS	LIONEL BARRYMORE	ROBERT BRUSTEIN
JACOB ADLER	HOWARD BAY	BILLIE BURKE
STELLA ADLER	NORA BAYES	ABE BURROWS
EDWARD ALBEE	JOHN LEE BEATTY	RICHARD BURTON
THEONI V. ALDREDGE	JULIAN BECK	MRS. PATRICK CAMPBELL
IRA ALDRIDGE	SAMUEL BECKETT	ZOE CALDWELL
JANE ALEXANDER	BRIAN BEDFORD	EDDIE CANTOR
MARY ALICE	S.N. BEHRMAN	LEN CARIOU
WINTHROP AMES	BARBARA BEL GEDDES	MORRIS CARNOVSKY
JUDITH ANDERSON	NORMAN BEL GEDDES	MRS. LESLIE CARTER
MAXWELL ANDERSON	DAVID BELASCO	GOWER CHAMPION
ROBERT ANDERSON	MICHAEL BENNETT	FRANK CHANFRAU
JULIE ANDREWS	RICHARD BENNETT	CAROL CHANNING
MARGARET ANGLIN	ROBERT RUSSELL BENNETT	STOCKARD CHANNING
JEAN ANOUILH	ERIC BENTLEY	RUTH CHATTERTON
HAROLD ARLEN	IRVING BERLIN	PADDY CHAYEFSKY
GEORGE ARLISS	SARAH BERNHARDT	ANTON CHEKHOV
BORIS ARONSON	LEONARD BERNSTEIN	INA CLAIRE
ADELE ASTAIRE	EARL BLACKWELL	BOBBY CLARK
FRED ASTAIRE	KERMIT BLOOMGARDEN	HAROLD CLURMAN
EILEEN ATKINS	JERRY BOCK	LEE J. COBB
BROOKS ATKINSON	RAY BOLGER	RICHARD L. COE
LAUREN BACALL	EDWIN BOOTH	GEORGE M. COHAN
PEARL BAILEY	JUNIUS BRUTUS BOOTH	ALEXANDER H. COHEN
GEORGE BALANCHINE	SHIRLEY BOOTH	JACK COLE
WILLIAM BALL	PHILIP BOSCO	CY COLEMAN
ANNE BANCROFT	DION BOUCICAULT	CONSTANCE COLLIER
TALLULAH BANKHEAD	ALICE BRADY	ALVIN COLT
RICHARD BARR	BERTOLT BRECHT	BETTY COMDEN
PHILIP BARRY	FANNY BRICE	MARC CONNELLY

Barbara Cook
Thomas Abthorpe Cooper
Katharine Cornell
Noel Coward
Jane Cowl
Lotta Crabtree
Cheryl Crawford
Hume Cronyn
Rachel Crothers
Russel Crouse
John Cullum
Charlotte Cushman
Jean Dalrymple
Augustin Daly
Graciela Daniele
E.L. Davenport
Gordon Davidson
Ossie Davis
Owen Davis
Ruby Dee
Alfred de Liagre Jr.
Agnes de Mille
Colleen Dewhurst
Howard Dietz
Dudley Digges
Melvyn Douglas
Eddie Dowling
Alfred Drake
Marie Dressler
John Drew
Mrs. John Drew
William Dunlap
Mildred Dunnock
Charles Durning
Eleanora Duse
Jeanne Eagels
Fred Ebb
Ben Edwards
Florence Eldridge
Lehman Engel
Maurice Evans

Abe Feder
Jose Ferrer
Cy Feuer
Zelda Fichandler
Dorothy Fields
Herbert Fields
Lewis Fields
W.C. Fields
Harvey Fierstein
Jules Fisher
Minnie Maddern Fiske
Clyde Fitch
Geraldine Fitzgerald
Henry Fonda
Lynn Fontanne
Horton Foote
Edwin Forrest
Bob Fosse
Brian Friel
Rudolf Friml
Charles Frohman
Daniel Frohman
Robert Fryer
Athol Fugard
John Gassner
Larry Gelbart
Peter Gennaro
Grace George
George Gershwin
Ira Gershwin
Bernard Gersten
William Gibson
John Gielgud
W.S. Gilbert
Jack Gilford
William Gillette
Charles Gilpin
Lillian Gish
Susan Glaspell
John Golden
Max Gordon

Ruth Gordon
Adolph Green
Paul Green
Charlotte Greenwood
Jane Greenwood
Joel Grey
Tammy Grimes
George Grizzard
John Guare
Otis L. Guernsey Jr.
A.R. Gurney
Mel Gussow
Tyrone Guthrie
Uta Hagen
Peter Hall
Lewis Hallam
T. Edward Hambleton
Oscar Hammerstein II
Walter Hampden
Otto Harbach
E.Y. Harburg
Sheldon Harnick
Edward Harrigan
Jed Harris
Julie Harris
Rosemary Harris
Sam H. Harris
Rex Harrison
Kitty Carlisle Hart
Lorenz Hart
Moss Hart
Tony Hart
June Havoc
Helen Hayes
Leland Hayward
George Hearn
Ben Hecht
Eileen Heckart
Theresa Helburn
Lillian Hellman
Katharine Hepburn

VICTOR HERBERT
JERRY HERMAN
JAMES A. HERNE
HENRY HEWES
GREGORY HINES
AL HIRSCHFELD
RAYMOND HITCHCOCK
HAL HOLBROOK
CELESTE HOLM
HANYA HOLM
ARTHUR HOPKINS
DE WOLF HOPPER
JOHN HOUSEMAN
EUGENE HOWARD
LESLIE HOWARD
SIDNEY HOWARD
WILLIE HOWARD
BARNARD HUGHES
HENRY HULL
JOSEPHINE HULL
WALTER HUSTON
EARLE HYMAN
HENRIK IBSEN
WILLIAM INGE
DANA IVEY
BERNARD B. JACOBS
ELSIE JANIS
JOSEPH JEFFERSON
AL JOLSON
JAMES EARL JONES
MARGO JONES
ROBERT EDMOND JONES
TOM JONES
JON JORY
RAUL JULIA
MADELINE KAHN
JOHN KANDER
GARSON KANIN
GEORGE S. KAUFMAN
DANNY KAYE
ELIA KAZAN

GENE KELLY
GEORGE KELLY
FANNY KEMBLE
JEROME KERN
WALTER KERR
MICHAEL KIDD
RICHARD KILEY
WILLA KIM
SIDNEY KINGSLEY
KEVIN KLINE
FLORENCE KLOTZ
JOSEPH WOOD KRUTCH
BERT LAHR
BURTON LANE
FRANK LANGELLA
LAWRENCE LANGNER
LILLIE LANGTRY
ANGELA LANSBURY
CHARLES LAUGHTON
ARTHUR LAURENTS
GERTRUDE LAWRENCE
JEROME LAWRENCE
EVA LE GALLIENNE
CANADA LEE
EUGENE LEE
MING CHO LEE
ROBERT E. LEE
LOTTE LENYA
ALAN JAY LERNER
SAM LEVENE
ROBERT LEWIS
BEATRICE LILLIE
HOWARD LINDSAY
JOHN LITHGOW
FRANK LOESSER
FREDERICK LOEWE
JOSHUA LOGAN
WILLIAM IVEY LONG
SANTO LOQUASTO
PAULINE LORD
LUCILLE LORTEL

DOROTHY LOUDON
ALFRED LUNT
PATTI LUPONE
CHARLES MACARTHUR
STEELE MACKAYE
JUDITH MALINA
DAVID MAMET
ROUBEN MAMOULIAN
RICHARD MANSFIELD
ROBERT B. MANTELL
FREDRIC MARCH
NANCY MARCHAND
JULIA MARLOWE
ERNEST H. MARTIN
MARY MARTIN
RAYMOND MASSEY
ELIZABETH IRELAND MCCANN
IAN MCKELLEN
SIOBHAN MCKENNA
TERRENCE MCNALLY
SANFORD MEISNER
HELEN MENKEN
BURGESS MEREDITH
ETHEL MERMAN
DAVID MERRICK
JO MIELZINER
ARTHUR MILLER
MARILYN MILLER
LIZA MINNELLI
HELENA MODJESKA
FERENC MOLNAR
LOLA MONTEZ
VICTOR MOORE
ROBERT MORSE
ZERO MOSTEL
ANNA CORA MOWATT
PAUL MUNI
BRIAN MURRAY
THARON MUSSER
GEORGE JEAN NATHAN
MILDRED NATWICK

Alla Nazimova
Patricia Neal
James M. Nederlander
Mike Nichols
Elliot Norton
Jack O'Brien
Sean O'Casey
Clifford Odets
Donald Oenslager
Laurence Olivier
Eugene O'Neill
Jerry Orbach
Geraldine Page
Joseph Papp
Estelle Parsons
Osgood Perkins
Bernadette Peters
Molly Picon
Harold Pinter
Luigi Pirandello
Christopher Plummer
Cole Porter
Robert Preston
Harold Prince
Jose Quintero
Ellis Rabb
John Raitt
Tony Randall
Michael Redgrave
Vanessa Redgrave
Ada Rehan
Elmer Rice
Lloyd Richards
Ralph Richardson
Chita Rivera
Jason Robards
Jerome Robbins
Paul Robeson
Richard Rodgers
Will Rogers
Sigmund Romberg

Harold Rome
Billy Rose
Lillian Russell
Donald Saddler
Gene Saks
Diana Sands
William Saroyan
Joseph Schildkraut
Harvey Schmidt
Alan Schneider
Gerald Schoenfeld
Arthur Schwartz
Maurice Schwartz
George C. Scott
Marian Seldes
Peter Shaffer
Irene Sharaff
George Bernard Shaw
Sam Shepard
Robert E. Sherwood
J.J. Shubert
Lee Shubert
Herman Shumlin
Neil Simon
Lee Simonson
Edmund Simpson
Otis Skinner
Lois Smith
Maggie Smith
Oliver Smith
Stephen Sondheim
E.H. Sothern
Kim Stanley
Jean Stapleton
Maureen Stapleton
Joseph Stein
Frances Sternhagen
Roger L. Stevens
Isabelle Stevenson
Ellen Stewart
Dorothy Stickney

Fred Stone
Peter Stone
Tom Stoppard
Lee Strasberg
August Strindberg
Elaine Stritch
Charles Strouse
Jule Styne
Margaret Sullavan
Arthur Sullivan
Jessica Tandy
Laurette Taylor
Ellen Terry
Sada Thompson
Cleon Throckmorton
Tommy Tune
Gwen Verdon
Robin Wagner
Nancy Walker
Eli Wallach
James Wallack
Lester Wallack
Tony Walton
Douglas Turner Ward
David Warfield
Wendy Wasserstein
Ethel Waters
Clifton Webb
Joseph Weber
Margaret Webster
Kurt Weill
Orson Welles
Mae West
Robert Whitehead
Richard Wilbur
Oscar Wilde
Thornton Wilder
Bert Williams
Tennessee Williams
August Wilson
Elizabeth Wilson

LANFORD WILSON   IRENE WORTH   STARK YOUNG
P.G. WODEHOUSE   TERESA WRIGHT   FLORENZ ZIEGFELD
PEGGY WOOD   ED WYNN   PATRICIA ZIPPRODT
ALEXANDER WOOLLCOTT   VINCENT YOUMANS

THE THEATER HALL OF FAME
FOUNDERS AWARD
○ ○ ○ ○ ○

ESTABLISHED IN 1993 in honor of Earl Blackwell, James M. Nederlander, Gerard Oestreicher and Arnold Weissberger, The Theater Hall of Fame Founders Award is voted by the Hall's board of directors to an individual for his or her outstanding contribution to the theater.

1993 JAMES M. NEDERLANDER	1999 NO AWARD	2004 NO AWARD
1994 KITTY CARLISLE HART	2000 GERARD OESTREICHER	2005 DONALD SEAWELL
1995 HARVEY SABINSON	2000 ARNOLD WEISSBERGER	2006 NO AWARD
1996 HENRY HEWES	2001 TOM DILLON	2007 *ROY SOMLYO*
1997 OTIS L. GUERNSEY JR.	2002 NO AWARD	
1998 EDWARD COLTON	2003 PRICE BERKLEY	

MARGO JONES
CITIZEN OF THE THEATER MEDAL

PRESENTED ANNUALLY TO a citizen of the theater who has made a lifetime commitment to theater in the United States and has demonstrated an understanding and affirmation of the craft of playwriting.

1961 LUCILLE LORTEL

1962 MICHAEL ELLIS

1963 JUDITH R. MARECHAL
GEORGE SAVAGE

1964 RICHARD BARR,
EDWARD ALBEE
CLINTON WILDER
RICHARD A. DUPREY

1965 WYNN HANDMAN
MARSTON BALCH

1966 JON JORY
ARTHUR BALLET

1967 PAUL BAKER
GEORGE C. WHITE

1968 DAVEY MARLIN-JONES

1968 ELLEN STEWART

1969 ADRIAN HALL
EDWARD PARONE

1969 GORDON DAVIDSON

1970 JOSEPH PAPP

1971 ZELDA FICHANDLER

1972 JULES IRVING

1973 DOUGLAS TURNER
WARD

1974 PAUL WEIDNER

1975 ROBERT KALFIN

1976 GORDON DAVIDSON

1977 MARSHALL W. MASON

1978 JON JORY

1979 ELLEN STEWART

1980 JOHN CLARK DONAHUE

1981 LYNNE MEADOW

1982 ANDRE BISHOP

1983 BILL BUSHNELL

1984 GREGORY MOSHER

1985 JOHN LION

1986 LLOYD RICHARDS

1987 GERALD CHAPMAN

1988 NO AWARD

1989 MARGARET GOHEEN

1990 RICHARD COE

1991 OTIS L. GUERNSEY JR.

1992 ABBOT VAN NOSTRAND

1993 HENRY HEWES

1994 JANE ALEXANDER

1995 ROBERT WHITEHEAD

1996 AL HIRSCHFELD

1997 GEORGE C. WHITE

1998 JAMES HOUGHTON

1999 GEORGE KEATHLEY

2000 EILEEN HECKART

2001 MEL GUSSOW

2002 EMILIE S. KILGORE

2003 NO AWARD

2004 CHRISTOPHER DURANG
MARSHA NORMAN

2005 NO AWARD

2006 JEROME LAWRENCE
ROBERT E. LEE

2007 NO AWARD

2008 DAVID EMMES
MARTIN BENSON

MUSICAL THEATRE HALL OF FAME

THIS ORGANIZATION WAS established at New York University on November 10, 1993.

Harold Arlen

Irving Berlin

Leonard Bernstein

Eubie Blake

Abe Burrows

George M. Cohan

Dorothy Fields

George Gershwin

Ira Gershwin

Oscar Hammerstein II

E.Y. Harburg

Larry Hart

Jerome Kern

Burton Lane

Alan Jay Lerner

Frank Loesser

Frederick Loewe

Cole Porter

Ethel Merman

Jerome Robbins

Richard Rodgers

Harold Rome

IN MEMORIAM
JUNE 2007–MAY 2008

○ ○ ○ ○ ○

PERFORMERS

Bergman, Ingmar (89) – July 30, 2007
Britton, Sherry (89) – April 1, 2008
Bruce, Carol (87) – October 9, 2007
Burmester, Leo (63) – June 28, 2007
Church, James Anthony (77) – March 25, 2008
Dabney, Augusta (89) – February 4, 2008
Dixon, Ivan (76) – March 16, 2008
Evans, Michael (87) – September 4, 2007
Fauvell, Timothy M. (50) – November 7, 2007
Fraction, Karen (49) – October 30, 2007
Frazier, Harry (77) – May 26, 2007
Gari, Roberto (87) – January 22, 2008
Ghostley, Alice (81) – September 21, 2007
Goulet, Robert (73) – October 30, 2007
Griffin, Merv (82) – August 12, 2007
Grizzard, George (79) – October 2, 2007
Hadley, Jerry (55) – July 18, 2007
Heston, Charlton (84) – April 5, 2008
Hutt, William (87) – June 27, 2007
Jones, Pattie Darcy (54) – June 16, 2007
Kerr, Deborah (86) – October 18, 2007
Kirkwood, Pat (86) – December 25, 2007
Lane, Charles (102) – July 9, 2007
Leath, Brennen (25) – September 22, 2007
Letts, Dennis (73) – February 22, 2008
Lister, Moira (84) – October 27, 2007
Kenwith, Herbert (90) – January 30, 2008
Kirkwood, Pat (86) – December 25, 2007
Maldonado, Jorge (30) – December 19, 2007
Marceau, Marcel (84) – September 22, 2007
Mose, Barry (89) – February 2, 2008
Murphy, Tom (39) – October 6, 2007
Nettleton, Lois (80) – January 18, 2008
Oliver, Robert (68) – February 4, 2008
Pelfrey, Linda Lawley (58) – November 24, 2007
Pleshette, Suzanne (70) – January 19, 2008
Pollack, Sydney (73) – May 27, 2008
Rodrigues, Percy (89) – September 6, 2007
Ryan, Steve (55) – September 3, 2007

Scheider, Roy (75) – February 10, 2008
Scofield, Paul (86) – March 19, 2008
Shaw, Joseph (87) – January 6, 2008
Sills, Beverly (78) – July 2, 2007
Smith, Lionel Mark (62) – February 13, 2008
Somers, Brett (83) – September 15, 2007
Stevenson, Allan (89) – October 24, 2007
Sundiata, Sekou (58) – July 28, 2007
Umeki, Miyoshi (78) – August 28, 2007
Van Slyke, Joe (55) – August 13, 2007
Widmark, Richard (93) – March 24, 2008
Windsor, Walter M. (89) – February 29, 2008

PRODUCERS, DIRECTORS, CHOREOGRAPHERS

Abbott, Michael (81) – January 24, 2008
Browning, Kirk (86) – February 10, 2008
Chapman, Lonny (87) – October 12, 2007
George, George W. (87) – November 7, 2007
Gilford, Madeline Lee (84) – April 14, 2008
Harmon, Charlotte (96) – July 29, 2007
Harris, Jay (69) – September 24, 2007
Hart, Bill (70) – January 20, 2008
Hine, Roy A. (51) – November 21, 2007
Hodge, Max (91) – August 17, 2007
Kidd, Michael (92) – December 23, 2007
Kravat, Jerry (72) – March 31, 2008
Minghella, Anthony (54) – March 18, 2008
Mirvish, Edwin (92) – July 11, 2007
Nagrin, Lee (78) – June 7, 2007
Posante, Jim (59) – January 13, 2008
Segal, Mort (76) – January 11, 2008
Sherrin, Ned (76) – October 1, 2007
Symonds, Robert (80) – August 23, 2007
Van Lente, Diane (57) – August 13, 2007
Walsh, Thommie (57) – June 16, 2007

COMPOSERS, LYRICISTS, SONGWRITERS

Campbell, Elaine (81) – August 11, 2007
Stockhausen, Karlheinz (79) – December 5, 2007
Wallis, Ruth (87) – December 22, 2007

Wallowitch, John (82) – August 15, 2007

PLAYWRIGHTS
Lampley, Oni Faida (49) – April 28, 2008
Levin, Ira (78) – November 12, 2007
Shaw, David (90) – July 27, 2007

OTHER NOTABLES
Colt, Alvin (92) – May 4, 2008
  Costume designer
De Santis, Anthony (93) – June 6, 2007
  Chicago theater owner
Gardner, Dean (55) – September 24, 2007
  Broadway treasurer
Howard, Peter (80) – April 18, 2008
  Music arranger
Lantz, Robert (93) – October 18, 2007
  Talent agent
Lasky, Floria (84) – September 21, 2007
  Talent lawyer
Leone, Leonard (92) – June 5, 2007
  Theatre Educator

Marlowe, Joan (88) – March 6, 2008
  Publisher of theater bulletin
Newman, Danny (88) – December 1, 2007
  Theater promoter
Ray, Timothy J. (47) – October 25, 2007
  Theater press agent
Siegel, Joel (63) – June 29, 2007
  Critic
Stephenson, Patricia Ziegfeld (91) – April 11, 2008
  Daughter of Florenz Ziegfeld
Sullivan, Amy (54) – June 10, 2007
  Executive director, Eugene O'Neill Theater Center
Traube, Beverly Anderson (77) – June 16, 2007
  Talent agent
Wright, Mark (77) – June 6, 2007
  Broadway stage manager

THE BEST PLAYS AND MAJOR PRIZEWINNERS
1894–2008

○ ○ ○ ○ ○

LISTED IN ALPHABETICAL order below are all works selected as Best Plays in previous volumes of the *Best Plays Theater Yearbook* series, except for the seasons of 1996–1997 through 1999–2000. During those excluded seasons, *Best Plays* honored only major prizewinners and those who received special *Best Plays* citations. Opposite each title is given the volume in which the play is honored, its opening date and its total number of performances. Two separate opening-date and performance-number entries signify two separate engagements when the original production transferred. Plays marked with an asterisk (*) were still playing June 1, 2008 and their numbers of performances were figured through May 31, 2008. Adaptors and translators are indicated by (ad) and (tr), the symbols (b), (m) and (l) stand for the author of the book, music and lyrics in the case of musicals and (c) signifies the credit for the show's conception, (i) for its inspiration. Entries identified as 94–99, 99–09 and 09–19 are late–19th and early–20th century plays from one of the retrospective volumes. 94–95, 95–96, 96–97, 97–98, 98–99 and 99–00 are late–20th century plays.

PLAY	VOLUME	OPENED	PERFS
ABE LINCOLN IN ILLINOIS—Robert E. Sherwood	38–39	Oct. 15, 1938	472
ABRAHAM LINCOLN—John Drinkwater	19–20	Dec. 15, 1919	193
ACCENT ON YOUTH—Samson Raphaelson	34–35	Dec. 25, 1934	229
ADAM AND EVA—Guy Bolton, George Middleton	19–20	Sept. 13, 1919	312
ADAPTATION—Elaine May; and			
NEXT—Terrence McNally	68–69	Feb. 10, 1969	707
*ADDING MACHINE—Jason Loewith and Joshua Schmidt	07–08	Feb. 25, 2008	97
AFFAIRS OF STATE—Louis Verneuil	50–51	Sept. 25, 1950	610
AFTER ASHLEY—Gina Gionfriddo	04–05	Feb. 28, 2005	35
AFTER THE FALL—Arthur Miller	63–64	Jan. 23, 1964	208
AFTER THE RAIN—John Bowen	67–68	Oct. 9, 1967	64
AFTER-PLAY—Anne Meara	94–95	Jan. 31, 1995	400
AGNES OF GOD—John Pielmeier	81–82	Mar. 30, 1982	599
AH, WILDERNESS!—Eugene O'Neill	33–34	Oct. 2, 1933	289
AIN'T SUPPOSED TO DIE A NATURAL DEATH—(b, m, l)			
Melvin Van Peebles	71–72	Oct. 20, 1971	325
ALIEN CORN—Sidney Howard	32–33	Feb. 20, 1933	98
Alison's House—Susan Glaspell	30–31	Dec. 1, 1930	41
ALL MY SONS—Arthur Miller	46–47	Jan. 29, 1947	328
ALL IN THE TIMING—David Ives	93–94	Feb. 17, 1994	526
ALL OVER TOWN—Murray Schisgal	74–75	Dec. 29, 1974	233
ALL THE WAY HOME—Tad Mosel, based on			
James Agee's novel *A Death in the Family*	60–61	Nov. 30, 1960	333

CONTRIBUTORS TO *BEST PLAYS*

○ ○ ○ ○ ○

Sheryl Arluck worked in healthcare administration, serving as director of continuing medical-education at New York University for more than 10 years, before becoming vice president of a special-events company. After September 11, 2001, she spent a year working with the New York recovery effort. In addition to her duties for *The Best Plays Theater Yearbook*, Arluck is a freelance event planner.

Dan Bacalzo is the managing editor of TheaterMania.com, to which he frequently contributes reviews, features and news stories. He has contributed to many publication including *In Theater, Stagebill, West Side Spirit* and *Theatre Journal*. Bacalzo holds a PhD in Performance Studies from New York University, where he is an adjunct faculty member in the Drama Department. The former artistic director of Peeling, an Asian-American performance collective, he is the author of the solo shows *I'm Sorry, But I Don't Speak the Language* and *Sort of Where I'm Coming From*. Bacalzo serves on the nominating committees of the Drama Desk Awards, Henry Hewes Design Awards and the GLAAD Media Awards.

David Cote is the theater editor and chief drama critic of *Time Out New York*. For the *Best Plays Theater Yearbook* series, Cote contributed essays on *Shining City* and *Blackbird*. He is a contributing critic for NY1's *On Stage* and has written for *The New York Times, Opera News, Salon, Maxim* and *The Times* of London. He has written popular companion books to the Broadway shows *Wicked, Jersey Boys* and *Spring Awakening*. A member of the New York Drama Critics' Circle, he is also a librettist and playwright. The one-act opera, *Fade,* for which he wrote the text, had its London premiere in October 2008. Cote also has a play in development commissioned by Gingold Theatrical Group. He received his BA from Bard College in 1992.

Christine Dolen has been *The Miami Herald*'s theater critic since 1979. She was a John S. Knight Journalism Fellow at Stanford University in 1984–85 and a senior fellow at Columbia University's National Arts Journalism Program in 1999. In 1997, she was a member of the Pulitzer Prize drama jury. Dolen's awards include the Green Eyeshade in criticism from the Atlanta Chapter of the Society of Professional Journalists and first place in arts writing in the Missouri Lifestyle Journalism Awards. In 2001, she received the George Abbott Award for Outstanding Achievement in the Arts. Her blog, Drama Queen, appears on *The Miami Herald*'s web site, and she has contributed to both *American Theatre* and *Inside Arts* magazines.

Garrett Eisler has written essays and criticism for *The Village Voice, The Journal of American Drama and Theatre, Time Out New York* and *Studies in Musical Theatre*. Since May 2005, he has also been writing The Playgoer, a theater news and commentary blog at playgoer.blogspot.com. Formerly literary manager of Syracuse Stage, Eisler holds an MFA in directing from Boston University and is completing a PhD in theater history at the Graduate Center of the City University of New York. He has taught at New York University, Boston University, Syracuse University and at the Dalton School in Manhattan.

Sylviane Gold began her career as a theater journalist at the *New York Post* in 1970 and continued at publications ranging from the *SoHo Weekly News* to *The Wall Street Journal* and *The New York Times*. Her reviews of New York theater for the *Boston*

Phoenix won the 1982 George Jean Nathan Award for Dramatic Criticism. She was a member of the New York Drama Critics' Circle from 1982 to 1989. Since 1999, she has written the "On Broadway" column for *Dance Magazine*. From 1990 to 2006, she chaired *Newsday*'s George Oppenheimer Award committee, which honored a new American playwright each year; she currently oversees the successor prize. She joined the editorial board of *Best Plays Theater Yearbook* in 2006.

John Istel has edited and contributed to a variety of performing arts, general interest and reference publications over the last 20 years including *American Theatre*, *The Atlantic*, *Back Stage*, *Contemporary Playwrights*, *Elle*, *Mother Jones*, *Newsday*, *New York*, *Stagebill* and *The Village Voice*. He has taught at New York University, Medgar Evers College and and currently teaches at New Design High School on Manhattan's Lower East Side.

Jeffrey Eric Jenkins became editor of *The Best Plays Theater Yearbook* series in 2001. Before joining *Best Plays* he served as theater critic, contributor and editor for a wide variety of publications. For many of the past 20 years, he has taught history, literature and performance at New York University, Carnegie Mellon University, the University of Washington and SUNY–Stony Brook. Jenkins received degrees in drama and theater arts from Carnegie Mellon University and San Francisco State University, and has directed more than two dozen productions in professional and educational theaters across the United States. He is a former chairman of the American Theatre Critics Association and now serves on the boards of the Theater Hall of Fame and the American Theatre Wing. He also chairs the Henry Hewes Design Awards, which is supported by the late critic's family and the American Theatre Wing.

Vivian Cary Jenkins spent more than twenty years as a healthcare executive and teacher before becoming an editor for *The Best Plays Theater Yearbook* series. Prior to her career in healthcare, she was a dancer and a Peace Corps volunteer in Honduras. During the 2007–08 season, she began working with Ping Chong and other artists as a performer in *Inside/Out: Voices From the Disability Community*

Chris Jones is the chief theater critic of the *Chicago Tribune*. For many years, he reviewed and reported on the Broadway road for *Variety*. Over the past two decades, his articles on theater and culture have also appeared in *The New York Times*, *American Theatre*, The Washington Post and the *Los Angeles Times*, along with many other newspapers, journals and magazines. He holds a PhD in theater from Ohio State University.

Robert Kamp is the owner of I Can Do That Productions, Inc., a graphic design company in New York City. Prior to starting his own business, Kamp worked for several arts and entertainment publications including *Stagebill* and *City Guide Magazine*. Kamp designed the *Best Plays* logo, and has worked on the book's photos and graphic images since the 2000–2001 edition.

Peter Marks is the theater critic for *The Washington Post*. Prior to joining the Post, he worked for a decade at *The New York Times*, where he served as the Off Broadway drama critic. At the *Times*, he also worked as a theater reporter, and covered media in the 2000 presidential campaign. He previously was a reporter for *Newsday* and the Bergen *Record*. He also teaches in the theater department and the honors program at George Washington University.

Charles McNulty is the chief theater critic of the *Los Angeles Times*. Before joining the *Times*, he was the theater editor of *The Village Voice*, chairman of the Obie Awards and head of Brooklyn College's program in graduate dramaturgy and theater criticism. A long time theater critic for the *Voice*, he was a member of the Obie Award panel for a decade. His writing has appeared in *The New York Times*, *Variety*, *Modern Drama*, *American Theatre* and *Theater*. He serves on the advisory board of Literary

Managers and Dramaturgs of the Americas (LMDA). He received his DFA in dramaturgy and dramatic criticism from the Yale School of Drama. He lives in West Hollywood with his partner, Alex Press, their two cats and one dog.

Nelson Pressley is a freelance critic and arts journalist whose work has appeared regularly in *The Washington Post* since 1999. His reviews and features have also appeared in *American Theatre, Irish Theatre Magazine, The Sondheim Review,* and other publications. He has taught theater and film at Shepherd University, served as a Helen Hayes Awards judge for three seasons, has moderated and participated in numerous public panels, and continues to be seen on *Around Town,* a Washington-based PBS arts roundup on WETA. He studied theater in London as an undergraduate, holds a BA in English from the University of Delaware, an MA in Theater History and Criticism from Catholic University of America, and is currently completing doctoral studies in English at the University of Maryland.

Christopher Rawson has been theater critic and theater editor at the *Pittsburgh Post-Gazette* since 1983. Along with writing local reviews, features, news and columns, he reviews regularly in New York, London and Canada. His BA came from Harvard, his PhD from the University of Washington and his love of theater from his father, actor Richard Hart. Since 1968, he has taught English literature at the University of Pittsburgh, where his subjects include Shakespeare and August Wilson. He coordinates the selection process for the Theater Hall of Fame and is currently chairman of the American Theatre Critics Association.

Michael Sommers writes reviews, features and news about the New York stage for *The Star-Ledger* of New Jersey and other Newhouse Newspapers publications. During his 27-year career in New York, he has also been an editor of *Back Stage* and *Theatre Crafts* magazine. He has served three terms as President of the New York Drama Critics' Circle and is a longtime judge for the Clarence Derwent and Theatre World Awards.

Jeffrey Sweet is a member of the playwrights' ensemble of the Tony Award-winning Victory Gardens Theater of Chicago, which has produced thirteen of his plays, many of which are included in the anthology of his work, *The Value of Names and Other Plays.* Two works were honored by the American Theatre Critics Association, and one received a Special Citation from *The Best Plays Theater Yearbook* (1993–94). He is the author of *Something Wonderful Right Away,* an oral history of Second City, and two widely used texts on playwriting, *The Dramatist's Toolkit* and *Solving Your Script.* He serves on the Council of the Dramatists' Guild, is an alumnus of New Dramatists and is a member of Ensemble Studio Theatre.

Jennifer Ashley Tepper is a graduate of New York University's Tisch School of the Arts. She has worked on shows such as *[title of show]* on Broadway, the world premiere of *The Intelligent Homosexual's Guide to Capitalism and Socialism With a Key to the Scriptures,* and *Things to Ruin: The Songs of Joe Iconis* and *Boys' Life* at Second Stage Theatre. Tepper was also a research assistant on *The South Pacific Companion* and *Make 'Em Laugh,* a documentary miniseries for public broadcasting. Other credits include projects with New York Musical Theatre Festival, York Theatre Company, the Rodgers and Hammerstein Organization, the Actors Fund, the Producing Office and the American Theatre Wing's Tony Awards.

Celia Wren is a former managing editor of *American Theatre* magazine. She currently reviews theater for *The Washington Post.* Wren is also the media critic for *Commonweal* and a frequent contributor to the *Richmond Times-Dispatch.* Her work has appeared in *The New York Times, The Village Voice, Newsday, The Boston Globe, The New York Observer, Talk* and *Smithsonian,* among other publications. She lives in Virginia with her husband and her cats.

Charles Wright has contributed essays to eight editions of *The Best Plays Theater Yearbook*. His writing has appeared in *Biography Magazine* (for which he was a columnist), *The New Yorker*, *Stagebill* and TheaterMania.com, among other publications. As a business affairs executive at A&E Television Networks, Wright has been involved in hundreds of hours of nonfiction programming, including *Jesus Camp*, produced by A&E IndieFilms, released by Magnolia Pictures, and nominated for a 2007 Academy Award as Best Documentary Feature, and *The September Issue*, produced by R.J. Cutler, awarded the Grand Jury Prize for Excellence in Cinematography at the 2009 Sundance Film Festival, and released by Roadside Attractions. A native of Tennessee and longtime resident of New York City, Wright holds degrees from Vanderbilt, Oxford, and the University of Pennsylvania.

Index

Play titles appear in bold. Asterisks (*) mark titles shortened for the index.
Page numbers in italic indicate essay citations.
Page numbers in bold italic indicate Broadway and Off Broadway listings.
Nouns or numbers in parentheses delineate different entities with similar names.